I0320772

LNDC
RON
STD

**Fourth Edition**

# TERRORISM AND ORGANIZED HATE CRIME

## Intelligence Gathering, Analysis, and Investigations

**Fourth Edition**

# TERRORISM AND ORGANIZED HATE CRIME

## Intelligence Gathering, Analysis, and Investigations

## Michael R. Ronczkowski

CRC Press
Taylor & Francis Group
Boca Raton London New York

CRC Press is an imprint of the
Taylor & Francis Group, an **Informa** business

CRC Press
Taylor & Francis Group
6000 Broken Sound Parkway NW, Suite 300
Boca Raton, FL 33487-2742

---

**Library of Congress Cataloging-in-Publication Data**

---

Names: Ronczkowski, Michael, author.
Title: Terrorism and organized hate crime : intelligence gathering, analysis, and investigations / by Michael R. Ronczkowski.
Description: Fourth edition. | Boca Raton : CRC Press, [2018] | Includes bibliographical references and index.
Identifiers: LCCN 2017011394| ISBN 9781138703469 (hardback : alk. paper) | ISBN 9781315203133 (ebook)
Subjects: LCSH: Hate crime investigation--United States. | Hate crime investigation. | Terrorism--United States--Prevention. | Terrorism--Prevention.
Classification: LCC HV8079.H38 R66 2018 | DDC 363.25/95--dc23
LC record available at https://lccn.loc.gov/2017011394

---

Visit the Taylor & Francis Web site at
http://www.taylorandfrancis.com

and the CRC Press Web site at
http://www.crcpress.com

# Dedication

*For my family, and all the hardworking men and women in law enforcement, both sworn and nonsworn, and the armed forces who make sacrifices every day in honor of their country. Keep up the fight!*

# Contents

# *APPENDICES*

# Foreword to the First Edition

As I write this foreword, the entire world is focused on the Middle East and the continuing threat of more terrorist attacks on Americans, both here and abroad. And while the military continues its deployment of troops and equipment to address the possibility of war, law enforcement personnel in this country scurry to hire and train analytical specialists—individuals essential to our ability to address matters of homeland security.

The present-day practice with regard to the hiring and use of analytical specialists in law enforcement agencies is in stark contrast to the common practices in 1965 when I began my law enforcement career with the Miami-Dade Police Department (MDPD) in Miami, Florida. Throughout my 27 years in South Florida, I witnessed firsthand how detectives were forced to rely on personal contacts and individual practices to gather and analyze information. I still remember how, as a young General Investigations Unit lieutenant, I would sit at my desk every morning plotting burglary trends from the previous day's crime reports. I would gather the information, try to put it into some type of usable format, push pins into a district map in the uniform roll call room, and then provide the data to the uniform lieutenants for dissemination to their officers. It was the best that we could do at the district level in the mid-1970s.

What few analysts the department hired were devoted to organized crime analysis and plotting the relationships among the various organized crime figures plying their trade in the Miami area. It was, in fact, the combination of the successes enjoyed in the organized crime investigations arena and the attendant frustration the rest of us were experiencing in analyzing crime data that finally caused the agency to recognize the need to have personnel specialized in gathering and analyzing information assigned throughout the department. I was the deputy director when I left MDPD in 1992. By then, the use of analysts in the agency was much more widespread. The intelligence unit began to realize the value of having professionally trained analysts, and so were many of the criminal investigative units both at headquarters and throughout the district.

As police chief in Tampa, Florida, I continued to recognize the need to have an effective medium in which to gather, analyze, and share information among agencies. The Tampa Police Department (TPD) had an effective analytical function. They did a great job of gathering and analyzing information and disseminating it to internal units. Unfortunately, and through no fault of the personnel, they did not do a good job of sharing information as it related to youth gangs. In spite of the plainly visible graffiti and gang tags on walls throughout the city, the city administration remained adamant in its position that there was no youth gang issue in Tampa. Through detailed briefings with the political structure, I was able to convince those in the administration of the importance of acknowledging the problem so that we could deal openly with other local authorities, law enforcement agencies, social service agencies, and the judiciary. The chief judge for the Circuit convened a summit on youth gangs, and we were well on our way to confronting this serious issue.

Local agencies have to not only share among themselves but also share with state and federal agencies. Local law enforcement frequently possesses information that may be germane to state and federal investigations, but the conduit to share it is lacking. In fact, many agencies still rely on personal contacts and friendships among detectives as means for sharing information. As director of the U.S. Marshal's Service (USMS) from 1993 to 1999, I observed just how many federal agencies are dependent on information from local, county, and state agencies to address matters of national security and interests. Terrorism and threats to homeland security have been major concerns in Washington, DC, for many years.

As director at USMS, I witnessed firsthand the impact that terrorists, foreign or domestic, can have on our society and way of life. The 1993 World Trade Center bombing, the Oklahoma City bombing, and the 1998 embassy bombings in Kenya and Tanzania strained the resources of dedicated federal investigators. And while I was not the director during the tragic and violent 1992 incident at Ruby

Ridge involving alleged members of the Patriot movement, I was involved in the subsequent review of the actions of the deputy marshals. I certainly came to recognize the continuing need to monitor and comprehend organized hate groups such as the Patriot movement in the United States. There has been a constant need for national intelligence and analysis after these tragic events, but also a new emphasis on information that can identify possible future attacks. However, much of the training and materials available to law enforcement has focused on preparing and responding.

There has been a training and analytical void in law enforcement on the full context of the terrorism and organized hate crime issues faced by officers and analysts. That was, until now.

This book is extremely topical and current. Mike Ronczkowski has spent more than 20 years in law enforcement—8 years managing and teaching intelligence analysts. He serves as an adjunct professor at a local university, teaching a course on how to recognize and deal with terrorism. As he worked on his lesson plans, he came to recognize the need for a book like this. This book is relevant for law enforcement personnel around the world and, at the same time, appropriate for students seeking to learn more about one of criminal justice's hottest topics.

Material in this book undoubtedly provides personnel with an understanding and approach for gathering intelligence and conducting analysis on terrorism-related matters. The reader will also find that many of the concepts are applicable to other law enforcement investigations.

From a management perspective, I believe that hiring and training analysts is essential. I have seen many agencies promote clerical staff members into analytical roles and just assume that they would learn on the job. This is a fallacy. As this book points out, law enforcement managers and policy-makers need accurate and quality intelligence. This will enable them to make informed decisions if they are to properly address issues. How can this be achieved without training and an understanding of the topic being analyzed?

I firmly believe that the author's approach, as detailed in this book, will greatly aid in addressing the analytical needs faced by agencies, filling in the gaps and voids that exist today.

In my current role as Commission Secretary for the Commission on Accreditation for Law Enforcement Agencies (CALEA), I have witnessed growth of an emphasis on agencies hiring, training, and even certifying analytical personnel to address such topics as homeland security, terrorism, and organized hate crime. The problem has been the lack of materials applicable to law enforcement—that is, until the author wrote this book. I congratulate him for addressing the needs of so many law enforcement agencies and for sharing his knowledge and experience with the rest of the law enforcement community. It has been an honor to review and write the foreword for this book, and I strongly recommend the use of it by law enforcement practitioners, managers, and students.

**Eduardo Gonzalez**
Commission Secretary for CALEA 2001–2004
Director United States Marshal's Service 1993–1999

# Foreword to the Third Edition

Following the events of September 11, 2001, the International Association of Chiefs of Police (IACP) held a Criminal Intelligence Sharing Summit in Alexandria, Virginia, in which participants posited that failures of the intelligence process contributed in no small measure to the events of that tragic day. They further concluded that the ability of law enforcement agencies—at all levels—to collect, collate, analyze, disseminate, and share intelligence was key to fighting the war on terror. The IACP thus proposed the development of a federal initiative to enable accomplishment of this objective. In response to this proposal, the U.S. Department of Justice, Office of Justice Programs, Bureau of Justice Assistance in 2002 created the Global Intelligence Working Group (GIWG) and tasked it with the responsibility of developing what is now known as the National Criminal Intelligence Sharing Plan. This plan provides a framework to improve our nation's ability to develop and share criminal intelligence information and to bolster the safety and security of our communities.

> A recommendation that IACP Summit participants identified as core to achieving the goals of the National Criminal Intelligence Sharing Plan was to 'promote intelligence-led policing through a common understanding of criminal intelligence and its usefulness.' Intelligence-led policing is defined as the collection and analysis of information to produce an intelligence end product designed to inform law enforcement decision-making at both the tactical and strategic levels. Intelligence-led policing is predicated on the production and application of intelligence information and products. For intelligence-led policing to be effective, the process must be an integral part of an agency's philosophy, policies, and strategies, and must also be integral in the organization's mission and goals.*

Embodied within the term "intelligence-led policing" is the underlying concept that decisions regarding the delivery of police services should, in fact, be led by intelligence. Yet for all of the acknowledgment given to the concept, few law enforcement agencies have embraced it to the extent that it truly influences, to any measurable degree, the decision-making process. As a result, many agencies, particularly those at the local level, continue to operate within the revolving door of the reactive "call-response" method of policing, forever letting the crises of the moment, instead of an intelligence-based plan, dictate the use of police resources.

Part of the reason for this phenomenon is that many agency administrators do not have a proper understanding of what intelligence is. As such, they will often use the terms "information" and "intelligence" interchangeably and make the mistake of assuming they are synonymous when they are not. When field officers and investigators take reports, they are collecting information. That is, they are collecting raw data that may or may not be accurate, up-to-date, or complete, and that, by themselves, do little to indicate what the overall crime problems may be within a jurisdiction. Intelligence, however, is produced when information has been analyzed by a competent professional who can provide officers, investigators, and agency administrators with assessments of what, based on their analyses, is likely to occur in the future. In other words, it is the task of the analyst to join together the individual pieces of a complex jigsaw puzzle (the information collected by officers) and transform them into intelligence products that provide the police administrator with one true picture of existing and emerging crime problems within the community.

Many agencies deliver police service based on perception rather than fact. Ask five officers their opinion of the greatest crime problem within the community and one is likely to receive five different answers based on the officers' perceptions of what has occurred in their areas during their tours of duty. But no one officer works all areas of town, works 24 hours per day, or has access to information gathered by other officers or obtained from community members, parole and probation departments, other

---

* U.S. Department of Justice, Office of Justice Programs, *The National Criminal Justice Sharing Plan,* October 2003, 3–4.

law enforcement agencies, and so on. As such, no one officer has all of the information relating to everything that has occurred, may be currently occurring, or is likely to occur within the jurisdiction.

In contrast, with access to—and through the analysis of—information that has been collected by officers, investigators, and the other entities mentioned above, the analyst is in a unique position to provide the agency administrator with a fact-based (as opposed to a perception-based) assessment of what existing and emerging community crime problems truly are, what the underlying causes of the problems may be, what current events may portend for community harm, and what might be done to ameliorate or eliminate them or to prevent their future occurrence. In possession of such an assessment, the police administrator can now make objective decisions as to what strategies should be used and what resources, both now and in the future, will be needed to effectively direct the delivery of police services throughout the whole of the jurisdiction.

Unfortunately, however, as the executive director of the Alpha Group Center for Crime and Intelligence Analysis, an organization that conducts training programs for crime and intelligence analysts throughout the world, it is disheartening to me and to our other instructors, including Michael Ronczkowski, the author of this book, to see the lack of importance given to the role of analysis function within many law enforcement agencies and the resulting lack of benefits that police administrators could be receiving were they more fully cognizant of the contributions that could be made by the analysts they employ—assuming that they do, in fact, employ a crime or intelligence analyst or at least dedicate someone to the task at all.

The reasons why benefits go unrealized are many and varied. But primary among them is that many administrators are simply unaware of the tasks an analyst should perform, the types of products and services they should provide, or even what they themselves should be receiving from the analyst. In short, although they may hire an analyst, they do so without any specific knowledge of the job they are to do. When this occurs, analysts frequently become little more than historians within an agency and they are used, at best, to crunch numbers in an effort to explain what has happened in the past. Crime and intelligence analysts are not—and should not be—historians used simply to explain what has happened in the past but to present scenarios, based on analyzed information, of what is likely to occur in the future. Armed with these scenarios, the police administrator is in a significantly enhanced position to plan not only for the future and orderly growth of the organization but also for the heightened safety and security of the community as well.

The ability of the analyst to provide useful intelligence to administrators to accomplish this goal, however, is dependent on several factors, not the least of which is the quality of the information on which intelligence is based. Field officers and investigators have the potential to perform an incalculably valuable function as the information gatherers within a law enforcement agency. Unfortunately, few recognize the value of this function, with the result that crime reports, arrest reports, and field interrogation or field contact reports are often completed with little regard for detail. Ask any analyst, or, for that matter, any investigator, and they will frequently bemoan the fact that modus operandi factors of crimes and physical descriptions of people have been omitted, questions of victims, witnesses, or suspects went unasked, or that even such basic things as dates and times of occurrences were recorded in error. In such situations, the old axiom of GIGO (garbage in, garbage out) prevents the analyst from creating the intelligence products necessary to accurately assess the potential threats to the community. Worse yet is the tendency of officers to "kiss off" reports and to fail to gather information in the first place. For analysts, GIGO—garbage in, garbage out—is bad, and NINO—nothing in, nothing out—is the kiss of death. Officers need to be reminded continually of their value as data gatherers, of their critical role in the subsequent analytical process, and of their need to collect accurate, up-to-date, and complete information to the greatest extent possible. Without information, there can be no analysis. And without analysis, there can be no intelligence. And without intelligence, there can be no basis to make objective decisions to guide the delivery of police services or to govern the effective use of law enforcement resources.

Another factor that will govern the quality and thus the value and usability of the intelligence product is the training the analyst has received to perform this type of work. Analysts are now being enlisted to help their agencies in the fight against not only crime but also terrorism as well. Yet, few have had any training to equip them with the skills needed to determine even the existence of terrorist threats, let alone the ability to provide any meaningful recommendations for how to respond to them. Sad to say, many police administrators have simply "knighted" people as analysts and given them the admonition to go forth and "analyze something." Without the requisite knowledge, skills, and abilities, however, the "analyst" fails to make a worthwhile contribution to the agency, with the result that the analysis function is relegated to a relatively low level of importance within the organization. In light of the world situation today, this is a luxury our law enforcement agencies can no longer afford.

In this age of global terrorism, today's analysts must be specifically trained to deal with new problems involving often previously unknown and shadowy figures whose objectives differ significantly from the traditional criminals we have come to know and understand. They must come to a knowledge of who the terrorists are, the groups and organizations they represent, and the motivations that drive them to commit their acts of mass violence. Moreover—and of vital importance—analysts must learn how to identify and interpret the often subtle yet critical clues that indicate the possibility of an impending terrorist action and be taught the techniques to gather information and produce intelligence that truly enhances homeland security efforts.

The need for competent professionals to perform the analytical function is recognized by the National Criminal Intelligence Sharing Plan, the Commission on Accreditation for Law Enforcement Agencies, the International Association of Chiefs of Police, and a plethora of other major law enforcement organizations worldwide. In light thereof, funds must be budgeted for and analysts must receive the training necessary for them to fulfill not merely a secondary but rather a primary and dynamic role within the agencies they serve. So, too, must the people who supervise and manage the analytical function receive training so that they can fairly evaluate the performance of the analyst and guide the direction of the analysis program. Finally, the National Criminal Intelligence Sharing Plan recommends that even police administrators themselves receive the training and education necessary to acquaint them with the philosophy of intelligence-led policing, the nature of the intelligence process, and its role in enhancing public safety.

In that regard, *Terrorism and Organized Hate Crime: Intelligence Gathering, Analysis and Investigations, Fourth Edition*, by Michael Ronczkowski, and his widely acclaimed *Homeland Security and Terrorism Analysis Course* are welcome additions to the educational arena because they provide a framework for exploring the many issues involved in the analysis of terrorism and organized hate crimes. Throughout this book, Ronczkowski identifies the traits and structures of multiple forms of terrorism and demonstrates how to recognize the indicators of an impending act of terrorism or mass violence, how to deter and prevent an attack, how to gather information, and, of significant importance, how to transform information into intelligence products to meet community demands for safety and security. Moreover, in clear and concise language, this book illustrates how to establish and effectively operate a homeland security program and how to develop an analytical approach to terrorism that all law enforcement agencies, regardless of size, can use to address matters of homeland security, terrorism, and organized hate crimes within their jurisdiction, region, state, or province. As such, it is an excellent resource for not only analysts and intelligence officers but also for police administrators as well.

**Steven Gottlieb**
*Alpha Group Center for Crime and Intelligence Analysis*

The Alpha Group Center is a premier provider of crime and intelligence analysis training to command- and line-level staff members of both civilian and military law enforcement organizations throughout the world. Offering onsite courses in Crime Analysis, Criminal Intelligence Analysis, Criminal Investigative Analysis, Homeland Security and Terrorism Analysis, Statement Analysis, Interview and Interrogation Techniques, and Law Enforcement Research Methods, the Alpha Group also serves as a training provider for the Certification Program for Crime and Intelligence Analysts, which is cosponsored by the State of California Department of Justice and the University of California and California State University Systems. This is currently the only certification program offered by—and with oversight from—a state governmental entity (as opposed to a private organization or association) that offers certification and confers the professional title of Certified Crime and Intelligence Analyst to program graduates. It is for this reason that this program is so well regarded throughout the law enforcement profession today. Furthermore, because the Alpha Group presents the curriculum to members of federal, state, local, military, and tribal law enforcement organizations throughout the world, this certification is available to people of any state or country who complete the program at any location at which it is offered.

# Preface

Since September 11, 2001, the U.S. Federal Bureau of Investigation (FBI) and law enforcement agencies nationwide have been thrust into the forefront of the "war" on terrorism. One may ask why law enforcement is fighting a "war" instead of "crime." For centuries, wars have been fought by the military. However, since the wave of "new terrorism" reaches beyond conventional boundaries by nonconventional methods, there is a need to attack from all fronts with all available resources. It has become apparent that a successful campaign against terrorism will require cooperation and coordination among military, law enforcement, and private civilian agencies. The subsequent passage of the USA PATRIOT Act in October 2001 gave the role of traditional law enforcement a new direction. This enhanced the parameters in which agencies can communicate and gather good intelligence information. Since October 2001, the FBI staff alone sought to hire nearly 900 agents and 400 crime and intelligence analysts, also known as investigative research specialists, in the wake of perceived deficiencies in the gathering, analysis, investigation, and dissemination of intelligence data. According to the FBI, in 2006, their agency doubled the number of intelligence analysts from 1,023 to 2,161. This initiative, coupled with collaboration and partnerships with state, local, and county law enforcement agencies, may thwart future attempts to attack the United States and its interests. Only time will tell.

In an October 18, 2002, *Miami Herald* article, these deficiencies were made apparent. During testimony taken before a joint congressional hearing on October 17, 2002, FBI director Robert Mueller stated that the FBI does well at collecting information "but will be the first to concede that we have not done a good job at analyzing it." This statement should not be viewed as an issue for only the FBI. Much of the information that the FBI gathers comes from the thousands of law enforcement agencies throughout the United States and other countries. Based on this, it can be argued that if the FBI has not done a good job of analyzing the information, then law enforcement has not done a good job of analyzing the same information. However, this is not the case. The public had not experienced any revelations that their domestic security was compromised or breached; the public only encountered criminals, organized hate groups, organized crime, gangs, and the occasional "wacko," all of which could be addressed by local law enforcement. Therefore, there was no precedent to look for or monitor "terrorists" or "terrorist-related" activity, and therefore no one to analyze this type of activity.

Terrorism, although not a new concept, is a relatively new variable for law enforcement agencies to consider on a regular basis. The need to effectively analyze terrorist-related and organized hate group information in a timely manner is critical. However, to analyze a topic, particularly terrorism and organized hate crimes, an analyst must have an understanding of the subject matter. This is perhaps the reason, as FBI Director Mueller stated, that the FBI has not done a good job of analyzing this type of information.

This book is written to bridge that gap to provide law enforcement agencies here—nearly 18,000 in the United States alone—as well as those in other countries, with an approach to analyzing homeland security needs and to aid the law enforcement community in understanding the vital role it plays in the war on terrorism. References to domestic terrorism cannot be construed as being specific to any one country. In this modern era of technology, communication, and transportation, placing boundaries on investigating and analyzing a topic such as terrorism is counterproductive. Based on history, terrorism is not going away any time soon. Therefore, law enforcement must develop methods and practices that address developing multifaceted links to local, regional, national, and international terrorism and hate crimes. Although many of the approaches detailed here focus on laws and practices in the United States, homegrown organized hate groups as well as domestic and international terrorism can strike in any country at any time.

New to this edition is an in-depth discussion on radicalization and recruitment as well as details on ISIS. Many struggle to recognize a terrorist and their motives. It is important to know the triggering factors that may cause an individual to support or join a radical, extremist, or violent cause and ideology. Chapter 5 provides insight from well-documented rescurces from some of the leading researchers throughout the world. While it is important to know and understand the overall topic of terrorism and what may constitute a terrorist act, it is just as important to understand the individuals involved.

# Acknowledgments

This book would not have been possible without assistance from a multitude of people and entities. In no particular order, I would like to extend my gratitude to everyone who aided, directly and indirectly, this project over the past year: Sergeant Sean Holtz for his expertise in the area of cyber-crimes and cyberterrorism matters as well as his technical wizardry; Dan Helms, Crime Analyst, National Law Enforcement and Corrections Technology Center, Rocky Mountain Region, and the Crime Mapping and Analysis Program (CMAP) for use of the GIS images; and Bair Software, Research and Consulting for the training project images. Thanks also to Julie Gonzalez for making the phone call and facilitating the foreword for the first edition; Florida Atlantic University for giving me the opportunity to instruct in the Department of Criminology and Criminal Justice—in particular, the Terrorism course; the Miami-Dade Police Department in Florida; Steve Gottlieb and the Alpha Group Center for Crime and Intelligence Analysis Training, as well as the staff at the National Law Enforcement and Corrections Technology Center–Southeast in Charleston, South Carolina, for providing working environments that allowed me to gain experience and hone my skills and abilities. A special thanks to the staff, particularly Mark Potok and Russell Estes, of the Southern Poverty Law Center for their assistance, immediate responses, and work on the Center's Intelligence Report.

# Author

**Michael Ronczkowski, MPA,** has over 30 years of law enforcement experience. He began his law enforcement career in 1983 with the Miami-Dade Police Department in Miami, Florida, where he rose through the ranks before his honorable retirement in 2010 as the Major overseeing the department's Homeland Security Bureau and Director and founder of the Miami-Dade Fusion Center, now known as the Southeast Florida Fusion Center, a DHS-recognized fusion center. During his tenure as commander of the Miami-Dade Fusion Center, he served on several Major Cities Chiefs Association and national initiatives related to fusion centers. Most notable was the establishment and development of the Nationwide Suspicious Activity Reporting (SAR) Initiative. He served as an adjunct professor and taught courses on terrorism and the criminal justice system at Florida Atlantic University in the Criminal Justice Department for 8 years. Recognized internationally for his analytical skills, techniques and practices, and crime-mapping expertise, Ronczkowski has presented analytical material at numerous conferences, training classes, and workshops for various international associations, the Department of Justice, the Department of Homeland Security, and the National Institute of Justice. Also, he has testified before both the United States Senate Homeland Security Subcommittee and the Congressional Homeland Security Subcommittee on the topics of Islamic extremism and emergency response. He managed a countywide analytical intelligence unit for more than 10 years and has written analytical policy, procedures, and training protocols, and has developed analytical databases and information resources. He also served as a certified Florida law enforcement instructor, field training officer, and supervisor. Ronczkowski has nearly 20 years of investigative experience and has supervised various criminal investigative units, including serving several years with the FBI and U.S. Marshals Service's fugitive task forces. He is an authorized Environmental Systems Research Institute (ESRI) ArcView® instructor, and he taught crime, and incident mapping and analysis for the National Law Enforcement and Corrections Technology Center for 6 years. In addition, he instructs the Homeland Security and Terrorism Analysis course for the Alpha Group Center (since March 2004). He currently serves with the Putnam County (TN) Sheriff's Office. In 2005, Ronczkowski became a board certification member for the United States Association of Professional Investigators (USAPI). Ronczkowski is the author of numerous writings on topics covering terrorism, analysis, and intelligence, including "The Robbery Clearinghouse: Successful Real-Time Intelligence Analysis" (*Police Chief Magazine*, September 1999), "Tactical/Investigative Analysis of Targeted Crimes" (*Advanced Crime Mapping Topics*, NIJ—Crime Mapping and Analysis Program, April 2002), "Terrorism" (*Encyclopedia of Criminal Justice*, December 2004), "Analysis and Intelligence Driven Enforcement: The Future for Law Enforcement and Homeland Security" (*CALEA Journal* 85, June 2004), and "Using Police Information" (CDAP Project Partnership—Bureau of Justice Assistance and John Jay College, June 2005). Ronczkowski is also a contributing author for the Encyclopedia of Police Science and The Sage Encyclopedia of Terrorism, Second Edition. He earned a bachelor of arts degree in criminal justice and a master's degree in public administration from Florida Atlantic University. Ronczkowski is also a graduate of the Federal Bureau of Investigation's National Academy, Session #217.

# Introduction

"Terrorism" is perhaps the one word that creates more controversy and thought-provoking research than any other word, no matter where it is discussed. Debated, defined, and studied for decades by scholars and academics, terrorism remains at the forefront of many discussions, government debates, and media outlets. Now those in the field of law enforcement are debating, defining, and studying what terrorism is and what it means to the first responders of the world.

World events have shaped public perceptions for years, and these events have aided in the establishment of a framework that law enforcement managers use in guiding their agencies. With the advent of modern technology, law enforcement has sought to enhance its security, ability to work faster, process, and analyze data, and develop avenues for sharing and consolidating information, working "smarter" and more efficiently.

Events surrounding recent terrorist activities now force law enforcement agencies to expedite and expand technological initiatives to aid in operational, tactical, investigative, intelligence, and deployment strategies. Facilitating methodologies with which to process these new demands within the law enforcement arena has led agencies across the country to hire specially trained criminal and intelligence analysts.

Since 1979, law enforcement agencies have sought to improve delivery of their services by standardizing practices and procedures through the development of the Commission on Accreditation for Law Enforcement Agencies (CALEA). The importance of crime analysis is noted in CALEA's documentation on accreditation. Based on this, many agencies have established crime analyst positions. The importance of these positions has not gone unnoticed. In 1996, crime analyst was listed as a "hot track" position in law enforcement, and the International Association of Crime Analysts was cited as saying, "The demand for these technical whizzes has risen 10-fold in 15 years." In a post-9/11 environment, the positions of crime and intelligence analyst continue to grow in not only the federal realm but also at many state, local, and county law enforcement agencies. Some estimates report that there are 6,000–9,000 such positions nationwide.

For individuals in the field of analysis, this was not a surprise. The International Association of Chiefs of Police (IACP) also recognized the importance of designing and implementing a standardized policy governing crime analysis and has developed a blueprint for agencies to follow. In this document, which became effective on October 1, 1993, the IACP outlined a model policy for law enforcement agencies to use as a guide in its development of analytical protocols. The IACP's model policy notes that crime analyst techniques began to emerge as early as 1972 in Dallas, Kansas City, and Sacramento. For nearly 20 years, analysts have honed their skills, usually on the job and with little managerial direction. Many analysts anecdotally stated that their agencies were uncertain of how to utilize the talents of those in this largely nonsworn position. They also failed to see the importance of having a dedicated unit responsible for identifying patterns, series, and trends, usually without going on the street and generating statistics, such as arrests. However, this changed with the IACP's model policy. The crime analysis process was organized into five categories: data collection, data collation, analysis, report dissemination, and feedback/evaluation. This policy provided direction and helped define the role of the analyst within the agency.

Now that the concept of crime analysis has been with law enforcement for at least 40 years and has been widely embraced in the past 20 years, why does it seem that agencies are still reactive rather than proactive? Perhaps, it is because although the law enforcement community has implemented methods to standardize and categorize the analytical process, lack of understanding, education, and training of personnel throughout the ranks has impeded the process. How can one provide analysis for a topic for which one lacks knowledge, understanding, or formal training?

Traditional law enforcement methods have tended to be reactive rather than proactive, with an emphasis on identification and arrest of an offender in a specific jurisdiction. Analytical practices have enhanced this process; however, through experience, training, and technological advances, analytical personnel can aid the law enforcement community in looking at crime from a proactive posture across jurisdictional boundaries. Now that law enforcement agencies accept and rely on analysts for the gathering, analyzing, and disseminating of "crime" information, a more exotic term has been added to the mix: "terrorism."

What is terrorism? How do we handle it? What information should we gather? How do we analyze it? What are we looking for? Why are crime analysts analyzing terrorism? These are just a few of the questions that an analyst outside a federal- or military-based agency might have. Analytical-based training for law enforcement analysts investigating crimes, although growing, has been limited during the past 40 years. Therefore, the importance of understanding "terrorism analysis" is exponential. The criminal relationships associated with crime, the knowledge and understanding of the topic, and the subject to be analyzed are of immediate importance if law enforcement agencies are to play a vital role in the war against terrorism. Waiting 30 days, or 30 years, runs the risk of missed information and perhaps many injuries or deaths. Provided in this book is a framework for answering and addressing these questions. Law enforcement now must target these much-debated issues and focus on understanding and defining its new and enhanced role in the war on terrorism.

Since 2010, there has been much emphasis placed on getting the community to provide information to law enforcement based on their observations. The see something—say something campaign—although successful at various levels, still relies on untrained observers to report information in a timely manner. While very important, this information must be vetted and still places law enforcement in a proactive posture that is often at the end of a potential terrorist act. Law enforcement must become more proactive and seek to identify terrorist acts early. To do this, they must gain further insight into those who join, support, and carry out the violence. Importance must be placed on understanding and interrupting the radicalization and recruitment process. Then, we can pursue the links and disrupt the funding sources, and thwart potential terrorist and extremist acts.

# 1 A Need for Understanding and Analysis

In the United States and the rest of the Western world prior to September 11, 2001, the terms "terrorist," "terrorism," and "terrorist activity" were reserved for "other" countries and third-world locations struggling for an identity. However, this perception could not have been further from the truth. Although only a country for 240 years, the United States, like many other countries, was born through the revolutionary acts of ordinary people. While viewed as revolutionary acts of citizens, according to modern definitions of terrorism these acts could be seen as terrorist activities today.

The United States, as well as other countries, has recognized the need to gather and monitor terrorist-related activity and intelligence for many years. In the United States, the Central Intelligence Agency (CIA) is tasked with this mission for locations and groups outside the country. However, the need for internal monitoring was not seen as critical until September 11, 2001. With the demise of the Soviet Union and the end of the Cold War, the United States was viewed as the only remaining superpower and in the eyes of some extremists, as Satan. After the fall of the Soviet Union in 1991, many believed the need for spying and in-depth intelligence was diminished. The need, however, may have become more urgent and the process more complex after the Soviet collapse. Being a super-power and a melting pot of cultures that is surrounded by two oceans and neighbored by two cordial and passive countries, it is easy to become complacent and develop an "it can't happen here (or to me)" attitude. Now that this myth has been shattered forever, law enforcement is redefining its mission and purpose not only locally but also with respect to the international crisis of terrorism.

What took us so long to wake up? The United States was aware of terrorist activity and its international reaches. It even convened a committee to conduct research on terrorism. The research was undertaken by a nonprofit institution, Rand, which formally initiated terrorism research in 1972 in response to two significant terrorist events that horrified the world: the Japanese Red Army's attack on Lod Airport in Tel Aviv, Israel, and Black September's attack at the Munich Olympic Games in Germany. This research was in response to President Richard M. Nixon's creation of a cabinet committee to combat terrorism.[1]

Nearly 50 years later, we are still struggling with defining, dealing with, and addressing terrorism and the roles of officials and agencies in combating terrorism. Why is this? Is it because of politics and legal concerns? It is certainly not due to a lack of academic and scholarly research, and writings on the subject. Countless publications have been written in the past 45 years covering virtually every aspect of the terrorism topic. However, outside the field of terrorism research or military arenas there is still a lack of awareness, especially among law enforcement personnel, as to how best to deal with and analyze terrorism and terrorist-related activity. Therefore, how can we expect law enforcement personnel to identify something about which they do not have a conceptual understanding? Law enforcement academies focus on training and developing individuals so they understand every aspect of what they can do and what is expected of them in local crime-based situations, according to state guidelines. So how can law enforcement personnel be expected to address the international reaches of terrorism effectively without proper training and adequate knowledge of what they are attempting to identify and analyze? Much of the current law enforcement training focuses on first responder handling of hazardous materials and weapons of mass destruction (WMDs) instead of obtaining information and gathering intelligence. However, the recently developed nationwide suspicious activity reporting (SAR) initiative provides local law enforcement personnel with insight into the behaviors associated with terrorism. Providing training and a clear understanding of what information needs to be gathered and analyzed are essential to effective management.

## THE MISSION

For years, many law enforcement agencies have employed civilian and sworn status personnel as crime and intelligence analysts. The role of these highly specialized individuals has gone largely unnoticed in the realm of law enforcement until now. Accredited law enforcement agencies currently follow the guidelines set out in the Communications Assistance for Law Enforcement Act (CALEA) standards manual,[2] as well as those set by the International Association of Chiefs of Police (IACP) model policy, as blueprints for their respective personnel assigned to performing crime and intelligence analysis. Chapter 15 of the CALEA standards manual refers to the mission of an analyst as being that of a "support" position, stating that "the information obtained by analyzing the data is used to support management and operations."[2] Additionally, it is noted that information obtained from such analyses must be used in strategic planning in areas such as crime prevention. However, is crime prevention the same as terrorism prevention? Much crime prevention is completed within the jurisdictional parameters of the respective agency. If this is the case and local agencies are focused on a limited geographic area, the chances are that terrorism prevention is not a part of this mission.

The barometer often used as a measure of effectiveness and analyzed by an array of personnel is the Federal Bureau of Investigation (FBI)'s Uniform Crime Report (UCR). Using UCR, law enforcement managers can perform statistical management to gauge the effectiveness of their mission to reduce crime, to instill a sense of security among their citizens and in the community they serve, and to follow a set of standardized procedures.

However, there is a flaw. There are just over 18,000 law enforcement agencies in the United States. According to the U.S. Department of Justice, the FBI has attempted to collect basic crime and arrest data since 1930 from these agencies, but only just over 17,000 of them have complied.[3] Although the procedure for submitting and using data is standardized, the voluntary nature of compliance and the various ways in which states compile and submit information to the UCR leaves a gap in the basic collection of raw numbers. Given this gap in the collection of basic raw crimes, the 18,000-plus independent law enforcement agencies are less able to define methods and practices designed to facilitate analysis of terrorism-related issues in a manner suitable to fit the immediate needs of concerned parties.

The missions and roles of analytical personnel and their duties need to be clearly defined in every agency's standard operating procedures for all employees to follow. Regardless of whether or not an agency employs analytical personnel, information gathering and analysis of data associated with terrorist-related activities or terrorists is vital to national security. Furthermore, it is imperative that this information is forwarded to concerned parties in an expeditious manner.

Actionable intelligence and real-time information is essential for preventing acts of terrorism. Thorough analysis and expedient dissemination of information about domestic and international terrorists and their activities will improve the government's ability to disrupt and prevent terrorist acts, and will provide useful warning to the private sector. Currently, the U.S. government does not have an institution (such as the CIA, which performs analysis regarding terrorist threats abroad) primarily dedicated to systematically analyzing all information and intelligence on potential terrorist threats within the United States. This will undoubtedly change with the establishment of the Department of Homeland Security, the instituting of a czar for intelligence, and the restructuring of numerous government agencies. According to documents establishing the Department of Homeland Security, this department, working together with the enhanced capabilities of other agencies such as the FBI, would make the United States safer by bringing in the ability to compile intelligence from a variety of sources.

Consolidation of resources is essential to any collective attack. In this mission, however, there are several underlying factors impeding the process that must be considered. The factors that stand in the way of ensuring effective homeland security and performing terrorism analysis are as follows:

- The U.S. Constitution
- The First Amendment: Freedom of speech, press, and religion
- The Fourth Amendment: Protection against unreasonable search and seizure

- Traditional law enforcement approach to investigating crimes
- Reactive versus proactive style of policing
- Lack of or insufficient number of crime and intelligence analysts
- Law enforcement that traditionally analyzes after the fact
- Politics and political correctness
- Media interpretations of events
- Proactive behavior or attitude when analyzing information or data, which is usually met with skepticism
- Local law enforcement that is often consumed with local, civil, and community issues, such as racial profiling and community-oriented policing initiatives
- Proactive attitude requiring a change in philosophy, which law enforcement has not been traditionally quick to change or accept

Currently, law enforcement analyzes and responds to the here and now. With homeland security, organized hate crime and terrorism analysts need to be proactive and ready for the long term (at least 18 months) and need to look for nontraditional suspects.

An often forgotten component that may stand in the way is history. A quick snapshot of the last six decades sheds some light into some of the skepticism surrounding intelligence as a whole:

1950s—McCarthy hearings and the Communist bogeyman. FBI investigations of politicians and members of the entertainment industry.

1960s—FBI investigates civil rights leaders and antiwar activists. Uniformed police deal with civil unrest and demonstrations at the 1968 Democratic Convention in Chicago.

1970s—Vice President Spiro Agnew resigns; Watergate; Pentagon papers; more civil unrest. Freedom of Information Act extended to law enforcement. Information surfaces about CIA assassination plots.

1980s—Iran–Contra investigation.

1990s—Ruby Ridge and the assault on the Branch Davidian compound at Waco.

2000s—9/11 World Trade Center; attack on Pentagon; Pennsylvania hijacking.

This brief comparison can be easily played out for earlier years with everything from the Prohibition era to the attack on Pearl Harbor. One can oversimplify and sum it up as politics. Everything from shrinking budgets, the government's willingness to rely heavily on electronic and satellite-based intelligence over human intelligence, and the aforementioned high-profile eras have forged uncertainty in the minds of the public when it comes to intelligence.

## INTELLIGENCE ANALYSIS UNITS

Intelligence analysis units have existed in law enforcement for several decades. In *Applications in Criminal Analysis*, Marilyn B. Peterson provides historical background on intelligence and reports that found their way into law enforcement in the 1920s and 1930s.[4] This was in response to the need to collect information on anarchists and mobsters. Intelligence units operated sporadically in the United States until the advent of computers and the adoption of analysis by many state and local agencies in the early 1980s. In the 1990s, perhaps the greatest growth and organization of intelligence units was seen. This was the decade that saw the birth of many professional associations dedicated to intelligence and analysis, many of which still operate today. There were also several books written on the topic, and training programs began to emerge. Then came the new millennium. Just prior to the end of the century, everyone was consumed with the Y2K bug and computer meltdowns. Law enforcement personnel were busy preparing for chaos and anarchy. Intelligence units, for those agencies that had them, were working around the clock in hopes of averting a catastrophic event. Today, these units are preparing for events related to terrorism and threats to homeland security. However, "today" has been taking place for at least 20 years. Peterson dedicated a section of her book to terrorism, noting that it had blossomed in the previous 25 years as a threat, and she pointed out that groups such as the Skinheads and the Ku Klux Klan were then being considered domestic terrorist groups.[4]

Although many agencies have intelligence units in place, many still do not. Or, if they do have intelligence units they fail to use their skills and abilities to the fullest. Calling a group of investigators or analysts an "intelligence unit" without embracing national standards and thinking globally is just another unit within a law enforcement agency. Another consideration is logistical. An informal cursory poll conducted of analysts throughout North America over the 3 years after 9/11 revealed that many analytical units are removed from the general investigative work area. They are usually relegated to a back room, or they work off-site in federal or state government intelligence centers. In order for their work to be effective, analysts must be accessible to those personnel performing the line-level investigation.

Whether seeking to develop an analysis unit or to optimize an existing one, police administrators should strive to place these units in open areas that are readily accessible to their personnel. This is true whether the unit is composed of one person or several squads. Another practice to avoid is the use of cubicle jungles. Besides their location and accessibility, the second most important factor for successful units is communication, which is greatly diminished by the use of any wall, including 6-foot cubicle walls. Interaction is essential to any intelligence unit.

With the logistics worked out, police administrators and managers—through the use of intelligence units—must be assisted in working smarter and aided in directing enforcement efforts of their organizations toward the right issues for the right reasons. Law enforcement is in the throes of an information age that is forcing the design or purchase of complex records management systems. Much of what law enforcement does is process information, but this does little to combat crime or to assist terrorism prevention in the absence of an effective intelligence analysis unit. To be effective, such units also require high-end computers, laser printers, plotters, and other peripheral devices and complex software packages. All these items are costly, and some managers fail to see the benefits of using scarce budgetary funds for a unit that does not produce traditional results, that is, arrests. However, these tools interpret the vast volumes of information collected annually. This interpretation pays dividends that indirectly drive a successful agency by providing direction that will ultimately lead to arrests and increased clearances. Properly outfitted units can also aid many facets of law enforcement, particularly special enforcement programs, including those dealing with terrorism, homeland security, and organized hate groups. This is done through analysis-driven enforcement (ADE) or analysis and intelligence-driven enforcement (AIDE). Some also refer to this as intelligence-led policing. All rely on technology and the use of advanced crime analysis techniques, such as crime mapping, to identify critical need areas of policing. Managers then use this information to make informed decisions that assist in dedicating resources to the endeavor at hand.

Intelligence analysis units will never lead an agency in statistical categories such as arrests, seizures, or citations. They will have few, if any, quantifiable measures. Intelligence units come with a high cost and require a professional, trained, and dedicated staff. Regardless of an agency's size, these units play an invaluable role with contributions that are realized indirectly. All local agencies are at the forefront of the information gathering process. Every agency can and should either have the dedicated staff or be involved in a regional task force to address issues of homeland security. The difficulty lies in managers' ability to remove themselves from the need for instant gratification and results as well as recognizing the need for overlooking jurisdictional limitations. This role becomes evident as managers embrace ADE or AIDE and analysts train to look for criminal occurrences that may be linked to terrorist and organized hate crime activities.

## DEFINING ANALYTICAL POSITIONS AND ROLES

With the mission defined, it is now necessary to standardize and establish working definitions for personnel assigned to perform duties essential to developing effective and timely intelligence.

This assignment might seem to be a relatively easy task. However, law enforcement agencies have spent the past two decades struggling with it. Job descriptions and requirements across the United States vary as much as the color and style of uniforms and badges.

Just as with uniforms, many agencies have written job descriptions and requirements to meet their particular needs. These have not impeded the level of service realized by any one jurisdiction; but if we as a country are to effectively tackle the issues surrounding homeland security and terrorism, it is essential that analytical requirements, practices, and procedures be standardized so that everyone is "speaking the same language." The importance of analysts has been realized locally by many agencies, and now this sentiment is being echoed in the halls of the nation's capital. Analysts help to protect the interests of the country through the development of useful high-quality analysis. The question that has remained unanswered for years is this: What is the difference between crime analysis and intelligence analysis?

For many years, analytical and law enforcement practitioners have accepted the working definitions detailed in *Crime Analysis: From First Report to Final Arrest* by Gottlieb et al.[5] as best practices for their personnel. Written in 1994, these definitions were insightful. However, some of the details mentioned in the book may have been overlooked at the time. One such detail that was probably overlooked, or even questioned, was the mention of terrorism in the working definition of intelligence analysis. This occurred some 7 years before most people realized that this would be something law enforcement had to consider, or even what the term "terrorism" meant. The definitions cited in the book are outlined as follows[5]:

**Crime analysis**: Allows the analyst to determine who is doing what to whom by focusing on crimes against persons and property (homicide, rape, robbery, burglary, theft, etc.).

**Intelligence analysis**: Aids in the determination of who is doing what with whom by focusing on the relationships between persons and organizations involved in illegal, and usually conspiratorial, activities (narcotics, trafficking, prostitution rings, organized crime, gangs, terrorism, etc.).

These definitions were incorporated into various job descriptions and policy protocols along with the premise that the world of analysis encompasses only administrative, strategic, and tactical practices. For law enforcement, this was true until September 11, 2001. We can now add another method of analysis—homeland security, which is actually a hybrid of the aforementioned types of analysis.

## INTELLIGENCE DISCIPLINES

Over the years, differences in analytical definitions could be attributed to the fundamentally different missions of various agencies employing analysts. The military, federal, state, and local law enforcement agencies employ analysts, but the job functions vary from one agency to another. No matter how different the daily functions concerning administrative, tactical, and strategic analysis are for the various agencies, they now have one thing in common to strive for, and that is homeland security analysis. Regardless of the definitions used, an effective analyst is part researcher, part psychologist, part historian, part investigator, and part linguist. In simple terms, any analyst is, or should be, a multitasker. As just mentioned, there are, and will continue to be, different missions. However, this can be overcome if we know how to apply them in our daily duties. Five of the most common forms of intelligence disciplines that are not specific to any one mission or agency are outlined as follows:

1. IMINT or imagery intelligence: The study and analysis of photos, videos, and satellite images.
2. SIGINT or signals intelligence: The study and analysis of signal communications (radios).

3. MASINT or measures and signatures intelligence: The study and analysis of unique signatures produced by just about anything on the ground (radars, motors, generators, etc.).
4. HUMINT or human intelligence: The oldest form of intelligence—study and analysis based on information from human sources such as informants.
5. OSINET or open source intelligence: The study and analysis of data from open press, Internet, technical industry documents, group literature, etc.

Every one of the aforementioned disciplines can be found in everyday law enforcement. For example, MASINT is often referred to as modus operandi (MO) and is used to find the unique characteristics of a crime and attribute it to an individual. HUMINT is simply confidential informants or snitches. No matter which discipline or what the mission at hand, it is easy to point out that many personnel focus strictly on one discipline. However, it is usually OSINET that is overlooked, misunderstood, and difficult to corroborate at most levels of crime and intelligence analysis. An issue to be realized with OSINET is that terrorists and terrorist organizations, as in al-Qaeda's training manual, note that approximately 80% of the information needed to formulate an attack can be found through open source means. Even the U.S. military's Operation Able Danger noted that they developed many of their links and associations from terabytes of open source information. Part of the problem being faced is a lack of clear understanding regarding the role and abilities of intelligence analysts.

In a 1997 document, 15 axioms for intelligence analysts were published by a member of the CIA Directorate of Intelligence,[6] which should be considered to provide valuable insight into what principles can be used in everyday analytical conduct. The principles that should be used as guidelines by all analysts in their daily duties regardless of agency size are outlined as follows[6]:

Believe in your own professional judgments.
Be aggressive, and do not fear being wrong.
It is better to be mistaken than to be wrong.
Avoid mirror imaging at all costs.
Intelligence is of no value if it is not disseminated.
Coordination is necessary, but do not settle for the lowest common denominator.
When everyone agrees on an issue, something is probably wrong.
The consumer does not care how much you know; just tell him what is important.
Form is never more important than substance.
Aggressively pursue the collection of information you need.
Do not take the editing process too seriously.
Know your community counterparts and talk to them frequently.
Never let your career take precedence over your job.
Being an intelligence analyst is not a popularity contest.
Do not take your job or yourself too seriously.

Not all 15 axioms are employed by everyone or are applicable in every agency all the time, but they should be used as guiding principles in defining the roles and missions of analytical personnel. There is, however, one more axiom that might be added to the list: possess a fundamental grasp of the topic. Many of the cited axioms are expanded on in detail in subsequent sections. Use of the axioms is directed at the analysts, but they are only one piece of the whole picture. Agency leaders and command staff personnel also play vital roles in defining analytical positions and how they are used. In *Psychology of Intelligence Analysis*,[7] former CIA employee Jack Davis states in the Introduction that "to ensure sustained improvement in assessing complex issues, analysis must be treated as more than a substantive and organizational process" (p. 7). Definitions mean little if an agency's leaders do not establish an organizational environment that utilizes analysts in their intended role. It is incumbent upon these leaders to ensure that analysts are used to their fullest capabilities, certified and trained properly, and not relegated to mundane data entry duties.

## WHAT IS HOMELAND SECURITY AND TERRORISM ANALYSIS?

Undertaking and employing analytical methods is a bold concept that can be construed as proactive and controversial. Both are contrary to traditional law enforcement practices of being reactive to crime and being wary of controversial situations. Now we are adding the exotic world of homeland security and terrorism that by necessity requires law enforcement personnel to be proactive. Waiting could have detrimental effects that would be felt beyond the traditional jurisdictional boundaries of any one particular agency. It is usually after a tragic event that we observe many different people and agencies analyzing the occurrence and looking for what went wrong, what could have been done prior to the event, as well as what a law enforcement agency had neglected to do in that particular case. Performing analysis after a significant event for law enforcement is done to identify deficiencies and best practices and to improve future performance. However, with the availability of modern training, technology, and professional analysts, law enforcement has the ability to make an informed and educated statement to predict or anticipate future behavior.

One way of looking at analysis is that it is to law enforcement what market research is to business. Just as market research investigates every aspect of a business from customer-based demographics to target market, analysts charged with homeland security and terrorism need to look at every available variable. Traditional analysis seeks to build a probable cause for substantiating criminal charges, usually after developing some sort of investigative lead. With homeland security and terrorism analysis, law enforcement personnel cannot afford to wait for any lead to come in. They need to proactively seek not only terrorist activity but also potential terrorists, links, and targets.

Traditional law enforcement has been reluctant to share information due to jurisdictional reasons, confidentiality constraints, and issues associated with case ownership. With a routine case, items such as case ownership are not seen as negatives and generally do not have detrimental effects on criminal cases. This is not the case with homeland security and terrorism. In homeland security, and terrorism analysis and investigations, these limitations need to be overcome. Due to the nature of the assignment and the sensitivity of the materials to be analyzed, information must be handled carefully. Personnel need to understand that the intelligence they are dealing with is not limited to any one jurisdiction. Knowledge may be power, but in the world of homeland security, failure to share this knowledge, understand what needs to be analyzed, and think globally could have a devastating impact.

### Understanding What Needs to be Analyzed

Since the advent of computer technology, law enforcement agencies have sought to enhance their capabilities to increase efficiency and effectiveness by implementing technological initiatives within their jurisdictions. However, due to bureaucratic and budgetary restrictions, many agencies strive to purchase the best systems possible from the lowest bidders. This has the potential of leaving an agency with outdated systems that meet the needs of the agency but lack compatibility with the systems of other agencies seeking to share information. Also, due to implementation phases and the need to work out the bugs, many analysts find themselves being trained only in the basics and forced to learn the rest on the job. It is one thing to know which buttons to push but another to understand the topic you seek to analyze. In order to completely understand the topic, one must have a basic understanding of history, theories, practices, and needs prior to analyzing.

Not all terrorists or their organizations are based overseas. In *Countering the New Terrorism*,[8] Ian O. Lesser states that "in the United States, right-wing militia and survivalist movements are a prominent source of terrorist risk, and are increasingly networked with like-minded groups worldwide" (p. 104). Law enforcement should therefore look in its own backyard before looking overseas for terrorists or terrorist-related activity. Terrorist groups, domestic and foreign, as well as organized hate groups constantly seek to enhance their membership and expand their reach of violence. What better way to reach the United States or any other country than by locating, associating with, and collaborating with local groups that have an antigovernment stand? This might be a shocking concept for some law enforcement agencies. After all, the media portrays a terrorist as someone coming from the Middle East who does not look or sound like the average American. Are we being publicly misled? Should we be looking in our own backyards or only overseas in search of terrorism? The answers to these questions probably vary from place to place, but one thing is certain. We are dealing with groups full of hatred that have a transnational reach or following. Therefore, law enforcement agencies will not be able to deal with terrorism in the same way that it deals with crime. Also, an analyst is more apt to identify activity in an expeditious manner if he or she is armed with a fundamental understanding of terrorism and a skill for reviewing variables without prejudice or bias.

David C. Rapoport (1988) points out that he started preparing a terrorism report for the Canadian Broadcasting Company in 1969. Fifteen years later when he wrote and edited the book *Inside Terrorist Organizations*,[9] he noted that the "academic enterprise" (p. 1) grew exponentially in a very short period of time. More than 30 years later, with considerably more academic research and publications available on the topic, law enforcement agencies are beginning to realize the magnitude of the field. Why reinvent the wheel? Many of the "who, what, where, when, why, and how" questions were answered for us. All we have to do now is understand how to implement and use this vast knowledge and research to our advantage.

## KEYS TO ANALYSIS

Analysts employed by law enforcement agencies throughout the country utilize various approaches, methods, and techniques when analyzing crime. These methods probably will not have a negative impact in the world of crime fighting. The fundamental approach is relatively simple. If we cannot prevent a crime, then we must do what we can to identify, apprehend, and prosecute the subject. In this approach, analysts review an array of crime reports and information usually submitted by their personnel. Whether this is done manually or through the latest technology is irrelevant, because unless a serial criminal is involved, time is often on the side of law enforcement when building a case. Many crimes go unreported, and agencies do not seek out this type of information. Even worse is that some law enforcement agencies even encourage the nonreporting of incidents as it helps to lower the published crime rate. This is more of a "how can we analyze something we don't know" issue. The same cannot be said for homeland security and terrorism analysis.

The six keys to analyzing information for intelligence that will remedy the need to get beyond street crimes are as follows:

1. Seek reported and unreported information in an expeditious manner in order to thwart any potential activity that may penetrate homeland security or cause terrorist-related activity.
2. Validate the authenticity and the accuracy of information received, and never discount anything without checking it against all variables or leads.
3. Know your data, resources, and capabilities.
4. Avoid becoming a one-dimensional analyst and instead look at all global factors, including the organization at hand.
5. Do not to jump to extremes.
6. Immerse yourself in the process.

The first key is to seek reported and unreported information in an expeditious manner in order to thwart any potential activity that may penetrate homeland security or cause terrorist-related activity. We are still seeking to deter, prevent, and arrest, but the difference is that we are doing it without delay.

Martha Crenshaw said, "Intelligence failures may preclude warning of impending attack, or paradoxically an overload of warnings, especially if they are imprecise, may induce complacency or the 'cry wolf' syndrome."[10] Although these are valid concerns, it is up to the analytical and intelligence community to maintain professional decorum, enhance training efforts, educate itself and its members, streamline and standardize practices, and validate and document all information.

The second key is to validate the authenticity and the accuracy of information received and never discount anything without checking it against all variables or leads. Specific tactical terrorist warnings of impending attacks are rarely received. According to Crenshaw, "governments often know that a terrorist attack is probable and what the likely targets are, but cannot predict the day or hour of the attack" (p. 15).[10]

Following this, the third key is to know your data, resources, and capabilities. An analyst who has an in-depth or intimate knowledge of the data is more likely to take a little bit of information and transform it into a viable piece of intelligence that may aid in operational and deployment strategies that can curb terrorist or hate crime activity. Also, the analyst is able to corroborate and challenge information as it is introduced, by analyzing it against a wide array of variables. Analysts who know what resources are available are able to identify potential targets and their associations as well as to recognize oddities.

The fourth key warns against becoming a one-dimensional analyst and exhorts instead to look at all global factors, including the organization at hand. Analysts who look at only one facet or variable will inevitably fail. With homeland security and terrorism analysis, analysts need to look beyond the potential of identifying a terrorist or a terrorist's target. Terrorist organizations cannot survive without the support and membership of like-minded individuals. Crenshaw states, "Organizational analysis explains not only why terrorism continues regardless of political results but why it starts" (p. 21).[10] We need to identify what would make it hard for such organizations to recruit and keep loyal members, and we need to identify their weaknesses. Many law enforcement agencies did this for years by tracking gang members and their affiliations. It can be argued that many groups classified as terrorist or hate organizations today may have been viewed as elaborate gangs or extremist movements just 10 years ago.

The fifth key warns against jumping to extremes. We cannot look only for those things that may lead to WMDs. In the 1970s, the U.S. Army developed a spectrum of conflict. As shown in Figure 1.1, terrorism is right after riots and disorders and before guerilla warfare on its spectrum of conflict. WMDs are at the end of the spectrum. So why is the public focusing on the end? Is it because WMDs are more sensational than terrorism? Whatever the views the public may have, law enforcement agencies need to remain focused and approach the situation systematically, with care, and caution. The media cannot be allowed to dictate the law enforcement analytical process when dealing with terrorism.

The sixth and final key to analyzing information for intelligence is to immerse oneself in the process. No matter what technology is used, the human factor is essential and cannot be replaced.

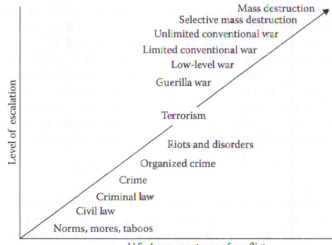

**FIGURE 1.1**    The U.S. Army spectrum of conflict.

Analysts possess experience, have preconceptions based on assumptions and expectations, and know the makeup and limitations of a jurisdiction.

## DETERRENCE, PREVENTION, ARREST, AND TARGET HARDENING

"In meeting a threat, government has two basic alternatives: defense and deterrence."[10] This statement was published in 1988 by Martha Crenshaw (p. 16) when speaking of terrorism, and it remains relevant to this day for the government and law enforcement. However, for law enforcement agencies the alternatives are often construed as prevention and deterrence. Crenshaw noted that "the exercise of prevention is based on estimates of an enemy's intention and of its capabilities" (p. 16).[10] In this section, a modern, all-inclusive approach to prevention that is used by analysts when aiding their agencies in dealing with the criminal element is expanded upon. This approach can be applied to terrorism-related matters as well as organized hate groups. Based on a review of early scholarly and academic publications, analysts are able to become multidimensional by looking for variables that enhance deterrence, prevention, arrest, and target hardening for homeland security, organized hate crime, or terrorist-related matters. These four components are also discussed in detail in a publication sponsored by the National Law Enforcement and Corrections Technology Center (NLECTC)'s crime mapping and analysis program. They are discussed in the context of tactical and investigative crime, but they are also applicable to matters of homeland security and organized crime. The publication *Advanced Crime Mapping Topics*[11] was the result of a symposium held in 2001 consisting of a panel of experts from around the country. These experts came from all areas of the criminal justice world and included analytical practitioners, police managers, cartographers, academics, and policy makers. The four concepts presented at the symposium are outlined in the following subsections.[11]

### DETERRENCE

"Analytically, deterrence of anything from street crime to biological terrorism may rely on fear of consequences such as prison or execution imposed by governments or on fear of social condemnation" (p. 28).[11] In the realm of law enforcement, when dealing with street crime, this statement is accurate and is often a goal set by agencies seeking to address a particular trend. Whether through the use of social programs, such as the Drug Abuse Resistance Education (DARE) program, or rehabilitation measures, law enforcement and governments continuously strive to deter crime. The above statement regarding biological terrorism should not be discounted, although this form of terrorism seldom occurs and will probably never be encountered by many of the thousands of law enforcement personnel. The best chance of deterrence when dealing with terrorism is the following of sound analytical practices designed to place a stranglehold on the financial means and access targets of terrorists and to limit their ability to recruit new members. Terrorists have little fear of social condemnation or execution. Their beliefs and their desire to be viewed as martyrs for their cause dramatically reduce the likelihood of any form of deterrence. If a person is willing to become a homicide bomber and die for his or her beliefs and group, there is little that government can do in the form of sanctions to curb it. However, by proactively analyzing all terrorist-related information without undue delay, law enforcement personnel should be able to indirectly deter potential terrorist activities.

### PREVENTION

Of the four areas of concern mentioned in the section "deterrence, prevention, arrest, and target hardening," prevention through proper and timely analysis of information is where law enforcement can have the greatest impact on terrorism. Due to the structure and management of terrorist organizations, which is discussed in depth in "terrorism: structure and management," (Chapter 2), the likelihood of law enforcement personnel infiltrating a cell or column is highly improbable. This, coupled with the concept of leaderless resistance or a lone wolf, would leave law enforcement personnel virtually handcuffed. However, through effective and accurate analysis, command staff and government personnel can be armed with intelligence that greatly aids operational and deployment strategies designed to prevent a future attack.

There are three methods of terrorist activity prevention[12]:

1. Monitor groups suspected of planning terrorist activities in order to prevent their actions or arrest and incapacitate them.
2. Deny such groups what they need to carry out acts of terrorism.
3. Monitor the acquisition of various supplies, information, or access required by terrorists, and then use this information to detect groups that are more likely to be contemplating acts of terrorism so the group can be watched.

These three methods of prevention, although broad-based, can be readily adapted by virtually any law enforcement agency by expanding databases and documenting all potential information received. With these methods, the initial step in identifying potential leads for developing further intelligence and for enhancing investigative practices can be realized.

Just as law enforcement agencies need to successfully identify and prevent terrorist-related activities, a terrorist needs to successfully complete his or her mission. Prevention of terrorism thus requires depriving terrorists of one or more of five specific conditions required to achieve their ends[12]:

1. Locate the target.
2. Get to the target.
3. Accomplish this with needed associates.
4. Have the necessary information, equipment, and facilities.
5. Expect enough safety to justify taking the risks.

Knowing that these conditions exist for a terrorist, it is important for analytical personnel to be aware of terrorists' needs when reviewing information for possible intelligence leads.

## ARREST

In the world of law enforcement, locating and arresting a subject is the goal. In the realm of homeland security and terrorism, an arrest may come too late. We cannot afford to wait for an incident to be planned or to occur. Therefore, every effort should be made to focus on prevention, deterrence, and target hardening.

Arrest with regard to organized hate group members can pose both logistic and intelligence problems. Hate group members are often investigated and monitored in the same fashion as gang members. For law enforcement agencies, opportunities for gleaning intelligence from the ranks of organized hate group membership are far greater than those for gleaning intelligence from a terrorist organization based overseas. This is partly because hate groups publicly expose their beliefs and sometimes their actions. Once arrested, a larger issue of where and how to detain these individuals is created. Foreign-based groups are often incarcerated on a military installation or in a maximum-security federal penitentiary. Organized hate group members usually end up in county jails and state prisons. Hatred permeates so much from the ranks of these groups that several correctional facilities have implemented extensive databases and geographic mapping applications to capture hate group information while members are incarcerated.

## TARGET HARDENING

The intent of target hardening is to reduce the possibility of attack by strengthening the perceived weakness of a given target. However, this is not a perfect science. Terrorists do not shy away from secure or fortified targets, which are also known as hard targets. This is evident from the numerous attacks conducted by terrorists on military installations and equipment such as the 1996 bombing of the Khobar Towers in Saudi Arabia or the attack on the USS *Cole* in October 2000, which killed 17 American sailors. Keeping this in mind, one should not overlook or underevaluate any potential target. Another group of targets that requires consideration is what can be referred to as soft targets, such as hotels, restaurants, and public venues. These potential targets are often taken for granted and are seen as locations that have little notoriety to offer if attacked. However, in the world of terrorism, nothing can be taken for granted.

By analyzing the array of information available to law enforcement agencies, it is possible for government officials to identify likely targets of potential terrorists. Armed with this information and with the use of a wide range of intelligence tools, officials charged with preventing possible attacks can make better informed decisions and can assist identified targets in strengthening the weaknesses that may cause them to be an attractive choice for a terrorist attack. When initiating a proactive target-hardening posture, all aspects should be reviewed. Physical as well as psychological targets need to be evaluated and addressed. Items such as access control, security, identifications, and ingress and egress are all part of target hardening. Terrorists are looking not just to inflict bodily harm, they also count on the psychological impact a tragic event will have on the public. Whether their intent is direct or indirect, terrorists know that through their course of actions they may injure or kill a small number of individuals in any terrorist incident. They know that their actions will be repeatedly played in the media, creating a psychological impression on the public. For instance, look at the impact felt by the airline industry after September 11, 2001, when the number of passengers dramatically decreased. The reason for this decrease in the number of passengers traveling by air was fear, and this is something that cannot be addressed with target hardening.

## CHAPTER CONCEPTS

The chapter concepts can be summarized as follows:

The mission of analytical personnel is that of support, and the information obtained from analysis is used for strategic planning. Also, the topic to be analyzed, as well as what is meant by homeland security analysis, needs to be understood.

Currently, the U.S. government has no institution primarily dedicated to the systematic analysis of intelligence on potential terrorist threats within the country.

Intelligence has been used by law enforcement agencies since the 1920s. There is also a need to define analytical roles within an agency and to know the difference in the working definitions of crime and intelligence analysts.

Fifteen axioms for intelligence analysts are described. They provide valuable insight into what principles can be used in everyday analytical conduct.

Six keys to analyzing information for intelligence remedy the need to get beyond street crimes.

## REFERENCES

1. Jenkins, B. M. 1999. Foreward. In *Countering the New Terrorism*, ed. I. O. Lesser et al. Santa Monica, CA: Rand, p. iii.
2. The Commission on Accreditation for Law Enforcement Agencies (CALEA). 1999. *Crime Analysis*. Washington, DC: CALEA.
3. U.S. Department of Justice, Bureau of Justice Statistics. 1999. *Bridging Gaps in Police Crime Data*. 1. U.S. Department of Justice Office of Justice Programs, Washington, DC.
4. Peterson, M. B. 1994. *Applications in Criminal Analysis*. Vol. 3. Westport, CT: Greenwood Press, pp. 115–17.
5. Gottlieb, S., S. Arenberg, and R. Singh. 1994. *Crime Analysis: From First Report to Final Arrest*. Montclair, CA: Alpha Publishing, p. 11.

6. Watanabe, F. 1997. How to Succeed in the DI: Fifteen Axioms for Intelligence Analysts. *Stud Intell* 1:1.
7. Heuer, R. J., Jr. 1999. *Psychology of Intelligence Analysis*. Center for the Study of Intelligence, Central Intelligence Agency. http://www.cia.gov/csi/books/19104/art1.html (accessed February 17, 2003).
8. Lesser, I. O. et al. 1999. *Countering the New Terrorism, Implications for Strategy*. Santa Monica, CA: Rand, pp. 104.
9. Rapoport, D. C., ed. 1988. *Inside Terrorist Organizations*. New York: Columbia University Press, p. 1.
10. Crenshaw, M. 1988. Theories of Terrorism: Instrumental and Organizational Approaches. In *Inside Terrorist Organizations*, ed. D. C. Rapoport, pp. 14, 15, 16, 21. New York: Columbia University Press.
11. Cooper, J., E. Nelson, and M. Ronczkowski. 2002. Tactical/Investigative Analysis of Targeted Crimes. In *Advanced Crime Mapping Topics*, eds., Sean Bair, Rachel Boba, Noah Fritz, Dan Helms, Steven Hick, p. 28. Denver, CO: National Law Enforcement and Corrections Technology Center.
12. Heymann, P. B. 1998. *Terrorism and America: A Commonsense Strategy for a Democratic Society*. Cambridge, MA: MIT Press, pp. xi, xii, 84.

# 2 Understanding and Defining Terrorism

In the late 1970s, Michael Stohl authored an introduction to the book *The Politics of Terrorism*[1] entitled "Myths and Realities of Political Terrorism." Referring to terrorism, he notes: "The burgeoning journalistic and scholarly literature that has resulted from this increased awareness has unfortunately not been accompanied by a commensurate increase in the understanding of the phenomenon" (p. 1).[1] Here we are some 40-plus years later, and has anything changed? Does the law enforcement community understand any better? The answer is no. If academics and scholars are continually struggling to understand terrorism and its repercussions, it is probable that law enforcement personnel are just beginning to understand and address the matter. This chapter is designed to aid the law enforcement community in understanding and defining terrorism, terrorist activity, and potential threats.

It has been explained that terrorists and their adversaries act in ways to change each other's behavior, and if a terrorist group fails in an activity it is because the government has virtually eliminated any possibility that the group's actions are rewarded. If law enforcement personnel, particularly analytical and intelligence personnel, have a sound foundation and understanding of terrorism, terrorist activity, and what a terrorist is, then government will be able to identify and change or eliminate the behavioral opportunities of those seeking to violate or encroach upon homeland security measures.

Leaders of terrorist organizations may be reluctant to see their purpose accomplished and the organization's utility ended. Terrorists may look for incremental gains to sustain group morale without ending the members' dependence on the organization, which is similar to how many street gangs work. It is important that law enforcement personnel are keenly aware of this because traditionally, with the arrest of a criminal there is closure to a crime series. Many crimes occur because there are opportunities for such activities to take place. However, with terrorism the activity or event is usually well planned, and once committed the organization will regroup and initiate a strategy for its next move. Just as the definition of terrorism has changed over the decades, the causes of some groups have changed with time. This affords them the opportunity to garner support from different sectors and reinvent themselves in an effort to sustain life, enlist new members, and gain financial means. Defining terrorism is extremely difficult because it changes with time and historical context.

## DEFINING TERRORISM

The definition of terrorism has been much debated and written about for decades. Countless books have entire chapters dedicated to this topic. There are many working definitions of terrorism. In *Terrorism: An Introduction*, Jonathan R. White gives six "official" definitions of terrorism. Five of these are from various U.S. government agencies. Which one is the most accurate? It depends on your position, mission, and the period in which you seek to define terrorism. Three of the more commonly cited definitions come from the Federal Bureau of Investigation (FBI), U.S. Department of State, and U.S. Department of Defense, and they are outlined here:

1. The FBI defines terrorism as "the unlawful use of force and violence against persons or property to intimidate or coerce a government, the civilian population, or any segment thereof, in furtherance of political or social objectives."[2]
2. The U.S. Department of State defines terrorism as "an activity, directed against persons involving violent acts or acts dangerous to human life, which would be a criminal violation if committed within the jurisdiction of the U.S.; and is intended to intimidate or coerce

    a civilian population; to influence the policy of a government by intimidation or coercion; or to affect the conduct of a government by assassination or kidnapping."[3]

3. The Department of Defense defines terrorism as "the calculated use of violence or threat of violence to inculcate fear; intended to coerce or to intimidate governments or societies in the pursuit of goals that are generally political, religious, or ideological."[3]

    The similarities are evident, but which is correct, and why is it that one government cannot have just one definition? The answer is simple: Each agency's mission is fundamentally different. However, one should not get hung up on having an all-inclusive definition of terrorism, but rather focus on an understanding of what makes up terrorism. Phillip B. Heyman[4] pointed out that there have "been many attempts to define 'terrorism' as clearly as we define murder, robbery, or rape. The effort has been less than successful" (p. 3). In this section, the analytical practitioner and law enforcement investigators are given a foundation from which to fulfill their daily duties concerning terrorism and terrorist activity apart from a historical perspective of the topic.

    Snow[5] gives us the logical and simple explanation that "the root of the term terrorism itself is from the Latin word *terrere*, which means 'to frighten'" (p. 1). Looking at modern criminal statutes such as those for robbery, one finds terminology like "the taking of property by force or fear." Has law enforcement been dealing with terrorism for many decades without realizing it? Lesser et al.[6] note, "Terrorism is, among other things, a weapon used by the weak against the strong" (p. 85). Again, using the robbery reference, many officers and detectives would argue that most robbers are intellectually and emotionally weak and use their social inabilities against those they see as financially strong in order to further their cause of financial gain.

    Providing a definition for the root of terrorism can cause much debate and confusion. Deciding which definition should be adopted is another dilemma. Therefore, it is suggested that law enforcement agencies and analysts use a standardized and broad definition if they must have one. The following definitions of terrorism, according to U.S. Code 22 USC, Sec. 2656f(d), are straightforward and can be used by all parties when dealing with terrorism and terrorist activity:

> The term "terrorism" means premeditated, politically motivated violence perpetrated against noncombatant targets by subnational groups or clandestine agents, usually intended to influence an audience.
>
> The term "international terrorism" means terrorism involving citizens or the territory of more than one country.

    Although having a written definition of terrorism can be helpful, agencies should not dwell on the definition. It is well to remember that the definition of terrorism has been debated for decades, changed throughout the years, and is not going to be changed by any one law enforcement agency overnight. Besides, this is just one facet that needs defining. Terrorist activity, and who is a terrorist, must also be defined.

## DEFINING TERRORIST ACTIVITY

Terrorist activity is designed to make a statement. This activity is a form of propaganda because the terrorist knows that the media will cover sensational and tragic events. Media coverage serves as a venue for expressing not only what physically can be done but also what will likely affect those who view the activity psychologically. Terrorist activity takes many forms, including assassinations, bombings, arson, sabotage, hostage taking, property damage, and anarchy. According to Gurr's empirical analyses as cited by White,[7] most terrorist activities last 18 months from the onset of violence. Preparation behind a terrorist activity may go on for months, if not years, before the actual first incident occurs. It is important that the law enforcement community takes note of this, because law enforcement has traditionally been reactive to events. With terrorist-related activity, if one is not proactive the community can be adversely affected. However, terrorist activity in the world of law enforcement has gone unnoticed—or has it? The fact is that many agencies have been gathering information on many activities classified under various other guises, such as labor movements, anarchy, social unrest, and anti-civil rights actions. The FBI does not measure criminal terrorism, but it has gathered information on numerous reported hate crimes since the 1990s. Looking back, is it possible that some of these crimes could have been viewed as terrorist activity then? Can they be viewed as such even now? What is a working definition of terrorist activity? The U.S. Department of State defines terrorist activity in section 212(a)(3)(B)[8] of the Immigration and Nationality Act as follows:

(ii)   TERRORIST ACTIVITY DEFINED—As used in this Act, the term "terrorist activity" means any activity which is unlawful under the laws of the place where it is committed (or which, if committed in the United States, would be unlawful under the laws of the United States or any State) and which involves any of the following:

(I)    The hijacking or sabotage of any conveyance (including an aircraft, vessel, or vehicle)

(II)   The seizing or detaining, and threatening to kill, injure, or continue to detain, another individual in order to compel a third person (including a governmental organization) to do or abstain from doing any act as an explicit or implicit condition for the release of the individual seized or detained.

(III)  A violent attack upon an internationally protected person (as defined in section 1116(b)(4) of title 18, United States Code) or upon the liberty of such a person

(IV)   An assassination

(V)    The use of any:
  (a)   Biological agent, chemical agent, or nuclear weapon or device, or
  (b)   Explosive or firearm (other than for mere personal monetary gain), with intent to endanger, directly or indirectly, the safety of one or more individuals or to cause substantial damage to property

(V)    A threat, attempt, or conspiracy to do any of the foregoing

Although some of these activities appear to be an obvious fit for terrorist activity, personnel on the front line—law enforcement and analytical personnel—should not overlook anything as a potential terrorist activity. When law enforcement strips down the above definition, most of the activities it covers appear to be crimes at nearly every state level. It does not take the actions of an entire group to justify terrorist activity; it only takes one. Just like a 1,000-piece jigsaw puzzle, at the beginning the picture appears confusing, but as the pieces are put together it becomes more obvious. Lose one piece and the picture is never completed. Analysts deal with the pieces right out of the box, so it is important to maintain them and arrange them without delay. Each piece of information is one piece of the puzzle. Work the information and you will be more successful at linking the pieces and less likely to overlook data as well as remaining open minded in your review of the data. Work the crimes, you will find yourself working to fit into the elements of the crime and striving to meet legal guidelines in your reviewing of data rather than remaining open minded. The elements of a crime can be viewed as a subliminal bias, which may cause delays in the linking of the pieces. One piece of the puzzle that must be identified is the form of terrorism or terrorist activity being investigated.

## FORMS OF TERRORISM

Terrorism comes in many diabolical forms that are as diverse as the definitions of terrorism. Whether to lessen the blow or to identify why a terrorist activity took place, being aware of the forms of terrorism assists the mainstream population in identifying and cataloging serious events. It is hoped that this knowledge will help to deter and apprehend suspects.

Over the years, the term terrorism has been redefined and reinvented on many fronts. One word that will often be at the top of the list of definitions is "political." In Alex Schmid's review and analysis of 109 terrorism definitions, he reported that "political" was the second most common element used when defining terrorism, with a frequency rate of 65%.[9] Only violence and fear had a higher frequency rate (83.5%).

Political terrorism is not the only form of terrorism. Most definitions of terrorism have an underlying tone of politics associated with them, but there is a need to expand on political terrorism as a direct form of terrorism. Terrorism comes in many different forms, styles, types, and methods. However, for the purposes of the law enforcement community only six forms of terrorism are discussed. These forms are the ones that most law enforcement officials are likely to encounter when fulfilling their duties. The working definitions of the six forms of terrorism enumerated in this section are outlined as follows:

1. *Political terrorism* refers to an act or a series of acts directed toward bringing about political or policy change through the use of force, intimidation, or threatened use of force.
2. *Ecological terrorism* refers to an act or series of acts designed to slow, impede, or halt the growth or harvesting of a nation's natural resources.
3. *Agricultural terrorism* refers to the use of chemicals or toxins (biological means) against some component of the agricultural industry in an attempt to disrupt distribution or consumption of goods by the general public.
4. *Narco-terrorism* refers to terrorist acts conducted in an attempt to divert attention from illegal drug and narcotic operations. This term is usually applied to activities of groups that use the drug trade to fund terrorism.
5. *Biological terrorism* refers to the threat of use of biological or chemical agents to injure, maim, or cause death.
6. *Cyberterrorism* refers to the use of computer resources to intimidate and infiltrate public, private, and government computer-based infrastructures through the use of viruses or through code breaking in an attempt to disrupt service, or destroy or compromise data.

## POLITICAL TERRORISM

In Ted Robert Gurr's[10] study on political terrorism, he noted several characteristics of groups that operated in the 1960s. Although this pertains to groups that operated roughly 50 years ago, many of the characteristics that he identified still ring true and are applicable to some modern-day groups.

Political terrorism has often been seen as a left-wing movement that virtually faded away in the United States after the 1970s. Individuals associated with these movements were considered political activists associated largely with underground movements. Although more prevalent during that era, political terrorism has existed for centuries. It is only now that we are coming to understand what makes up this form of terrorism and are identifying and developing methods of stymieing its activities.

Based on Gurr's characteristics of groups that operated in the 1960s, activities associated with political terrorist or left-wing groups can be misclassified and labeled as other forms of terrorism. This is due to their methods of operation and their use of explosive and incendiary devices, which are the archetypical weapons of political terrorism.[10] In order to avoid this confusion, Gurr identified three objective elements associated with political terrorism and stated that all three elements must be present for a terrorist activity to be classified as political terrorism. The three objective definitional elements based on his definition of political terrorism are as follows[10]:

1. Destructive violence is used by stealth rather than in open combat.
2. Some of the principal targets are political.
3. Actions are carried out by groups operating clandestinely and sporadically.

Gurr[10] went on to state that many of the targets of political terrorism are politicians, the military, and the police, and that most terrorist campaigns are short-lived.

## ECOLOGICAL TERRORISM

Incidents of ecological terrorism are sometimes reported publicly as random acts of destruction and are seldom seen as having an underlying agenda or cause. Individuals operating in these groups are viewed as radical environmentalists (tree huggers and elves, as in the Earth Liberation Front [ELF]). These groups and individuals are not necessarily interested in garnering public support. They have little belief that any policy or legislative changes posed by the government can bring about sufficient social changes. They follow the premise that ecosystems have an inherent worth that cannot be judged in relation to human needs and that if action is not taken to effect changes there will be mass extinctions of the human population.

Two of the most prevalent target groups of ecological terrorists are the U.S. Forest Service and the logging industry. Many groups that carry out this form of terrorism dismiss the fact that they are violent and deny being terrorists. They consider actions such as setting large fires or inserting metal spikes into trees slated for harvesting as deterrents required to keep logging companies from cutting down trees and destroying the environment. Their intentions are allegedly not designed to injure or kill individuals, but they cannot control the fires that are set or the lack of precautionary measures that could be employed to suppress their illegal actions.

## AGRICULTURAL TERRORISM

Agricultural terrorism, or agroterrorism, is a relatively new form of terrorism that has many potential deadly scenarios. This form of terrorism has the potential to cause a far greater impact on the multibillion-dollar economic and international trade of a country by contaminating goods and disrupting the export of goods, than the bombing of a single building. Opportunities to target designated sites are plentiful. There are approximately 1,912,000 farms and 87,000 food processing plants in the United States alone.[11] Most locations, for example, farms, are considered soft targets, and a terrorist act may go undetected for days or even weeks. Potential targets for agroterrorists include food handlers, processing facilities, grocery stores, restaurants, farms and ranches, livestock, crops, and food or agriculture transportation systems. This form of terrorism also includes the introduction of diseases to livestock.

## NARCO-TERRORISM

Narco-terrorism, or narcotic-related terrorism, is performed to further the aims of drug traffickers. These aims include financial gain, avoiding detection and apprehension, and establishing control over territories. This form of terrorism has been the focus of law enforcement personnel and militaries of a large number of countries for many years. Activities of narco-terrorists are often directed toward judges, prosecutors, politicians, and law enforcement officials in the form of assassinations, extortions, hijackings, bombings, and kidnappings.

## BIOLOGICAL TERRORISM

Biological or chemical terrorism has received much media attention in recent years largely due to its association with weapons of mass destruction. Just the thought of anthrax, smallpox, or some form of plague being spread can have crippling psychological implications. Biological agents attract a lot of media and Internet attention. Nearly 350,000 recorded results were returned in a recent Internet query with just one search engine. In reality, bioterrorism opportunities are perhaps the least likely scenarios to be encountered by law enforcement personnel. However, due to the catastrophic potential of biological or chemical terrorism, law enforcement personnel need to become familiar with, and be prepared for, the many different types of hazards that exist and the methods by which toxins can be ingested.

## CYBERTERRORISM

Cyberterrorism provides terrorists with the ability to operate in distant locations and to gain access to identities and financial records anywhere in the world. Terrorists operating in cyberspace are capable of accessing secure data banks, stealing or altering information, or destroying valuable data. Access to law enforcement, government, or military data files can aid a potential terrorist in avoiding detection. Cyberattacks may be geared toward disruption or denial of Internet service, or financial gain. Financial gain is sometimes associated with identity theft or reallocation of funds from accounts, both of which are considered white-collar crimes and do not receive much attention from law enforcement agencies or the general public. Cyberterrorist acts, although void of mass physical casualties, have the potential to inflict mass hysteria and economic fallout that can be detrimental to the global economy.

# HISTORY AND ROOTS OF MODERN TERRORISM

With a working definition of terrorism and terrorist activity in hand, it is important to know some of the history behind the evolution of terrorism. This will provide insight into the growth of the term terrorism as well as how terrorism became a modern-day obsession.

The Latin meaning of terrorism was explained in the section "Defining terrorism." However, the French are often credited with coining the term terrorism. The term terrorism originated in revolutionary France in the late 1700s period known as the Reign of Terror, and it has its roots in the Enlightenment period of the eighteenth century. Reign of Terror was the name given to the bloody violence imposed upon the French citizens by their revolutionary leader, Maximilien Robespierre.

By the mid-1800s, the term changed to describe violent revolutionaries who revolted against governments. In the early 1900s in the United States, the term was used to describe labor organizations and anarchists. The anarchists garnered perhaps the most attention from law enforcement agencies. At that time labor organizations were fighting for the working class, and they sought improvement in the work environment, employee rights, and financial equality. Although some labor organizations disrupted the normal flow of society through their demonstrations, they generally did not create mass hysteria or death. Anarchists, on the other hand, did what they could to disrupt societal law and order by whatever means possible in order to achieve their ends, regardless of who got in their way. Many of these anarchists were eventually rounded up and deported.

After World War II, the term terrorism changed again to be associated with nationalistic groups revolting against European domination. During the turbulent 1940s and 1950s, known as the postcolonial era, Europeans felt the repercussions of terrorism through nationalists seeking to end colonial rule. The two hardest hit countries were France and England—both had colonial settlements on various continents. Two of the major problem areas of the time were Algeria and Kenya. The French suffered greatly from terrorist attacks in Africa against colonialism in Algeria by the National Liberation Front (FLN). The English colonies in Kenya were targeted by the Mau Mau. Also during the 1940s, the State of Israel was formed in the Middle East. When the British replaced the Ottomans as the governing colonial force over the Palestinians and Jews in Palestine in what became known as the Balfour Declaration of 1917, they promised the Jews a home in Palestine. Over time, this grew into a conflict that saw the Jews trying to remove the British. They turned to urban terrorism and established the Irgun Zvai Leumi (national military organization), commonly referred to as the Irgun, as an underground terrorist organization to conduct terrorist activities against the British. These terrorist activities continued until about 1948, when Israel was recognized as a nation. Becoming a nation did not end the problem in the Middle East for Israel. Various groups, particularly the Palestinian Liberation Organization (PLO), continue to struggle against non-Arabs in the region.

Over the years that the Middle East conflict continued, much of the world saw a rise of the left wing. From the mid-1960s to the early 1980s, the term terrorism was associated with activities of left-wing groups worldwide, many of which were opposed to conflicts such as the Vietnam War.

Much of the activity experienced in the United States during this period was viewed as the work of left-wing groups, also referred to as "radicals," revolutionaries, or "extremists," such as the Symbionese Liberation Army. As left-wing groups diminished in number and importance, the rise of religious extremists was seen with the Iranian Revolution in 1979 and the transformation of Iran into an Islamic republic. Shortly after the transformation, Ayatollah Khomeini of Iran declared a holy war against Westerners. Iran is also said to have had an important role in the establishment of two terrorist organizations that are in existence to this day: (1) Hezbollah and (2) Islamic Jihad. Today, terrorism is associated with large groups, such as Hezbollah, al-Qaeda, the Islamic State in Iraq and Levant (ISIL), and Islamic State (IS). The last two are commonly referred to simply as ISIS by many in the public and media. These organizations are capable of working independently from a state, with members who are considered to be violent religious fanatics or extremists.

Terrorism was also once characterized by changes in the ways intellectuals approached social problems and class-based revolutions or revolts, such as the Russian Revolution. One thing is certain: the meaning and style of terrorism has changed with society over time. Regardless of who defines terrorism, this fact is agreed upon consistently. Other driving forces that changed the meaning of terrorism over time are the media, advancement in communication capabilities and sophisticated weapons, and various socioeconomic factors.

## THE EVOLUTION OF DOMESTIC TERRORISM

Domestic terrorism is not a new phenomenon, and it did not suddenly appear on the shores of the United States on September 11, 2001. It has been around for over two centuries. The meaning of terrorism has changed with time. The differences in the definitions of terrorism and in social viewpoints of the topic have led to many incidents of domestic terrorism being categorized as actions of extremists, anarchists, radicals, revolutionaries, and even unions. Depending on the time and era, incidents we would now consider as terrorism were seen as antigovernment or antisocial behaviors, or were perceived as improving the way of life for a fledgling nation.

One of the first incidents of antifederal behavior in the United States occurred in 1791, when the federal government levied an excise tax on the production of whiskey. It has been said that this led to many revolutionary acts, and this might be construed as the first terrorist threat faced by the country. However, actions against the king of England that occurred during this era were seen as revolutionary, and not terroristic, activities. Revolutionary, martyr, leader, and terrorist are all subjective labels.

Throughout the history of the United States, there have been numerous incidents of antigovernment behavior that by today's standards would be considered terrorist activities. Prior to the American Civil War that took place in the early 1800s, an anarchist group known as the "Know-Nothings" operated in the eastern United States. They were a secret society with an anti-immigrant agenda, which was committed to a white Protestant ruling class. No matter how many anarchist incidents they initiated, the membership regularly claimed that they were not involved, thereby avoiding apprehension by law enforcement agencies. Deborah Able[12] reports that the nativist movement associated with the Know-Nothings became the basis for a conservative political party known as the American Party. This is the same party under whose auspices Millard Fillmore ran for president in 1856.

Violent ideological extremism also dominated many issues in the 1800s, up to and during the Civil War. Much of the war activity was geared toward Southern states seeking to preserve their rights. Most Southerners were not fighting to preserve slavery but to preserve the power of local governments. With the end of the Civil War, revolutionary terrorism and repressionist terrorism made their appearances as labor movements and grew in the post-Civil War era. Primarily during the 1870s and 1880s, rural movements were complemented by labor violence and anarchism from the left wing began to emerge. In the early 1900s, anarchists wreaked havoc in the United States with one incident that led to the assassination of a president. The response at the time was to round up the anarchists and deport them, usually to Europe. The assassination of President William McKinley in 1901 by anarchist Leon Czolgosz is just one instance of the long history of political violence in the United States; but until recently, this action was not interpreted as terrorism.

In the era immediately preceding World War II, groups behind nationalistic movements were viewed as terrorist groups since they revolted against European authority. Through the decades, particularly in the 1960s, the character of American terrorism began to change. It became known as a radical phenomenon, although the antigovernment behavior went beyond mere picketing and demonstrations. Left-wing terrorism began to lose its importance after the Vietnam War and modern right-wing extremism began to emerge, which came to fruition around 1984 with the violent activity of the hate movement. With the arrival of the new millennium, the term terrorism came to be associated with large groups possessing strong beliefs based on religion and violent fanaticism based on some particular causes such as the environment.

Domestic terrorism has been present in the United States for decades in many forms. Although there have been numerous changes over the years, the structure and makeup of domestic terrorist groups and classifications of domestic terrorists have remained relatively consistent for the past 25 years. Based on this consistency, the FBI has ultimately developed a broad listing for the types of terrorist groups or terrorists found in the United States. The three types of domestic terrorists according to the FBI are as follows:

1. Left wing
2. Right wing
3. Special interest (e.g., abortion clinic bombings)

Table 2.1 demonstrates the characteristic and demographical differences between left-wing and right-wing members.[13] Special interest terrorists are often seen as lone wolves or members of a leaderless resistance with views that are extreme and skewed and may be originally based on either the left or the right wings. Such radical or extremist domestic groups or individuals randomly select their targets based on the presumption that they are associated with a segment of the population that opposes their point of view.

Domestic right-wing terrorist groups often adhere to the principles of racial supremacy and embrace antigovernment and antiregulatory beliefs. They generally engage in activity that is protected by constitutional guarantees of free speech and assembly. Many of these groups attempt to tame their rhetoric in order to appeal to a broader segment of the population. Left-wing groups, on the other hand, generally profess a revolutionary socialist doctrine and view themselves as protectors against capitalism. Special interest groups in the 1980s through the 1990s were often associated with abortion

---

**TABLE 2.1**
**Profiling Terrorists**

| Characteristic | Right Wing | Left Wing |
|---|---|---|
| Social change perspective | Reactionary | Revolutionary |
| Social class membership | Lower/middle | Lower/middle/upper |
| Leadership | Male dominated | Egalitarian |
| Marital status | Married | Single/divorced/separated |
| Age | 16–76 | 25–45 |
| Educational level | High school | College |
| Religious belief | Fundamental | Agnostic/atheist |
| Criminal planning | Impulsive | Meticulous |

*Source*: T. O'Connor, http://faculty.ncwc.edu/toconnor/392/spy/terrorism.htm (November 2002), North Carolina Wesleyan College.

---

clinic attacks. Today, these groups are seen as anarchists and extremist socialist groups seeking to resolve specific issues rather than effect widespread political change. Groups and individuals often emerge from the extreme fringes of the animal rights, pro-life, and environmental movements. Although much of the terrorist activity seen in the United States can be grouped into the aforementioned categories, terrorist activity is too broad to be limited to just three types.

In 1987, the FBI expanded on these three types of terrorism. In the *FBI Law Enforcement Bulletin*,[14] John Harris named five categories of domestic terrorist groups. These groups, which were recognized by the FBI in 1987, are still applicable today. The five groups are summarized as follows:

1. Left wing (white leftists)
2. Right-wing extremists
3. Puerto Rican leftists
4. Black militants
5. Jewish extremists

When reviewing the list of existing domestic terrorist groups, one can readily associate a group to a category. But just as with the FBI's types of domestic terrorists, a sixth group category can be suggested as that of "special interest."

In the United States, there are as many as 400 right-wing groups that can be classified as domestic terrorist groups, with anywhere from 10,000 to 100,000 members. In a speech before the Senate Select Committee on Intelligence[15] on February 6, 2002, Dale L. Watson, executive assistant director of counterterrorism and counterintelligence for the FBI, reported that in the preceding decade right-wing extremism overtook left-wing terrorism as the most dangerous domestic terrorist threat to the United States. He went on to note that two special interest extremist groups, the Animal Liberation Front (ALF) and the ELF, had committed approximately 600 criminal acts in the United States since 1996 resulting in damages in excess of $42 million.[15] Interestingly, in this statement to the Senate these two extremists groups were viewed as domestic terrorist threats, although their actions were described as criminal. This can be attributed to the lack of coordinated and direct information available on domestic groups.

According to MILNET, which was an open-source military information database and a research tool used by researchers, historians, and academics, no U.S. government agency maintains a formal list of domestic terrorist groups. However, there are two private nonprofit organizations that monitor groups in the United States under the designation of organized hate groups, (1) the Anti-Defamation League (ADL) and (2) the Southern Poverty Law Center (SPLC). The SPLC[16] documented 676 active hate groups in the United States in its 2001 Intelligence Report. In 2002, this number increased by nearly 5% to 708 organized hate groups (M. Potok, personal communication, March 10, 2003). This is a dramatic rise from the 240 reported in 1996. The actual active membership numbers for hate groups are tough to ascertain because although conservative estimates reflect 25,000 members, there are possibly as many as 150,000 "armchair racists" who espouse the beliefs without necessarily taking any action.[17] The fact that there is no officially designated government agency that maintains a formal list is significant. Should some intelligence be developed regarding a domestic terrorist group, it may be hard to qualify and quantify this information within official government ranks.

In recent years, although much has been written about international terrorist groups, little information is available on known domestic terrorist groups. Domestic terrorist groups may be dismissed as conglomerations of radicals, whiners, extremists, fanatics, and hate groups. No matter what the reference, they are dangerous. In a statement for the record before the U.S. Senate on May 10, 2001, the then director of the FBI Louis J. Freeh remarked that domestic terrorist groups represent interests that span the full spectrum of political and economic viewpoints as well as social issues. He stated that FBI investigations into groups are based on information regarding planned or actual criminal activity and not on information regarding beliefs.[18] This may be the reason why there is little officially documented data concerning domestic terrorist and hate groups. Based on Freeh's remarks, it is possible to suggest that local and state law enforcement agencies are more cognizant of groups that fall into the category of domestic terrorists, especially organized hate groups, because they may have operated in or near the jurisdictions of such agencies.

A sampling of known domestic terrorist groups,[19] many of which are also viewed as organized hate groups, is outlined in the following list; they are further explained in detail in Appendix A:

American Coalition of Life Activists
Animal Liberation Front
Army of God
Aryan Nation (aka Aryan Republican Army)
Branch Davidians
Christian Identity Movement
Citizens of the Republic of Idaho
Colorado First Light Infantry
Colorado Militia
Covenant (aka Sword and Arm of the Lord)
Earth Liberation Front
Freeman
Ku Klux Klan
Michigan Militia
Militia of Montana
Mountaineer Militia
National Alliance
North American Militia of Southwestern Michigan
Patriot's Council
Phineas Priesthood
Posse Comitatus
Reclaim the Seeds
Republic of Texas
Southern California Minuteman
The Order (aka The New Order)
Unnamed California and Texas Militias
Viper Militia
World Church of the Creator (also known as the Creativity Movement)

The sheer number of groups or movements in the United States is alarming, and it remains unconfirmed. A concern for law enforcement personnel is that any one of the domestic groups can be seen as a potential place to recruit an extremist. An Internet search on general topics such as militias provides over 200,000 results with the use of just one search engine. Militia groups are scattered throughout the United States, and their numbers are growing. Bruce Hoffman,[20] citing works from the mid-1990s, states that there are "an estimated 800 other similarly oriented militias—with a total membership claimed to be over 5 million, though more realistically put at no more than 50,000" (p. 107). According to SPLC's 2004 Intelligence Report,[21] there were 152 identified active patriot groups (see Appendix B of this book) having cells in many states, compared to 171 in 2003. In 2004, SPLC showed that 45 were classified as militias.[21] These numbers were much lower in 2002, with the number of patriot groups equal to 143 and militias to 54 (M. Potok, personal communication, March 10, 2003). By the end of 2016, the Intelligence Project reported a dramatic increase in the number of antigovernment groups including a significant increase in militias. Barbara Perry,[17] in her book

*In the Name of Hate: Understanding Hate Crimes*, cited the militia movement as being fueled by religious fanaticism and the willingness to kill, and referred to it as a "full-scale terrorist underground." Despite not having a definite number to work with, law enforcement personnel need to exercise caution when monitoring information on such groups. It does not take a group to commit an act of terrorism; a single person acting alone can do a lot of damage. You only have to consider the case of a homicide bomber to be convinced of this. Just as important, not all groups or group members have terrorist ties nor do all expound violence, but they are at best unstable and pose fertile ground for the growth of domestic terrorism.

## DOMESTIC TERRORISM

With the ambiguity in defining terrorism, how can we possibly define domestic terrorism? In many parts of Europe, there is no differentiation between domestic terrorism and foreign terrorism. There are factions of United States-based domestic groups that have overseas bases of support and operation. One of the few working definitions of domestic terrorism comes from the MILNET website[22]:

> Domestic terrorism is the actions by persons seeking to persuade or dissuade the government or people of their home country using violent means that intend to frighten or coerce, ranging from threats to outright acts of violence such as kidnapping, beatings, or murder.[22]

This definition clearly fits many groups from as early as the 1960s to this day and everything from abortion clinic bombings to the Oklahoma City, Oklahoma, bombing. However, much attention has been, and continues to be, focused on international terrorism and groups that are based overseas. Although the federal government has the means and authority to investigate and follow up terrorist-related activity overseas, local law enforcement agencies do not, and they may fail to see the correlation between domestic or local events in the big picture of terrorism. The media tend to focus on terrorist subjects from other countries as being the bad guys who are at the root of the entire epidemic known as terrorism. This may make a more attractive news angle to follow, and our citizens may find it easier to deal with this angle rather than reading about one of their own siding with the enemy. After all, terrorists cannot look like mainstream law-abiding citizens, right? The truth is that domestic terrorism has taken place for many years and it is usually carried out by those who fit the mainstream citizen category. However, it is often classified as a routine crime somewhere in the criminal justice system.

It was not until the passage of the *Uniting and strengthening the United States by providing appropriate tools required to intercept and obstruct terrorism* (USA PATRIOT) Act in October 2001 that many American citizens came to understand a working definition of domestic terrorism. Although the text is laden with many enhancements designed to increase the effectiveness of law enforcement in the war on terrorism, domestic terrorism is not directly addressed until about three-quarters into the document. For the purposes of this book, the following definition of domestic terrorism from the USA PATRIOT Act[23] is suggested for use in law enforcement:

(A)  Involves acts dangerous to human life that are a violation of the criminal laws of the United States or of any state;
(B)  Appear to be intended
    (i)  To intimidate or coerce a civilian population;
    (ii)  To influence the policy of a government by intimidation or coercion; or
    (iii)  To affect the conduct of a government by mass destruction, assassination, or kidnapping;
(C)  Occur primarily within the territorial jurisdiction of the United States.

This second definition is specific to the United States and its citizens, whereas the MILNET definition is more broadly based and can be adopted by almost any country. A third definition that must be considered is the one presented by Louis J. Freeh[18]:

> The unlawful use, or threatened use, of violence by a group or individual that is based and operating entirely within the United States or its territories without foreign direction and which is committed against persons or property with the intent of intimidating or coercing a government or its population in further-ance of political or social objectives.

It is becoming increasingly more complicated to define domestic terrorism and what constitutes domestic terrorism. Therefore, it is suggested that the definition overwhelmingly adopted in the USA PATRIOT Act be established as the standard to be used by law enforcement agencies through-out the country.

The complex nature of terrorism and the ability of virtually every person in the world to easily travel are increasingly eroding traditional boundaries. Many so-called international terrorist organizations have sprouted roots in many countries, including the United States, and all are trying to enter the main-stream to avoid detection, reap financial gains, or exploit laws designed for law-abiding citizens. Elaine Landau[24] points out that there are not many differences between domestic terrorists and the highly publicized terrorist bands operating in other parts of the world. This also muddies the waters when trying to define domestic terrorism; caution should be used when monitoring such groups, and the best way is to categorize and monitor them with link analysis in order to develop associations.

As noted in the section "The evolution of domestic terrorism," domestic terrorism has been pre-valent in the United States for several years, although it has often been classified as something else in the criminal justice system. Walter Laqueur[25] advised that statistics concerning terrorism should focus on international terrorism. He said that terrorism statistics collected over the years are dependent on who is collecting the figures and what criteria are being used; he also notes, "This is not to argue that statistics on terrorism are altogether useless" (p. 335).[25] Terrorism statistics are no different from many law enforcement statistics, which are at times subjective and completely dependent on the reporting or collection criteria. What is important about statistics is that they are cited and compared with like variables. Some statistics and examples of domestic terrorism, accord-ing to the Council on Foreign Relations,[26] that show how prevalent it has been in the United States before September 11, 2001 are outlined as follows:

Between 1980 and 2000, Americans accounted for about three-quarters of the 335 terrorist acts committed in the United States.
Weapons of mass destruction were used. In 1984, followers of the Bhagwan Shree Rajneesh cult sprayed salad bars in Oregon with salmonella, causing 751 people to become ill, in an attempt to change the outcome of a local election.
In April 1995, the Oklahoma City bombing took place.
In July 1996, the Atlanta Centennial Park, Georgia, bombing took place.
In the summer of 1999, shooting sprees targeting minorities in Chicago, Illinois, and Los Angeles, California, took place.

In December 2002, former FBI associate deputy director Buck Revell[27] pointed out several factors that are changing and increasing the domestic terrorist threat. One point of particular interest men-tioned by him is that "antigovernment reactionary extremists have proliferated and now pose a sig-nificant threat to the federal government and to law enforcement at all levels." This point is well taken, but today's reactionary extremists were the anarchists of the turn of the century. People clas-sified as anarchists were seen as opposing all forms of organized authority, including government, and they advocated the use of violence in order to improve a class of society, usually the working or lower class. Revell also notes that had it not been for modern-day nongovernmental agencies such as SPLC and ADL, the federal government would have been totally clueless about right-wing extremists. It is these extremist or organized hate groups that can provide a conduit to international terrorist organizations seeking to expand their terror campaign into a country such as the United States.

Americans do not have immunity to the lure of violent ideologies or hatred. At the beginning of the new millennium, there were several U.S. citizens allegedly associated with known terrorist organizations such as al-Qaeda. Two of the more prevalent groups were the individuals who came to be known as "the American Taliban" and "the dirty bomber." The connection for each of these individuals was said to be religion. The dirty bomber reportedly converted or was exposed to an extreme version of Islam while being incarcerated in a Florida prison. This does not mean that every disenchanted prisoner will join an international terrorist group, but prisoners' hatred often runs deep and represents a valuable recruitment source of potential candidates to join organized hate groups and antigovernment movements.

## ORGANIZED HATE GROUPS AND CRIMES

As alluded to in the evolution of domestic terrorism, organized groups such as gangs and crime families have a long-standing presence in the United States. The roots of modern hate groups have been around for centuries. From the early settlers of the United States to one of the first organized hate groups, the Ku Klux Klan, which has been around for over 145 years, hate has festered and been a contributing factor to many illegal actions. However, the presence of these groups was once seen as a crime threat and not as a terrorist threat, but times have changed. In a speech before the U.S. Senate, Louis J. Freeh reported that on a national level, formal right-wing hate groups such as the World Church of the Creator, also known as the Creativity Movement, and the Aryan Nation represent a continuing terrorist threat. These two groups have formal followings throughout the country and probably have even more informal followers. Small splinter factions, such as the South Florida Aryan Alliance, spawned from these larger groups. These groups have become more vocal nowadays and blatantly display their cache of weapons in photographs, social media networks, or public domains. Concern over hate crimes and actions of hate groups such as the aforementioned ones prompted the FBI to initiate data collection on hate or bias with the Hate Crimes Statistics Act of 1990 through the uniform crime reporting system.

In 2001, the FBI reported that there were nearly 10,000 reported incidents of hate crimes within the United States. According to some private nonprofit associations that monitor hate crimes, this number may actually be as high as 50,000 per year. By 2014, the FBI was reporting just under 5,500 incidents of hate. This discrepancy in numbers can be largely attributed to changes in reporting practices and lack of training or awareness on the part of law enforcement personnel. Measures are in place to remedy this discrepancy, but only time will tell if the issue has been addressed. However, hate crime statistics for 2004 chronicle even fewer (7,649) criminal incidents reported by law enforcement agencies as being motivated by bias against a race, religion, disability, ethnicity, or sexual orientation, and the statistics include information on 9,035 offenses, 9,528 victims, and 7,145 known offenders. Many reported hate crime incidents are focused on gender, race, and ethnicity, and they are reported as being committed by individuals rather than groups. In 2014, race was the leading bias reported in the incidents of hate with just under 50% of the incidents reported in this manner. It should be noted that when we speak of gathering and analyzing information, analysts should remain cognizant of the detailed information found in hate crime reports and consider it in their analysis. This is contrary to the way terrorism-related actions are reported. In such instances, one hears more about the group than the individual who actually committed the act.

During her tenure as Attorney General of the United States, Janet Reno identified a need and requested that the FBI work in concert with state and local law enforcement agencies to develop a model hate crime training curriculum. This was in response to her deep concern about the problem of increasing hate crime incidents in the United States, as well as to address the alleged differences in data. The result was four new training curricula for patrol officers, detectives, policy-level officers, and a mixed audience of all three levels. Interestingly, analytical personnel were not included. Regardless of this criticism, many personnel were trained on a variety of topics, including group characteristics that should be shared with analysts tasked with analyzing hate groups. Some known characteristics of organized hate groups are outlined as follows:

Group structure is loose on a local level but highly structured internationally.
A substantial number of members are white males under the age of 30 years.
Leaders tend to project a mainstream image.
Many are technologically savvy and use such devices as cable television and computers to promote their rhetoric.
Group members are often loosely affiliated (e.g., Skinheads).
Groups focus on issues of concern to Middle America as a way of cloaking and marketing hate.
Members of these groups believe in an inevitable global war between races.

Another matter that needed to be addressed was a definition for hate crime. Much like terrorism, hate crime has numerous working definitions. Some of the more prominent definitions are those from the Hate Crimes Statistics Act of 1990, Bureau of Justice Administration (1997), the ADL, and the National Education Association. For purposes of law enforcement, the FBI definition is widely used as a standard[28]:

A criminal offense committed against a person, property or society, which is motivated, in whole or in part, by the offender's bias against a race, religion, disability, sexual orientation, or ethnicity/national origin.

Louis Freeh, in his statement before the Senate, also noted that anarchists and extreme socialist groups have an international presence and pose a potential threat to the United States. This is important to note, because foreign-based terrorist organizations that wish to attack American soil must first gain access to the United States. As demonstrated by some disenfranchised American citizens such as those who joined the Taliban and al-Qaeda in Afghanistan, foreign-based groups recruit Americans and thereby reach American soil. Monitoring hate groups and their members, publicly and in prison, is vital. These groups represent potential recruitment grounds for well-financed, foreign-based terrorist organizations that have hatred toward the United States and who can build on this cause in an effort to solicit members of domestic groups to perform acts of terrorism. Law enforcement should also remain cognizant of members and leaders of groups conducting business behind bars either through visitors or communications. This has happened for years; just consider some of the larger-than-life organized crime figures. The hatred of domestic groups did not evolve overnight. It has been around for decades; without a doubt it poses a great risk to homeland security and there are many potential recruiting grounds.

American organized hate groups are not proprietary to the United States. Several groups have established chapters overseas and have recruited members in many European countries, including UK, Germany, and Austria. This is similar to the actions of terrorist organizations that are extending their reach from overseas to the United States. The roles played by these various groups in the terrorism theater are expanding both domestically and internationally.

## ROLE OF ORGANIZED HATE GROUPS IN DOMESTIC TERRORISM

Terrorism of any magnitude has an underlying tone of hate. All organized hate groups have beliefs or practices that attack or malign an entire class of people, and such is the case with terrorist groups like al-Qaeda, whose members overwhelmingly hate Americans and Jews.

Membership numbers concerning known militias and patriot groups are staggering. With potentially hundreds of homegrown organized groups active in the United States, law enforcement agencies should strive to categorize groups along the following suggested domestic ideological parameters, in addition to the FBI's domestic types, rather than treat them as individual organizations:

White supremacy
Hate groups
Neomilitia or patriot movements
Sovereign citizen movements
Militias
Tax protestors
Foreign- or state-sponsored groups

Use of the suggested parameters will aid analytical and investigative personnel in narrowing their criteria when tracking and monitoring activity as well as members of various groups. There are other categories available, but for analytical purposes most groups will fit into the aforementioned list. Categorizing domestic groups along these lines will also aid in identifying splinter groups, membership transfers, or groups that may associate with one another based on a common belief or hatred. Law enforcement is accustomed to using labels for such groups as career criminals. The difference is that most career criminal labels have structured guidelines and are usually progressive, so there is no need to change the category. When categorizing organized hate groups, law enforcement agencies need to be aware that members may change groups or associate with multiple groups. Therefore, as new information concerning changes becomes known, it is important that a mechanism exists to facilitate the change in order to keep intelligence accurate.

Figure 2.1 depicts a hate map. Symbols are used to identify groups, following SPLC categories. The information demonstrates how virtually every area of the United States has been touched by organized hate groups. Categories used by the SPLC differ slightly from those just outlined. The SPLC's categories are valid but broad-based, and they may be too limiting for future analytical consideration. However, they should not be discounted. The organized hate group categories and definitions used by SPLC are discussed as follows[29]:

Ku Klux Klan—The Ku Klux Klan with its mystique and long history of violence is the oldest and most infamous of American hate groups. Although blacks have typically been the Klan's primary target, it has also attacked Jews, immigrants, homosexuals and, recently, Catholics. Since December 1865 when it was formed, the Klan has seen itself as a

**FIGURE 2.1**    Hate map. (Courtesy of the Southern Poverty Law Center, Intelligence Report, 2003.)

Christian organization. However, in modern times Klan groups are motivated by a variety of theological and political ideologies.

Started during Reconstruction at the end of the Civil War, the Klan quickly mobilized itself as a vigilante group to intimidate Southern blacks (and any whites who would help them) and to prevent blacks from enjoying basic civil rights. Outlandish titles (like Imperial Wizard and Exalted Cyclops), hooded costumes, violent night rides, and the notion that the group comprised an invisible empire conferred a mystique to the group that only added to the Klan's popularity. Lynching, tar-and-featherings, rape, and other violent attacks on those challenging white supremacy became hallmarks of the Klan.

After a short but violent period, the "first era" Klan disbanded after Jim Crow laws secured the domination of Southern whites. However, the Klan enjoyed a huge revival in the 1920s when it opposed (mainly Catholic and Jewish) immigration. By 1925, when its followers staged a huge Washington, DC march, the Klan had as many as five million members and considerable political power in some states. A series of sex scandals, internal battles over power, and newspaper exposés quickly reduced its influence.

The Klan arose for the third time during the 1960s to oppose the civil rights movement and to preserve segregation in the face of unfavorable court rulings. The Klan's bombings, murders, and other attacks took a great many lives, including those of four young girls who were killed while preparing for services at the 16th Street Baptist Church in Birmingham, Alabama.

Since the 1970s, the Klan has been greatly weakened by internal conflicts, court cases, and a seemingly endless series of splits and government infiltration. Whereas some factions preserved an openly racist and militant approach, others tried to enter the mainstream, cloaking their racism as "civil rights for whites." Today, SPLC estimates that there are a total of 5,500–6,000 Klan members split among the scores of different and often warring organizations that use the Klan name. The total number of groups counted in 2002 was 133 compared to 109 in 2001, a 22% increase.

Neo-Nazi Groups—Neo-Nazi groups share a hatred for Jews and a love for Adolf Hitler and Nazi Germany. Although they also hate other minorities, homosexuals, and sometimes Christians, they perceive Jews as their cardinal enemy and trace social problems to a Jewish conspiracy that supposedly controls governments, financial institutions, and the media. While some neo-Nazi groups emphasize simple hatred, others are more focused on the revolutionary creation of a fascist political state. Nazism has its roots in Europe, of course, and links between American and European neo-Nazis are strong and are currently growing stronger. American neo-Nazi groups, protected by the First Amendment to the U.S. Constitution, often publish material and host Internet sites that are aimed at European audiences. These materials are illegal under European antiracism laws. For this reason, many European groups have their Internet sites on American servers to avoid prosecution under the laws of their native countries. The most important neo-Nazi group in the United States is National Alliance, founded by William Pierce who is the infamous author of the futuristic race war novel *The Turner Diaries*, a book believed by some to have served as the blueprint for the 1995 Oklahoma City bombing. The total number of groups counted in 2002 was 220 compared to 209 in 2001.

Racist Skinheads—Racist Skinheads form a particularly violent faction of the white supremacist movement and have often been referred to as the "shock troops" of the hoped-for revolution. The classic Skinhead look is a shaved head, black Doc Martens boots, jeans with suspenders, and an array of typically racist tattoos.

The Skinhead phenomenon began in the industrial cities of Britain in the 1960s as a working-class movement strongly marked by contempt for hippies and middle-class youth. Although drugs and violence was always part of the Skinhead scene, Skinheads originally embraced

Afro-Caribbean music and were of different races. British fascists were able to precipitate a split in the movement between racist and antiracist elements, a split that has endured to the present day in Britain and in the United States where "Skins" arrived in the early 1980s. Racist Skins are referred to by their enemies as boneheads. Antiracist Skins are often referred to as SHARPS, a reference to a group known as Skinheads against Racial Prejudice that is now essentially defunct.

Racist Skinheads in the United States, like those in other countries, often operate in small crews that move from city to city with some regularity. The largest and most dangerous Skinhead group today is Hammerskin Nation, with thousands of members and extremely violent track records in North America and Europe. The total number of groups counted in 2001 was 43, and in 2002 this number was found reduced to 18.

Christian Identity—The Christian Identity religion asserts that whites, not Jews, are the true Israelites favored by God in the Bible. In most of its forms, Identity theology depicts Jews as biologically descended from Satan, whereas non-whites are seen as soulless "mud people" created with the other biblical "beasts of the field." Christian Identity has its roots in a nineteenth-century English fad called British Israelism, which asserts that European whites are descended from the 10 "lost tribes" of Israel and are thus related to Jews, who are descended from the other two Hebrew tribes mentioned in the Bible. However, British Israelism, which was initially friendly to Jews, was adopted and transformed in the twentieth century into a rabidly anti-Semitic creed by a number of racist preachers in the United States.

For decades, Identity has been one of the most important ideologies for the white supremacist movement. In its hardest-line form, it asserts that Christ will not return to Earth until the globe is swept clean of Jews and other Satanic influences. In recent years, intense doctrinal disputes, the lack of a central church structure, and a shift among white supremacists toward agnosticism and racist variations of neo-paganism weakened the Identity movement and reduced its number of adherents. The total number of groups in 2001 was 31, whereas in 2002 it was 27.

Neo-Confederate Groups—Many groups celebrate traditional Southern culture and the dramatic conflict between the Union and the Confederacy during the Civil War, but some go further and embrace racist attitudes toward blacks and, in some cases, white separatism. Such groups are listed in this category.

The League of the South, which was founded in 1994 and had some 9,000 members in 2001, is at the center of the racist neo-Confederate movement. Calling once again for Southern secession, the League's leaders opine minorities are destroying the Anglo-Celtic (white) culture of the South. They oppose most non-white immigration and all interracial marriages. Michael Hill, the founder of the League and a former college professor, called blacks a deadly and compliant underclass and embraced the ideas of well-known white supremacists such as North Carolina attorney Kirk Lyons. The total number of groups in 2001 was 124; in 2002 it was 91.

Black Separatist—Black separatists typically oppose integration and racial intermarriage, and they want separate institutions—or even a separate nation—for blacks. Most forms of black separatism are strongly anti-white and anti-Semitic, and a number of religious factions assert that blacks, not Jews, are the biblical "chosen people" of God.

Although SPLC recognizes that the rise of black racism in the United States is at least in part a response to centuries of white racism, its members believe that racism must be exposed in all its forms. White groups espousing beliefs similar to Black Separatists would be considered clearly racist. The same criterion should be applied to all groups, regardless of their members' color. The total number of groups counted in 2001 was 51 and in 2002 the number reached 82, a 61% increase.

Other groups—Included in this category are hate groups following a hodgepodge of doctrines. Some, like the National Association for the Advancement of White People, are white supremacist groups masquerading as mainstream groups, with an interest in issues such as black crime, busing, and affirmative action. Others embrace racist forms of neo-pagan religions such as Odinism, a pre-Christian theology that is largely focused on the virtues of a tribe or race.

The Council of Conservative Citizens is a reincarnation of the White Citizens Councils that sprang up in the South in the 1950s and 1960s to oppose school desegregation. Like the League of the South, to which it has many links, the 15,000-member Council tried without success to mask its white supremacist ideology to promote a right-wing political agenda. The total number of groups counted in 2001 was 109 and in 2002 this number had increased to 137.

Calculations and determinations that make up the SPLC's categories are based on group activities such as criminal acts, marches, rallies, speeches, meetings, and publications. Whether a group advocates or engages in violence or criminal activities is not considered. Therefore, use of the first seven domestic categories might be more applicable for matters of homeland security and terrorism analysis. However, for informational purposes and general relationship correlations, the SPLC categories would be of value pending further analysis.

As reflected in its maps, the SPLC also uses symbols to demonstrate the type of group being identified. Although these symbols are generic, few people have not seen these and almost everyone knows what they are intended to reflect. Although these symbols are used generically, they are hybrids of actual symbols used by the various organized hate groups located within the United States (Appendix C). Symbols have played an important role in groups for decades and are used as badges of honor, often worn on clothing and uniforms, reflected on flags and banners (such as the ones depicted in Figure 2.2), or painted on buildings. Some members go as far as tattooing the symbols on their bodies. Many symbols have been modified even further and adopted by street-level gang members and inmates incarcerated in correctional institutions. Symbols, however, are not proprietary to United States-based organized hate groups. They have also been used by numerous international terrorist groups, such as the Irish Republican Army (IRA), and they can be found prominently displayed on buildings in areas controlled by the related organizations.

The use of symbols and their meanings are discussed in Appendix C. Identification of symbols in large international groups, organized hate groups, or even street gangs may provide information into associations, relationships, or terrorist activity signatures. It is also important for law enforcement personnel to remain cognizant of international or foreign-based terrorist organizations, such as those listed in Appendix D, which may have relationships with or the support of domestic groups, or may be active in the United States. If a foreign-based terrorist organization is looking for a way to infiltrate the borders of a country, gaining access to an organized group of malcontents filled with extreme hatred within the country opens new horizons for recruitment.

Now that we have an understanding of the types of terrorists and terrorist groups that exist, and where they exist, there is one last general question for law enforcement agencies. What is a terrorist? After all, there is no stereotypical appearance, race, religion, or ethnicity for a terrorist.

FIGURE 2.2    South Florida Aryan Alliance banner.

## WHAT IS A TERRORIST?

One person's terrorist is another's freedom fighter. In some cases, a terrorist may be seen as a leader, martyr, or visionary. However, in the world of law enforcement this argument is not necessarily a concern. "Criminal" is not usually thought of as an option for how a terrorist is seen. According to Brent Smith, terrorists remain criminals but they are motivated by ideology, religion, or political cause. If one were to look at just eight pictures—those of Osama bin Laden, Timothy McVeigh, Yasser Arafat, Muhammad Atta, Che Guevara, Menachem Begin, Yahweh Ben Yahweh, and William Pierce—there would be much debate as to who the terrorists are. The perception would depend greatly on the year and the definition of the term terrorist that is used. Two of the individuals, Timothy McVeigh and Yahweh Ben Yahweh, were not viewed as terrorists at the time of their alleged atrocities. These individuals were seen as radicals, extremists, and criminals. All one has to do is check their criminal records and you will not find them labeled there as terrorists, the way we label sexual predators or career criminals. They were charged with crimes and sentenced accordingly. On the other hand, bin Laden, Arafat, Atta, Guevara, and Begin do not have criminal records, at least not in the United States. Menachem Begin, the former prime minister of Israel, is described in the media, published documents, and the Internet as being active in Jewish guerilla activity, as fighting for Jewish independence, and as being a member of the Irgun. The Irgun was considered one of the more relentless groups of the 1940s. The Irgun can be classified as a terrorist group, yet Begin is not referred to as a terrorist. As for Arafat, Atta, and Guevara, their descriptors run the gamut. Arafat and Guevara are described as guerilla fighters, freedom fighters, revolutionaries, martyrs, and terrorists. William Pierce, who is also known as Andrew MacDonald and is the writer of *The Turner Diaries* (1978), was perhaps one of America's most notorious neo-Nazis. Timothy McVeigh was allegedly in possession of this book at the time of his arrest. Pierce was the leader of the West Virginia-based National Alliance. To some, he was known only as a professor holding a PhD in physics, which he once taught at the Oregon State University—not one's stereotypical vision of a terrorist. This listing of eight individuals is just a sample of the controversy that can be generated on the topic of what a terrorist is.

When it comes to identifying a terrorist, one area that is alluded to is organized hate group leaders or members. This is not an indictment that all individuals associated with these groups are terrorists, but many of those in the leadership ranks expound extremist beliefs in the United States similar to those of terrorist leaders in the Middle East. There are also some similarities between many hate group leaders and terrorists. The education, personae, and exposure to military tactics are similar for many known terrorists. A recent review of 20 individuals seen as leaders and associated with extremism in the United States, according to ADL, showed that most of them were highly educated and had authored several publications and books. In addition, some sought to enter the mainstream by running for political office. The party ticket of choice was often the Populist Party. However, some ran under the traditional Republican and Democratic parties. Two ran for the presidency. One was elected, and the person served as a state representative in the Louisiana legislature. One ran and won a primary in California, whereas another won a large percent of the first ballot when running for the Arkansas office of lieutenant governor. Several served in the armed forces. There is no definitive way to identify a terrorist, hate group member, or potential recruit. They come from all walks of life, social classes, and educational levels. Regardless of their diverse backgrounds or locales, there are approaches that can be employed by analysts or investigators that aid them in identifying a terrorist.

In order to initiate any form of analytical or intelligence-based undertaking, law enforcement personnel need to have a starting point for gathering and cataloging individuals and their activities. One starting point is beliefs. In 1988, essentially three types of terrorist beliefs were identified that apply to virtually any individual who can be construed as being a terrorist or belonging to a terrorist group:

1. Nationalistic
2. Ideological
3. Theological

   The U.S. military recognizes and describes nationalistic and theological beliefs in its general terrorism training courses, both of which are applicable for use in law enforcement. "Nationalist terrorists seek to form a separate state for their own national group, often by drawing attention to a fight for 'national liberation' that they think the world has ignored."[3] Many members of nationalist groups are not viewed as terrorists, rather they are seen by the populous as freedom fighters. An example of a nationalist group would be the IRA whose members began their struggle not as a Catholic versus Protestant religious conflict, but as a fight for independence and establishment of an Irish state. As for ideological terrorists, their actions are simply based on their beliefs. The differences between nationalist and ideological groups are usually found in their goals. Many ideological terrorists express frustration toward social structures and capitalism, and they seek a new order. The third type of belief group is theological or religious terrorists who believe they speak and work for their chosen deity. They "seek to use violence to further what they see as divinely commanded purposes, often targeting broad categories of foes in an attempt to bring about sweeping changes."[3]

   Once a belief or point of view is established, analytical personnel need to avoid grouping these individuals in general terms based on membership in a left- or right-wing movement. Terrorists are multifaceted. They often approach their mission much like they approach a business. They have beliefs, and businesses have mission statements. They have economic needs and seek funding, and a business is always looking at the financial bottom line. They develop geographic bases of support, and businesses look for locations. Terrorists develop tactics to take advantage of others, and businesses develop tactics to outdo competition and convince the consumer to buy their product. Terrorists selectively choose their targets, and businesses look for a target audience. Another consideration is that both may even change affiliations or beliefs. With this said, how can analytical personnel in the field of law enforcement differentiate between a terrorist and a criminal?

## TERRORIST VERSUS STREET CRIMINAL

Jonathan White[7] offers a comparison of a terrorist versus a typical street criminal. Although it may not be all-inclusive or fit every situation, the information provided will greatly aid analytical personnel in categorizing individuals. This categorization is done much the same way as agencies decide what constitutes a gang member or a career criminal. The difference is that we are now looking for characteristics that might constitute a terrorist.

### Differences Between Typical Street Criminals and Terrorists

The differences between typical street criminals and terrorists can be outlined as follows[7]:

*Terrorist*
   Fights for political objective
   Motivated by ideology or religion
   Group focused
   Consumed with purpose
   Trained and motivated for the mission
   On the attack

*Typical street criminal*
   Crimes of opportunity
   Uncommitted
   Self-centered
   No cause
   Untrained
   Escape oriented

Members of the law enforcement community would probably readily agree about what constitutes a typical street criminal. It is the terrorist whom those in the law enforcement community are unfamiliar with, and whom they, except for a select few, have never encountered. The aforementioned list is useful in that law enforcement personnel can inquire about these variables when determining whether to document someone as a terrorist. This information will also enhance opportunities for developing interrelationships. Determining whether or not a suspect fits the category of terrorist requires investigators and analysts to ask the fundamental questions—who, what, where, when, why, and how—when encountering such individuals. Chances of developing a profile that fit most terrorists are highly unlikely. Asking the proper questions is essential when encountering individuals in order to identify differences, but these differences will not always be apparent. Such was the case with the September 11, 2001 terrorists.

## September 11, 2001: Are the subjects criminals or terrorists?

The 19 subjects of the September 11, 2001 attack on the United States were undoubtedly terrorists as opposed to criminals. However, in order to demonstrate the effectiveness of the terrorist versus criminal comparison mentioned in the section titled "Differences between typical street criminals and terrorists," all one has to do is look at the activity that led to the tragic events and at a profile of the September 11, 2001 terrorists. These terrorists did not commit any violations of state or federal statutes (other than traffic and immigration violations) that would have classified them as criminals in a traditional law enforcement sense. The following is a profile of the terrorists involved in the attack:

Ranged in age between their early 20s and mid-30s

Primarily from Middle Eastern countries; have traveled and resided in several different countries.

Affiliated with an international group, al-Qaeda, known for its dislike of the United States government

Motivated by religious beliefs and extreme ideology

Usually had one spokesperson for the group

Mainly used bank branches located in highly populated Muslim areas

Usually came into banks as a group to open an account

Wanted to deal with one person at the bank

Nineteen hijackers, twenty domestic bank accounts, four different bank branches

Opened bank accounts having a few thousand dollars within 30 days of arriving in the United States, with three to four members present

No social security cards, and nonpermanent addresses

Lived within the same region, although not all in one jurisdiction, in rented apartments.

Primarily had wire transfers from United Arab Emirates (UAE), Saudi Arabia, and Germany, and used identification from these countries.

Made numerous balance inquiries

Made overall transactions that were below federal banking guideline reporting requirements

Purchased traveler's checks overseas, brought them to the United States, and deposited a portion of them in the bank accounts

Consumed with their mission and purpose; even willing to die for it

Trained at several aviation schools as well as known terrorist camps

Based on the limited information provided in the aforementioned list, there would be little if any reason for the law enforcement community to be concerned, especially if it was only looking for evidence of a crime. These terrorists were not what traditional law enforcement personnel were trained to detect and monitor; the personnel are trained to detect and monitor only street criminals. There were no red flags raised in the case of the 9/11 attackers. Analytical and investigative personnel need to be cautious when reviewing and discounting any information. What appears to be legitimate activity by law-abiding individuals may turn out to be something more if monitored over time or from a certain perspective. Just as is noted in the profile of the 9/11 subjects, religion played a role.

The perspective of religion is something new for law enforcement personnel to consider. In many law enforcement circles, there is little, if any, reference to religion when dealing with crime. There is also a reluctance to engage in any religious discussion. Understanding the religious perspective whether Islam or Judaism is just another aspect that the law enforcement community needs to consider.

## UNDERSTANDING THE RELIGIOUS CONNECTION

Since September 11, 2001 many in the Western world have started focusing on one of the fastest growing religions in the world with 1.3 billion adherents—Islam. However, it is important to note that the majority practicing the faith are peaceful people and do not condone the tragic events of 2001. Additionally, following this thought process will create a bias that will negatively impact any analysis. Although it may be simple to blame the majority, law enforcement personnel must not forget that religion is used as a reason by many terrorists, both foreign and domestic. All you need to do is refer to the number of domestic terrorist groups who adhere to the Christian Identity religion.

With much focus on Islam, this section will attempt to shed light on this religion and those who follow it, much like the 9/11 subjects. The Arab world is made up of approximately 22 countries and 300 million people of which about 3 million live in the United States; the vast majority, who are of Lebanese descent, live within the urban areas of Los Angeles, Chicago, Detroit, New York, and Washington, DC.

Islam is a monotheistic afterlife religion that follows Allah as the eternal all-powerful who sees all and knows all. God also has no physical description or gender connotation. There are several significant events in Islam, following an Islamic lunar calendar, many of which take place around the year AD 630. There are also many references to angels and at least 25 prophets are noted by name in the holy book called the Quran. Islam follows a system of rituals. They serve as a way to transform religious beliefs into reality. The main reference is to the Pillars of Islam or what is commonly referred to as the Five Pillars. The Five Pillars, in order, are as follows:

1. Shahadah: The creed of Islam that declares allegiance to God
2. Salat or daily prayer: The most important of all duties
3. Zakat or annual charity: Addresses disparity (2.5% prescribed by Muhammad)
4. Saum or month-long fasting: In the ninth month of the Islamic lunar calendar—Ramadhan
5. Hajj or pilgrimage: One journey to Mecca in a Muslim's lifetime

## ISLAMIC EXTREMISM

The U.S. Army has studied Islamic religious extremism extensively and has declared it the most dangerous of all terrorist threats to U.S. interests. The focus of this section is on the word extremism. Islam is an Arabic word meaning "submission" in the context of submitting to the word of God. It has its beginning in the early seventh century when the religion was founded by Muhammad ibn Abdulah. Muhammad was born in Mecca, Saudi Arabia, in AD 570, and began his ministry in Mecca around AD 620. Muhammad spent much of his life in his ministry converting the then pagan population to Islam. As he converted the regional city-states, he left behind a religious institution and a religious form of civil government.

Religious extremist ideology in any religion can be dangerous. However, it is the Islamic religious extremist ideology that appears to be particularly dangerous to the West. Adherents to Shiism, for example, the members of the Revolutionary Guard of Iran, have manifested themselves as the international terrorist organization known as Hezbollah. However, extremism is not limited to the Shia component of Islam. Within the Sunni community, there are several organizations that are a threat to Western democracies, for example, the Muslim Brotherhood and Hamas. They seek to further the goal of a true Islamic state and promote the Islamic revolution and the formation of Islamic republics worldwide. At this level of extremism, there appears to be no or little strife between the Shia and Sunni branches of Islam.

Hamas, the Palestinian branch of the Muslim Brotherhood, was born of the Intifada (uprising), which was a series of demonstrations, riots, and violence led by Palestinians against the rule of Israel. The Intifada began in 1987 in the Gaza strip and spread throughout the Israel-occupied territories. Hamas was founded on the principle of Islamic nationalism and the elimination of the State of Israel. Hamas was loosely affiliated with the PLO and the Islamic Jihad, but the group became bitter enemies of the PLO when the latter endorsed the concept of coexistence between the Palestinian state and Israel with the intent that there should be a gradual phased creation of a Palestinian homeland. Hamas wanted an immediate and unrelenting frontal assault on Israel. In 1991, Hamas split from the PLO when the PLO refused the group's request for a Hamas presence at the Palestinian National Council.

Since the former leader of Iran and initiator of the Islamic revolution Ayatollah Khomeini died in 1989, the political and religious leadership of Iran claims to have moderated its views on the West, worldwide Islamic revolution, and overt direct involvement in terrorist activities. This perception deserves skepticism and the claim remains to be proved. Regardless of the religious role that modern-day leaders such as Khomeini have played, it will continue to be the teachings and writings of Muhammad that will be interpreted by conservatives, moderates, and extremists in the religion.

## ISLAMIC SECTS

Upon Muhammad's death, there was controversy over the religious leadership, resulting in a division of Islam into the two commonly referenced sects, Sunni and Shia. It should be noted that Muslims prefer to be referred to simply as Muslims. However, Sunni and Shia are often two principal terms associated with Muslims. Additional sects do exist, such as Wahhabis, but this will be explained further in Chapter 8. Some of the behavior or belief traits of Sunnis and Shias are outlined as follows:

Sunni—The term Sunni is used to denote those Muslims who practice Islam according to authentic traditional Islamic sources. There is unanimous agreement among them regarding the Quran's authenticity; the Quran is neither temporal nor newly created, but is eternal. The Sunnis believe that believers will be blessed with the sight of Allah in the hereafter, as is mentioned in the Quran. Since this religion has been completed, no one has the right to formulate new legislation or directives. However, one must refer to the qualified Muslim scholars who must work solely within the bounds established by Allah's Book and the Sunnah of the Prophet.

Shia—To some Shiites, the Quran's authenticity is doubtful and appears to contradict many of their sectarian beliefs or doctrines. The views and opinions of their imams are the primary source of their jurisprudence. Shiites believe that to see Allah is not possible in this world or in the hereafter. The Shiites consider their imams to be infallible and to have the right to create new rulings and directives in contradiction to the revealed law.

Many terms need to be understood if one is to make an informed decision. Perhaps the most important thing to know is that extremists exist in every religion. Some of the terminology associated with Islam is highlighted in Appendix I.

Monetary transactions are regulated in Islam. Muslims are forbidden from engaging in interest-based borrowing or lending. They are required to make written contracts for business dealings and to be honest in all financial exchanges.

It is apparent that financing played an important role in the activities of the 9/11 terrorists. Much of the money they obtained came via other operatives, also known as supporters and sleeper cells, operating in various European countries. These individuals obtained the money through legitimate businesses and employment, such as masonry work and automobile sales and repair. Other terrorists with al-Qaeda affiliations stated that they received training on criminal activities such as bank robberies and fraud schemes to fund their activities. They were also instructed in street crimes, such as residential and vehicle burglaries, as well as the use of stolen telephones and credit cards in order to facilitate their communication needs.

What appears to be noncriminal and run-of-the-mill may just be that piece of the puzzle required to avert a catastrophic event. It is important to remember that one is not looking for just street criminals any more, and terrorists do not work alone. An infrastructure of support exists for every active terrorist. One must look at the big picture based on verified information and avoid stereotypes. Terrorist groups are not just a ragtag bunch of individuals with fanatical or extreme religious beliefs. They are organized groups with structure and management components.

## TERRORISM: STRUCTURE AND MANAGEMENT

Much like corporations, businesses, governments, and paramilitary or military organizations, terrorist groups have structure and management components, as loose as they may appear to be.

In the 2003 government document *National Strategy for Combating Terrorism*[30] a basic structure of terror was presented, which is demonstrated in Figure 2.3. "At the base, underlying conditions such as poverty, corruption, religious conflict, and ethnic strife create opportunities for terrorists to exploit" (p. 6).[30] Terrorists use these conditions to justify their actions and expand support. An organization's structure, membership, resources, and security determine its capabilities and reach. Open borders, and to some extent advanced technology, allow access to international resources and new recruitment arenas. But no matter what, an organization must have a base of operation. Some organizations receive such bases of support, either physical or virtual, from states and countries all over the world. Groups such as al-Qaeda were able to establish and maintain bases and terrorist training camps in Afghanistan, and many others have done likewise in Bekka Valley, Lebanon.

The leadership component becomes the catalyst for terrorist action. Regardless of size or structure, most organizations tend to utilize a chain-of-command style of management. Many terrorist groups, domestic and foreign based, and hate organizations tend to follow a paramilitary or military organization when it comes to their training, structure, and tactics. The corporation or business world component is often displayed on the financial side of a terrorist organization. A tremendous financial need exists for an organization to keep a handful of operatives in the field, let alone to sustain the entire group. Therefore, many groups have turned to traditional criminal methods for gaining the capital they need to survive, committing crimes such as flimflams, credit card fraud, Internet scams, and robbery. However, these methods bring unwanted law enforcement attention to the members of an organization. Therefore, many groups turn to business ventures, such as nonprofit organizations. Law enforcement personnel and scholars would probably argue that these so-called business ventures

**FIGURE 2.3**    National strategy for combating terrorism structure.

are an exploitation of a capitalistic and free society. Many international groups that have pure hatred for the United States and everything that it stands for exploit the use of nonprofit religious and aid groups within the United States in order to add to their financial coffers.

Similar to Maslow's hierarchy of human needs, terrorists have needs too. Jonathan White[7] demonstrated the use of James Fraser's (former U.S. Army counterterrorist specialist) and Ian Fulton's analyses and writings from 1984. This was done in the form of a pyramid, similar to the national strategy for combating terrorism and to Maslow's hierarchy, to explain the structural needs of terrorist organizations. Fraser points out that terrorist organizations are divided into four distinctly separate levels dependent on each other: (1) command, (2) active cadre, (3) active supporters, and (4) passive supporters.[7]

Figure 2.4 shows the four levels of an organization as developed by Fraser and Fulton. The command level is at the top and is the smallest level. Just like many businesses, it does not exercise direct day-to-day operational control over activities and individuals. Command-level members would be well-educated planners, financial monitors, and target selectors. The second level is the active cadre. This is the hard-core component of the organization that consists of the field soldiers and, as some communities have come to experience, suicide/homicide bombers. It is at this level that the mission gets carried out. Active cadre members are aware of the existence of other members and the organization's beliefs, but they have limited knowledge of missions beyond their roles. The third tier in the hierarchal structure is made up of active supporters. These are the individuals charged with logistics, field support, and intelligence gathering for the active cadre. In order to keep one terrorist in the field, it takes several individuals to actively support the mission. The largest group is composed of passive supporters. They are used to muster political or financial support. Many of these individuals do not even know they are supporting an active terrorist organization. Therefore, it is difficult to capture and identify verifiable intelligence on individuals who fall into this classification.

Organizational size varies from group to group. Terrorist organizations may have a handful of members or may have as many as 10,000 or more. Dealing with and managing such numbers of personnel is difficult enough in a legitimate business, but in a covert terrorist organization of large size opportunities for leaks exist. Leaders within these organizations realize the importance of being inconspicuous. Therefore, leaders keep communication, access to information, and mission details on a need-to-know basis and often use small units, referred to as cells. The use of cells restricts the likelihood that law enforcement agencies or spies can gain access to an organization. Cells are generally composed of four to six members, all having specialties to enhance the mission, and each member has limited knowledge of the overall mission. This ensures that if one is captured or intelligence is leaked, the entire mission is not jeopardized. It also makes infiltration of the group by law enforcement personnel or a source of human intelligence nearly impossible. Similar to the military, where squads make up units and units make up divisions, a group of terrorist cells makes

**FIGURE 2.4** Command, active cadre, active supporters, and passive supporters.

up columns. This form of command structure allows many individuals with various specialties to come under a single command. This is important for an analyst or investigator to know when developing leads and initiating a link analysis.

The makeup and structure of a terrorist organization make it ripe for dissent and problems. Management is difficult enough in the public sector, but once it is coupled with a cloak of secrecy one has a recipe for potential failure. Understanding the problems associated with terrorist management will give the law enforcement community the knowledge necessary to exploit the weaknesses of the enemy and to potentially use these weakness to its advantage.

Terrorist groups face several managerial problems. Some of the common problems of terrorist management are outlined as follows[7:]

Communicating within an infrastructure of secrecy
Coordinating activities despite decentralization
Maintaining internal discipline
Avoiding fragmented ideologies
Maintaining logistics
Training
Financing

Terrorist leaders face many special operational problems. Communicating within an infrastructure of secrecy is perhaps a terrorist organization's primary weakness. Even with technological advances such as satellite telephones and the Internet, terrorists find it difficult to communicate because they are decentralized. With every communication they run the risk of being intercepted and compromised. Although secrecy is a tactical advantage, terrorists still need some form of communication to survive.

The second problem faced by terrorists involves coordinating activities in the absence of centralization. This is something to which many law enforcement agencies can relate. Decentralization creates potential logistical nightmares and mishaps. Large-scale terrorist operations require a coordinated effort in order to be successful. Decentralization combined with the first problem, communication, increases the likelihood of errors and detection.

Third, maintaining internal discipline poses several difficulties because organizational leaders must continuously strive to keep the members focused on the mission as well as on the group's ideology in order to prevent defection. This overlaps with the fourth problem, avoiding fragmented ideologies. For a terrorist group, it is important that all members share a common ideology. Regardless of their education, economic status, or nationality, the one factor that often bonds a group's membership is a common ideology or belief system.

The fifth problem faced by terrorist organizations is that of maintaining logistics. It takes 35–50 support personnel to keep one terrorist active in the field.[31] Support personnel are essential for providing food, transportation, funding, communications, and housing. Housing is perhaps the greatest challenge, because in order to avoid detection it may be necessary for a terrorist to relocate numerous times before completing a mission.

Training, the sixth problem faced in terrorist management, is as vital to a terrorist as it is to a law enforcement official. It is one thing to adopt a belief system and entirely another matter to be effectively trained in how to handle situations. Many law enforcement officials who have survived deadly scenarios are cited as a credit to their training. They understand that their training caused their instincts to take over. The same holds true for just about anyone with an extensive training background, including a terrorist. However, the problem of providing training for a terrorist is compounded by logistics and secrecy. Establishing a training facility especially for conducting a deadly terrorist act is no easy task and can bring unwelcome attention to the group.

Financing is the seventh and final problem faced in terrorist management, and it applies to all managers, both legitimate and terrorist-related. Financing lies at the heart of any operation. Terrorist attacks do not materialize overnight; they must be planned and organized in advance. They require considerable funding to sustain momentum. Financial means are needed for travel, lodging, food, supplies, training, and payoffs.

Using the aforementioned information, analysts and investigators must consider and evaluate the weaknesses of terrorist organizations. For every weakness in a terrorist organization, there is strength to be gained by law enforcement personnel. It is up to the law enforcement community to become cognizant of terrorists' needs when gathering and analyzing information in order to effectively exploit a weakness and seize the opportunity to thwart a tragic terrorist event.

## CHAPTER CONCEPTS

The chapter concepts can be summarized as follows:

- For years, the definition of terrorism has been debated without concurrence on its meaning. This is because it has been defined within political and social contexts and has been influenced by history.
- Terrorism has many different forms, including political, ecological, agricultural, narco, biological, and cyber.
- Domestic terrorism is not a new phenomenon. It has evolved since 1791 and has gone through several different stages.
- Different types of domestic terrorist groups are left-wing groups, right-wing groups, Puerto Rican leftists, black militants, Jewish extremists, and special interests groups.
- Organized hate groups play a role in the context of domestic terrorism. These groups are categorized as white supremacy groups, hate groups, patriot movements, sovereign citizen movements, militias, tax protestors, and foreign-sponsored groups.
- There are three types of terrorist beliefs: (1) nationalistic, (2) ideological, and (3) theological. Further, there are many differences between a terrorist and a street criminal.

## REFERENCES

1. Stohl, M., ed. 1979. *The Politics of Terrorism*. New York: Marcel Dekker, p. 1.
2. Justice Department. 2003. *Federal Bureau of Investigation*. http://www.fbi.gov/publish/terror/terrusa.html (accessed February 21, 2003).
3. General Military Training, Terrorism, n.p., n.d., p1-3-10, pl-3-14, and pl-3-16.
4. Heymann, P. B. 1998. *Terrorism and America: A Commonsense Strategy for a Democratic Society*. Cambridge, MA: MIT Press, p. 3.
5. Snow, D. M. 2002. *September 11, 2001, The New Face of War?* New York: Longman, p. 1.
6. Lesser, I. O., et al. 1999. *Countering the New Terrorism, Implications for Strategy*. Santa Monica, CA: Rand, p. 85.
7. White, J. R. 2002. *Terrorism: An Introduction*. 4th ed. Belmont, CA: Thomson Wadsworth, pp. 23, 33, 36, 39.
8. United States Department of State Immigration and Nationality Act, Section 212(a)(3)(B).
9. Hoffman, B. 1998. *Inside Terrorism*. New York: Columbia University Press, pp. 40, 107.
10. Gurr, T. R. 1979. Some Characteristics of Political Terrorism in the 1960s. In *The Politics of Terrorism*, ed. M. Stohl, pp. 25–49. New York: Marcel Dekker.
11. President. 2003. *The National Strategy for the Physical Protection of Critical Infrastructures and Key Assets*. White House, p. 9.
12. Able, D. 2000. *Hate Groups*. Berkeley Heights, NJ: Enslow Publishers, p. 26.
13. O'Connor, T. 2002. *Profiling Terrorists*. North Carolina Wesleyan College. http://faculty.ncwc.edu/toconnor/392/spy/terrorism.htm (accessed November, 2002).
14. Harris, J. W. 1987. Domestic Terrorism in the 1980's. *FBI Law Enforc Bull* 56:5–13.
15. Senate Select Committee on Intelligence. 2002. *The Terrorist Threat Confronting the United States*. Statement for the Record of Dale L. Watson, p. 2.

16. Southern Poverty Law Center. 2001. *Intelligence Report*. Hate Groups. http://www.tolerance.org/maps/hate/index.html (accessed February 28, 2003).

17. Perry, B. 2001. *In the Name of Hate: Understanding Hate Crimes*. New York: Routledge, pp. 138, 174.

18. U.S. Senate Committees on Appropriations. 2001. *Armed Services, and Select Committee on Intelligence, Threat of Terrorism to the United States*. Statement for the Record, Louis J. Freeh.

19. MILNET, Known Domestic Terrorist Groups. 2002. Profiles of Domestic Terror Groups. http://www.milnet.com/milnet/tgp/tgpmain.htm (accessed October 25, 2002).

20. Hoffman, B. 1998. *Inside Terrorism*. New York: Columbia University Press, pp. 107.

21. Southern Poverty Law Center. 2001. *Intelligence Report*. Known Active Patriot Groups. http://www.splcenter.org/intelligenceproject/ip-index.html (accessed February, 2006).

22. MILNET. 2002. *Domestic Terror: What It Holds for the Millenium*. Domestic Terrorism a Definition, p. 2. http://www.milnet.com/milnet/domestic/Dom-Terror.htm (accessed October 25, 2002).

23. Uniting and Strengthening America by Providing Appropriate Tools Required to Intercept and Obstruct Terrorism (USA PATRIOT) Act of 2001, 107th Congress, 1st session, HR3162 (October 24, 2001).

24. Landau, E. 1992. *Terrorism: America's Growing Threat*. New York: Lodestar Books (E.P. Dutton), p. 45.

25. Laqueur, W. 1987. *The Age of Terrorism*. Boston, MD: Little, Brown, p. 335.

26. Council on Foreign Relations. 2003. T*errorism: Questions & Answers*. American Militant Extremists United States, Radicals. http://www.cfrterrorism.org/groups/ (accessed March 3, 2003).

27. Revell, B. 2002. *A Long Path of Terror*. On the Beat, p. 1. http://www.adl.org (accessed February 20, 2003).

28. U.S. Justice Department. 2003. *Federal Bureau of Investigation*. http://www.fbi.gov/ucr/Cius_98 (accessed February 21, 2003).

29. Southern Poverty Law Center. 2003. *Hate Groups*. Hate Group Definitions. http://www.tolerance.org/maps/hate/index.html (accessed March 6, 2003).

30. President. 2003. *National Strategy for Combating Terrorism*. 6.

31. Bodansky, Y. 1999. *Bin Laden: The Man Who Declared War on America*. Rocklin, CA: Forum.

# 3  Homeland Security and Analysis

Although the Symbionese Liberation Army (SLA) operated in the 1970s and targeted banks, initiated kidnappings, and bombed and killed law enforcement personnel, it was seen as a revolutionary or radical group that was disgruntled with the government. Even after the final arrests and convictions were made and the remaining members were sentenced in 2002 and 2003, approximately 30 years after the crime spree and killing began, they were still viewed as a fad or leftist group. They were also described as a group whose time had passed, and its members were described as criminals who were convicted and sentenced for traditional crimes. What makes this group different from al-Qaeda, apart from al-Qaeda's international ties and large size? Perhaps it is the fact that members of the SLA were citizens of the United States and often looked and acted like the majority of other criminals or gang members.

For years, many groups like the SLA have operated within the country dissatisfied with the government or the politics of the United States. Throughout the 1960s and into the 1970s, many individuals and groups demonstrated in various ways against the United States and its political points of view. The war in Vietnam was frequently used as a reason behind these antigovernment sentiments. Whether in the United States or in Europe, many factions sought to terrorize those associated with the war initiative. An example can be found in Germany in the form of the relatively small Baader-Meinhof Gang whose members had anti-Vietnam beliefs. However, much of the activity surrounding these rather small groups was seen more as a social or political nuisance rather than as terrorism. It was not until Ted Robert Gurr published the chapter "Some Characteristics of Political Terrorism" in *The Politics of Terrorism*[1] that what was taking place was shown to be more far-reaching than a mere nuisance: it was terrorism. Gurr noted that terrorist activity such as that demonstrated in the Vietnam era was conducted by very small groups and was ephemeral.

Regardless of the size of the group, terrorists and terrorism have a dramatic effect on the world, wherever the activity takes place. The victims or their family members are not concerned about the size of the group or whether the group's activity was short-lived. However, they would have wanted some level of warning that an attack was imminent. Although the U.S. government cannot provide a warning system based on intelligence for the entire world, it has been able to design and impose a system in the United States known as the Homeland Security Advisory System (HSAS). This system is designed to provide a comprehensive and effective means by which information regarding the risk of impending terrorist attacks can be disseminated to federal, state, and local law enforcement authorities, as well as to the American public. When the system was instituted in March 2002, the federal government initiated numerous press releases and garnered a massive amount of media attention in order to inform the public about the new advisory system. However, many individuals in the public sector as well as in the law enforcement community even today have only a vague awareness of the system and what each level on the continuum means. This chapter presents a standardized approach to and awareness of the advisory system.

## DEFINITION OF HOMELAND SECURITY

Just like the terms terrorism, terrorist activity, and terrorist, homeland security has many meanings to different people. The U.S. federal government defines homeland security as follows:

> Homeland security is a concerted national effort to prevent terrorist attacks within the U.S., reduce America's vulnerability to terrorism, and minimize the damage and recover from attacks that do occur. (p. 8)[2]

The government elaborated on each phrase in this definition. "Concerted national effort" is based on the principles of shared responsibility and partnership with Congress, state and local governments, the private sector, and the American people. "Terrorist attacks" covers kidnappings; hijackings; shootings; conventional bombings; attacks involving chemical, biological, radiological, or nuclear weapons; cyber attacks; and any number of other forms of malicious violence. "Reduce America's vulnerability" refers to constantly evolving the way in which the government works with the private sector to identify and protect the critical infrastructure and key assets of the country, detect terrorist threats, and augment the defenses of the country. "Minimize the damage" requires efforts on the part of citizens to focus on the brave and dedicated public servants who are first responders. To "recover," we must be prepared to protect and restore institutions needed to sustain economic growth and confidence, rebuild destroyed property, assist victims and their families, heal psychological wounds, and demonstrate compassion, recognizing that we cannot return to a pre-attack norm.

Regardless of how homeland security is defined, a terrorist threat can come from anywhere. Based on the *National Strategy for Combating Terrorism* report,[2] a terrorist threat is flexible, transnational, enabled by modern technology, and characterized by loose interconnectivity within and between groups. These groups operate on three levels: The first level consists of those who operate within a single country and have a limited reach. The second level comprises the terrorist organizations that operate regionally. These operations transcend at least one international boundary. Organizations with global reach constitute the third level. Their operations span multiple regions, and their reach can be global. The United States is subject to attack from all the three levels; therefore, it is imperative that intelligence analysis is expedited and advisories posted as soon as possible.

## HOMELAND SECURITY ADVISORY SYSTEM

HSAS was instituted in March 2002 by the U.S. government to provide different levels of awareness of the likelihood of terrorist attacks to state and local governments and to ordinary citizens, regardless of their locale. The determination of each level is decided upon by high-ranking government officials based on a wide range of information and intelligence received and corroborated by a multitude of sources worldwide. Once intelligence is developed, it is verified and corroborated against multiple variables and scenarios to determine whether it is credible, whether there is a specific threat, or whether there is a grave threat. Only then is it presented for proper advisement and color designation, following the Homeland Security Presidential Directive.[3] The hierarchy used with the now defunct HSAS is demonstrated in Figure 3.1. This system, which was used as a guide,[4] is an intelligence-driven system designed to aid law enforcement personnel and the public in responding to or preparing for a terrorist threat. One question that arises at this point is as follows: Where does the intelligence come from, and whose information is used?

The advisory system was well publicized during its inception, but the public even today lacks finite understanding as to what each level represents. A summary of each level as posted on the Department of Homeland Security (DHS)'s website[5] is outlined as follows:

Low condition (green)—This condition is declared when there is a low risk of terrorist attacks.
    Federal departments and agencies should consider the following general measures in addition to agency-specific protective measures that they develop and implement:
    Refining and exercising, as appropriate, preplanned protective measures
    Ensuring that personnel receive proper training on HSAS and on specific preplanned department or agency protective measures
    Institutionalizing a process to ensure that all facilities and regulated sectors are regularly assessed for vulnerabilities to terrorist attacks and all reasonable measures are taken to mitigate such vulnerabilities
Guarded condition (blue)—This condition is declared when there is a general risk of terrorist attacks. In addition to the protective measures taken under the previously mentioned threat

**FIGURE 3.1**   Original Homeland Security Advisory System.

condition, federal departments and agencies should consider the following general measures
along with the agency-specific protective measures that they develop and implement:
Checking communications with designated emergency response or command locations
Reviewing and updating emergency response procedures
Providing the public with any information that would strengthen its ability to act appropriately
Elevated condition (yellow)—An elevated condition is declared when there is significant risk of
terrorist attacks. In addition to the protective measures taken under both the previously men-
tioned threat conditions, federal departments and agencies should consider the following gen-
eral measures along with the protective measures that they specifically develop and implement:
Increasing surveillance of critical locations
Coordinating emergency plans, as appropriate, with nearby jurisdictions
Assessing whether the precise characteristics of the threat require further refinement of pre-
planned protective measures
Implementing, as appropriate, contingency and emergency response plans

High condition (orange)—A high condition is declared when there is a high risk of terrorist attacks. In addition to the protective measures taken under the previously mentioned threat conditions, federal departments and agencies should consider the following general measures along with the agency-specific protective measures that they develop and implement:
Coordinating necessary security efforts with federal, state, and local law enforcement agencies; the National Guard, or other appropriate armed forces organizations
Taking additional precautions at public events and possibly considering alternative venues for or even cancellations of such events
Preparing to execute contingency procedures, such as moving to an alternative site or dispersing the workforce
Restricting access to the threatened facility to essential personnel only
Severe condition (red)—A severe condition reflects a severe risk of terrorist attacks. Under most circumstances, the protective measures for this condition are not intended to be sustained over substantial periods of time. In addition to the protective measures adopted under the previously mentioned threat conditions, federal departments and agencies should consider the following general measures along with agency-specific protective measures that they develop and implement:
Increasing or redirecting personnel to address critical emergency needs
Assigning emergency response personnel and prepositioning and mobilizing specially trained teams or resources
Monitoring, redirecting, or constraining transportation systems
Closing public and government facilities

Many terrorist acts are aimed at political change. "Closing public and government facilities," which is mentioned under the severe condition (red) of HSAS, might be construed as an act of submission. Terrorists would probably consider an attack to be successful if the United States, or any other government, closes down its facilities.

HSAS is managed by the U.S. Attorney General in concert with the Secretary of the Department of Homeland Security. They are responsible for developing, implementing, and managing the system for the federal government based on the latest verified intelligence. Again, whose intelligence? A concern regarding the system, which is not publicly addressed, is whether the information and intelligence being used to make informed decisions include domestic terrorist activities or do they deal with foreign-based activities alone? Also, it is not public knowledge whether the intelligence used is a derivative of local and state law enforcement information or is just from federal and military sources. Despite this concern, it is imperative that law enforcement agencies submit all intelligence as soon as it is developed. In addition, state and local governments are encouraged to implement the advisory system and modify it to meet the needs of their agencies.

Use of such a system is vital to standardizing practices, approaches, and contingency plans when dealing with homeland security or terrorism risks. However, one should not become consumed with the national advisory system or wait until a particular level is announced. This would be reactive, just like the system that is designed to help in preparing and responding to attacks. The system is full of suggestive reactionary practices that will aid any agency or its citizens in responding to threats, but law enforcement personnel today are looking to identify the threat and not just to respond. Waiting for the federal government or anyone else to initiate a threat level before doing anything would be neglect of duty. Every agency and its members are part of the solution and analytical practices should be undertaken and be continuous, whether or not agency staff members feel they have anything to bring to the homeland security table.

Furthermore, this system is based on "national" intelligence. Nothing prevents local jurisdictions or regions from implementing their own systems. Regardless of the advisory level, information gathering and analysis should be continuous and should be routinely reconciled in order to paint the clearest picture. Analysis should be continuous and heightened as the advisory level is raised. Analysts must work in a well-rounded fashion, look globally, and have an acute awareness of their roles and how their duties can benefit homeland security.

## THE UPDATED HOMELAND SECURITY ADVISORY SYSTEM

On July 14, 2009, DHS Secretary Janet Napolitano announced the formation of a task force to conduct a 60-day review of the HSAS. The mission of the task force was to assess the effectiveness of the system in informing the public about terrorist threats and communicating protective measures to be followed within the government and throughout the private sector.

Secretary Napolitano appointed Fran Townsend, former assistant to President George W. Bush for Homeland Security, and Judge William Webster, former director of the Federal Bureau of Investigation (FBI) and Central Intelligence Agency (CIA), to cochair the task force and lead the review. The review included a broad consideration of HSAS and the system's impact on state, local, tribal, territorial, and international law enforcement partners; the private sector; and the American people. The task force consulted with the Department of Justice—under which HSAS was originally created—and provided opportunities for public input. Following the 60-day review period, the task force presented its findings to Secretary Napolitano, who in turn discussed the findings with other cabinet officials before making a recommendation about the future of the system to the White House.

On January 27, 2011, the DHS announced that it was beginning a 90-day phasing out of the initial HSAS. When the task force produced its report in September 2009, it noted that the national threat level was changed only 17 times since the inception of HSAS. The members further noted that it was never at the green or blue levels and was at the red level only once, on August 10, 2006. The times that were noted in the report as to when HSAS was impacted during the period from 2002 to 2009 are outlined as follows:

2002

September 10, 2002—raised from yellow to orange: The U.S. intelligence community received information, based on debriefings of a senior al-Qaeda operative, of possible terrorist attacks timed to coincide with the anniversary of the September 11, 2001, attacks on the United States. Information indicated that al-Qaeda cells were established in several South Asian countries in order to conduct car-bomb and other attacks on U.S. facilities. These cells had been accumulating explosives since around January 2002 in preparation for the attacks.

September 24, 2002—lowered from orange to yellow: Based on a review of intelligence and an assessment of threats by the intelligence community, as well as the passing of the anniversary of the September 11 terrorist attacks and the disruption of potential terrorist operations in the United States and abroad, the Attorney General in consultation with the Homeland Security Council returned the threat level to an elevated risk of terrorist attack, or yellow.

2003

February 7, 2003—raised from yellow to orange: Intelligence reports suggested that al-Qaeda leaders were planning for attacks on apartment buildings, hotels, and other soft or lightly secured targets in the United States.

February 27, 2003—lowered from orange to yellow: Threat level was lowered based on a careful review of how specific intelligence evolved, as well as counterterrorism actions taken to address specific aspects of the threat situation.

March 17, 2003—raised from yellow to orange: The intelligence community believed that terrorists would attempt multiple attacks against U.S. and coalition targets worldwide in the event of a United States–led military campaign against Saddam Hussein.

April 16, 2003—lowered from orange to yellow: Following a review of intelligence and an assessment of threats by the intelligence community, DHS, in consultation with the

Homeland Security Council, lowered the threat advisory level to an elevated risk of terrorist attack.

May 20, 2003—raised from yellow to orange: In the wake of terrorist bombings in Saudi Arabia and Morocco, intelligence reports indicated that terrorists might attempt attacks against targets in the United States.

May 30, 2003—lowered from orange to yellow: Following a review of intelligence and an assessment of threats by the intelligence community, DHS, in consultation with the Homeland Security Council, lowered the threat advisory level to an elevated risk of terrorist attack.

December 21, 2003—raised from yellow to orange: The U.S. intelligence community received a substantial increase in the volume of threat-related intelligence reports.

2004

January 9, 2004—lowered from orange to yellow: Following a review of intelligence and an assessment of threats by the intelligence community, DHS, in consultation with the Homeland Security Council, lowered the threat advisory level to an elevated risk of terrorist attack.

August 1, 2004—raised from yellow to orange: The threat level was raised specifically for the financial services sector in New York City, northern New Jersey, and Washington, DC, as a result of receiving new and unusually specific information about where al-Qaeda would like to attack.

November 10, 2004—lowered from orange to yellow: The threat level was lowered for the financial services sectors in New York City, northern New Jersey, and Washington, DC. State and local leaders as well as the private sector strengthened security in and around specific buildings and locations as well as throughout the financial services sector after the threat level was raised on August 1, 2004. Permanent protective measures were put in place that did not exist before this date.

2005

July 7, 2005—raised from yellow to orange for mass transit: In light of the attacks in London, the U.S. government raised the threat level in the mass transit portion of the transportation sector, including regional and inner city passenger rail, subways, and metropolitan bus systems.

August 12, 2005—lowered from orange to yellow for mass transit: Since raising the threat level for mass transit systems on July 7, 2005, DHS worked with federal, state, and local partners to develop and implement sustainable mass transit security measures tailored to the unique design of each region's transit system. In light of these increased long-term measures, the department lowered the national threat level for the mass transit portion of the transportation sector.

2006

August 10, 2006—raised from yellow to red for flights originating in the United Kingdom bound for the United States; raised to orange for all commercial aviation services operating in or bound for the United States: The U.S. government raised the nation's threat level to the highest for commercial flights originating in the United Kingdom and bound for the United States, and raised the threat level for general aviation to high for all inbound international flights, other than flights from Great Britain, and all flights within the United States.

August 13, 2006—lowered from red to orange for flights originating in the United Kingdom bound for the United States; remains at orange for all domestic and international flights: The DHS lowered the aviation threat level from red to orange for flights from the United Kingdom bound for the United States. The U.S. threat level remained at orange for all domestic and international flights. The ban on liquids and gels in carry-on baggage still remained in full effect.

## NATIONAL THREAT ADVISORY SYSTEM

HSAS was introduced on March 11, 2002. Seven years later in July 2009, Secretary Napolitano formed a bipartisan task force of security experts, state and local elected officials, law enforcement officials, and other key stakeholders—cochaired by Fran Townsend and Judge William Webster—to assess the effectiveness of HSAS. The results of this assessment formed the basis of the National Terrorism Advisory System (NTAS).

Under the new system, DHS is responsible for coordinating with other federal entities to issue formal, detailed alerts when the federal government receives information about a specific or credible terrorist threat. These alerts include a clear statement that there is an "imminent threat" or "elevated threat." The alerts also provide a concise summary of the potential threat, information about actions that are being taken to ensure public safety, and recommended steps that individuals, communities, businesses, and governments can follow.

The NTAS alerts will be based on the nature of the threat: in some cases, alerts will be sent directly to law enforcement agencies or affected areas of the private sector, whereas in other cases alerts will be issued more broadly to the American people through both official and media channels, including a designated DHS web page as well as social media channels such as Facebook and Twitter.

Additionally, NTAS will have a "sunset provision," meaning that individual threat alerts will be issued with a specified end date. Alerts may be extended if new information becomes available or if the threat evolves significantly. The new alert system was implemented in April 2011. For more information on NTAS, see www.dhs.gov/alerts.

Types of advisories issued under NTAS:

*Bulletin*—Describes current developments or general trends regarding threats of terrorism.
*Elevated Alert*—Warns of a credible terrorism threat against the United States.
*Imminent Alert*—Warns of a credible, specific, and impending terrorism threat against the
  United States.

## HOMELAND SECURITY AND ANALYSIS

Several factors are considered when assessing a potential homeland security or terrorist threat. These considerations include whether the threat is credible, whether it is corroborated, whether it is specific and imminent, and how grave it is. These four factors should be at the immediate crux of any form of real-time intelligence analysis that is conducted. In the realm of law enforcement, the approach is often to follow a hunch or gut feeling, based on training and experience, when seeking out criminal activity or developing a trend or pattern. With homeland security, there is no such opportunity. When analyzing traditional crime many analysts attempt to forecast, often based on probability, when and where the next incident in a serial crime will take place. Although this has its place in law enforcement, it is fair to say that the likelihood of predicting the next terrorist attack with any degree of certainty is slim. Rather than attempting to forecast the next attack, there should be a concerted effort to identify weaknesses and understand how to anticipate behavior based on an array of known variables. When dealing with the traditional criminal element, there is rarely a situation that negatively and tragically impacts more people or countries than terrorism. Therefore, there is no room for anything less than credible, corroborated, timely, and well-defined information.

According to DHS's White House website[5] on information analysis and infrastructure protection, "The CIA will continue to gather and analyze overseas intelligence. Homeland Security will continue to require interagency coordination."

Imposing vague terminology such as "require interagency coordination" reduces the chance that all law enforcement agencies will work together in a real-time fashion. The fact that there is no mention of gathering and analyzing domestic intelligence, only overseas intelligence, is greatly disturbing and may cause law enforcement personnel to overlook potential threats to homeland security that may arise from factions in their own backyards. As alluded to in the White House's March 12, 2002 press release concerning HSAS, states and localities are encouraged to adopt and implement compatible systems. The question is, how many states and localities have adopted or implemented compatible systems? This question is not meant as a criticism but is designed to demonstrate the need for self-initiated and documented processes and systems that will aid all parties involved in the war on terrorism. Since September 11, 2001 communication and intelligence processes have come to the forefront of any successful anti-terrorism campaign. However, these processes vary from agency to agency. International or foreign-based terrorist organizations can never be overlooked, and there is a great deal of information available from myriad resources on such groups; however, there is little information available on domestic terrorists or organized hate groups. Due to the lack of domestic intelligence coordination and communication, it is incumbent upon law enforcement personnel, analysts included, to provide real-time intelligence analysis, effectively disseminate it, and provide accurate advisories without delay.

Up to now, homeland security and terrorism analysis has been addressed largely by federal law enforcement and military analysts. Although these well-trained analysts have a lot to offer, their traditional duties and practices do not always translate easily into effective local and state law enforcement procedures. The primary reason for this is that they have two distinctly different missions. Law enforcement analysts use federal and state guidelines, and they operate in defined jurisdictional areas. Military analysts use directives, treaties, resolutions, and international laws, and they operate in an international theater. Simply put, it is crime versus war. Therefore, it is incumbent upon law enforcement personnel to incorporate the best of both worlds into methods that can be readily adapted and retrofitted in order to enhance the capabilities of analysts and investigators charged with handling homeland security issues.

One way to adapt is by developing a base from which to start. The *National Strategy for Homeland Security* report developed such a base. This strategy identifies a strategic framework based on three national objectives that are also applicable to any law enforcement agency. In order of priority, these objectives are to prevent terrorist attacks within the United States, to reduce America's vulnerability to terrorism, and to minimize the damage and recover from attacks that occur.[6] The first two objectives are those that law enforcement personnel, particularly analysts, can be successful at achieving. The third objective seems to be the focus of many lectures and training courses that are given to law enforcement officials. As interagency and intergovernmental coordination is enhanced, the first two proactive objectives will overshadow the third, which is partially reactive. All these objectives are made slightly more attainable, in part, by legislative enhancements such as the Uniting and Strengthening America by Providing Appropriate Tools Required to Intercept and Obstruct Terrorism (USA PATRIOT) Act.

## THE UNITING AND STRENGTHENING AMERICA BY PROVIDING APPROPRIATE TOOLS REQUIRED TO INTERCEPT AND OBSTRUCT TERRORISM ACT

The USA PATRIOT Act of 2001[7] from the 107th Congress, HR 3162, was established to deter and punish terrorist acts in the United States and around the world, and to enhance law enforcement investigatory tools. The passing of the USA PATRIOT Act of 2001 was unprecedented. National and world events surrounding September 11, 2001, were the driving force behind the evolution and passing of what has come to be known simply as the Patriot Act. These events were the stimuli for the possibly record-breaking pace at which this act was passed and subsequently signed by President George W. Bush on October 26, 2001. This was just one month after the act was initiated and passed in the Senate by a 98-to-1 vote. This massive sweeping legislation positively impacted law enforcement agencies and their roles in combating terrorism, and it covers a broad range of topics.

Some of the topics covered by the USA PATRIOT Act include the following:

Enhancing domestic security against terrorism
Enhancing surveillance procedures
International Money Laundering Abatement and Antiterrorist Financing Act of 2001
Protecting the borders
Removing obstacles to investigating terrorism
Providing for victims of terrorism, public safety officers, and their families
Increasing information sharing for critical infrastructure protection
Strengthening criminal laws against terrorism
Improving intelligence
Protecting critical infrastructures

Interestingly, although the content of the act appears all-encompassing, domestic terrorism is not defined until about three-quarters of the way into the document. Although this is not necessarily viewed as a negative trait, it is important that all law enforcement personnel remain cognizant of the numerous domestic-based organizations as well as the foreign-based ones that have other bases, outreach, and supporters within the United States. The act was a product of international terrorist actions. However, it is also worth noting that this act is not meant just for investigating and analyzing exotic foreign-based terrorist groups. It applies to all groups, domestic and international, and all forms of terrorism.

Passage of this act greatly improved the tools available for law enforcement. Beyond the immediate benefit of the act, which is availability of enhanced surveillance procedures, law enforcement at all levels will reap the greatest investigative rewards from enhanced money-laundering and financial tracking capabilities as well as increased information sharing among agencies. However, it is important to note that forfeiture aspects and associating them or identifying them with terrorists will lead to long, tedious, and arduous investigations that require a great deal of expertise. This will pose great difficulty for the majority of law enforcement agencies that have fewer than 25 officers. The act is geared toward the one thing that no terrorist organization can do without—finances.

## IMPORTANCE OF FINANCES IN TERRORIST ACTIVITIES

Tracking, monitoring, and cutting off finances are tremendously important tools in the war on terrorism. As of October 2002, an aggressive international law enforcement effort resulted in the freezing of $113 million in terrorists' assets in 500 bank accounts around the world, which had significant activity in Western countries, including $35 million in the United States alone.[8]

The use of sleeper cells and the activities associated with their efforts for financial gain are key components of terrorist-related activity. However, other forms of funding are used, such as funding from nongovernmental organizations (NGOs) and charitable organizations. Many of these are passed off as legitimate business ventures, but things are not always what they appear to be. International fundamentalist terrorists increasingly use NGOs and charitable organizations as a way to gain finances to fund terrorist activities. The NGOs are used much in the same manner as active supporters. They may offer logistical support in the forms of employment, documents, travel, and training. Uses of "fronts" by terrorist organizations (such as Hamas) in the United States uncovered charities, humanitarian foundations, and relief organizations that were used to raise funding in support of terrorist activities. Speaking in 1995 on the topic of protecting America, Oliver Revell[9] stated, "Numerous front groups supporting Hamas have been established in the United States, and several collect funds as tax exempt 501(C)(3) organizations" (p. 4).[9] Tremendous challenges exist for law enforcement personnel investigating terrorist fund-raising through the use of NGOs and alleged charitable humanitarian organizations. The line between legitimate and what appears to be legitimate is often blurred.

Financing efforts by terrorist organizations have ranged from basic to sophisticated. There probably is not a financing method known that has not been tried at least once. Use of correspondent bank accounts, private bank accounts, offshore shell banks, *hawala* (see section "Hawala system") transactions, cash smuggling, identity theft, credit card fraud, drug trafficking, money laundering (which is explained in further detail under enhanced analysis in the section "Crimes and incidents that may yield information or links," in Chapter 5), and flimflams are prevalent. The terrorist's goal is to seek financial gain while remaining undetected. That is why the USA PATRIOT Act plays an important role with its emphasis on financial topics. Regardless of the form of terrorism being investigated, the Patriot Act opens new avenues for law enforcement. As law enforcement agencies target traditional financial methods, terrorists are more apt to use ancient and informal methods to transfer money, such as the hawala system.

## Hawala System

The word hawala means "transfer" in Arabic and in some circles hawala is referred to as *hundi*. In some contexts, the word hawala is used synonymously with "trust." Hawala is an ancient alternative or parallel remittance system that originated in South Asia and is processed with the assistance of a *hawaladar* or agent. It is based largely on trust and extensive use of connections, such as family members and other known affiliations, and is generally void of formal financial institutions such as banks. It was developed in India before the introduction of traditional banking practices and is often referred to as an underground banking system. There is little documentation and record keeping in this system. There are many motivations for using the hawala system, including its effectiveness, efficiency, reliability, lack of bureaucracy, lack of a paper trail, and ability to evade taxes. In some instances two terms are associated with transactions: (1) "black" hawala and (2) "white" hawala. Simply put, black hawala refers to illegitimate transactions, particularly money laundering, whereas white hawala refers to legitimate transactions. Many dealings associated with the hawala system are done in the areas of import and export businesses, travel services, jewelry, and currency exchanges. Transactions are usually completed in 1 to 2 days. There are many locales that rely or use the system. Some of the most common ethnic locations where the system is prevalent are Pakistan, India, Somalia, and the Persian Gulf States. Three countries that tend to show up on the radar screen are Great Britain, Switzerland, and Dubai.

There are several other common aspects to hawala: First, in most cases hawala transactions go across international lines, such as with worker remittances to their home countries. Second, hawala usually involves more than one currency, although this is not absolutely required. Third, a hawala transaction usually entails principals and intermediaries. To accommodate requests of the principals, the intermediaries usually take financial positions. Later, much as in the case of conventional banking practices, these transactions will be cleared among the units to balance their books.

Transactions involving tens of thousands of dollars are frequent. The only real limitations of a hawala system are the willingness and abilities of the parties involved. Invoice manipulations can be used to cover payments. For example, if an individual owes $10,000 to another, a purchase of goods is arranged at $7,000 and an invoice is sent for $17,000. This conceals the purchase of the goods as well as the money owed. Quite often, the hawala system does not use any sort of negotiable instrument. Money transfers take place based on communications among members of the hawala network.

This brief section is meant to provide an awareness of alternative forms of financial transactions that exist in the world. It is important to note that while there are documented incidents of the use of hawala in terrorist events, the bulk of transactions are legitimate. Some scholars suspect that hundreds of billions of dollars are transacted in hawala networks every year. The most obvious legal problem with hawala in remitting countries is the lack of any registration or licensing, although the operations themselves are generally harmless. In receiving countries like India, there is in addition the more subtle potential clash between hawala operations and exchange controls whereby hawala transactions often result in increased black market transactions and expanded underground activity. Further details and references on hawala systems can be attained by law enforcement personnel through the U.S. Department of Treasury Financial Crimes Enforcement Network (FinCEN) and Interpol. Knowledge of the various methods that a group may use to conduct financial affairs is another tool that will aid law enforcement agencies in dealing with terrorism.

## Benefits of Hawala System

In June 2003, the World Bank noted significant benefits of a hawala transaction. The benefits noted by the World Bank are as follows:

A hawala is anonymous and therefore very hard to detect. The hawala system often utilizes coded notations only understood by the hawala brokers (known as hawaladars) to identify both the transaction and the parties.

There is a lack of transparency due to the fact that the transactions often occur over the phone or via e-mail between the hawaladars, relying on the local dialect and cultural nuances to communicate.

Hawala transactions are considered safe and reliable. There is next to no history of fraud or embezzlement. This is in no small part due to the reliance on trusted family and tribal relationships to carry out the transaction.

The transaction is effected quickly, because it transpires in the space of one or two short phone calls or e-mails.

The hawala system offers instant global coverage, in particular to remote parts of Asia and the Middle East.

It is inexpensive when compared with the money transmitter fees charged by, for example, Western Union or HSBC.

There is little to no paper trail. There is at best a cryptic note and an outside reference in a ledger. All of this makes investigations very difficult.

There is the practice of mixing hawala activities with other business activities, as well as the commingling of funds. These practices make auditing and prosecution almost impossible.

No money ever changes hands. The first hawaladar merely gives the instructions, and the second hawaladar using his or her own local funds delivers the money to the recipient, often to his or her home or office. At a later date, accounts between hawaladars are reconciled, often using gold or diamonds.

## Charitable Contributions—Zakat

Much like hawaladars use of gold, an Islamic form of charity has a history in gold and silver—*zakat*. One of the most important principles of Islam is that all things belong to God and wealth is therefore held by human beings in trust. The word zakat means both "purification" and "growth." Possessions are purified by setting aside a proportion for those in need, and, like the pruning of plants, this cuts back balances and encourages new growth.

Zakat is the amount of money that every adult, mentally stable, free, and financially able Muslim, male and female, has to pay to support specific categories of people.

The obligatory nature of zakat is firmly established in the Quran, the Sunnah (or Hadith), and by the consensus of the companions and the Muslim scholars. Over the years, many Muslims have agreed that the obligatory nature of paying zakat in gold and silver has grown to include other forms of modern currency.

According to Islamic Internet sites, zakat is obligatory when a certain amount of money, called the *nisab*, is reached or exceeded. Zakat is not obligatory if the amount owned is less than this nisab. The nisab (or minimum amount) of gold and golden currency is 20 mithqal; this is approximately 85 g of pure gold and 1 mithqal is approximately 4.25 g. The nisab of silver and silver currency is 200 dirhams, which is approximately 595 g of pure silver. The nisab of other kinds of money and currency is to be scaled to that of gold, that is, 85 g of pure gold. This means that the nisab of money is the price of 85 g of 999-type (pure) gold, on the day in which zakat is paid.

When is zakat due? Zakat is due under the following two conditions:

1. The passage of one lunar year: Zakat is obligatory after a time span of one lunar year passes with the money in the control of its owner. Then the owner needs to pay 2.5% (or 1/40) of the money as zakat. (A lunar year is approximately 355 days.)
2. Deduction of debts: The owner should deduct any amount of money he or she borrowed from others, check if the rest reaches the necessary nisab, and then pay the zakat for it.

If the owner had enough money to satisfy the nisab at the beginning of the year but the money increased (in profits, salaries, inheritance, grants, etc.) later in the year, the owner needs to add the increase to the nisab amount owned at the beginning of the year and then pay zakat, 2.5%, of the total at the end of the lunar year. Each Muslim calculates his or her own zakat individually. For most purposes, this involves the annual payment of 2.5% of one's capital.[10]

The purpose for giving a detailed explanation of zakat here is to provide an understanding of the cultural norms experienced in the Islamic culture. An additional purpose is for law enforcement officials to understand another opportunity that may exist for financial exploitation regarding tracking or monitoring finances. Just like any other charitable opportunity, there are known examples of subversive activities being funded under the guise of zakat. However, law enforcement agencies investigating the financial aspects of a criminal activity often look at bank records, Internal Revenue Service records, and other known financial resources of the Western world. To deal with terrorism effectively, law enforcement officials should be well-versed in the norms of other cultures.

## DEALING WITH TERRORISM

One of the greatest frustrations faced when dealing with terrorism is the wide variety of forms that terrorist activities can take.[11] Terrorism assumes many guises, such as those noted in Chapter 2—for example, political and cyber. These forms are compounded by the various types and styles of attacks beyond conventional bombings. If dealing with terrorist acts is so frustrating, how are the investigative and analytical communities to make sense of it? Traditionally, analysts and investigators have looked for common links and approaches that aided them in concluding their criminal investigations. An analyst who is assigned a case to monitor and gather intelligence leads and information utilizes various analytical techniques, often through the use of sophisticated software, to link common variables (also known as link analysis). Analysts have criminal and statutory guidelines to assist in developing probable cause and securing a criminal conviction. The numerous off-the-shelf intelligence programs are designed to expedite the intelligence process and graphically illustrate interrelationships that otherwise may be overlooked. When dealing with homeland security and terrorism, these luxuries are not as available as they are for traditional crimes. There are thousands of law enforcement agencies in the United States, with 50 sets of varied state statutes, and much of what may be construed as a homeland security incident or terrorism is usually classified as a crime. An all-inclusive database or intelligence system that all agencies can agree upon does not exist. Whether it is a hijacking or a bombing, the first inclination of law enforcement personnel is to treat it as a violent crime that needs immediate response and attention, and not as a homeland security or terrorist action. This was true until September 11, 2001. How can we be sure that everyone is on the same page and is keeping an open mind as to the potential for terrorism to strike anywhere? The answer is simple: Through open communication, availability of detailed information, proactive investigations, and the use of highly trained analytical and intelligence personnel.

Enforcing cooperation between the CIA, FBI, and the Immigration and Naturalization Service (INS) is essential in dealing with terrorism.[11] This is unarguably true; however, the same premise should be enforced among municipal, county, state, and federal law enforcement agencies. All levels of response, including investigation and information gathering, are crucial pieces to the puzzle when dealing with homeland security and terrorism. After all, it is not just international terrorist organizations overseas that need to be monitored. There are many domestic groups actively or passively operating in everyone's own backyard. Whether an investigation is local, state, or federal based, money is one nexus that, if exposed, can bring all agencies together. Foreign- and domestic-based terrorist organizations generally have one feature in common—the need for financing. As documented in Steven Emerson's remarkable video documentary for the Public Broadcasting System (PBS) that aired in November 1994, titled *Jihad in America,* terrorist organizations regardless of how much they despise and loathe the United States have no problem seeking support and financial backing in the United States. Based on this critical need, perhaps the best approach for dealing with terrorism is to track the flow of money and finances in such organizations.

It can be detrimental to be one-dimensional and to not consider global approaches to homeland security and terrorist-related information. It has been demonstrated that terrorist activity can occur anywhere and at any time, but financial support is an ongoing process with many guises. This need exists and poses perhaps the greatest opportunity for law enforcement to expose and exploit in order to gain the upper hand in tracking and monitoring potential homeland security threats.

Homeland security and terrorism have received a great deal of public attention over the past couple of years. Most of the attention comes from the federal government and the media. Law enforcement agencies, based on this attention, were force-fed a multitude of methods and practices for dealing with matters of homeland security and terrorism. Some local and state agencies established homeland security units in an attempt to keep up with the growing concerns regarding the ever-evolving world of terrorism. Traditional managers and administrators also reacted to this crisis, predictably, by having their agencies develop plans of action and contingency and by identifying potential targets that exist within their jurisdictions in case of an attack. However, this can be construed as nothing more than window dressing. Something near and dear to all managers is the budget, and this is perhaps the leading reason why only window dressing has been applied.

Agencies nationwide are continually being asked to do more with less. Homeland security and terrorism analysis is just another opportunity to do more with less. Overnight, agencies began assigning investigative and analytical personnel to address agency-specific homeland security needs and to serve as points of contact. It has become the responsibility of these points of contact to expeditiously educate themselves in their new roles and to pass this knowledge and insight to other personnel. Limitations were imposed on training and capital equipment purchases for numerous newly established units. Allocations were based on previously established budgets, and for many agencies the prospect looks bleak for the expansion of these monies. No matter what, law enforcement agencies have to deal with terrorism and continue to address concerns as they arise without excuses.

This has been only a cursory overview of some of the concerns facing government agencies in their attempts to deal with terrorism. The number of concerns needing to be addressed is yet to be determined, but there are some issues that can be overcome without draining the budget.

## Law Enforcement Concerns

There are many concerns beyond budgetary ones faced by law enforcement personnel and agencies regarding homeland security and terrorism analysis. Throughout the decades, law enforcement personnel and academia have done a respectable job of educating and promoting awareness of criminal concerns across the board. There have been many models designed to standardize an array of law enforcement concerns, ranging from community-oriented policing (COPS) to the New York Police Department's computerized statistics performance-based management approach (COMPSTAT). One model that is known to virtually every sworn law enforcement person is the SARA (scan, analyze, respond, and assess) model (Figure 3.2). The components of SARA were readily understood, but before the regular use of analytical personnel law enforcement circles often joked that the As were overlooked or forgotten.

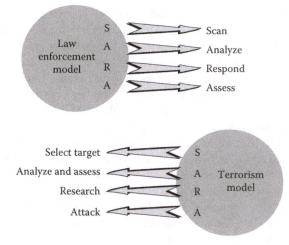

**FIGURE 3.2**   Scan, analyze, respond, and assess and terrorism models.

Just as law enforcement agencies organize practices into a model context, the same can be done with terrorism. In Figure 3.2 the use of the SARA model as a terrorist model is demonstrated. Terrorists have a planning stage (target selection, analyzing and assessing the mission), a research (reconnaissance) and planning stage, and an execution stage (the attack). For a terrorist, the use of all these stages is integrated and inseparable. In the absence of this integration, the mission will fail. Terrorist activity is not designed to help anyone other than the terrorists themselves or the terrorist organization in promoting their perceptions in the name of their cause. Terrorists do not randomly and spontaneously pick their targets. As history demonstrates, terrorists are often selective in their targets and seek to maximize the tragedy in physical and psychological terms in order to make a statement. This requires extensive analysis and assessment. It may take years, but when they are ready they regroup and implement their plan of action. Dealing with individuals who have the patience and capability to undertake extensive campaigns poses a new concern for law enforcement personnel who are used to dealing with people who commit crimes of opportunity and greed.

The American law enforcement community is also worried about local issues and concerns, and most police managers do not think abstractly but pride themselves on a pragmatic approach.[12] Critical thought inevitably focuses on local issues. Issues of displacement and how actions may impact other jurisdictions are often overlooked. Terrorism is viewed as too exotic for most agencies to be concerned with. This is not necessarily the fault of chiefs of police or their staff. The political and budgetary concerns of all government entities, not just law enforcement, drive the way these businesses are run. This has led many managers and leaders to stay focused on issues specific to their jurisdictions and, when necessary, on the immediate region but seldom beyond that. This attitude permeates from the unwillingness of the constituents being served to pay for services rendered outside their jurisdictional boundaries. It is important for the law enforcement community to educate not only its personnel but also the public and government officials on the vital need to work outside any one particular jurisdiction and to work in concert with regional, state, and federal agencies on matters of homeland security and terrorism.

Information and intelligence sharing by analysts, investigators, and counterterrorism agents is essential and probably poses the greatest concern for law enforcement at all levels. Jurisdictional haggling, credit claiming, and unnecessary secrecy permeate the counterterrorist and law enforcement communities. A sense of ownership and zeal to handle a case is commendable, but when dealing with homeland security and terrorism issues there is no time for agencies to play games; time is of the essence. Interagency cooperation also fragments on jurisdictional grounds, the perceived level of threats, and the immediacy of response needed. Most agencies have specific guidelines outlined in their policies and procedures manuals covering traditional law enforcement response and investigation, but such guidelines fail to cover intelligence gathering and matters of homeland security. Procedures and practices must be put in writing and not left to word of mouth or on-the-job training. The magnitude of homeland security investigations and the need to corroborate information are dependent on details and documentation; therefore, proven and standardized practices must be used. Once standardized practices are put in place, agencies must arrive at some sort of consensus on a database structure before developing one. Use of existing systems may not suffice due to limited data fields, too many narrative fields, or lack of compatibility with other agencies. Minimum database requirements need to be established. Not every agency will have the same database software, but by following predefined requirements investigations can be enhanced and time saved.

Law enforcement agencies typically separate what would today be classified as a terrorist into such categories as criminal, political, or mentally challenged, and these classifications may be too simple. As demonstrated in the section, "Differences between typical street criminals and terrorists" in Chapter 2, terrorist behavior differs from that of ordinary street criminals. Criminal investigation techniques must be modified to reflect these differences when examining terrorist cases. Another factor to consider is how agencies and the FBI have captured data on terrorist acts in the past. The FBI has labeled the majority of domestic terrorist activities under nonterrorist headings in the Uniform Crime Reporting (UCR) system. Many incidents were investigated, classified, and reported as hate crimes or under the routine UCR classifications of part 1, part 2, and noncriminal. The use of the FBI classification "hate crimes" is expressly valid when dealing with domestic-based terrorist groups. This can possibly be attributed to a group's lack of leadership, infrequency of action, and members being "single-event wonders" or to the hatred of some groups toward a specific segment of the population. American law enforcement officers routinely deal with significant homeland security and terrorism issues, and unintentionally dismiss any correlation with the same by referring to the incidents as routine crimes. This can be largely attributed to a lack of coordination, training, and awareness.

## COORDINATION, TRAINING, AND AWARENESS

Paramilitary organizations such as law enforcement agencies have long prided themselves on their expertise, training, and adaptability. Training is the foundation on which law enforcement practices are built. From day one, officers are trained in detail on everything from report writing to firearms. However, this training is generally geared toward handling only typical street crimes and the closest the personnel get to terrorism—on the U.S. Army spectrum of conflict—is riots and disorders through field force or special event response team training. On the other hand, many agencies go to the other extreme by providing training on law enforcement response to weapons of mass destruction, which is the last item on the U.S. Army's spectrum of conflict. It is commendable that training is being provided concerning weapons of mass destruction, especially to first responders, but what about the rest of the spectrum, particularly terrorism? Although there are no hard numbers to go by, it is more likely that an officer encounters a member of any one of the hundreds of organized hate and terrorist groups before he or she encounters a weapon of mass destruction.

How does one train 600,000–700,000 American law enforcement personnel, and where does one start? One starts with the basics. Many basic law enforcement training initiatives relating to terrorism are focused on response. This is indicative of being reactive, and when dealing with homeland security and terrorism one needs to be proactive. Education on topics such as what to look for, what questions to ask, identity concerns, and the definitions of homeland security and terrorism should be emphasized. In addition to the training, many educational and reference materials available for law enforcement personnel are geared toward response topics and some preventative scenarios.

There is currently one federally funded program, the State and Local Anti-Terrorism Training (SLATT), that since 1996 has been addressing the law enforcement training on terrorism matters and is designed to aid intelligence gathering and investigations relating to domestic terrorism.

However, until September 11, 2001, many agencies were probably unaware of the existence of this program, or even if they were aware, they saw no need to attend it. This deficiency caused many local and state agencies to turn to training provided by the military and federal agencies. Cooperation such as this is commendable, but agencies need to be mindful of the inherent differences in the style, mission, and type of law enforcement being practiced.

Coordination of law enforcement activities among various agencies is something that is done daily. Agencies often work under cooperative work agreements or memorandums of understanding (MOUs) and joint regional task forces. When operating under an MOU, agencies clearly spell out the guidelines to be followed and who will be in charge. The same cannot be said for homeland security, terrorism, and some routine investigations. It is these gray areas that often lead to confusion and, more importantly, loss of information or intelligence. To demonstrate this point, several general incident categories are outlined in the following list. Information and intelligence data are often routed to specific (different) locations or agencies whose members do not necessarily share all aspects of an investigation or all information:

Terrorist related: FBI
Bomb related: Alcohol, Tobacco, and Firearms (ATF)
Bomb hoaxes: Police general investigation units
Biohazardous materials: Fire departments
Arson: Fire departments, fire marshals, arson investigators, ATF
Explosive devices or chemicals: Bomb squads
Deaths involved: Homicide investigators
Fugitives: U.S. Marshal's Service, FBI, County Sheriff's Office
Miscellaneous: Gang units, robbery units, task forces, other jurisdictions, and county- or state-level law enforcement agencies

Unless a terrorist-related event has a red flag associated with it, there is a great likelihood that the pieces of the puzzle can be scattered across multiple jurisdictions and databases.

The lack of awareness concerning homeland security, terrorism, and organized hate groups on many fronts is prevalent throughout law enforcement. Some of this is attributed to a lack of training matter and some to the lack of intelligence. The "I'll know it when I see it" approach will not work. In order to facilitate effective information gathering and analysis, all members of an organization must be on the same page. Even if an agency has investigators dedicated to information gathering and analysis, these investigators cannot be everywhere and know everything. All members in an agency are part of the solution, and to be of value they need to have knowledge of the issue being faced and need to be trained to identify the pieces of information that should be gathered. Once the logistics and educational issues are addressed, agencies can focus on gathering information.

## CHAPTER CONCEPTS

The chapter concepts can be summarized as follows:

Despite the brevity of the definition of homeland security, each phrase is replete with meaning and can be adopted by any government agency.
The HSAS consists of five levels—green, blue, yellow, orange, and red, each representing varying degrees of alert, preparation, and response.
The USA PATRIOT Act has many roles to play in the war on terrorism, particularly with respect to finances.
Dealing with terrorism is a novel experience for the law enforcement community, and there are many new concerns being faced by agencies and government managers to this effect.

Government and law enforcement agencies investigating crimes must be cognizant of the need to coordinate and train their personnel, as they must encounter potential terrorist and organized hate crime activities.

## REFERENCES

1. Stohl, M., ed. 1979. *The Politics of Terrorism*. New York: Marcel Dekker, p. 1.
2. President. 2003. *The National Strategy for Combating Terrorism*. White House, Washington, D.C., p. 8.
3. President. 2002. *The National Strategy for Homeland Security*. Office of Homeland Security, Washington, D.C., p. 2.
4. Ridge, T. 2002. *Gov. Ridge Announces Homeland Security Advisory System*. White House, TN: Office of the Press Secretary.
5. Department of Homeland Security. *Homeland Security Advisory System*. http://www.whitehouse.gov/ (accessed February 21, 2003).
6. President. 2003. *The National Strategy for the Physical Protection of Critical Infrastructures and Key Assets*. White House, Washington, D.C., p. 1.
7. Uniting and Strengthening America by Providing Appropriate Tools Required to Intercept and Obstruct Terrorism (USA PATRIOT) Act of 2001, 107th Congress, 1st session, October 24, 2001.
8. Congressional Research Service. 2002. Report IB95112, Terrorism, the Future, and U.S. Foreign Policy, R. Lee, and R. Perl, Issue Brief for Congress, December 12, 2002, CRS-2.
9. Revell, O. 1995. Protecting America: Law enforcement views radical Islam. *Middle East Q* 4. http://www.meforum.org/article/235 (accessed March 11, 2003).
10. Zakat Information Center. http://www.islamicity.com/mosque/zakat/ (accessed January 22, 2011).
11. Snow, D. M. 2002. *September 11, 2001, The New Face of War?* New York: Longman, p. 11.
12. White, J. R. 2002. *Terrorism: An Introduction*. 4th ed. Belmont, CA: Thomson Wadsworth, p. 207.

# 4 Behavioral Traits and Suspicious Activity

There have been many attempts to study and analyze behaviors associated with terrorism. Many actions or behaviors can be construed as having a terrorism nexus. The ambiguity that can exist is the reason why several researchers have attempted to learn from the past, much like terrorists have done. Several efforts in this direction are highly informative such as the reports published by Dutch and New York law enforcement agencies.

Working with the National Institute of Justice (NIJ), Brent Smith from the University of Arkansas launched a series of projects to explore the behavior patterns of terrorists worldwide. Through these projects, hundreds of terrorists were studied covering a period of more than two decades. What they learned was published in the *NIJ* journal, journal number 260 in July 2008, and it was considered intriguing: The cases of McVeigh, the September 11 hijackers, and Eric Rudolph discussed in the journal are quite unusual. In fact, they suggested that most terrorists live close to their selected targets and engage in a great deal of preparation—often over the course of months or even years—that has the potential of coming to the attention of local law enforcement.

According to Smith's analysis, almost half (44%) of all studied terrorists lived within 30 miles of their targets. In the July 2008 publication, Smith noted that terrorists most commonly prepared for their attacks with surveillance and intelligence gathering, robberies, and thefts to raise funding for the group, weapons violations, and bomb manufacture. Again, most of these events took place relatively near their homes, which in turn were close to the targets. Terrorists may stay close to home because of new immigration status, lack of transportation, lack of knowledge of the urban landscape, or a desire to avoid attention. Among single-issue terrorists in particular, 71% of the preparatory acts occurred within 12 miles and 92% within 28 miles of the targets. This finding may also be attributed to the use of "uncoordinated violence" tactics by environmental and antiabortion extremists, which often results in local targeting by "lone wolves" sympathetic to the cause.[1]

A separate follow-up NIJ project that analyzed the distance between more than 250 environmental and international terrorists' homes and their targets confirmed the earlier preliminary findings that their spatial patterns are fairly similar. The analysis found that about half of the environmental terrorists and nearly three-fifths of the international terrorists lived within 30 miles of their targets. It should be noted that temporal data used in the study are limited due to the small number of international incidents that have taken place in the United States.

The efforts undertaken by Smith and the NIJ to study terrorist activities should also be viewed in concert with that of terrorist groups. It is easy to put a blanket description on either a terrorist or a terrorist group, but analysts need to be cognizant of the fact that one size does not fit all. The other pitfall to avoid is one that puts a person or a group in a silo. What this means is that analysts should remain alert and understand that there may be some cross-pollination of ideologies, groups, or individuals. Identifying a subject as a member of group A and then transferring the case to the squad of investigators that handles only members of group A is a shortsighted practice. Analysts should strive to work the information in an effort to identify the behaviors associated with terrorism. Looking at the information as domestic or international, or looking only for the elements of a particular crime, leads to delays in investigation.

Many of the individual and group behaviors that analysts have been looking for over the years for crimes, gangs, and organized criminal organizations are applicable also to terrorists. Outlined in Figure 4.1 are several behaviors that are indicative of terrorist organizations. These behaviors or activities will likely be exhibited by one or a group of individuals in their preparation for an attack.

Flowchart of terrorist group activity

FIGURE 4.1    Behaviors associated with terrorist group activity.

Although the information is represented as a progressive flowchart, analysts should remain cognizant of the fact that rarely, if ever, will information be gleaned in such a manner. It is very important that law enforcement personnel strive to identify activities listed in the recruitment and preliminary planning stages. Identification of behaviors recognized in the first two activity categories will be representative of a proactive analyst since the last two categories will be learned upon a reactive response.

Smith's research highlights the importance of having a proactive law enforcement commitment. Figure 4.2 demonstrates the temporal patterns of terrorist group activities as seen from the research. As one can easily discern, time is of the essence. Furthermore, it is evident that should law enforcement agencies expand their understanding of behavioral traits associated with terrorist activity they will have more time to develop relationships. Too many times, law enforcement officials at numerous levels look for behaviors associated with destructive actions. Expanding behavioral traits beyond

Temporal patterns of group activities

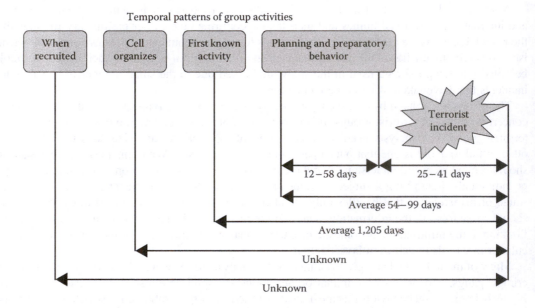

FIGURE 4.2    Temporal patterns of terrorist group activities based on Brent Smith's research.

what has been often referred to as the "seven signs of terrorism" will enhance the ability of law enforcement agencies to identify patterns and relationships. However, personnel should be reminded that not everyone is a "bomb thrower" and that the identified patterns or relationships may include lesser offenses. Regardless, it is the cumulative actions of the activities that need to be understood, and if it is done effectively one can realize a far greater timeframe in which to work.

For law enforcement, the study and understanding of behaviors has been dramatically effective in curbing various crimes involving narcotics and gangs, and even street crimes. Analysts have played an effective role in identifying behavioral patterns through temporal and spatial analytical techniques. Investigators have successfully used behavioral patterns to observe drug smugglers and burglars. Officers in police academies are often instructed that a burglar will commit crimes within 1 mile of his or her residence. When one examines his or her own behaviors, it is not hard to understand the principles of behavioral traits. Smith's research noted the correlation to 30 miles. This can be construed as a comfort range. Noncriminals often find that their activities and daily habits range within 30 miles as well. It must also be noted that individuals revert to what they know best at some point. An example of this would be tourist destinations. Once you understand the norm, it is not difficult to identify tourists and maybe even where they are from. Aspects such as mannerisms, eating habits, foods, attire, and even speaking patterns tell a lot. Just understand that one will never be 100% successful and analysts often strive for 68%, 80%, and 93% accuracy. Considering that many crimes have clearance rates in the 20% range, behavioral analysis can be highly effective. Make no mistake, behavioral analysis is seen by some as profiling, and it is. The difference is that behavioral analysis does not include, and should never include, race, or religion. One must seek to identify norms and understand behavioral traits that have been demonstrated by research to be a nexus of terrorism. Just expand beyond the immediate obvious areas and seek to understand them within a 30-mile radius. Behavioral trait information can be derived from an array of sources, but there is a strong likelihood that they will come from the public and road law enforcement personnel.

## NATIONAL INFORMATION SHARING AND SUSPICIOUS ACTIVITY REPORTING

In recent years, two topics have garnered significant attention, both good and bad: (1) information sharing and (2) suspicious activity reporting (SAR). Everyone with a stake in homeland security matters agrees that in order to be successful in such investigations these two topics are priorities. However, the same people, both in the private and public sectors, face challenges on how it is to be accomplished and implemented. Then there are the questions of who will manage the initiatives and privacy.

Presidential Executive Order 13311 of July 29, 2003, assigned the functions of the President under Section 892 of the Homeland Security Act of 2002 to the Secretary of Homeland Security; the order was titled Homeland Security Information Sharing. Executive Order 13356 of August 27, 2004, strengthened the sharing of terrorism information and established the Information Systems Council. The mission of the Council was to plan for and oversee the establishment of an interoperable terrorism information sharing environment (ISE). This order also called for the establishment of requirements for the collection of terrorism information inside the United States. Part II of Executive Order 13356 was instituted to further the sharing of information on October 27, 2005, under Executive Order 13388.

When the program manager for the information sharing environment (PM-ISE) was established and placed within the Office of the Director of National Intelligence (ODNI), the information sharing process was defined and the SAR program developed. The nationwide SAR initiative (NSI) supported one of the core principles of the 2007 National Strategy for Information Sharing. This information sharing strategy was woven into all aspects of counterterrorism activity. The NSI responded to the strategy's mandate that the federal government support the development of a nationwide capacity for suspicious activity. In December 2008, a concept of operations for the NSI program was published and standards were set out. Pursuant to the ISE—suspicious activity report functional standard—SAR is the process of documenting the observation of behavior that may be indicative of intelligence gathering or preoperational planning related to terrorism, criminal, or other illicit intentions. The NSI is not a single monolithic program, rather it is a coordinated effort that leverages and integrates all ISE-SAR related activities into a national unified process. This is a process that is based on 12 discrete steps and is driven by identified behavioral traits.

Many behavioral traits or activities associated with terrorism are generally First Amendment-protected activities. They should not be reported in SAR or ISE-SAR without articulable facts and circumstances that support the source agency's suspicion that the behavior observed is not innocent. The facts and circumstances should be indicative of criminal activity associated with terrorism, including evidence of preoperational planning related to terrorism. Race, ethnicity, national origin, or religious affiliation should not be considered as factors that create suspicion (although these factors may be used as specific suspect descriptions). Additional details pertaining to behaviors used to identify terrorism-related activity can be found in the ISE-SAR Functional Standard, which is at www.ise.gov.

## WHY SUSPICIOUS ACTIVITY REPORTING, AND THE ROLE OF LOCAL LAW ENFORCEMENT

There is much debate about how SAR came about and how local law enforcement became involved in it. The Intelligence Reform and Terrorism Prevention Act of 2004 required the creation of the ISE, which uses SAR as the backbone to many of its efforts. Two organizations played an instrumental role in the development of the SAR program. They are the Los Angeles Police Department, and the Major Cities Chiefs Association (MCCA). In 2008, the Suspicious Activity Report Support and Implementation Project noted the support and guidance of the project sponsors: the Bureau of Justice Assistance, U.S. Department of Justice (DOJ), DOJ's Global Justice Information Sharing Initiative (Global), Criminal Intelligence Coordinating Council, U.S. Department of Homeland Security (DHS), and the MCCA. The guidance and leadership of representatives from these organizations were paramount in the development of a common national standard for the reporting of suspicious activity.

The ISE defines a suspicious activity report as the official documentation of observed behavior that may be indicative of intelligence gathering or preoperational planning related to terrorist, criminal, or other illicit intention. The SAR process focuses on what law enforcement agencies have been doing for years—collecting information and establishing a process whereby information can be shared to detect and prevent criminal and terrorist activity. Standardizing the SAR process will help law enforcement agencies build and improve their individual SAR processes and provide for a more consistent method to collect and piece together the information puzzle so that precursors of terrorist and criminal activity can be identified.

As already noted earlier in this section, many agencies and individuals played an integral role in the development of the SAR process, but it was four agencies and their respective homeland security units that had the greatest influence on SAR process development: the (1) Los Angeles, (2) Miami-Dade, (3) Boston, and (4) Chicago police departments. The efforts of the Los Angeles Police Department under then Chief William Bratton and the staff from the Counter Terrorism and Criminal Intelligence Bureau paved the way for much of the development and findings of SAR. One person who garnered much attention in the development of SAR was Commander Joan T. McNamara of the Los Angeles Police Department who became known as the "mother of SARs." Relied on by several federal, state, and local agencies, Commander McNamara and her staff were often called upon by lawmakers at several levels.

McNamara, assistant commanding officer for the Los Angeles Police Department's Counter Terrorism and Criminal Intelligence Bureau, testified before the Subcommittee on the Intelligence, Information Sharing, and Terrorism Risk Assessment of the U.S. House of Representatives Committee on Homeland Security, on March 18, 2009. Her testimony detailed the new role of local police in counterterrorism efforts.

Front-line officers, with their intimate knowledge of their communities and their keen observational skills, have traditionally been thought of as first responders. This perception changed with the 9/11 terrorist attacks. Policymakers, law enforcement executives, and others increasingly called for police to be redefined as "first preventers" of terrorism and the emphasis at the local level shifted from response to prevention. Local police were now considered an integral part of the efforts aimed at protecting the nation from a variety of threats, including those posed by domestic and international terrorists. Local law enforcement is now considered an integral part of our national security effort. In the years following the 9/11 attacks, enhanced collaboration and revolutionary new sharing protocols have been forged with federal partners to increase knowledge, awareness, and information flow. Still, a critical gap existed in the information sharing cycle.

Tasking local law enforcement personnel with the policing of traditional crime and the prevention of terror attacks in their local jurisdictions constituted a dramatic paradigm shift, both for the federal government and for the local and state agencies. If this shift in established thought and practice were to be successful, it would require law enforcement agencies nationwide to adopt universal guidelines for effective communication with federal partners, and effective information sharing. This was far easier said than done. There was no system in place at any level to facilitate this crucial and necessary exchange.

The SAR program was the Los Angeles Police Department's answer to this problem and it now serves as a national model for the American law enforcement community as it is being institutiona-lized through the NSI. The underlying premise of SAR is very simple: A police officer's observation and reporting of just one event could be the vital "nugget" of information needed to focus attention in the right place or to connect seemingly unrelated dots and predict or prevent a terrorist act. The SAR program takes the emphasis off racial or ethnic characteristics of individuals and places it on detecting behaviors and activities with potential links to terrorism-related criminal activity. Coupled with extensive training, this approach ensures that citizens' civil and privacy rights are protected.

The SAR program is built on the foundation of behaviors and activities that have been historically linked to preoperational planning of, and preparation for terrorist attacks. They include actions such as acquiring illicit explosive material, taking measurements or drawing diagrams, abandoning suspicious packages or vehicles, and testing security measures. This is the first program in the United States to create a national standard for terrorism-related modus operandi (MO) codes. By creating and assigning numbers, or codes, to terrorism-related behaviors, terrorist activities can be tracked by date, time, and location, just as other crimes are tracked currently. With the advent of coding, an agency's records management system has been transformed into a valuable and viable terrorism prevention tool.

When the preliminary information contained on a SAR report is analyzed using these codes, the system can be utilized to map, chart, and graph suspicious behaviors, and allows counterterrorism personnel to run specific queries based on a particular behavior, location, or time frame in order to identify emerging patterns. The eventuality of a nationwide application of this behavioral coding, uni-form reporting, and tracking method will provide the revolutionary basis for linking behaviors and indicators, and for revealing emerging patterns of terrorism throughout the United States. These stan-dardized codes also enable local agencies across the country to share information in a systematic and uniform fashion that enables trends, spikes, and patterns to be identified and placed in a national con-text. The SAR methodology has the potential to revolutionize how the American law enforcement community reveals the emerging patterns of terrorism-related indicators and behaviors. In addition, SAR provides police with the capability to search through previously reported suspicious activities and identify important links to behavior that might otherwise be overlooked. This ability to query is crucial to law enforcement personnel's ability to successfully analyze and synthesize information and to produce actionable intelligence toward terrorism prevention. Fusing the SAR-related informa-tion with an all-crimes picture provides decision makers with the statistical support they need to allo-cate resources and police officers in a more strategic way; it closes gaps in training, investigation, enforcement, and protection; it reveals potential patterns that extend beyond the region of interest to the rest of the country and, potentially, overseas. Once information is shared vertically and horizontally throughout the region and nation, activities previously viewed as having happened in isolation can be placed in a national context.

## SUSPICIOUS ACTIVITY REPORTING AND THE NATIONAL LANDSCAPE

The SAR program is representative of the tremendous strides that local law enforcement has made in the area of counterterrorism. The SAR program enables police to paint their own rich picture of what is happening on the ground in their communities in relation to terrorism, rather than relying solely on their federal partners for information. This goes a long way toward closing what were previously wide gaps in information sharing. The program also makes local law enforcement agencies stronger partners in the national effort to prevent terrorism and other crimes on U.S. soil. It essentially flips the age-old paradigm in which information is pushed from the federal to the local level with very little push the other way. Now local police departments are valuable players in the information sharing process and are increasingly relied upon to provide their federal partners with an accurate picture of what is happening at the local level.

Fusion centers also stand to benefit from the SAR program. Reports about suspicious activity that contain comprehensive data provided by a trained workforce result in more informed analytical products, valued dissemination, and more stringent investigative requirements. Leveraged properly, the SAR program stands to become one of the essential threads that ensure seamless information flow that is critical to cooperation on the national and international levels. In order to effectively counter a threat such as terrorism, we must first know where these activities are taking place and at what frequency. Law enforcement personnel must have situational awareness that is enabled by standardized processes with strong civil liberties protections that are shared by most, if not all, across the nation. The time has come for local police to contribute to this process in a significant way. The SAR program is one such contribution that stands to make this vision a reality.[2]

One developmental challenge of NSI was to create an orderly flow of information and to identify a concept of operations that could be adopted and followed by any law enforcement agency. Figure 4.3, which was developed over a course of several months by an array of law enforcement executives, represents five SAR activity processing steps: (1) planning, (2) gathering and processing, (3) analysis

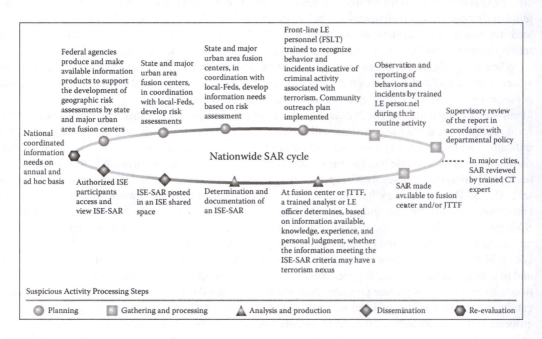

**FIGURE 4.3**  Nationwide suspicious activity reporting cycle.

and production, (4) dissemination, and (5) re-evaluation. There are also some key principles that apply across the cycle:

The process represents a cycle that responds to SAR requirements as set out in the national strategy for information sharing.

It incorporates multiple levels of review and vetting to ensure that the information has been gathered and managed legally and has a potential nexus to terrorism.

The process relies on a distributed system of sharing that maintains agency control over ISE-SAR information.

The process is not static, but it will be modified to incorporate lessons learned and best practices.

To foster collaboration across all levels of government, the process enables greater awareness of information needs among federal, state, and local agencies.

Where possible, SAR handling will be incorporated into existing processes and procedures used to manage other crime-related information and criminal intelligence.

The ISE-SARs containing personal information that are later determined to have no terrorism or criminal nexus will be removed from the ISE shared space and other participants notified.

The nationwide SAR cycle however does not have a defined starting or ending point. This is not a design error, rather it a realization that the process is continuous and has many participants at various levels. It must be remembered that a SAR is not intelligence or necessarily an act of terrorism, but a refined piece of information that needs to be analyzed and made available to other law enforcement (LE) personnel; it should not be just pushed to a joint terrorism task force (JTTF).

A goal of the ISE was that by 2014 every federal, state, local, tribal, and law enforcement entity operating domestically would participate in a standardized integrated approach to gather, document, process, analyze, and share terrorism-related suspicious activity.

## SUSPICIOUS ACTIVITY REPORTING BEHAVIORAL INDICATORS

All department employees, regardless of position or title, play a vital role in identifying and reporting suspicious activity that may be indicative of behavioral traits or patterns related to homeland security threats. To assist in the identification of suspicious activity related to homeland security threats, departments should adopt the baseline of the seven signs of terrorism as a guide. The seven signs comprise the following: (1) surveillance, (2) elicitation, (3) testing security, (4) acquiring supplies, (5) suspicious persons, (6) trial runs, and (7) deploying assets. Along with recognizing suspicious activity or behavior patterns, it is very important to have the information documented in full detail.

When encountering suspicious activity, personnel are reminded that protection of civil liberties is essential. Every attempt should be made to expedite the verification and validation of the information presented by the encountered suspect. Some examples of the behavioral traits that may exist or are identified by personnel and are clearly delineated and documented in an offense incident report are provided in the following subsections. It must be noted that the actions and mere possession of the items listed in these subsections do not in themselves necessarily constitute a violation of law.

### ACTIONS AROUSING SUSPICION

Some examples of suspicious actions pertaining to an individual that may be reported by law enforcement personnel are as follows:

Engages in suspected preoperational surveillance (uses binoculars or cameras, takes measurements, draws diagrams, etc.)

Appears to engage in countersurveillance efforts (doubles back, changes appearance, evasive driving, etc.)

Engages security personnel in questions focusing on sensitive subjects (regarding security information, hours of operation, shift changes, and so on; questions such as "what do the cameras film?" and "do these cameras record?")

Takes measurements (counts footsteps; measures building entrances or perimeters, distances between security locations, and distances between cameras, etc.)

Takes pictures or video footage with no apparent aesthetic value (i.e., camera angles, security equipment, security personnel, traffic lights, building entrances, etc.)

Draws diagrams or takes notes (building plans, location of security cameras or security personnel, security shift changes, notes of weak security points, etc.)

Abandons suspicious packages or items (suitcase, backpack, bag, box, package, etc.)

Abandons vehicle in a secured or restricted location (i.e., the front of a government building, airport, sports venue, etc.)

Attempts to enter secured or sensitive premises or areas without authorization (i.e., "official personnel," closed off areas of airports and harbors; secured areas at significant events such as presidential speeches and inaugurations; etc.)

Engages in testing existing security measures (i.e., dry run, security breach of outside fencing/security doors, false alarms to observe reactions, etc.)

Attempts to smuggle contraband through access control points (airport screening centers; security entrance points at courts of law; entrance points at venues of sports, games, and entertainment; etc.)

Makes or attempts to make suspicious purchases, such as large amounts of otherwise legal materials (i.e., pool chemicals, fuels, fertilizers, potential explosive device components, etc.)

Attempts to acquire sensitive or restricted items or information (plans, schedules, passwords, etc.)

Acquires or attempts to acquire uniforms without a legitimate cause (service personnel uniforms, government uniforms, etc.)

Acquires or attempts to acquire official or official-appearing vehicles without a legitimate cause (i.e., emergency or government vehicle, etc.)

Pursues specific training or education that indicates suspicious motives (flight training, weapons training, etc.)

Stockpiles unexplained large amounts of currency

In possession of multiple passports, identification cards, or travel documents issued to the same person

Espouses extremist views (verbalizes support of terrorism, incites or recruits others to engage in terrorist activity, etc.)

Brags about affiliation with, or membership of, an extremist organization (white power, militias, Ku Klux Klan, etc.)

Engages in suspected coded conversations or transmissions (over e-mail, radio, telephone, etc., e.g., information found during a private business audit is reported to police)

Displays overt support for known terrorist networks (in possession of posters of terrorist leaders, etc.)

## POSSESSION AROUSING SUSPICION

The following items may arouse suspicion if found in the possession of individuals:

Coded or ciphered literature or correspondence
Event schedules for sporting venues, performing art centers, and theaters
Appearance or travel schedules of VIPs
Multiple forms of identification items from multiple governments
Security schedules

Blueprints
Evacuation plans
Security plans
Weapons or ammunition
Explosive materials
Illicit chemical agents
Illicit biological agents
Illicit radiological material
Other sensitive or military materials
Hoax/facsimile explosive device
Hoax/facsimile dispersal device

The Los Angeles Police Department was one of the first law enforcement agencies in the country to formalize the SAR process and issue a general order to all their personnel regarding behavior documentation. Some agencies have expanded the behaviors to one hundred traits, whereas others use just the base of seven. Regardless of the number used, it is important to document the behavioral traits in full detail in official reports that are used in the analysis process. Figure 4.4 demonstrates the behavioral traits identified by the ISE for use in SAR documentation.

## RETRIEVING THE SUSPICIOUS ACTIVITY REPORT FOR ANALYSIS

It is important to remember that although the SAR initiative may reside at the local level, it is part of a nationwide program. Figure 4.5 demonstrates the SAR program as it was instituted in 2009 with a series of shared space servers, which include participation from federal, state, county, and local law enforcement communities. A handful of shared space servers were put in place in the ISE program; further, law enforcement personnel not directly connected to these servers have the options of collaborating with a sponsoring agency or utilizing the FBI's eGuardian program through one of the sensitive but unclassified portals. The primary method by which investigative leads are sent to the JTTF is the FBI's eGuardian system. The eGuardian system functions as another server in the ISE-networked shared space.

Once an agency establishes and adopts the NSI-SAR guidelines, including an approved privacy policy, they are eligible to participate in the program. This gives them access to SAR data and the ability to perform queries across the nation. It affords them the opportunity to expand their efforts to identify local behaviors that may have a nexus to terrorism and compare these behaviors to those that may be experienced, observed, or identified elsewhere in the country.

## TERRORISM INFORMATION NEEDS

Suspicious activity reports are not the only source of clues to terrorism information. Terrorism information needs (TINs) were developed in response to the National Strategy for Information Sharing of October 2007, which directed the U.S. government to "facilitate the exchange of coordinated sets of requirements and information needs across the federal and non-federal domain ..."[3] These information needs are a product of the collaboration between federal, state, local, and tribal law enforcement partners.

Information needs are intended to inform federal, state, local, and tribal entities on terrorism topics, behaviors, and activities that are important to the counterterrorism community. The information that is responsive to these needs may or may not constitute foreign or counterintelligence, since not all terrorists are affiliated to a foreign power or a foreign terrorist organization. The TINs must be adapted to the specific mission, authorities, and circumstances of each organization in order to promote information sharing. They should be retained and disseminated pursuant to the existing, lawful authorities of that entity.

| Category | Description |
|---|---|
| *Defined criminal activity and potential terrorism nexus activity* | |
| Breach/attempted intrusion | Unauthorized personnel attempting to or actually entering a restricted area or protected site. Impersonation of authorized personnel (e.g., police/security, janitor). |
| Misrepresentation | Presenting false or misusing insignia, documents, and/or identification, to misrepresent one's affiliation to cover possible illicit activity. |
| Theft/loss/diversion | Stealing or diverting something associated with a facility/infrastructure (e.g., badges, uniforms, identification, emergency vehicles, technology or documents [classified or unclassified], which are proprietary to the facility). |
| Sabotage/tampering/vandalism | Damaging, manipulating, or defacing part of a facility/infrastructure or a protected site. |
| Cyber attack | Compromising, or attempting to compromise or disrupt an organization's information technology infrastructure. |
| Expressed or implied threat | Communicating a spoken or written threat to damage or compromise a facility/infrastructure. |
| Aviation activity | Operation of an aircraft in a manner that reasonably may be interpreted as suspicious, or posing a threat to people or property. Such operation may or may not be a violation of Federal Aviation Regulations. |
| *Potential criminal or noncriminal activity requiring additional fact information during investigation* | |
| Eliciting information | Questioning individuals at a level beyond mere curiosity about particular facets of a facility's or building's purpose, operations, security procedures, etc., that would arouse suspicion in a reasonable person. |
| Testing or probing of security | Deliberate interactions with, or challenges to, installations, personnel, or systems that reveal physical, personnel, or cyber security capabilities. |
| Recruiting | Building of operations teams and contacts, personnel data, banking data, or travel data. |
| Photography | Taking pictures or video of facilities, buildings, or infrastructure in a manner that would arouse suspicion in a reasonable person. Examples include taking pictures or video of infrequently used access points, personnel performing security functions (patrols, badge/vehicle checking), security-related equipment (perimeter fencing, security). |
| Observation/surveillance | Demonstrating unusual interest in facilities, buildings, or infrastructure beyond mere casual or professional (e.g., engineers) interest such that a reasonable person would consider the activity suspicious. Examples include observation through binoculars, taking notes, attempting to measure distances, etc. |
| Materials acquisition/storage | Acquisition and/or storage of unusual quantities of materials such as cell phones, pagers, fuel, chemicals, toxic materials, and timers, such that a reasonable person would suspect possible criminal activity. |
| Acquisition of expertise | Attempts to obtain or conduct training in security concepts; military weapons or tactics; or other unusual capabilities that would arouse suspicion in a reasonable person. |
| Weapons discovery | Discovery of unusual amounts of weapons or explosives that would arouse suspicion in a reasonable person. |

**FIGURE 4.4**    Behavioral traits that were identified by the information sharing environment's law enforcement panel and adopted as part of the nationwide suspicious activity reporting initiative

Information needs must be considered only in relation to a person, group, or organization "known or appropriately suspected to be or have been engaged in conduct constituting, in preparation for, in aid of, or related to terrorism." This standard also applies to information needs associated with human factors related to radicalization. Any questions regarding the appropriateness of sharing specific information should be coordinated with legal or privacy counsel prior to sharing the information.

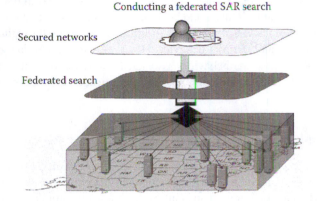

Conducting a federated SAR search

Secured networks

Federated search

**FIGURE 4.5** Overlay of how the federated searching of the nationwide suspicious activity reporting initiative is conducted.

Although TINs will experience modifications over the years, there are several core principles that are needed in order to provide a clear picture. Some TIN overarching categories are outlined as follows:

Imminent and emerging threats to U.S. interests and infrastructure
Terrorist leadership, strategies, plans, and intentions
View, background, biographical information, psychological assessment, influence
Financial resources
Expertise and specialized skills
Roles and responsibilities
Physical description, health, and biometrics
Location
Travel
Contacts and associates
Senior personnel MO
Access to sensitive areas
Terrorist operational capabilities and activities
Terrorist communications
Terrorist finances and financial networks
Sponsors of terrorism and terrorist safe havens
Terrorist radicalization and countering violent extremism
Socioeconomic and cultural factors
Demographics and migration
Religious identification
Role of religious enablers of jihadist terror
Psychological factors
Perception of secular state institutions
Resonance of extremist (al-Qaeda; other Sunni and Shia) message and globalization of jihad
Use of Iraq or Afghanistan to fuel jihadist strategic, operational, tactical, and propaganda goals
Political factors (lawlessness, insurgencies)
Role of familial, personal, tribal, or other connections
Role of educational or state-supported institutions
Role of charities
Weapons of mass destruction: chemical, biological, radiological, and nuclear

Whether law enforcement officials understand the totality of the SAR initiative and the principles of TINs is essentially irrelevant. What should be understood is that information that is not reported in detail cannot be properly analyzed. References to information needs throughout this chapter have been centered on terrorism and terrorist behavior. However, experienced law enforcement officials will note striking similarities to the behaviors associated with various crimes. It is important for all personnel to remember that detailed reports and early identification are the keys to planning, preventing, and protection.

## RADICALIZATION AND BEHAVIORS

According to the DHS report published on March 26, 2009, *Domestic Extremism Lexicon*,[4] radicalization is the process by which an individual adopts an extremist belief system leading to his or her willingness to advocate or bring about political, religious, economic, or social change through the use of force, violence, or ideologically motivated criminal activity. Beyond definitions, which are a good base to work from, the law enforcement community has come to realize that behavioral traits are learned in a variety of fashions such as upbringing, self-learning (Internet), and even incarceration. They are also a golden opportunity for early identification. Law enforcement has spent years targeting the youth in an effort to reduce the likelihood that they become criminals or even gang members in the future.

In 2007, the New York Police Department (NYPD) Intelligence Division produced and published a report titled *Radicalization in the West: The Homegrown Threat*. Although the report details the radicalization process, it is not the first report detailing characteristics associated with the radicalization process. The NYPD report was dynamic and brought tremendous insight to the radicalization process particularly with respect to the domestic front within the United States. However, analysts and investigators should be cautioned about operating in a vacuum. Other domestic reports have been published in other countries such as Canada, Great Britain, and the Netherlands. In March 2006, the Algemene Inlichtingen en Veiligheidsdienst (AIVD),[5] formerly known as the BVD (Binnenlandse Veiligheidsdienst; domestic security service), which is the general intelligence and security service or the secret service of the Netherlands, published a report titled *Violent Jihad in the Netherlands*. This report noted that radicalization, recruitment, and terrorism are seen as interrelated elements of one dynamical continuum within radical networks. The AIVD's report noted that these characteristics lead it to the following definition of a jihadist network:

> A jihadist network is a fluid, dynamic, vaguely delineated structure comprising a number of interrelated persons (radical Muslims) who are linked both individually and on an aggregate level (cells/groups). They have at least a temporary common interest, that is, the pursuit of a jihadism-related goal (including terrorism). Persons within such a network are referred to as members. A member is a person who contributes actively and consciously to the realization of the aforementioned goal within the bounds of the network (p. 14).[5]

Regardless of the domestic origins of a report, one can argue that all reports bring valuable information to the table. The AIVD report noted that by the end of the 1990s jihad veterans and radical ideologists began to approach members of the local Muslim communities in Europe. They noted that recent migrants and young second- and third-generation Muslims proved particularly receptive to the extremist ideology of the jihadists. Although the report is focused on the European connection, there appear to be similarities to such communities within the United States. Some law enforcement communities have seen that second and third generations in strong ethnic communities are receptive to extremist and gang recruitment activities.

Within the AIVD report, it was cited that since 2003 the service had observed a so-called grassroots radicalization gaining ground largely among young Muslims in Europe. This was triggered by itinerant preachers via radical websites. The increasing radicalization was reported as being fueled by children born and bred in Europe whose parents were North African and Pakistan migrants. It was also noted that the growth of what they referred to as autonomous networks was stimulated by triggers such as the war in Iraq, which garnered considerable media attention. Beyond the Netherlands, the report also expanded the emergence of this radicalization to include neighboring countries in Europe. One can proffer that it stretches beyond Europe to include the United States. This statement is based on the AIVD report, NYPD report, and other documents such as the *U.S. Senate Committee on Homeland Security and Governmental Affairs Majority and Minority Staff Report* published on May 8, 2008.

Chapter 5 will provide greater detail on the methods, tactics, and concerns related to the radicalization and recruitment of extremists and jihadists.

## EARLY INDICATORS OF TERRORISM

The December 2007 edition of the *FBI Law Enforcement Bulletin* focused on terrorism; it included an article titled *Countering Violent Islamic Extremism: A Community Responsibility*. The authors provided valuable insight into the path one undertakes to radicalization, which is noted verbatim here in an effort to avoid misquotes or misrepresentation of material.

Conversion to Islam is not radicalization. The FBI defines violent extremists as persons who engage in, encourage, endorse, condone, justify, or support in any way the commission of a violent act against the U.S. government, its citizens, or its allies to achieve political, social, or economic changes, or against others who may possess opinions contrary to their own radicalized ideology.

The FBI assesses the radicalization process as four stages: preradicalization, identification, indoctrination, and action. Each one is distinct, and a radicalized individual may never reach the final stage. The chart (Figure 4.6) identifies different aspects of the stages and provides indicators to help determine when an individual is likely to be in a certain one.

*Preradicalization*

Conversion may be to a religion or a commitment to another form of the religion. An individual's motivation is critical to the process and not always static. For example, people who initially convert to gain acceptance may reinterpret their faith if the group they join is composed of Muslim extremists.

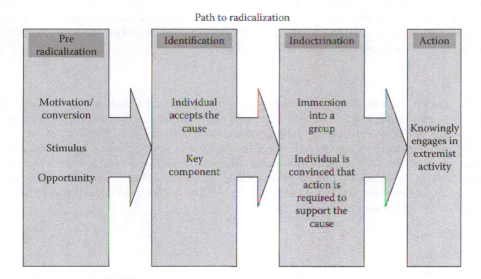

**FIGURE 4.6**   Four-step path of the stages and indicators associated with terrorism radicalization.

*Motivation*

In a jilted-believer conversion, internal frustration and dissatisfaction with the current religious faith leads the individual to change belief systems. The new system can be initially religious in tone or secular. Conversion attempts to resolve inconsistencies between what the person has come to believe and was taught to believe. For example, Adam Gadahn (aka Azzam the American), a California native who converted to Islam and supports al-Qaeda and Islamic extremism, wrote in his conversion story that Jesus was, at best, the Son of God and not someone whom individuals should revere and pray to.

A protest conversion may be an attempt by people to identify themselves apart from or to rebel against a society or circumstances they perceive as oppressive. Additionally, faith reinterpretation is another form of an intrinsically driven conversion where individuals alter their religious tradition through introspection and evaluation. This motivation refers specifically to those born into Muslim families but choose to follow a more extremist form of Islam, including such individuals as Faysal Galab, Tasein Taher, and Shafal Mosed of the Lackawanna Six. Galab, Taher, and Mosed drank alcohol, used drugs, and had relationships with non-Muslim women—all forbidden by the Koran—before converting. After this transition, it was easier for Kamal Derwish, who primarily influenced their newfound Islamic path, to convince them to participate in jihad as a way of absolving their sins.

Acceptance seeking, a form of extrinsic conversion, is a fundamental human motivation. Individuals have a pervasive drive to form and maintain at least a minimum quantity of lasting and significant interpersonal relationships. However, the product of these relationships can have positive or negative consequences for the people involved. Those with weak social ties may benefit from the solidarity that extremist groups provide.

*Stimulus and opportunity*

Converts who proceed through the radicalization process often are driven by a respected, frequently older, extremist with whom they have come into contact. Kamal Derwish played a key role in the radicalization of the Lackawanna Six. In the case of the Virginia Jihad Network, spiritual leader Ali Al-Timimi convinced a group of individuals, including a technology expert from Pakistan, a decorated Gulf War veteran and member of the National Rifle Association, a Korean immigrant, a son of a Yemeni diplomat, and a Muslim who had converted from Catholicism, to engage in violent jihad against U.S. troops. Interactions between converts and Islamic extremists can occur in a variety of venues. For example, in mosques, extremists can observe other Muslims' commitment to the faith and their reactions to the Islamic message given by extremist religious leaders. In prisons, extremist recruiters can identify a population disaffected with society and use their operational skills and propensity for violence to further their cause. In Islamic and secular universities, they can find curious individuals who question society, as well as their own beliefs. Further, extremists can interact with others in businesses, which provide a private setting to conduct meetings and further indoctrinate new converts, and in Internet chat rooms where vulnerable individuals from around the world can gather to discuss the Islamic doctrine.

*Identification*

In this stage, individuals identify themselves with a particular extremist cause and accept a radicalized ideology that justifies violence or other criminal activity against perceived enemies. Accepting the cause leads people to become increasingly isolated from their former lives. New converts often seek and follow guidance from imams, more senior followers, on how to live every detail of the religion, becoming more committed to the newfound faith. Converts' social connections with other like-minded individuals can strengthen this dedication. In addition, overseas travel may accelerate the radicalization process by providing networking and experience (e.g., religious or language instruction and basic paramilitary training) that later may support operational activity.

*Indoctrination*

Indoctrination can involve becoming an active participant in a group or being initiated within the recruit's self-created jihadist environment. Through various activities with the group and increasingly demanding and significant roles within it, converts see their potential as a jihadist and, ultimately, can become convinced of the need for further action to support the cause.

Formal recruitment into a terrorist group usually will occur before or during indoctrination. Recruitment plays an important role in any terrorist organization, and radicalized individuals can use their experience to spot, assess, and encourage potential recruits to follow the same path. This process also could include vouching for new recruits or helping them establish their extremist credentials. A charismatic recruiter with limited training or participation in jihad can transform that experience into a particularly enticing recruitment tool for individuals susceptible to an extremist message. Extremist Islamic clerics can play a major role because of their knowledge of Islam, their ability to provide religious justification for terrorist attacks, and the emotional hold they can have over impressionable recruits.

In the case of Jam'iyyat Ul-Islam Is-Saheeh (JIS), Kevin James, the group's founder, propagated JIS ideology and recruited adherents inside and outside prison mainly by disseminating the JIS manifesto and through direct meetings with inmates. James also sought new recruits without prison records who could benefit the group through their occupations, abilities, or access to sensitive locations.

*Action*

The final stage consists of supporting or engaging in terrorist activities. Although this action can be violent or nonviolent (e.g., financing), it always intends to inflict damage on the enemy. Some individuals who reach this stage will attempt to participate in a terrorist attack. Every action has three stages: preparation, planning, and execution. During any of these, recruits can try to stop participating. However, they may be so caught up in the group's activities that they will engage in behaviors they otherwise would not consider. Attack preparations can include target selection, casing, financing, and forming distinct operational cells.

Facilitation, a key component of any terrorist attack, can be accomplished by operatives dedicated to the support role or waiting for a separate attack, supporters unwilling or unable to perpetrate a terrorist attack, or unwitting participants. It can include providing financial assistance, safe houses, false documents, materials, attack plans, surveillance, or travel assistance. Individuals unable or unwilling to carry out a violent terrorist attack still can further the goals to which they subscribe. For example, facilitators play a key role in obtaining funding for a terrorist operation through such criminal activities as fraud, scams, embezzlement, or theft, and some may even involve violence. The JIS case included three homegrown Islamic extremists in Los Angeles, California, who robbed gas stations allegedly to fund their planned operations in support of the JIS cause.

An assessment of the aforementioned radicalization process of various reported models in the 2007 NYPD bulletin confirmed the four distinct phases. The NYPD report also noted that each of the four phases is unique and has specific signatures. It was also discovered that all individuals who begin the process do not necessarily pass through all the stages, and they may stop or abandon the process at different points and may be involved in the planning or implementation of the terrorist act. NYPD personnel also pointed out that although the model is sequential, the individuals involved do not always follow a perfectly linear progression.

The lexicon associated with domestic extremism and that may be discovered in the radicalization process can be found in Appendix I. Although the information contained in this appendix is not all-inclusive, it is applicable to many domestic extremist investigations and is derived from a DHS document that was produced in March 26, 2009.

## WOULD-BE WARRIORS

A 2010 Rand publication titled *Would-Be Warriors*[6] looked at terrorist radicalization in the United States since September 11, 2001. It noted that as long as America's psychological vulnerability is on display, jihadists will find inspiration, and more recruitment and terrorism will occur. The author of this insightful occasional paper, Brian Michael Jenkins,[6] reported that the recruitment will continue and that the homegrown jihadist threat in the United States today consists of tiny conspiracies, lone gunmen, and one-off attacks. The same report summarized the cases of domestic radicalization and recruitment to jihadist terrorism that occurred in the United States between September 11, 2001, and the end of 2009. Jenkins[6] noted that of the 46 publicly reported cases, 13 occurred in 2009. Most of the would-be jihadists were individuals who recruited themselves into the terrorist role. It is the last reference that has been the focus of much debate from the media to the U.S. Senate. In May 2008, Senators Joseph Lieberman and Susan Collins chaired a committee that looked into the emerging threat of homegrown terrorists and their connection and use of the Internet to radicalize. The committee's own investigation identified ways in which the Internet campaign can play a significant, if varying, role in each of the four stages of the radicalization process previously discussed in the section "Early indicators of terrorism." Self-radicalization in the modern era is easily achieved through a medium such as the Internet. Lieberman and Collins detailed the terrorist Internet campaign, which includes propaganda and the use of chat rooms. Their committee report referred to the Internet as a virtual training camp that allows extremist leaders to talk directly to those who may be vulnerable to the influences of the core terrorist enlistment message.

Use of the Internet for the radicalization process may be growing. The Internet allows the facilitation of communications that helps to identify and connect with networks around the world. These opportunities can help in building relationships and gaining expertise that previously were possible only through participation in overseas training camps. A key piece to the law enforcement identification puzzle can be found in the last sentence: relationships. It is the relationships that law enforcement must come to understand and identify if they are to be successful in limiting the radicalization process.

Additional locales where law enforcement can expose relationships related to radicalization are jails and prisons. Anecdotal information derived from various law enforcement officials indicates that inmates seek a sense of belonging, and one place they may find it is in ideologies that exist in institutional facilities like jails and prisons. Inmates who convert to Islam tend to garner the attention of homeland security investigators. However, it should be pointed out that not every conversion is done with the intent of becoming radicalized. Some correctional personnel state that they have experienced inmates converting for religious reasons. Some also convert for convenience, acceptance (survival), or meals.

Regardless of the origin of their radicalization recruitment, groups fail to exist without membership and therefore they rely heavily on sustained recruitment. Recruits are not necessarily born terrorists; they become radicalized at some point in their lives. It is the radicalization process and the behaviors associated with it that need to be understood, linked, and perceived weaknesses identified by law enforcement officials.

## RELATIONSHIPS OF PEOPLE, PLACES, AND THINGS

As the details within reports bring to light the characteristics associated with the radicalization process, they also shed much light on the need for identifying the relationships affiliated with the process. Beyond the fundamental need to understand the topic being analyzed, there is also the need to understand the behaviors that are indicative of relational building. There are several kinds of data that can be developed and used to identify relationships, but this section focuses on three overarching areas: (1) people, (2) places, and (3) things.

Perhaps the primary key to developing relationships is one component that is noted even in subversive materials—information gathering. The 1956 Irish Republican Army's *Handbook for Volunteers of the Irish Republican Army* not only cites the need for information but also notes that the information gathering process is a continuous operation. There are no time limits for the process. To develop clear, concise, and accurate relationships, law enforcement officials must look at information that may span years. Sure, software programs and modern technology help cull through volumes of data, but it is still the analyst or investigator who is responsible for making sense out of the results. Fuzzy logic tools provide assistance, but it is the need to understand the characteristic norms that may yield the greatest relationships. Traditional law enforcement personnel develop relationships often centered on hierarchical structures where there is a well-defined vertical chain of command.

Many homeland security investigations have observed networked structures wherein the result of the criminal element has demonstrated an understanding of law enforcement efforts to link information, therefore they have been shown to exhibit what can be called a flat structure. It also can be that there is less need for hierarchical structures. There are at least three networked structure types that have been observed: (1) chain, (2) hub or star wheel, and (3) all-channel networks. Networked structures are successful when they share a unifying interest and their responsibilities are distributed. Organizationally, networked structures, particularly all-channel networks, are flat and hard to disrupt.

Identifying relationships is important, and certainly suspicious activity reports and other initiatives help to identify relationships. However, a truly successful identification is the one that is done without delay and in an expedited manner. Therefore, software and technology are going to be the keys in churning through terabytes of data. There is no singular profile that exists and no predictive test that can guarantee one's success in the identification of terrorists or their actions.

Today's law enforcement agencies consist of multiple sharing environments designed to serve three communities: (1) intelligence, (2) investigations, and (3) analysis. Historically, each community has developed its own policies, rules, standards, architectures, and systems to channel information to meet its mission requirements. This, coupled with a multitude of legacy databases has left these communities struggling to identify solutions to access the databases in order to enable the data as actionable. Their efforts have led to the procurement of an array of software solutions that have extensive sustainment expenses and, in many instances, limited use by a small number of authorized users.

The future of a cost-saving solution depends on a vision based on national policies, priorities, and partnerships, and a clear understanding of the investigative framework, roles, and responsibilities for effective information sharing. Envision a solution that represents a trusted partnership among all levels of the law enforcement community to detect, prevent, disrupt, preempt, and mitigate the effects of criminal activity. Realizing this vision will impact the numerous departmental entities participating in the solution and will require achievement of the following six goals:

1. Facilitate the establishment of a trusted partnership among all levels of the department's investigative and analytical contingent.
2. Promote a collaboration culture among departmental personnel by facilitating the improved sharing of timely, validated, protected, and actionable investigative information.
3. Function in a centralized, distributed, and coordinated manner.
4. Develop and deploy incrementally, leveraging existing departmental information resources, an all-inclusive tool that will eliminate the need to search data independently.
5. Enable the department to speak with one voice on investigative matters and ensure that identified data sources are leveraged in order to further investigations in an expedited manner, ensure collaboration, and promote the ability to enhance case clearances.
6. Ensure that sharing procedures are identified, training at all levels is furthered, and investigative tools are standardized.

Enhancing operational capabilities will further the business process and function of any agency. The areas of emphasis include—but are not limited to—improving the access to and sharing of criminal-related alerts and notifications, enhancing the ability of recipients of criminal information to search information databases better, and improving collaboration across all levels of the department. The objective is to add value to current and future processes (criminal cases) in the following three dimensions:

1. Offering an all-inclusive solution of collaboration tools and the ability to search disparate databases across the department, and providing an all-crimes/threats interdiction solution
2. Discovering and identifying data and their relationships
3. Providing the policies, processes, training, and technical means for introducing new capabilities into the department

Through the use of various technologies and national standards, law enforcement has begun to realize just how much data are available to them. The problems that continue to persist are that nearly every law enforcement agency is sitting on numerous legacy systems that are full of data and that new technology is too expensive for the majority of agencies throughout the country. As for legacy systems, some in the law enforcement field have advocated randomly defining a time period to start new. Well, what about the data in legacy systems? This data is valuable when developing and defining relationships and patterns. Some have advocated that in order to collaborate, the data must be put in a central repository so that all agencies can search for them. This is antiquated thinking and it delays investigations. Besides, investigators and analysts search numerous agency systems, the Internet, and commercial data providers in order to get a clear and concise picture.

An example of relational building software that has been deployed in the law enforcement arena and addresses many of the aforementioned issues is a solution produced by GuideSTAR (GS) Technologies, Inc., Colorado.

Figures 4.7 and 4.8 demonstrate the interface of GS's investigative and collaborative data solution. Some examples of properly using collaborative tools such as GS's solution with new and developing data along with legacy system data are outlined as follows:

GuideSTAR reveals murder suspect and victim relationship: A gang member being interviewed by homicide detectives regarding a murder conducted earlier that morning swore he did not know the victim. One of the detectives left the interview room. The detective entered the member's name into GS and came back minutes later with pictures of him with the victim on a social networking website page that had not been visible as it resided on a cache, as well as other relational data from other databases. The verification assisted the detective in confirming the relationship and thus he was able to obtain a confession.

GuideSTAR searches and links data to clear cases: A large metropolitan police department integrated several databases with GS, including those containing more than 50,000 warrants, tens of thousands of field interview cards, and over 15 million call for service records. Investigators used the GS solution to automatically access and link massive amounts of data to identify relationships in a number of seemingly unrelated cases. This intelligence resulted in viable leads and an increase in case clearances.

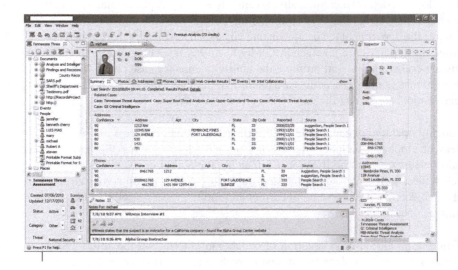

**FIGURE 4.7**   GuideSTAR's (redacted view) data returned from commercial, government, and open sources that show metadata, associated cases, and notes. (From GuideSTAR Technologies, Ron Fournet, CEO, GuideStar Technologies RAPTOR Solution, Software Screen Images, January 7, 2011. With permission.)

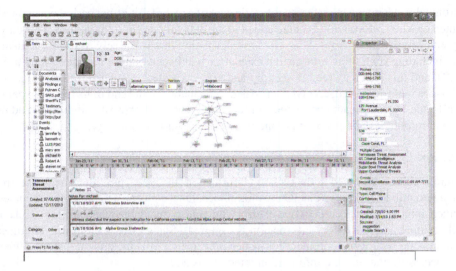

**FIGURE 4.8** GuideSTAR's (redacted view) data returned from commercial, government, and open sources that show relationships via their Whiteboard interface, timeline of events, history, and data/threat scoring. (From GuideSTAR Technologies, Ron Fournet, CEO, GuideStar Technologies RAPTOR Solution, Software Screen Images, January 7, 2011. With permission.)

GuideSTAR collaboration exchange leads to arrests: Two sheriff's offices were utilizing GS independently of each other. One was using the solution to monitor sexual predators and the other was working an organized theft case involving over 30 locations and 200 subjects. Behind the scenes, the GS collaboration tool identified a common address and alerted the respective offices to a common object of interest. The resulting collaboration produced several leads confirming the identity of two subjects and providing sufficient verification of addresses to ultimately lead to a search warrant and several arrests.

GuideSTAR identifies criminal ties to an airline worker suspected of stealing luggage: A worker at an international airport was suspected of stealing items from the luggage of hundreds of individuals after airport police observed the worker taking two boxes from a luggage conveyor belt and removing their contents. Using the GS solution, airport police discovered that the man had several ties to known criminals and was suspected of running a major theft ring. The GS solution provided police with numerous nonobvious relational leads to pursue. Police ultimately recovered stolen personal items worth hundreds of thousands of dollars.

## DATA AND INFORMATION QUALITY

Regardless of the solutions or programs such as SARs used by an agency, the underlying key to accurate analysis is data or information quality (IQ). In January 2010, the Global Justice Information Sharing Initiative produced a publication called the *Information Quality Program Guide*.[7] This guide was intended to help justice managers develop an IQ program for their organizations. The guide features a step-by-step approach to the development and implementation of an agency-wide IQ program and details the information life cycle.

### INFORMATION LIFE CYCLE

According to the 2010 *Information Quality Program Guide*, information is handled at every phase of an information cycle—creation and receipt, maintenance, use, and disposition phases. The creation and receipt phase refers to the creation or receipt of information, documents, or data, either manually or electronically. Maintenance refers to the static care of a record—it is that period when data is being maintained or when information is being added to the data for current or future use. This may require security and privacy protections. Use refers to information that is actively in use for a justice entity purpose (including continuing information exchanges within and outside the agency and use by multiple staff), and this also may require security and privacy protections. Disposition refers to the purging or disposal of (destroyed, archived, or sealed) information at the end of its retention period. IQ is further affected by significant components of the aforementioned phases: within roles and responsibilities, within policies and procedures, and within information technology.[7]

## INFORMATION QUALITY

The program guide mentioned in the section "Information life cycle" provides a self-assessment tool for agencies to utilize. It is noted that IQ is a multidimensional concept. Traditionally, agencies looked at IQ dimensions as being accuracy (free of error), timeliness (available when needed), and completeness (all required and mandatory information is captured). Since there is almost no circumstance in which there is no security requirement for justice information, it is incumbent that the dimension of security (access limitations and information integrity) is added.

Beyond these core dimensions, there are other requirements that must be met to ensure data quality. These dimensions are termed contextual IQ dimensions. The contextual IQ dimensions highlighted in the 2010 publication are outlined as follows[7]:

Accessibility—extent to which data is available or easily and quickly retrievable
Concise representation—extent to which data is compactly represented
Consistent representation—extent to which data is presented in the same format
Ease of manipulation—extent to which data is easy to manipulate
Objectivity—extent to which data is unbiased, unprejudiced, and impartial
Relevancy—extent to which data is applicable and helpful for the task at hand
Reliability—extent to which data is regarded true and credible
Reputation—extent to which data is highly regarded in terms of its source or content
Understandability—extent to which data is easily comprehended
Value added—extent to which data is beneficial and provides advantages from its use
Verifiability—degree and ease with which information can be checked for correctness

Why place so much importance on data quality? Simple, you can reap only what you sow. Software solutions can only do so much and investigators and analysts need accurate and immediate information if they are to draw effective assumptions or conclusions from it.

## CHAPTER CONCEPTS

The chapter concepts can be summarized as follows:

Understanding and defining behavioral traits associated with terrorism and their correlation with traits associated with crimes
National information sharing and the SAR process; how the process has been formulated and used by law enforcement agencies within the United States
Use of the SAR process and handling of SAR data according to NSI
The SAR behavioral indicators and how they are documented and retrieved for use in investigations
Indicators of the radicalization process and its four stages: (1) preradicalization, (2) identification, (3) indoctrination, and (4) action
Use of the Internet in the radicalization process
The key uses of identifying relationships associated with people, places, and things

## REFERENCES

1. Smith, B. *A Look at Terrorist Behavior: How They Prepare, Where They Strike.* http://www.ojp.usdoj.gov/nij/journals/260/terrorist-behavior.htm (accessed January 2, 2011).
2. McNamara, J. 2009. *Suspicious Activity Reporting, U.S. House of Representatives, Committee on Homeland Security, Subcommittee on the Intelligence, Information Sharing and Terrorism Risk Assessment.* March 18, 2009.
3. President. 2007. *National Strategy for Information Sharing Successes and Challenges in Improving Terrorism-Related Information Sharing.* White House, Washington, D.C., p. 11.
4. U.S. Department of Homeland Security, Office of Intelligence and Analysis. 2009. *Domestic Extremism Lexicon.* Washington, DC, p. 7.
5. Ministry of the Interior and Kingdom Relations. 2006. Algemene Inlichtingen-en Veiligheidsdienst (AIVD). In *Violent Jihad in the Netherlands: Current Trends in the Islamist Terrorist Threat,* General Intelligence and Security Service Communications Department, The Hague, p. 14.
6. Jenkins, B. M. 2010. *Would-Be Warriors, Incidents of Jihadist Terrorist Radicalization in the United States Since September 11, 2001.* Santa Monica, CA: Rand, pp. iii, ix.
7. Bureau of Justice Assistance. 2010. *Information Quality Program Guide.* Washington, DC, pp. 48, 49.

# 5 Radicalization and Recruitment

Many organizations throughout the world seek to recruit. Whether it is gangs, terrorist organizations, religious institutions, social groups, or employers, there is an age-old desire to bring members of society to join a cause, purpose, ideology, or group. In Chapter 4 the topic of radicalization and behaviors were discussed. The focus of this chapter is specifically centered on the 2007 New York Police Department's radicalization report and various reports produced by the United States government. Although this section is fairly comprehensive and provides a very solid primer, it essentially looks at the path to radicalization from a perspective of behaviors.

In an effort to expand the topic of radicalization and recruitment, this chapter will present principles and facts from worldwide research and studies. This chapter will look at many factors that are found in the recruitment of individuals for the purpose of pursuing a radicalized agenda.

## DEFINING THE TOPIC OF RADICALIZATION

"Radical" is a term that many find concerning and others seek to identify the process to become one. Radicalization is not a new term. It has been in use since the eighteenth century, the Enlightenment period, and throughout the French and American revolutions. Just like the term of terrorism, radicalization's definition has evolved over time. In the nineteenth century it was often referred to as "political agenda."

While some may believe it is important to have a steadfast definition of the three recurring terms that are found throughout research and agencies, it is not that simple. Outlined below are "working" definitions for the three principle terms: radicalization, recruitment, and conversion. Simply, many dictionaries provide an academic definition. This section will provide working definitions that are easily adapted and have been derived from a wide variety of governments from across the world. Since 2004, after the Madrid and London terrorist attacks, the term "radicalization" has been brought to the forefront when it comes to the discussion of terrorism for individuals who turn to terrorism. Terrorism studies, policymakers and the general public have often construed the radicalization process to be a concept that stems from the actions of homegrown terrorists. In reality, the radicalization process is not something that should be applied to radical Islamic extremists or homegrown terrorists. The actions related to radicalization do not occur in a vacuum and are prevalent throughout the world.

Based on the topic, context, and group, these terms may be fluid and ever changing. Since there is no universally accepted definition in academia or government, the definitions listed below may seem open-ended or vague to some. These terms are being defined in the context of terrorism and extremism.

- Radical—Applies to one who carries his theories or convictions to their furthest application. It implies not only extreme beliefs, but extreme actions.[1]
- Radicalization—A gradual process by which individuals are introduced and encouraged to pursue an extremist belief system or ideology. These beliefs and ideologies are frequently driven by personal concerns, political events, or religious differences. Individuals often accept and use violent means to reach a specific objective based on extreme beliefs. This can lead to social polarization and an intolerant isolationist point of view. Behaviors and attitudes can be violent and non-violent when presented.

- Recruitment—In the context of radicalization, recruitment is often driven by social and individual factions. It requires an interaction between the "recruit" and the recruiting system that can be in the form of person-to-person or through virtual means.
- Conversion—A noticeable change in a person's religious identity. This may take the form of a change from one faith to another, a secular belief to a formal faith, or a recommitment to an existing faith.

It should be noted that the aforementioned terms do apply across all religious and ideological beliefs. Furthermore, the term conversion should be used with caution. As will be discussed in this chapter, there are many reasons individuals seek to "join" a group or belief. In the context of conversion, law enforcement should be cognizant that not all those who convert are recruited or seek a radical agenda. It has been reported that some individuals who convert for religious reasons do so to expand or realign their personal belief systems. There are also those who may be confined in an institution who convert for convenience such as better meals or in order to adapt to the constraints present in their environment, or as a form of self-perceived survival. Conversion can frequently have positive influences such as increased self-esteem.

Having established a baseline for the principle terminology, this chapter will delve into many aspects of the recruitment and radicalization process. The references used throughout the remainder of the chapter will not be germane to any one specific religion or ideology. However, it will focus on those factors used to recruit individuals for the purpose of furthering an extremist radical agenda or belief.

## FACTORS CONDUCIVE TO RADICALIZATION

Extremists and terrorists do not fall from the sky. They grow and develop from their experiences and various external factors that aid in the facilitation of their radicalization process. There are many factors and triggering events that are conducive to the radicalization process. These factors are not mutually exclusive. It is not possible to combine specific factors to equal a predefined result of whether someone has been radicalized. Investigators and analysts will need to consider the factors such as the individual's background, upbringing, social environment, education, economic status, behavior, and beliefs. It is important to note that radicalization is a prerequisite to terrorism, but radicalization does not automatically propel one to violence.

Dr Alex P. Schmid authored a research paper in March 2013 for the International Centre for Counter-Terrorism—The Hague, regarding all aspects of radicalization. Schmid reported that academics cannot agree on the root causes of terrorism in general. He continues to state that research identified more than 50 different alleged causes. Here is a sample:

- Terrorism is rooted in political discontent.
- A culture of alienation and humiliation can act as a kind of growth medium in which the process of radicalization commences and virulent extremism comes to thrive.
- A collective or individual desire for revenge against acts of repression may be motive enough for terrorist activity.
- The failure to mobilize popular support for a radical political program may trigger the decision to employ terrorism in order to engineer a violent confrontation with authorities.
- Modern terrorism occurs because modern circumstances make terrorism methods exceptionally easy.
- The choice of terrorism represents the outcome of a learning process from one's experiences and the experiences of others.[2]

The purpose of presenting varying academic and government points of view is important to demonstrate that you cannot simply categorize causes of radicalization. Schmid notes that much of the academic research does not involve listening to the explanations of the terrorist or extremist themselves. Therefore, several points of view and opinions will continue to be presented in this chapter and it will be up to the reader to determine what is applicable to their situation or purpose.

In December 2013, the *Journal of Psychology and Behavioral Science* published an article titled *Understanding Violent Radicalization among Muslims: A Review of the Literature* authored by Rahimullah, Larmar, and Abdalla. The article starts by pointing out that terrorism is a by-product of radicalization and poses a significant threat. The authors identified several risk factors of radicalism that could be among Muslims: religious risk factors, Muslim identification, association with radicals, socioeconomic factors; experienced deprivation, experienced affluence, and perceived relative deprivation, personal experiences, criminal activity, globalization, racism and Islamophobia, cultural identities, and anomie and psychological aspects.[3] The article notes that the various aforementioned factors are thought to place an individual at risk of radicalizing. The authors report that there are several catalysts of radicalization. They note that these catalysts are a key feature of Veldhuis' and Staun's model.[3]

- Recruitment—the need to have a consolidated relationship with the group's members
- The role of radical media and the Internet—the use of these media to expose individuals to their propaganda and promote their radical agenda
- Trigger events of radicalization—issues at either the social or individual level that act as triggers, which might call for revenge or action and may be numerous, and include:
  - Disruptive events like the death of a loved one
  - Experience of discrimination, injustice, or imprisonment
  - Inability to gain employment
  - Social events that might be important and relevant depending on how the individual perceives them and their environment such as an influential speech or publication

The depth of the research in the article is well noted. It is worth reporting that the authors highlighted various models that have been widely used to explain radicalization. They focused on six models of radicalization.[3]

- Integrated model—Savage and Lihn (2008) integrated three theories: terror management, uncertainty reduction, and social identity theory to develop a six stage model of radicalization.
- Witorowicz's model—developed in 2004, shows radicalization as a four-step process.
- PET model—developed and published by the Danish Intelligence Services, this is a four-phase, top-down model.
- NYPD model—unlike the PET model, the NYPD model is a bottom-up process where the individual instigates radicalization in a four-phase model.
- Root cause model—formulated in 2009 by Veldhuis and Staun, this model is based on root causes, not stages, and it cites three levels; macro, macro social, and macro individual.
- Roy model—formulated in 2004 and similar to the Veldhuis and Staun model. It emphasizes macro factors.

Many aspects of the various models noted above will become apparent throughout the material presented in this chapter. One thing is clear: there is no one-size-fits-all when it comes to identifying anyone involved in the radicalization process.

Models are good to present and understand the overall concept of radicalization. As it was noted above, much of the academic research lacks an explanation derived from the terrorists or extremists themselves. It can be argued that this may not be possible since many of the actors perpetrating radical acts have been permanently removed from society and existence. There are several papers that seek to explain the point of view of radicalized individuals. One that this writer considers worthy of mentioning is the April 2009 publication by the Foundation for Defense of Democracies (FDD) Center for Terrorism Research. The principle authors, Gartenstein-Ross and Grossman, identified six indicators of jihadist radicalization which were derived from examination of data from 117 homegrown jihadist terrorists in the United States and the United Kingdom. It was reported by these authors that indicators do not necessarily make a terrorist, but they help to explain how they are radicalized. While someone can question the upbringing location of those studied, it is worth noting that the authors reported that individuals studied in their report spent a significant portion of their formative years in the West.

Gartenstein-Ross and Grossman identified six indicators of jihadist radicalization. The first three of these have to do with how rigidly one interprets one's religion, how they view relations between the West and Islam, and on their level of trust. The second three indicators are more easily observable and comprise of manifesting a low tolerance for religious deviance, imposing beliefs on others, and expressing radical views. In the authors' study, they found that the six steps outlined below differ in prevalence, but they found that all of them occurred frequently enough to consider them significant.

1. Adopting a legalistic interpretation of Islam—this refers to how believers interpret their rights and obligations in relation to Islam's holy texts and adopts rules based on strict guidelines of the Quran and sunnah.
2. Trusting only select religious authorities— homegrown terrorists come to trust only the interpretations of a select and ideologically rigid set of religious authorities.
3. Perceived schism between Islam and the West—as homegrown terrorists radicalize, they often come to perceive an inherent schism between Islam and the West—believing that the two are at odds.
4. Low tolerance for perceived theological deviance—as homegrown terrorists internalize rigid interpretations of Islam, many come to view alternate interpretations and practices as not just incorrect theologically, but as personal affronts.
5. Attempts to impose religious beliefs on others—another significant step is when individuals attempt to impose their religious beliefs on others.
6. Political radicalization—homegrown terrorists in this study evince a considerable amount of political radicalization and was the factor found most frequently.[4]

The paper's authors note that their research had several specific conclusions about homegrown terrorists' radicalization. First, religion was a significant factor in their radicalization. Second, like other studies, they found there to be no single terrorist profile. Third, they found there was an importance on international connections. Fourth, they found prisons not to be as important in international terrorism as some researchers have feared. Only 7 out of the 117 cases demonstrated a connection.

Although several researchers argue that there is no one specific homegrown terrorist profile, there is one respected research report that does present such a profile. In 2007, Tomas Precht authored *Home Grown Terrorism and Islamist Radicalisation in Europe* which was funded by the Danish Ministry of Justice. Precht presents that the radicalization process starts with individuals who are frustrated with their lives, society, and governments. He further reports that there is no single cause or catalyst for radicalization and that it is a multidimensional process influenced by a complex array of factors. Precht states that homegrown terrorist groups might form and grow autonomously up to a certain level. However, in European cases, overseas travel and international contacts were contributing factors in more advanced phases of radicalization. Presented for discussion, there were three categories of motivational factors that influence radicalization which are outlined below.

Background factors such as:

- Muslim identity crisis
- Personal traumas
- Experience of discrimination and relative deprivation factors
- Living environment and peers (segregation and parallel society)
- Alienation and perceived injustices
- Relative absence of a critical Muslim debate on Islamist terrorism

Trigger factors such as:

- Western foreign policy and single provocative incidents
- The myth of Jihad and desire for activism
- Presence of a charismatic person or spiritual adviser

Opportunity factors (places to meet like-minded people) such as:

- The Mosque
- Internet and satellite channels
- School, universities, youth clubs, or work
- Prison
- Sporting activities
- Cafes, bars, or bookstores[5]

Again, it is important to remember that identifying and understanding extremism and radicalization is a complex undertaking. There is no simple cause and effect. The individuals we seek to understand come from all areas of society and diverse backgrounds.

Having discussed the radicalization process in broad terms and provided a general understanding of the factors, it is important to drill down to the individual. Many have studied and sought to understand the reasons a person becomes radicalized. While the overall arch of radicalization usually involves multiple, reinforcing processes, scholars have identified a series of individual pathways to radicalization. These pathways were presented by Clark McCauley and Sophia Moskalenko in their 2011 publication *Friction: How Radicalization Happens to Them and Us*. In this book, the authors discuss individual, group, and mass radicalization. This compilation will solely focus on the following individual pathways which strike similar components that have been discussed earlier in this chapter:

- Personal grievance—this pathway emphasizes revenge for real or perceived harm inflicted upon oneself by an outside party.
- Group grievance—this is similar to the dynamics primed by personal grievances, with the difference being the individual perceives the harm inflicted on a group to which they belong.
- Slippery slope—this represents gradual radicalization through activities that incrementally narrow the individual's social circle and their mindset and in some cases, desensitizing them to violence.
- Power of love—romantic and familial engagement is an often overlooked factor but these can serve as a connection factor to connect individuals to influential figures with a radical ideology.
- Status and thrill seeking—high-risk behavior, if successful, offers a pathway to status insofar as it becomes construed as bravery and commitment to a cause.
- Unfreezing—loss of social connection can open an individual to new ideas and a new identity that may include political radicalization.[6]

It can be easy to use any of the models or factors discussed to this point. However, there are those who argue that radicalizing is a strategic choice made by a sole individual. This may be true to some point but the whole process of radicalization cannot be summed up by adding one factor with another to get a concrete understanding of why someone has become radicalized. According to the Veldhuis and Staun root cause model, participation in terrorist activity requires an active, conscious decision, whereas radicalization is a gradual process that generally does not have a clearly defined beginning or end state.[7]

When we discuss radicalization we must look beyond the process and relationships of groups to have a full awareness of what governments face. The underlying piece to the puzzle that is key and common to any of the models discussed is the individual. It can be argued that perhaps it is the ease of access to material that enables and fosters the growth of radicalization. There has been consensus among many researchers that two factors facilitate the radicalization process: the two factors are a spiritual mentor and the Internet. It is the latter that perhaps poses the greatest concern to law enforcement throughout the world. The threat and likelihood of radicalization appears to have increased in today's global society thanks to technology. The topic of the Internet and recruitment will be discussed in depth later in this chapter. However, there are those who seek answers through the Internet and further their radical thoughts based on the material presented. Often, these individuals self-identify with a group's ideology and self-radicalize but they fail to actually belong to a group, and act on their own accord. It is these individuals who are often referred to as homegrown lone wolf actors.

## SELF-RADICALIZATION

Self-radicalization is often mentioned by members of the media and researchers but it is held in the context of Muslims or Islamic extremist groups. However, self-radicalization is highly applicable to all groups, foreign or domestic. This was apparent when FBI Director Robert Mueller provided testimony before the Senate Select Committee on Intelligence of the United States Senate on February 11, 2003. Director Mueller stated,

> I am particularly concerned about loosely affiliated terrorists and lone offenders, which are inherently difficult to interdict given the anonymity of individuals that maintain limited or no links to established terrorist groups but act out of sympathy with a larger cause.[8]

The nature of the threat posed by radicalized individuals is complex. Many of the federal, state, and local law enforcement investigations since 9/11 have revealed militant Islamic and domestic affiliated extremists throughout the United States. Although there have been numerous violent acts by extremist groups and individuals, it is important to note that the focus of many of their activities centers primarily on fundraising, recruitment, and training. In order to achieve this, individuals sympathetic or supportive of extreme radical ideologies or agendas are needed. On September 20, 2006, Deputy Assistant Director of the FBI, Donald Van Duyn, provided testimony to the House Homeland Security Committee Subcommittee on Intelligence where he noted that the key to success of stopping the spread of radicalization is identifying patterns and trends in the early stages. This starts with individuals who self-radicalize.

Researchers and academics throughout the world have spent decades trying to understand the radicalization process and strategies to prevent the causes. One report, published in February 2015 and written by Mark Hamm and Ramon Spaaj from Indiana University, provides insight to lone wolf terrorism in America. The report document is titled *Lone Wolf Terrorism in America: Using Knowledge of Radicalization Pathways to Forge Prevention Strategies*. Although the report is America centric, it is not difficult for the reader to see the similarities with the same problem in other parts of the world.

Hamm and Spaaj discovered 98 cases between 1940 and 2013 that fit their definition of lone wolf terrorism. Of the 98 cases, 38 cases occurred before 9/11 and 60 took place after 9/11. Of interest in their report was the continual fact that they report lone wolf terrorism in America is not on the rise—in the terms of lethality. One could argue that this is due to law enforcement successes or the fact that there are many "unknowns." Prior to 9/11 there was not much focus on radicals or extremists beyond Federal law enforcement. Of interest was the author's reference to lone wolf terrorism being a multifaceted crime and that there is no specific profile of the American lone wolf terrorist. They note that the evidence indicates that most of them are unemployed, single white males with a criminal record. Compared to members of terrorist groups, lone wolves are older, less educated, and more prone to mental illness.[9] Data presented by the authors in the report sought to explain the pathways to

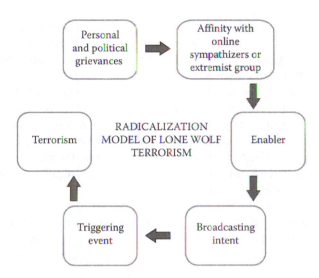

**FIGURE 5.1**    The radicalization model of lone wolf terrorism.

radicalization by noting that it is important to understand the locus (or place) of radicalization. I will present the material from the report collectively and will not differentiate the data points as pre- or post 9/11 since, as an investigator, it is important not to overlook the modus operandi. If we follow "current" trends and overlook "past" trends we may miss data. With regards to lone wolf actors, data presented in the report showed pathways listed below, highlighted and demonstrated in Figure 5.1:

- Loci of radicalization—individuals that belonged to an extremist group but had since abandoned it and moved to informal online social networks, the civilian workplace, and mass media.
- Motives—these tend to combine personal grievances with political grievances.
- Affinity with extremist groups—seeking direction through venues via networks of like-minded activists found online or on cable television.
- Enablers—this is enabled through either direct means in the form of people who unwittingly assist in planning attacks, or indirectly by people who provide inspiration for terrorism.
- Broadcasting intent—while they physically isolate from society, at the same time they communicate with outsiders through spoken statements, threats, letters, manifestos, and video-taped proclamations.
- Triggering event—the triggering event is a catalyst for lone wolf terrorism and may be personal or political, or some combination of the two.

## THE COMMONALITIES OF LONE WOLF TERRORISM: A SUMMARY

The commonalities form a radicalization model indicating that lone wolf terrorism begins with personal and political grievances, which become the basis for an affinity with an extremist group. Moreover, radicalization is caused by an affinity with online sympathizers in a post 9/11 era.[9]

Now that we have discussed radicalization from broad terms down to the individual from various areas of the world, it is evident that radicalization is not a cookie-cutter process. In 2006, an article was written by the Canadian Centre for Intelligence and Security Studies regarding militant jihadism radicalization, conversion, and recruitment. The authors report that terrorism is the extreme consequence of radicalization that shows signs of early involvement in support activities including crimes. The Canadian report cites empirical work by Marc Sageman and they concluded that individual profiles based on such personal characteristics as sex, age, national origin, religion, education, and socioeconomic background are of little value in identifying future terrorists.[10] This should not be construed to mean that investigators or analysts should overlook these variables but rather weight them and put them into context with the particular case they are working.

So, one may ask, if the "traditional" variables used by law enforcement have little value, then what else is there that can be viewed to give some insight to the radicalization process? There are several researchers who have looked at the psychology of radicalization in order to answer this question. In September 2014, Dr Arie W. Kruglanski and Mr David Webber from the University of Maryland, College Park, presented a psychological model of radicalization. Their model identified three crucial components that lead to extreme commitment in which the most radicalized individuals are extremely dedicated to their goal. These three components are:

1. The motivational component that identifies the goal to which the individual is highly committed (the quest for significance)
2. The cultural component that defines the role of group ideologies in identifying violent means as appropriate in a goal pursuit
3. The social component that identifies the group dynamics through which an individual comes to endorse the group ideology[11]

In the same paper, the authors propose that the following three factors comprise the radicalization process that leads to intense commitment to radical means.

1. Individual motivation and identification of the goal trying to be achieved
2. Group ideology which approaches radicalization from the cultural level and acknowledges that an individual's choices are determined by the cultural milieu in which they are embedded
3. Social level which understands it as a process steeped in group dynamics[11]

Having looked at the radicalization process from a multitude of angles, a few key areas continually emerge: ideology, social relations, and criminal activity. We will continue to delve further into many of these areas throughout this chapter. Comparing the aforementioned key factors with the prevailing components found in other models—grievance, ideology/narrative, and mobilization—one can start to see distinct data points that may be useful for law enforcement.

As we have seen, the topic of radicalization is a very elusive and a dynamic process. Regardless how it is viewed and the context in which it is placed, there are some conditions conducive to radicalization when looking at an individual. Here is a list of some conditions:

- Socioeconomic and political environments of the individual
- Social interactions and relationships
- Psychological and even cognitive factors such as trauma and displacement
- Exposure to ideas and narratives that legitimize terrorism or radical violent actions

## CONVERSION

According to the *Converts and Islamist Terrorism* paper published in June 2016 by the International Centre for Counter-Terrorism—The Hague, it is noted that converts to Islam represent a small percentage of the Muslim community in Western countries. This paper is careful to note that converting to Islam by itself should not be seen as the only factor used to raise a security concern. The authors state that many people frequently use conversion as a positive influence and it increases self-esteem for some. One hypothesis that exists holds that converts are more vulnerable to radicalization because they lack knowledge of Islam, or due to their zeal and dedication to their newfound faith.

In 2006, the FBI produced the first in a series of analytical products that dealt with the radicalization process. In May of 2006 they focused on the radicalization process looking at it from conversion to jihad. A key takeaway from this product is that conversion to the Islamic faith does not always lead the convert down the path to being radicalized. The FBI noted that the conversion process places the convert in a position to be influenced by Islamic extremists which is more important than the convert's initial motivations for converting. While much of the research data focuses on the conversion from one formal faith to the Islamic faith, it is extremely important to mention that the same principles can and do apply to other extremist causes in other religions. We need to remember the religious foundation of the many right- and left-wing extremist/religious organizations such as the Christian Identity Movement, Yahweh, and Nation of Islam. When it comes to conversion, especially in correctional facilities, there are those who convert for convenience or even survival. This topic will be explored further in subsequent sections in this chapter.

## PROFILES OF INDIVIDUAL RADICALIZATION

Profiling may be a taboo term to some but it does provide valuable insight to many issues and enables researchers to catalog many data points. The National Consortium for the Study of Terrorism and Responses to Terrorism (START) recently conducted an in-depth research project pertaining to individual radicalization. Preliminary findings from START's Profiles of Individual Radicalization in the United States (PIRUS) project highlight interesting and policy-relevant trends among individuals radicalized in the United States since World War II.

According to the START October 2015 research brief, the PRIUS project is a database of Islamist, far left and far-right individuals who have radicalized to violent and non-violent extremism in the United States. Data collection for this project occurred over three waves, beginning in summer 2013 and concluding in spring 2014. Over that period, researchers and student interns gathered data for over 1,500 individuals and authored over 100 qualitative case studies. The research showed a several "waves" of radicalization in the United States since World War II. Here is a summary of the research presented:

- Numerous extremists were arrested, killed, or died in action from the late 1960s to early 1970s as a result of the surge in far left extremism in that period.
- Another peak in radicalization occurred in the 1990s with significant far-right extremist activity, which spiked again in the mid-2000s.
- Soon after the 9/11 attacks, a new wave of radicalization occurred comprised primarily of Islamist extremists.
- Among Islamist extremists, demographic factors—such as being between 18 and 28 years of age, not married, and/or not closely integrated into U.S. society—were related to the use of violence, as well as having been abused and having a criminal history.
- Among far-right extremists, demographic factors and a criminal history related to using violence.
- For far left individuals, a history of abuse was a significant factor in predicting the likelihood for violence as well as criminal and demographic risk factors.
- Interestingly, participation in religious activities as well as the consumption of radical media was negatively correlated with the use of violence among both far-right and far left extremists.

A few specific characteristics seemed to correspond to violence among radicalized individuals. Loners and individuals with psychological issues were more likely to commit violence. Similarly, individuals who experienced a drop in social standing prior to their illegal extremist activity were more likely to use violence. However, those individuals who spent a longer time radicalizing before engaging in illegal extremist activities were less likely to commit an act of violence.

Some specific conditions and events were more common among certain ideologies:

- Extremist group affiliation was most common among Islamist extremists. Islamist extremists radicalized in the United States were also more likely than far-right or far left extremists to have been actively recruited into an extremist group. Islamist extremists were commonly part of insular cliques, and experienced low levels of intragroup competition.
- Far-right and far left extremists demonstrated more diverse characteristics. Far-right extremists had the longest duration of radicalization and experienced the most intragroup competition. Far left extremists, in turn, were more likely to have experienced a change in performance—in either work or education—prior to radicalization than those from the other ideological backgrounds. Far left extremists were also more likely to be students, although this is not surprising given the prevalence of far left extremism among college students in the 1960s.
- A few conditions prominent in policy and academic debates over radicalization were similar among far left, far-right, and Islamist extremists. Radicalization appears to be a very social phenomenon, regardless of ideology. Approximately half of the individuals in the dataset belonged to a clique—a tight-knit, insular group of people. There was little significant difference among ideologies in the prevalence of psychological issues, loners, and a loss of standing. However, all of these elements were more common among violent individuals. This suggests that individuals that demonstrate these risk factors are equally predisposed to violence regardless of their ideological background. Finally, there was no difference in the role of prison in the radicalization processes across ideologies. Given the recent concerns about the radicalization of Muslim prisoners, this suggests that the risk of prison radicalization is roughly equal for far-right and far left extremists.[12]

## CRIMINAL ROOTS

Researchers and governments alike often cite the connection between radicalization and criminal activity. This section will discuss the factor of criminal roots as it relates not only to the radicalization, but also how it is contextually connected to the recruitment process.

The commitment to violence is what distinguishes a terrorist from other extremist or criminals. However, as law enforcement officials are aware, many criminals are already prone to acts of violence which may make them potential candidates for radicalization and recruitment. Criminals have the potential to be drawn to various illicit activities as a way to identify with others, or to join or affiliate with a group to fulfill their need for belonging.

Connections to criminal activity by radical extremists are not new or applicable to any one specific country. Many researchers have noted how criminals may be viewed as fertile ground for those seeking individuals to join their cause or ideology. The one-stop shops that some see as prime ground are correctional facilities. This will be discussed in detail later. However, the criminal roots connection is a topic that groups such as ISIS see as ripe for picking. Some researchers have noted that the Islamic State is finding fruitful recruiting among Europe's street gangs and criminals. Whether it is predominately in poor Muslim neighborhoods or in non-Muslims who are attracted by a group's violent ideology, all levels of criminals are seen as attractive potential accomplices. It was reported by a former FBI counterterrorism official that some criminals are just looking for any opportunity to justify their violence and criminal actions.

The Islamic State membership, like many criminals, is seen as having a thuggish pedigree. One country that has garnered attention regarding the Islamic State and its activities is Belgium. Security authorities in Belgium have described the Islamic State's use of criminal links as symbiotic since they rely on their criminal associations to hide from the authorities. They also use criminals to procure supplies such as explosives. Belgian Foreign Minister Didier Reynders noted that there are many links between criminals and Islamist militants who use the same tools, cars, and apartments. Counterterrorism experts in

Europe have documented a profound shift in the profile of terrorist recruits. They have asserted that their key characteristics are closer to those of urban street gangs than religious extremists.

The overwhelming majority of studies related to radicalization and violent extremism are predominately focused on those following or adhering to an Islamic-based doctrine. One recently published report provides new data from a 2-year study concerning radicalization and recruitment among U.S. far-right terrorists. In November 2016, START produced the *Recruitment and Radicalization among Far-Right Terrorists* research report. This report examined multiple aspects of recruitment and radicalization. The 144-page report looks at many aspects of the radicalization process and demonstrated an emphasis on violent extremism and motivations. The authors provide a highly academic and research-driven thematic assessment which focuses on family socialization prior to extremist involvement. Of interest in the summary was that participants in the study felt the "group" offered them protection from bullies and rival gangs in their neighborhoods.

There are several risk factors that can push or pull an individual toward deviant behavior, for example, family, peer, school, and community. The START report notes that in the field of criminology, violent extremism and "normal" crime are traditionally studied separately. They cite that violent extremism is often characterized as unique compared with conventional crime for two principal reasons. First, violent extremism is inherently an overtly political act, motivated by clear ideological commitment and convictions. Generally, extremists use violence to express a particular grievance. Second, the group nature of violent extremism often aids in the separation from conventional crime because researchers focus on group dynamics while neglecting a person's earlier experiences. Thus, there is a tendency to neglect how extremists have been influenced by a variety of internal and external factors.[13] The report notes that generic offending and violent extremism are disproportionately committed by young males. Another similarity that street gangs and organized crime syndicates share with violent extremists is their adherence to an ongoing organizational structure. Finally, similar to violent extremists, street gangs are not defined by a single act but are rather the amalgamation of multiple violent crimes over the course of that individual's criminal career.[13]

## THE GANG CONNECTION

Gangs continue with criminal activity, and recruit new members in urban, suburban, and rural regions across the United States. While this section will be U.S. centric, it is important to note that it is still applicable throughout the many parts of the world. Gangs develop criminal associations that expand their influence over criminal enterprises, particularly street-level drug sales. It may be these associations, criminal enterprises, or the experiences of individual gang members that make them attractive recruits for violent extremist or terrorist organizations. It is also possible to draw connections to many radicalization factors noted earlier in this chapter to those affiliated with gangs. Various *National Gang Threat Assessment* reports published by the National Gang Intelligence Center provide valuable insight to the state of gangs and their connections in the United States.

According to the 2011 National Gang Threat Assessment, there are approximately 1.4 million active street, prison, and motorcycle gang members comprising 33,000 gangs in the United States.[14] These numbers are presented as an overall baseline designed to demonstrate the magnitude of individuals involved in gang activities. Gangs are responsible for an average of 48% of violent crime in most jurisdictions, and as will be discussed, they are shown to be a growing number and concern in correctional institutions. The concern by many regarding gangs is their emergence in nontraditional gang crimes, such as alien smuggling and human trafficking. There is also growing concern related to the potential growth in gangs being involved in various financial crimes such as counterfeiting and identity theft. All the aforementioned crimes pose a possible connection for extremists and terrorists to exploit and seek to gain financial resources with little visibility.

Beyond the street level, gang alliances and collaboration between rival factions and criminal organizations are becoming a concern for law enforcement. Modern technology and ease of transportation have enabled local or national level gangs to expand and develop relationships with various organizations, groups, and individuals worldwide. While some of this may not be for overt violent acts, it is possible that it may be for supportive functions such as recruiting, finances, training, and logistics. Another concern that emerges centers around the expansion of ethnic-based and nontraditional gangs. Law enforcement officials have reported to the National Gang Intelligence Center that they have experienced an expansion of African, Asian, Eurasian, Caribbean, and Middle Eastern gangs. Reports of those targeted for recruiting or seen as ripe for recruitment are those defined as "second-generation." The parents or other family may have immigrated to a country for specific reasons or freedoms but it is the second generation who may not assimilate into their adopted country and seek to identify a way to belong. These individuals may look for a cause to join, and encounter conflicting views and ideologies which recruiters use to their advantage. While there may not be an obvious direct correlation to gang membership and radicalization, once they are incarcerated law enforcement must remain cognizant of their background especially with ethnic-based gangs. These members can easily be construed as susceptible to radicalization and recruitment efforts.

In 2015, William Sturgeon published an article on corrections.com concerning radicalization and intelligence gathering. He stated that "… there are a great many similarities in the early stages of joining a gang and being radicalized."

Some examples of "similarities" between gang recruitment and radicalization:

- The recruits begin to hang around with the group they are aligning with at that time.
- The recruits either grow their hair/beard or they cut their hair and keep their beards, again depending on the group they are aligning with at that time.
- They distance themselves from the correctional staff, unless instructed to become more familiar with "certain" personnel. These are usually staff who the group believes can assist them in getting jobs, better living conditions, favors, etc.
- The recruits for gangs may start to use the vernacular, acquire tattoos, wear certain clothing in certain ways of the group they are aligning themselves with at that time.[15]

## CAUSES OF EXTREMISM

What are the causes of extremism? This is a simple question that has varying points of view. Adam Sinicki published an article for Health Guidance titled *The Psychology of Extremism* that sought to answer this topic. He addressed the matter by stating that extremism describes any kind of exaggerated view. An obvious example of this is political extremism, wherein a person or group of people holds highly extreme and black-and-white views regarding their politics and often incorporates ideals and attitudes which the rest of us would find offensive, impractical, or plain wrong.

Other examples might be an extreme obsession with one idea or hobby, religious fanaticism, or some kind of debilitating belief. A very right-wing, neo-Nazi could be accused of extremism on the one hand, but equally so could someone who takes their concern for the environment so far that they are willing to burn down factories and forego washing.

Extremism is highly dangerous because it often results in views that are detached from reality, or that are destructive to the ideals of others. But how does this come about?[16] The author looked at several factors of this phenomenon for which a synopsis is listed below:

- Spectrums—all beliefs and ideas can be put onto a spectrum
- Confirmation bias—tendency to ignore information that contradicts our beliefs and only take on the information that confirms and enforces it
- Convergence and divergence—to become similar to members of a group and less similar to other groups
- Religious zeal—experiencing an extreme emotional response when you are preaching your cause or engaging in its practice
- Deep seated psychological issues—some are prone to more extreme views than others and some develop them free of any environmental factors

Believing there are multiple ways to examine the root causes of violent extremism, the Radicalization Awareness Network (RAN) produced an issue paper in April 2016 to address the topic. The issue paper, which was written by Magnus Ranstorp, reported that there is a wide array of factors on the macro-, meso-, and microlevels of analyst. Terrorism research has indicated that neither poverty nor socioeconomic deprivations are direct root causes of terrorism. Ranstorp stated that violent extremism can be best conceptualized as a kaleidoscope of factors. He identified nine factors that cause violent extremism which are outlined below:

1. Individual socio-psychological factors—includes grievances and emotions
2. Social factors—includes social exclusion, marginalization, and discrimination
3. Political factors—includes grievances framed around victimhood against Western foreign policy and military intervention
4. Ideological/religious factors—includes beliefs that Western society embodies immoral secularism
5. Culture and identity crisis—relates to cultural marginalization which produces alienation
6. Trauma and other trigger mechanisms—involves psychological trauma or other complex psychological problems
7. Group dynamics—involve charismatic leadership, pre-existing friendship, and kinship ties
8. Radicalizers/groomers—involve hate preachers and those who prey on vulnerabilities and grievances
9. Social media[17]—provides connectivity, virtual participation, and an echo chamber for like-minded extremist views

All the aforementioned data points, factors and research variables presented to this point provide a foundation for a myriad of reasons why a person may become radicalized, or seek an extremist agenda. While some may become radicalized on their own accord, it is more likely that some active external influence will persuade or pursue an individual to join forces with a particular extremist ideology, agenda, or group. Recruitment is a term used by virtually every civic organization or company throughout the world. However, it is the use of recruitment that will be explained as it relates to those who seek to further radical extremist agendas.

## RECRUITMENT APPROACHES

Initiating a group or specific ideology may not be as challenging as some may think. Individuals routinely gather, initiate, or join organizations daily. They come together for common causes, experiences, or to further actions based on an ideology. The big difference is these individuals do it for social and civic reasons, and it is done within the bounds of existing laws. However, many of the recruitment approaches used by these organizations and even companies have been bastardized by extremist and radical groups to ensure their ranks are sustained and grow. There is no single, uniform recruitment process for a group or ideology. Evidence suggests most recruiting is accomplished by personal friends or those who can establish a bond with the extremist ideology or belief. Recruiters will often emphasize the brotherhood, the bonds, and the sense of belonging when seeking to recruit individuals.

In 2006, policy analysts from the RAND Corporation authored a detailed report on terrorist selection and recruitment that highlighted recruitment approaches. The authors, Gerwehr and Daly, stated that,

> Any attempt at recruitment makes use of persuasive instruments, direct (e.g., a face-to-face (FTF) invitation to participate in paramilitary training) or indirect (e.g., political pronouncements and exhortations posted on a website). These instruments include every form of mass media in use today (e.g., newspapers, radio, television, and the Web) as well as interpersonal social influence (e.g., sermons, rumors, education, and training). Often a group with some reach and resources will use several instruments in concert for

added effect, such as writing textbooks that support the ideology of the group and then creating a school in which those textbooks may be made required reading.[18]

The same authors continue by presenting a perspective on communication that is used in the recruitment process. They demonstrate one perspective on types of communication used in recruitment but note that the recruiting pattern will continue to evolve. Four recruitment approaches cited in their paper were centered on al-Qaeda and global jihad, but are applicable across other ideologies and religions. They are presented by the authors in quadrants for consideration.

1. Public and proximate—recruiting in this quadrant is conducted face-to-face or in small groups, in a setting visible to the general public or authorities. Prisons, refugee camps, and large-scale wartime experiences are prime examples of this setting. Recruiters commingle with the population and target individuals or small groups that they deem ripe for recruitment.
2. Public and mediated—recruiting in this quadrant tends to be broader, more akin to propaganda than to a sales pitch. Mass media is used, including those within the reach of legislation and government as well as illicit media. The target for these media efforts is usually some stratum of the regional demographic or psychographic, such as young, single men gathering in a particular café, or devout members of a particular religious congregation.
3. Private and proximate—recruiting in this quadrant is used out of the public eye and in intimate settings, as a rule. Individuals recovering from addictions in private clinics, attending prayer sessions in a neighbor's living room, attending a paramilitary training program, or receiving vocational instruction from a tutor are all examples of venues where these types of recruiting are undertaken. This suits those groups who are operating out of sight or in opposition to local authorities.
4. Private and mediated—recruiting in this quadrant combines a mass-media approach with intimacy or clandesinity. Techniques include producing dissident literature on someone's basement printing press and circulating it covertly to a broad audience. This includes password-protected websites, restricted Internet chat groups, and the clandestine propagation of digital video.[18]

Much focus today centers on the need to further methods to access and penetrate a group or individual's electronic media. While this is very important, law enforcement must remain cognizant that the radicals and extremists are well aware of this and may still revert to the "old-school" way of conducting business—face-to-face or non-electronic means. Regardless of the technology used, terrorists, radicals, and extremists will continue to attract new recruits and will use marketing skills and techniques to achieve their goals.

## MODELS OF RECRUITMENT

Law enforcement investigators and analysts have many "check lists" that they use in their efforts to expedite the investigative process and ensure they look at all variables. The problem lies with the fact that these lists are derived from past practices and experiences. They are also not very fluid or adaptable. Gerwehr and Daly noted that the specific characterization of any recruitment process may be called its shape—a combination of overall pattern and specific descriptors. In their writing, they report that recruiting reveals a few common structures and they present four models of recruitment: the net, the funnel, the infection, and the seed crystal. The authors effectively demonstrate the models with figures and present the following explanations.

1. The net—In the "net" pattern a target population may be engaged equitably (e.g., every member of a congregation may be sent a videotape or every student invited to a weekend retreat). Some members will respond positively, others negatively; but in general, the whole population is viewed as primed for recruitment.

2. The funnel—A recruiter may use an incremental or phased approach when he or she believes a target population is ripe for recruitment yet requires a significant transformation in identity and motivation. As the term funnel implies, potential recruits start at one end of the process and are transformed, after some culling along the way, into dedicated group members when they emerge at the other end.

3. The infection—Frequently a target population is so insular or so difficult to reach that the most effective method is to recruit from within. A trusted agent can be inserted into the target population to rally potential recruits through direct, personal appeals. This method leverages the significant persuasive strength of (1) source credibility, (2) social comparison and validation, and (3) specifically tailored appeals. At least in its early stages, this method of recruiting suits groups which are actively opposed by governments, lending itself to clandestinity and operational security.

4. The seed crystal—Often a target audience is so remote or so inaccessible that a trusted agent cannot be put into it, nor can a media net be cast over it. In this case recruiters may seek to provide a context for self-recruitment.[18]

Surprisingly there is little specific research on the characteristics of those who are targeted to be the foot soldiers of a radical or extremist agenda. To understand the recruit requires one to understand the group who is doing the recruiting and their cause. This will often reveal insight into which individuals they may target for recruiting. Beyond the foot soldier who will be more of a follower than a doer, it is important to know that many groups target specific individuals for their knowledge, experiences, and skill sets to further their agenda.

## CATEGORIES OF RECRUITS

In 2006, the Canadian Centre for Intelligence and Security Studies, The Norman Paterson School of International Affairs, Carleton University, published a series of trends in terrorism reports. They presented a section that described some of the common groups or categories from which mujahideen emerge. Outlined below is a synopsis of the eight categories of recruits that this research presented.

1. Young volunteers—The youth of every generation are idealistic and believe they have the power to change the world. It is this intellectual and psychological development that recruiters seize and manipulate so insidiously.

2. Religious nationalists—Many intelligence agencies once felt confident that by tracking local and regional nationalist struggles, they could identify radical Islamist networks and activities.

3. Homegrown terrorists—In the charged atmosphere of distrust and suspicion following 9/11, Muslim diaspora communities have become fertile recruiting grounds for radical Islamism. Keppel maintains that the battle for Muslim minds is likely to be waged not in the Middle East, but in European diaspora communities where Muslims tend to be less prosperous and more confined to ghetto areas than in North America. Roy describes Islamist fundamentalism as a product of the diaspora and a consequence of reaction to sociological changes rather than cultural or historical factors. While genuine grievances and resentments exist as immigrants struggle to obtain citizenship and are faced with racism and unemployment, such preconditions for radicalism are not new; what is new is that they are now being used by extremists to recruit recent immigrants for confrontation with the West.

4. Friendship and kinship networks—Sageman's research on known Islamist extremists indicates that peer group friendship and kinship connections have been influential factors in the radicalization process, whether as a means of introducing radical ideas, maintaining commitment to them through comradeship in jihad, or providing trusted contacts for operational purposes. A degree of "radical oneupmanship" between friends can lead incrementally to extremist actions.

5. Reverts—This concerns those individuals, likely second-generation immigrants, who are born and raised in a Western country and apparently assimilated into society but they revert back to following a radical ideology.
6. Converts—French authorities have reported an increase in the number of converts to Islam whom they say are not only being recruited as foot soldiers for al-Qaeda but are taking on leadership roles in planning and directing attacks. al-Qaeda now considers converts as full members.
7. Women—While for years women have committed suicide attacks in places such as Chechnya and the Palestinian territories, European networks aligned to al-Qaeda have been shaped by fundamentalism and strict separation of the sexes. Nonetheless, a youthful Dutch militant extremist network has included aggressive European female extremists who were suspected of plotting suicide attacks, either alone or with their husbands. The Dutch group had links to a Belgian network which was responsible for sending Muriel Degauque, a native European female convert to Islam, to carry out a suicide bombing in Iraq—the first to do so for a network affiliated to al-Qaeda.
8. Prisoners—Muslims represent a disproportionate share of the populations of prisons in many Western countries, and Islamist activists often have criminal records. In France it has been suggested that Muslim youth represent over 20% of the prison population. Radical Muslim clerics have been very active in visiting prisons to mobilize alienated and angry youths for the jihadist cause and to proselytize Islam among prisoners of other ethnic and faith communities. In addition, where prisons contain a number of extremists, they can become "schools" where al-Qaeda militants pass on or impose their violent ideology on others.[10]

Radicalization is a strategic choice. Individuals may turn to radicalism for different reasons and some may be more conscious than others, and their motivations are abundant and unique.

## INDICATORS AND ELEMENTS

When it comes to Islam, conversion to Islam is not radicalization. The same can be said about nearly every other radicalized religion or ideology. Converts who proceed through the radicalization process often are driven by a respected, frequently older, extremist with whom they have come into contact. The key to countering violent extremism lies in identifying patterns, trends, indicators, and elements of the behaviors in the early stages. In October 2010, the Mississippi State University Office of Research Security posted a report that listed potential counterintelligence (CI) risk indicators that attempt to assess the risk that an individual may become, or may already be, involved in espionage or terrorism. This list and categorization of counterintelligence risk indicators is prepared for two purposes: (1) to assist the training of personnel security investigators and adjudicators in the recognition of risk indicators and the assessment of counterintelligence risk and (2) to assist in developing guidance for what actions should be taken when potential counterintelligence risk indicators are recognized or discovered at various stages of the personnel security process.

The personnel security investigation and subsequent adjudication provide an opportunity to identify and evaluate these indicators. As described here, there are three broad categories of potential CI risk indicators with multiple subcategories.

- Potential indicators that the subject may be or become a target for recruitment
  - Circumstances beyond the subject's control
  - Behaviors that may attract foreign intelligence attention
  - Indicators of already being a target
- Potential indicators of susceptibility to espionage or terrorist activity
  - Indicators of conflicting interests
  - Indicators of vulnerability to pressure or duress

- Indicators of competing identities
- Indicators of personal weaknesses
- Potential indicators of espionage, terrorism, or subversive activity
  - Indicators of recruitment
  - Indicators of information collection
  - Indicators of information transmittal
  - Indicators of illegal income
  - Indicators of terrorist activity
  - Indicators of support for terrorism
  - Other behavioral indicators

These are called "potential" indicators because no single indicator constitutes evidence of terrorism, espionage, or any other unauthorized use of classified or other protected information. The significance of any single indicator is greatly influenced by the presence of certain other indicators, and various combinations of indicators may form a pattern that is a valid basis for doubt or suspicion. Two types of interaction between risk indicators are especially important.

- An indicator that an individual may be a target for recruitment is far more significant if there is also some indication of susceptibility to recruitment, and either one or both of these enhance the significance of any indicator that this same individual may already be engaged in espionage or terrorism.
- If an individual has family, friends, or professional associates in a foreign country, the significance of these foreign contacts is increased if there is also some indication of susceptibility to recruitment, and especially if there is any indicator that this individual may already be engaged in some improper activity.[19]

A review of recent cases involving individuals who were recruited and radicalized reveals that jihadist tactics are evolving. We know that some of the individuals involved in terrorist actions in various locations such as Paris and Brussels were supplied benefits from welfare. Milking the system and gaining financial support from government programs appears to be a strategy employed by some radical extremists. While we strive to develop a comprehensive list of indicators, it is important to note that denial, deception, and diversion techniques employed by radical extremists make this effort challenging. It is the observable activities that provide the best insight to the indicators that law enforcement seeks to identify. Potential indicators of violent extremist radicalization may include communicating with known extremists using email or social media, providing material support, glorifying extremist acts, and encouraging others to engage in violence.

The greatest challenge, for a myriad of reasons such as resources and financial limitations, facing law enforcement is the role of social media and new technology in the recruitment and radicalization process.

## RECRUITING IN THE DIGITAL AGE

Attempting to understand and address American jihadist terrorism, the Congressional Research Service prepared a report, authored by Jerome P. Bjelopera, for members and committees of the U.S. Congress in 2013. Bjelopera discussed many aspects of homegrown violent jihadist plots and also discussed the radicalization process and the forces driving violent extremist activity. He noted that radicalization and recruitment, particularly of Islamist terrorists in the Western world, in the current era has experienced resurgence in part due to the Internet. Just like companies and others who rely on the Internet to spread their word and market to a wide audience, Islamist terrorists and extremists have embraced digital media to gain influence.

Regardless of whether jihadist online activity drives individuals to violence, the Internet arguably serves to spur radicalization in three ways. First, it allows jihadists to augment their messages with suggestive audio and video. Second, it makes it easier for would-be jihadists to find and interact with like-minded people around the world. Finally, the Internet normal[izes] behaviors considered unacceptable or inappropriate in real-world environments. Terrorists publish rhetoric online that displaces culpability for their violent actions, which they commonly describe as inevitable responses when faced with overpowering enemies such as the West.

Radicalizing material is readily accessible online, as are virtual communities in which one can discuss violent jihad. Since 2005, video-sharing websites have broadened the availability of jihadi video material. All sorts of other texts and graphic images supporting violent jihad exist on the Web, as does a great volume of tradecraft, such as bomb-making guides. Social networking, now inherently part of the Internet, is likely a tool that is used in the development of contacts among radicalized individuals and recruitment into violent jihadist groups. Before he died, Anwar al-Awlaki circulated jihadist lectures online and managed his own popular Facebook page and blog. The five Virginia men convicted on June 24, 2010, in Pakistan on terrorism charges allegedly contacted an al-Qaeda operative via social networking websites, according to press coverage of their trial in the city of Sarghoda.[20]

In September 2011, Ryan Hunter and Daniel Heinke authored an article for the FBI *Law Enforcement Bulletin*. The authors provided a perspective of radicalization and delineated the role the Internet plays in the process. This was viewed in their suggested prevailing radicalization model which they report is composed of three main components: grievance, ideology/narrative, and mobilization. They presented the role of the Internet by stating online that radicalization presents a primary concern. Extremists use a variety of tools that range from dedicated password-protected jihadist websites, forums, blogs, social networking resources, and video-hosting services to professionally produced online English-language propaganda magazines, such as Inspire magazine, established by al-Qaeda in the Arabian Peninsula (AQAP). These online assets, serving as a sort of "virtual jihad university," can play a role in all three radicalization components.

- Grievance: The Internet allows rapid and widespread dissemination of information about events that may fuel grievances. Often, such propaganda is intensified by highly emotional images combined with an amplifying comment or soundtrack. Because anyone can post content online, individuals have a forum to present the material in a way that supports their point of view no matter how extreme.
- Ideology/narrative: Similarly, the Internet allows the extremist narrative to spread globally. Anwar al-Awlaki, a Yemen-based American citizen and member of AQAP, is perhaps the best example for English-speaking audiences. His lectures and contributions to Inspire magazine are widely available online. It no longer is necessary to have an ideologue at a local mosque or gathering place to inspire future extremists.
- Mobilization: How online interaction impacts mobilization poses pressing questions inside the United States and Europe. Because extremists interact online with other like-minded individuals despite geographical differences, can they develop the group dynamics that lead to violence? How effective are social networking sites as a venue for terrorists to spot and assess would-be extremists? In a recent case in Germany, a 21-year-old extremist accused of fatally shooting two U.S. soldiers and wounding two others at Frankfurt airport on March 2, 2011, claimed to be radicalized through the Internet and motivated to take action after seeing propaganda videos.[21]

The goal of many radical and extremist groups is to build an army of believers. To achieve this goal they must communicate their message and reach as many individuals as they can while operating in a covert manner. These groups cannot easily hold face-to-face interviews and use physical facilities to hold "rallies" or mass gatherings. Therefore, radical and extremist organizations have turned to use of the Internet to communicate their message which is largely targeted toward a youthful audience. It is this youthful audience and their reliance and use of social media and other Internet resources to communicate that groups rely upon. Groups use the Internet as the primary vehicle and tool for disseminating the organization's propaganda and operational guidance. Brian Michael Jenkins noted in a paper prepared for RAND in 2011 that the Internet serves as a source of inspiration, but it may also become a substitute for action, allowing would-be terrorists to safely engage in vicarious terrorism while avoiding the risks of real action.[22]

In 2010, several researchers from the University of Grenoble collaborated to author a report dealing with the social influence in the online recruitment of terrorists. These researchers cited that for terrorist organizations, perhaps the most attractive feature the Internet has to offer is that of relative anonymity. The Internet offers its users relatively anonymous social interactions—if they so choose—in instant messaging, email, chat rooms, message boards, games, and personal websites. Specifically, the ability to be relatively anonymous in an online social interaction reduces accountability and leads to the depersonalization and deindividuation of users. Depersonalization is a state in which a normal sense of personal identity and reality is lost. Deindividuation is a state in which the impacts of an individual's internal standards for behavior are decreased, while the saliences of situational cues are heightened. Both depersonalization and deindividuation lead to elevated group salience and polarization between groups by taking the focus off the self and thus increasing adherence to group, rather than individual, norms which then become predictive of behavior. Thus, individuals may be more likely to engage in questionable behaviors and may interact differently than they otherwise would because of the anonymous nature of the online communication medium. Furthermore, when deindividuated, individuals will experience a decreased sense of personal responsibility for their actions. Research on deindividuation indicates that when an individual is deindividuated the following emerges: uninhibited behaviors, reduced self-evaluation (i.e., a reduction in focus and scrutiny of one's own behaviors and mental states), as well as reduced evaluation of others. A reduction in accountability and increase in depersonalization make it increasingly likely that individuals will engage in antinormative behaviors (i.e., outside both external societal norms and the internal norms of the individual). Thus, terrorist recruitment efforts that begin using computer-mediated communications (CMC) are likely to have greater success than other methods, such as those that begin face-to-face, because the recruit's perception of increased anonymity and likely state of deindividuation removes attentional resources away from internal standards of behavior, allowing for greater propensity to engage in negative behavior.[23]

The aforementioned paper, which can be found on the CAIRN Info International Edition website, delineates a proposed model of online terrorist recruitment progression that explains behaviors in contrast with the social identity process, self-perception process and computer-mediated communication (CMC) factors. In summary, the authors present five behaviors proposed in the model which are presented below.

1. Initial request—an invitation for the recruit to visit a particular website. Social identity as a member of terrorist group is not salient to the recruit. Recruit perceives themselves as an ordinary individual in the self-perception process phase. The initial request can be made face-to-face via CMC, or through a religious magazine, journal, or flyers.
2. Initial commitment—the recruit visits a website, just to look around. Social identity as a member of the terrorist group is made salient as the recruit explores the website. Recruit perceives themselves as someone willing to learn about the terrorist group from the source. Commitment is anonymous, at a safe distance, with time/pace controlled, and no complications from nonverbal cues.
3. Escalating commitment—the recruit expresses a desire for more information /access. Social identity as a member of a terrorist group becomes more salient as the recruit begins to support the group and see themselves as a member. The recruit perceives themselves as a new member of an important online community that supports the terrorist group's agenda.

Commitment is primarily anonymous, based on login usernames and aliases, and is still at a safe distance and controlled.

4. Escalating commitment—the recruit proves his loyalty by posting in online forums, disseminating radical propaganda, videos, etc. Social identity as a member of the terrorist group becomes more salient and important to the recruit as they become a sympathizer. The recruit perceives himself as a full-fledged terrorist sympathizer who supports the group's larger mission. Desire for anonymity within in-group dissipates; anonymity remains as protection from the out-group.

5. Final commitment—the recruit meets face-to-face with other terrorists, engages in group prayers, foreign travel, and training exercises. Social identity as a member of the terrorist group is most salient and important, as the recruit becomes an established member. The recruit perceives himself as a full-fledged terrorist group member willing to carry out violence on command to meet the group's goals. Anonymity remains as temporary protection from the out-group. The recruit gives up control of own behavior to authoritative terrorist leaders.

Al-Qaeda is seen by some researchers to be one of the first groups to embrace modern technology. They used the Internet as a tool to build the support base and recruit new terrorists and terrorist sympathizers. Al-Qaeda's use of the Internet allows them to provide audio and video streams, forums, and chat sessions, which were often translated into English, French, and other languages to enlist supporters in Western nations. Through their efforts, they were able to increase the number of jihadist websites and further their recruitment efforts to develop active sympathizers. It is the last aspect that some researchers believe is a required precursor to becoming an active terrorist.

The Australian government notes that the freedom to voice political, religious, or ideological beliefs is an important and healthy part of any democracy. While the majority of people use the Internet as a tool for good it does present an opportunity that it may affect a small number of people in a community to become vulnerable to radicalization efforts. It is important to state that there is no checklist to recognize people who may be radicalized by material viewed online. However, they have presented bulleted material that is listed below as a summary of signs. They note that behavioral signs may be useful to help family members, friends, and members of the public to seek assistance if they are concerned that somebody they know may be radicalizing.

These signs may include:

- Becoming increasingly secretive about online viewing habits
- Using online social networking platforms such as Facebook or Twitter to promote violence or other criminal behavior to advance a cause
- Downloading large amounts of violent extremist content such as:
  - Online instruction and training manuals about making explosives or other methods to undertake violence
  - Violent extremist literature, images and/or video clips that advocate the use of violence or other illegal behavior to promote a cause

Extremist material can include:

- Articles, images, speeches, or videos that encourage hate or violence
- Statements or posts made on social media, chat rooms, or blogs that encourage hate or violence
- Content encouraging people to commit acts of terrorism
- Websites created or hosted by terrorist organizations
- Terrorist training materials
- Suspicious content regarding use or sale of chemicals online
- Videos or images of terrorist attacks.[24]

## SOCIAL MEDIA

In October 2016, in a joint effort of the Center for Complex Operations (CCO) and the Peacekeeping and Stability Operations Institute (PKSOI), several authors collaborated on a 400-page publication titled *Impunity: Countering Illicit Power in War and Transition*. One author, Maeghin Alarid, wrote a contributing article titled *Recruitment and Radicalization: The Role of Social Media and New Technology*. Alarid states that terrorist groups have good reason to use social media, whose popularity suits them in many ways. It is the fact that most social media platforms are easy to use and cost little or nothing. This allows them to tailor their message and reach the homes of millions of people. In the report, Alarid notes that the common denominator seems to be that everyone who is radicalized and recruited online feels sympathetic toward that group's cause, and people who feel there is "something missing" from their lives appear to be more susceptible than others. A candidate for recruitment may come to the group's attention by making a financial donation, downloading extremist propaganda, entering a jihadi chat room, or visiting radical pages on Facebook. In today's environment, we see numerous examples of the radicalization process, from interest to recruitment, through execution of an actual mission, happening entirely online. Radicalizing and recruiting online has great advantages over the traditional (and riskier) public communications. Terrorist groups can reach out to an incalculably vast audience. With no travel required, cost is minimal—no logistics or transportation support is needed, and the odds of detection are low. And the newly radicalized need not necessarily pack up and head for the Middle East—jihadi groups encourage attacks at home to avoid the risk of infiltration while traveling. The threshold for engaging in cyber jihad is markedly lower than for someone who gives up a familiar, comfortable life to travel to an actual battle zone and risk death or capture. If the notion of online activism as a proper, respectable, and sufficient form of jihad wins wide acceptance within radical circles, we can expect ever-increasing efforts in online propaganda and cyber attacks. This could further inspire yet more individuals, facilitating both radicalization and recruitment, and lead to a new cycle of attacks.[25]

Social media, like most digital material, lives on forever online and reaches a huge audience. Terrorist and extremist organizations understand this and have sought to exploit recruitment and radicalization opportunities especially in the past decade. Beyond recruitment efforts, terrorists, according to Alarid, use many innovative methods to communicate online. The Impunity article states:

- Terrorists can draft an email message and save it as a draft rather than sending it, so that anyone with access to that email account can log in and read the message. Known as "dead drops," these communications are less subject to interception (than an email that has been sent).
- Terrorists can post training manuals online or even hack into a legitimate website and hide training materials "deep in seemingly innocuous subdirectories of the legitimate site," a process known as "parasiting."
- Terrorists can conduct research on potential targets online, where both text and imagery, including satellite photography, is frequently available. Google Earth, for instance, has been used to target British soldiers in Iraq with increasing accuracy.
- Terrorists can appeal anonymously for donations of financial or other support via websites.[25]

## ONLINE PUBLICATIONS, VIDEO GAMES, LIVE STREAMING, AND DIRECT MARKETING TACTICS

As technology advances so do the efforts of terrorist and extremist groups in their use of these tools. Online publications have become a signature communications platform for both al-Qaeda and the Islamic State (ISIS/ISIL). The magazines Dabiq and Inspire are easily found in open source forums on the Internet and are published in English to reach a vast Western audience. In November 2016, Inspire magazine was released via Twitter in English and Arabic. This was a 48-page issue that included an installment of the Inspire Guide—a publication that provides lessons learned from terrorist attacks in the West. Issues often seek to capitalize on recent tensions and events in an effort to demonstrate and promote their cause as well as trigger an event-based response. Many of these publications will provide tactical guidance for the readers to follow. It should be noted that many organizations utilize publications beyond Islamic extremist groups. Other publications such as *Bite Back*, *Earth First! Journal*, and *The Good Citizen* are used by "domestic" extremist groups in the United States on behalf of their respective causes.

As it was alluded to earlier, Twitter is another social network used by groups to their advantage. It allows these groups to further their radical message and agenda in real time but not necessarily for recruitment. Alarid's report showed the potential power of one of the largest social media network sites, Facebook. In the report it was noted that by January 2014, the average age of Facebook users was 30 years, with almost half of all users logging in daily. As of April 2015, the online social network had roughly 1.3 billion active accounts every month, and 54.2 million individual and group pages. Terrorist groups understand that if they want to reach out to the younger generation, this is an excellent vehicle. A 2010 report by the Department of Homeland Security listed several ways that terrorist groups use Facebook, and we have seen both al-Qaeda and ISIL use them all:

- As a way to share operational and tactical information, such as bomb recipes, AK-47 maintenance and use, tactical shooting, etc.
- As a gateway to extremist sites and other online radical content by linking on Facebook group pages and in discussion forums
- As a media outlet for terrorist propaganda and extremist ideological messaging
- As a wealth of information for remote reconnaissance for targeting purposes[25]

Two other digital and social media tools being used by terrorist organizations are YouTube and video games. YouTube is a popular platform to produce high tech videos that are dubbed with modern and hip music. These videos are geared toward attracting viewers and are carefully crafted to avoid YouTube's filtering efforts that are designed to identify and remove terrorist content. To further efforts to appeal to younger generations, terrorist groups have used computer savvy members to produce video games for their websites. Video games such as Quest for Bush, Jihad Growing Up and Americans' Hell are examples of extremist games produced by terrorists groups to further their message and train members. ISIS/ISIL has adapted a very popular video game, Grand Theft Auto, so that players can role-play as a member of their group while engaged in combat. There have even been instances where extremists have used maps from video games, even if they are dated, to aid in their planning and logistical attempts. Video games are also used as a forum to communicate verbally by using voice over Internet protocol technology through the device's Internet connection.

Beyond communication, terrorists and extremists use marketing skills to attract new recruits online. ISIS/ISIL uses digital media to direct target select audiences to further the spread of their propaganda or message. They use denial, deception, and diversion techniques to mask their efforts. Pro-ISIS/ISIL accounts overtly consuming and propagating a pro-ISIS/ISIL messaging often attempt to mask their support by using deceptive disclaimers in their account descriptions such as "For research/analysis." Many social media companies will often suspend accounts associated with subversive sites, but they frequently reappear on various Internet platforms, sometimes with varying account names. One such site is centered on a pro-ISIS/ISIL video series known as *The Light Series*. Masked as education, research, and analysis, this series has been associated with many platforms such as Twitter and YouTube under various monikers. Besides marketing the material as education and research, these groups will "welcome" others such as cat lovers and use symbols such as a green bird. One may ask, why? One of the most searched video topics happens to be cats and they hope that an individual will land on their page and follow their links. The green bird symbol is representative of the Islamic symbol for martyred souls and is seen as the "highest level of paradise."

Recruiters are very skilled at targeting and infiltrating certain types of Facebook pages—including anti government, religious, and education forums—as well as exploiting socially isolated and marginalized individuals. In May 2015, an Australian researcher, Robyn Torok, authored a paper on how terrorists use marketing skills to attract new recruits. She noted that propaganda material is presented on a variety of social media platforms, including Twitter and Facebook which are often linked into YouTube videos.

In addition, recruitment also involves joining networks of radicalized individuals online by becoming "friends" with them or following trending issues. Once an individual becomes part of these networks they are then exposed to certain marketing techniques such as "future pacing."

This is a technique whereby a seller speaks to a potential buyer using language that suggests that they have already accepted a product. Sellers use language such as "when you use this…" or "you will notice the difference …" that imply the idea that the product is already purchased in order to create this acceptance in a buyers mind. The aim here is to create a connection between the buyer and the product. While this is not a guarantee of success, it does increase the probability of a sale.

Torok's research found that in online interactions, this pattern of language that uses future pacing is also present when extremists are seeking to recruit an individual. This is done in a number of ways including challenging those with existing religious beliefs, such as Catholicism, about the oneness of God and the abhorrence of idols.

From innocent foundations, radicals use future pacing to plant the seed for actively making a difference about injustices to fellow Muslims. The goal is to create a belief in an individual that they need to be active in their faith which can then be subsequently directed toward violent acts. Key statements are planted both early and often, and significantly before a person is recruited to radical discourse.

Locating profiles, pages, links on Facebook and YouTube are done easily by using key terms that ISIS or radicals use, or by following profile trending of accounts that adopt a future pacing mentality. Since information is very accessible, it makes it part of the problem in preventing new people being recruited and radicalized.

Future pacing is just one technique that is part of a package of strategies with one clear objective: to create change. Terrorist groups such as ISIS use future pacing to try to create a new reality or acceptance of their "product," which is a set of ideas or ideologies. The most significant way that ISIS has been able to do this is to create the extremist goal of an Islamic Caliphate. In other words, "living the dream" of many extremist Muslims in creating and maintaining a "pure" Islamic state under Sharia law.[26]

In an effort to fool or trick artificial intelligence programs and algorithms from identifying their subversive sites, many groups have started to use code words. By some, use of the code words has become part of what is known as "Operation Google," an online campaign meant to circumvent censorship algorithms. Many code words have gained popularity and are currently being used by white supremacy extremists on social media, particularly Twitter. These same groups may even employ symbols such as the use of triple parentheses which is known as "echoes" and is used to represent Jewish persons. An example of this would be (((Rosenberg))). Outlined below are some code words that are being used to circumvent censorship:

n-word = google
Jew = skype
Mexican = yahoo
Asian = bing
Muslim/Arab = pop rocks
Conservatives = reagans
Gay (men) = skittles
Lesbian = fishbucket

Use of code words is not new and has been employed in many organizations, and is widely used in prisons. However, it is important for investigators to be aware of trending terms and to be cognizant of the context that these terms are being used. It has been said that if you, as an adult, do not know these terms, you should ask a teenager.

ISIS/ISIL online jihadist targeting strategies do not show a specific socioeconomic, religious, or educational common background found in foreign recruits. They will often target the weak, the lonely, and those who feel they have no other purpose, and provide them with a new life that makes substantial promises. Targeting and marketing will be routinely centered on a key target demographic—the youth. They are impressionable and easily targeted with digital means.

## YOUTH TARGETING

Targeting the youth of a community is seen as an attractive recruiting ground for them to spread their message and ideology. Children are impressionable and can easily be manipulated by authority figures. Palestinian youth, for example, have grown up with the images of martyrdom and have been subject to the mantra of terrorists and extremists most of their lives. Madrassas (institutions of learning) are also seen by some as prime breeding grounds particularly the lower levels of education because the youth are impressionable. Use of children by terrorists organizations is not new. Documents have been discovered that reveal organizations should actively lure and prepare the youth to further their radical agenda. Al-Qaeda recruited from madrassas in the 1980s, the Real IRA recruited teenagers in the 1990s and other groups such as Boko Haram and ISIS/ISIL have used children insurgents to carry out missions. Other groups that have used school-aged youth in some capacity are Hamas, Hezbollah, Al-Shabaab, and Jemaah Islamiyah. This is done because a child is less likely to arouse mistrust and suspicion.

The Real IRA referred to the youth with no prior police records as "clean skins." They believed that use of these youths allowed them operational freedom and reduced the likelihood of arrest. Similar to criminal enterprises, youths may be given more dangerous tasks on the assumption that if they are caught they would receive a lighter sentence. Also, most National governments do not retain records or investigate cases involving individuals viewed as a juvenile—under the age of 18. These cases are thus left for the "local" investigative agencies to pursue but quite often due to time, resources, and lack of potential incarceration they are not a high priority.

Recruitment of youth can be found to take place across a wide range of venues, for example, schools and after-school activities, religious institutions or events, youth groups, summer camps, and the Internet. In an April 2009 Homeland Security Institute report, four broad categories were identified to describe the way in which young persons were recruited or became members of the groups studied. These approaches—"born into a radical environment," forced into it, recruited or persuaded, and self-radicalization—are not inclusive of all the ways in which young persons are recruited, and are likely to occur in various combinations.[27]

## PRISON AND JAIL RADICALIZATION

Documented European and American experience shows that prisons are venues where extremists have radicalized and recruited among the inmate population. In 2006, the FBI Deputy Assistant Director advised a House Homeland Security Committee that prison radicalization primarily occurs through anti-U.S. sermons provided by contract, volunteer, or staff imams, radicalized inmates who gain religious influence, and extremist media. The ideologies that radicalized inmates most often appear to embrace include the Salafi form of Sunni Islam (including revisionist versions commonly known as "prison Islam") and an extremist view of Shia Islam similar to that of the government of Iran and Lebanese Hezbollah.

Most cases of prison radicalization appear to be carried out by domestic Islamic extremist groups with few or no direct foreign connections, like the Sunni Islamic extremist group in California, the Jam'iyyat Ul-Islam Is-Saheeh, identified in July 2005. However, not all prison radicalization is Islamic in nature. Domestic groups such as white supremacists also recruit in prisons.

As was noted in the Anti-Defamation League (ADL) publication, *White Supremacist Prison Gangs in the United States*, there is no agreement among prison officials as to what constitutes a prison gang. Some locales use terms such as groups and cliques when describing them. Some of the first prison gangs came into existence in the 1950s in the U.S. but it was in the formation of the Aryan Brotherhood in the 1960s that prison officials noticed the infusion of ideology. As social media sites have grown, so have the connections among extremists. Use of social media on the outside of prison walls fosters a base for an individual to carry forward and develop relationships once they are incarcerated. Ideology, close quarter living, and religions such as Odinism serve as vehicles for inmates to join together and further extremist thoughts. It should be noted that some individual actions that may seem extremist are actually ways for that person to survive and engage in a form of organized crime within the facility. Many incarcerated individuals were street gang members prior to being incarcerated and continue to engage in gang activities while locked behind bars. A street gang member's incarceration often prompts opportunities for them to be used for continuing the gang's recruitment efforts or to be radicalized to an extremist ideology. Gang members' vulnerability to radicalization and recruitment for involvement in international and domestic terrorism is a growing concern to law enforcement. In the 2015 National Gang Report it was reported that over one quarter of jurisdictions and nearly half of prison facilities reported that gang members joined domestic extremist groups. Much of the prison gang and extremist group problems are classified as security threats groups (STGs). There are variations of what may construe a STG but it is most often associated with any group of three or more with recurring or threatening behavior. Some jurisdictions may refer to STGs as a disruptive group. STGs can be any organization—club, association, or group of formal or informal individuals. They often have a common name, identifying symbols, or they share an ideology all of which are viewed to be related to potential disruptive activities within the prison.

Tony Parker noted in his 2013 thesis for the Naval Post Graduate School that security threat groups continue to be a significant security concern inside correctional facilities and they provide a model for radicalization. He used Figure 5.2 as a means to show the model of how the influence in promoting inmate radicalization is demonstrated. He continued to write that Hamm reflected in a 2008 article, the radicalization process within the correctional setting often follows the gang model. Inmates join gangs for many reasons including protection, to promote and participate in illicit activity, or to

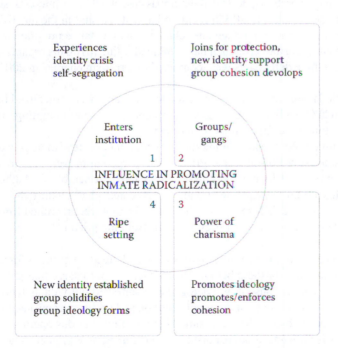

**FIGURE 5.2**    Model of influence in promoting inmate radicalization.

promote a particular ideology or agenda. Inmates entering the correctional setting often find themselves without a support structure. In 2011, the National Gang Intelligence Center reported that, compared to other inmates, prison gang members were much more susceptible to radicalization. Gangs or security threat groups, led by a charismatic leader, provide inmates the support structure and protection they desire as long as the inmate supports the agenda of the in-group. Hamm's research of the Florida and California prison system, and a study of the Kevin James case, identified inmate leadership as the most important factor in prisoner radicalization. Security threat groups have crossed racial lines as well as joined forces with traditional enemies to unite under a common goal of destroying a mutual opponent.[28]

According to a 2006 report by the George Washington University Homeland Security Policy Institute, there have been a number of publicized connections between former prisoners and terrorism:

- Jeff Fort, a gang leader in Chicago, Illinois, converted to Islam while incarcerated in 1965. Fort went on to found a group called El Rukn, which made a name for itself in 1985 when it brokered a deal with the Libyan government to carry out attacks on U.S. police stations, government facilities, military bases, and passenger airplanes in exchange for $2.5 million and asylum in Tripoli.
- James Ellison, the founder of the extremist Christian group Covenant, Sword and Arm of the Lord (CSA), met Robert G. Millar while incarcerated. Millar, a leader in the radical "Christian Identity" movement, became Ellison's spiritual advisor in prison. After Ellison was released, he recruited for CSA and established a compound with his followers. When the compound was eventually raided, authorities found homemade landmines and U.S. Army anti-tank rockets. In addition, they found a large supply of cyanide that the CSA was apparently planning to use to poison a city's water supply.
- Sheik Omar Abdel Rahman, the emir of Egypt's Gama'at al Islamia (the Islamic Group), is the radical cleric who plotted to bomb New York City landmarks in 1993. Upon being sentenced to a life term, he issued a decree from federal prison, declaring of Americans that "Muslims everywhere [should] dismember their nation, tear them apart, ruin their economy, provoke their corporations, destroy their embassies, attack their interests, sink their ships … shoot down their planes, [and] kill them on land, at sea, and in the air. Kill them wherever you find them." Osama bin Laden later claimed that this fatwa provided religious authority for the 9/11 attacks. Abdel Rahman has continued trying to run his organization while incarcerated—and three defendants were convicted of terrorism charges in 2005 for helping him do so.
- Richard Reid is believed to have converted to Islam and been radicalized by an imam while incarcerated in Great Britain. He was later apprehended while attempting to detonate a bomb on a U.S. commercial flight in December 2001.
- A recently foiled plot to attack numerous government and Jewish targets in California was devised inside New Folsom State Prison. The perpetrators were members of an inmate-founded group called Jami'iy yat Ul-Islam Is-Saheeh (Assembly of Authentic Islam). The leader of this group, Kevin Lamar James, advocated jihad against the U.S. government and supporters of Israel. Two men implicated in the plot were recruited from a local mosque by a disciple of James who had been released from the prison.[29]

Prisons are often thought to be a fertile environment and breeding grounds for radicalization. Many possible explanations exist for these beliefs. Researchers seem to agree that jail time may accelerate the radicalization process because it brings together disaffected individuals who can be receptive to antisocial messaging that presents an intolerant solution and fits an extremist agenda. Terrorist groups do not view prison as an obstacle because some of the operative modus operandi such as carrying out clandestine activity is the same as being outside prison. Terrorists approach incarceration as an opportunity to advance the interests of their groups through forming new connections or reinforcing existing ones. The universal operating code among prison inmates is familiar ground. They promote an opportunity to align with a group as a brotherhood. Investigators and analysts who monitor groups within correctional institutions should remain cognizant that merely categorizing individuals to a specific group may appear to be relevant but it can lead to overlooking data points. Correctional facilities also provide a venue for contacts and cooperation between disparate groups which could prove valuable later. There have been documented instances in Italy, London, and Pakistan where elements of disparate groups such as extreme right and left came closer together and even discussed creation of a shared ideological platform.

## SHARED CHARACTERISTICS AND BACKGROUNDS

In August 2015, Professor Robert Winters published an article related to violent extremism and its roots in the U.S. correctional system. He cited that "prison provides fertile ground for radicalization because of the unique set of circumstances it represents. First, inmates are often angry at the system that incarcerated them, and in many cases that anger may be generalized blame of "the government" or American society. Second, incarceration represents a personal crisis for most offenders (especially those incarcerated for the first time), and such crises often prompt a personal search for spiritual understanding—what was long colloquially called "finding God in prison." Third, offenders may well seek acceptance by a group which will provide some degree of protection in the prison environment. Fourth, in many cases charismatic leaders have extensive, repeated, and virtually undisturbed opportunities to teach their particular brand of ideology to converts. This fourth factor was the most significant at Camp Bucca, which one military veteran called a "virtual terrorist university." Naturally, conversion to a religious ideology in a correctional setting may not be entirely sincere, and even if it is sincere at the time, that dedication may not survive the offender's subsequent release from prison. Researchers for the Office of Justice Programs at the U.S. Department of Justice in 2007 who interviewed numerous prison chaplains as part of the study, found that those chaplains divided prison converts into five general categories. The "crisis convert" is responding to the trauma of incarceration. The "protection-seeking convert" is looking for security. The "searching convert" is an offender with little pre-incarceration experience with religion who, now exposed to many different faiths and with plenty of time to examine them, embarks on a "spiritual quest." Many such converts end up as "serial joiners," experimenting with a number of different religions. The "manipulating convert" is seeking the benefits of prison religious programming such as special diets, attendance at meetings and classes, the opportunity to wear religious garb or symbols, or simply the perceived advantage of being viewed as "moral, pro-social, and law-abiding" by correctional (and parole) officials. Finally, the "free-world recruited convert" is influenced not by fellow inmates but by a religious leader who visits the facility from outside, such as through a prison ministry program."[30]

A 2013 Journal of Human Security research article presented one theory that the authors state could help us understand prisoner vulnerability. The authors note that most studies are focused on demographic variables to look for vulnerabilities. They stated that psychographic variables that have been cited in empirical studies seem to matter most. In support of this, they presented the transformative learning theory (TLT) developed in the 1990s by Jack Mezirow. The article states that:

> This is a framework for understanding how change (learning) occurs in individuals—more specifically, how adults learn and adapt to new environments. In this instance we are using it to understand the behavioral changes prisoners undergo while in prison and how this learning transformation makes them more vulnerable to radical extremists. When an individual goes through some sort of crisis (known as the transformative trigger), the individual uses pre-existing habits to make sense of the event. However, when the individual cannot make sense of the situation and resorting back to their habitual ways fails to help them manage the event, this becomes known as a 'distortion'. As a result, the individual reacts to the meaning distortion by exploring new experiences and undergoing critical reflection (e.g., turning to religion for guidance). These new perspectives help the individual cope with the new environment by helping to create

new behaviors, roles, and relationships. Overall, this transformation allows individuals to manage their new environment, adapt to a new daily routine and ultimately help an individual learn how to get past a crisis. However, going through a crisis can make the individual easier to persuade and even more open to manipulation and brainwashing, thus making them very susceptible to extremist recruitment. TLT can help shed light on the process and precursors of prison radicalization. Individual radicalization is not only associated with particular socio-political contexts (e.g., prison) and personal characteristics, but is also a combination of reflection, knowledge acquisition, and identity reassessment. As individuals begin to develop self-doubt or experience confusion over identity or intense personal debate, eventually a point is reached whereby the individual comes to the realization that their old identity no longer exists and a new one must be established. Therefore, when radicalized individuals socialize and are validated by other "like-minded" individuals, their transformation is reinforced and the new identity is strengthened. Ultimately, those individuals who become violent, radicalized inmates not only justify their actions but such actions are also expected among the greater group of radicals.[31]

In 2010, Peter R. Neumann authored a policy report titled *Prisons and Terrorism Radicalisation and De-radicalisation in 15 Countries* for The International Centre for the Study of Radicalisation and Political Violence. The report offers a wide-ranging analysis of the role prisons play in radicalizing individuals. This chapter has largely been focused on the radicalization and recruitment process within correctional institutions. However, we must remember that there are already individuals in the facilities that foster terrorism and extremism to perform these tasks. Whether they are officially recognized as a gang member based on formulated criteria, or documented as a known terrorist, there is a likelihood that a "terrorist" may be in prison. Neumann stated that in the prison context, most difficulties in dealing with terrorists are caused precisely by the fact that these offenders do not see themselves as criminals. Rather than quietly serving their sentence, many regard their time in prison as an opportunity to continue the "struggle," and involve themselves in activities ranging from passive resistance to turning prison into a "battleground" from which to support the wider campaign. Typical behaviors include:

- Refusing to cooperate with the prison authorities. Politically motivated offenders believe they have been incarcerated for their beliefs rather than their actions, and that the process that led to their incarceration is illegitimate. As a result, they may choose not to cooperate with prison staff, or even attempt to establish parallel structures.
- Developing the movement's strategy and ideology. Unable to participate in operations and planning, imprisoned terrorists may want to use their time in prison to help develop their movements' strategy or ideology. From Gerry Adams' Brownie columns to Mohammed Al Maqdisi's theories of "jihadist" warfare, some of the most influential tracts and articles in the history of militant and/or terrorist movements were written while their authors were in prison.
- Mobilizing supporters. Prisons can provide an environment from which to continue the confrontation with the state, especially by highlighting and/or exaggerating the kinds of grievances and injustices that are also fueling the movements' campaigns on the outside. This can involve allegations of discrimination, mistreatment and torture, and result in negative media coverage, protests, and even dramatic confrontations such as hunger strikes.
- Participating in violent campaigns. Terrorists will consider it their duty to attempt to contribute to their movements' violent campaigns. The most obvious way is to try to escape from prison and rejoin their groups. Where this is impossible, they may seek to become involved in strategic and operational planning, or issue operational guidance, or authorization.

Implicit in this description is a further difference between politically motivated offenders and "ordinary" prisoners. Political offenders are more likely to have a constituency in the form of vocal supporters on the outside, who—like the offenders themselves—refuse to accept the legitimacy of their incarceration. They regard them not as perpetrators of crimes but as victims of injustices and discrimination.[32]

Characteristics, backgrounds, politics, nationalism, and ideology may vary as to why someone recruits or becomes radicalized. When we speak of triggering events, it can be easy to label someone using the aforementioned but it is when the variable of religion is introduced that things change. The topic of religion, more so than politics, is one that many will shy away from especially in a politically correct world. Religion may be a topic that some do not discuss but when it comes to correctional facilities, religion is something routinely discussed.

## RELIGION IN CORRECTIONAL INSTITUTIONS

In the past several years, governments, experts, researchers, and law enforcement personnel have shown interest in jihadist prison radicalization. Research on this topic is not clear and concise. Some scholars have conducted research in Europe, others in the Middle East and Asia, and they note that jail or prison time potentially accelerates the radicalization process for some individuals. As countries and laws vary, it is perhaps the makeup of prison populations that may pose the greatest difference. Countries such as Pakistan appear to be riper for developing a radical jihadist than that of the United States. By sheer volume the population demographic fails to have a diverse religion or ideology. Thus it may lead to a greater likelihood that jailhouse jihadism is more prevalent in such environments. When it comes to U.S. correctional facilities, experts have sounded warnings about the unknown level of threat posed by radicalization.

When it comes to religion in correctional facilities, there is consensus among many groups that spiritual rehabilitation plays an important role. Many of these groups represent different faiths and share a belief in the importance of spiritual rehabilitation. This philosophy was stated in 1870 by the American Prison Association (now called the American Correctional Association): "We have a profound conviction of the inefficiency of all measures of reformation except as such are based on religion."[33]

When it comes to religious groups, there is a 1982 report that states religious groups currently active inside prisons—particularly those representing the Muslim faith and Christian evangelicalism—are in fact changing some prisoners' lives by helping them to see themselves as contributing members of a community rather than as outcasts. Outside prison walls, religious groups are involved in efforts to liberate prisoners from what is portrayed as a basically unjust and inhumane criminal justice system that encourages rather than deters criminal behavior.

A third aspect of religion's relationship with the prison system is the trend, beginning in the early 1970s, toward more recognition of prisoners' rights. Alvin J. Bronstein, Executive Director of the National Prison Project of the American Civil Liberties Union, credits the September 1971 riot at the Attica Correctional Facility in New York with creating the prisoners' rights movement. As a result of this and other riots in the early 1970s, prison officials began to pay more attention to prisoners' rights, including the right to freely exercise religious beliefs as guaranteed by the Constitution's First Amendment.

Providing materials, services and special diets for sometimes as many as eight religious groups with vastly different requirements has not been easy for most prisons and their chaplains. According to Father Richard A. Houlahan, chaplain director for the Federal Bureau of Prisons, a much larger percentage of the prison population regularly participates in religious activities than does the population outside, probably because "the prisoners develop a relationship with the cha-plaincy people." Anthony Travisono, Director of the American Correctional Association, has a more cynical explanation. Being active in a religious group "makes a great deal of interesting reading for the parole board," he told Editorial Research Reports. "If I'm the top macho guy inside of a place and I take part in religious ceremonies, it looks good on my record."

The author of this 1982 report continues to note that sometimes inmates are attracted to the "perks" of a particular religion rather than the religion itself. Travisono said black inmates often will join a sect of the Muslims if they are worried about their physical well-being, since Muslims have a reputation for being tough and loyal and are well-respected by both inmates and officials. At the maximum-security federal prison at Leavenworth, Kansas, hundreds of prisoners reportedly flocked to see pretty girls sing at gospel concerts, but showed little interest in Bible study classes. "Overall the trend has not been a bad one," Travisono said. "If someone can get his head together by the use of religion, most correctional officials are very much for that. Religion also stems the violence in an institution; it has a calming influence. [But] to my knowledge, there is no statistic suggesting that anyone who starts all of this in prison follows it through on parole."

Over 80 % of the Muslim prison population (estimated to be around 12,000) converted after they were incarcerated. In an article published in 1978, freelance writer Keith Butler estimated that for every 1,000 black prisoners in an institution, at least 200 will call themselves Muslims—about 150 belonging to the sect founded by Elijah Muhammad and the other 50 belonging to sects like the Sunni or Hanafi Muslims. According to the Islamic chaplain for the D.C. Department of Corrections, Imam Mikal Huda Ba'ath, the factors responsible for the growth of Islam in prison include "conditions associated with inmate power, the circumstances surrounding the disproportionate percentage of black inmates in today's penal institutions, inmate group hostility toward ... society ... and the employees who are paid to keep them, the fear of death within the institution and ... the necessity ... to belong to something powerful, strong, and fraternal."

Muslim involvement in prisons began when Elijah Muhammad was sent to a federal prison in Michigan in 1942 for refusing induction into the military. He began preaching the message that blacks needed to build a separate nation, free of the "white devils" that enslaved them in America. As Muhammad's followers joined him in refusing the draft, prison became a part of life for committed Muslims who saw going to jail as simply moving from one community in the Nation of Islam to another. But the Muslims' fiery rhetoric did not sit well with prison officials, who routinely condemned them to solitary confinement, barred their ministers from visiting and refused to honor their requests for Muslim literature and pork-free diets. In 1959, after 38 Muslims in Washington, D.C.'s main prison in Lorton, Virginia, were locked in solitary confinement for 90 days, the Muslims sued. A federal court ruled in 1961 that they had a right to practice their religion.

Since then the Muslims have resorted more frequently to litigation than any other religious group. In 1967 they were awarded the right to have their own ministers visit them in prison and in 1978 they won the right to a pork-free, specially prepared diet. In the 1960s and 1970s, the Muslims seemed to become less militant. When Elijah Muhammad's son Wallace assumed leadership after his father's death in 1975, he dropped the black supremacist version of the Koran and announced that American Black Muslims would practice Islam as it was practiced around the world. For Muslims in prison, the emphasis is now on education and self-discipline, making the Muslims model prisoners in the eyes of many officials.[34]

## PRISLAM

Many have viewed prison radicalization as a phenomenon that predominately occurred outside the United States. In a recovered al-Qaeda manual, use of prison as a vehicle for recruitment was promoted along with it being a time for personal growth and a means to stage protests in an attempt to disrupt the institution. The latter may not be as difficult as some may think. Approximately half of American prisons are operating at overcapacity and the same can be said about prisons in Europe. The United Kingdom allegedly houses the most terrorism suspects in Europe and it has been estimated that al-Qaeda targets one in ten Muslim prisoners for recruitment.

Parker's thesis prepared for the Naval Post Graduate School states "the prison environment is multifaceted and heavily influenced by the many factors. The research related to prison radicalization provides an insight into components that could facilitate prison radicalization. The negative effects of

**FIGURE 5.3** Environmental factors conducive to prison radicalization.

gangs in prison, inadequate vetting of chaplains and volunteers, loss of family support, and poor information sharing and staff training are target areas that must be addressed."[28] Parker used a variation of Figure 5.3 to demonstrate environmental factors conducive to prison radicalization.

In a 2011 paper authored by Melissa Jane Kronfeld, she cited that today, "Islam is described by inmates as a good way of 'doing time'; it serves as a coping mechanism that provides psychological relief. Today, the U.S. has the largest prison system in the world, with over two million people currently incarcerated and another four million who have served their time and/or are currently on parole. Islam, once considered by penal authorities as a 'passing fad,' is now the fastest growing religion in American prisons, mostly via the 30,000 to 40,000 annual jailhouse conversions, and could represent anywhere between 5% and 10% of the prison population, but upwards to 20% in the penal institutions of New York, Pennsylvania, California, and Maryland, although no nationwide statistics exist. In 1995, it was estimated that approximately 4,000 inmates reported being Muslim. The number had remained stable for almost a decade but it has since doubled. It is estimated that 80% to 90% of those who convert while in prison choose Islam, and 20% of those who do convert continue to practice. The Muslims are predominately African-American, a group that also represents the racial majority in the American prisons, and the majority of these inmates are under forty-five years of age. Among the more than 30% of inmates who seek religious services, a large percentage seek out Muslim services. These numbers increase if one considers those inmates who convert or pursue Islam outside of the formal prison structure."[35]

## OTHER RELIGIONS AND TRENDS

In 2001 researchers produced a paper that looked at religion in prisons within England and Wales. This document presents data on the religious affiliation of prisoners in Prison Service establishments in England and Wales for the years 1999–2000. Authors noted that the British prison service recognizes more than 40 different religious denominations. They studied patterns and trends in faiths followed by prisoners between 1993 and 2000. Outlined below are what they determined to be the main points of their research.

- In 2000, the largest groups of prison inmates were Anglicans, who formed 39% of the prison population. Next in size was the group with No religion (32%), followed by Roman Catholics at 17% and Muslims at 7% of the prison population. Buddhists, Hindus, and Sikhs each accounted for around one half of 1% of the population.
- Prisoners with No religion were the fastest growing group of the prison population. This group more than doubled in size, growing by 181% between 1993 and 2000; the prison population as a whole grew by 55% over the same period.
- The number of Muslims in prison doubled between 1993 and 2000. The population of Buddhists, although relatively very small, also grew faster than average, increasing by 60% over the same period.
- The number of all Christians grew more slowly than the average over this period, falling from 75% of the total population in 1993 to 59.5% in 2000. The fastest growing Christian denomination in prisons was Roman Catholicism, whose adherents accounted for approximately one sixth of the prison population in each year between 1993 and 2000, but whose actual numbers grew by 45% over this period.
- Inmates with No religion were most likely to be young (under 30 years) white males on short sentences (of less than 3 years).[36]

Within the United States there have been several studies that examined inmate faith preferences and sought to understand religion in prisons as well as whether there were potential ties to radicalization. An August 2007 inmate faith preference survey conducted by the California Department of Corrections and Rehabilitation showed that Protestants represent the largest faith group followed by the Catholic faith. This same survey showed the Islamic faith to be less than 3% of the inmates. The same percentages found in the California study were somewhat representative of a self-reported Federal prison report which showed Protestants to represent half of the inmates followed by Catholic and "None." Muslims or the Islamic faith did show a percent greater than the California study but it still failed to reach double digits. One organization that is often cited for its work on the matter of religion and religion in prisons is the Pew Research Center.

In 2007, the Pew Research Center conducted the first ever, nationwide, random sample survey of Muslim Americans. This survey provides a baseline in an attempt to further the discussion regarding the matter of radical jihadism in prisons if it is true that prison communities are reflective of the community in which they exist. Pew's study demonstrated that more than three-quarters (77%) of Muslim Americans say they have always been Muslim, while 23% say they converted to Islam; nine-in-ten (91%) converts to Islam were born in the United States, and almost three-fifths (59%) of converts to Islam are African-American. Two-thirds (67%) of all converts to Islam in the United States came from Protestant churches, 10% came from Catholicism, and just 5% from other religions. Nearly one-in-seven converts to Islam (15%) had no religion before their conversion. A 55% majority of converts identify with Sunni Islam and another quarter (24%) identify with no specific tradition. Only 6% of Muslim converts in America identify themselves as Shia.[37]

In a survey that was conducted from September to December in 2011, the Pew Forum attempted to contact all 1,474 professional chaplains working in state prisons across the country. They received responses from approximately 50% of the people queried. The vast majority of inmates are housed in state institutions. Overwhelmingly, state prison chaplains consider religious counseling and other religion-based programming an important aspect of rehabilitating prisoners. According to the Pew report, nearly three-quarters of the chaplains (73%), for example, say they consider access to religion-related programs in prison to be "absolutely critical" to successful rehabilitation of inmates. Seventy-eight percent say they consider support from religious groups after inmates are released from prison to be absolutely critical to inmates' successful rehabilitation and re-entry into society. Among chaplains working in prisons that have religion-related rehabilitation or re-entry programs, more than half (57%) say the quality of such programs has improved over the last 3 years and six-in-ten (61%) say participation in such programs has gone up.

At the same time, a sizable minority of chaplains say that religious extremism is either very common (12%) or somewhat common (29%) among inmates. Religious extremism is reported by the chaplains as especially common among Muslim inmates (including followers of the Nation of Islam and the Moorish Science Temple of America) and, to a substantial but lesser degree, among followers of pagan or earth-based religions such as Odinism and various forms of Wicca. An overwhelming majority of chaplains, however, report that religious extremism seldom poses a threat to the security of the facility in which they work, with only 4% of chaplains saying religious extremism among inmates "almost always" poses a threat to prison security and an additional 19% saying it "sometimes" poses a threat.[38]

Radicals and extremists are not born, nor do they fall from the sky. Whether on the outside or on the inside of a correctional facility, radicalization and recruitment efforts abound. These efforts have either a direct or indirect leadership component. There are those leaders of a cause or ideology to whom radicals and extremists will often turn to in their research when incarcerated.

## RADICAL EXTREMIST GROUPS WITH A PRESENCE IN PRISONS AND JAILS

Correctional facilities throughout the world are in strife with many challenges, for example, overcrowding, understaffing, insufficient financial resources, and the rise of organized gangs and extremist groups. These groups cover a broad spectrum of religions, ethnicities, and ideologies. Since the 1970s many of the groups within institutions have become more organized, ideologically educated, and coordinated. Many groups throughout the world have used prisons to their advantage. Groups like ETA and the IRA used ideology coupled with a nationalistic undertone to recruit and develop a network of paramilitary political prisoners. Within the United States there have been many "groups" such as the Aryan Brotherhood and the Nation of Islam that are often cited as examples of religiously oriented prison gangs/groups that aggressively recruit and radicalize inmates. The reality is there are many examples that have fostered hatred, racism, discrimination, and violence toward others and the Western world. Outlined below are some of the groups that are often noted as a concern to law enforcement.

- JIS and Kevin James: Jami'iy yat UI-Islam Is-Saheeh (JIS) founded and headed by a charismatic Black Muslim convert named Kevin James hatched terrorist plots from within California's New Folsom prison. The group's actions embody many of the factors discussed that contribute to convicts being led to terrorism through conversion. James propagated JIS ideology and recruited adherents inside and outside prison, mainly through disseminating the JIS manifesto and direct meetings with inmates. According to a 2006 FBI report, James also provided guidance for members to recruit outside prison. He sought new recruits without prison records, who could benefit the group through their occupations, abilities, or access to sensitive locations.

  Kevin Lamar James grew up and became a street gang member in Los Angeles. He was a member of the 76th Street Crips and in the 1990s he received a 10-year sentence for robbery. It is believed that during this sentence that James was first exposed to Islam according to the Nation of Islam and eventually associated with a fringe group of Sunni Muslims known as JIS. In the late 1990s, James used his past experience as a gang member to spread the message of JIS and create a network through the prison system. James' efforts brought together and united members of rival groups and gangs in the name of Islam.

  In 2009, two members of JIS were sentenced for their involvement in a plot to attack Jewish and Israeli institutions in the Los Angeles area, as well as the Los Angeles airport and military recruiting offices. It is important to note that James was calling the shots for the criminal acts outside of the prison walls by others from within prison by following one of the central tenants of JIS, remain clandestine.

- Muslims of America: In Chapter 10, under the section on homegrown terror, Jamaat al-Fuqra and the Muslims of America (MOA) are discussed in context of general membership and activities. MOA is known to have recruited many of its members from within prisons. MOA is considered by some to be a corporate front for the Islamic extremist group known as al-Fuqra who seeks to purify Islam through violence.

MOA is loosely structured with some members openly recruiting converts, raising money, organizing activities, and distributing propaganda. Recruitment by MOA is very selective and allegedly requires individuals to be born into the group, be in approved marriages, or seek approval through a review board. While they do have a presence in correctional facilities it should be noted that they focus recruiting efforts toward those recently released from prison who demonstrate aggressive behavior. They are fairly diverse in their recruiting efforts but they have been shown to have a propensity to pursue Blacks and Hispanics.

- Moorish Science Temple Nation: The Moorish Nation is a type of sovereign citizen movement in which adherents believe that descendants of Moors were fraudulently brought to the United States by European colonists, and therefore not subject to federal and state laws.

Some of the earliest law enforcement investigations concerning the Moorish Science Temple and its leadership come from the FBI. Archival documents show the FBI received information and conducted investigations concerning sects of this group can be found as far back as 1940. Informants for the FBI were concerned that the group was conducting subversive activities that would be detrimental and hostile to the United States government.

The group was founded in 1913 and according to the Southern Poverty Law Center it fragmented rapidly after Drew Ali's death in 1929. Offshoots have since formed and other black nationalist and black Muslim groups took to adding suffixes like "Ali," "El," "Dey," "Bey," and "Al" to their last names. Sovereign ideology has leaked into some of the Moorish offshoot groups and they preach for their members not to cooperate with police, courts, and government officials. According to the Anti-Defamation League, since 2009, the sovereign citizen movement has experienced a major resurgence, and this includes African-Americans. Both Moorish and non-Moorish sovereign citizen ideas have spread rapidly within the African-American community, aided by social media websites such as YouTube and Facebook. Moorish and non-Moorish sovereign ideas alike have also spread in prisons and jails across the country.

Most sovereign citizens are still white, but in a number of cities with large African-American populations such as Chicago, Detroit, Philadelphia, and others, African-Americans now comprise the majority of sovereign citizens. Today Moorish sovereign citizens can be found in any area with a substantial African-American population.[39]

- Sovereign Citizens Movement: According to the FBIs 2015 National Threat Report, the threat from white supremacy, sovereign citizens, and abortion extremism have experienced an increase. They contribute the increase in the number of deaths caused by followers to be caused by lone offenders. The Sovereign Citizens Movement has its roots in the Posse Comitatus movement and in racialist philosophies such as the Christian Identity Movement. It is important to note that the sovereign citizen ideology has spread without a national leader or organizational structure and some of the informal groups are led by self-appointed ideologues espousing diverse doctrines. Noteworthy is the fact that a significant segment of sovereigns do not follow any religious doctrine as part of their sovereign stance.

The same 2015 FBI report stated that sovereign-citizen criminals continued to communicate, share tradecraft, and recruit adherents in prison environments as well as through other means. Other reports show that recruiters often look for people who are financially stressed, angry with the government, or have a personal problem and they believe by joining the movement their problems will be solved. They also seek out con artists and people who want something for nothing. Law enforcement officials have expressed concerns of anti-government extremism as being one of their top terrorist threats they face. The FBI supports this by considering sovereign-citizen extremists as compromising a domestic terrorist movement.

In a 2011 FBI Law Enforcement Bulletin it was noted that even when sovereign citizens go to prison for crimes, they continue criminal activity behind bars. Inmates provide a new population for them to sway to adopt the sovereign-citizen ideology; they then can train these inmates to help them defraud banks, credit institutions, and the U.S. government. They can create fraudulent businesses from inside prison walls and complete fraudulent financial documents to receive lines of credit from legitimate banks. The learning system goes both ways—inmates can teach sovereign citizens new criminal methods that they can use either from inside the prison or when they are released.

The FBI article presented possible indicators used by the sovereign citizens. They often produce documents that contain peculiar or out-of-place language. In some cases, they speak their own language or will write only in certain colors, such as in red crayon. Several indicators can be:

- References to the Bible, The Constitution of the United States, U.S. Supreme Court decisions, or treaties with foreign governments
- Personal names spelled in all capital letters or interspersed with colons (e.g., JOHN SMITH or Smith: John)
- Signatures followed by the words "under duress," "Sovereign Living Soul" (SLS), or a copyright symbol (©)
- Personal seals, stamps, or thumb prints in red ink
- The words "accepted for value"

They also carry fraudulent drivers' licenses to indicate their view that law enforcement does not have the authority to stop their vehicle or may write "No Liability Accepted" above their signature on a driver's license to signify that they do not accept it as a legitimate identification document.[40]

There are several ways in which sovereign citizens try to recruit and spread their ideologies. Within a correctional facility sovereign citizens may try to become religious volunteers in order to hold "services" for inmates. These services are actually a type of seminar that they use to recruit and teach other inmates. Another means would be to become instructors or teachers to avoid any extra scrutiny of religious practices.

Support for the movement is not just found in the United States. It can be found in Canada, New Zealand, Australia, and the United Kingdom. Tactics employed by sovereign citizens are diverse. Some of their more notable actions have been deemed "paper terrorism" because they will often file bogus or legitimate documents against governments.

## LEGAL CONCERNS AND CHALLENGES

Liability is the one word that evokes concern and caution especially in a government setting. One setting that is especially ripe is the correctional facility. You have an environment where individuals are gathered, housed, and interact, that have idle time and often create self-perceived needs or deficiencies. They will then translate these needs and deficiencies into legal action against the institution.

### RELIGIOUS FREEDOM AND RESTORATION ACT

Kelly Gower, the Lead Notes Editor for the *Rutgers Journal of Law and Religion* prepared a paper in 2005. The paper notes that in 1993, Congress passed the Religious Freedom and Restoration Act (RFRA). RFRA restored strict scrutiny as the standard for free-exercise claims, largely as a reaction to the Court's decision in Smith. Congress passed RFRA to "restore the compelling interest test as set forth in *Sherbert v. Verner* and *Wisconsin v. Yoder*, and to guarantee its application in all cases where free exercise of religion is substantially burdened." Congress based its authority to enact RFRA on Section 5 of the Fourteenth Amendment. The RFRA balancing test provided that the government may "substantially burden a person's exercise of religion only if it demonstrates that the burden to the person (1) is in the furtherance of a compelling government interest; and (2) is the least restrictive means of furthering that compelling governmental interest." However, only 4 years after RFRA's enactment, the heightened level of scrutiny established by RFRA was held unconstitutional by the Supreme Court in *City of Boerne v. Flores*. Prior to the enactment of RLUIPA, the Religious Liberty Protection Acts of 1998 and 1999 (RLPA) were introduced; however, they failed to pass congressional muster. RLPA and RFRA shared the same underlying purpose: to restore the compelling interest test for state actions that substantially burden free exercise. In the wake of City of Boerne, RLPA was not sufficiently narrow to gain the required congressional support. The Religious Land Use and Institutionalized Persons Act (RLUIPA) was enacted in 2000.

Unlike the RLPA which failed to pass in both houses of Congress, the RLUIPA generated the necessary support to become law despite the fact that it advocated the same standard articulated in both RFRA and RLPA. RLUIPA's focus, however, is limited: it only applies to burdens associated with land use regulation and institutionalized persons. In these two specific areas, the Act forbids state and local governments from imposing a substantial burden on the exercise of religion unless they can demonstrate that imposition of such burden is the least restrictive means of furthering a compelling interest. Unlike the standard articulated by the Supreme Court, which affords prison officials immense leeway in limiting the free exercise of prisoners under the First Amendment, RLUIPA restores the proper compelling interest/least restrictive means analysis.[41]

## THE RELIGIOUS LAND USE AND INSTITUTIONALIZED PERSONS ACT

In a 2012 report published by the National Gang Crime Research Center and authored by George Knox, the problem of gangs and security in security threat groups was surveyed. Knox reported that there are a myriad of problems involving religion that overlap with gangs, STGs, racial conflict, extremism, and other challenges to the correctional system. The correctional system has to maintain safety and security as a foremost goal. We will see that there are new challenges facing corrections today from the abuse of religious practices behind bars.

Knox's report noted that few correctional facilities have reported abuse of RLUIPA. RLUIPA stands for Religious Land Use and Institutionalized Persons Act. Persons wanting to know more about how this impacts on corrections can go to the website sponsored by the Becket Fund—www.RLUIPA.com—and see that many correctional agencies have been sued over this federal law that went into effect in the year 2000. What this new law did was extend certain new statutory rights to prison inmates, said inmates quickly learned they had a new weapon to use against correctional administrators, and a massive onslaught of frivolous lawsuits were soon unleashed against correctional agencies nationwide. Additionally, gangs got into the "prisoner religious rights" business and began to operate as a religious front, using RLUIPA as the basis for holding their meetings.

It is helpful to summarize the recent case from Ohio regarding this statute. Basically, what RLUIPA did for adult correctional institutions was to increase the review requirements for placing any restrictions on inmates that might pertain to religion. Prior to the passage of RLUIPA the rational review doctrine applied. This meant that disciplinary measures and restrictions could be placed on inmates regarding religion simply if the prison administration rationally decides it is in the best interests of safety and security to do so. After 2000, though, RLUIPA established the strict scrutiny doctrine under which the burden of proof shifts from the inmate needing to prove his rights were violated, to the prison needing to prove it is not violating the rights of inmates. In other words, under the strict scrutiny doctrine, American prisons are under strict scrutiny and assumed to want to systematically violate the rights of inmates, such that any restriction on an inmate's religious practices is assumed to require extra special scrutiny.

In establishing the strict scrutiny doctrine, RLUIPA also created two classes of inmates: those whose rights are protected when they operate under the cloak of a religion, and those whose rights are not protected when they do not. Thus, those inmates who might want to advance a hatred of anything but Caucasian people could easily do so by organizing their religious service under a wide variety of banners (Christian Identity, WCOTC, etc.), and when they possess inflammatory materials along these lines, they are a religion and the inmates can claim it is constitutionally protected. At the same time, an ordinary neo-nazi who does the same thing, but who does not claim it is a religious practice, will face summary disciplinary procedures under the rational review doctrine. Over the years it appears that inmates have learned that it "pays off" to take on the special status of a religion.

The Ohio adult prison system won a major victory against RLUIPA: the portion of the law applying to prisoners was found to be unconstitutional in the Sixth Circuit.

The survey question in the 2012 NGCRC National STG Survey was constructed as follows: "has your facility experienced any abuses of religious freedoms as a result of the RLUPA?." Some 18.7% reported "yes," in fact they had experienced abuses of RLUIPA.[42]

To establish a claim under RLUIPA, a prisoner must show that a prison receiving federal funds has enacted a regulation that renders his exercise of a religious practice effectively impractical.

## REQUESTS FOR RELIGIOUS ACCOMMODATIONS AND LIBRARIES

Requests for religious accommodation are not uncommon in many locations. However, it is the requests for religious accommodation within a correctional facility that bring new challenges—security. There is also the challenge of dealing with frivolous requests that are submitted by inmates seeking to be a "paper terrorist" and clog the justice system with legal challenges. There are also those inmates seeking a better way of getting through the day by getting what they perceive to be better treatment, food, or access to the outside world. A jail administrator once stated that a person making the request for religious accommodation had better plan on being a full-time follower of the religion he/she is citing and not just a part-time member for convenience.

Based on the American Civil Liberties Union (ACLU) National Prison Project, courts often disagree about what qualifies as a religion or a religious belief. So-called mainstream belief systems, such as Christianity, Islam, and Judaism, are universally understood to be religions. Less well-known or non-traditional faiths, however, have had less success being recognized as religions. While Rastafari, Native American religions, and various Eastern religions have generally been protected, belief systems such as the Church of the New Song, Satanism, the Aryan Nations, and the Five Percenters have often gone unprotected. The Supreme Court has never defined the term "religion." However, in deciding whether something is a religion, lower courts have asked whether the belief system addresses "fundamental and ultimate questions," is "comprehensive in nature," and presents "certain formal and external signs."[43]

According to a 2012 Pew Research Center 50-state survey of prison chaplains, it was discovered that "the diversity of faith groups in the inmate population underscores the challenges the prison system faces in meeting the religious needs of all inmates." The Pew Forum survey included several questions designed to probe the kinds of requests that inmates make for accommodation of their religious beliefs and practices, as well as the frequency with which they are granted. An overwhelming majority of chaplains who responded to these questions say that inmates' requests for religious texts (82%) and for meetings with spiritual leaders of their faith (71%) are usually approved. And about half of chaplains say that requests for a special religious diet (53%) or for permission to have sacred items or religious clothing such as crucifixes, eagle feathers and turbans (51%) also are usually granted.

But one kind of request appears to be less routinely granted. Only about three-in-ten chaplains (28%) say that requests for special accommodation related to hair or grooming are usually approved in the prisons where they work, while 36% say such requests are usually denied and 36% say the decisions can go either way."[38]

When it comes to prison libraries there are a multitude of publications that should draw a closer look. Governments such as Saudi Arabia have made the propagation of radical Islam in America and around the world a top priority. To achieve this, under the moniker of National Islamic Prison Foundation, they have shipped tens of thousands of Korans to U.S. jails. They have also provided financial support under the auspices of prison outreach programs that some believe seek to convert inmates to Islam. In 2008 an article was published on the Investigative Project website that there was a nearly 400 page inventory of Islamic books and videos available to federal inmates and chaplains just in federal penitentiaries. The article notes that numerous examples of radical texts and videos from extremists include Wahhabi and Muslim Brotherhood scholars, Sayyid Qutb, and a couple hundred volumes by a noted Pakistani jihadist. The aforementioned is just an example of publications available. The same might be said of other domestic ideologies and others. The difference might be that with domestic groups there is more of an obvious connection to extremist ideologies and a greater understanding of the topic by jail administrators. It might be the unknown, such as Islam, that allows extremist materials to enter the controlled environment of prisons. The example above is just about federal facilities. In the 2012 National Gang Crime Research Center survey, it was noted that the Satanic Bible and Book of Shadows have been requested or possessed in nearly one quarter of the correctional facilities they surveyed. The local jail systems may have a varying degree of what might be construed as extremist materials in their libraries and it they might go overlooked due to resources and knowledge of the topic. There might also be the fear of what can be perceived as denial of religious materials or access that could lead to legal action. The local jails lack the financial means to defend legal actions.

## IDENTIFYING THE RADICAL VISUALLY

A question posed to many in the law enforcement field investigating terrorism and extremists is often in the context—how do you know they are terrorist, or how do you know it is a threat? Another question that comes about is—what have you seen that confirms it to be a concern? A return question might be—how do you know that it is not? Well, it is not a simple task to identify a radical. You must be able to combine visual observations and comingle it with other variables such as behaviors, actions, statements, relationships, and known environmental concerns to develop a clear picture to identify potential radicals. However, there are some visual observations that may help identify concerns and it is not based on bald headed or bearded males. Group logos, flags, and other extremist imagery are prevalent. They are used as visual representation of groups and possibly their ideology. Print, Internet, propaganda, tattoos, clothing and accessories, and other graphic media are the most common representations. While correctional facilities control many of the aforementioned within a facility, it is the tattoos that might provide the best insight to potential extremist concerns.

Many gangs and right-wing extremist group members will brand themselves with symbols, numbers and acronym tattoos/markings to demonstrate their allegiance or support of subversive groups. Appendix C, Symbols of Hate, demonstrates some of the more common symbols used by domestic extremist groups. When it comes to Islamic terrorist tattoos and markings, it is important to note that tattoos traditionally are not acceptable within the Muslim world. However, tattoos were still found in countries such as Iraq primarily on younger men, and current and former military members. Quite often, the tattoos appeared on hands, shoulders, and upper arms so that they could be covered to avoid criticism. Some of the overseas tattoos are not necessarily a high quality product but they do share symbols and some wording that when properly translated raise concerns. Some wording that translates possibly into "a thousand crying eyes" or "army to free Iraq" were found on members of Jaish Taharir Al-Iraq group members in Iraq. The same group's members could be identified by a cross within a diamond with a crescent above, both of which were blue in color, and a black snake within a red triangle. Other tattoos that have been identified on the hands of mujahedeen and individuals engaged in jihad were three green/black dots with a square or crescent moon as part of the tattoo. In Iraq there was even a suicide bomber tattoo that people referred to as "ghosts." The tattoo was an outline of an angel with wings and the body consisted of a heart with the letter "F" inside denoting a Fedayeen Martyr.

It is important to remember the application of body art, including symbols commonly associated with extremist ideology, may be an exercise of the right of free speech or expression. It is the combination of suspicious behavior and or requests that should lead to the possible need for further investigation. It is also just as important for law enforcement personnel to capture and document full details and locations of not only the tattoos or other visuals but it is just as important to discuss the context of other observable behaviors.

Figures 5.4, 5.5, and 5.6 provide examples of the type of tattoos that have been found in prisons and jails within the United States.

**FIGURE 5.4**    Radical jail tattoos.

**FIGURE 5.5**    Radical jail tattoos 2.

**FIGURE 5.6**    Sharia compliant tattoos.

When it comes to members or supporters of the Sovereign Citizen Movement, there is an array of indicators that may be observed beyond tattoos. Many of the indicators are actual documents or materials carried by the individual. Items often found are listed below:

- Pocket-sized constitutions
- Magna Carta
- Bibles
- License plates with odd names
- Fraudulent identification documents
- Driver's license with the term "No Liability Accepted" above their signature
- The 14th Amendment

- References to the 1933 Gold Standard
- Anti-government materials

In Sturgeons 2015 publication he provided some examples for "intelligence gathering":

- When an offender begins to associate with those offenders who have been identified as already radicalized and/or gang members, correctional personnel making this observation should write reports stating
  - The name(s) of the offender (s) being observed
  - The name(s) of the radicalized offenders
  - The time(s) that they were seen together
  - State when these offenders started meeting/hanging around together, or when it was first observed by correctional staff
  - Identify every location where they were seen together, for example, eating together, walking together in the yard, changing seat in the school areas so that they could sit closer to each other.
- Research has demonstrated that those offender-recruiters who would radicalize other offenders use a series of methods and techniques.
  - The recruiters look for those offenders who are the most vulnerable. Some of the experts use the word "disenfranchised." From my years of experience, I would say that the recruiters look for those who are afraid, looking for protection, looking to belong to "something," and who are vulnerable to kindness.
  - The steps/phases are similar to these:
    - Recruiters make their approach in an open setting (yard, dayroom, gym, school).
    - Recruiters engage in light conversation.
    - Conversations will discuss the benefits of the group/gang (protection, belonging to something that is bigger than self, believing in a higher spiritual being, becoming someone, to mention a few). Of course these examples will manifest themselves differently, depending on whether the recruits are joining a gang, subversive group, or if they are being radicalized as part of joining a terrorist group.
    - Once the recruit demonstrates an interest, the recruiter becomes more and more engaging. The conversation will become more focused on religion and the recruit's relationship with God, the cause, the religion, etc. It should be noted that many of the recruiters are NOT trained in the study of Islam, and in many cases what they are preaching/teaching is their interpretation of the Quran.
    - In the case of the recruit being radicalized, the recruiter will start to share literature with the recruit; again, the literature may not be based on official teachings contained in the Quran.
    - Once the recruiter believes that he/she has the recruit's confidence and trust, he/she will make the move to fully involve the recruit in the movement.
    - From the time that the recruit is fully engaged, the recruiter will continue to bring the recruit further and further into the fold.[44]

Much of the material up to this point has been derived from numerous worldwide research efforts. As with anything, the material that is used or found to be applicable for a position must be placed in proper context. Beyond the references cited, there are many studies that can be found on the topics discussed.

## REVIEW OF WORLDWIDE RESEARCH STUDIES

Radicalization and recruitment is not something that is a concern to any one specific country. Many of the world's top academics, researchers, and law enforcement minds have sought to understand all aspects of the radicalization and recruitment processes. There are many great research efforts that have been undertaken and published in an effort to possibly help identify an issue before it becomes a big problem. Just like a recipe for your favorite food, you can easily find different variations for the "same" visual outcome while using different methods and means available to the preparer. Every country has different laws, resources and law enforcement tactics available to them to address the radicalization and recruiting topic but you must remember that they present it in the way that fits their knowledge base. That is why it is important to review and understand the various respected publications available from a wide variety of researchers and data sets. To this end, outlined below is a summary of the more noted papers available that have been prepared by some of the leading researchers on the topic. Although there are many anecdotal research writings, they should be carefully considered and viewed in the context in which they are presented.

No one can say that any one particular country is immune from terrorism, terrorists, or radical extremists. Worldwide caution and awareness is important. Europe has experienced continual credible threats arising from ISIS/ISIL and al-Qaeda. In the past couple of years extremists have carried out attacks in France, Belgium, Germany, and Turkey. The Middle East and Africa continue to be a hotbed of activity especially toward Westerners. South and Central Asia continue to be affected by insurgent activities that are directed toward civilian, government, and foreign targets. Simply, there is no shortage of individuals or regions of concern that seek to use violent extremist activity to further their cause or ideology.

## NEW YORK POLICE DEPARTMENT

Initially published by the New York Police Department in 2007, *Radicalization in the West: The Homegrown Threat*, garnered a wide array of attention in the law enforcement community. Prepared by Senior Intelligence Analysts Mitchell Silber and Arvin Bhatt, this report gave law enforcement in the United States some insight into the radicalization process. As was noted in the report's executive summary, in order to test whether the same framework for understanding radicalization abroad applied within the United States, we analyzed three U.S. homegrown terrorism cases and two New York City based cases:

- Lackawana, New York • Portland, Oregon • Northern Virginia • New York City—Herald Square Subway • New York City—The Al Muhajiroun Two

The same radicalization framework was applied to a study of the origins of the Hamburg cluster of individuals, who led the September 11 hijackers. This assessment, almost 6 years after 2001, provides some new insights, previously not fully grasped by the law enforcement and intelligence community, into the origins of this devastating attack.

## DUTCH/DANISH

*Home-Grown Terrorism and Islamist Radicalization in Europe* is a report prepared in 2007 and is a research report funded by the Danish Ministry of Justice. It is an assessment of the factors influencing violent Islamist extremism and suggestions for counterradicalization measures. The project is the result of a 6-month research grant from the Danish Ministry of Justice (Research and Documentation Unit). During the research process, the author, Tomas Precht, had the opportunity to have insightful meetings with both the General Intelligence and Security Service of the Netherlands (AIVD) and the Danish Security and Intelligence Service (PET) including the Centre for Terrorism Analysis (CTA) regarding specific elements of the report. The project intends to give an assessment of the factors influencing homegrown terrorism and violent Islamist extremism in Europe. The purpose is to identify the specific phases, major characteristics, and catalysts of the radicalization process as well as suggesting relevant counterradicalization measures.

A second report published in October 2009 by the Netherlands Institute of International Relations Clingendael is titled *Islamist Radicalisation: A Root Cause Model*. The authors suggest that it is essential to examine the causes rather than the courses of radicalization, and in so doing, to perceive radicalization as an "embedded individual process" that occurs in the individual within a specific social and environmental context. For that purpose, they introduce a theoretical model of the causes of radicalization that sheds some light on the sociological and (socio-) psychological circumstances under which radicalization is likely to occur, as well as on the circumstances under which it is less likely to occur. With their explanatory model, they aspire to provide researchers and policy-makers with a solid foundation from which to further analyze the causes of radicalization and, subsequently, to develop measures to counter their negative effects.

## UNITED KINGDOM

Various reports have been prepared either by UK researchers seeking to understand the topic of radicalization and recruitment in the United Kingdom. Many law enforcement agencies will often cite efforts of the British intelligence agency's MI5 behavioral science unit. While they present some excellent points in their 2008 in-depth case studies on several hundred individuals involved in violent extremist activity, it too must be viewed broadly. Even though they note that there is no single demographic profile or pathway, it was interesting that the individuals tend to be either converts or second-generation, native-born children of legal immigrants.

Numerous reports in the United Kingdom provide some of the world's top insights to the topic of radicalization and recruitment. In late 2006, the European Commission charged one of the International Centre for the Study of Radicalisation and Political Violence (ICSR)'s partners, King's College London, with conducting an in-depth study of the ways in which Islamist militants in Europe were being recruited and mobilized. The resulting ICSR study—*Recruitment and Mobilization for the Islamist Militant Movement in Europe*—was published in October 2008. Another insightful report was published in late 2013. The UK's Prime Minister's Task Force on Tackling Radicalisation and Extremism set out to tackle all forms of extremism. The report sets out practical proposals to tackle extremism in the following areas:

- Disrupting extremists
- Countering extremist narratives and ideology
- Preventing radicalization
- Integration
- Stopping extremism in institutions, including schools, universities and further education, and prisons

Originally published in 2009 by the FDD's Center for Terrorism Research, the paper *Homegrown Terrorists in the U.S. and U.K.: An Empirical Examination of the Radicalization Process*, authors examined six manifestations of the radicalization process that can be observed in homegrown terrorists. Though the six steps differ in prevalence, they found that all of them occurred frequently enough within the sample to be considered significant. As noted by the authors, "several studies have examined the demographics of homegrown Islamic terrorists, and a lesser number of studies have examined their social affiliations. But to date, no study has empirically examined the process through which these terrorists are radicalizing, which constitutes a substantial gap in the literature. This study addresses the present gap through an empirical examination of behavioral manifestations of the radicalization process in 117 homegrown "jihadist" terrorists from the United States and United Kingdom."[4]

## EUROPE

For many reasons, going back generations and decades, numerous European countries have been at the forefront of terrorist activities, including radicalization. Two that have been seen by some to having allowed radicalization to fester are Belgium and France. This is for a variety of reasons, many of which are associated with political posturing. Some cite the nearly 15-year exile of the Ayatollah Ruhollah Khomeini from Iran where he spent the last several months in France before returning to Iran, as leading to the growth of radical Islam in France. When it comes to Belgium, they have been viewed as a center for Islamic terrorism since the mid-1990s. Many of the initial extremist activities in Belgium were associated with the Armed Islamic Group (GIA) that is based in Alergia. Today, many associate the topic of conversion to Islam and growth of ISIS/ISIL in Europe as being the top threat.

Beyond the two reports mentioned above that provide insight to Europe, there are two other reports that shed insight to current trends in terrorism within Europe. Published by RAND in 2011, Lorenzo Vidino authored the report *Radicalization, Linkage, and Diversity Current Trends in Terrorism in Europe*. Based on a survey of legal documents, intelligence reports, academic literature, and media sources, and on conversations with experts and government officials, this paper provides an overview of current trends in jihadism in Europe from an operational perspective. Its main finding is that, although most European plots appear to have been independent, the most serious ones tended to involve extensive operational connections to groups operating outside of Europe. In an earlier report published in 2008, the European Commission's Expert Group on Violent Radicalisation prepared a concise report on the radicalization process. This report is one of the products of an expert group constituted by the European Commission to provide policy advice on fighting violent radicalization. It reports specifically on the current state of violent radicalization academic research.

Radicalization leading to acts of terrorism is context-specific. It thrives in an environment characterized by a shared sense of injustice, exclusion, and real or perceived humiliation. In general, all forms of radicalization exhibit the following characteristics:

- People who feel left behind in the progress of mankind and resent injustice are more prone to radicalization. Kinship, friendship, group dynamics, and socialization all trigger an individual's association with radicalization.
- People involved in terrorism come from a variety of social backgrounds. The use of violence involves a limited number of individuals who undergo diverse paths of radicalization.
- Profiling to identify possible terrorists is not productive, as no profiling measures fit all variables at work. It is possible to identify several positions which individuals may move toward or away from radicalization or deradicalization.
- Preventative strategies require tailoring to specific terrorist activity drivers and specifics of the groups involved.
- The constant use of ideology helps consolidate violent ideas and attitudes, and reduces potential moral inhibitors in order to generate a subculture of violence.
- Propaganda is key, as it offers doctrinal arguments that legitimize extremist positions. Radical/terrorist propaganda is generally framed around ideological, utilitarian, emotional, and identitarian considerations.

## WHAT CAN BE DONE TO PREVENT RECRUITMENT AND RADICALIZATION

Recommendations are akin to opinions—everyone seems to have one. Deradicalization efforts that may be found in Asia or Saudi Arabia may be considered successful but they are based on their laws and cultural considerations. There are profound differences between countries and cultures. In most Western world countries, tactics used to reduce or limit radicalization and recruitment that are used in the Middle East or Asia are not legally plausible.

Radicalization in Western countries is most effectively mitigated through preventative strategies like promoting a pluralistic religious environment rather than forceful interventions. Fostering a diverse marketplace of ideas, developing more effective methods of reintegrating released inmates, and ensuring that officials are able to distinguish personal beliefs from actual criminal behavior are some of the regularly cited recommendations. However, the most often cited recommendation is to provide staff with basic religious competency training.

In 2015, experts including prison wardens and administrators, representatives of international organizations, policy makers, and program managers working on correctional reform programs came together. Their discussion focused on what are some of the universally accepted good practices and standards that would help in countering prisoner radicalization. The culmination of their efforts was captured and put into a 2016/2017 publication titled *Prison Management Recommendations to Counter and Address Prison Radicalization*. One common theme that the experts emphasized is "the need to focus on sound correctional practices such as communication, accountability, vigilance, and effective supervision in "actively managing" facilities and its population and not simply "guarding" the prisoners."[45]

In 2014, the Community Oriented Policing Services (COPS) of the U.S. Department of Justice in concert with the International Association of Chiefs of Police (IACP) published a report on using community policing to counter violent extremism (CVE). In the report they stated that leveraging available resources from the community allows law enforcement to help mitigate the grievances that can lead to radicalization to violence and recruitment. Community policing principles have been used by many law enforcement agencies to address a host of crime and quality-of-life issues and can easily be repurposed to address CVE. The following key principles focus on how state, local, and tribal law enforcement agencies can continue to effectively deliver services and proactively respond to community concerns, while also addressing violent extremism of all types.

Key Principle #1: Foster and enhance trusting partnerships with the community
Key Principle #2: Engage all residents to address public safety matters
Key Principle #3: Leverage public and private stakeholders
Key Principle #4: Utilize all partnerships to counter violent extremism
Key Principle #5: Train all members of the department

In September 2011, authors provided a perspective into radicalization of Islamist terrorists in the Western world in an article prepared for the FBI Law Enforcement Bulletin. Ryan Hunter and Daniel Heinke state that "law enforcement activities directed solely against an individual's illegal activity after radicalization likely start too late and do not provide a sufficient answer to the complex phenomenon of homegrown Islamist terrorism. An effective counterradicalization program has to confront one, preferably all, of the components of the radicalization process and involve a variety of participants beyond the law enforcement and intelligence communities.

It seems that in each component, efforts of government and nongovernment actors can address issues at the level of the individual or the external environment. While potential counterradicalization activities and actors are wide and varied, a few highlights stand out.

- Prevent or properly handle grievances: On an individual level, efforts should focus on improving young Muslim immigrants' participation in society regarding their social, educational, and economic situation. Externally addressing discrimination and other issues that give rise to grievances also must be taken seriously.
- Counterideology: Individually, potential young extremists should be provided clear, descriptive, and unbiased information. Misleading or agitating propaganda should be countered aggressively. At the external level, to educate Muslims and address possible misunderstandings, authorities should provide open information on extremist Islamist trends and government programs to these communities, preferably in concert with respected Muslim citizen representatives. Proposed steps to prevent the spread of violent ideologies, such as website disruptions, also have to be evaluated while addressing questions of free speech and effectiveness.
- Countermobilization: Efforts include the classic antiterrorism approach of intelligence and law enforcement agencies collecting and analyzing information on extremist persons or

groups, enacting early detection programs, identifying potential threats, and disrupting plots and other extremist activities. At one level, these activities may target individual would-be operatives or recruiters and known communication or facilitation nodes."[21]

It is clear that there is no definitive answer on what should be done to prevent or counterradicalization and recruitment efforts that lead to terrorism. There are several publications that attempt to address this topic but there are two that this author believes are worth further review. First, *Preventing Terrorism and Countering Violent Extremism and Radicalization that Lead to Terrorism: a Community-Policing Approach* which was published by the Organization for Security and Co-operation in Europe in February 2014. Second, *Countering Radicalization and Recruitment to Al-Qaeda: Fighting the War of Deeds* written by Paul Kamolnick which was published in 2014 by the Strategic Studies Institute of the U.S. Army War College.

## CHAPTER CONCEPTS

The chapter concepts can be summarized as follows:

- Working definitions for the topics of radicalization, recruitment, and conversion are presented in the context of dealing with terrorists and extremists.
- Factors conducive to radicalization are considered in an effort to determine root causes of terrorism.
- Several models of radicalization are discussed and presented as well as it being demonstrated that there is no one-size-fits-all when it comes to identifying anyone involved in the radicalization process.
- The radicalization model of lone wolf terrorism is presented as it relates to self-radicalization and the common variables are discussed.
- Recruiting in the digital age is determined to be important and use of the Internet, social media, video games, and other means are discussed.
- Prison and jail correctional facilities have been seen as breeding grounds for radicals and extremists. The chapter identifies shared characteristics, gang connections, religion, and various groups within institutions and the roles they may play in the radicalization and recruitment processes. Legal concerns are also discussed.

## REFERENCES

1. Jenkins, B. M. 2009. *Outside Expert's View, Homegrown Terrorists in the U.S. and U.K.* FDD's Center for Terrorism Research, Washington, D.C., p. 7.
2. Schmid, A. 2013. *Radicalisation, De-Radicalisation, Counter-Radicalisation: A Conceptual Discussion and Literature Review.* The Hague: International Centre for Counter-Terrorism, pp. 2–3.
3. Rahimullah, R., S. Larmar, and M. Abdalla. 2013. Understanding Violent Radicalization Amongst Muslims: A Review of the Literature. *J Pychol Behav Sci* 1(1):19–31.
4. Gartenstein-Ross, D. and L. Grossman. 2009. *Homegrown Terrorists in the U.S. and U.K.: An Empirical Examination of the Radicalization Process.* FDD's Center for Terrorism Research, Washington, D.C., pp. 11–13.
5. Precht, T. 2007. *Home Grown Terrorism and Islamist Radicalisation in Europe from Conversion to Terrorism.* Danish Ministry of Justice, p. 5.
6. McCauley, C. and S. Moskalenko. 2011. *Friction: How Radicalization Happens to Them and Us.* Oxford University Press, New York, pp. 13–75.
7. Veldhuis, T. and J. Staun. 2009. *Islamist Radicalisation: A Root Cause Model.* The Netherlands Institute of International Relations Clingendael, The Hague, p. 59.
8. Senate Select Committee on Intelligence. 2003. War on Terrorism. In *Statement for the Record of Robert S. Mueller, III.*

9. Hamm, M. and R. Spaaj. 2015. *Lone Wolf Terrorism in America: Using Knowledge of Radicalization Pathways to Forge Prevention Strategies.* Indiana State University, pp. 6–11.

10. Gendron, A. 2006. *Militant Jihadism: Radicalization, Conversion, Recruitment.* Vol. 7. Trends in Terrorism Series Volume 2006-4. Canadian Centre for Intelligence and Security Studies, The Norman Patterson School of International Affairs, Carleton University, Ottawa, Ontario, pp. 9–14.

11. Kruglanski, A. and D. Webber. 2014. *The Psychology of Radicalization.* Zeitschrift für Internationale Strafrechtsdogmatik, pp. 379, 380. http://www.zis-online.com/dat/artikel/2014_9_843.pdf, 379, 380 (accessed January 18, 2017).

12. Jensen, M., James, P. and H. Tinsley. National Consortium for the Study of Terrorism and Responses to Terrorism, Maryland. 2015. *Profiles of Individual Radicalization in the United States: Preliminary Findings.*

13. National Consortium for the Study of Terrorism and Responses to Terrorism, Maryland. 2016. *Recruitment and Radicalization among US Far-Right Terrorists.* pp. 10, 11.

14. National Gang Intelligence Center. 2011. *2011 National Gang Threat Assessment,* Washington, D.C., p. 9.

15. Sturgeon, W. 2015. *Radicalization and Intelligence Gathering in Correctional Institutions—Part 2.* http://www.corrections.com/news/article/38882-radicalization-and-intelligence-gathering-in-correctional-institutions-part-2 (accessed January 28, 2017).

16. Sinicki, A. 2016. *The Psychology of Extremism.* Health Guidance. http://www.healthguidance.org/entry/16426/1/The-Psychology-of-Extremism.html (accessed January 20, 2017).

17. Ranstorp, M. 2016. *The Root Causes of Violent Extremism.* RAN Issue Paper. Radicalisation Awareness Network Centre of Excellence, Brussels, pp. 3–4.

18. Daly, S. and S. Gerwehr. 2006. *Al-Qaida: Terrorist Selection and Recruitment.* Santa Monica, CA: RAND Corporation, 2006.

19. Mississippi State University Office of Research Security. *Potential CI Risk Indicators.* http://www.ors.msstate.edu/ci/ (accessed January 22, 2017).

20. Bjelopera, J. 2013. Congressional Research Service: American Jihadist Terrorism: Combating a Complex Threat, Report R41416, Washington, D.C., p. 22.

21. Hunter, R. and D. Heinke. 2011. Perspective Radicalization of Islamist Terrorists in the Western World. *FBI Law Enforce Bull* 80(9):29–31.

22. Jenkins, B. M. 2011. *Stray Dogs and Virtual Armies: Radicalization and Recruitment to Jihadist Terrorism in the United States Since 9/11.* Santa Monica, CA: RAND Corporation, p. 17. http://www.rand.org/pubs/occasional_papers/OP343.html (accessed January 24, 2017).

23. Guadagno, R., A. Lankford, N. Muscanell, B. Okdie, and D. McCallum. 2010. Social Influence in the Online Recruitment of Terrorists and Terrorist Sympathizers: Implications for Social Psychology Research. *Rev Int Psychol Soc* 23(1):25–56.

24. Australian Government. 2017. *Radicalisation and the Internet.* https://www.livingsafetogether.gov.au/informationadvice/Pages/what-is-radicalisation/radicalisation-and-the-internet.aspx (accessed January 24, 2017).

25. Alarid, M. 2016. *Recruitment and Radicalization: The Role of Social Media and New Technology, Impunity: Countering Illicit Power in War and Transition.* Peacekeeping & Stability Operations Institute, Carlisle, PA, pp. 314, 317, 320–321.

26. Torok, R. 2015. *Terrorists Use Marketing Skills to Attract New Recruits Online.* The Conversation. http://theconversation.com/terrorists-use-marketing-skills-to-attract-new-recruits-online-39497 (accessed January 25, 2017).

27. Homeland Security Institute. 2009. *Recruitment and Radicalization of School-Aged Youth by International Terrorist Groups.* Report RP08-37-01, Homeland Security Institute, Arlington, VA, p. 14.

28. Parker, T. 2013. *Establishing a Deradicalization/Disengagement Model for America's Correctional Facilities: Recommendations for Countering Prison Radicalization.* Naval Post Graduate School, Monterey, CA, pp. 16–17, 24.

29. Homeland Security Policy Institute (HSPI) and Critical Incident Analysis Group (CIAG) Prisoner Radicalization Task Force. 2006. *Out of the Shadows: Getting Ahead of Prisoner Radicalization.* George Washington University, Washington, D.C., 2006, pp. ii–iii.

30. Winters, R. 2015. *Violent Extremism and Its Roots in the U.S. Corrections System.* http://www.corrections.com/news/article/40631-violent-extremism-and-its-roots-in-the-u-s-corrections-system (accessed January 26, 2017).

31. Mulcahy, E., S. Merrington, and P. Bell. 2013. The Radicalisation of Prison Inmates: Exploring Recruitment, Religions and Prisoner Vulnerability. *J Hum Secur* 9(1):7.

32. Neumann, P. 2010. *Prisons and Terrorism Radicalisation and De-radicalisation in 15 Countries*. London: International Centre for the Study of Radicalisation and Political Violence, pp. 14–15.

33. Taft, P. 1978. Whatever Happened to that Old-Time Prison Chaplain? *Corrections Magazine*, The American Correctional Association, December, p. 55.

34. Rosenblatt, J. 1982. *Religious Groups and Prison Reform*. Editorial research reports 1982 (Vol. I). Washington, DC: CQ Press. http://library.cqpress.com/cqresearcher/cqresrre1982022609 (accessed January 27, 2017).

35. Kronfeld, M. 2011. *Prislam: The Recruitment and Radicalization of Terrorist Operatives in the Prison System and the Threat to American Homeland*. pp. 34–35. https://www.academia.edu/5467166/Prislam_ The_Recruitment_and_Radicalization_of_Terrorist_Operatives_in_the_Prison_System_and_the_Threat_ to_the_American_Homeland (accessed January 27, 2017).

36. Guessous, F., N. Hooper, and U. Moorthy. 2001. *Religion in Prisons 1999 and 2000*. http://webarchive. nationalarchives.gov.uk/20110218135832/rds.homeoffice.gov.uk/rds/pdfs/hosb1501.pdf (accessed January 27, 2017).

37. Pew Research Center. 2007. *Muslim Americans: Middle Class and Mostly Mainstream*. Pew Research Center. http://www.pewresearch.org/daily-number/converts-to-islam/ (accessed January 27, 2017).

38. Pew Research Center. 2012. *Religion in Prisons—A 50-State Survey of Prison Chaplains*. Pew Research Center. http://www.pewforum.org/2012/03/22/prison-chaplains-exec/ (accessed January 29, 2017).

39. Anti-Defamation League. 2016. *The Washitaw Nation and Moorish Sovereign Citizens: What You Need to Know*. http://blog.adl.org/extremism/the-washitaw-nation-and-moorish-sovereign-citizens-what-you-need-to-know (accessed January 29, 2017).

40. FBI. 2011. Sovereign Citizens a Growing Domestic Threat to Law Enforcement. *FBI Law Enforce Bull*. https://leb.fbi.gov/2011/september/sovereign-citizens-a-growing-domestic-threat-to-law-enforcement (accessed January 29, 2017).

41. Gower, K. 2005. Religious Practice in Prison & the Religious Land use and Institutionalized Persons Act (RLUIPA): Strict Scrutiny Properly Restored. http://lawandreligion.com/sites/lawandreligion.com/files/ Gower.pdf (accessed January 29, 2017).

42. Knox, G. 2012. *The Problem of Gangs and Security Threat Groups (STG's) in American Prison and Jails Today: Recent Finding from the 2012 NGRC National Gang/STG Survey*. National Gang Crime Research Center. http://www.ngcrc.com/corr2012.html (accessed January 29, 2017).

43. American Civil Liberties Union. 2017. *Know Your Rights Freedom of Religion*. National Prison Project. https://www.aclu.org/files/images/asset_upload_file78_25744.pdf (accessed January 29, 2017).

44. Sturgeon, W. 2015. *Radicalization and Intelligence Gathering in Correctional Institutions—Part 2*. http:// www.corrections.com/news/article/38882-radicalization-and-intelligence-gathering-in-correctional-institu-tions-part-2 (accessed January 28, 2017).

45. Global Counterterrorism Forum. 2017. *Prison Management Recommendations to Counter and Address Prison Radicalization*. https://toolkit.thegctf.org/document-sets/prison-management-recommendations-counter-and-address-prison-radicalization/document (accessed January 30, 2017).

# 6 Gathering Information
## *The Key to the Process*

Several definitions of what constitutes the duties of an intelligence or crime analyst have been debated throughout the law enforcement community since at least 1972. This was noted in a review of numerous job descriptions from around the United States in March 2000. Although at all levels and professions these analysts perform a wide range of tasks and possess different skill sets, researchers consistently noted that gathering, analyzing, and disseminating crime information are among the daily duties of those they examined.

When gathering crime information for a law enforcement agency concerned with predefined jurisdictional limitations, most information is derived from one source, that is, the offense and incident report. The inherent restriction here is that the information reported is limited by the fact that it must be reported. Therefore this information is reactive; it must be written from the perspective of the responding officer, thus it is subjective. Other forms of information used by law enforcement agencies come from a variety of sources. Some additional information sources along with their restrictions or potential concerns are outlined as follows:

Confidential informants
*Concerns*: What is the source? Is the source documented? Has the source been blackballed? What is the source's motivation?
Covert operations
*Concerns*: What is the format of the operation? What are the jurisdictions' legal requirements? What are the time constraints or periods?
Interview and interrogation
*Concerns*: What is the legal basis for the interview? Is the case criminal or informational? What are the limitations or arrangements?
Open sources
*Concerns*: What is the source? Has the source been validated and corroborated? Is it being used as a basis for the furtherance of a case? How is it accessed?
Equipment
*Concerns*: What is the type of equipment used? What is the training of the operator of the equipment? What are the legal requirements of its use? Is it automated or manual?
Professional interchange
*Concerns*: What is the relationship? Are there any biases? Is the information factual and based on documentation or just hearsay?
In dealing with terrorism, these restrictions must be exploited and exposed. Being proactive is a must, and in order to spawn intelligence one needs as much information as possible, for without information one cannot have intelligence. There is no such thing as a bad source; there is only bad information. Information equals intelligence, and it is not the other way around. Gathering or obtaining good, clean, timely, and accurate information is the key.

## INTELLIGENCE GATHERING

The primary objective of intelligence gathering "is to deal with future danger, not to punish past crimes" (p. 129).[1] This rings especially true in the world of terrorism. Although one is not seeking to punish past crimes, one cannot discount their usefulness when attempting to understand the future.

In the world of law enforcement, intelligence has often been used in a reactive manner to formulate and establish policy.

Information is endless in terms of quantity. There are no limitations to the resources that can create useful and viable information. Perhaps the best sources of information are human sources. However, in law enforcement the use of undercover officers and informants is limited. The costs and risks associated with such operations are exponential. Also, many of the terrorist groups and organized hate groups are closed societies and difficult to infiltrate. Therefore, much of the information gathered about them comes from traditional sources such as reports, search warrants, anonymous tips, sources in the public domain, and records management systems. This information is used to populate various investigative databases.

When investigating a crime or developing answers to ongoing criminal patterns, series, or trends, law enforcement personnel often rely on numerous databases and records management systems. These systems, the majority of which are based on offense reports, are used to gain information about and insight into prior incidents with similar signatures or modus operandi. Police reports, field interview cards, property pawn transactions, public records, and traffic citations are some additional common sources of information on known criminals. Ordinary street criminals often have lengthy arrest histories and numerous encounters with law enforcement officers documented in their criminal records. Criminals do not seek to have run-ins with the law, but they do not shy away from law enforcement officers. Terrorists, on the other hand, go to great extremes to avoid detection. As noted in the profiles of the September 11, 2001, hijackers, other than a traffic infraction they had little contact with the law enforcement community. Therefore, gathering information on these individuals requires analysts to think outside the box and to identify nontraditional sources of information. One example of these sources is purchases that perhaps an ordinary person would not make, especially if in bulk. Other sources are the Internet, published material, court records, handouts, radio (including citizen band and ham radios), and self-published books such as *The Turner Diaries* and *Hunter* by Andrew MacDonald.

There are inherent difficulties in categorizing terrorism that are compounded by the shaping of policy for a type of behavior that fits poorly into more familiar categories. "Terrorist acts are both crimes and forms of warfare, and in both respects are unlike what we are used to" (p. 7).[1] With an understanding of the larger possibilities, such as warfare, law enforcement personnel are able to make informed decisions on matters concerning data collection. When gathering information, it is important to document and standardize every step of the process. This alleviates any complications when categorizing behaviors or activities and ensures that all participants in the process are on the same playing field.

Terrorism is different from street crime on many fronts. "Most crimes are the product of greed, anger, jealousy, or the desire for domination, respect, or position in a group, and not of any desire to 'improve' the state of the world or of a particular nation" (p. 7).[1] When gathering information or intelligence for homeland security, one must be cognizant of the difference between most crimes and terrorism. For terrorism-related activities, it is important for law enforcement personnel to think globally and not just make decisions about collection based on jurisdictional parameters. When dealing with terrorism, most law enforcement databases are not structured to capture information from a wide array of sources. Intelligence databases, if designed for a single-use agency, should be designed with the understanding that the information they contain may be exported for use outside the jurisdiction; otherwise, information may need to be integrated from other sources. In addition to the jurisdictional restrictions placed on an analyst and those that are self-imposed, other restrictions may include politics, interpretation of regulations, exotic military operations, and fear of impending actions.

The gathering of information can be complex or rudimentary. Regardless of the degree to which an agency is willing to develop a database, there are nine basic considerations that should be captured in detail:

1. Individuals
2. Associates

3. Relatives
4. Employers
5. Telephone subscribers
6. Organizations, groups, or gangs
7. Businesses
8. Corporations
9. Educational records/background (missing in most law enforcement data sets)

Use of these nine basic considerations for gathering detailed information on matters of homeland security, terrorism, or hate crimes will greatly aid the investigative and analytical processes, especially if the information is shared with multiple jurisdictions. It must be remembered to include owned or leased properties, for example, vehicles, office space, and the like, with respect to individuals. By doing this one can identify other potential variables to use in link analysis. These nine considerations allow for immediate link analysis and readily demonstrate interrelationships and associations. In order to do this in an expeditious manner, analysts often turn to their records management systems. There are some inherent problems with relying on only one system. If an agency is using an off-the-shelf records management system, it is generally insufficient for use as a criminal intelligence database. These systems do not usually automatically capture all the nine basic considerations. Many systems capture dispatch and self-initiated activities, but more in-depth information is needed and this will probably come from documents prepared by the first responder. Other problems center on the method or style of tabulation of data fields. Bad addresses, incorrect zip codes, and the inability to capture information from outside a particular jurisdiction are prevalent in most databases.

## ROLE OF THE FIRST RESPONDER

The gathering of information must start somewhere. In the field of law enforcement, information gathering is initiated when a responding officer, or first responder, is dispatched to, or comes upon, an incident or scene. The first responder is the eyes and ears of intelligence analysis. Traditionally, the starting point for the formal process of data gathering for most law enforcement agencies is the moment at which documentation begins and an offense incident report is generated. For years, officers have been responding to incidents, recording relevant facts, and documenting the incidents in a manner designed to encompass all elements of the crime being investigated. The importance of detailed data gathering in a post-9/11 world cannot be emphasized enough (as a once-famous fictional television character used to say, "just the facts"). Although critically important, facts are routinely centered on criminal statutes and utilized to fulfill the requirements of probable cause in order to successfully prosecute an offender. Although this is extremely important and should not be overlooked, first responders need to expand their reporting repertoire to include details that may seem mundane or inconsequential to the incident being addressed. Link analysis and corroboration of information are dependent on details, for example, telephone numbers for cell phones and pagers, addresses, apartment numbers, and property. If analysts and investigators cannot link similarities, have only generalities with which to work, or have to follow up an investigation to gain details, valuable time is wasted. Time is money, and in matters of homeland security and terrorism, time can save lives.

Officers must be trained in what to look for and on how to accurately portray or explain details in a police report in order for it to translate properly to databases. As outlined in Chapter 4, suspicious activity reports also can play a vital role in homeland security investigations. Officers should be well versed and trained in behavioral traits associated with terrorist activity. However, for awareness and training to be effective, personnel must be able to articulate the details well in writing. Everything from observations, dispatched calls, or self-initiated activity that demonstrates terrorist-related behavioral traits should be written down and processed without delay. One area that garners much information is traffic stops. Traffic stops provide perhaps the best opportunity to harvest information. Some traffic stop indicators that may provide assistance and warrant further investigation are outlined as follows:

Driver entering through a minor border checkpoint (Washington State "millennium bomber").
Driver mainly drives rental cars (Japanese Red Army and 9/11 skyjackers).
Driver adheres to major interstates.
Driver uses valid driver's license and state identification card (need to integrate with society).
Invalid or expired visas, or possession of passports.
Vehicle contains weapons, propaganda, or chemical residue.
Vehicle plates or registration differ from driver's license.
Presence of peculiar license plates or homemade plates, or absence of plates.
Bumper stickers (saying, e.g., "Abolish the IRS" or "Remember Waco").
Decorations or militia identification numbers.
Vocal resistance to documentation (citing the Constitution or the Bible)
Possession of antigovernment literature.

Human intelligence is usually the most desirable form of gathering information, but this can be extremely difficult in the world of terrorism. Officers are essentially forms of human intelligence that if trained properly without resorting to shortcuts can yield leads and details that may prove beneficial in the future. This should be evident from the reviews of some of the more notable leads and arrests that have been made possible by traffic stops initiated by road officers. A few samples of some high-profile traffic stops are outlined as follows:

2007—Interstate transportation of explosives without permits by Ahmed Abdellatif Sherif Mohamed and Youssef Samir Megahed, both Egyptian nationals.
2002—al-Aqsa Martyrs' Brigade Suicide Bombers (Israeli National Police) stopped en route to a mission.
2001—Mohammed Atta (Tamarac, Florida) ticketed for invalid driver's license and ultimately had a bench warrant issued for his arrest.
2001—Zaid Jarah (Maryland State Police), al-Qaeda 9/11 skyjacker, stopped for speeding on September 9, 2001; car was found at airport following the attacks.
2001—Hani Hanjour (Arlington, Virginia), al-Qaeda 9/11 skyjacker, stopped in vehicle with New Jersey tag and a Florida driver's license; stopped for speeding.
1999—Ahmed Ressam (Port Angeles, Washington) stopped by U.S. Customs; he possessed two Canadian driver's licenses and an airline ticket from New York to London, had a hotel reservation in Seattle, and used a route that did not require him to go through Victoria, British Columbia—millennium bomber.
1994—Timothy McVeigh (Oklahoma state trooper); he had no license plates, had a copy of *Turner Diaries*, carried a weapon, and wore a shirt that read "The tree of liberty must be refreshed from time to time with the blood of patriots and tyrants."
1988—Yu Kikumura (New Jersey state police), Japanese Red Army bomber; vehicle stopped for routine violation; led to the discovery of bomb materials.

Address data, which often come from traffic stops or details, are crucial in just about any law enforcement database. Quite often, address data are not verified or questioned. Knowledge of one's jurisdiction is something most officers have ingrained in their minds from day one. Knowledge of the community should give officers an advantage over subjects and they must possess the insight to question addresses and other information provided by subjects. A post office box number, cluster box number, packing company group box number, shelter address, or "refused" or "unknown" as a residential address is not sufficient and will only delay investigations. Another problem is the number of reports that show addresses of occurrence as being the police department, jail, impound lot, hospital, or as vague as "Smith's Department Store on Main Street." All these scenarios not only delay investigations but also negatively impact the use of analytical databases, link analysis software, and geographical information systems.

Details are the most important factor in developing quality intelligence that can be readily validated. When dealing with a typical street criminal or investigating a street crime, many investigative leads are developed through generalities such as a subject being described as a white male with a specific tattoo or mark. This is because many street criminals have encountered law enforcement officials at some point through arrests, field interviews, pawned property transactions, or traffic stops, and law enforcement systems are laden with known subject descriptors obtained from the various encounters. Thus, criminal justice information systems are lined with a wide array of relational attributes on these suspects, which once queried will provide numerous workable leads for investigators. The same cannot be said of potential homeland security and terrorist suspects. These suspects go through great pains to avoid law enforcement encounters and attempt to fit into the mainstream as everyday law-abiding citizens. Perhaps the greatest chance for a first responder to encounter potential suspects is through traffic crashes, traffic stops, or random calls for service, when potential suspects may only be seen as witnesses or neighbors at the time. Timothy McVeigh, the Oklahoma bomber, was initially apprehended for a traffic stop. Based on this, it is vitally important that first responders document in detail all encounters with individuals, including place of work, educational facility currently attended, phone numbers (beeper and cell phone), alien card, passport, driver's license, and license plate numbers. It is equally important to document details about associates who may accompany a suspect. It is just as important for investigators to remember that many road officers keep informal notes for traffic stops and encounters either on their copy of the citation that they issue or in their notebooks. Items such as mannerisms and conversations may also be noted in detail.

First responders or road officers routinely conduct traffic stops, subject checks, and field interviews. These are golden opportunities to gather information that will dramatically enhance any homeland security database. In order for this to be effective, questions must be asked in detail. One thing an officer asks for is identification. For many officers, presentation of any form of a driver's license or state-issued identification card suffices as authentic and legitimate and causes little concern or need for further questioning. However, this is a new era in law enforcement. Officers should question all forms of identification and should look for multiple sets of documents, use of different addresses, and any evidence of tampering. If other individuals are accompanying the subject, questions should be asked for the purpose of comparing intentions and knowledge of one another. Also, information obtained by the examination of vehicles or residences, in accordance with applicable laws, for signs of foreign travel (i.e., photographs, maps, video cameras and tapes, airline and hotel receipts, training manuals, and radical or questionable writings) is extremely important and should be recorded in reports, as further questions may be warranted. These items are just the beginning. Many crimes can yield further links or, through the use of search warrants, corroborate previously received information.

## CRIMES AND INCIDENTS THAT MAY YIELD INFORMATION OR LINKS

Just about any encounter with law enforcement may yield a link to the missing piece of the homeland security and terrorism analytical puzzle. The key is to have the opportunity to attain that piece, no matter how mundane or insignificant it may appear at the onset. Many crimes or incidents that first responders encounter provide the greatest opportunity for gathering valuable details for inclusion in their reports. The information received by first responders is fresh, and any reported scene is likely uncontaminated. Several types of crimes and incidents that warrant careful review and consideration in the analytical process are explored in the following subsections.

## STOLEN IDENTITIES

One type of reported crime that can be directly associated with those in the terrorism trade is that of stolen identities (use of someone else's personal information) and the issuance of fake or stolen identification papers, for example, social security cards, driver's licenses, passports, resident alien cards, military identification, and credit cards. Modern technology has made counterfeiting identification about as easy as desktop publishing. Identity crimes provide criminals access to financial venues and a way to fit into the mainstream. Identity theft is often considered a nuisance and a crime that is a challenge to investigators. This type of crime is not one that attracts the attention of the media or high-ranking members of the law enforcement community. It is viewed as a white-collar crime that lacks the violence of homicides and home invasion robberies. However, if you analyze the potential direct and indirect relationships that are possible in this type of crime, it is not difficult to fathom the potential gains that may be realized by a terrorist. One attractive feature of identity theft is that chances of detection and arrest are minimal. If apprehended, the time for which the culprit is sentenced might be minor, and the crime can be carried out by street criminals or organized enterprises using technology from just about anywhere in the world. This makes the crime more complex for local law enforcement personnel to pursue.

## FALSE IDENTIFICATION

Other problems related to the manufacture or sale of false or altered identification are possession of false identification and the lack of supporting documentation. Incidents such as these are often encountered by first responders in traffic stops or field interviews. Officers do not question the identification's authenticity unless there is some obvious indicator to do so. Although response times and minimizing the time calls are being held for dispatch are areas of concern for road patrol officers, failure to question a document's authenticity may make the critical difference. Documentation of the identification in question and responses to questions should be noted in an incident report. In the case of an arrest, impoundment of the document and making of copies, as well as notification of concerned government entities, are crucial to follow-up investigations. In the case of foreign residents, visitors, and registered aliens, identification items such as passports, alien cards, visas, airline tickets, and hotel bills are all forms of supporting documentation that should be readily accessible.

## Counterfeiting of Goods

Today, it is difficult to tell what is real and what is not because of the sophistication of today's counterfeiters. Counterfeiting to many is seen as a business, an illegal one, which has a high profit margin and low probability of apprehension. Everything from clothing, leather goods, alcohol, toys, electronic media, and pharmaceuticals are routinely counterfeited and sold worldwide. The problem is so widespread that Fortune 500 companies spend millions of dollars each year to fight counterfeiters. Some of the more popular countries that are the originating points of counterfeiting are Hong Kong, Peoples' Republic of China, Mexico, and Korea. In Asia the problem is so bad that a museum of counterfeit goods was built in 1989. Estimates demonstrate that the counterfeiting problem is worth over $500 billion in sales each year. Bogusly branded items are found displayed on the World Wide web, flea markets, businesses, and street corners. Outside of customs inspectors and trained investigators, few officers know how to differentiate a counterfeit item from a real one.

## Illegal Trafficking of Cigarettes

One type of crime associated with activities aiding terrorist groups is illegal trafficking of cigarettes and smuggling of cheap cigarettes across state lines. This is done to avoid paying taxes and to resell them at great profits. In the early 1990s, law enforcement personnel in the Miami, Florida, area conducted several operations, known as Operation Gaza Strip, targeting illegal cigarette sales and government-subsidized food stamps. The targets of the operations were mom-and-pop convenience stores, most of which were owned and operated by individuals of Middle Eastern descent and were located in low-income and high-crime areas. Allegations were raised that profits gained from the illegal acts of the subjects were being routed to individuals in the Middle East, possibly to support fundamentalist causes. State and federal charges were eventually brought against a multitude of individuals, but charges of supporting terrorism were never brought because such a possibility was not even considered at that time. Today, the climate has changed. More than 10 years after the aforementioned incident, in Charlotte, North Carolina,[2] nearly 20 individuals were charged with numerous crimes, some of which included smuggling cheap cigarettes to Michigan. The individuals were characterized as being from a Charlotte-based cell that aided terror. At least one individual of Middle Eastern descent was found guilty of sending $3,500 to the militant (terrorist) Lebanese group Hezbollah. He was also convicted on 16 separate counts and was sentenced to a series of consecutive prison terms that add up to 155 years.[2]

Cigarette traffickers can easily make somewhere between $50 and $70 per carton of cigarettes sold illicitly. Because of its great potential to make money and low penalties if apprehended, cigarette trafficking to support terrorism is quite popular. More important is the fact that various terrorist organizations have been found to be involved in such activities. Groups such as Hezbollah, Real Irish Republican Army (RIRA), Islamic Jihad, and the Kurdish Workers Party (PKK) have directly or indirectly benefited and made millions of dollars from the cigarette trafficking trade. It is important to note that research indicates Internet sales of cigarettes are somewhat prevalent in places such as Gibraltar and the Colón Free Trade Zone.

## Misappropriation

Thefts of any magnitude should be reviewed in order to identify potential internal leakages or outright misappropriation of items that can be used for illegal activities, such as construction of explosive devices. Large-scale theft, in particular, is a type of crime that poses a potential problem. Many of these crimes take the forms of truck hijackings, cargo thefts, construction thefts, industrial thefts or losses, in-transit (airlines, shipping, and railway) thefts, and military-related crimes. These crimes are attractive because of two factors: (1) Criminals are often found in, or go through, remote areas and (2) there is little or no security. Whether the theft is done to further a campaign of terror or to sell something for financial profit, large-scale thefts provide an opportunity to gain access to massive quantities of chemicals, fertilizers, explosives, fuel, technical equipment, logistical support items, and items used in the making of explosives. Items classified as explosives pose the greatest concern. However, most law enforcement personnel are unaware of the numerous items that can be used as explosives or in developing explosives, and there should be concern that any theft of these items may be classified as theft of chemicals or merely be lost in the shuffle. In addition to thefts, the mere possession of any of the explosive compound materials warrants immediate attention, but again what should law enforcement personnel be looking for? This question is addressed in the provisions of section 841(d) of title 18, *United States Code* (USC), and title 27 of the *Code of Federal Regulations* (CFR) 55.23. The director of Alcohol, Tobacco, and Firearms must publish and revise at least annually in the Federal Register a list of explosives determined to be within the coverage of Chapter 40 of 18 USC, *Importation, Manufacture, Distribution, and Storage of Explosive Materials* (Appendix E). Chapter 40 of 18 USC covers not only explosives but also blasting agents and detonators, all of which are defined as explosive materials in section 841(C) of title 18, USC. Although the list is comprehensive, it is not all-inclusive. The fact that an explosive material is not on the list does not mean that it is not within the coverage of the law if it otherwise meets the statutory definitions provided in section 841 of title 18, USC. Also, some chemicals may be inert, and if they are stolen in one jurisdiction the theft may not receive further immediate attention. The counterpart to the inert chemical may be stolen from another location by other members of a group, and the combination of the parts can create an explosive. This is why it is imperative that possession or theft of any material listed on the ATF list is identified and investigated immediately.

## Cargo Crimes

Cargo crimes, a largely unregulated area due to lack of statutory coverage, are often documented as thefts, burglaries, or robberies. There is no precise data collection process in place for cargo crimes within the United States. According to the South Florida cargo theft task force, there is as much as $25 billion in cargo direct merchandise losses each year. A single tractor-trailer can have between $1 and 2 million in merchandise that can be easily sold or used by the person who steals it, and if the culprit is captured the risk of being jailed for an extended period of time is likely to be less than that for a bank robbery. Also, robbing a bank has a high risk factor associated with it and for the most part a low return, usually about a couple of thousand dollars. Analysts should be cautious when dealing with cargo crimes. Most cargo crimes are the result of tractor-trailer thefts. This seems simple, but on many occasions the tractor is recovered in one jurisdiction and the trailer in another without the cargo. The problem with such cases is that the reporting agency may consider the case closed once one component is recovered and further review or investigation is discounted.

Another consideration regarding cargo crime is what is referred to as leakage. This is the removal of property or insertion of articles, including explosives, without tampering with or removing the container's seal. There are many methods for doing this, but the two most common are by removing bolts and panels or by drilling out rivets. Once access is gained, the subjects conduct the illegal act and reinstall the hardware without the knowledge of the driver, who may be picking up the trailer or container from a port. This process can also be reversed, and individuals may place items into a container outside the country without tampering with the seal.

Cargo crimes come in several different forms and involve a wide variety of merchandise. Some items that are routinely targeted due to their high ticket value are computers and peripheral devices, cellular telephones, cigarettes, alcohol, perfume, and designer clothing. In a 1998 publication,[3] a cargo security expert noted that access to automated computer files is of serious concern because these files contain sensitive shipping information that allows criminal insiders to case entire shiploads of containers for the most lucrative cargoes. Shipments can even be electronically passed to other destinations via computers and this may go undetected for weeks, especially if the shipment is transnational. This same article noted several emerging trends in cargo crimes. The first trend involves an insider who is part of a criminal conspiracy or is paid off. The second is international infiltration of cargo transportation systems. The third is fraud. Fourth is the widening intelligence information gap on cargo theft. The stealing-to-order phenomenon is the fifth trend, where specific items are taken in order to fill a specific request. Besides their lucrative financial advantages, cargo crimes provide an international nexus for foreign-based terrorist organizations to exploit. One area of concern focused on by cargo theft detectives is seaports. This is because seaports are critical gateways for the movement of international commerce. More than 95% of non-North American foreign trade arrives by ship. According to JayEtta Z. Hecker's[4] testimony concerning container security in 2001, approximately 5,400 ships carrying multinational crews and cargoes from around the globe made more than 60,000 U.S. port calls. More than six million containers (suitable for tractor-trailers) enter the country annually.[4]

An additional form of cargo is humans. Human trafficking or smuggling has recently been making a blip on the federal radar. Law enforcement personnel should not dismiss or overlook the amount of funding associated with human trafficking and should understand the laws associated with this form of modern slavery.

## Suspicious Vehicles

Incidents involving suspicious vehicles (especially rental vans and trucks) and suspicious persons should be immediately reviewed. Instead, these incidents are often filed away as information for future reference or are "not reported" by the responding officer, as no police action is taken. Also, civil matters such as landlord and tenant disputes or defaulting on a lease should be given consideration, particularly if they occur at strange hours or involve instances where no apparent justification is given. Reports for incidents such as those just cited should be written in great detail and include complete suspect and associate information, identification used by the suspect, actions taken by the suspect, time periods covered, vehicle information, method or form of payments made, and the existence of security monitoring videotapes, if any.

## Found or Abandoned Property

The last type of incident that may yield leads is found or abandoned property, particularly if there are symbols or foreign writings on the property. Such items often go straight to "property and evidence" rooms pending claim by the rightful owner, or they undergo some form of legal destruction. These items should not be overlooked. Property items that deserve further review are computers, packages and letters, baggage, photographs and drawings, contraband, weapons, and anything labeled with foreign markings or symbols. Certain guidelines, limitations, and restrictions must be followed regarding the entry of these items into a criminal intelligence database.

### GATHERING LIMITATIONS AND RESTRICTIONS

Gathering intelligence information and entering it into a criminal intelligence database, whether for the purposes of homeland security, monitoring terrorism, or monitoring hate groups and criminal enterprises, is governed by state and federal legislation. The predominant regulation in the United States is set out in 28 CFR Part 23, and is interpreted in guidelines updated and maintained by the U.S. Bureau of Justice Assistance. It is noted that 28 CFR Part 23 is a guideline for law enforcement agencies operating federally funded multijurisdictional criminal intelligence systems under the Omnibus Crime Control and Safe Streets Act of 1968. It provides information for submission and entry of criminal intelligence information, security, inquiry, dissemination, and review and purging. It does not provide specific information on how standards should be implemented by individual agencies.

The CFR makes it clear that entry of information into a criminal intelligence database must be supported by reasonable suspicion. This applies to databases that are shared with other law enforcement agencies; they may be classified under criminal intelligence, intelligence case information, or similar designations. On an evidentiary scale, as shown in Figure 6.1, reasonable suspicion is just above mere suspicion (a hunch) and just below probable cause, which is the standard for initiating an arrest.

The federal regulation 28 CFR Part 23, 23.20(c) defines reasonable suspicion as follows:

> Reasonable Suspicion or Criminal Predicate is established when information exists which establishes sufficient facts to give a trained law enforcement or criminal investigative agency officer, investigator, or employee a basis to believe that there is a reasonable possibility that an individual or organization is involved in a definable criminal activity or enterprise.

Case law suggests that reasonable suspicion as applied in the context of whether information should be entered into a criminal intelligence database is not necessarily the same as when applied to situations supporting the stop and frisk of a suspect. In court cases, reasonableness should be judged objectively from the perspective of a cautious and prudent law enforcement officer based

**FIGURE 6.1**   Evidentiary scale.

on the officer's experience and training. Additional guidance and information relating to reasonable suspicion can be found in the following court cases:

*Ornelas v. United States*, 517 U.S. 690, 696 (1966)
*Illinois v. Wardlow*, 528 U.S. 119, 124 (2000)
*U.S. v. Jimenez-Medina*, 173 F.3d 752, 756, 9th CA (1999)
*U.S. v. Garzon*, 119 F.3d 1146, 1451, 10th CA (1997)
*Jackson v. Sauls*, 206 F.3d 1156, 1165, 11th CA (2000)

Federal regulation 28 CFR 23.20(a) goes on to state that "a system will only collect information on an individual if there is reasonable suspicion that the individual is involved in criminal conduct or activity and if the information is relevant to that criminal conduct or activity." A 1998 policy clarification removed any ambiguity regarding information not supported by reasonable suspicion, declaring that the entry of individuals, entities, organizations, and locations that do not fall under reasonable suspicion can be included providing this is done solely for the purposes of criminal identification or is germane to the criminal suspect's activity. However, three requirements must be met prior to entering such information into a criminal intelligence database:

1. Appropriate disclaimers must accompany the information noting that it is strictly identifying information and carries no criminal connotations.
2. Identifying information may not be used as an independent basis to meet the requirement of reasonable suspicion.
3. The individual who is the criminal suspect identified by this information must meet all requirements of 28 CFR Part 23.

There is no limitation on nonintelligence information being stored on the same computer system as criminal intelligence information, provided that sufficient precautions are in place to separate the two types of information and that access is limited to appropriate personnel. Law enforcement agency personnel should be cognizant of various state public record (sunshine) laws before storing information on the same computer system. These standards are applicable only to agencies that enter information into a multijurisdictional intelligence database, such as with task forces investigating matters relating to homeland security, terrorism, and hate groups. Single-agency databases where no information is supplied outside the agency may maintain information in their agency. They would be subject to internal policies and procedures as well as state public record laws. In either scenario, personnel should be cognizant of record-purging requirements. Some locations require information and intelligence not currently active or having no activity during a specified time period, often between 2 and 5 years, to be purged.

## Gathering Information from Tips

Gathering information from tips is another gray area that should be reviewed cautiously. Limitations and restrictions concerning tips vary from state to state; but if they are entered into a multijurisdictional criminal intelligence database, they are subject to many of the same guidelines enumerated in the section titled "Gathering limitations and restrictions."

Tips are vital sources of information. They can come from a variety of sources, internal and external, such as informants; anonymous letters; tip lines such as Crime Stoppers; and e-mails and online forms, such as the one established by the Federal Bureau of Investigation (FBI) that allows anyone to submit information via the FBI website. However, it is important to remember that tips are stand-alone pieces of information that need to be evaluated, verified, and corroborated prior to being acted upon and entered into a criminal intelligence database. Tips should be kept separate or be denoted as pending verification. Every detail of the tip, including the date and time received, caller (if known), nature of the information, and investigator assigned for follow-up, should be entered into a data form in order to avoid miscommunication.

Once a tip is received, it must be assigned for a timely investigative follow-up so that a determination of status can be made promptly. If it is determined that the information does not have lasting value, it should be removed from the database. Tip information should be reviewed every 90–120 days after database entry to determine whether reasonable suspicion has been developed, thus justifying its move to the criminal intelligence database. Review processes can be continuous if warranted. However, if no real developmental activity is demonstrated on a tip, it should be purged from the system after 2 years. This ensures that a data set remains relevant to the mission at hand and is not a conglomeration of information that can possibly result in erroneous leads or links.

Regardless of whether a law enforcement agency has only an internal database, a database in which information is shared with multiple jurisdictions, or a database just for the purpose of tracking tips, there should be a written protocol to follow, as well as formal training. In addition, agencies should back up their data daily and have security measures in place to limit access and to avoid being compromised.

## INTELLIGENCE GATHERING AND INFORMATION INTERPRETATION

Interpretation of the information gathered is dependent on analytical and investigative techniques that are used to transform it into intelligence. In a publication by the Central Intelligence Agency (CIA),[5] the following was reported: "Major intelligence failures are usually caused by failures of analysis, not failures of collection. Relevant information is discounted, misinterpreted, ignored, rejected, or overlooked because it fails to fit a prevailing mental model or mindset" (p. 1). Analysts and investigators need to keep open minds, be creative in their approaches, and avoid assumptions that are not based on fact and corroboration.

Information that has been gathered according to the aforementioned guidelines, which has been properly standardized, formatted, and entered into a secure criminal intelligence database, is the starting point for the intelligence interpretation phase. However, no matter what the quality of the data or the magnitude of the database, it is analytical processes that extract the intelligence. One workflow process that is followed is referred to as the "intelligence cycle."

As noted in Figure 6.2, there are five steps that constitute the cycle: (1) planning and direction, (2) collection, (3) processing, (4) all source analysis and production, and (5) dissemination. These five steps are used to transform raw information into a finished intelligence product for use

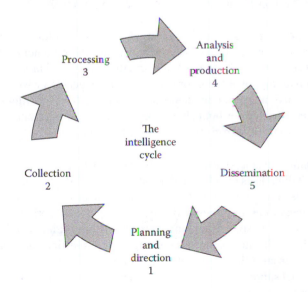

**FIGURE 6.2**    Intelligence cycle.

by policymakers. Many law enforcement and investigative entities follow this cycle, including the CIA. Regardless of who employs the intelligence cycle, the approach is the same. However, differences are likely to occur in the volume of information available, manpower, law enforcement mission, technology, and legal limitations. There are several pieces of the intelligence cycle that will remain constant but the steps will vary based on the depth of analysis. These items are jurisdictional concerns, problems, or personalities in various contexts—political, geographic, economic, military, scientific, or biographic. Also, current events, capabilities, and future trends should be examined.

In order to attain success when using the intelligence cycle, there are several basic data collection techniques as well as goals that law enforcement personnel can pursue. The goals of basic intelligence analysis are as follows:

Identify and define existing conditions
Identify, rapidly, changes in existing conditions
Accurately anticipate trends from existing conditions

In addition to pursuing the goals, analysts generally categorize or pursue leads based on three identifiable pre-incident indicators. Three of the more common breakdowns that are used for the purpose of link analysis or intelligence gathering are as follows:

1. Group related
   Ongoing campaigns
   Protests against the treatment of members
   Names, dates, commemorative actions
   Visible group preparations for activity
2. Target related
   Specific collection of threats against a target
   Actions by the target that places it in focus
   Prior activity directed against the target
3. Incident related
   Previous threats and announcements of intent
   Tips from other sources
   Equipment stolen, logistic movements, rehearsals, prior attacks

Regardless of the goals or incident indicators used, it is essential for analysts to have an approach and to know the data. Random querying based on a mere hunch or memory is like driving with one's eyes closed. Analysts must have a hypothesis or a structured analytical problem as their road map, and then they can start breaking down the information into manageable or working parts. Four general intelligence gathering and interpretation factors are outlined in the following list.[6] These four factors or the aforementioned variables or both should be used as a starting point when initiating analysis concerning homeland security, terrorism, or organized hate groups:

1. *Group information*: Name(s), ideology (political or social philosophy), history, and significant dates (including dates on which former leaders were killed or imprisoned); publications (some groups also have a Bible or manifesto that outlines their activities; current, future, or hypothetical); gatherings, meetings, and rallies (often posted in periodicals or on the Internet).
2. *Financial information*: Sources of funds, proceeds from criminal activities, bank account information (domestic and foreign); the group's legal and financial supporters (generally, anyone who writes an official letter of protest or gathers names on a petition for a terrorist is a legal–financial supporter, and sometimes an analysis of support will reveal links or mergers with other terrorist groups).

3. *Personnel data*: List of past and current leaders; list of active members and former members; any personnel connections between its members and other groups of similar ideology; group structure, particularly if the organization's pattern is based on columns and cells; skills of all group members, for example, weapons and electronics expertise and explosive training. Knowing the skills of a group is an important part of threat assessment. If the group's philosophy revolves around one leader, it is important to know what will occur if something happens to that leader. Often, an analysis of family background is useful to determine how radically a leader or member was raised and to identify military tenure or training of that person.

4. *Location data*: Location of a group's headquarters and safe houses; training facilities owned or attended; stash houses, where weapons and supplies may be stored. It is important to specify the underground to which terrorists of a group can flee. This is more difficult than determining safe havens. Terrorists usually prefer to live in communal homes rather than alone.

One way of conceptualizing the information is through the use of a table. This information when tabulated is an at-a-glance reference for investigators and analysts who view the data and an easy reference for future reports. This is demonstrated, using the data pertaining to four well-known international terrorist organizations, in Table 6.1.

Besides giving a starting point to the intelligence process, the four working parts allow for the sharing of workload among agencies or personnel. Once the intelligence gathering process is initiated and completed in detail, the basic interpretation process can be undertaken. One analytical method that can be used is referred to as the "loop effect."[7] This method was initially employed as a tactical and investigative tool, but with some minor adjustments it is easily adaptable to investigations concerning terrorism and organized hate groups, as shown in Figure 6.3. The loop effect is a step process for analysts to ensure continuous follow-through, hence the reference to loop.

Every piece of information, case, or report has a starting point, referred to as case initiation. The first two steps in the loop effect are the gathering of raw information manually and electronically. Analysts receive and categorize information as it arrives, seeking to prioritize it according to protocols and attempting to identify items that need immediate attention. Steps one and two are the triage of analytical work.

The third step of the loop effect is also an information-gathering component, but the information gathered here comes from an investigator or an analyst asking questions and looking for initial associations and verifications. Questions asked center on the five Ws, who, what, where, when, and why, and usually on how. Once the questions are satisfactorily answered, the analyst begins preliminary analysis, looking for pattern identification.

The fourth component of the loop effect is identification and documentation, and is also characterized as basic analytical techniques. These first four components, coupled with basic analytical techniques and followed by the four intelligence-gathering and interpretation parts, are only the beginning. Up to this point in the process, an analyst undertakes massive amounts of information, striving to validate and identify patterns as early as possible in the process. Tentative conclusions should not be drawn until further investigation is done to substantiate any findings and enhanced analytical steps are initiated.

Step 5 consists of enhanced analysis. During this step, an analyst transforms the information and preliminary intelligence into a viable intelligence product. Relationships and associations are elaborated and inferences drawn. Many variables are examined using a wide range of analytical techniques including spatial and temporal analyses; victim, offender, and target analyses; threat and vulnerability assessments; and financial and toll record analyses. The list of techniques and tools employed is virtually unlimited and depends greatly on the skills, abilities, and data awareness of each analyst.

**TABLE 6.1**
**Sample Intelligence Table**

| | Tupamaros (Uruguay) | Irish Republican Army (Ireland) | ETA (Basque) | Red Brigade (Italy) |
|---|---|---|---|---|
| Type and history | Revolutionary; urban student radicalism | Nationalist; second-class treatment | Nationalist; unique language | Revolutionary; economic change |
| Aim | Socialist economy | United Ireland | Own nation | Societal betterment |
| Organization | Students organized sugar workers into cells | First tried military battalions and then cells | Shadow government, central committee | Pyramidal paired cells called "brigades" |
| Strength | 2 per cell, 3,000 members | 5 per cell, 2,000 members | 700 members | 800 actives, 8,000 underground |
| Attacks | Sabotage, demonstrations | Protests, clashes, executions | Demonstrations, assassinations | Kidnapping, robbery, extortion |
| Social | Students and sympathizers | Average age 21, married with children | Average age 25, middle class | Average age 27, radicalized students, criminals |
| Support | Ideological neo-Marxist support | Relatives and friends abroad | One-third mass support, some ideological Marxist support | Many sympathizers; ideological Maoist support |
| External aid | Cuba | Russia, United States, Palestine Liberation Organization, others | France, Cuba, Russia, Libya, links to IRA, PLO | Czechoslovakia, links to Sicilian mafia |

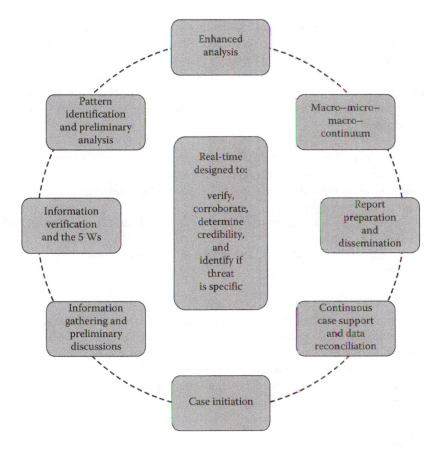

**FIGURE 6.3** Loop effect and follow-through.

Once all available resources are examined, step 6 comes into play—the macro-micro-macro continuum, which is explained in depth in Chapter 8. Analysts and investigators have traditionally gathered information, reviewed it, investigated it, drawn conclusions, and reacted. The macro-micro-macro continuum phase does not discount the work already performed, but as a precautionary measure it provides for a second look at the data to ensure that conclusions are consistent with the available variables and that the intelligence is corroborated.

Step 7 generates the end product. Analysts prepare reports, maps, and bulletins designed to aid management in making informed decisions. The final step is a given for most intelligence units: continuous case support and data reconciliation. These two steps are explained in detail in Chapter 8.

The entire loop effect is designed to work in real-time environments in order to ensure verification and corroboration of information, determine credibility, and identify specific threats and their severities. Once the basic requirements are fulfilled, analytical personnel are ready to begin the enhanced stage, that is, transforming information into intelligence.

## EVALUATING THE INFORMATION USED

Information that is retained either in an intelligence file or in an intelligence database should be continually evaluated and determined to ensure it is reliable and the content valid, prior to entering and using it in the analytical process. Source reliability can often be noted as one of four categories: (1) reliable, (2) usually reliable, (3) unreliable, and (4) unknown. Content should also be checked for validity and confirmed where known. Considering these factors, it is the classification of criminal intelligence information that is the greatest challenge when dealing with data. Classifications evolve continually and are subject to change, and the agency determines the category in which to place the data. Items classified as restricted should be based on credible facts not just because it is under the guise of homeland security. Classification systems and dissemination criteria should be defined and consistently implemented. The Law Enforcement Intelligence Unit (LEIU) recommends the following classifications:

> *Sensitive*—significant case currently under investigation, informant identification data, or reports that require strict dissemination requirements
> *Confidential*—information that is received through official law enforcement channels and is for law enforcement personnel only
> *Restricted*—reports that were previously classified as confidential or sensitive and no longer require those classifications
> *Unclassified*—information to which the general public can obtain direct access, or open-source information

It is the last classification, unclassified, that is often overlooked. On many occasions, agencies fail to check the reliability of their source, start in a higher classification listing, and work downward. The flow should go upward and be based on credible, reliable, and valid information regardless of the nature of a case. The aforementioned classifications are not all-inclusive. Chapter 7 details the proper handling of classified materials and includes particulars related to national security information. The aforementioned material is largely germane to local and state law enforcement agencies.

## CHAPTER CONCEPTS

The chapter concepts can be summarized as follows:

> The gathering of information can be complex or rudimentary. Therefore, everyone involved developing an understanding of the topic and using a standardized approach are essential.
> There are nine basic considerations when gathering information: (1) individuals, (2) associates, (3) relatives, (4) employers, (5) telephone subscribers, (6) organizations, (7) businesses, (8) corporations, and (9) educational records/background.
> Thorough gathering of information is the role of the first responder. Detailed questions including the five W's need to be asked.
> Analysts and investigators need to look beyond routine street crimes in order to identify incidents that may yield information or links to terrorist activities.
> State and federal laws and guidelines govern intelligence-gathering limitations. For entering information into a criminal intelligence system or database, reasonable suspicion is required.
> There are four types of information classifications—sensitive, confidential, restricted, and unclassified, when working with criminal intelligence information.

## REFERENCES

1. Heymann, P. B. 1998. *Terrorism and America: A Commonsense Strategy for a Democratic Society*. Vol. 7. Cambridge, MA: MIT Press, p. 129.
2. Associated Press. 2003. N. Carolina Man Gets 155 Years in Scheme that Aided Terror Group. *The Miami Herald*, final edition, March 1, 2003, p. 22A.
3. Badolato, E. 1998. Current and Future Trends in Cargo Security. *Secur Technol Des* 15:16.

4. Hecker, J. Z. *Container Security Current Efforts to Detect Nuclear Materials, New Initiatives, and Challenges*. U.S. General Accounting Office, Washington, D.C., p. 2.

5. Heuer, R. J., Jr. 1999. *Psychology of Intelligence Analysis*. Washington, DC: Center for the Study of Intelligence, Central Intelligence Agency, p. 1.

6. O'Connor, T. Counterterrorism Analysis, Intelligence Gathering and Information. http://faculty.ncwc.edu/toconnor/392/spy/terrorism.htm (accessed November 20, 2002).

7. Cooper, J., E. Nelson, and M. Ronczkowski. 2002. Tactical/Investigative Analysis of Targeted Crimes. In *Advanced Crime Mapping Topics*, eds. S. Bair, R. Boba, N. Fritz, D. Helms, and S. Hick, p. 31. Denver, CO: National Law Enforcement and Corrections Technology Center.

# 7 Enhancing Investigations
## *Going Beyond the Traditional*

Terrorist groups, regardless of their ideological ilk, geographic location, or organizational structure, have certain basic needs in common, such as funding, security, operatives/support, propaganda, and means and/or appearance of force. In order to meet these needs, terrorists engage in a series of activities, some of which are legal and many of which are not. Terrorist precursor crimes, offenses committed to facilitate a particular attack or promote a terrorist campaign's objectives, are thought to be often carried out far away from the primary theater of conflict associated with a terrorist group. Many of the precursor activities, especially regarding crimes conducted for the purpose of fundraising, take place in wealthy Western countries, including the United States. Precursor crimes, known or alleged or both, include various fraud schemes, petty crimes, identity and immigration crimes, counterfeiting of goods, narcotics trade, and illegal weapons procurement, among others.[1]

## MIDDLE EASTERN CRIMINAL ENTERPRISES

Since the 9/11 terrorist attacks, the United States has taken a new look at the various threats originating in the Middle East and from Middle Eastern communities in the United States. Contrary to a notion that prevailed prior to 9/11, the Federal Bureau of Investigation (FBI) and law enforcement community in general have come to recognize that some Middle Eastern criminal groups have no nexus to terror. Instead, these groups have the same goal as any traditional organized crime ring—to make money through illegal activities.

The groups have been active in the United States since the 1970s in areas with significant Middle Eastern or Southwest Asian populations. These organizations are often loosely organized theft or financial fraud rings formed along familial or tribal lines. They typically use small storefronts as bases for criminal operations.

What kinds of crime schemes do these enterprises engage in? They engage in many kinds of crimes: automobile theft, financial fraud, money laundering, interstate transportation of stolen property, smuggling, drug trafficking, document fraud, health care fraud, identity fraud, cigarette smuggling, and the theft and redistribution of infant formula. These enterprises rely on extensive networks of international criminal associates and can be highly sophisticated in their criminal operations. Organizations often engage in joint criminal ventures.

In the United States, Middle Eastern criminal enterprises are most prevalent in Illinois, Ohio, New Jersey, and New York. Internationally, they thrive in Afghanistan, Pakistan, Iran, Turkey, the United Arab Emirates, and Canada. Middle Eastern criminal enterprises often include criminals from Afghanistan, Algeria, Bahrain, Egypt, India, Iran, Iraq, Israel, Jordan, Kuwait, Lebanon, Libya, Morocco, Oman, Pakistan, Qatar, Saudi Arabia, Syria, Tunisia, Turkey, the United Arab Emirates, and Yemen.[2]

On March 17, 2010, FBI Director Robert S. Mueller III[3] provided a statement before the House Committee on Appropriations, Subcommittee on Commerce, Justice, Science, and Related Agencies, that furthered the aforementioned thoughts that were posed in 2007. Although the focus was on FBI priorities, concerns, and budgetary posture, the director noted that his agency's concerns included criminal organizations and enterprises. The information noted here should not be viewed as just a priority for federal law enforcement. Priorities for state and local law enforcement agencies should also include the same level of concern since the majority of the information needed to work these types of cases is found at the local level.

## FINANCING TERRORISM THROUGH VARIOUS FORMS OF CRIMINAL ACTIVITY

In 2010, the FBI director stated in his testimony that transnational/ national organized crime is an immediate and increasing concern for domestic and international law enforcement and intelligence communities. Geopolitical, economic, social, and technological changes that have taken place in the last two decades have allowed these criminal enterprises to become increasingly active worldwide. Transnational/national organized crime breaks down into six distinct groups: (1) Eurasian organizations that have emerged since the fall of the Soviet Union (including Albanian organized crime), (2) Asian criminal enterprises, (3) traditional organizations such as La Cosa Nostra (LCN) and Italian organized crime, (4) Balkan organized crime, (5) Middle Eastern criminal enterprises, and (6) African criminal enterprises. Due to the wide range of criminal activity associated with these groups, each distinct organized criminal enterprise adversely impacts the United States in numerous ways. For example, international organized criminals control substantial portions of the global energy and strategic materials markets that are vital to the national security interests of the United States. These activities impede access to strategically vital materials, which has a destabilizing effect on the geopolitical interests of the United States and places the country's businesses at a competitive disadvantage in the world marketplace. International organized criminals smuggle people and contraband into United States, seriously compromising the country's border security and, at times, national security. Smuggling of contraband/counterfeit goods costs United States businesses billions of dollars annually, and the smuggling of people leads to exploitation that threatens the health and lives of human beings. International organized criminals provide logistical and other support to terrorists, foreign intelligence services, and hostile foreign governments. Each of these groups is either targeting the United States or acting in a manner that is against the nation's interests.

International organized criminals use cyberspace to target individuals and the United States infrastructure, using an endless variety of schemes to steal hundreds of millions of dollars from consumers and the nation's economy. These schemes also jeopardize the security of personal information, stability of business and government infrastructures, and security and solvency of financial investment markets. International organized criminals are manipulating securities exchanges and perpetrating sophisticated financial frauds, thereby robbing consumers and government agencies of billions of dollars. International organized criminals corrupt and seek to corrupt public officials in the United States and abroad, including countries of vital strategic importance to the United States, in order to protect their illegal operations and increase their sphere of influence.

Finally, the potential for terrorism-related activities associated with criminal enterprises is increasing, as evidenced by the following: occurrence of alien smuggling across the southwest border by drug and gang criminal enterprises; Columbia-based narco-terrorism groups influencing or associating with traditional drug trafficking organizations; prison gangs being recruited by religious, political, or social extremist groups; and major theft criminal enterprises conducting criminal activities in association with terrorist-related groups or to facilitate the funding of terrorist-related groups. There also remains the ever-present concern that criminal enterprises are, or can, facilitate the smuggling of chemical, biological, radioactive, and nuclear weapons materials.[3]

Regardless of the crime, scheme, or scam, there is one consistent component. Criminal enterprises need funding to survive. Another truism that can be proffered is that law enforcement lacks the time, resources, and knowledge (training) to pursue financial investigations. Some law enforcement agencies, largely at the federal level, hire professional financial or fraud investigators to tackle the need to identify financial relationships. The challenge is that there are too many cases to work and too few financial investigators (FIs) to stem the tide.

## ROLE OF THE FINANCIAL INVESTIGATOR IN THE INTELLIGENCE PROCESS

The role of a police FI likely varies by agency and respective mission. However, there are some standard objectives that an FI can provide when assisting a detective and intelligence analyst:

Provide financial analysis for a variety of white-collar crime and other investigations, which involve businesses and corporations of a large complex nature, individuals, etc.

Define objectives and analyze the allegations to identify the issues and the type of evidence needed to prove criminal financial activity

Analyze a variety of records to reconstruct partial or complete histories of accounts obtained from third-party records, banks, insurance companies, etc. Cases may involve international as well as domestic records.

Determine the nature of the scheme, determine the identity and roles of subjects or victims, and provide insight into relationships

Identify and calculate the monetary value of the fraud over the defined time period.

Gather facts through such methods as interviews and analyses of financial documents and use this evidence to substantiate findings and conclusions.

Identify leads that may be beneficial to the detective for the disposition of the case.

Develop financial profiles of subjects and alerts detectives of additional findings that surface when analyzing records, including net worth analysis.

Formulate findings by compiling and reconciling reports, accounts, and bank statements using original documents and records.

Prepare reports, summarizing findings in various formats used by investigative and legal personnel in preparation for court trials.

Testify as a subject matter expert before a grand jury, trial jury, etc., as to the information obtained, chain of custody of evidence, and conclusions.

Although it has been alluded to earlier, there are numerous financial crimes for which FIs can provide valuable insight into not only the finances but also relationships. The crimes that are time consuming to investigate but for which the use of FIs can be very fruitful are outlined as follows:

Mortgage fraud
Narcotics
Organized schemes to defraud
Insurance fraud
Bribery
Mail/wire fraud
Lottery clubs
Food stamp fraud (electronic benefit cards)
Medicare fraud
Credit card fraud
Kickbacks
Money laundering
Conspiracy
Embezzlement

Thus far, the benefits of using FIs in investigations have been delineated and the types of criminal investigations that benefit from the efforts of FIs have been elaborated. An investigator or intelligence analyst must identify ways to locate assets and financial accounts. The obvious way to locate assets is by the review of bank accounts, which is done via the use of a court-ordered subpoena. There are several data components required by an FI in order to perform a comprehensive analysis, for example, check number; the nine-digit American Banking Association (ABA) number, also known as the "routing" number; account number (fractional number); front and back of the check; and credit/debit slips. Another commonly used financial resource is the Financial Crimes Enforcement Network (FinCEN) where the police financial investigator (PFI) can attain currency transaction reports (CTRs); suspicious activity reports; and Form 8300, a report of cash payments over $10,000 received in a trade business. The aforementioned methods can be construed as conventional methods to attain asset information, but there are also the less known unconventional ways to locate assets such as trash pulls, mail covers, phone tolls, and public records. Depending on the jurisdictional location, there may be specific requirements that must be met in order to use or perform the unconventional methods. Other means of identifying assets include buying something from the subject covertly, discussions with the landlord seeking applications, rent or security deposit checks, wages and earning statements, state sales tax reports (Department of Revenue), and divorce court records.

## ROLE OF FUSION CENTERS IN THE INTELLIGENCE PROCESS

Before delving into the role of fusion centers in the intelligence process, one must understand that the fundamentals of a fusion center have been practiced and have been in place at many law enforcement agencies for years. For instance, in 1993 the Miami-Dade Police Department initiated the robbery clearinghouse. Today, many agencies have initiated real-time crime centers as well as virtual fusion centers to address crime incidents within their jurisdiction.

### INTELLIGENCE-LED POLICING

The robbery clearinghouse was instituted under the auspices of a resolution adopted by the Dade County Association of Chiefs of Police and it currently serves as the department's and the county's robbery intelligence component. The clearinghouse staff's primary goal is to support investigative, operational, and deployment strategies through the collection, analysis, and dissemination of countywide robbery-related intelligence. Analytical and intelligence technological resources employed by the clearinghouse enables a forum that provides countywide "one-stop shopping" for robbery detectives. It is through the use of real-time countywide robbery intelligence that patterns are identified for immediate attention.

The clearinghouse collects and analyzes robbery-related information throughout Miami-Dade County and provides a variety of investigative services to local, state, and federal agencies that was previously unavailable. This is accomplished by the development and linking of computerized information systems, all designed to be operated within a short time frame. Details regarding the clearinghouse can be found in the September 1999 *The Police Chief* magazine under the article titled "The Robbery Clearinghouse: Successful Real-Time Intelligence Analysis."

Since the publication of that article, which denotes how successful intelligence and collaboration can be beneficial, numerous articles have been published. Some of the most heavily cited intelligence material comes from the U.S. Department of Justice's Global Justice Information Sharing Initiative. In April 2009, the department produced a document titled *Navigating Your Agency's Path to Intelligence-Led Policing*. Intelligence-led policing (ILP) seems to have many working definitions depending on the agency. The Bureau of Justice Assistance (BJA)[4] defines ILP as follows: "A collaborative law enforcement approach combining problem-solving policing, information sharing, and police accountability, with enhanced intelligence operations" (p. 4).

For the purposes of the April 2009 publication,[4] the definition was narrowed to the following:

> ILP is executive implementation of the intelligence cycle to support proactive decision-making for resource allocation and crime prevention. In order to successfully implement this business process, police executives must have clearly defined priorities as part of their policing strategy. (p. 4)

According to the April 2009 publication, ILP is a business process for systematically collecting, organizing, analyzing, and utilizing intelligence to guide the making of law enforcement operational and tactical decisions. ILP aids law enforcement agencies in identifying, examining, and formulating preventative, protective, and responsive operations for specific targets, threats, and problems. It is important to note that ILP is not a new policing model; rather, it is an integrated enhancement that can contribute to public safety. The ILP process can provide a meaningful contribution by supporting an agency's existing policing strategy, whether it is community-oriented policing, problem-oriented policing, or some other methodology. ILP is a proactive application of analysis, borrowing from the established processes of the intelligence analytic function and using the best practices from existing policing models. The ability to collect, examine, vet, and compare vast quantities of information enables law enforcement agencies to understand crime patterns and identify individuals, enterprises, and locations that represent the highest threat to the community and concentration of criminal and/or terrorist-related activity. Using this method, law enforcement agencies can prioritize the deployment of resources in a manner that efficiently achieves the greatest crime reduction and prevention out-comes. Assessment and vetting of criminal information and intelligence over a continuum also enables law enforcement agencies to examine the effectiveness of their responses, monitor shifts in the criminal environment, and make operational adjustments as the environment changes. Intelligence-led policing encourages the development and use of analytical products and tools (assessment reports, statistics, and maps) to aid personnel in defining strategic priorities for the agency (i.e., what the agency needs to do and what resources are needed to do it). It also encourages the use of both overt and covert information gathering. This approach maximizes the use of available resources and partnerships, such as those capabilities available through state and local fusion centers and local/regional intelligence centers.

The ILP philosophy centers on several key elements: executive commitment and involvement; collaboration and coordination throughout all levels of the agency; tasking and coordination; collec-tion, planning, and operation; analytic capabilities; awareness, education, and training; end-user feed-back; and reassessment of the process. These planning, organizational, and administrative steps are vital to ensure that the ILP framework is implemented in the way most appropriate for each agency's needs. The ILP philosophy is not and should not be confused with CompStat or other statistical man-agement tools; ILP is purely a complementary process to these tools.[4]

## FUSION CENTERS

With the continual focus on law enforcement intelligence and the growth of fusion centers, one may ask the question: What is a fusion center? The information provided above in intelligence-led policing demonstrates that law enforcement agencies have used intelligence for targeting crimes, developing a collaborative work environment, and instituting a framework that addresses a need.

A working definition for fusion centers can be found in the U.S. Department of Justice's Justice Information Sharing Program. The department defines a fusion center as an effective and efficient mechanism to exchange information and intelligence, maximize resources, streamline operations, and improve the ability to fight crime and terrorism by merging data from a variety of sources.

Perhaps the biggest difference between the robbery clearinghouse, ILP, and fusion centers can be found in the goals of each approach. The ultimate goal of a fusion center is to provide a mechanism by which law enforcement, public safety, and private partners can come together with a common purpose and improve the ability to safeguard the United States and prevent criminal activity. The largest differ-ence comes with the multidiscipline public safety approach to addressing man-made and natural disasters and the need to include the private sector, which may or may not be vetted to receive sensitive data.

In 2004 and 2005, many states began creating fusion centers with various local, state, and federal funds. Homeland security grant funding from the Department of Homeland Security (DHS) is per-haps the largest funding stream that sustains fusion centers, which is above and beyond the personnel commitments that individual agencies provide. Many fusion centers were derived from state agency offices of statewide intelligence or other units that performed similar functions. As of 2010, there were 72 DHS-designated fusion centers in the United States and as of 2016 there were 78, which are outlined in Appendix J.

At the time when fusion centers began to flourish, no standards or guidelines were in existence to address interoperability and communication issues with other centers at the state, regional, and federal levels. As a result, centers designed to share information were actually silos of information, incapable of information exchange. Between 2006 and 2008 various baseline capabilities and guidelines pertaining to fusion centers have been produced by an array of federal, state, and local law enforcement consortiums. The guidelines are used to provide a common operating base for centers to strive for or adhere to.

Data fusion involves the exchange of information among different sources—including law enforcement, public safety, and private sector components—and with analysis it can result in meaningful and actionable intelligence and information. The fusion process turns this information and intelligence into actionable knowledge. Fusion also allows the relentless re-evaluation of existing data in context with new data in order to provide constant updates. The public safety and private sector components are integral to the fusion process because they provide fusion centers with crime-related information, including risk and threat assessments, and subject matter experts who can aid in threat identification. Because of the privacy concerns associated with personally identifiable information, it is not the intent of fusion centers to combine federal databases containing personally identifiable information with state, local, and tribal databases into one system or warehouse. Rather, when a threat, criminal predicate, or public safety need is identified, fusion centers allow information from all sources to be readily gathered, analyzed, and exchanged based on the predicate. This is accomplished by providing access to a variety of disparate databases that are maintained and controlled by appropriate local, state, tribal, and federal representatives at the fusion center. The product of this exchange is stored by the entity taking action in accordance with any applicable fusion center or department policy or both, including state and federal privacy laws and requirements.

Many fusion centers, particularly at the state level, have adopted an all-crimes, all-hazards approach to their core mission. Large urban area fusion centers tend to be all-crimes centric, but they do maintain situational awareness to all hazards since many have a direct or indirect impact on crimes. Trying to monitor and process too much information brings many challenges to fusion centers. It is akin to trying to boil an ocean versus a pot of water. The need for executives to be in the know creates additional challenges such as staffing fusion centers 24 hours a day. Without second-guessing any one center, one can ask the simple question: Is it necessary to man and staff fusion centers 24 hours a day in today's technologically advanced world? To provide an answer or insight for this question, an agency should look no further than South Florida and its four-county (comprising Miami-Dade, Palm Beach, Broward, and Monroe) effort to develop and institutionalize what has come to be known as the "virtual" fusion center.

## Virtual Fusion Centers

Not every fusion center needs to be staffed 24 hours a day. With today's technology a virtual environment is possible. In 2008, law enforcement officials in South Florida created the South Florida Virtual Fusion Center (SFVFC), which incorporates the information sharing aspect of traditional fusion centers with the accessibility of virtual connectivity using a Microsoft SharePoint platform. The SFVFC brings relevant partners together to maximize the ability to prevent and respond to terrorism and criminal acts. By embracing this all-crimes all-hazards concept, the SFVFC is able to effectively and efficiently safeguard the region and maximize all anticrime efforts. The following is a list of partners:

Law enforcement partners
Monroe County
Miami-Dade County

Broward County
Palm Beach County
Florida Department of Law Enforcement
FBI and other federal law enforcement agencies
Regional partners
Fire/rescue
Emergency management
Health
Private partners

The SFVFC is a unique model that relates to fusion centers. Although virtual in nature, the center leverages information from its regional partners to produce a comprehensive view of the situational awareness of the region. The goals of SFVFC are to establish, enhance, and maintain collaborative relationships with all information-sharing entities in the region to create and maintain a seamless flow of communication. By reaching out to disciplines other than law enforcement, a level of cooperation and coordination is created that assists in the protection of the citizens, visitors, and critical infrastructure of the region. This leverages all possible sources of information and technology for SFVFC partners.

The core functions of SFVFC are to enable compilation and make available information from all relevant sources to anticipate, identify, prevent, and/or monitor criminal and terrorist activity.

Users are able to post their own alerts to provide situational awareness to other members of the community or to specialized work groups. These alerts can be customized by the user so that information can be disseminated in a timely and accurate manner. Information can range from finished products where all information has been checked and verified for accuracy to raw data that is provided for situational awareness as it is being developed.

## HANDLING OF CLASSIFIED MATERIALS

Information regarding handling of classified material that is available in an open forum is limited. A search on the Internet brings back limited information of value. One such website, *Defense Human Resources Activity*,[5] is the source of the following overview:

As an approved custodian or user of classified information, you are personally responsible for the protection and control of this information. You must safeguard this information at all times to prevent loss or compromise and unauthorized disclosure, dissemination, or duplication. Unauthorized disclosure of classified material is punishable under the federal criminal statutes or organizational policies.

Your security officer or supervisor will brief you on the specific rules for handling classified information that apply to your organization. Here are some standard procedures that apply to everyone:

Classified information that is not safeguarded in an approved security container shall be constantly under the control of a person having the proper security clearance and need to know. An end-of-day security check should ensure that all classified material is properly secured before closing for the night.

If you find classified material left unattended (e.g., in a rest room, on a desk), it is your responsibility to ensure that the material is properly protected. Stay with the classified material and notify the security office. If this is not possible, take the documents or other material to the security office, a supervisor, or another person who has authorized access to that information, or if necessary lock the material in your own safe overnight.

Classified material shall not be taken home, and you must not work on classified material at home.

Classified information shall not be disposed of in the waste basket. It must be placed in a designated container for an approved method of destruction such as shredding or burning.

| Proper handling of classified information | | | |
|---|---|---|---|
| Classification | Impact if compromised | Storage requirements | Transmission of information |
| Confidential | Possible damage to national security | Must be secured at the end of the work day in a GSA-approved storage container or area | Registered U.S. mail Federal Express Secure message Secure fax Authorized courier Defense courier service |
| Secret | Could cause serious damage to national security | Must be secured at the end of the work day in a GSA-approved storage container or area | Registered U.S. mail Federal Express Secure message Secure fax Authorized courier Defense courier service |
| Top secret | Could cause exceptionally grave damage to national security | Must be secured whenever not in use in a GSA-approved storage container | Secure message Secure fax Authorized courier Defense courier service |

**FIGURE 7.1**    United States Federal Government's Standards for the handling of classified materials.

E-mail and the Internet create many opportunities for inadvertent disclosure of classified information. Before sending an e-mail, posting to a bulletin board, publishing anything on the Internet, or adding to an existing web page, you must be absolutely certain none of the information is classified or sensitive unclassified information. Be familiar with your organization's policy for use of the Internet. Many organizations require prior review of any information put on the Internet.

Classified working papers such as notes and rough drafts should be dated when created, marked with the overall classification and with the annotation "working papers," and disposed of with other classified waste when no longer needed.

Computer diskettes, magnetic tape, compact discs (CDs), carbon paper, and used typewriter ribbons may pose a problem when doing a security check, as visual examination does not readily reveal whether the items contain classified information. To reduce the possibility of error, some offices treat all such items as classified even though they may not necessarily contain classified information.

Top secret information is subject to continuing accountability. Top secret control officials are designated to receive, transmit, and maintain access and accountability records for top secret information. When information is transmitted from one top secret control official to another, the receipt is recorded and a receipt is returned to the sending official. Each item of top secret material is numbered in series, and each copy is also numbered.[6]

Sensitive controlled information (SCI) is subject to special handling procedures not discussed here. Figure 7.1 summarizes and denotes the federal standard for the handling of classified material.

## SECURITY AND NONDISCLOSURE

The information provided in the section "Handling of classified material," although applicable to non-federal law enforcement personnel, is generally not applicable for most law enforcement officials. Basic security and nondisclosure of records is something that is easily adopted as a base for most law enforcement agencies. The basics to consider and utilize are outlined in this section.

Sensitive information includes the following categories:

- Active criminal intelligence—information that relates to an identifiable person or group of persons collected in an effort to anticipate, prevent, or monitor possible criminal activity
- Active criminal investigation—information gathered by a criminal justice agency in the course of conducting an investigation of a specific act or omission
- Law enforcement sensitive (LES)—information that could adversely affect ongoing investigations, create safety hazards for officers, divulge sources of information, and/or compromise the identities of investigating officers
- For official use only (FOUO) or sensitive but unclassified (SBU)—information that warrants a degree of protection and administrative control.

Personnel must acknowledge and understand that the unauthorized disclosure to unauthorized personnel or the negligent handling of sensitive information could jeopardize sources of information, damage or irreparably injure ongoing or future investigations, or place persons at risk. Accordingly, personnel should not disclose, publish, release, transfer, copy (whole or in part), or otherwise make available any information obtained in the scope of their law enforcement function, except as provided by agreement or general orders, and must keep all relevant information made available in confidence and prevent its unauthorized disclosure. But this restriction does not apply to information that was in the public domain at the time it was disclosed, or information that is disclosed pursuant to the provisions of a court order.

However, personnel should acknowledge that any information obtained from the public domain is not disseminated if, in its dissemination, relevant and sensitive information regarding a criminal or intelligence investigation may be compromised or plans pertaining to the mobilization or deployment of tactical operations involved in responding to emergencies are thwarted.

## SOURCE DEVELOPMENT AND USE IN INVESTIGATIONS (HUMAN INTELLIGENCE)

Use of informants is a basic weapon in the fight against crime and informants are a judicially recognized source of information. An informant's motivation should be carefully evaluated in determining the extent to which information provided by the individual can be relied on. Some work for money, some for revenge, some for court-ordered requirements, and others for the pursuit of doing the right thing.

A source is a person who provides information of an investigative nature to law enforcement personnel either confidentially or overtly. Many are compensated financially, whereas some are compensated otherwise through means such as court-ordered sanctions. A source is also encouraged, controlled, or directed by a law enforcement officer either overtly or covertly. Using the aforementioned material, law enforcement personnel should note the differences between a true source and those personnel who report to have snitches or informants. Without downplaying the use of such individuals, this section refers to the use of controlled and documented persons as sources.

There are essentially four categories of sources used by law enforcement personnel:

1. Anonymous source
2. Nonconfidential source (open)
3. Confidential source
4. Unwitting source

In an effort to avoid the release of industry practices, information pertaining to source development and handling procedures has been streamlined and limited to information gleaned from open sources.

## SOURCE DEVELOPMENT AND HANDLING PROCEDURES

Source development and handling procedures should be developed and used to augment already existing confidential informant procedures being used by law enforcement agencies. There are numerous terms that need to be identified and are routinely used when working with sources. Terms noted in this section are not all-inclusive, and they should be used in the context of applicable laws. Some of the terms used are outlined as follows:

Domain—sector, assignments, or groups that have an impact on the jurisdiction
Source—person who is knowledgeable in a field of interest and is not handled by any one detective
Informant—implies a criminal nexus and procedures governing such are in accordance with
    departmentally established procedures
Levy—tasking of source; every contact should end with a tasking

## SOURCE MANAGEMENT

Training of agency personnel is essential when working with and understanding sources. Biannual assessments should be conducted on current domains to determine resource allocation for source and intelligence development. Personnel should utilize domain assessments provided by analysts, current local and international events/changes affecting the domain, detective assessment/opinion, and other pertinent data to make proper adjustments in resource allocation. It is also important to maintain awareness of possible conflicts with other cases, and source report deconfliction should be done on a routine and continual basis. Source deconflicters should be tasked with meeting to discuss source reporting and meeting with other agencies to ensure efforts are not duplicated. This maximizes the effective utilization of resources.

Analysts should create and maintain fluid domain assessments to ensure accurate and effective data as it pertains to the domain. Data should comprise all available resources of information and must be noted along with the deriving source, date acquired, and location and name of originating source. Efforts should be made by analysts to identify intelligence gaps within domains and create target packages by providing all pertinent data to assist detectives in filling the gap. Domain assessments should remain fluid and be reviewed every 14 days to ensure the data is current, and pertinent information is updated. Changes should be noted in detail and all prior information should be retained in order to document continuity. Domain assessments are sensitive documents and must be treated as such following existing procedures and protocols. Release of assessments outside the concerned agency requires the approval of a supervisor and must be documented. Assessments should be treated as sensitive material and carried by hand during any transmission. Under no circumstance should assessments be transmitted via electronic correspondence unless in an approved and secure venue.

## OPEN-SOURCE REPORTING

Investigators should identify open sources by name and provide basic contact information for the open source. Other biographical information is helpful, although not required. A confidential source manager (CSM) should be used and established. A CSM is responsible for all sources and overall source dossier management, as well as ensuring that confidential sources are being utilized properly and contact is being maintained by managing detectives.

An agency's command staff should have a clear picture of source capabilities and the source network. In the event a detective needs a source in a certain community or has access to a certain job, field, or group, the CSM can help identify a possible match and guide the detective toward the source's handling detective. Responsibilities of the CSM also include maintaining a dossier sample and keeping the format up to date. The CSM needs to identify sources by source number and basic demographic information, including

Sex
Age range (e.g., 20–25 years)
Ethnicity
Physical characteristics
Access (what do they do, what domain they have access to, member of which specific group, etc.)
Educational level
Languages spoken
Handling detective
Source dossier procedures should be amended to include the following source biography data:
Level of education
Languages spoken
Membership in organizations
Hobbies
Extended family relationships
Detective inquiries into source biases, motivations, training progress, effectiveness, and perso-
    nal opinion to facilitate source use by another detective
Religious and political affiliations
Personality assessment

## CONFIDENTIAL SOURCE MANAGEMENT AND REPORTING

Analysts need to utilize confidential source reporting to update domain assessments. Identify confidential sources by "Source" and source number in reports. Any inquiries to source information need
to be referred to the handling agent for further clarification and applicability. Sources should be developed to meet the needs of intelligence gaps in agency-identified domains. Sources need to be identified as open and confidential sources.

Open sources include human sources who routinely provide information of value to the law enforcement community. They require little or no anonymity and a low level of protection. On the other hand, a
confidential source requires a high level of anonymity and protection. Open and confidential sources
should be contacted every 14 days (by telephone or personal) at a minimum. All contacts must be documented in a source dossier and should include type of contact, times, and synopsis of conversations. All
information needs to be reported, regardless of perceived or real investigative value. Detectives should
remember to continually test, train, evaluate, and levy their source during every contact.

In the November 2010 edition of the *FBI Law Enforcement Bulletin*, Dreeke and Sidener[6] highlight some attributes of proactive human source development that coincide with the aforementioned
procedures. They cite a hierarchal relationship-building process that starts with identifying the need
and progresses toward creating the ideal resume for the person or thing that is needed. The handler,
who should be open to and observant of opportunities, then observes where the sources live, work,
and play. The authors point out that once they understand the stages of the relationship-building process, detectives should remind themselves of the following ideals[6]:

Exhibit selflessness, tolerance, genuineness, sensitivity, integrity, and humility.
Refrain from correcting or improving anyone else with whom they are speaking.

Regardless of the legal process and procedures used when developing or working with human
sources, detectives should remember the importance of ongoing subject assessments. People change
over time and subject assessment is the cornerstone that will help to yield the most reliable information.

## CHAPTER CONCEPTS

The chapter concepts can be summarized as follows:

Middle Eastern criminal enterprises have the same goals as traditional organized crime rings, which is to make money through illegal activities.

Transnational/national organized crime is an immediate and increasing concern for law enforcement and intelligence officials.

An FI can be valuable to law enforcement officials for identifying criminal enterprise financial schemes.

Intelligence-led policing is a business process that has been around, in various forms, and continues to be used by law enforcement officials through clearinghouses and fusion centers.

Fusion centers have a set of developed baseline standards that are being adopted by 72 recognized centers of the DHS.

Handling of classified materials must be understood, and the various classifications associated with sensitive national security information.

Source development, handling, and procedures associated with using information for investigations need to be understood.

## REFERENCES

1. O'Neil, S. 2007. *Terrorist Precursor Crimes: Issues and Options for Congress*. CRS Report for Congress. Congressional Research Service, Washington, DC, p. summary.
2. Federal Bureau of Investigation (FBI). 2007. *Middle Eastern Criminal Enterprises*. Washington, DC. http://www2.fbi.gov/hq/cid/orgcrime/middle_eastern.htm (accessed January 18, 2011).
3. Nylan, L. 2010. *Mueller Prepared Testimony on FBI's Fiscal 2011 Budget*. Washington, DC. http://www.mainjustice.com/2010/03/17/mueller-prepared-testimony-on-fbis-fiscal-2011-budget/ (accessed January 18, 2011).
4. Bureau of Justice Assistance. 2009. *Navigating Your Agency's Path to Intelligence-Led Policing*. Washington, DC, pp. 3–7.
5. Defense Human Resources Activity. 2011. *Handling Classified Information*. Arlington, VA. http://www.dhra.mil/perserec/csg/s1class/handling.htm (accessed January 18, 2011).
6. Dreeke, R., and K. Sidener. 2010. *FBI Law Enforcement Bulletin, Proactive Human Source Development*. Washington, DC, p. 7.

# 8 Working the Puzzle One Piece at a Time
## *Learning to Anticipate Behavior*

No single profile exists for terrorists with regard to background or personal characteristics. The differences in the origins of terrorists in terms of their society, culture, and environment preclude such a universal approach as a single profile for foreign or domestic terrorists.[1] Much like understanding or interpreting languages, analysts and investigators need to have a familiarity with, if not a total understanding of, the cultures of the individuals they are investigating. Many open-source information venues exist that can provide invaluable assistance in this matter. No matter how much someone attempts to assimilate into a society outside their own, there is a likelihood that they will revert back to something from their culture. It is law enforcement personnel's job to identify these behavioral differences.

Chapter 2 contains an analogical reference to building the investigative or intelligence puzzle one piece at a time. The reference has to do with an analyst or investigator putting a picture together one piece at a time, using various tools of the trade. But this is not true for all cases, and a bit more clarification is needed. Cases having a nexus to homeland security are inherently going to be different in that personnel will be working with a piece that is not a corner or a straight edge. Figure 8.1 demonstrates a piece in the middle of the puzzle, and traditional crime analysis as puzzle pieces with corners and straight edges. Even this may not always be true; it is more likely that homeland security cases are going to fall in the gray areas of standard investigative techniques. These gray areas will not have straight edges or corners with which to initiate the building of puzzles. The complexity, sensitive nature, and political nature of homeland security or terrorism cases present challenges not regularly seen by law enforcement personnel since the days of organized crime and large-scale narcotics rings. Modern law enforcement personnel may have lost some of their strategic investigative prowess over the last several decades and transcended into an environment of instant gratification through arrests and case clearances, thanks in part to the use of computers. This is evident from the impact that the CompStat process has had on agencies, many of which worked solely on analyzing Uniform Crime Report Part I crimes—statistical management, if you will.

Today, there is a need to prevent the next terrorist attack. One of the leading intelligence agencies in the world, the Central Intelligence Agency (CIA), encourages the use of alternative analytical approaches in understanding complex transnational issues such as terrorism. In traditional crime analysis, analysts have struggled with forecasting crime patterns, often based on historical events. With homeland security threats, forecasting is not necessarily successful. The use of alternative analytical approaches is more beneficial than just the use of technology in such cases. New approaches such as using calendars, tracing e-mails and Internet protocols, and restructuring data sets shed new light on topics. Analysts must also be mindful of potential failures when conducting analysis and testing hypotheses. Whether thinking out of the box or pursuing the use of new technology or tools, analysts are likely to be working with deficit data. The reasons for this are a lack of specific variables with which to work, missing data, as well as a worldwide theater. Techniques such as timelines, association matrices, link analysis, and data sorting are, and will continue to be, staples in the analytical toolbox. These initiatives and forecasting events will continue to be frequently used techniques. However, instead of just forecasting the next attack or performing automated processes, an analyst or investigator should strive to look for behavioral patterns. Anticipating behavior patterns can be done at both the individual and the group levels. People are predictable and are creatures of habit, if one is patient and skilled enough to locate the cues. There are a multitude of possible places to look for the puzzle pieces, usually in a data set.

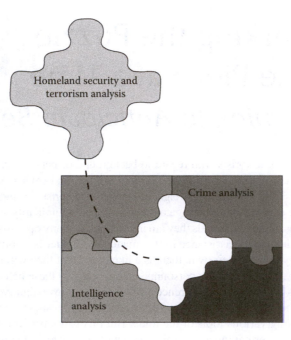

**FIGURE 8.1** A piece in the middle of a puzzle: In homeland security and terrorism analysis, the law enforcement community will likely not have the luxury of corners or straight lines. They must work the complex maze of information often from just one piece that may rest in the middle.

Since the days of organized crime and narcotics, arguably the biggest change in law enforcement investigative techniques and tools has been the advent of the personal computer and office networks. With this change, agencies have had the opportunity to mine and further data capturing and extraction initiatives. However, the instant gratification component and the decades that have passed may have weakened the law enforcement strategic skill set, including inductive and deductive reasoning skills.

## DATA SET CHALLENGES

Perhaps the greatest challenge in the information, analysis, and intelligence process is that of obtaining clean data. Imagine working with somewhere between 30% and 80% of the information from your jurisdiction—and probably even less if data is obtained from another agency that you are hoping to merge with yours. This is the situation faced by many law enforcement agencies. The reason is that data systems, for example, computer-aided dispatch (CAD) and data tables, are geographically specific to a jurisdiction. For traditional Part I crimes this is a challenge, but for homeland security this can be detrimental.

## NAMES AND ADDRESSES

Data in many analytical systems stem from CAD imports. The data are raw and limited to the accuracy at the time of reporting and the accuracy of the data entry specialist. Some agencies validate their data against geographic layers and addresses that do not match are, at times, removed from their data set. Addresses from outside the jurisdiction, such as those of visitors from outside the country, are sometimes entered into the comments section. This translates into the data dump that is requested, now lacking these addresses because the extraction is made from the primary data table and not the comments section. Figure 8.2 shows a fairly detailed data entry format and query screens that are used by an analyst. In this figure, which is comparatively typical in many law enforcement agencies, there are some

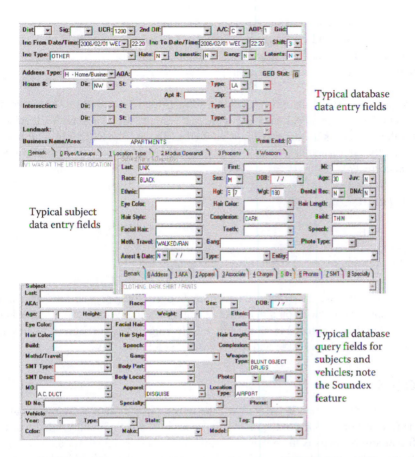

**FIGURE 8.2**    Traditional law enforcement databases are often agency/jurisdiction specific.

inherent problems: First, where and how would one enter a hyphenated name, a name with a suffix such as "Jr." or "III," and a multipart Hispanic or Arabic name? Second, where would one enter an address from outside the home country or, for that matter, an address from Washington, DC, for example, 2950 Constitution Avenue, NW, Suite 303? Third, there is no designated field for a country code or formatting for a postal code, which is the sister to the United States zip code. Fourth, in this world of political correctness, there are no identifying fields for religion or schooling. Fifth, where would one enter multiple known addresses, and which one gets designated as the primary? Finally, what about post office boxes or military addresses?

The first item deals with the mainstay of many law enforcement endeavors: names. Many names throughout the world have long-standing cultural origins. Some denote the region or city where they are based, whereas others provide a descriptor denoting the family's line of work. It is likely to be the cultural aspect of naming conventions that poses the greatest obstacle for law enforcement. Although analysts like to categorize names as belonging to a country, it is the culture that may disclose the information needed to successfully understand the links. One group of names that has received little attention is Arabic names. Some of the issues that should be understood when dealing with Arabic names are outlined as follows[2]:

Arabic names include given name, father's name, grandfather's name, and last name.
Women's names are the same, but with a female first name.
After marriage, women's names include female first name, husband's name, and husband's last name.
*Bin* or *ibn* in a name refers to "son of."

Hyphens are used in Arabic names to draw associations.

Names with KH, DH, and GH in them denote that the name is composed of Arabic characters without a Roman alphabet or phonic equivalent.

Many names note city of origin, for example, Tikrit in Iraq = Al-Tikrit.

These are just some of the daunting challenges regarding names that law enforcement personnel must come to understand and deal with. In Figure 8.2, note the use of a Soundex feature. This is used to deal with the numerous spelling mishaps as well as the multiple ways in which a name can be spelled, especially Arabic names. Just look at the variations that can be found for Sayyed Qutb. Which one is correct?

a. Syed Qutb
b. Sayed Qutb
c. Sayyad Qutb
d. Sayad Qutb
e. Sayyid Qutb

Addresses and locations are perhaps the next challenge. Not everyone follows a world atlas and observes geographic boundaries on a map. Many cultures in the world are, and have been for centuries, nomadic, clannish, and tribal in nature, often following different religious values and traits. For instance, where are Czechoslovakia and the U.S.S.R. on a map today?

## DATA TOOLS

Data come from many sources. Besides CAD, the most common data source is documentation prepared by the first responder. One of the most comprehensive, but underanalyzed, documents prepared by law enforcement officials is the traffic accident report. Figure 8.3 shows an example of the information collected from many traffic accidents. These forms are scrutinized largely due to their financial (insurance) implications and may not be entered in detail to a database outside of raw CAD data. From a law enforcement perspective, these forms are cumbersome and require a fair amount of time to complete. The forms are rarely analyzed for much more than identifying problem intersections, or as a base for studies such as racial profiling. However, from an analytical point of view, especially when seeking out individuals trying to avoid law enforcement encounters, these forms provide a tremendous amount of detail on both parties as well as all the individuals involved directly or indirectly, including witnesses. Names, addresses, identification, insurance carriers, relatives, associates, photographs, and vehicles are just some of the details that can be accessed.

Computers and numerous software packages (e.g., Pen-Link, I2, and GuideSTAR Technologies' Raptor™) are all powerful and excellent analytical tools that aid in everyday analysis as well as in developing strategic intelligence. They can even assist in overcoming some of the aforementioned obstacles. However, for some agencies these software packages and suites are cost prohibitive due to licensing, support, training, and hardware issues. Other tools such as the Microsoft Office suite, primarily Microsoft Access, Share Point, and Excel are readily available, but like most software packages they are not utilized to their fullest potential. This is generally due to the operator's comfort level with the product and overall knowledge of the tool's capabilities, as well as lack of training. Regardless of which software or hardware tools are used, reliance on any of them to perform analysis should be carefully monitored. Any analytical/intelligence tool is good, but one should not let the tools or limited knowledge of them drive the analytical process. It must be remembered that someone programmed the tools to perform a task or identify relational data. The primary problem that exists is the lack of knowledge concerning the data table. Users get too comfortable with the data entry interface and fail to see the true power of the query capabilities of such tools. The most powerful query tool and computer is already built into all analysts: the brain and common sense. Computers are great but

**FIGURE 8.3**  Typical representation of details collected in most traffic crash/accident reports.

they only do what someone directs or programs into them. Prior to the age of computers, strategic cases were successfully made, and when one started learning math, calculators were not allowed. One first learned to do things the hard way. Many analytical/intelligence training courses and scenarios are heavily focused on computers and software packages; thus analysts are forgetting to employ their own computer as another tool. With homeland security and terrorism analysis, it is important to use Soundex features, Boolean strings, and wildcard queries. These are invaluable tools but few understand how to use them, largely due to letting the software perform the link analysis.

## IDENTIFYING WHAT IS NEEDED

In Heuer's analysis of competing hypotheses (ACH), which is explained further in Chapter 9, there is a reference to making a list of significant evidence. The only caution here is that personnel should do everything possible to shy away from checklists. The reason for this is that checklists are seen as milestones and can give a false sense of security, because as they are checked off it is easy to assume that the issue has been addressed and put to rest. Just as in ACH and the macro-micro-macro continuum, all aspects should be reconsidered or reevaluated. One way to bring all aspects of the two approaches—common sense and the desire for a checklist—together is through an approach referred to by the author as KNED (known, needed, and expected direction) (Figure 8.4). The KNED diagram is used as an approach to extract information that is often overlooked when visualized. This approach trains the visual senses into seeing the entire picture.

Computer programs are limited in their logic capabilities. As simple as the KNED process appears on the surface, the author has noted over the past 2 years of teaching this approach through the use of real cases, that many analysts and investigators who rely heavily on computer-based programs struggle with it. Those who grasp the concept, however, actually match and outdo computer software in the classroom. Another difficult issue is the desire of personnel with arrest authority to develop probable cause and establish the elements of a crime. There is nothing wrong with this desire, but one should be

| KNOWN | NEEDED | EXPECTED |
|---|---|---|
| | | |
| | | |
| | | |
| | | |
| | | |
| | | |
| | | |
| | | |
| DIAGRAM WORKING AREA | | |

**FIGURE 8.4**   The known, needed, and expected direction (KNED) approach.

cautioned that there is an underlying desire to focus on the crime and when the elements are not clear the information will be dismissed or forgotten, or other variables will not be pursued. Law enforcement personnel are faced with information overload. Therefore, one must be able to process and make sense of information as it becomes available. One caution though is not to put the most recently received piece of information on the top of the pile. Information should be processed in its entirety as it is received. By jumping ahead, the validation of data suffers and something will eventually be forgotten or overlooked.

To demonstrate the use of Figure 8.4, the following small sample statement can be used: April 2006—an off-duty sheriff deputy working as a security guard at a cigarette wholesaler reports that four men have come into the business and purchased 299 cases of cigarettes. The entire transaction cost was just under $30,000.

This example is from a real case, and while teaching this approach the author has found that many law enforcement personnel immediately focus on the significance of the 299 cases and the $30,000, whereas others want details on the four men. They immediately surmise that they are dealing with cigarette smuggling or a financial crime. When queried about what information they want regarding the four men, the response often is "a complete workup." Can someone please define complete workup or even advise what systems or resources they would check? This varies depending on the person's skill set, knowledge of data resources, and the available technology. In this scenario, there is no mention of a crime anywhere. And why focus on the four men? Is there enough to work with, and is there any relevance? Is someone striving for an arrest to close the case? There are many other opportunities to glean information, if one knows where to start. Traditional law enforcement training focuses on the subject, and this variable is often described as a male between the ages of 16 and 24 years. Additional training exploits the use of technology and use of computers. However, personnel have leaped into the computer age and often forget to use the most powerful computer available to them, their brain. Reliance on computers and software can be detrimental if they are not seen as what they are—analytical tools. There is a need to understand the process just like when first learning mathematics. One does not start learning with the use of a calculator.

Let us break down the aforementioned scenario: (1) We know that a deputy reported something he thought was unusual or suspicious. We need to speak with this deputy. We expect to understand the circumstances through the deputy's eyes—subjectivity is always involved. (2) We know the deputy is working off duty. We need to know how long he has been working there. We expect to understand what is considered normal and the time frames involved. (3) We know that we have a cigarette wholesaler. We need to obtain the corporate and business records, and know who hired the off-duty deputy. We expect to identify principal parties and understand the volume of business being conducted. (4) We know that four males entered and made a purchase. We need a description of the males, who of the four made the purchase, how it was made, and the method of transportation used to get to the business. (5) We know that 299 cases were purchased. We need the significance of 299. Is there a different reporting requirement for 300? We also need to know the weight and how much is contained in a case. We expect to identify a possible violation threshold as well as the possibility of a method of transportation, if we are dealing with significant weight. (6) We know that the entire transaction cost just under $30,000. We need to know the significance of the dollar amount and how the transaction was completed, whether in cash, check, or credit. We expect to identify whether there is a reporting threshold and to identify account ownership information. (7) We know that we are dealing with a business in which large monetary transactions are common. We need to know if there was a surveillance or camera system and what types of recorded documents are kept. We are expecting possible identifications.

As can be seen, there is a tremendous amount of information that can be extracted from just a brief description. Is this overkill? Not if one is working on homeland security cases. The experience and training of the law enforcement professional and available time when working the KNED process will come into play, and overkill will be avoided. If we had just worked the typical reaction of looking for a crime, this information may have languished somewhere until further obvious developments had taken place. Once the "needed" column is compiled, one has a working list of leads that fellow investigative team members can work on. Once this is worked on, the information gleaned from the needs are brought back to the team and reevaluated using the macro-micro-macro continuum. The process is then initiated again, based on the reconciled and validated information. There will also be a method to confirm whether a lead has been worked or not; documented details are essential. If this information had gone directly to a data entry clerk and been entered into a database, it may never be directly reviewed. Should the information have come in through a tip, there is another chance that it would be assigned for follow-up and eventually taken at face value, usually within 30–120 days.

It has been suggested by some law enforcement officials that a fourth column titled "Outcome" could be added to KNED. The problem with this column is that someone could easily see that an outcome is noted and dismiss the entire line item as being completed. Also, one should always have an "expected direction" for every line item. The reason is, without this entry one is just fishing. Whoever is assigned the particular needed item needs direction since they may not be familiar with the case details. Each line item should be done completely from left to right. The author has witnessed individuals tackle this initiative one column at a time. By doing so, one is driving with one eye open and will eventually struggle when it comes to completing the last column. One can spend an inordinate amount of time applying this approach to all data. That is where experience and training kicks in, and one knows where to the draw the line.

## FORMS OF ANALYSIS THAT CAN BE USED TO IDENTIFY THE MISSING PIECE

There are many different ways in which to view and contrast data variables. There is no one right way that works for every occasion. Analysts are encouraged to use multiple forms, usually three, in an attempt to validate their hypotheses. Not all forms utilize or draw from the same data set, and various software packages that perform the same base function can result in different outcomes. Some of the more common forms of analysis are outlined as follows:

Spatial: Geographic information systems (GISs) use techniques to examine and explore data from a geographic perspective to develop and test models, and to present data in ways that lead to greater insight and understanding, largely from a visual perspective. This is done through layering geographically matched data over a base map.

Temporal: An attempt to understand items that are related by, or limited in time, as well as time patterns within data.

Tempo: Looking for a characteristic or rate of activity, or pace, in a data set. This can be done by time, day, date, or other events such as lunar and solar events.

Victim: Attempt to understand behavior or characteristics that can be attributed to the target of the incident. This applies to individuals or a group of individuals.

Subject: Attempt to identify behavioral characteristics or traits of a person responsible for a particular action. This may include ideological beliefs, statements, direct actions, and associations.

Target: Attempt to understand weaknesses or vulnerabilities attributed to a location or symbolic venue. Applies primarily to physical structures; however, this can be applied to individuals who have a strong correlation with, or can be construed as being the same as, the venue either through name or address.

Tactic: Means to achieve a goal, or a course of action followed in order to achieve an immediate or short-term goal. This includes type or methodology used to pursue or obtain a goal.

Homeland security and terrorism analysis places emphasis on items that have significance. Terrorists perform their own analysis and develop intelligence. They learn from their predecessors; therefore, analysts need to identify past events. In this section, the focus is on two of the aforementioned analytical forms employed when reviewing prior events: (1) temporal and (2) tempo. The most common is temporal. The approach to these efforts often centers on the use of a calendar. However, there is more to consider when it comes to dates, and they are, or may not be, what they appear.

## USE OF CALENDARS AND SIGNIFICANT DATES IN ANALYSIS

Calendars and dates have been used in crime analysis fairly consistently in order to represent crime patterns or trends. The identification of days that have historically had occurrences has been utilized in the development of operational and deployment strategies. Use of calendars and dates has been parlayed into many aspects of homeland security and terrorism analysis. One problem is that there are differences between the analyses.

Calendars and dates, although used routinely in analysis and intelligence, can potentially be misused and provide misinformation. The reason for this can be found in the 40-plus calendars currently in use as well as the lack of understanding by many of this matter. Also contributive is the inherent nature of a person to use what is known, and subliminally adopt as a standard something that everyone uses. Many other variables can be found when using different calendars, such as years, dates, eras, and religions. When working with calendars it is important to remember there are essentially three types of calendars:

1. Calendars based on rules. These calendars are specified completely in terms of rules that are independent of astronomical events. Examples are the Gregorian, Julian, and Mayan calendars.
2. Calendars based on astronomical observation. These require the observation of celestial phenomena (e.g., the first appearance of the crescent moon after a dark moon, the astronomical conjunction of sun and moon). The Islamic calendar is of this type.
3. Calendars based on astronomical calculation. These calendars have been based on astronomical observation, but the development of astronomical theory calculation of the times of astronomical events has replaced observation. Examples are the Jewish and Chinese calendars.

The Islamic calendar has drawn a considerable amount of attention. It is lunar in nature and follows astronomical observations. Figure 8.5 demonstrates the difference between an Islamic and a Gregorian calendar for the calendar year 2006 (there are about 33 Islamic years to every 32 Gregorian). Having brought this aspect to light, is there any significance as to why September 11, 2001, was chosen for one of the most catastrophic terrorist events?

## When is 9/11 Not 9/11?

The title of this section can cause one to believe that there are only a handful of possibilities. In fact, there are over 40 calendars in use throughout the world. A sampling of some of the dates associated with the question posed in the title of this section is outlined as follows:

Gregorian
9/11/01
Julian
8/29/01
Mayan
12.19.8.10.1
Persian
1310 Shahrivar 20
Indian
1923 Bahadra 20
Hebrew
5761 Elul 23
Bahá'í

## SAMPLE COMPARISON OF ISLAMIC CALENDAR VS. GREGORIAN
### ISLAMIC DATES BEGIN AT SUNSET THE PRECEDING EVENING

| NY = NewYear | Aa = Aashurah | MN = Miladun-Nabi | IM = Isra/Me'raj | NS = NisfuSha'ban | RM = Ramadan | LQ = Lailatul-Qadr | EF = Eidul-Fitr | YA = Yaum-Arafah | EA = Eidul-Adha |
|---|---|---|---|---|---|---|---|---|---|

Solar Eclipses
T = Total  A = Annular  H = Hybrid(Tot./Ann.)  P = Partial

Lunar Eclipses
t = Total(Umbral)  p = Partial(Umbral)  n = Penumbral

**January**
*ZHJ 1426/MHM 1427*

| S | M | T | W | T | F | S |
|---|---|---|---|---|---|---|
| 1 | 2 | 3 | 4 | 5 | 6 | 7 |
| ZH | 2 | 3 | 4 | 5 | 6 | 7 |
| 8 | 9 | 10 | 11 | 12 | 13 | 14 |
| 8 | YA | EA | 11 | 12 | 13 | 14 |
| 15 | 16 | 17 | 18 | 19 | 20 | 21 |
| 15 | 16 | 17 | 18 | 19 | 20 | 21 |
| 22 | 23 | 24 | 25 | 26 | 27 | 28 |
| 22 | 23 | 24 | 25 | 26 | 27 | 28 |
| 29 | 30 | 31 |  |  |  |  |
| 29 | 30 | NY |  |  |  |  |

**February**
*Muharram 1427*

| S | M | T | W | T | F | S |
|---|---|---|---|---|---|---|
|  |  |  | 1 | 2 | 3 | 4 |
|  |  |  | 2 | 3 | 4 | 5 |
| 5 | 6 | 7 | 8 | 9 | 10 | 11 |
| 6 | 7 | 8 | 9 | Aa | 11 | 12 |
| 12 | 13 | 14 | 15 | 16 | 17 | 18 |
| 13 | 14 | 15 | 16 | 17 | 18 | 19 |
| 19 | 20 | 21 | 22 | 23 | 24 | 25 |
| 20 | 21 | 22 | 23 | 24 | 25 | 26 |
| 26 | 27 | 28 |  |  |  |  |
| 27 | 28 | 29 |  |  |  |  |

**March**
*Safar/Rabi-1*

| S | M | T | W | T | F | S |
|---|---|---|---|---|---|---|
|  |  |  | 1 | 2 | 3 | 4 |
|  |  | SF | 2 | 3 | 4 |  |
| 5 | 6 | 7 | 8 | 9 | 10 | 11 |
| 5 | 6 | 7 | 8 | 9 | 10 | 11 |
| 12 | 13 | 14 | 15 | 16 | 17 | 18 |
| 12 | 13 | n | 15 | 16 | 17 | 18 |
| 19 | 20 | 21 | 22 | 23 | 24 | 25 |
| 19 | 20 | 21 | 22 | 23 | 24 | 25 |
| 26 | 27 | 28 | 29 | 30 | 31 |  |
| 26 | 27 | 28 | T | ?? | RA |  |

**April**
*Rabi-I/Rabi-II*

| S | M | T | W | T | F | S |
|---|---|---|---|---|---|---|
|  |  |  |  |  |  | 1 |
|  |  |  |  |  |  | 2 |
| 2 | 3 | 4 | 5 | 6 | 7 | 8 |
| 3 | 4 | 5 | 6 | 7 | 8 | 9 |
| 9 | 10 | 11 | 12 | 13 | 14 | 15 |
| 10 | 11 | MN | 13 | 14 | 15 | 16 |
| 16 | 17 | 18 | 19 | 20 | 21 | 22 |
| 17 | 18 | 19 | 20 | 21 | 22 | 23 |
| 23 | 24 | 25 | 26 | 27 | 28 | 29 |
| 24 | 25 | 26 | 27 | 28 | 29 | RT |
| 30 |  |  |  |  |  |  |
| 2 |  |  |  |  |  |  |

**September**
*Sha'ban/Ramadan*

| S | M | T | W | T | F | S |
|---|---|---|---|---|---|---|
|  |  |  |  |  | 1 | 2 |
|  |  |  |  |  | 8 | 9 |
| 3 | 4 | 5 | 6 | 7 | 8 | 9 |
| 10 | 11 | 12 | 13 | p | NS | 16 |
| 10 | 11 | 12 | 13 | 14 | 15 | 16 |
| 17 | 18 | 19 | 20 | 21 | 22 | 23 |
| 17 | 18 | 19 | 20 | 21 | 22 | 23 |
| 24 | 25 | 26 | 27 | 28 | A | 30 |
| 24 | 25 | 26 | 27 | 28 | 29 | 30 |
| RM | 2 | 3 | 4 | 5 | 6 | 7 |

**October**
*Ramadan/Shawaal*

| S | M | T | W | T | F | S |
|---|---|---|---|---|---|---|
| 1 | 2 | 3 | 4 | 5 | 6 | 7 |
| 8 | 9 | 10 | 11 | 12 | 13 | 14 |
| 8 | 9 | 10 | 11 | 12 | 13 | 14 |
| 15 | 16 | 17 | 18 | 19 | 20 | 21 |
| 15 | 16 | 17 | 18 | 19 | 20 | 21 |
| 22 | 23 | 24 | 25 | LQ | 27 | 28 |
| 22 | 23 | 24 | 25 | 26 | 27 | 28 |
| 29 | 30 | EF | 2 | 3 | 4 | 5 |
| 29 | 30 | 31 |  |  |  |  |
| 6 | 7 | 8 |  |  |  |  |

**November**
*Shawwal/Zul-Qa'dah*

| S | M | T | W | T | F | S |
|---|---|---|---|---|---|---|
|  |  |  | 1 | 2 | 3 | 4 |
|  |  |  | 9 | 10 | 11 | 12 |
| 5 | 6 | 7 | 8 | 9 | 10 | 11 |
| 13 | 14 | 15 | 16 | 17 | 18 | 19 |
| 12 | 13 | 14 | 15 | 16 | 17 | 18 |
| 20 | 21 | 22 | 23 | 24 | 25 | 26 |
| 19 | 20 | 21 | 22 | 23 | 24 | 25 |
| 27 | 28 | 29 | 30 | ZQ | 2 | 3 |
| 26 | 27 | 28 | 29 | 30 |  |  |
| 4 | 5 | 6 | 7 | 8 |  |  |

**December**
*Zul-Qa'dah/Zul-Hijjah*

| S | M | T | W | T | F | S |
|---|---|---|---|---|---|---|
|  |  |  |  |  | 1 | 2 |
|  |  |  |  |  | 9 | 10 |
| 3 | 4 | 5 | 6 | 7 | 8 | 9 |
| 11 | 12 | 13 | 14 | 15 | 16 | 17 |
| 10 | 11 | 12 | 13 | 14 | 15 | 16 |
| 18 | 19 | 20 | 21 | 22 | 23 | 24 |
| 17 | 18 | 19 | 20 | 21 | 22 | 23 |
| 25 | 26 | 27 | 28 | 29 | ZH | 2 |
| 24 | 25 | 26 | 27 | 28 | 29 | 30 |
| 3 | 4 | 5 | 6 | 7 | 8 | WA |
| 31 |  |  |  |  |  |  |
| A |  |  |  |  |  |  |

**FIGURE 8.5**   Islamic calendar versus Gregorian (traditional Western) calendar—1427 versus 2006.

Izzat Azamat Vav
Islamic
1422 Jumada t'Tania 22
French Republican
209 Frucitdor III
Unix time value
1000166400
International Organization for Standardization (ISO) ISO8601 week and day, and day of year
Day 2 of week 37 of 2001
Excel serial date numbers
1900 date system (PC) Excel serial day: 37145
1904 date system (Macintosh) Excel serial day: 35683

As demonstrated by the aforementioned sample, there are clear inconsistencies. The U.S. Armed Forces follow a Julian calendar; so, depending on which calendar format is used in any analysis and by whom, it is possible to draw more than one conclusion. Analysts and law enforcement personnel may spend too much time analyzing dates for significance. After all, what is significant? This will vary based on the person, culture, and definition. Following the tragic train bombing events in Madrid, Spain, some analysts and academics looked for significance. It was noted that both events occurred on the eleventh day of a month, if one uses a Gregorian calendar. Both took place during months that through their numeric equivalent are divisible by three. One last piece of information that was observed was the continuation of the number three, in the number of years between the two. Is any of this significant? What about the fact that 2004 was a leap year? What is the significance of that, if any?

## Dates of Terrorism Significance

There are many significant dates in the world of terrorism beyond September 11, 2001. A list of dates that may have potential significance in terrorism based on a traditional Western Gregorian calendar is outlined in this section. The significance of any date is based on several variables, including personal perception, personal ideology, group ideology, calendar used, religion followed, and culture. Items such as celebrations, major events, or even the weather should be noted when monitoring dates.

This list is not all-inclusive and is largely based on events that have occurred since 1968. It is also devoid of many events that have occurred in North America such as abortion clinic bombings; ecological events; and many incidents attributed to domestic-based, Puerto Rican, Jewish Defense League, and anti-Castro groups. The list is as follows:

*January*
1, 1964: The Palestinian Liberation Organization (PLO) is formed.
1, 2001: A Hamas suicide car bomb wounds 54 in Netanya, Israel.
5, 1996: Hamas bomb maker Yehiya Ayyash (The Engineer) is killed.
5, 2003: The al-Aqsa Martyrs' Brigade detonates simultaneous suicide bombs in Tel Aviv, Israel.
6, 1963: The Columbian National Liberation Army (ELN) is founded.
8, 1998: Ramzi Yousef is given life plus a 240-year sentence for the 1993 World Trade Center bombing.
12, 2000: The execution of the Kurdistan Workers' Party (PKK) leader Abdullah Ocalan is stayed in Turkey.
17, 1991: Operation Desert Storm air offensive begins.
18, 1982: An American University president is assassinated by Islamic Jihad.
20, 1981: Hostages taken in November 1979 from the U.S. Embassy in Iran, are released.
22, 1999: In France, Armed Islamic Group (GIA) ringleaders get 8 years for terrorist acts, and 84 others are sentenced in a mass trial.
23, 2003: Daniel Pearl is murdered in Pakistan.
25, 1993: Mir Aimal Kasi kills two and wounds three outside CIA headquarters.
31, 2001: A Scottish court finds Libyan al-Megrahi guilty in the Pan Am 103 bombing.

*February*
2, 2000: In France, Euskadi Ta Askatasuna (ETA) leader Iglesias Chauvas and member Chonchita Alvarez are arrested for a 1995 plot to assassinate the king of Spain.
3, 2000: Syria and Sudan sign an agreement on fighting terrorism in compliance with the Arab Antiterrorism Convention.
6, 2000: In the United Kingdom, Ariana Afghan flight is hijacked with 20 hostages who are eventually released; the hijackers surrender on February 11, 2000.
7, 1991: In the United Kingdom, the Provisional Irish Republican Army (PIRA) is responsible for a three-round mortar attack on No. 10 Downing Street—the prime minister's home.
13, 2000: In Columbia, the Revolutionary Armed Forces of Columbia (FARC) and ELN stage a series of attacks, killing 12 and kidnapping 16.
15, 1984: U.S. diplomat Leamon Hunt is murdered by the Red Brigade in Italy.

15, 1999: PKK leader Ocalan is arrested and returned to Turkey, which sets off Kurdish protests throughout Europe.

16, 1992: The Hezbollah general secretary is killed in a helicopter ambush.

17, 1988: Marine Lt. Col. William R. Higgins is kidnapped and hanged in Lebanon.

17, 1998: Four al-Gama militants are hanged for attacks in 1994 and 1995, in Egypt.

20, 1998: Japanese Red Army member Tustomu Shiosaki is sentenced to 30 years for an attack on the U.S. Embassy in Indonesia.

21, 1970: A Swissair jet is bombed by the Popular Front for the Liberation of Palestine— General Command (PFLP-GC) in Israel: 47 killed.

22, 1969: The Democratic Front for the Liberation of Palestine is founded.

24, 1998: Osama bin Laden issues a fatwa that allows attacks on Americans worldwide.

25, 1991: A ground offensive is launched in Operation Desert Storm.

25, 1994: In Israel, 39 worshippers at the Tomb of Patriarchs are massacred.

25, 1996: Hamas bombs buses in Jerusalem, killing 28.

26, 1993: First World Trade Center bombing kills 6 and wounds 1000.

27, 1980: M-19 seizes the Dominican Embassy in Columbia; it ends on April 21, 1980.

*March*

1, 2001: In the United Kingdom, 21 groups are banned under a new terrorism law; Liberation Tigers of Tamil Eelam (LTTE)'s office is the first one closed down.

1, 2003: Khalid Shaykh Mohammed (KSM) is arrested in Pakistan.

3, 2005: In the Philippines, the Moro Islamic Liberation Front (MILF) explodes a bomb in a crowded terminal, killing 21.

4, 1999: A PKK suicide bomber injures four in Turkey.

5, 1998: In Sri Lanka, LTTE is blamed for a bus bomb that kills 37.

5, 2003: A Hamas suicide bomber explodes a bomb on a bus, killing 15.

7, 1999: In Bangladesh, a bomb kills 10; Harkatul Jihad backed by bin Laden is blamed for the incident.

9, 2002: A suicide bomb in Jerusalem kills 11; Hamas claims responsibility.

10, 2000: LTTE conducts a suicide motorcade attack in Sri Lanka, killing 29.

11, 1999: FARC founders Miguel Pascua and Commandant Oscar are killed in a raid.

11, 2004: In Madrid, Spain, al-Qaeda detonates 10 of 13 backpack bombs on a train, killing nearly 200.

12, 1993: Bomb attacks in India kill 250.

15, 2001: In Turkey, a Russian plane is hijacked.

16, 1984: William Buckley, a U.S. citizen, is kidnapped and killed by Hezbollah.

16, 1985: U.S. journalist Terry Anderson is kidnapped in Lebanon.

20, 1995: Aum Shinrikyo commits a sarin gas attack that kills 12 on a Tokyo subway.

20, 2002: Islamic Jihad detonates a bomb on an Israeli bus killing seven.

21, 2002: A suicide bomber detonates a bomb in a crowd of shoppers in Jerusalem.

22, 1945: The Arab League is founded.

23, 1998: In Algeria, seven GIA militants are sentenced to death for assassinating an archbishop.

26, 1978: Egypt and Israel ratify the Camp David peace accords.

27, 2001: In Algeria, Abdelmajid Dahoumane is arrested for a New Year's bomb plot.

27, 2002: In Israel, Hamas claims responsibility for killing 29 via a suicide bomb.

*April*

2, 1986: The Hawari group is blamed for a bomb that explodes on Trans World Airlines (TWA) Flight 840 killing four.

2, 2003: Jemaah Islamiah explodes a bomb on a crowded passenger wharf killing 16 in the Philippines.

4, 1986: In Germany, the La Belle disco is bombed, killing three.

5, 1988: Hezbollah hijacks Kuwait Airways and kills two.

6, 2001: An Algerian named Ahmed Ressam (the Millennium Bomber) is convicted for a New Year's bomb plot.

10, 2002: Hamas kills eight in Israel by detonating a suicide bomb on a bus.

11, 1968: The PFLP-GC is formed.

12, 2002: The al-Aqsa Martyrs' Brigade kills six in Jerusalem.

18, 1983: A car bomb explodes in front of the U.S. Embassy in Lebanon, killing 63; Hezbollah is responsible.

19, 1993: At Mount Carmel at the Branch Davidians compound in Waco, Texas, a shootout with the Bureau of Alcohol, Tobacco, and Firearms kills 79.

19, 1995: Timothy McVeigh detonates a truck bomb at the Alfred P. Murrah Federal Building in Oklahoma City, killing 168.

23, 2000: Abu Sayyaf kidnaps 21 in the Philippines.

26, 2001: The Columbian government withdraws its troops and allows ELN to claim territory.

*May*

1, 1993: A suicide bomber kills Sri Lankan President Premadasa during a May Day celebration.

7, 2002: Hamas kills 15 in a Tel Aviv suicide bombing at a club.

8, 1985: The firebombing of U.S. Citibank and Xerox in Spain.

10, 2002: Chechen separatists are suspected in a remote-control mine attack that kills 41.

12, 2001: ETA is suspected in a car bomb attack in central Spain that wounds 14.

13, 1991: In Italy, Mehmet Ali Agca attempts the assassination of Pope John Paul II.

13, 2003: al-Qaeda bombs three housing compounds in Saudi Arabia, killing 20.

15, 1948: Founding of the State of Israel.

16, 1978: Italian Aldo Moro is murdered by the Red Brigade.

16, 2003: Simultaneous attacks at five locations in Casablanca kill 42.

17, 1989: Mohammed Ali Hamadei is convicted in Germany of the 1985 hijacking of TWA Flight 847.

21, 1991: The Prime Minister of India, Rajiv Gandhi, is killed by a female LTTE suicide bomber.

21, 2002: Shining Path is suspected of detonating a car bomb outside the U.S. Embassy in Peru, killing nine.

22, 1962: A Continental Airlines flight from Chicago to Kansas City becomes the first suicide bombing of an American aircraft; 44 killed.

22, 2001: Abu Sayyaf raids a beach resort and kills two.

24, 2000: Israeli troops pull out of Lebanon.

25, 2001: Hamas and Palestinian Islamic Jihad (PIJ) set off two suicide bombs at a bus station on the anniversary of the pullout of Israeli troops from Lebanon.

26, 1998: A Japanese doctor is convicted in connection with the Aum Shinrikyo sarin gas attack in 1995.

27, 2001: Abu Sayyaf kidnaps 20 in a raid on a resort.

28, 1964: FARC is founded.

28, 1997: A ship owner is slain in an ambush by 17 November (17N).

29, 1997: Mohammed Abouhalima is found guilty of the first World Trade Center bombing.

*June*

1, 2001: Hamas claims responsibility for the Tel Aviv disco suicide bombing that killed 20.

3, 1989: Ayatollah Khomeini dies after a 10-year rule in Iran.

5, 2002: Islamic Jihad uses a car bomb to ram a bus and kills 17.

6, 2001: In Canada a bomb maker is charged for the 1985 Air India bombing and jailed in Japan.

6, 2003: A taxi rigged with explosives rams a bus carrying Germans in Kabul, killing five.

7, 2000: An LTTE suicide bomber kills 22 in Sri Lanka.

9, 1997: The suspected leader of al-Gama is killed in Cairo; 40 members arrested.

11, 1985: A Jordanian flight is hijacked in Lebanon, and the plane is eventually destroyed.

12, 2001: Abu Sayyaf claims the beheading of U.S. hostage.

12, 2001: Abu Nidal and three others are tried in absentia in Jordan for a murder committed in 1984.

13, 1999: Shining Path kills eight in a village raid.

14, 1985: Hezbollah hijacks TWA Flight 847 and murders a U.S. Navy diver.

15, 1972: A Cathay Pacific Airways flight from Thailand to Hong Kong explodes from a suitcase bomb that kills 81.

18, 2001: An Islamic Jihad suicide bomber kills 19 passengers on a bus.

19, 2002: The al-Aqsa Martyrs' Brigade kills seven in a suicide attack at a bus stop in Israel.

21, 1994: Sarin gas attacks by Aum Shinrikyo kill seven.

21, 2001: The United States indicts 14 members of Hezbollah for the Khobar Towers bombing attack in Dahahran, Saudi Arabia, that killed 19 U.S. airmen.

23, 1985: An Air India flight off the coast of Ireland explodes due to plastic explosives, killing 329.

24, 2000: FARC leader Rey Palacios is captured in Columbia.

25, 1995: Khobar Towers is bombed by Hezbollah.

27, 1976: An Air France flight is hijacked by PFLP.

29, 1999: A PKK leader is sentenced to be hanged in Turkey.

*July*

4, 1976: The Israeli raid at Entebbe, Uganda, rescues 246 hijacked hostages.

4, 1995: In India, al-Faran guerillas kidnap U.S. and U.K. citizens.

7, 1998: A GIA leader in Algiers is among the 11 rebels killed by the Algerian government.

7, 2005: Four bombs explode and kill 56 passengers on underground trains and a bus in London.

8, 1965: A Canadian Pacific Airlines explosion kills 52.

10, 2001: The ETA carries out a car bomb attack in Madrid.

11, 1998: Abu Nidal is responsible for the attack on a Greek island ferry, killing nine.

12, 2000: An ETA car bomb wounds 10 in Madrid's Callao Plaza.

13, 1999: Muslim militants storm a Kashmir camp in India, killing four.

16, 2000: In Japan, Aum Shinrikyo members are sentenced to death for sarin gas attacks.

17, 2002: Greek police arrest the leader and founder of 17 November.

18, 1994: Hezbollah is found responsible for the Buenos Aires Jewish Community Center bomb that killed nearly 100.

21, 2005: In London, bomb attacks are attempted at three underground stations and on one bus; only the detonators explode and cause one minor injury.

22, 2002: Hamas leader and 14 others killed in an Israeli airstrike.

22, 2003: Uday and Qusay Hussein killed in a U.S. raid in Mosul, Iraq.

23, 2001: A bicycle bomb kills seven in Kashmir.

24, 2001: An LTTE attack on an international airport and air force base in Sri Lanka, kills 18.

25, 1995: The GIA is suspected in the Paris metro station bombing that killed seven.

27, 1996: Army of God follower Eric Rudolph detonates a bomb in Centennial Park, Atlanta, during events for the Summer Olympic Games, killing 1 and injuring 100.

30, 1997: Hamas is found responsible for a double suicide attack that kills 16 in Israel.

30, 2001: Former ETA leaders are sentenced to 1000 years each.

31, 2002: Hamas is found responsible for bombing at the Hebrew University, Jerusalem, that kills seven.

*August*

2, 1990: Iraq invades Kuwait.

2, 2000: Hindu pilgrims are killed in India on their way to a shrine and 102 are killed in Kashmir.

3, 1998: FARC and ELN coordinate attacks, killing 106 soldiers.

3, 2001: A London railway station is targeted with a car bomb and the Real Irish Republican Army (RIRA) is blamed.

4, 2002: Hamas uses a suicide bomber to kill nine passengers on an Israeli bus.

5, 2003: A car bomb explodes in front of the Indonesian Marriott Hotel; Jemmah Islamiya is responsible.

6, 1991: A former Iranian prime minister is assassinated in Paris.

6, 2002: Militants attack Hindu pilgrims in New Delhi, killing eight.

7, 1998: Two blasts at U.S. embassies in Kenya and Tanzania kill 224.

8, 2000: Chechen rebels suspected in the Moscow Pushkin Square bombing that killed 12.

9, 2002: A grenade blast kills four at a Christian missionary hospital in Islamabad, Pakistan.

10, 1987: 17 November detonates a bomb near a bus of U.S. airmen.

11, 1982: A member of a Palestinian terror group, 15 May, is responsible for the bomb found on the Pan Am flight from Tokyo to Hawaii; 1 killed and 15 wounded.

12, 2001: A suicide bomb in a Haifa restaurant kills 21 and the PIJ is suspected.

14, 1994: Carlos the Jackal is arrested in Sudan and extradited to France.

15, 2001: Lashkar-e-Tayyiba is responsible for the Handwara bombing, India, that killed 18.

17, 1995: A bomb explodes near the Arc de Triomphe in Paris.

18, 2001: ETA are responsible for a car bomb near a tourist area in Barcelona, Spain.

19, 2003: A Hamas suicide bomber detonates a bomb on a bus, killing 20.

21, 1995: A Hamas suicide bomber on a bus kills five.

23, 2001: The ELN is blamed for a car bomb outside a police station that kills one.

28, 1999: A car bomb in Yemen kills six.

29, 2001: Mahmoud Haballah is arrested in Canada for his involvement in the al-Qaeda bombings of U.S. embassies.

30, 2001: An LTTE bomb outside a building in Kalunai kills three.

*September*

4, 1999: The bombing of an apartment block in Russia kills 64.

5, 1972: Israeli athletes are held hostage at the Munich Olympics by Black September, and 11 are killed on September 6, 1972.

6, 1970: The PFLP begins the simultaneous diversion of a Swissair DC-8 and a TWA Boeing 707 to Jordan, followed 6 days later by the hijacking of a BOAC VC-10. The aircraft are forced to land at Dawson Field, 30 miles from Amman, which was quickly renamed Revolutionary Airport. The planes are blown up on September 12.

6, 1986: Abu Nidal attacks a synagogue in Istanbul, killing 21.

7, 1995: The GIA is suspected in a car bomb explosion outside a Jewish school in Lyon, France.

8, 1999: The bombing of an apartment block in Russia kills 94.

11, 1978: Camp David accords.

11, 2001: al-Qaeda is responsible for four hijackings: two of the aircraft crash into the World Trade Center towers, one crashes into the Pentagon, and one crashes into a Pennsylvania field; this results in nearly 3000 casualties.

13, 1993: Israel and PLO sign a peace agreement.

14, 1986: A bomb at Kimpo airport in Seoul, South Korea, kills five.

14, 2003: The ELN kidnaps eight in Columbia.

15, 2003: A truck bomb detonates outside a security building in Moscow.

18, 1997: A bomb in a Cairo tourist bus kills nine.

19, 1989: UTA Flight 772 to Paris explodes over Niger, killing 170.

20, 1984: Islamic Jihad is responsible for a truck bomb explosion at the U.S. Embassy in Beirut, Lebanon, killing 23.

23, 1983: An Omari Gulf aircraft is bombed in the United Arab Emirates, killing 111.

24, 2004: Lashkar-e-Tayyiba is suspected of a Hindu temple attack in India that kills 31.

27, 1987: 17 November is responsible for the U.S. commissary bombing in Greece.

29, 1998: LTTE is blamed for shooting down a Lionair flight in Sri Lanka, killing 55.

29, 2003: FARC is blamed for a motorcycle bombing that kills 10.

Between September and October in 1984 the town of Dalles, Oregon, about 80 miles from Portland, experiences a bioterrorist attack when followers of the Indian guru Bhagwan Shree Rajneesh spike salad bars at 10 restaurants in a town with salmonella and make about 750 people sick, with the goal of changing the results of a political election.

*October*

1, 1995: Shaykh Omar Abdel-Rahman is convicted in the New York bomb plot.

1, 2001: Jaish-e-Mohammed is responsible for a suicide bomb in Srinagar that kills 38.

2, 2000: An LTTE suicide bombing kills 23 in Sri Lanka.

3, 1996: 17 November is blamed for the Greek NATO bomb attack.

4, 2000: The Shining Path leader is captured in Peru.

5, 2000: An LTTE suicide bomber kills 10 in Sri Lanka.

6, 1973: The Yom Kippur War begins.

6, 1981: Egyptian President Anwar Sadat is assassinated by Egyptian Islamic Jihad.

7, 1985: The Achille Lauro cruise ship is hijacked.

12, 2000: Boat bombing on the USS *Cole* kills 17 in Yemen; al-Qaeda is responsible.

12, 2002: Multiple car bombs explode outside nightclubs in Bali, killing 202; Jemaah Islamiah is responsible.

15, 2003: Palestinian terrorists bomb a U.S. Embassy motorcade, killing three.

16, 1997: An LTTE truck bomb at a hotel next to the Trade Center in Colombo, Sri Lanka, kills 18.

17, 1995: The GIA is suspected in a Paris subway bombing.

19, 2000: An LTTE suicide bomb wounds 23 in Sri Lanka.

20, 1981: An Antwerp synagogue is bombed, killing two.

21, 2002: A car bomb explodes next to a bus in Karkur, killing 19; the PIJ is suspected.

23, 1983: Islamic Jihad bombs U.S. Marine barracks in Beirut, killing 299.

23, 2002: Chechens seize a theater in Moscow, taking over 800 hostages.

29, 1975: Three Black September members hijack a Lufthansa flight.

*November*

1, 1955: A dynamite bomb kills 44 on a United Airlines flight from Denver to Portland, Oregon.

4, 1979: The U.S. Embassy in Tehran is seized and 66 are taken hostage.

4, 2001: The PIJ is responsible for a shooting attack on a Jerusalem bus.

6, 2001: The ETA is suspected in a Madrid rush-hour car bomb that wounds 100.

7, 1985: M-19 captures the Supreme Court building in Columbia; more than 100 killed.

8, 1987: The PIRA bombs a Remembrance Day celebration in the United Kingdom, killing 13.

9, 2003: al-Qaeda is suspected in the Riyadh residential compound attack that kills 18.

10, 2003: A luxury residential compound in Saudi Arabia is bombed, killing 17.

13, 1995: A car bomb at U.S. military facility in Riyadh kills seven.

14, 2002: Mir Amai Kasi executed for the 1993 attack outside the CIA building.

17, 1973: The group 17 November takes its name from the student uprising on this date in Greece that kills 34.

19, 1995: Egyptian Islamic Jihad bombs the Egyptian Embassy in Islamabad.

20, 2000: Hamas is responsible for a roadside bomb targeted at an Israeli school bus.

20, 2003: al-Qaeda is responsible for a vehicle bomb in front of the British Consulate-General in Istanbul, Turkey, killing 30.

23, 1985: Egyptian plane is hijacked by Abu Nidal en route to Malta; 60 killed.

23, 1996: A hijacked Ethiopian plane crashes in the Comoros Islands, killing 127.

25, 1984: The 25 April Movement is responsible for the U.S. Embassy mortar round attack in Portugal.

28, 2002: Three suicide bombers drive vehicles into the front of the Paradise Hotel in Kenya, killing 15.

29, 1987: Korean Airlines Flight 858 is blown up, killing 115.

*December*

1, 2001: Hamas is responsible for two suicide bombing attacks in a mall that kill 10.

3, 1984: Hezbollah Islamic Jihad hijacks a plane bound for Tehran.

6, 2000: The LTTE is suspected in a landmine attack that kills four bus passengers in Sri Lanka.

12, 1983: Hezbollah is responsible for U.S. and French Embassy attacks in Kuwait.

14, 1987: The founding of Hamas.

16, 1983: The PIRA bombs Harrod's department store in London, killing nine.

17, 1996: MRTA rebels take 700 hostages at Japanese ambassador's residence in Lima, Peru.

18, 1999: LTTE is blamed for two bombings in Sri Lanka, killing 34.

21, 1975: Carlos the Jackal kidnaps 11 Oil and Petroleum Exporting Countries (OPEC) ministers in Vienna.

21, 1988: Libya is responsible for the Pan Am Flight 103 bombing over Scotland, killing 259.

23, 2001: Richard Reid attempts to ignite an explosive device concealed in his shoes on an American Airlines flight from Paris to Miami, Florida.

25, 2000: Bomb blasts in India and Pakistan by Jamiat-ul-Mujahedin kill 11.

27, 1985: Abu Nidal attacks Rome and Vienna airports, killing 18.

27, 2002: Chechens are blamed for two suicide bombers with truck bombs, killing 72.

28, 1972: Black September seizes Israeli Embassy in Thailand.

30, 2000: Abu Sayyaf is blamed for the series of bombs set off in Metro Manila, Philippines, that kill 16.

## LEARNING FROM PAST BEHAVIOR

Regardless of the group, terrorists have historically learned from their predecessors. Whether a significant date or a failed attack, a terrorist can garner information about prior incidents quite easily, especially in the United States. Entrepreneurs and the corporate world have exploited the use of the Freedom of Information Act or sunshine laws to gather case records and files. They then consolidate, link, and repackage the information that some agencies already had with them and sell it back to law enforcement personnel and others. Figure 8.6 demonstrates an example of repackaging. This reference is not meant to be negative. Law enforcement agencies do not always have the skill set or time to prepare such information.

One reason why a terrorist or terrorist group would find such information attractive is the detail. A cursory review of law enforcement personnel with security clearances working in homeland security over the past 2 years reveals an interesting fact as to how many people refused to discuss case information; but once an arrest was made, they failed to pursue sealing the court record. The author has walked into classes with an affidavit and information from agency cases that provided what may be considered too much detail. Some even provided the who, what, where, and when information. There are websites that exploit these documents and sell them for as little as $2.

A terrorist group would seek out these documents to learn details such as what brought the group's actions to the attention of the law enforcement community, what techniques were used by investigators to gather information, and what locations and individuals were used. They are essentially looking for the same things that the investigators are: skills, knowledge, and resources. In an open society information is often too readily available, and there is a hesitancy to seal documents.

## LOOKING FOR SKILL, KNOWLEDGE, RESOURCE, ACCESS(IBILITY), MOTIVE

Analysts and investigators need to be cognizant of what goes into developing a terrorist activity or event. Many variables and individuals will ultimately come into play. The issue of variables has been discussed. When looking at individuals, or subjects, there are five components that should be explored in depth. It is important to be aware of not only the individual but also the group.

| | | | | | |
|---|---|---|---|---|---|
| Airmen Databases | Al Qaeda Jihad Manual | CBW Information | FBI Watch List | Flight School Information | Newswires |
| Al Qaeda Data | Analyses | Court Documents | FBIS | Miscellaneous Articles | Tri-Folds |
| Embassy Bombings | USA vs Abdi | USA vs Al Aboudy | USA vs Alandon | USA vs Al-Atabi (Hatef) | USA vs Al-Atabi (Wathek) |
| USA vs Al-Baraa | USA vs Albred | USA vs Aldraibi | USA vs Al-Hachami | USA vs Alibrahimi | USA vs Ali-Haimoud |
| USA vs Al-Khaledy | USA vs Al-Maleky | USA vs Almazaal | USA vs Al-Obaidi | USA vs Al-Saraf | USA vs Al-Shiblawy |
| USA vs Alshomary | USA vs Aulbeldy | USA vs Awadaiiah | USA vs Badri | USA vs Galica | USA vs Gurung |
| USA vs Hannan | USA vs Hussein | USA vs Khoury | USA vs Koubriti | USA vs Lopez-Flores | USA vs Martinez-Flores |
| USA vs Moussaoui | USA vs Pervez | USA vs Raissi | USA vs Raissi & Dahmani | USA vs Reic | USA vs Villalobos |
| | | USA vs Walker-Lindh | | | |

**FIGURE 8.6**   Public records laws affording opportunities for individuals and businesses to gather data. These data are then repackaged, computerized, and sold publicly in easy-to-use formats such as the example shown in the figure.

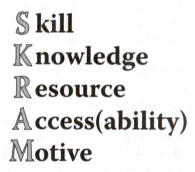

S kill

K nowledge

R esource

A ccess(ability)

M otive

**FIGURE 8.7**   The five key components analysts should look for when identifying terrorist activity.

The five components are outlined in Figure 8.7, as skill, knowledge, resource, access(ibility), and motive (SKRAM).

Behavior patterns of individuals and groups are to some degree dependent on SKRAM. Many organizations and their affiliated groups (such as the Irish Republican Army [IRA] and PLO) have remained fairly consistent, still employing tactics they have employed for years. When putting the pieces together one will be continually looking for items that comprise SKRAM. Say that a terrorist organization is going to deploy a "dirty bomb" somewhere in a particular country. Without the skill and knowledge within their membership to build a dirty bomb, there is little chance this can occur. If this scenario was in question, one should determine whether they have the resources necessary to build a dirty bomb or have access to one. Access to a location and/or ability to carry out the attack is also essential. The last piece, motive, is probably the easiest to develop. All aspects of SKRAM can be attained if one knows where to gather the information needed for successful analysis. The SKRAM components can often be found in recruiting attempts, techniques, and locations.

## RECRUITING OPPORTUNITIES

Perhaps one of the greatest opportunities for law enforcement personnel to regularly thwart terrorist activities is at the recruitment level. If terrorists cannot recruit successfully, their activities will be stymied or altogether eliminated. This tactic followed by the law enforcement community has been successful on many fronts. From street gangs to organized crime, membership is the key. One place to find many malcontents (potential recruits) in a single location is a jail or prison. Typical street gang members to organized crime figures, including the drug cartel type, can be found in an institution designed to rehabilitate. Although these groups might appear to have little in common, they tend to find a common ground in ideology and religion. Many already have hatred toward the government or some segment of the population.

Chapter 5 details many recruitment aspects associated with radicalization within correctional institutions. However, there are other considerations that an investigator should look at when it comes to identifying possible recruitment signs. Outlined in the following section are items that should be evaluated as they arise. Many of these items are not necessarily precursors to terrorism but are presented as thought-provoking points to evaluate.

## PRISONS—RECRUITMENT AND COMMUNICATION

According to *The Sociology and Psychology of Terrorism: Who Becomes a Terrorist and Why?*,[3] individuals who become terrorists are often unemployed, socially alienated individuals who have dropped out of society. This describes most people incarcerated in prisons. Religion is rapidly growing behind bars, beyond the aspects of ideology and social adjustment. One of the fastest growing religions is Islam. Couple this with the years that idle minds have to formulate thoughts or be molded and there is little doubt as to why the prison population provides fertile ground for recruitment. However, from the law enforcement perspective prisons are overlooked largely due to the perception that the arrest is complete. The amount of information available at the prison level is phenomenal. Accuracy and details prevail, in most instances. There is little expectation of privacy outside of legal or religious interactions. Essentially, the law enforcement community has a venue in which individuals must find covert ways to communicate internally and externally. Organized crime figures have for years continued to run their criminal enterprises from within the prison system. The same is true of terrorists. An example is an Egyptian man named El-Sayeed Nosair who is serving a life sentence in New York for the 1990 murder of Rabbi Maier Kahane in Manhattan, New York City. Nosair was also indicted for his involvement in the plotting of the 1993 bombing of the World Trade Center while in prison.

### ABILITY TO COMMUNICATE FROM WITHIN

Nosair was not the first and will certainly not be the last to communicate from behind prison walls. Another example of terrorism continuing to operate behind bars is the case of Sheikh Omar Abdel-Rahman, also known as the Blind Sheikh. In October 1995, Sheikh Abdel-Rahman was convicted of engaging in a seditious conspiracy to wage urban terrorism in the United States, which included the 1993 World Trade Center bombing and plots to blow up landmarks (a Federal Bureau of Investigation [FBI] building, and the Lincoln and Holland tunnels). In January 1996, he was sentenced to life plus 65 years in prison. In 1997, the U.S. Bureau of Prisons imposed special administrative measures (SAMs) on the sheikh, who was serving his sentence at the U.S. Penitentiary Federal Medical Center in Rochester, Minnesota. These measures limited specific privileges such as access to mail, media, telephone, and visitors for the purpose of protecting others (Figure 8.8). Despite this, he still found a pipeline by which to communicate with members outside prison.

**RESTRICTIONS ON SHEIKH ABDEL RAHMAN'S**
**COMMUNICATIONS FROM PRISON**

16. Beginning in 1997, and continuing to the present day, the Bureau of prisons (at the direction of the Attorney General) pursuant to 28 C.F.R. $ 501.3, imposed Special Asministrative Measures ("SAM") upon SHEIKH ABDEL RAHMAN. I have reviewed the SAM and related documents. A summary of certain provisions of the SAM is set forth below.

17. Among other things, the SAM limited certain of his privileges, including his access to the mail, the media, the telephone, and visitors, for the express purpose of protecting "persons against the risk of death or serious bodily injury" that

**FIGURE 8.8**    Court record limiting Abdel-Rahman's access to the world outside the prison.

Federal prosecutors charged four associates of Abdel-Rahman with helping the Islamic militant to continue to direct terrorist activities from his U.S. prison cell, as noted in the indictment shown in Figure 8.9. Abdel-Rahman's lawyer, Lynne Stewart, an Arabic translator, and two others were charged with providing material support of a terrorism organization by helping Abdel-Rahman pass and receive messages while incarcerated in a federal prison cell.

UNITED STATES DISTRICT COURT
SOUTHERN DISTRICT OF NEW YORK
- - - - - - - - - - - - - - - - - - - - - - - - - - - - - - - - - X

UNITED STATES OF AMERICA

---v.---

AHMED ABDEL SATTAR,                                    INDICTMENT
   a/k/a "Abu Omar,"                             02 Cr.
   a/k/a "Dr. Ahmed,"
YASSIR AL-SIRRI,
   a/k/a "Abu Ammar,"
LYNNE STEWART, and                         02 CRIM. 395
MOHAMMED YOUSRY,

    Defendants.

- - - - - - - - - - - - - - - - - - - - - - - - - - - - - - - - - X

INTRODUCTION

The Grand Jury charges:

Background: The Islamic Group

1. At all relevent times described herein, the Islamic Group, a/k/a "Gama'a al-Islamiyya," a/k/a "IG," a/k/a "al-Gama' at," a/k/a "Islamic Gama' at," a/k/a "Egyptian al-Gama 'at al-Islamiyya," (hereinafter, "IG") existed as an international terrorist group dedicated to opposing nations, government, institutions, and individuals that did not share IG's radical interpretation of Islamic law. IG considered such nations, governments, institutions and individuals as "infidels," and interpreted the concept of "jihad" (struggle) as waging opposition against infidels by whatever means necessary, including force and violence.

**FIGURE 8.9**    Federal indictment for associates or acquaintances of Abdel-Rahman.

Communication from within prison walls is neither new nor limited to terrorists. Over the past several decades, organized crime figures and street gangs have sought out methods by which to continue their criminal enterprises from behind bars. Everything from tattoos to sign language has been used. Analysts must not rely solely on modern technology to intercept communications. Old methods of communication such as international Morse code or the use of Mayan images are now used by prison inmates and others. Individuals using these methods are acutely aware of the technology employed by the law enforcement community, and they may even know the community's weakness, which is the inability to understand "old" methods of communicating. To find this in practice today, one just needs to visit a prison or review tattoos used by street gangs.

Prisons and other correctional facilities and their potential for recruitment were highlighted as a concern in an April 2004 U.S. Department of Justice report.[4] In this report, which reviewed the FBI's counterterrorism program post 9/11, it was noted that correctional intelligence is essential for joint terrorism task forces (JTTFs). In Operation Tripwire, an initiative designed to identify sleeper cells, JTTF members are identifying existing or former sources who are incarcerated and are involved with radical elements. The report notes that between September 2001 and April 2004 the efforts of Operation Tripwire in gathering correctional intelligence led to the identification of approximately 370 connections between inmates and various terrorism investigations, as well as potential terrorism-related activity within the prisons.[4]

## GANGS—TODAY'S STREET TERRORISTS

According to the National Drug Threat Assessment 2004 Executive Policy Summary,[5] there are an estimated 850,000 active gang members in the United States alone. Anyone can be seen as a potential recruit for a terrorist organization. Many gangs have received notoriety over the past 20 years, for example, Latin Kings, Bloods, and Crips. It has been alleged that some groups have ties to terrorist organizations. One such group is El Rukn. In 1986, members of the El Rukn street gang in Chicago plotted with the Libyan leader Muammar Abu Minyar al-Qaddafi to obtain rocket launchers and to perpetrate terrorist acts against the United States in exchange for money. On the European and German fronts, the gang that set the stage for interacting and training with terrorist organizations such as the PLO and IRA was the Baader-Meinhof Gang, which eventually came to be known as the Red Army Faction (RAF). The RAF referred to its members as "urban guerrillas." It operated from the 1970s to 1998, causing great civil unrest, especially in the autumn of 1977. The RAF killed dozens of high-profile Germans in its more than 20 years of existence.

However, in the era of trained and violent organizations, one stands above all: the MS 13.

### Mara Salvatrucha 13 and Sureño 13

Mara Salvatrucha (MS) or MS 13, an El Salvadorian street gang that grew out of the El Salvadorian civil war, emerged in Los Angeles during the 1980s in an area heavily populated with Mexican gangs. The group adopted the number "13" in its name (M is the thirteenth letter of the alphabet). Since its beginning, the gang has successfully migrated from Southern California to the East Coast, with a significant presence in over 30 states including Virginia; Maryland; North Carolina; Pennsylvania; Texas; Washington, DC; and New York City. They are also spreading to Nicaragua, Panama, Guatemala, Mexico, and Honduras.

During the 1980s, California gangs were divided into *sureños* (southerners) and *norteños* (northerners). These were umbrella terms used mainly in the prison setting for Hispanic gangs in California. Sur 13, also known as Sureño 13, originated in Southern California; however, its formation is different from that of MS 13. As gang members began to appear in the Southwest and on the East Coast, they referred to themselves as both Sur 13 and sureños. However, as California gang members representing various southern gangs migrated from the state, many began to unite under the name Sureño.

Some of the differences between MS 13 and Sur 13 are that MS 13 migrated to the East Coast, maintaining ties with California-based members and members of La Mara in El Salvador. Sur 13 gangs on the East Coast are emulators and are rarely connected to the West Coast Sureño gangs. The MS 13 tattoos and graffiti include both "eme" and "ese" (Spanish for the letters M and S), whereas Sur 13 does not include "ese." Although both are Hispanic, MS 13 membership tends to be El Salvadoran, whereas Sur 13 consists mostly of Mexican nationals. However, these differences may not always remain constant, and change or adaptation is always possible.

In March 2005, federal agents together with local law enforcement personnel brought about the arrests of over 100 members of MS 13 in seven cities throughout the United States. The reach and membership of the group are largely unknown. Cliques of the MS 13 are prevalent in the United States, Canada, and Central America. The actual membership numbers are not known, but it has been suggested by federal law enforcement authorities that the numbers in the United States alone may be in the region of 50,000. Law enforcement officials have expressed concern about the emergence of MS 13 and its potential to partake in terrorist activities either independently or as part of a larger organization such as al-Qaeda.

MS 13 criminal activities have included homicide, robbery, drug trafficking, money laundering, illegal exports, and automobile theft. In encounters with members of this formidable gang, law enforcement personnel have noted numerous identifying features of members, for example, large gothic style tattoos, the presence of the area code where the clique originated in the tattoos, theatrical happy or sad faces, three dots on the hands or face signifying "*mi vida loca*" (my crazy life), as well as the number 13. The reference to number 13 may indicate a mathematical component such as the numbers 6 and 7, which add up to 13. The wearing of bandanas and the colors blue and black are also prevalent.

Street gangs are not the only recruiting grounds for potential terrorists. Many organizations claim to be student organizations or associations, and are often found near or on the campuses of higher education. Much like gangs, they seek to exploit their ideology and find individuals who may be weak-minded or who seek a sense of belonging.

Besides traditional methods such as lectures and writings, modern-day anarchists, extremists, and radicals have found a new medium to propagate their ideologies—music.

## MUSIC—ANOTHER MEANS TO RECRUIT

Rap, hip-hop, religious, and rock music are some music genres that can be used to spread ideology, hate, and extremist points of view. Some people feel that the biggest difference between themselves and the prior generation is the music. This is true. During the explosion of rap artists, many young people thought it was chic to be, or follow, "gangsta." Now some are following a jihad, terrorist, or extremist point of view and associating with some questionable parties.

In February 2004, a Great Britain–based group calling themselves Sheikh Terra and the Soul Salah Crew produced a rap video called Dirty Kuffar; *kuffar* is an Arabic term that refers to a nonbeliever. Distributed by the British Muslim extremist Mohammedal-Massari, many aspects of this propaganda video are geared toward a jihad and recruiting point of view. Some striking images splash across the screen, and words such as "peace to Hamas and Hezbollah." Images such as those of the Ku Klux Klan (KKK) and Nazi members seem out of place in a jihad rap song, unless you are seeking to recruit.

Dirty Kuffar is not the only song with a questionable existence. Many other music groups, particularly in the hip-hop genre, can be considered extremist. A Puerto Rican group from Brooklyn, New York, the Mujahideen Team or The M-Team, has appeared at the Islamic Circle of North America (ICNA) and Muslim American Society events. Like Sheikh Terra and the Soul Salah Crew, the Mujahideen Team refers triumphantly to the September 11 attacks. This group exploits the world of electronic media and even has a site on myspace.com, a favorite among thousands of youths. Electronic forums owned by these fringe elements should be monitored. Besides chat rooms, websites, and instant messaging, groups can exploit the use of hidden code within music disks to launch website videos. Regardless of the means or purpose, there is much to be learned in this formidable venue. Use of music is not without controversy, though.

There is some debate with regard to music in the Islamic religion and Muslim culture. Perhaps the largest debate surrounding music in Islam is the issue of whether it is allowed or forbidden. Some people believe that music is pure and a beautiful creation of God Almighty, who set the tone for everything in the universe. Therefore, if it is a creation of God it should be enjoyed. According to the same segment of the population who believe the Quran is complete and perfect, there is no prohibition of music or singing. Prohibition of music is allegedly attributed to some scholars and clerics who interpret the Quran and follow human-made laws and books of Hadith and Sunnah.

One thing that cannot be debated is the use of music to sway the youth, regardless of the country. Music is a powerful and inspiring tool. Every group, from white supremacists to jihad extremists, uses music and songs to express its beliefs. The Palestinian government used music on a grand scale, complete with an orchestra, to celebrate the life of their first female suicide bomber Wafa Idris. This event was broadcast on television on July 24, 2003. Idris had detonated a 22-pound suicide bomb in Jerusalem in late January 2002 that killed her and an 81-year-old Israeli man, and injured more than 100 others.

## CHAPTER CONCEPTS

The chapter concepts can be summarized as follows:

The complexity, sensitive nature, and political nature of homeland security cases present new challenges necessitating new ways to look at data.

Data and data sets pose challenges such as the way in which information is collected, database field structure, data relationships, and data cleanliness.

Arabic names present unique issues in databases due to naming conventions and spelling inconsistencies.

A process for reviewing and analyzing information is KNED, which stands for known, needed, and expected direction.

The seven common forms of analysis are spatial, temporal, tempo, victim, subject, target, and tactic.

In homeland security and analysis, dates are considerations to understand, such as the need to understand that there are 40-plus calendars. Law enforcement personnel should not get locked in on dates as they have numerous meanings depending on the calendar used.

The importance of knowing past initiatives in the effort to understand current and future behavior is emphasized.

It is important to look for SKRAM in homeland security analysis and investigations as well as in recruiting efforts; it is also important to look for additional recruiting and SKRAM variables in gangs, prisons, and music.

## REFERENCES

1. Deputy Chief of Staff for Intelligence. 2005. *Military Guide to Understanding Terrorism in the Twenty-First Century. 2–1.* Fort Eustis, VA: U.S. Army Training and Doctrine Command.
2. Anonymous. 2003. *A Law Enforcement Guide to Understanding Islamist Terrorism.* Baton Rouge, LA: First Capital Technologies, LLC, pp. 82–7.
3. Hudson, R. A. 1999. *The Sociology and Psychology of Terrorism: Who Becomes a Terrorist and Why?* Washington, DC: Federal Research Division, p. 20.
4. U.S. Department of Justice Federal Bureau of Investigations. 2004. *The FBI's Counterterrorism Program Since September 2001, Report to the National Commission on Terrorist Attacks Upon the United States,* p. 15.
5. National Drug Intelligence Center. 2006. *National Drug Threat Assessment 2004 Executive Policy Summary.* http://www.usdoj.gov/ndic/pubs10/10330/#Gangs.

# 9 Enhanced Analysis
## *Transforming Information into Intelligence*

Enhanced analysis is where "the rubber meets the road." Up to this point in the analytical process, personnel have primarily been cleaning data and analyzing information using broad approaches. Transforming the information into quality intelligence requires time and skill. Whether some forms of analysis are art or science is debatable. In the case of homeland security and terrorism analysis, it is both. Methods employed by an analyst can be replicated for use on many different fronts. In addition, there are numerous scientific models and tools available for analysts that can be utilized by anyone to prove or verify information. Data should yield the same results whoever undertakes the process.

Use of a checklist is encouraged but should not be relied on, due to the magnitude of events that can be faced by an analyst conducting terrorism or organized hate group investigations. Too many steps are involved in the intelligence process and information often arrives intermittently, making organization of information difficult. Matrices, link charts, timelines, and maps also play important roles in transforming information into enhanced intelligence. Whatever techniques are used to analyze the information, it is crucial to know a subject's criminal data and what information is available. In warfare, one needs to know the enemy, and in the analytical world one needs to know the enemy (subject or target) as well as the data. If one does not know what one has, how can it be transformed into intelligence? What an analyst sees in data is determined to a large degree by the sum total of his or her knowledge, experience, and training.

## ANALYZING: TRANSFORMING INFORMATION INTO INTELLIGENCE

Philip B. Heymann[1] pointed out the following in his book about international terrorism: "A primary objective of intelligence acquisition abroad is to anticipate the action of terrorist groups" (p. 25). This is also true for domestic groups. In order to apply this premise to the realm of law enforcement, it requires some adjustment. For years, analysts and investigators have spent the majority of their time on linking, locating, and reacting to a suspect's action in hopes of facilitating an arrest. Forecasting and predicting a particular course of action for a suspect and responding to it is not the norm for many law enforcement managers, who usually focus on certainty, control, and the bottom line. Managers must alter their styles of operation when addressing homeland security and terrorism analysis. If the law enforcement community does not take the next step and anticipate the actions of terrorist groups, the results may be catastrophic.

The following comprises information used to develop a group's modus operandi:

Capabilities
History
Statements
Support
Intentions/causes/motivation
Current and future capabilities
Vulnerabilities of the organization
Location of operation
Dates of meaning or significance
Membership

Leadership (noting that there may be a leaderless resistance)
Threatening calls or any other messages
Attacks
Financing or aid

New generations of terrorists learn from their predecessors. They analyze the mistakes made by former comrades who were killed or apprehended. "Press accounts, judicial indictments, courtroom testimony, and trial transcripts are meticulously culled for information on security force tactics and methods, and then absorbed by surviving group members" (p. 25).[2] In other words, they analyze records for intelligence much like law enforcement personnel should. The information gleaned from scrutinizing court proceedings is often overlooked or taken for granted by law enforcement personnel, partly because the law enforcement community traditionally considers a case as closed once a defendant stands trial and all court matters are over. Detailed information, including indictments and affidavits, is widely available for the taking, thanks in part to freedom of information or sunshine records requests. Without the sealing of records, what good is a secret clearance if one only needs to wait for a case to be closed in order to understand how a law enforcement body pursues a case and identifies the tools used to secure the warrant or arrest? These measures can no longer be ignored if one is to completely understand and analyze terrorism. When transforming information into intelligence, one is continually trying to corroborate, advance, and reconcile data. Analysts and investigators must keep their minds open when transforming information and they should not discount learning from the enemy. Use of the aforementioned list, especially court-related documents and press information, will not always yield leads, but the list items mentioned should be monitored and routinely compared with other variables. However, one must not limit oneself to media accounts and court cases in the individual's immediate region. Terrorist organizations and organized hate groups are transnational, as represented by the list of known active patriot groups, and are located in many cities and states. Therefore a global approach is essential, where applicable. This is one aspect that the law enforcement community can learn from the enemy. In a terrorism training document seized in Manchester, England, from a disciple of jihad titled *Military Studies in the Jihad against the Tyrants* (based on translation), also known as the al-Qaeda training manual, information sources, both public and secret, are detailed. It is stated that by using public sources openly and without resorting to illegal means, it is possible for an operative to gather at least 80% of the information needed about the enemy. Sources cited include newspapers, magazines, radio, and television. If terrorists believe they can get 80% of the information they need from legal sources, then law enforcement personnel should have an advantage on the remaining 20% through quality use of criminal intelligence databases and from considering all available factors.[3]

Another factor to consider is links to common crimes, such as theft, that may have hidden variables associated with them. One such factor is the collection of components required to make homemade bombs, such as fertilizer, icing sugar, and diesel fuel. The designation "stolen" for these items does not normally set off bells and whistles. These are common items that anyone can purchase and possess legally in contrast to the theft of military ordnance, such as plastic explosives or dynamite, which would immediately alarm law enforcement personnel and initiate notifications. Whether these items are stolen separately or collectively, there is a potential for disaster. Which items might a potential terrorist seek to obtain without being detected? Although the answers to this question could be endless, analysts need to document detailed and finite descriptions of items that are located, stolen, or purchased, and are in the possession of suspects. These items can then be weighed against other variables in order to develop potential links or leads.

## ANALYTICAL AND INVESTIGATIVE VARIABLES

Once the form, type, classification, and modus operandi are established, there are a multitude of analytical and investigative variables to consider. These variables are used in link analysis or in charting an individual, group, or activity. Some of the variables that should be used when corroborating information for groups and offenders are outlined in this section. The components of a group or an organization profile, as listed in this section, should also be included in terrorism and organized hate crime intelligence databases. However, these variables can be expanded upon, and an analyst can freely search narratives or miscellaneous fields. The components of an offender profile are described in *Crime Analysis: From First Report to Final Arrest*,[4] and these components are now commonplace in many analytical databases.

The components of a group or organization profile comprise the following:

Culture
Cause
Sponsor
Religion
Ideology and beliefs
Symbology, if any
Membership
Makeup
Numbers
Recruitment
Origin
Prior arrests or detainments of members
Financial considerations
Income generation
Supporters
Hierarchy
Chain of command
Political position
Target selection
Method of attacks
Weapons used
Current and future capabilities
Modus operandi
Base of operation, for example, local, regional, national, international, or transnational
Court records
Media records
Historical references, for example, records, reports, and news
Training
Where
By whom

The components of an offender profile comprise the following[4]:

Age, sex, race
Marital status
Level of intelligence
Sexual adjustment
Social adjustment
Appearance
Employment history
Emotional adjustment
Work habits

Location or residence in relation to crime scene
Personality/characteristics

The analysis of a criminal act must take into consideration the following factors:

Motive
Lifestyle
Prior criminal history
Sequence of events during the offense
Mood of the offender before, during, and after committing the offense

When considering the use of variables, personnel are cautioned on the importance of verifying the sources and differentiating between information obtained as tips and that obtained as actual cases. It is also imperative that the information is obtained and entered in compliance with federal, state, and local laws. Use of any of the aforementioned variables for weighing, comparing, or linking is best done with intelligence-based software, provided that the data entry methods are standardized in the database. Attempting to analyze organized groups and their supporters through manual methods and matrix charts may be possible, but this will only delay intelligence development and investigations. No matter what methods are undertaken to analyze and use the variables, it is vital that personnel document their actions. Methods and variables must be documented as well as dates, times, and software used. This will allow other personnel to replicate results, if necessary, and to know if additional information was received that needs to be analyzed.

Analysts and investigators usually focus the most attention on linking individuals, telephone numbers, and addresses. With terrorism and organized hate group crimes, these variables are not always easily available or accurate, but there is one variable that drives all groups—financial considerations. Financial considerations should weigh heavily when gathering information. Without financial backing, terrorist organizations or individuals will have difficulty in succeeding. Terrorist and organized hate groups are committed for the long haul and they often have elaborate support systems that require funding. It has been demonstrated in criminal and some terrorist cases that trailing the money will lead to the source, but this can be laborious. Money laundering plays a role in terrorism support as much as it does in ordinary criminal activity. The three stages of money laundering as follows[5]:

1. Placement—Entry of bulk money into a business-based financial system
2. Layering—Conduction of a series of transactions designed to conceal an audit trail
3. Integration—Legitimization of illegal proceeds

The different methods for completing the stages are as follows[5]:

Structuring (also known as smurfing): This is possibly the most common method used; many individuals deposit cash or buy bank drafts in amounts under $10,000.
Bank complicity: A criminally co-opted bank employee may facilitate the money laundering.
Currency exchanges: Allow customers to buy foreign currency that can be transported out of the country.
Securities brokers: A stockbroker may take in large amounts of cash and issue securities in exchange.
Asset purchases with bulk cash: Big ticket items are purchased, such as automobiles and real estate, and are often registered in a friend's name.
Postal money orders
Telegraphic or wire transfers of funds
Gambling in casinos

Credit cards: Credit card bills are overpaid, and a high credit balance that can be turned to cash at any time is kept.

Travel agencies: Cash is exchanged for travel tickets, which is a common method of moving money from one country to another.

When tracking the money, it is important to be aware of the aforementioned stages and methods. However, not all currency flows through money laundering arenas, traditional banking, or financial market systems. One system that is used legally and illegally is the *hawala* remittance system that is mentioned in Chapter 3.

## WEBSITES AND OTHER RESOURCES

Analysts and investigators must be creative and constantly look for new media from which to harvest information. Advances in cable and satellite television have provided international terrorist organizations, such as the Palestinian Liberation Organization (PLO), opportunities to exploit the media to their advantage and to promote their positions in the Middle East. What may be perceived as just another news broadcast or interview can provide insight into locations, individuals, and direct or indirect messages. However, this method places investigators at the whim of terrorist organizations and at the subjectivity of the news. More proactive and real-time measures are needed. The Internet is a good source of information. Organization and membership websites, especially hate groups, often post their beliefs, causes, calendars for upcoming events, propaganda, flyers, and even their manuals of operation. One can learn a great deal by viewing the world through their eyes. Figures 9.1 and 9.2 show examples of flyers created and distributed by groups. The two groups with flyers depicted are the World Church of the Creator (Figure 9.1) and the National Alliance (Figure 9.2). They readily demonstrate how concerns and topics can be conveyed to an international audience. Flyers such as these are meant to stir controversy and enlist new members. Rallies also arouse many emotions and create contention. Rallies or gatherings are held for the purposes of recruiting, promoting beliefs, and gathering attention. They may be held publicly or privately, as depicted in Figure 9.3. These venues are valuable sources of information with uniforms and symbols displayed (Figure 9.4). Speeches given at rallies provide additional information. Many groups utilize signs (Figure 9.5) to communicate their beliefs.

There are many websites associated with organized hate groups. These are promulgated by individuals and educational institutions and provide a wide range of information on, and insight into, activities and events that may prove helpful to law enforcement personnel. These sites should be viewed with some level of skepticism, however, because their content is often skewed and subjective. Other than a group's official website or websites operated by its leadership and members, there are two sites that are dedicated to the collection of detailed and reliable hate crime and hate group information: (1) the Southern Poverty Law Center (SPLC) Intelligence Report (http://www.splc.org) has resources on symbols, hate groups, attacks, legislation, and government resources and (2) the Anti-Defamation League (ADL; http://www.adl.org) has resources directed toward law enforcement personnel and training, postings of upcoming extremist events, a terrorist attack database, and listings of extremism by state. Both of these are nonprofit organizations that aid law enforcement agencies. Raymond A. Franklin's[6] *The Hate Dictionary* is also available on the Internet. It provides links to a tremendous number of Internet sites as well as servers, chat rooms, groups, and several other locations.

There are thousands of Internet sites that can provide insight into a group or an individual, as well as information geared toward law enforcement. Some of the many resources available concerning intelligence on terrorist groups or threats are as follows:

http://www.dhs.gov—U.S. Department of Homeland Security
http://www.fbi.gov/terrorinfo/counterrorism/waronterrorhome.htm—Federal    Bureau    of    Investigation (FBI) terrorism information

FIGURE 9.1    World Church of the Creator "End Muslim Immigration Now" flyer.

http://www.terrorism-research.com—terrorism research
http://www.rand.org—terrorism research
http://www.start.umd.edu/start/—National Consortium for the Study of Terrorism and
    Responses to Terrorism (START)
http://www.whitehouse.gov/homeland—homeland security contact listing
http://www.state.gov/s/ct—U.S. Department of State
http://www.nipc.gov—National Infrastructure Protection Center
http://www.justice.gov—U.S. Department of Justice
http://www.naco.org—National Association of Counties
http://www.defense.gov—U.S. Department of Defense
http://www.counterterrorism.com—examines the counterterrorism tools available to law
    enforcement agencies and first responder personnel

# COMING SOON
## TO A NEIGHBORHOOD NEAR YOU

- Black savages are flooding in from Africa.
- They will spread the HIV virus to every corner of the United States.
- They will reproduce like cockroaches; despite being poor, uneducated, and jobless.
- They will bring murder, rape, and robbery to every community in which they are placed.

TOP LEFT: BLACK AFRICANS LINE UP TO BE TAKEN TO THE UNITED STATES. TOP RIGHT: CHILDREN LAUGH AND PLAY AMONG THE CORPSES LEFT TO ROT IN THE STREET; A COMMON SIGHT IN AFRICA.

A campaign has been launched to bring more non-Whites to the United States. Recruiting teams are being sent to Africa to persuade Blacks to move here as government-approved immigrants.

The Jews want as many non-Whites as possible mixed in with the White population as quickly as possible. They believe that once they have done that it will be too difficult a task for us to unmix what they have mixed. They'll be surprised at what we are willing to do to repair the damage they have done.

## WHITE REVOLUTION: IT'S COMING TOO!

# NATIONAL ALLIANCE
**P.O. Box 90 • Hillsboro, WV 24946 • USA • 304-653-4600**
**www.natvan.com • www.natall.com**

**FIGURE 9.2**   National Alliance "Coming Soon" flyer.

http://www.nlectc.org—National Law Enforcement and Corrections Technology Centers; daily terrorism update newsletter

http://www.terrorism-info.org.il/site/home/default.asp—Intelligence and Terrorism Information Center, Israel

Although it is impossible to provide an all-inclusive listing, the aforementioned sites provide a good starting point and direction to many other online resources. If past behavior is an indication

**FIGURE 9.3**    Ku Klux Klan followers in Florida gathering at a public park.

**FIGURE 9.4**    Alleged member of a branch of the Ku Klux Klan: The military-style uniform and symbols of hate are proudly displayed and worn.

of future behavior, law enforcement personnel should routinely review the many online calendars of significant terrorist events and meaningful dates for the numerous groups all over the world. Dates of significance, anniversaries, and holidays may assist in forecasting or validating the possibility of future threats. Also, many groups or their members have published online memoirs, diaries, and books that may cite specific dates. These publications are available through various rogue websites as well as through some popular online bookstores.

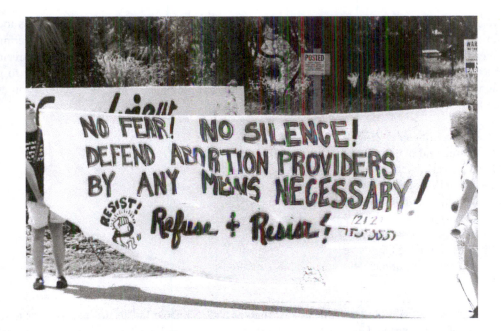

**FIGURE 9.5**    The left-wing group Refuse and Resist, with suspected relations to a Ku Klux Klan faction, at a rally in Florida allegedly advocating disobedience.

What is critically needed is an awareness of the various media venues available to the general public. Venues such as the Internet, shortwave radio, print media (magazines, papers, and books), and independent nonmainstream publishing companies offer an array of how-to guides that virtually anyone can purchase for $30 or less. Although some of these media may have a legitimate target audience, it is the quick and easy access to these items by potentially dangerous individuals that should be considered by any analyst. One such example is a publishing company in Colorado that is referred to as the publisher of the "action library." This publisher operates legally under state and federal laws. However, law enforcement agencies should be aware of many of this publisher's publications for insight into the information they provide. There are hundreds or more of such publications of which law enforcement personnel should be aware. One such book invites the reader to tap into a unique storehouse of forbidden knowledge, with information on building weapons and explosives, opposing big governments, changing one's identity, and sniping. This is just one book. Many other books are available that give instructions on forging identity documents. Numerous writings on building bombs and silencers, sniping, explosives, and ammunition are also available.

These books are not necessarily written with malicious intent. Some are written by individuals who do not have any relationships with terrorist or organized hate group organizations. Some books are how-to manuals authored recently, whereas some books are decades old that were written by individuals with direct ties to terrorist and organized hate groups. One such book, a fictional publication that recently claimed revisited notoriety, was *The Turner Diaries*. After the Oklahoma City bombing and the subsequent apprehension of Timothy McVeigh, the FBI reported that McVeigh was in possession of *The Turner Diaries*. This easily obtained publication was allegedly used as a blueprint for his illicit activities. There are many eerie similarities to the bombing and the book's content, including the type of bomb used. If one person can use this writing as a blueprint for destruction, how many others are using a multitude of other books available for providing information about illegal and illicit activities? How many law enforcement personnel, including analysts, have read or are even aware of these publications?

Law enforcement personnel strive to prevent crime and identify weaknesses in their jurisdictions through analyses that may be exploited by the criminal element. This information is then used to develop operational and deployment strategies. The criminal element does not have access to this information, which gives law enforcement personnel the analytical advantage. However, the criminal element has access to many publications that it may use to self-train, so why should law enforcement ignore the obvious? Analytical personnel should be aware of these publications in order to gain insight into the thinking of potential terrorists and related individuals, and their activities in areas such as the following:

Robberies (financial gain)
Gathering and making weapons and ammunition
Leaderless resistance
Cause and ideology
How to hide and avoid authorities
Use of disguises
Hideout needs (supplies)
Making and using explosives
Column and cell organizations as well as supporters
Symbols

Another set of published documents that may provide valuable insight for terrorists or terrorist groups is official court and criminal case documents, as described in Chapter 7. Many investigators and analysts overlook the amount of information that becomes publicly available at the conclusion of their cases or during subsequent prosecution. Virtually every aspect of a case, including testimonies of plaintiffs and defendants, is available for the taking. Those engaged in terrorism-related activities can easily obtain unsealed documents and use them to gain information that can have detrimental effects on future law enforcement endeavors. Analytical personnel should be aware of the availability of this information and should include a review of these documents in their postcase analysis. An example of one such document is a how-to terrorism manual that was admitted as evidence by prosecutors during the federal trial of four men for their alleged involvement in the 1998 bombing of the U.S. Embassies in Kenya and Tanzania. This document included 18 chapters on how to operate as a terrorist. Topics that were covered in detail included counterfeiting currency and documents, communication, use of apartments, transportation, training, kidnapping and assassinations, espionage, explosives, use of poisons, and interrogations. Although this material was written for potential terrorists, law enforcement personnel could use this information against them. In addition, law enforcement personnel should consider these publications important to future intelligence-gathering initiatives and, where applicable by law, they should strive to have the information sealed from public review.

Another concern for law enforcement, particularly with organized hate groups and their members, is information available in jail, prison, probation, and parole databases. Information in these systems is often overlooked, probably because many law enforcement personnel view this part of the criminal justice process as being out of their hands. Stockpiles of information are waiting to be harvested in these untapped databases. Institutions capture a great deal of detailed information about inmates' activities and associations. This resource is an excellent source of information, and many correctional agencies are more than willing to share the insight they may possess about these groups.

## MACRO–MICRO–MACRO CONTINUUM

Armed with an arsenal of databases, resources, checklists, and variables, an analyst must begin to validate inferences, probabilities, and hypotheses. In order to avoid tunnel vision on any one piece of data, analysts should employ the "macro-micro-macro continuum."[7] This technique aids analysts in re-evaluating and double-checking initial results.

**FIGURE 9.6**   Macro–micro–macro continuum.

   The first macro includes the numerous pieces of information, intelligence, and variables present in a case. It gives the big picture. Figure 9.6 shows six potential sources of information that flow into the analytical resources. This includes raw computer-aided dispatch (CAD) or records management system (RMS) data that are available to local law enforcement agencies and form the first macro step. The problem often encountered is that many data sources, with the exception of the aforementioned two, stand alone and create delays. Therefore, use of data warehouses is encouraged where feasible.

   Providing there are no database connectivity issues or data sharing restrictions, the data are then extracted, transported, transformed, and loaded into the appropriate criminal intelligence data tools. Once the data are consolidated, any number of analytical techniques can be initiated. This starts the micro step of the continuum. During this step, analysts seek to identify potential targets, relationships, associates, and supporters. The micro step requires definitive answers and results. Every piece of information is scrutinized from every angle, and nothing is left out. However, this is not the end of the process. The use of results obtained from the micro step may lead to incorrect assumptions. These results must be extracted and re-evaluated against the big picture in order to validate them. Caution must be exercised at the micro level, especially with terrorism groups, because of their use of sleeper cells and their widespread networks of supporters. This is why the third step, macro, is used as a validation step. The results from the micro stage are re-evaluated and analyzed using analysis methods such as spatial, temporal, target, victim, and subject methods, in order to look for outcomes that may contradict the first step.

   Throughout the process, analysts should continually search for one-to-many and many-to-one relationships. Too often, analysts focus on one-to-one relationships alone, thus creating a potential void that leaves associations undetected. Once all three steps are performed, the final analytical reports are completed and submitted for consideration. However, this is not the end of the analysis. The process is continuous and is never complete unless there is definitive proof to the contrary. By using the macro-micro-macro continuum, analysts will be following many of the same methods that have been used for years, but now they will be taking a step back after their initial findings and will be comparing their data again, with a fresh look. However, this continuum is only a technique with which one can avoid errors and omissions. Analysts must still follow some type of approach or method.

   Analysts cannot rely on only one method. For the purposes of verification, a minimum of two methods should be utilized. Four of the more prevalent methods used by analysts to verify leads and substantiate information are as follows: (1) link analysis, (2) matrix tables, (3) timelines, and (4) flowcharts. Three of these methods are described below.

## LINK ANALYSIS CHARTS

Link analysis charts provide visual or graphical overviews of interrelationships. They are great analytical resources for long-term and complex investigations. Although there are many software packages available that provide link charts, this can be done manually with the use of virtually any software package that allows the drawing of graphics. Some basic rules for developing link charts, such as the one shown in Figure 9.7, are as follows:

> When connecting relationships by using lines, it is important that only confirmed relationships are connected with solid lines and arrows to demonstrate the direction of the relationship, where applicable. When a relationship cannot be confirmed, the use of a dashed line is appropriate.
> Groups or businesses are reflected using boxes, and in some cases individuals are drawn as individual circles within a larger circle.
> Individuals are reflected as circles, with the appropriate annotations reflected in same.

Link charts can be drawn using link analysis pictograms, such as the one shown in Figure 9.8, to reflect individuals, telecommunications, currency, and computers. Use of link charts becomes cumbersome when there are many relationships and a large organization. When this occurs, there is the likelihood that relationship lines overlap. This is not necessarily a concern, but when there are too many relationships the charts can be difficult to read. This can sometimes be remedied by using a curved line where the lines intersect, as if it were jumping the other line.

**FIGURE 9.7**  Link chart.

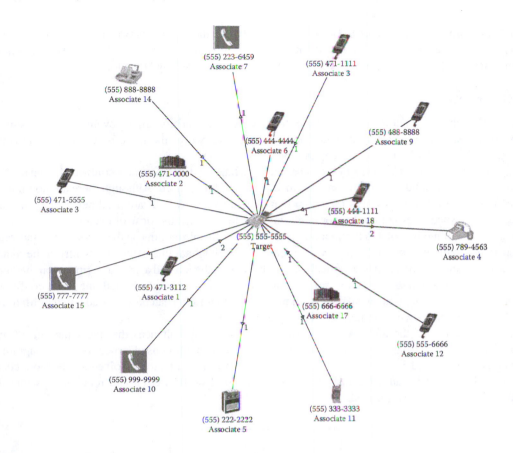

**FIGURE 9.8** Link analysis chart using pictograms.

## ASSOCIATION AND DIRECTIONAL MATRICES

The second analytical method is the use of association and directional matrices. An association matrix, as shown in Figure 9.9, is often used to support a link analysis chart. The names of individuals are entered alphabetically, with the group name on the bottom line. As associations are uncovered criteria symbols are entered into the appropriate boxes, with a legend identifying the symbols provided. The most commonly used symbols are circles, shaded and unfilled; plus signs; equal signs; and check marks. A directional matrix is commonly used to track the flow of goods, money, and weapons. If there is a substantial intelligence case being worked, it may be necessary to compile a separate chart for each commodity being monitored. The directional matrix looks similar to an accountant's ledger and is compiled for

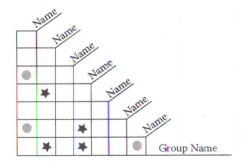

**FIGURE 9.9** An association matrix.

the same purpose as a link chart, but it shows commodity and money flow between relationships. The left axis represents where the commodity originates, and the top indicates where it goes. The right axis has a column reflecting the "total from" and the bottom a column reflecting "total to."

## EVENT FLOWCHARTS

Event flowcharts are another tool that helps to visualize relationships among events. They are similar to timelines. Several charting methods are available, but two of the more prevalent are the Birch method (Figure 9.10) and the Mercer method (Figure 9.11).[5]

The Birch method uses some of the same rules as a link chart. If an event is confirmed, then the box is drawn using a solid line. If it is unconfirmed, a dashed line is used. Although there are no limits to the number of event boxes, it is important that directional arrow lines are used between events and solid and dashed lines are used accordingly in order to establish the flow of events.

The Mercer method places the year on the top line, applicable months on the second line, and years separated on the month line, using two vertical lines. A diagonal line is then drawn from the month downward and is connected to a vertical line, with dates on the left and a brief description on the right. As with the other charts, an unconfirmed connection is marked using a dashed line and a confirmed one using a solid line. If an event date is unknown, the month span can be specified (such as March to July) and the unknown date marked with a question mark.

Use of either of the aforementioned two methods greatly enhances the understanding of any intelligence case. Usually, personal preference dictates the method used. Once the final diagram is generated, it should be reviewed by someone who was not directly involved in its production. This is important because an analyst can become too close to a case, and relationships may be taken for granted or overlooked.

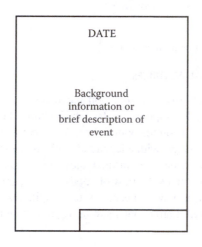

**FIGURE 9.10**   Birch method event chart.

**FIGURE 9.11**   Mercer method event chart.

## Heuer's Analysis of Competing Hypotheses (ACH)

Another assessment method is Heuer's[8] analysis of competing hypotheses (ACH). The ACH is an eight-step procedural tool used to enhance judgment on important issues and to minimize common analytical pitfalls; the eight steps are listed as follows[8]:

1. Identify the possible hypotheses to be considered. Use a group of analysts with different perspectives to brainstorm the possibilities.
2. Make a list of significant evidence and arguments for and against each hypothesis.
3. Prepare a matrix with hypotheses across the top and evidence down the side. Analyze the "diagnosticity" of the evidence and arguments, that is, identify the items that are most helpful in judging the relative likelihood of the hypotheses.
4. Refine the matrix. Reconsider the hypotheses, and delete evidence and arguments that have no diagnostic value.
5. Draw tentative conclusions about the relative likelihood of each hypothesis. Proceed by trying to disprove the hypotheses rather than prove them.
6. Analyze how sensitive a conclusion is to a few critical items of evidence. Consider the consequences for the analysis if that evidence were wrong, misleading, or subject to a different interpretation.
7. Report conclusions. Discuss the relative likelihood of all the hypotheses, not just the most likely one.
8. Identify milestones for future observation that may indicate events are taking a different course than the one expected.

Heuer's list is comprehensive. It also complements the two methods already discussed, the macro-micro-macro continuum and the loop effect, by demonstrating a consistent approach to tackling complex issues.

Use of any one of these methods alone or together will greatly enhance the quality of a report as well as aiding in threat and vulnerability assessments.

## ASSESSING THE THREAT

Terrorists are strategic actors. They choose their targets based on the weaknesses they see in the victim's defenses and preparedness. This is where threat assessments come into play. Government agencies have used threat assessment models and reports to identify sources and potential threats for many years. Assessments also assist in identifying the likelihood of occurrence of a threat. Assessments should emphasize well-documented events in terms of dangers or opportunities that exist due to a terrorist or organized hate group against an agency's interests. Agencies have a tremendous need to detect and intercept security threats that may impact their jurisdiction. However, gathering information and analyzing it solely based on individuals or groups creates a void. The void is the target that may be threatened. These threats should be measured against venues within a jurisdiction by law enforcement agencies using a set of predefined standards to ensure that all communities are evaluated in like terms.

In a post-9/11 International Association of Chiefs of Police (IACP) project response report,[9] a team of law enforcement experts identified a four-level standardized system for locating and measuring community risk. The four tiers of the risk system are as follows:

1. First priority level—fatal (functions that on failure could result in death, severe financial loss, or legal liability)
2. Second priority level—critical (functions that would be difficult to do without for any length of time)

3. Third priority level—important (functions that are not critical to an agency)
4. Fourth priority level—routine (functions that are not strategically important and that, if they fail, would only cause inconvenience)

The IACP four-tier system is more of a criticality assessment than a threat assessment, but it should be included as part of a threat assessment. According to a U.S. General Accounting Office publication,[10] a criticality assessment is a process designed to systematically identify and evaluate important assets and infrastructure in terms of various factors, such as the mission and significance of a target. For example, nuclear power plants, key bridges, and major computer networks might be identified as "critical" in terms of their importance to national security, economic activity, and public safety (p. 6).

Criticality assessments or the IACP's four-tier system should be used to bolster a threat assessment because they provide a basis for identifying the assets and structures that are the most likely to be at risk.

The purpose of a threat assessment is to evaluate the likelihood of terrorist activity for a given asset or location. It is a support tool for making decisions concerning how to establish and prioritize security program requirements, planning, and resource allocations. Raymond J. Decker, Director of Defense Capabilities and Management, stated, "A threat assessment identifies and evaluates each threat on the basis of various factors, including capability, intention, and lethality of an attack" (p. 3).[10] For several years, the Department of Defense has been utilizing threat assessments in its antiterrorism program for its military installations.

Threat assessment approaches involve many factors, but three of the most common are a terrorist group's intentions, past activities, and capabilities. These factors are detected throughout the analytical and investigative processes and should be applied when developing threat assessments.

Threat assessment models are designed to be generic in nature unless specific details dictate otherwise. They are not based on worst-case scenarios, as are vulnerability assessments. It is impossible to develop a model for every feasible threat scenario or group, but threat assessments provide a foundation on which to build. Developing a threat assessment model requires knowledge and survey of the jurisdiction or region in order to identify potential threats or areas of concern. Much focus of threat assessments is tailored toward buildings. Personnel should not forget the significance of key individuals. Heads of Fortune 500 companies can make attractive targets, as they have in the past, for terrorist groups seeking to weaken an economy. In order to emphasize this point, just imagine the repercussions of the stock market should one of these individuals be targeted.

Threat assessment reports usually begin with an introduction, a description of the geographic area being considered, and a list of reporting or participating agencies. This is followed by the report body, and the report usually concludes with related activities, a synopsis, and a forecast. The following layout is suggested for regular assessments in matters of homeland security. It should be followed by the completed site survey in the body text:

List identified targeted groups, members (suspects), and incidents.
Report results from checking websites and publications; report target and suspect analyses.
Initiate link analysis.
Provide link charts and matrices; sort based on numerous variables.
Provide results of reviewing against other link charts and older data.
Report data search results on victims, suspects, groups, and targets (based on findings).
Identify specific details: groups, members, targets, and geographic limitations.
Verify leads and information (should be done at all steps).
Report results of site file reviews and visits.
Determine posture of the sites' physical security status.
Report results of briefings conducted (should be done at all steps, as needed).

Identify all splinter groups.
Identify all supporter groups (active and passive).
Identify financial links.
Continually update all links and information without delay.
Perform final analysis review of all available data.

Threats or terrorist activities do not occur overnight. They are often elaborate and well financed, and are planned months or years in advance. This is to the advantage of law enforcement. The chances of gaining information on, or insight into a group are enhanced by time and by attending certain gatherings, and investigating propaganda for potential threat indicators. Some types of gatherings and propaganda that could be beneficial to law enforcement personnel in terms of gaining information are as follows:

Public demonstrations
Meetings, rallies
Unrest at colleges and public speeches advocating violence
Training
Antigovernment posters and leaflets
Publications and compact discs (CDs)
Phone threats

Evaluation and assessments should be continuous. Because threat assessments are invaluable decision-making tools, they need to be updated at least annually. Threats can change and new threats emerge; failure to reconcile assessment data can produce invalid information. Although assessments are key decision-making support tools, it is important to understand that they might not properly capture emerging terrorist threats.

## VULNERABILITY ASSESSMENT

Vulnerability assessments help to provide in-depth analyses into the inner workings of a facility or designated site in order to identify components that may be at risk for attack. The following is the U.S. General Accounting Office's[10] working definition of a vulnerability assessment:

> A vulnerability assessment is a process that identifies weaknesses in physical structures, personnel protection systems, processes, or other areas that may be exploited by terrorists and may suggest options to eliminate or mitigate those weaknesses.
>
> Vulnerability assessments are related to a current period of time and should be performed at least annually. All possible what-if and worst-case scenarios should be researched. The what-if scenarios involve security, design, engineering, mitigation, response, and damage buffers. Once an assessment is initiated and the site to be protected is identified, the perimeter of the identified target should be expanded to ensure that all possible ingresses and egresses are secured (p. 5).

Typically, vulnerability assessments are conducted by teams of skilled experts. Areas such as engineering, security, finance, and information systems are generally beyond the scope of law enforcement personnel. Therefore, experts and those with an intimate working knowledge of the site conduct the assessment. The level of protection needed should be determined, and the site in question should be evaluated against different threat levels. Some factors to consider when determining threat levels are national security, critical infrastructures, on- and off-site hazards, proximity to population centers, and adequacy of the site's existing preparedness plans. These factors help law enforcement personnel to make key management and deployment decisions should the need arise.

Government facilities are not the only facilities that should have vulnerability assessments performed annually. Many private-sector facilities could be attractive targets for terrorists and organized hate groups. Therefore, law enforcement officials should try to get copies of private industry assessments, especially for high-risk businesses such as power plants, natural gas facilities, and schools. Conducting an assessment is only one part of the process. Any identified exposures should be addressed and rectified before concluding the assessment or within a specific time frame.

With the information from threat and vulnerability assessments, law enforcement managers and government officials can be armed with sufficient information to make judgments concerning risks posed by terrorist attacks. Threat and vulnerability assessments can be expedited and made readily available through the use of spatial analysis geographic information systems (GISs). Examples of how a GIS can aid law enforcement personnel are shown in Figures 9.12 through 9.14. These figures can be used to demonstrate the vulnerability of a dirty bomb in an urban setting. Figure 9.12 is a bird's-eye view of a metropolis before the scenario begins. A 1,000-pound conventional high-explosive device contained in a sport utility vehicle and laced with powdered and liquid radioactive waste is detonated in an intersection. Figure 9.13 shows the fallout pattern of the device 1 hour after detonation, demonstrating the vulnerability of numerous buildings having close proximity to the blast site, which helps law enforcement personnel to evacuate and quarantine the area. Figure 9.14 reveals the extent to which radiation levels can reach within the blast area. Using the results of GIS modeling algorithms such as these, it is possible to conduct detailed vulnerability assessments that go beyond the mere recognition of a building or a specific target. Analysts are thus able to immediately assist homeland security plans with command center and staging area logistics, establishment of perimeters, and model contamination of soil and groundwater.

**FIGURE 9.12**  Bird's-eye view of a metropolis. (Courtesy of Dan Helms, Bair Software Research and Consulting, 2003.)

**FIGURE 9.13**    Fallout pattern. (Courtesy of Dan Helms, Bair Software Research and Consulting, 2003.)

## SPATIAL REFERENCING AND ITS USE IN HOMELAND SECURITY ANALYSIS

Geography and space are substantial variables to consider in analysis, threat assessment, response, recovery, and investigation. A GIS can provide decision makers with the data needed to confront a wide variety of threats including disasters, sabotage, and terrorist attacks. It also provides decision makers with a better understanding of data. Mapping, or spatial referencing, of current and future terrorist threats and capabilities is done with specific facilities and vulnerable targets. This allows authorities to determine the organizations that pose the greatest threats and the facilities and sectors that are at the greatest risk. It also allows planners, managers, and policy makers to develop thresholds for preemptive or protective action through the use of attribute data via what are referred to as layers. Layers of data in geographic software allow the user to paint a picture in a wide variety of patterns by activating one layer against another in order to visualize and identify important factors that may otherwise go undetected.

Spatial analysis, although growing in popularity with the analytical community in the form of crime mapping, is often bypassed by agencies due to the perceived complexity of operation and associated costs. This may be why law enforcement and military personnel rely so heavily on tabular data and matrices. Although the military uses satellite imagery as well as other forms of spatial referencing, the law enforcement community lags behind. In recent years, this has started to change, partly due to the funding and training for GIS offered by numerous federal agencies such as the National Law Enforcement and Correction Technology Centers and several private corporations. The law enforcement community has also recently begun to reap the benefits of spatial analysis through the use of affordable and user-friendly desktop GIS. However, personnel need to understand GISs.

**FIGURE 9.14** Radiation levels. (Courtesy of Dan Helms, Bair Software Research and Consulting, 2003.)

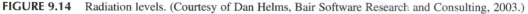

According to the Federal Interagency Coordinating Committee on Digital Cartography,[11] a GIS is "a system of computer hardware, software, and procedures designed to support the capture, management, manipulation, analysis, and display of spatially referenced data for solving complex planning and management problems." The latter part of the definition, "solving complex planning and management problems," is appropriate when dealing with homeland security and terrorism cases, because terrorism is complex and poses a variety of management problems for law enforcement managers.

Through the use of a GIS, law enforcement and government agencies can share information on several different platforms. This is particularly important when analyzing data from locales outside traditional jurisdictional boundaries. With a GIS, law enforcement personnel are able to map incidents or potential targets at various levels, from statewide level (small scale) to street level (large scale). Virtually the only restriction placed on this capability is the projection, or real-world reference, at which base map data are displayed, but this is easily transformed via most desktop GIS applications. Issues such as not having a neighboring jurisdiction's base map can be easily rectified through the use of free resources such as the U.S. Census Bureau's topologically integrated geographic encoding and referencing (TIGER) files. These files provide a wide variety of geographic layers available on the Internet that when downloaded (and projected if needed) can enhance the analysts' abilities to visualize areas with which they are unfamiliar. In addition, there are many Internet sites and resources, some free and some fee-based, that show new ways to view intelligence and the world. This is just the beginning. A GIS has an extensive range of applications, some of which have been used for decades and are just now being discovered by the law enforcement community. However, it is important to note that the majority of the data used to formulate spatial analysis in law enforcement is the agencies' own data. Herein lies the problem. The geocoding (address-matching) process used in GISs often demonstrates that many law enforcement agencies only attain an 80% accuracy rate, which translates into potential decisions being made knowing that possibly 20% of the data is missing.

## RANGE OF GEOGRAPHIC INFORMATION SYSTEM USES

The range of uses and benefits of a GIS is very broad. Beyond the obvious use of enhanced information sharing, a GIS offers an integrated analysis for law enforcement personnel. The ability to map a city's infrastructure against a wide range of potential homeland or security targets enables personnel to make informed decisions based on the whole picture.

A GIS can assist in homeland security analysis through many facets: The first facet is detection, deterrence, and identification. It is essential that all potential at-risk locations are identified and properly referenced on a map. This allows an analyst or first responder to visually detect other potential indirect targets, thereby enhancing the likelihood of deterring future attacks. Additionally, first responders would be able to instantly identify a potential field of fire if a gunman or sniper were to open fire from any given location. This capability is also helpful during the evidence collection process, because it limits the search area.

The second facet is preparing and planning. Law enforcement personnel, regardless of their assignments, are trained in planning and preparing for worst-case scenarios. This is particularly important in homeland security cases. Proper preparation and planning are crucial at all levels. Through a GIS, all personnel involved in a plan of action can gain a multidimensional view of various layers of data. By developing layers that account for the what-if scenarios, analysts are able to readily call upon and visualize a variety of data without interfering with any one aspect of an operation.

The remaining three facets are resource deployment, response and evacuation, and recovery. All are critical to any emergency preparedness plan, but they can easily go unnoticed by an analyst who is not looking at the global picture. Deployment and evacuation are two facets that pose perhaps the greatest concern for local and state law enforcement agencies. Deployment scenarios, depending on the seriousness of an operation or incident, are something for which most agencies have contingency plans. These usually occur during civil disorders or demonstrations, but they can be adjusted to fit most plans. In addition to basic deployment planning and monitoring, GIS software enables managers to estimate response times of field units.

Evacuations add a new dimension, because most agencies do not have control over civilians and outside parties. Evacuation plans are often established when a particular segment of the population is affected, as in the case of natural disasters or nuclear accidents. These plans are frequently used by emergency operation command centers that have a specific criterion for evacuation and predefined locations to which the evacuees are sent. In a terrorist situation, law enforcement does not have the luxury of dictating all the evacuation or deployment criteria. The use of real-time spatial data can greatly enhance an ad hoc plan of action.

The Federal Geographic Data Committee (FGDC),[12] a 19-member interagency committee composed of representatives from the executive office of the president and cabinet-level, and independent agencies, posted a document titled *Homeland Security and Geographic Information Systems* on its website detailing how GIS and mapping technology can save lives and protect property in post-9/11 America. The article cites several uses for a GIS in ensuring homeland security, some of which have been described earlier in this section, and expands on the topic.

According to the FGDC, the following characteristics that make up geographic information technologies, combined with appropriate sets of geospatial information, constitute an invaluable tool for handling, displaying, and analyzing information involved in every aspect of homeland security. The characteristics, as cited by the FGDC, are as follows[12]:

Detection: Geospatial information provides the spatial and temporal backdrop upon which effective and efficient threat analysis is accomplished. By linking and analyzing temporally and spatially associated information in real time, patterns may be detected that lead to timely identification of likely modalities and targets.

Preparedness: Emergency planners and responders must often depend on geospatial information to accomplish their mission. Current, accurate information that is readily available is crucial to ensuring the readiness of teams to respond. Geospatial information access and interoperability standards are essential elements, as they support the means for the nation's response units to react to terrorist attacks, natural disasters, and other emergencies.

Prevention: Geospatial information provides a means to detect and analyze patterns regarding terrorist threats and possible attacks. This information, coupled with information about borders, waters, and airspace, in turn may lead to disruption of terrorists' plans or prevention or interdiction of their attacks.

Protection: Geospatial information is an important component in the analysis of critical infrastructure vulnerabilities and in the use of decision support technologies such as visualization and simulation. This anticipates and protects against the cascading effects of an attack on one system as it relates to other interdependent systems.

Response and recovery: Geospatial information is used by many organizations in response to, and recovery from, natural disasters. Similarly, this information is invaluable for emergency response services of all kinds, as well as for carrying out long-term recovery operations. The Federal Response Plan, developed by 26 federal agencies and the Red Cross, identifies overall responsibilities and the concept of operations for presidential-declared disasters. A number of emergency support functions are identified, with the Federal Emergency Management Agency (FEMA) in the lead for coordinating response to natural disasters and the federal wildland agencies responsible for coordinating response to wildland fires.

These are examples of the potential benefits of using a GIS. The GIS is a relatively new tool for many law enforcement agencies that are just beginning to discover and harness the power of these systems. Powerful GISs are now available that quickly render one to several layers of digital geospatial data into map-like products. These systems can facilitate near real-time performance for a wide range of relevant geospatial analyses. They can also be used to access and process digital geospatial data virtually anywhere because digital data, unlike analog data, can be instantly transmitted. This ability is of great benefit during the preparation and planning stages.

## PREPARATION AND PLANNING

Use of a GIS in homeland security is dependent on good, clean, accurate, and timely data. The two fundamental components for using a GIS are incident data and base map data. Clean incident data, particularly addresses, are extremely important and are one of the leading reasons why information does not get geocoded or mapped. This is why it is essential for all participants to have a complete understanding of the importance of standardized data. The second component of a GIS is the quality of the base map used by the analyst. Analysts often have to work with layers of data that are maintained and updated by independent contractors or other departments. These can contribute to the learning curve associated with mastering the use of GIS-based programs. No matter who is charged with maintaining or updating the numerous GIS layers, updates must be done consistently and with a sense of urgency. Changes need to be shared with all end users, through word of mouth or preferably through formal means such as metadata (data about the data). The national spatial data infrastructure (NSDI) is a working example of compiling metadata to facilitate integration of data and support decision-making. The NSDI is a network of federal, state, and local geospatial information databases that provide metadata for all information holdings to make information easier to find and to use.

Effective planning and analysis require officials to anticipate the future while remaining cognizant of the past. When assessing and evaluating potential hazards and risks spatially, the integration of historical incidents against current issues may provide a vision for the future. Terrorists often seek to learn from those they consider to have achieved some level of success with their tactics. Their continuous review of historical material, such as writings and court material, is designed to assist them in developing future plans of attack. Law enforcement personnel must not overlook the same tactic of learning from the past, locally and nationally.

## GEOGRAPHIC INFORMATION SYSTEM LINKING

In the field of GISs, three words are commonly used: (1) points, (2) lines, and (3) polygons. Points are often referred to as dots or pins. They are known to law enforcement personnel as the locations of crimes, but they can also be residential locations and potential targets. Lines usually represent street center lines, roadways, and property lines. Polygons are often used to depict building footprints, land use and zoning, and jurisdictional boundaries. Perhaps one of the greatest benefits of a GIS is its capability to link images, documents, data tables, building floor plans, operational plans, points of contact, and guidelines through a process known as "hot linking." Hot linking provides a valuable tool for all law enforcement officials. It allows the use of the full power of technology by incorporating a mechanism designed to reduce or eliminate manual efforts and incorporate multiple sources of data within a single project or file. Once information is plotted within the GIS and saved as a project, law enforcement officials have a venue in which they can link a wide array of documents and images. The end user can simply point and click on a map location in order to gain access to all the linked items.

## ADDITIONAL BENEFITS OF A GEOGRAPHIC INFORMATION SYSTEM

Additional benefits to be gained from a GIS include the ability to anticipate and visualize fields of view that may be available to field commanders as well as the ability to see other possible points of interest and dispersion patterns for chemical and toxic plumes. The latter is a critical aspect of the planning stage when anticipating and developing evacuation models, as well as when developing deployment strategies that ensure the safety of all first responders. Figure 9.15 shows a hypothetical scenario of a chemical plant along a waterway and possibly within 5 miles of residential areas. In this scenario, responding officers and managers would be able to readily identify areas affected by toxic plumes through the use of 1- and 3-mile buffers. This includes the waterways and railways that may otherwise go undetected because they might be perceived as barriers, but toxic plumes do not recognize such barriers. The ability to identify potential exposure areas is one facet. Another is the ability to identify potential targets that terrorists and organized hate groups may seek out.

### Identifying Potential Targets

A GIS is a powerful tool that allows views other than a simple one-dimensional view. It can depict orthophotography images, satellite images, three-dimensional (3-D) modeling (as demonstrated in Figure 9.16), and elevations. However, before enhanced models or projects are built, law enforcement personnel should consider all potential targets and vulnerable areas. Although no list can be all-inclusive, the following list of potential targets and vulnerable areas may be used for review, analysis, and geographic consideration when developing and conducting spatial analyses for purposes of homeland security and terrorism initiatives. Figures given in parentheses for list items are approximate for the entire United States as reported in *The National Strategy for the Physical Protection of Critical Infrastructures and Key Assets*[13]:

Utilities—aboveground and underground
Water treatment (1,800 federal reservoirs and 1,600 municipal wastewater facilities)
Well fields (water and oil)
Oil and gas
Energy and nuclear (104 commercial nuclear power plants)
Government buildings (3,000 government-owned and operated)
Government officials
Informational resources/infrastructure
Landmarks (5,800 historic buildings)
Skyscrapers (460)
Transportation: land, air, and sea (5,000 airports; 120,000 miles of railway; 300 inland/coastal ports; 590,000 highway bridges)
Banking and financial institutions (26,600 FDIC-insured institutions)

**FIGURE 9.15**   Radius buffers.

Schools
Military bases or personnel
Private-sector defense contractors
Law enforcement buildings or personnel
International corporations
Shopping areas
Sports arenas

**FIGURE 9.16** Three-dimensional modeling of a target. (Courtesy of Dan Helms, National Law Enforcement and Corrections Technology Center—Rocky Mountain Region, Crime Mapping and Analysis Program.)

Sporting events
Special or symbolic events
Media spectacles
Annual special events, for example, boat and automobile shows, art festivals
Symbols of capitalism
Judicial facilities
Items associated with dates of significance
Cellular telephone tower sites
Agriculture (1,920,000 farms)
Postal and shipping sites (137 million delivery sites)
Chemical industry (66,000 chemical plants)
Pipelines (2 million miles of pipeline)
Public health and emergency services (5,800 registered hospitals)
Religious institutions
Air and seaports
Bridges and dams (80,000 dams)
Amusement parks

When identifying potential targets, law enforcement agencies need to coordinate with other government entities or private-sector groups that work directly with the areas of concern. Protection of infrastructures and assets "requires coordinated action on the part of federal, state, and local governments; the private sector; and concerned citizens across the country" (p. vii).[13] The lion's share of these assets are owned and operated by the private sector. An example of this coordination would be the identification of a water-pumping station. A law enforcement agency may see the need to identify and secure only the pumping station, but an employee of the water department may have additional concerns such as the need for electricity to operate the pump, which may be overlooked and lead to extensive flooding.

Mass transit systems are targets that present a challenge for law enforcement. Bus and rail systems are mobile, cover enormous areas, and travel through densely populated regions. This makes them attractive soft targets due to their accessibility and their often unsecured nature. For this reason, buses have been popular targets for terrorist groups for years in places such as Israel. In the United States it is virtually impossible to guard and secure every bus and rail system with law enforcement personnel. The GIS can help fill the void by identifying weaknesses or high-risk areas that may appear attractive to potential terrorists. Soft government targets such as mass transit systems may be selected for acts of sabotage or violence in response to government actions such as declaration of a war. However, soft targets are not always chosen. Hard targets are also selected for the impact that will be felt by the victim country.

Terrorists often select targets in order to make a statement. In addition, they want to minimize exposure and maximize casualties. Security measures at a facility or site should not be used as a variable when deciding whether or not to identify a location. Terrorists are not afraid of maximum security, as shown by the bombings of the Khobar Towers in Saudi Arabia, the USS *Cole* in Yemen, and embassies throughout the world. Once identified, maps, just like any other intelligence product, are of little value if they are not disseminated and used.

## DISSEMINATION OF INTELLIGENCE

Intelligence has no value if it is not disseminated. No matter how good the analysis and intelligence are, if management and other government officials do not review, consider, and respond to them with open minds and in a timely manner, they will be of no use. The public will only hear, after a man-made or natural disaster, anecdotal testimonials of warnings that had been made but were ignored. Past history demonstrates this to be true, as illustrated by three devastating events in the history of the United States: (1) the bombing of Pearl Harbor (December 7, 1941), (2) the attack on the World Trade Center (September 11, 2001), and (3) the Columbia shuttle disaster (February 1, 2003). The signs, and possibly some documentation, were allegedly present prior to all these events. Information was gathered and reviewed but not acted upon. This demonstrates the need for accurate, timely, and verifiable intelligence. Information should not be ignored because it lacks any of these three conditions (accurate, timely, and verifiable), but an open mind must be kept to all possible scenarios.

In November 2001, the U.S. attorney general reported that sharing information with all government employees is critical in preventing and disrupting terrorist acts. Many law enforcement agencies traditionally disseminated intelligence information based on need to certain segments of the force. With homeland security, everyone shares the need for information. There are some instances when intelligence must be restricted, but on many occasions there is no reason for having such constraints.

In the Antiterrorism Act of 1996, the FBI was the agency charged with gathering terrorist information. During the same year, the FBI Counterterrorism Center was established to combat terrorism on three fronts: (1) international, (2) domestic, and (3) countermeasures relating to both. Joint task forces also play a role in nation's response to terrorism. As of 2003, FBI Director Robert Mueller[14] reported that there were 56 joint terrorism task forces (JTTFs) in operation within the United States. The JTTFs are the conduits used by many local and state law enforcement agencies to introduce the information or intelligence that they harvest. Questions remain as to whether they will remain the sole conduits or if regional-level task forces will be used, much like a chain of command. There are two other avenues for disseminating information and it depends on the state as to which, if any, is utilized. They are offices of statewide intelligence units and designated state homeland security units. On the White House website, a map with a link to a contact name, telephone number, or e-mail address for each state and territory in the Union is provided. This information has been compiled into a reference list in Appendix F.

Dissemination of information or intelligence should be done with an eye toward security so as not to jeopardize a case. Personnel should remember that public records laws vary by jurisdiction and state. Although there are many standard terms such as "for official use only" (FOUO) and "law enforcement sensitive" (LES), they are not always applicable across jurisdictions. In addition, personnel should be cognizant that digital transmission such as e-mails may be subject to varying laws governing retention and public records.

## COMMONLY USED ANALYTICAL REPORTS

Regardless of the venue, it is critical that information is reported and disseminated immediately. Many styles of analytical reports have been in common use in the past several years. There is no need to reinvent the wheel just because it now deals with terrorism or organized hate, and analysts should stay with proven methods.

Various types of analytical reports are outlined here. Each has a place in the analytical world and should be applied accordingly:

Assessments: Threat and vulnerability assessments are two of the more common assessments.

Briefings: These reports are not case studies, but are designed to provide a summary overview of the case in question. They are usually delivered to command staff members and address only the basic facts.

Bulletins: These short reports are often in the form of "be on the lookout" (BOLO), identifying areas of concern and wanted subjects. They are direct and concise.

Chronological reports: These are commonly referred to as timelines and include confirmed and unconfirmed information, noted accordingly.

Commodity flowcharts: These are used to track the flow of currency and goods. A separate chart is often kept for each item.

Event flowcharts: These charts come in different styles, two of which were described in the events flowcharts section of this chapter, and are used to visually depict a series of events or occurrences. Only a summary of the event is noted.

Frequency distribution lists: These use a table of numbers, indicating the number of event occurrences. These events are often analyzed and weighted with respect to a case.

Link analysis: This method is used to identify and establish interrelationships among activities, events, individuals, corporations, finances, and telephone records by visual means.

Maps: They are also referred to as spatial analysis, spatial referencing, and geographic distribution analysis. The potential use of geographical information is virtually endless and includes the use of orthophotography and satellite imagery.

Matrix charts: These charts are used to identify connections or relationships among people and organizations using a series of grids and symbols.

Net worth analysis: These reports are also referred to as financial analysis reports. The documents show the financial affairs of the target in question as well as its assets and expenses.

Profiles: These are comprehensive reports on an individual, group, or corporation and include virtually every aspect of their existence, including behavior.

Statistical reports: These reports are often used for comparative purposes and they aid management in identifying shifts in activity.

Strategic reports: These reports are often used to monitor, track, and project long-range activities.

Tactical reports: These reports are designed to meet the immediate needs of a case and are used by management to develop operational and deployment strategies.

Telephone and toll record analysis: These reports are often compiled with the assistance of complex computer programs that establish links, track incoming and outgoing calls, and aid in identifying locations.

Warnings: These are used to forecast or predict the occurrences of future behavior based on
   validated and corroborated threat analysis information.

One report produced by the federal government is the *FBI Intelligence Bulletin*. According to FBI
Director Robert Mueller,[14] "a new FBI Intelligence Bulletin is sent to more than 17,000 law enforcement agencies virtually every week" (p. 8). The question that should be posed to the members of an
agency is, how many people have seen this bulletin or how many even know it exists? It is commendable that a bulletin is being prepared and disseminated; however, if it is not reaching personnel beyond
the command staff, how much value is there in producing it? The FBI has done its part. A survey of
several personnel working in analytical units in a large metropolitan area revealed that no one had
ever seen this document or even knew of its existence. These are the employees who will be asked
to analyze matters surrounding homeland security. Dissemination practices have to be direct and concise, and information must reach those in the trenches.

Special requests for dissemination, such as "for internal use only" or "in-house distribution,"
should be avoided. Once a document is disbursed, it is no longer under the sender's control. It
must be assumed that every document will end up in court, be subject to public record laws, or be
innocently distributed out of the sender's intended circle. There is also the chance that the information
may be leaked to individuals without clearance.

When preparing a report, questions should be answered, not created. The reader of the document
should be able to clearly understand the content of the report and he or she should not feel the need to
return to the preparer for further clarification. Documents should include the preparer's name or initi-
als, date prepared, source or sources of the data used to compile the report, and a document identification number; if any revisions have been made, these also should be noted in the document. For every
document there should be supporting documents. Analysts must log requests as they come in, document the actions taken, and maintain copies of all analytical subproducts (queries). When compiling
these records, it is important to maintain their true form as they evolve. Storage of these records,
whether manual or electronic, is an issue dependent on public record laws of a jurisdiction. In
some locales, storing records on a local unsecured personal computer may subject the entire case
to public review. This can lead to the leakage of intelligence through completely legal means.
Caution has to be used at every step. Nothing should be taken for granted.

Dissemination of the report is what an analyst is working toward. Therefore, it is important that the
proper personnel are on the receiving end. Within an agency, the two most common methods of dissemination are through photostatic copies and e-mail. Use of e-mail poses a whole new set of concerns. When distributing documents via e-mail, the size of the document is important. If it is
difficult for a recipient to access the information, he or she may delete it. Another consideration is
the use of electronic tracking and expirations. Electronic tracking provides assurance that the document was received and opened. Intelligence reports should never be typed directly into an e-mail.
Analysts should prepare an independent document and insert it as an attachment. This aids in divert-
ing improper viewing. Expiration dates should be established when disseminating information electronically. These measures help to ensure that information is reviewed in a timely manner and that
information is not reviewed for possible action after it is no longer valid.

## CHAPTER CONCEPTS

The chapter concepts can be summarized as follows:

   Information is transformed into intelligence. It is important to use various sources to develop a
      group's modus operandi, for example, capabilities, history, statements and intentions,
      causes, and motivations.
   When investigating terrorist and organized hate groups, it is essential that the components of a group
      or organization profile and the components of an offender profile are analyzed thoroughly.

Various nontraditional resources for analytical consideration are available. When analyzing these resources, tunnel vision can be avoided by the use of the macro-micro-macro continuum.

The role of threat and vulnerability assessments in homeland security is discussed. These assessments need to be current and conducted via partnering with the private sector.

Valuable insight can be gained through the use of spatial referencing and analysis, and through identifying potential targets.

Commonly used analytical reports are described. The ways in which intelligence is disseminated are discussed.

## REFERENCES

1. Heymann, P. B. 1998. *Terrorism and America: A Commonsense Strategy for a Democratic Society.* Cambridge, MA: MIT Press, p. 25.
2. Hoffman, B. 1999. Countering the new terrorism. In *Terrorism Trends and Prospects*, ed. I. O. Lesser, p. 25. Santa Monica, CA: Rand.
3. The Smoking Gun. 2003. *Bin Laden's Terrorism Bible.* Terrorism 101: A How-To Guide. http://thesmokinggun.com/archive/jihadmanual.html (accessed February 27, 2003).
4. Gottlieb, S., S. Arenberg, and R. Singh. 1994. *Crime Analysis: From First Report to Final Arrest.* Montclair, CA: Alpha Publishing, p. 59.
5. Sweeney, W. J. 2002. *Intelligence Analyst's Source Book.* Montclair, CA: Alpha Group Center.
6. Franklin, R. A. 2003. *The Hate Directory: Hate Groups on the Internet.* Release 7.1. http://www.bcpl.net/~rfrankli/hatedir.html (accessed January 15, 2003).
7. Cooper, J., E. Nelson, and M. Ronczkowski. 2002. Tactical/investigative analysis of targeted crimes. In *Advanced Crime Mapping Topics*, eds., S. Bair, R. Boba, N. Fritz and S. Hick. p. 32. Denver, CO: National Law Enforcement and Corrections Technology Center.
8. Heuer, R. J., Jr. 1999. *Psychology of Intelligence Analysis.* Washington, DC: Central Intelligence Agency, p. 2.
9. International Association of Chiefs of Police Project Response. 2003. *Leading from the Front: Law Enforcement's Role in Combating and Preparing for Domestic Terrorism.* Alexandria: IACP. http://www.theiacp.org (accessed February 28, 2003).
10. Decker, R. J. 2001. *Homeland Security Key Elements of a Risk Management Approach.* Washington, DC: United States General Accounting Office. *Homeland Security.* pp. 3–6.
11. Federal Interagency Coordinating Committee on Digital Cartography. 1988. Washington, DC: Geographic Information Systems.
12. Federal Geographic Data Committee. 2003. *Homeland Security and Geographic Information Systems.* http://www.fgdc.gov/publications/homeland.html (accessed March 12, 2003).
13. President. 2003. *The National Strategy for the Physical Protection of Critical Infrastructures and Key Assets.* Washington, DC: White House, p. vii.
14. Mueller, R. S., III. 2003. Teamwork is our future. In *The Police Chief.* ed., Charles E. Higginbotham, Alexandria, VA. p. 8. International Association of Chiefs of Police.

# 10 The Threat

## *The Future Is Here Today—Learning from the Past*

Bombings, or what are referred to today as improvised explosive devices (IEDs), are nothing new. "Traditional" bombs have been, and will likely continue to be, the leading weapon of terrorists and extremists alike. Much talk and law enforcement focus today has centered on chemical, biological, and nuclear attacks. Although these possibilities should not be overlooked, analysts must look for the skills, knowledge, resources, access/ability, motive (SKRAM) components outlined in Chapter 8, as well as the fact that terrorists learn from their predecessors. One of the more common skill sets in the world of terrorism centers on man-made IEDs.

Tactics among the majority of some of the largest terrorist organizations or their spin-offs of the past century, for example, the Irish Republican Army (IRA) and Palestinian Liberation Organization (PLO), have demonstrated the consistent use of IEDs in their attacks. Perhaps the biggest difference over the past century has been the refinement or capacity in which attacks are executed. For instance, vehicles instead of packages have been packed with explosives by the IRA in their attacks. This method has been taken further by groups such as Hezbollah through the use of truck bombs. Suicide bomb vests can carry a limited amount of explosive, but car and truck bombs can carry thousands of pounds. What method of transportation will be used or attacked next? This question will depend largely on the SKRAM variables of the individuals involved and the group's desire to make a larger statement.

A solid open-source resource for those seeking to learn from past events is the National Consortium for the Study of Terrorism and Responses to Terrorism (START) at the University of Maryland. START manages the Global Terrorism Database (GTD) which is an open-source database including information on terrorist events around the world from 1970 through 2015 (with additional annual updates planned for the future). Unlike many other event databases, the GTD includes systematic data on domestic as well as transnational and international terrorist incidents that have occurred during this time period and now includes more than 150,000 cases. For each GTD incident, information is available on the date and location of the incident, the weapons used and nature of the target, the number of casualties, and—when identifiable—the group or individual responsible.

Statistical information contained in the GTD is based on reports from a variety of open media sources. Information is not added to the GTD unless and until they have determined the sources are credible.

The National Consortium for the Study of Terrorism and Responses to Terrorism makes the GTD available via an online interface in an effort to increase understanding of terrorist violence so that it can be more readily studied and defeated. This resource can be found by going to https://www.start.umd.edu/gtd/ where the below listed characteristics can be found.

Characteristics of the GTD

- Contains information on over 150,000 terrorist attacks
- Currently the most comprehensive unclassified database on terrorist events in the world
- Includes information on more than 75,000 bombings, 17,000 assassinations, and 9,000 kidnappings since 1970
- Includes information on at least 45 variables for each case, with more recent incidents including information on more than 120 variables
- Includes reviews from over 4,000,000 news articles and 25,000 news sources to collect incident data from 1998 to 2015 alone

**FIGURE 10.1** GTD World Map: 45 Years of Terrorism. (Courtesy of the National Consortium for the Study of Terrorism and Responses to Terrorism, 2016).

The START site has detailed charts, graphs and maps available for use. Figure 10.1 was updated in 2016 and demonstrates 45 years of terrorism that displays the concentration and intensity (combining fatalities and injuries) of terrorist attacks that occurred worldwide across 45 years of data. One particular area of study is that dealing with the top targets of terrorist attacks such as modes of transportation.

## TRANSPORTATION TARGETED

Modes of transportation have been either the target of terrorist attacks or used to facilitate attacks for over a century. One of the first examples of this is the attacks on Alexander II, Czar of Russia. Leaders of Narodnaia Volia decided to assassinate Czar Alexander. Their initial plan was to blow up the Czar's train. They split into two groups and, disguised as shopkeepers, rented two buildings along the Imperial route. The explosion on the railway from Livadia to Moscow never materialized because they missed the Czar's train.

Narodnaia Volia, more commonly referred to as the "People's Will" or "Will of the People," a precursor to the Socialist Revolution Party, originated in Russia during the fall of 1879. Members of this organization were ultimately responsible for the death of Czar Alexander II. In 1881, after several unsuccessful attempts, a member of the People's Will assassinated the Czar with a hand-thrown bomb. On March 1, 1881, the Czar was returning by horse-drawn carriage to the Winter Palace. When he reached Catherine Quay, two bombs were thrown by a member of the People's Will. The first bomb was unsuccessful, but the second bomb satisfied the populists' objective. The Czar died a short time later. This event can be seen as a precursor of attacks on modes of transportation.

## TRANSPORTATION AND TERRORISM

According to the Terrorism Knowledge Base (TKB) website, between January 1, 1968, and January 1, 2006, there were 988 terrorist incidents targeting transportation that were committed by 95 terrorist groups worldwide.[1] The TKB is now known as the Global Terrorism Database which can be found by going to the National Consortium for the START which is based at the University of Maryland. Transit systems are common terrorist targets and the numbers continue to grow, and are now in excess of 6,500. These numbers are just an example of incidents that highlight the fact that transit vehicles are a target of choice for many terrorists. Terrorism waged against transit systems allows the terrorists to meet their prime objectives easily and with a high likelihood of casualties. Millions of people pass through transit facilities every day, and in some locations, it is the primary mode of transportation. Besides the volume of people passing through, transit systems are potential targets because they provide:

Easy access—systems are hard to secure
Large concentrations of people in vehicles, trains, and terminals
A vital component of the economic and social infrastructure
Service disruption that could affect millions of people
A target-rich environment

Although people seem fearful, almost paranoid, over chemical, biological, and radiological threats, bombs in the form of IEDs are the most common. Finding an IED in a transit attack is a much more likely scenario than finding anything else. Surface transportation systems cannot be protected as easily as airplanes. Trains, buses, subways, and light rail systems must remain readily accessible, convenient, and inexpensive for the traveling public. Therefore, they make attractive targets.

In the United States, use of Transportation Security Administration (TSA) officials at airports throughout the country was an effort to standardize and solidify air security. However, for every pro, there is a con. Just like with cyber security, there is no foolproof means of security. Terrorists are calculative and patient in preparing for attacks. Although the TSA performs admirably, there are still weaknesses that can be exploited. The same can be said about any form of transportation, regardless of which agency protects it. There are many transportation system vulnerabilities largely because most fixed transportation infrastructure lies unguarded.

Few countries in the world have seen more weaknesses exploited and fallen prey to more attacks on transportation than the United Kingdom, primarily London. The primary foe, the IRA, is widely known for their attempts, hoaxes, or direct terrorist attacks on buses and railways.

The Irish Republican Army Tactics Manual—How they became the father of many modern terrorists

In 1956, the General Headquarters of the IRA produced a handbook for its operatives to follow. Titled *Handbook for Volunteers of the Irish Republic Army – Notes on Guerrilla Warfare* it is a 38-page handbook that starts with an explanation of their tradition and covers many aspects of what is to be expected from its recruits. Covered in the handbook are the topics of strategy, organization, tactics, bases, attack, defense, general techniques and a final section titled "battle notes."

Although the handbook is 60 years old, it is evident that many of the tactics explained and put forward by their leadership are still widely in use and have been adopted by many terrorists and organizations in the modern era. As much as the media and others may focus on dirty bombs and the use of chemical, biological, and nuclear-based devices it is clear that the preferred weapon of choice is a homemade bomb. There is a saying that to understand the future that you need to know the past. This saying certainly comes into play in understanding the role, direct or indirect, that the IRA plays in the realm of terrorism. Everything from their tactics to their target types is still widely used by an array of terrorists and terrorist organizations.

As noted earlier in the book, the terms and references associated with terrorism have changed with various cultures, political environments, and terminology. What is viewed as terrorism today used to be termed as anarchy, radical movements, and guerrilla warfare. It is the last that has been widely associated with the IRA.

The IRA handbook starts out by ensuring that their recruits know and understand the context in which they frame their justification for actions. Under the auspices of "our tradition," Chapter 1 begins by proudly noting that no nation has a greater tradition of successful guerrilla warfare than Ireland. In fact, the first four pages of the handbook are a historical walk through actions they deem supportive of their guerrilla warfare actions. Starting with the kerne of old and their harassing of the Normans, Chapter one points out influential leaders of the Irish guerrilla warfare movements such as Art Og

Mac Morrough Kavanagh, Fiach MacHugh O'Byrne, Rory O'More, Michael Dwyer, Fintan Lalor, Mackey Lomasey and Hugh (The Great) O'Neill who were all noted to be successful leaders in their actions and guerrilla tactics to repel opposing forces. The fact that the IRA emphasizes the role of the aforementioned leaders at the start of the handbook is a testament that they are considered role models for others to learn from or follow. Perhaps the most notable guerrilla warfare component of the IRA over the last 100 years is the Black and Tans.

Chapter three of the handbook brings to light the guerrilla strategy. It is noted that the essence of all strategy is to bring, by the use of surprise and mobility, the greatest possible strength. They noted that the guerrilla attempts to do three things:

1. Drain the enemy's manpower and resources
2. Lead the resistance of the people to enemy occupation
3. Break down the enemy's administration

The main principles of war can be boiled down to:

1. Concentration—or economy of force
2. Protection—to guard against being taken unawares by the enemy
3. Surprise—to catch the enemy in such a situation that he is unable to switch his forces to meet the attack
4. Aggressiveness—determination to knock out the enemy in the attack
5. Objective—to pursue the objective to the end despite the enemy's countermeasures and never to be sidetracked

Chapter 6 notes that successful operations involve the people. It is strongly stated that there should be constant contact and coordination between the guerrillas and the local population. The handbook notes that this is aided by:

1. Recruiting volunteers from the territory in which they operate
2. Use of civil political committees among the people whose function it would be to agitate against the oppressor and get new members
3. Have guerrilla agents working among the civilian population collecting information
4. Use of part-time guerrillas who would continue in civilian occupations but be available for active service when called upon
5. Building up liaison between guerrillas and people until such time as it was perfect

The importance of accurate information is clearly emphasized throughout the handbook. However, it should also be noted that there are no time frames mentioned on how quickly efforts must be made. Being methodical and integrated into the population is important and will lead to a more successful campaign. In contrast to a post 9/11 environment, one can see the parallels of how modern terrorist organizations follow similar principles.

The final 17 pages of the handbook focuses on guerrilla attacks, tactics, intelligence methods, and general guerrilla techniques and demonstrate how germane they are to successful operations. Emphasis is placed on how guerrilla attacks are fluid and how there is a large measure of decentralization of efforts being carried out by "battle teams." One can compare the battle teams to what is referred to today as cells.

The importance of targeting transportation can be seen in Chapter 11 of the handbook titled "General techniques." Details on explosives and their applicable use are demonstrated throughout the chapter. The focus of the use of explosives is directed toward the targeting of transportation. It is even noted that being short of explosives is not deterrence and a guerrilla operative can go as far as placing felled trees across roads. However, the primary examples of guerrilla targets are clearly roadways and methods of transportation. It is easy to see how modern day terrorists have learned from the IRA and how their handbook is still used today.

## THE IRA CAMPAIGN AGAINST TRANSPORTATION

In the modern era of terrorism, the IRA can be construed as leading the way in attacks against surface transportation. According to a Mineta Transportation Institute report in 2001, between 1972 and 2000, the IRA exported their terrorist acts to the British mainland targeting surface transportation in England at least 45 times.[2]

> The focus of attacks was on the rail system but buses on the mainland were not immune.
> From 1991 to 1999 alone, 81 explosive devices, 6,589 bomb threats, and 9,430 suspicious objects. Security measures implemented during the campaign reduced threats and incidents and effectively reduced "ordinary" crimes such as robbery and vandalism, too.
> Of the 81 explosive devices that were placed at transport targets, 79 were hand-placed time bombs. Fifty percent of them did not work as intended. Altogether, three people were killed by IRA bombs on the rail system.
> In all, 17 persons were killed, and 200 were injured between 1991 and 1999.

However, the IRA is not the only terrorist organization to target transportation. Many have learned from their tactics and continue to exploit the ease of utilizing and targeting surface transportation in terrorist endeavors. Another country that has experienced a significant number of attacks against transportation is India. Between 1920 and 2000, India had the most fatalities as a result of attacks on modes of transportation, with more than twice as many attacks as most countries.

## PLANES, TRAINS, AND AUTOMOBILES—BUT THERE ARE MORE

Modes of transportation pose difficulties for law enforcement personnel dealing with terrorism. Virtually everyone in the world uses, or is likely to use, a mode of motorized transportation. Dependency, accessibility, and reliability of transportation create unique opportunities for terrorists to exploit weaknesses. Everything from rescue vehicles, taxis, limousines, trucks, and motorcycles often gain, or can gain, immediate access to a number of venues in the United States or abroad.

Transportation attacks are a grave concern to most investigators dealing with terrorism. On July 18, 2002, the Federal Bureau of Investigation (FBI) formally created the National Joint Terrorism Task Force (NJTTF) to act as a conduit for information. In an April 2004 federal report, it was noted that the NJTTF works with the FBI's Office of Intelligence to coordinate interagency intelligence-gathering initiatives dealing with transportation, such as the following[3]:

Foreign flight crew vetting
Maritime threat project
Operation dry dock
Agricultural aviation threat project

It is evident that transportation and terrorism is and will continue to be a concern in the United States and abroad.

## UNITED STATES: TERRORISM AND TRANSPORTATION

Besides unattended IEDs, there have been numerous terrorist attacks against various forms of transportation in the United States. Most were classified and handled as crimes. According to Dunham of the Anser Institute, during the early 1990s, the United States experienced several attacks on public transportation, including a 1992 attack in which someone left a hand grenade on a railroad station platform in Chicago.[4] He also noted other attacks that were reviewed by researchers in Florida. Based on a 2002 study conducted by researchers at the University of South Florida, there is a history with regard to major violent attacks on mass transportation in the United States, some of which are outlined below.[5]

August 6, 1927: Two bombs explode in two New York City subway stations. The bombs injured many persons, one of them, it was believed, fatally.

December 7, 1993: Armed gunman Colin Ferguson kills 6 and injures 17 passengers aboard a Long Island Railroad train during rush hour.

December 15 and 21, 1994: Edward Leary explodes two homemade bombs on the New York City subway system, injuring 53 people, in an apparent attempt to extort money from the New York Transit Authority.

October 9, 1995: "Sons of the Gestapo" sabotage Amtrak's Sunset Limited train, causing a derailment in the Arizona desert, killing 1 and injuring 65 others.

Although these incidents may have been lost in the annals of law enforcement history, they should be reviewed by entities working in terrorism in order to learn from the past. Americans inherently have short memories. This is probably why U.S. citizens are unaware of the aforementioned events and were in utter disbelief that the hijacking of aircraft could originate from their own country and further dismayed by the use of them as bombs. Short memories and lack of historical knowledge may be the reason for the disbelief. September 11, 2001, was not the first or even the second attack on New York City, and it certainly was not the first hijacking or multiple hijacking to take place. Planes, trains, automobiles, and even bicycles have been used in numerous terrorist attacks. Just remember that the mode of transportation has not always been motorized. Just like the attack on Czar Alexander II, there have been carriage or cart attacks, even in the United States.

One of the first cart attacks in the United States occurred on September 16, 1920, at the corner of Wall and Broad streets, the hub of American capitalism. Just after noon, as workers poured onto the street for their lunchtime breaks, a horse-drawn cart exploded into the crowd. The people believed to be responsible for this yet unsolved event, were members of Bolshevist or anarchist movements. Such an event today would lead to the designation of these members or groups as terrorists.

To New Yorkers and to Americans in 1920, the death toll of more than 30 people from the blast seemed incomprehensible. When Americans in 1920 heard of the carnage on Wall Street, many believed they had encountered a type of violence never before seen. There had been bomb explosions before at Chicago's Haymarket Square in 1886 and at the Los Angeles Times building in 1910, but they were attributed to specific labor movements. The blast on Wall Street, by contrast, seemed to be purely symbolic, designed to kill as many innocent people as possible in an assault on American power.

## SYMBOLIC GOVERNMENT TARGETS

There are many venues that can be considered symbolic for potential attack, many of which have involved a mode of transportation. One of the more common symbolic targets has been that of Western government facilities outside their respective country. Over the decades many government buildings, embassies, and official residences have been the target of numerous terrorist-related attacks. Arguably, the United States' facilities have been perhaps one of the more attractive targets of terrorists and terrorist organizations. Diplomatic installations have been well documented and targeted in Africa, but they are not an anomaly. Between 1987 and 1997, according to information from an after-action report on the African embassy bombings, there were more than 230 attacks on U.S. diplomatic and consulate installations throughout the world. The majority of the attacks took place in the late 1980s, and the weapons of choice for attacks were bombs and rockets. Diplomatic installation attacks took place on virtually every continent. Countries such as Spain, Peru, Dominican Republic, South Korea, Ecuador, Columbia, Italy, Pakistan, Australia, Serbia, and Algiers have all experienced and seen the carnage that can be achieved through pure hatred targeting symbolic facilities.

There have also been attacks that symbolically mentioned or were focused on government issues. These attacks have come in a variety of ways but, quite often, the common variable that they share is a mode of transportation.

## NOTABLE TERRORIST CASES AND ATTACKS WITH A TRANSPORTATION NEXUS OTHER THAN 9/11

### AVIATION (FIGURE 10.2)

In 2003, United States Secretary of State Colin Powell noted that one of the greatest threats to aviation was the use of man-portable air defense systems (MANPADS). Use of MANPADS against civilian aircraft came to the forefront in November 2002 in an attack against an Israeli Air Arikia Boeing 757 as it departed Kenya. This event is not limited to those outside the United States. In 2003, a criminal complaint was filed in New Jersey against Hemant Lakhani for import and transfer of a shoulder-fired surface-to-air missile (Figure 10.3). Although the use and range of MANPADS make them an attractive weapon for a potential terrorist, they have not been shown to be the preferred tactic. Bombings and hijackings have largely been the methods of attack.

According to James Poland, statistics on explosions aboard aircraft between 1949 and 2001 demonstrated that 80 aircraft were damaged or destroyed as the result of an explosive device. During the same time frame, the United States recorded the damage or destruction of 15 aircraft.[6]

### Popular Front for the Liberation of Palestine—The Masters of Airplane Hijacking

The Popular Front for the Liberation of Palestine (PFLP) was founded on December 11, 1967, by Dr George Habash, a Palestinian Greek Orthodox Christian, when it broke away from the Arab Nationalist Movement. The PFLP forged international relationships, even on the operational level, with the Japanese Red Army and the Lod Airport attack on May 30, 1972, and with the Baader Meinhof Gang in Germany and the Air France hijacking to Entebbe in 1976. The organization quickly specialized in showcase, large-scale terrorist operations beginning on July 23, 1968, with a hijacking to Algeria of an El Al flight en route from Rome to Tel Aviv. The PFLP quickly switched to non-Israeli carriers, including the simultaneous triple hijacking of TWA, Swissair, and Pan Am aircraft to Jordan on September 6, 1970. In a media spectacle, the three aircraft were emptied of passengers and blown up as cameras rolled.

### Pan Am 103

Pan American World Airways (Pan Am) flight number 103, traveling from London's Heathrow Airport to New York's John F. Kennedy International Airport exploded on December 21, 1988,

**FIGURE 10.2**    757 aircraft commonly used throughout the world.

UNITED STATES DISTRICT COURT                     ORIGINAL FILED
DISTRICT OF NEW JERSEY                            AUG   11   2003

| UNITED STATES OF AMERICA | : | CRIMINAL COMPLAINT |
|---|---|---|
| | : | SUSAN D. WIGENTON |
| v. | : | U.S MAG. JUDGE |
| | : | |
| HEMANT LAKHANI, | : | |
| | : | |
| a/k/a "Hemad Lakhani" | : | Mag. No. 03-7106 |

I, James J. Tareco, being duly sworn, state the following is true and correct to the best of my knowledge and belief.

Count One

From in or about December, 2001, to on or about August 12, 2003, in the District of New Jersey and elsewhere, defendant HEMANT LAKHANI, a/k/a "Hemad Lakhani," did knowingly and willfully attempt to provide material support and resources, and to conceal and disguise the nature, location, source, and ownership of material support and resources, intending that they were to be used in preparation for, and in carrying out, a violation of Title 18, United States Code, Sections 32, 2332a, and 2332b.

In violation of Title 18, United States Code, Sections 2339A and 2.

Count Two

From in or about December, 2001, to on or about August 12, 2003, in the District of New Jersey and elsewhere, defendant HEMANT LAKHANI, a/k/a "Hemad Lakhani," did knowingly and willfully engage and attempt to engage in the business of brokering activities with respect to the import and transfer of a foreign defense article, namely a shoulder-fired surface-to-air-missile of foreign origin, which was a non-United States defense article of a nature described on the United States Munitions List, without having first registered with and obtained from the Department of State's Directorate of Defense Trade Controls a license for such brokering or written authorization for such brokering.

In violation of Title 22, United States Code, Section 2778(b)(1) and (c), Title 22, Code of Federal Regulations, Sections 121.1, 127.1(d), 129.3, 129.6 and 129.7, and Title 18, United States Code, Section 2.

I further state that I am a Special Agent of the Federal Bureau of Investigation and that this complain is based on the following facts:

SEE ATTACHMENT A

continued on the attached pages and made a part hereof.

_____
James J. Tareco, Special Agent Federal Bureau
of Investigation

Sworn to before me and subscribed in my
presence, August 11, 2003 in Essex County,
New Jersey

HONORABLE SUSAN D. WIGENTON
UNITED STATES MAGISTRATE JUDGE                   _____
                                                 Signature of Judicial Officer

**FIGURE 10.3**    2003 criminal complaint against Hemant Lekhani.

while at 31,000 feet, killing 270 people. The aircraft, a Boeing 747-121 with registered tail number N739PA, and named "Clipper Maid of the Seas," was blown up as it flew over Lockerbie, Dumfries and Galloway, Scotland, when 12–16 ounces (340–450 g) of Semtex-H plastic explosive was detonated in its forward cargo hold, triggering a sequence of events that led to the rapid destruction of the aircraft. Two Libyan intelligence officers were eventually charged with the incident. However, some speculate that there may have been ties to the PFLP-GC.

## Pre-Incident Indicators

In the subsequent investigation dubbed Operation Autumn Leaves, and headed in the United States by the FBI, several motives were considered. There were two primary motives publicly speculated.

The first was the April 1986 bombing of Tripoli and Benghazi on April 15–16, 1986, by U.S. war-planes. The bombings were allegedly done in retaliation for the bombing 10 days earlier of a Berlin nightclub used by U.S. soldiers, which had killed 3 and injured 230. The second was the July 1988 downing of Iran Air 655, a passenger jet incorrectly identified by an American warship, the USS *Vincennes*, as a hostile military aircraft.

According to Simonsen and Spindlove, the intelligence community had received warnings of trou-bles in Europe. A total of nine security bulletins that could have had relevance to the Pan Am incident were issued between June and December 1988. One bulletin even described how a Toshiba radio cas-sette player and a barometric trigger could be used as a bomb.[7] West German police authorities had recovered a similar device in a vehicle belonging to a member of the PFLP-GC.

## Richard Reid

On December 22, 2001, Richard Reid, an Islamic convert, also known as the shoe bomber, boarded American Airlines flight number 63, a Boeing 767-300 aircraft, en route from Paris to Miami. While in flight he attempted to ignite the fuse of a bomb (plastic explosives) concealed in the heel of his shoe and was subsequently arrested. Following his nine-count indictment (Figure 10.4) and being found guilty, Reid openly stated that he was an Islamic fundamentalist and an enemy of the United States, similar to al-Qaeda. Reid was fined and sentenced to 110 years in prison.

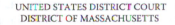

UNITED STATES DISTRICT COURT
DISTRICT OF MASSACHUSETTS

UNITED STATES OF AMERICA

           v.

RICHARD COLVIN REID,
a/k/a ABDUL-RAHEEM,
a/k/a ABDUL RAHEEM,    ABU
IBRAHIM

CRIMINAL NO. 02-10013-W & Y

VIOLATIONS:
18 U.S.C. §2332a(a)(1)
    (Attempted Use of a Weapon of Mass
    Destruction)
18 U.S.C. §2332
    (Attempted Homicide)
49 U.S.C. §§46505(b)(3) and (c)
    (Placing Explosive Device on Aircraft)
49 U.S.C. §46506(1) and 18 U.S.C. §1113
    (Attempted Murder)
49 U.S.C. §46504
    (Interference with Flight Crew
    Members and Attendants)
18 U.S.C. §§32(a)(1) and (7)
    (Attempted Destruction of
    Aircraft)
18 U.S.C. §924(c)
    (Using Destructive Device During
    and in Relation to a Crime of
    Violence)
18 U.S.C. §1993(a)(1) & (8)
    (Attempted Wrecking of Mass
    Transportation Vehicle)

INDICTMENT

COUNT ONE:         (18 U.S.C. §2332a(a)(1)—Attempted Use of Weapon of Mass
              Destruction)

The Grand Jury charges that:
    1.  At all times relevant to this count brought under Title 18, United States Code, Chapter 113B—
Terrorism, al-Qaeda was a designated foreign terrorist organization pursuant to 8 U.S.C. §1189.
    2.  At various times relevant to this count, Richard Colvin Reid received training from
Al-qaeda in Afghanistan.

**FIGURE 10.4**   Nine-count indictment against Richard Reid.

## MARITIME

The legal issues related to maritime security, in particular hijackings and piracy, are convoluted and complex. International maritime laws only recognize piracy if the vessel is in international waters. Should the vessel be within the territorial waters of a country, then that country is responsible for pursuing and investigating the incident, usually under the crime of robbery. Other issues arise when you consider that many vessels that regularly traverse a country's waterways are often registered and bear the flags of other lands (Figure 10.5).

Crews of cargo and passenger vessels emanate from many countries, and the ships are flagged in various lands throughout the world, all of which pose security difficulties. Although there has been much focus on passenger vessels, due to obvious reasons, it may be the use of cargo containers that poses a great risk to national security. These ships often arrive from countries with less than stellar security measures in place as well as coming from what many consider to be shallow draft ports. It is these ports that cannot accommodate many of today's secure and modern vessels; therefore older, less secure vessels are used. With thousands of cargo ships arriving in the United States alone each year, law enforcement should be cognizant of the hazardous possibilities that may lie within one, or more, of the 4,000 steel 40-foot containers. Officials at many ports utilize what is referred to as a gamma ray device to scan containers. However, it is highly unlikely that more than 5% of the containers arriving in the United States are scanned. Besides the sheer volume of containers arriving, one must remember that these containers are then loaded on the backs of trucks and often driven through the heart of many cities.

According to a report from the International Maritime Bureau (IMB), a total of 23 vessels were hijacked in 2005, the highest in 4 years, and 440 crew members were taken hostage, the highest number since IMB started compiling statistics in 1992. They further noted that the number of reported piracy attacks reduced from 329 in 2004 to 276 in 2005, the lowest recorded figure in 6 years. It was also noted that locations such as Somalia, Iraq, Tanzania, and Vietnam reported increases in piracy.

In spite of accounting for nearly 30% of all reported attacks, figures for Indonesia showed a drop from 94 reported attacks in 2004 to 79 attacks in 2005. Attacks in the Malacca Straits fell from 38 in 2004 to 12 attacks in 2005. Malaysia, Thailand, Brazil, Venezuela, Colombia, Haiti, Nigeria, and Guinea also all recorded a fall in the number of reported piracy and armed robbery attacks.[8]

Many of the aforementioned vessels targeted in the referenced statistics were largely cargo and goods-carrying ships. The rise in maritime criminal activity and the potential for a catastrophic attack on passenger ships has been creating much debate about how vulnerable cruise ships, a virtual floating city, may be to attack. With the size of vessels growing and the exponential increase in cruising passengers, there should be concern. Some cruise ships carry a crew of 1,000 and approximately 3,000 passengers. Even military vessels have not been void of attacks from terrorists. Should a cruise or military ship fall prey to a terrorist attack in the future, it will not be the first.

**FIGURE 10.5**    Cruise liners carry thousands of people and make attractive targets for terrorists.

## Achille Lauro

On October 7, 1985, a well-publicized cruise ship, *Achille Lauro*, was pirated with all aboard held hostage by four heavily armed Palestinian terrorists off the coast of Egypt. The hijackers were members of the Palestine Liberation Front (PLF), which broke away from the PFLP-GC in the late 1970s and later split again into pro-PLO, pro-Syrian, and pro-Libyan factions. The pro-PLO faction was led by Muhammad Abbas (aka Abu Abbas), the leader of the hijackers, and was based in Baghdad prior to Operation Iraqi Freedom.

The Italian cruise ship *Achille Lauro* was on a 12-day Mediterranean cruise and carrying about 680 passengers and a mostly Italian and Portuguese crew of about 350.

The hijackers demanded that Israel free 50 Palestinian prisoners. During the siege, the terrorists killed a disabled Jewish-American tourist, 69-year-old Leon Klinghoffer, and threw his body overboard with his wheelchair. After a two-day drama, the hijackers surrendered in exchange for a pledge of safe passage.

The hijackers boarded an Egyptian jet and attempted to fly to freedom when U.S. Navy F-14 jet fighters intercepted it and forced it to land in Sicily, Italy. The terrorists were taken into custody by Italian authorities.

## USS Cole

On October 12, 2000, the United States naval destroyer Cole was attacked by a small boat loaded with explosives while in port in Yemen. As part of the USS George Washington Battle Group, the USS Cole was in transit from the Red Sea to a port in Bahrain when the ship stopped in Aden for routine refueling. Yemen was the Defense Fuel Support Point that had been open just over a year when the attack occurred.

According to a Congressional Research Service (CRS) Report for Congress, before arriving in Aden, the ship's crew had filed a required force-protection plan and was at a heightened state of readiness. The condition of readiness included steps that were specifically intended to provide protection against attack by small boats.[9]

The USS Cole had just completed mooring operations at 9:30 a.m. and began the refueling process, which started at 10:30 a.m. At 11:18 a.m. local Bahrain time, a small boat approached the port side of the destroyer and detonated an explosion that caused a 40-foot by 40-foot gash in the port side of the Cole. It was reported that two suicide bombers aboard the boat were seen standing at attention just before the blast that killed 17 of the USS Cole's 320 sailors and injured 39 others.

The FBI investigated a report out of London that a Yemeni Islamic group, the Jaish-e-Mohammed (Mohammed's Army) and the Aden-Abyan Islamic Army, both with ties to, or off-shoots of Islamic Jihad, had claimed responsibility for the attack. The individuals responsible are also an alleged part of bin Laden's network of terror—al-Qaeda. Attacks against military targets either by land, sea, or air are not new. Nearly all the Islamic terrorist groups have expressed one thing in common: they want all U.S. and Western forces out of the Middle East, which they consider to be holy Muslim land.

### BUSES AND TRAINS/RAILWAYS

As alluded to earlier in this chapter, buses and railways (Figures 10.6 and 10.7) have been, and will probably continue to be, targets of terrorists. Accessibility and ease of boarding, with little or no screening, make them attractive assets for the terrorist to breach and exploit.

Although many jurisdictions have laws that forbid the carrying or introduction of weapons such as guns and knives on board mass transit, the fact remains that little is done to prevent it. Furthermore, one does not require a gun, knife, or even explosive to overtake a mode of transportation. An item that has little regulation and is largely not prohibited on public transportation is the paintball marker also known as a paintball gun. These devices are used by the law enforcement and military communities in many training exercises because of their ability to simulate real-life scenarios. They have even been

**FIGURE 10.6**    Buses and vans can carry hundreds of pounds of explosives. The three vehicles pictured here could pose a great danger to this airport terminal.

**FIGURE 10.7**    Trains have been attractive targets for terrorists for years.

used by jihad followers. In 2000 and 2001, nine individuals with terrorist ties conducted military-style training with these devices in preparation for holy war in Fredericksburg, Virginia. Randall (Ismail) Royer, an American citizen who converted to Islam and a former alleged official of the Council on American-Islamic Relations (CAIR), and the other men are believed to be linked to the Pakistan-based religious organization, Lashkar-e-Taiba (Tayyiba), a Kashmir separatist group that the United States designated a terrorist organization in 2001. With paintball markers, a form of compressed gas (e.g., a dive tank), and a case of paintballs (2000 balls), or more, it would not be difficult for a terrorists to commandeer a mode of transportation. Should the paintballs be frozen and fired at an unprotected individual, there is a chance that the attack could be deadly. Based on the aforementioned, it is important for the law enforcement to remain cognizant of opportunities beyond conventional weaponry.

## Israel Bus 405

On July 6, 1989, a fanatical follower of Hamas, Abd Al-Hadi Hganayem, boarded bus number 405 from Tel Aviv to Jerusalem after allegedly checking to confirm no Arabs were on board. The bus was filled with passengers and nine Israeli soldiers. Just before reaching the ravine at the village of Abu Gosh, the suspect rose up and reached the driver's seat, and chanted loudly "Allah akbar, Allah akbar" as he forced the bus over the cliff. Sixteen passengers, including one American, were killed and nearly 30 injured.

## London, 2005

On July 7, 2005, four explosions occurred in Central London between 8:51 a.m. and 9:47 a.m. (local time) using IEDs, three detonated on trains and one on a double-decker bus by four suicide bombers.

According to the TKB, the three train blasts occurred within moments of each other, and the bus bombing happened about an hour after the first three. One of these attacks targeted a train on the Piccadilly line, train 311 traveling south from Kings Cross station to Russell Square at 8:50 a.m. One bomber, identified as Jamaican-born Germaine Lindsay, detonated his explosives in the first car of the train near a set of double doors. The blast was strong enough to cause major damage to the second carriage of the train as well. Twenty-six passengers, plus the bomber, were killed in this attack. Because the train runs deep into the ground at this point of the line, it took rescue workers days to remove all the bodies from the wreckage. All four attacks occurred at the height of rush hour and on the same day that the G8 summit was scheduled to begin in Scotland.[10]

Initially the blasts claimed 55 lives: 26 died at Kings Cross, 13 died on the bombed bus at Tavistock Square, and the attacks at Edgware and Aldgate each killed six people. London officials investigated a Pakistani and al-Qaeda connection that three of the four bombers visited Pakistan and the fourth purportedly toured Afghanistan before the attacks. One of the suspects, Germaine Lindsay, was known to another terror suspect in the United States, Iyman Faris.

## Tokyo, 1995

On March 20, 1995, members of the Japanese religious cult Aum Shinrikyo released sarin (nerve gas) on Tokyo's subway system, killing 12 persons and making more than 5000 ill. It was the first large-scale use of a poison gas by a nongovernmental group, and although Aum Shinrikyo previously had not been identified as a terrorist group in the traditional sense of that term, the incident was promptly labeled an act of terrorism.

*Tokyo's subway system: Arguably the most comprehensive metro system in the world, Tokyo's first line opened in 1927 during the capital's rapid urbanization and today operates 21 lines owned by two principal operating companies. In addition to the subway, a number of monorail, tram, and private lines also serve the city. Tokyo's vast subway network comprises two separate subway systems. According to the Mineta Transportation Institute, the Teito Rapid Transit Authority (TRTA) is the older and larger system. It began operations in 1927 and currently runs 1677 motor cars and 536 trailer cars over eight lines with a total mileage of 154.6 km (96 miles). Three of its lines, Marunouchi, Hibiya, and Chiyoda, were the targets of the 1995 chemical attack. The second system, the TOEI, is run by the municipal government. It operates 524 cars on four lines with a total mileage of 64.4 km (40 miles). In addition, Japan Rail operates an extensive commuter network, and the adjoining city of Yokohama has two of its subway lines.[11]*

Public transportation is vital in the huge metropolitan area of Tokyo. Millions use it daily, encouraged by the fact that the majority of Japanese companies pay the full travel costs of their employees. Without its subways, the city would stop. During peak hours, the subways are fantastically overcrowded, with station staff sometimes literally pushing passengers into the cars. This too may have been a factor on March 20. The attack took place at the height of the morning rush hour, when passengers are accustomed to boarding the trains rapidly, without necessarily heeding what is going on. This not only provided concealment for the attackers, but also meant that even as ill passengers were stumbling off the contaminated coaches, new passengers were shoving their way on board. Within minutes, more than a thousand people had been exposed to the poison gas left behind by members of Aum Shinrikyo.

*Aum Shinrikyo. The base of operations for the Aum Shinrikyo cult is primarily in Japan, their home country, but the cult is said to have had operations and followings overseas in countries such as the United States, Australia, Russia, Germany, Taiwan, Sri Lanka, and the former Yugoslavia.*

Aum Shinrikyo (Supreme Truth) began operating as a religious organization in July 1987, having been founded as the Aum Shinsen no Kai organization in 1984. The head of the cult was Chizuo Matsumoto, also known as Shoko Asahara, a partially blind, charismatic former acupuncturist. He is currently incarcerated on death row in Japan. Shoko Asahara faced 27 murder counts in 13 separate indictments. The prosecution argued that Asahara gave orders to attack the Tokyo subway in order to overthrow the government and install himself in the position of king of Japan. He developed his group and organized it along quasi-government lines, with its own ministries and departments, all under the Supreme Leader Asahara. The empire included a diverse business conglomerate bringing the cult an estimated net worth in the billions. In August 1989, the cult formed its own political organization, the Shinri Party, which contested the 1990 general election. None of the 25 candidates won seats.

*Pre-incident indicators: Much of the cult's intrinsic paranoia reflected the hypochondriac paranoid fantasies of its supreme leader, who claimed that he and his followers were themselves being attacked by chemical weapons. The group published its own magazine/articles and made continuous threats against the Japanese Government, as well as others. To battle against its numerous enemies and to prepare for its role in the fantastical future imagined by its members required that the cult obtain the most advanced weapons of mass destruction and various assault weapons such as the AK-47 rifle. The weapons of mass destruction component required scientists, technicians, secret laboratories, front companies, a covert arms-acquisition program, international connections, and huge sums of cash. Aum allegedly spent more than $10 million on the development of biological agents. In October 1992, Aum leader Shoko Asahara and 40 followers went to Zaire, ostensibly to help treat Ebola victims but the real intention for the group, determined in 1995, was to obtain virus samples for a biological weapon. Before the 1995 subway attack, Aum had sprayed botulinum toxin over Tokyo several times in 1990 and conducted similar activities with anthrax spores in 1993. It was Aum's escalating attacks and criminal efforts that brought them to the attention of law enforcement before their big sarin attack.*

Although stripped of its legal status and tax privileges as a religious organization, following the poison gas attack in Tokyo, Aum Shinrikyo revived its activities in early 1997. The group raised and continues to raise funds through an array of sources. Two of their more common business methods have been the selling of cheap computers and the attendance of individuals at their seminars. They also raise funds from their membership.

## Highlights of Aum in Other countries

United StatesIn 1987, the cult started a company in New York by the name Aum USA
   Company.
In 1993, two Aum members attended flight school in Dade County, Florida.
In 1994, Aum developed a business relationship with an export business in California.

Early in 1995, members of Aum inquired about survival equipment at a trade show in Nevada.
Australia
Records confirm that Aum was in Australia from April 1993 to October 1994.
Aum formed two companies in Australia: Clarity Investments and Maha Posya.
Aum purchased a 500,000-acre sheep farm.
The Australian Justice Minister stated that Aum members tested sarin gas in Australia before
the Tokyo attack.
Taiwan
The presence of Aum in Taiwan was primarily business oriented.
Aum established a company in Taiwan in June 1993 by the name of Dai Hanei (Great
Prosperity) as a purchasing agent, supposedly for the purchase of computer parts.
Sri Lanka
Relatively little is known about Aum's activities in Sri Lanka.
The cult reportedly owns considerable assets there including a tea plantation that Aum began
operating in 1992.

*Aum today, Although the group's founding father is incarcerated, it still exists. Today, it is under the lea-
dership of Fumihiro Joyu. At his release on December 29, 1999, Joyu became the de facto head of the organization. As a result of being Aum Shinrikyo's spokesperson, Joyu was arrested and tried for libel for
publicly naming a third party as responsible for the sarin gas attack. Under his leadership, the group
has changed its name to Aleph, the first letter of the Hebrew alphabet, which means to start anew, and
has an estimated membership/following of 65,000. Although membership has been declared illegal in
Russia, it has been suggested that approximately two-thirds of the group's followers live in Russia.*

## Madrid, 2004

On March 11, 2004, citizens of Spain experienced one of the largest and deadliest terrorist attacks on
their soil, which killed nearly 200 and injured hundreds more (Figure 10.8). Between 7:30 a.m. and
7:45 a.m. local time, 10 explosive devices were detonated in four trains along the C-2 commuter train
line, which runs through Madrid, Spain. The total number of IEDs that were planted was 13 (backpacks or sports bags). Ten detonated on the trains, and the Spanish National Police explosives detonation team detonated the remaining three.

**FIGURE 10.8**    Madrid train bomb blast, March 11, 2004.

The bombs were allegedly placed in passenger cars on four Madrid-bound trains. The suspected terrorists boarded the trains outside Madrid during the morning rush hour and between 7:00 a.m. and 7:15 a.m. planted the explosive devices. The devices were set to explode 35 minutes after being placed on the trains and were located and detonated in such a manner to maximize casualties. Estimates are that up to 700 people were on each of the trains, with an average of 100 people in each of the passenger cars. In addition, it was theorized that the devices were set to explode at or near the railway stations. Three of the four trains were near or at the station when the explosions took place, but the fourth was behind schedule and was outside the station area.

The first explosives, a total of three, detonated at 7:39 a.m. on a commuter train that had already arrived at the Madrid Atocha Train Station, with 34 deaths. The second explosion occurred at 7:42 a.m., on a commuter train that was running two minutes behind schedule. This train was actually moving into the main station, and was approximately 500 m away from the first. The train came to a halt near the C/Tellez, as four bombs exploded, causing 64 deaths. The third train, with two bombs detonating at 7:42 a.m., was approximately 1000 m away from train #2, at the Pozo del Tio Raimundo station. This was the bloodiest, with at least 67 deaths. Finally, the fourth train was several hundred meters away at the Santa Eugenia station, where one bomb exploded at 7:42 a.m., causing 16 deaths. Three further explosive devices hidden in backpacks were destroyed in police-controlled explosions. Open sources report that the IEDs had been planted to hit emergency services as they arrived on the scene.

*Operational factors: After investigators began their initial investigation, Spanish authorities suspected the Basque Separatist Nation, also known as ETA, was involved because of earlier threats against the railway and the pending national election. As the investigation developed, it became evident that ETA, if involved directly or indirectly, was not the principal party responsible for this catastrophic event. The investigation ultimately led to the identification of primarily Moroccan Islamic extremists who had immigrated to Spain. The authorities surmised that the members of the cell responsible for the attack were associated with the Moroccan Islamic Combatant Group or an offshoot of Salafiya Jihadia who shared ideology with al-Qaeda.*

Within approximately one month, Spanish authorities arrested, detained, and questioned hundreds of individuals. They arrested and brought charges against 18 individuals of whom 14 were of Moroccan descent. Several suspects, including the alleged mastermind, blew themselves up when Spanish authorities went to their apartment.

There were reportedly few operational or pre-incident indicators of the attack such as surveillance. Osama bin Laden had threatened Spain for its role in the war on terror in the months prior to the attack. Cell members appear to have operated independently and supported their activities through criminal acts such as illegal narcotics. The explosive devices detonated by the suspects were made of sports type bags, Goma-2 ECO explosives (gelatin dynamite), and bolts and nails, and were activated by a modified cell phone. It was learned that the explosives and detonators used were obtained by theft with the assistance of a Spaniard with ties to the mining community and they were transported in a stolen van. It appears that the terrorists made use of local and readily available material in developing their plot.

Strategically, there were a few pre-incident indicators including previous threats, knowledge of extremist Islamic activity, prior knowledge of railway attempts from a known terrorist group in the country, and the pending national election. Although likelihood of mass casualties was an obvious target, it appears that a second event, the national elections, may have played a dramatic role. It has been speculated that this event single-handedly changed the Spanish political landscape when the incumbent party lost the election.

## TRUCKS, CARS, VANS, TAXIS, LIMOS, AND RESCUE VEHICLES

This section encompasses most forms of day-to-day transportation (Figure 10.9). These modes of transportation are plentiful and have a common denominator—the ability to gain access to a

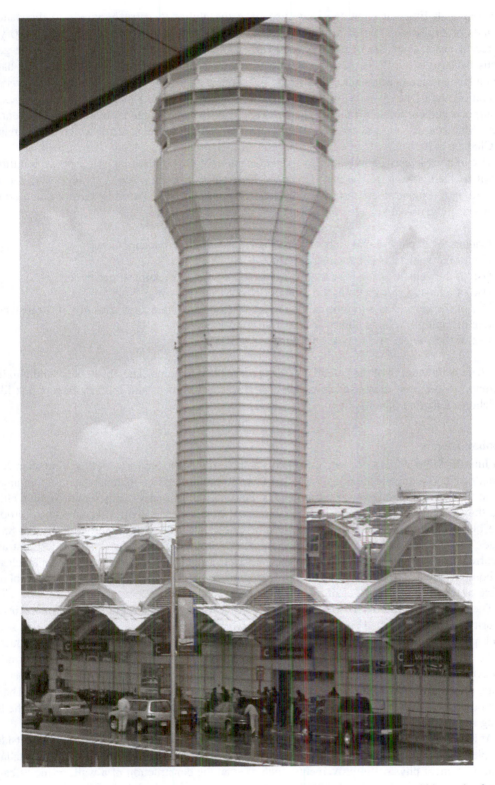

**FIGURE 10.9**    Trucks, taxis, SUVs, and cars are potential hazards. Note how many are within yards of an air traffic control tower, using public access.

location with little questioning. They also have the ability to carry hundreds to thousands of pounds of explosives. Truck bombs have been used to attack U.S. targets for at least 20 years. In recent years, there has been some focus on taxis and rescue vehicles. Taxis may have gained focus because of the large number of foreign nationals who operate them. It would be hard to find a law enforcement member who would question or even stop a rescue vehicle. However, consideration should be given to limousines. These vehicles often have more access to facilities such as airports and corporate offices. Limousines are also rarely encountered by law enforcement officials. Many cases have a nexus to common forms of transportation, some of which are enumerated in Chapter 8.

Use of a vehicle as a bomb delivery system is not new. One of the first groups to exploit this and use it to their advantage, in the amount of devastation that they could achieve, was the IRA. According to Poland, there have been the following methodologies used by terrorists and criminal bombers in the use of vehicle bombs.[6]

Placing the explosive materials on or in the car to kill the occupants
Use of the vehicle as a launching system
Use of the vehicle as a booby trap or antipersonnel device to ambush personnel
Use of a hostage for the transportation or delivery of explosives
Use of the vehicle as a fragmentation device when detonating a large quantity of explosives
Use of multiple vehicle bombs in a coordinated strike
Use of the vehicle in a suicide attack

There is little doubt of the potential in using a vehicle as a bomb. They have been, and will likely continue to be, used to deliver devastating blows to government and military targets just like in Oklahoma City and Saudi Arabia.

## Khobar Towers

On June 25, 1996, a fuel truck converted into a bomb estimated to have a "yield" of more than 20,000 pounds of TNT-equivalent explosives killed 19 U.S. military service members and injured an additional 500 service members housed at Khobar Towers. It also injured many Saudi Arabian citizens and third-country nationals, and severely damaged or destroyed a significant amount of property. The blast formed a crater that was between 15 and 35 feet deep and approximately 55–85 feet wide. This was the second bombing in Saudi Arabia in less than a year. The first terrorist attack occurred on November 13, 1995. Five Americans were killed when terrorists exploded a much smaller bomb (estimated to be between 200 and 250 pounds of TNT-equivalent explosives) in front of the office of the Program Manager of the Saudi Arabian National Guard.

The bombing of Khobar Towers on June 25, 1996, was a hideous act of terrorism. An Air Force security policeman spotted suspects backing up what appeared to be a cylindrical-shaped sewage truck perpendicular to the north perimeter fence, near Building 131, outside the American sector of the Khobar Towers complex (Khobar Towers also housed British, French, and Saudi military forces). After noticing two men run from the truck and jump into a waiting car, which then sped away, the security police immediately ordered personnel to begin evacuating the building. The evacuation was conducted using a floor-by-floor notification system. Within four minutes of the truck being spotted, the bomb detonated.

At Khobar Towers, Saudi Arabia as the host nation, exercised sovereignty both inside and outside the complex. Saudi Arabia did not permit the United States latitude in its activities within the installation; even permanent physical improvements, such as even the construction of a wall, or modifications to buildings, required Saudi approval. Internal security was a shared responsibility between the United States, coalition forces, and the Saudi Arabian military police. Security outside the fence was the responsibility of the Saudis.

*Pre-incident indicators: Ten suspicious incidents, including four of possible surveillance, were reported by military personnel in April, May, and June 1996. These incidents were subsequently reported in summary form in the June 17, 1996, issue of the Military Intelligence Digest, which stated that the incidents led to increased security measures. Many were during the period of the Hajj. These incidents were investigated by the Saudi military and local police. None indicated an attack on Khobar Towers was imminent. These suspicious incidents near the Khobar Towers in the Spring of 1996 were also thoroughly evaluated by the entire military chain of command.*

There were earlier incidents even though the military had hardened and secured the facility on numerous occasions. These incidents included one possible threat indicator when a suspect rammed a Jersey barrier on the east perimeter of the facility. It was reported to Saudi authorities. There were four incidents of possible surveillance, which were reported to local Saudi authorities for further investigation. These occurred on April 1, 4, 17, and 25, 1996, and all involved reports, by military personnel, of Middle Eastern men driving by or parked and observing the compound. Of the five remaining incidents, two were inconclusive, and three were completely discounted.

The military staff discussed these incidents with the Saudis, who did not view them as threatening. They attributed the incidents of possible surveillance to natural curiosity on the part of the Saudi populace about the activities of Americans inside the perimeter. Just outside the northern perimeter of Khobar Towers is a parking lot that was used by people visiting a nearby mosque. It also serviced a recreational area. During the month-long period of the Hajj, it was not unusual for many people to congregate in this area in the evenings. Most of the reported incidents took place during this time, and this may have caused the Saudi police to dismiss them as nonthreatening. The Saudis said they had undercover security personnel in the area and they were not concerned.

## Embassy—Nairobi, Kenya

On August 7, 1998, at approximately 10:30 a.m. local time, terrorists driving in a truck detonated a large bomb in the rear parking area, near the ramp to the basement garage of the American Embassy in Nairobi. A total of 213 people were killed, of whom 44 were American Embassy employees (12 Americans and 32 Foreign Service national employees). Twenty-two embassy employees were seriously injured. An estimated 200 Kenyan civilians were killed and 4,000 were injured by the blast in the vicinity of the embassy.

The security systems and procedures relating to actions taken in Nairobi appear to have been to some extent adequate. The fact that the suicide bomber failed in his attempt to penetrate the embassy's outer perimeter, thanks to the refusal of local guards to open the gates is a testament to this. In Dar es Salaam, the suicide bomber likewise failed to penetrate the perimeter, apparently stopped by a blocked entry point by an embassy water truck.

## Embassy—Dar es Salaam, Tanzania

On the morning of Friday, August 7, 1998, a truck laden with explosives drove up Laibon Road to one of the two vehicular gates of the U.S. Embassy in Dar es Salaam. According to physical evidence and reports from persons on the scene just prior to the bombing, the truck was unable to penetrate the perimeter because it was blocked by an embassy water tanker. Faced with being unable to breach the interior perimeter, the suicide bomber detonated his charge at 10:39 a.m. at a distance of about 35 feet from the outer wall of the chancery.

The bomb attack killed more than 10 people and another 85 people were injured. No Americans were among the fatalities, but many were injured, two of them seriously. The chancery suffered major structural damage and was rendered unusable, but it did not collapse. No one inside the chancery was killed, in part because of the strength of the structure and in part because of simple luck. A number of third-country diplomatic facilities and residences in the immediate vicinity were also severely damaged, and several American Embassy residences were destroyed, as were dozens of vehicles.

The American Ambassador's residence, a thousand yards distant and vacant at the time, suffered roof damage and collapsed ceilings.

*Pre-incident indicators: There were no credible intelligence reports that provided an immediate or tactical warning of the August 7 bombings. A number of earlier intelligence reports cited alleged threats against several U.S. diplomatic and other targets, including the embassies in Nairobi and Dar es Salaam. All of these reports were disseminated to the intelligence community and to appropriate posts abroad, but were largely discounted because of doubts about the sources. Other reporting, while taken seriously, was imprecise, changing, and nonspecific as to dates, diminishing its usefulness. Indeed, for eight months prior to the August 7 bombings, no further intelligence was produced to warn the embassies in Nairobi and Dar es Salaam.*

Although there was never an indication of when or how the U.S. embassies in Nairobi, Kenya, and Dar es Salaam, Tanzania would be attacked, there was mounting intelligence to suggest that the embassies were not adequately secure and were potentially targets of terrorist plots. Consequently, while certain threats were identified and intelligence had been collected and disseminated in some cases, they were often discounted before reaching high-level officials and determined to be unfounded.

In the summer of 1997, the CIA identified Wadih el-Hage as a key figure in al-Qaeda's leadership in Kenya. In August, 1997, the Kenyan police, CIA, and FBI raided el-Hage's house in Nairobi, downloaded files from his computer, and confiscated a number of written correspondences. He was extensively questioned three times by the FBI, but the documents from his home were not translated because of the unavailability of Arab-speaking staff and the low priority given to their contents.[12]

In examining the circumstances of these two bombings, the Accountability Review Boards for Nairobi and Dar es Salaam determined that the security systems and procedures for physical security at the embassies were generally met and, in some cases, exceeded the systems and procedures prescribed by the Department of State for posts designated at the medium or low threat levels. However, these standard requirements had not sufficiently anticipated the threat of large vehicular bomb attacks and were inadequate to protect against such attacks. For example, neither the embassy in Nairobi nor the one in Dar es Salaam met the department's standard for a 100-foot setback/standoff zone. Both were "existing office buildings" occupied before this standard was adopted, so a general exception was made—a weakness that was exploited.

## Bicycles

In the significant date list in Chapter 8, there was probably one event that went largely unnoticed. The event was on July 23, 2001, and involved the use of a bicycle as a bomb that killed seven in Kashmir.

On December 10, 2004, 11 persons, including 2 army personnel, were killed and 26 others sustained injuries when a bomb attached to a bicycle exploded at Quetta in the Baluchistan province of Pakistan. Fifteen members of the Frontier Corps and Baluchistan Reserve Police personnel were injured by a remote-controlled bicycle bomb in the southwest city Quetta when they passed by.

These are just examples of direct attacks that have taken place using bicycles (Figure 10.10). This mode of transportation has also been used in several suicide attacks. Between 1996 and 2000, there were at least three suicide bombing attacks in Sri Lanka by members of Liberation Tigers of Tamil Elam (LTTE).

Bicycle frames are often made of hollow aluminum tubing, which can be packed with explosives. Many have saddle bags that can carry a fair amount of explosive material. Law enforcement personnel often x-ray and inspect bags, but the bicycle often goes without inspection. In many large metropolitan areas, bicycles are allowed into buildings and on trains and buses. This weakness can be exploited by the terrorist and should not be overlooked in analysis or threat and vulnerability assessments.

The sheer magnitude of possibilities with regard to the use of transportation will prove to be a formidable challenge for law enforcement. The use of vehicle-borne improvised explosive devices

**FIGURE 10.10**    Bicycles are a common form of transportation and are allowed in buildings and mass transit systems.

(VBIED) will be the likely scenario encountered. There are, however, some situations that may afford personnel the opportunity to gain insight into a group's activities or even thwart a future attack with regard to transportation. Outlined below are some situations that may serve as pre-incident indicators:

  Person renting a vehicle is nervous, overly private, or does not appear to have a demonstrated need
  Vehicles parked for extended period of times at government, military, or other high-risk targets
  Inquiries about vehicle modifications, payload capabilities, or speed
  Desire to pay by cash and the need to get a deposit back without delay
  Theft of delivery, military, cargo, or civil service vehicles
  Inquiries about deliveries including timeline and routes
  Theft or purchase of paint, decals, or lighting equipment that can be used to modify a vehicle to appear as an emergency, delivery, or security vehicle

Incidents such as those noted above may come through law enforcement reports or even anonymous tips called into police departments. These events should be taken seriously and reviewed in the analytical process.

## SUMMARY OF RECENT TRANSPORTATION TARGETS

Between 1997 and 2000, there were more than 110 terrorist incidents targeting buses, bus depots, or bus stops (Figure 10.11). During this same time period, the second target of choice appears to be railways. There were at least 65 train- or railway-related terrorist attacks throughout the world in the 3-year time span. It is apparent that no one single country is immune from these attacks. From 2000 through 2008, the Global Terrorism Database reports that there were 763 additional terrorist incidents that targeted transportation. During this time frame, there are four countries that appear

**FIGURE 10.11**    The power and devastation of a bomb that was brought on a bus.

to be victimized the most: Afghanistan, Columbia, India, and Iraq. Some of the more prevalent countries experiencing attacks on transportation have been:

Israel
India
Tajikistan
Germany
Guatemala
Pakistan
Russia
Georgia
Philippines
Sri Lanka
United Kingdom

Regardless of the location, there have been several methods of attacks used on transportation. Everything from hijacking, handgun attacks, and bombings has been used to commit the majority of terrorist incidents involving transportation. One method that receives much attention is that of the suicide or homicide bomber.

## USE OF SUICIDE BOMBERS

Although not the staple in the terror repertoire, suicide bombing demonstrates how no one is safe, and how easily a terrorist can penetrate locations and create death and destruction (Figure 10.12). Islamic fundamentalist suicide bombers are discussed and highlighted on most modern media outlets as the main perpetrators of suicide attacks. Prior to the satellite and 24-hour cable explosion, suicide bombers were committing their atrocities throughout the world in regions outside the Middle East. According to Hudson, the unrivaled world leaders in terrorist suicide attacks are not the Islamic fundamentalists but are the Tamil Tigers of Elam in Sri Lanka also known as LTTE. LTTE are extremely committed and so dedicated to carrying out their mission that they carry cyanide capsules to avoid capture. In the wake of the Rajiv Ghandi assassination, no fewer than 35 LTTE operatives committed suicide rather than be questioned by authorities.[13] One of the more notable attacks against a Western country came at the U.S. Embassy in Beirut, in April 1983, when a suicide bomber detonated a van,

**FIGURE 10.12**   Hamas suicide bombers.

killing 63 people. According to the U.S. Army, there have been at least 300 separate suicide terrorist attacks worldwide since the Beirut attack. However, this report notes that suicide terrorism has been on a continuous decline during the past 20 years.[14]

## WHO ARE THE BOMBERS AND THEIR GROUPS?

With little debate, most would argue that the leaders in suicide bombing today are the members of Hamas in Palestine. An Israeli media outlet in late 2001 reviewed the makeup of 100 Palestinian suicide bombers and they noted the following.[15] Of the 100 suicide bombers, 75 were killed while perpetrating 67 different missions. In several attacks, like the one at Beit Lid in 1995, several suicide bombers participated in the same mission. The other 25 bombers were either intercepted by Israeli or Palestinian security forces before carrying out their attack or were captured after their explosives failed to detonate. Seven of the 30 suicide bombers sent on missions during the past year were arrested. Outlined below are some characteristics or traits:

66 belonged to Hamas, 34 were members of Islamic Jihad
67 were between the ages of 17 and 23 and most of the others were also under the age of 30
54 came from Gaza, 45 from the West Bank, and 1 was an Israeli Arab; the Israeli Arab who carried out the attack in Nahariya in September, 2001, was also an exception in his advanced age—53
23 had elementary education, 31 were high school graduates, and 46 had higher education
86 were unmarried and 14 were married

According to Martin, approximately 125 suicide bombings were carried out between 2001 and 2004, with 53 of these attacks occurring in 2002.[16] He noted that there was a marked increase in the number of females being used to carry out suicide missions. One of the more well-known female suicide bombers is Wafa Idriss. Wafa was a nurse with the Red Crescent, the Palestinian version of the Red Cross. On January 27, 2002, the 28-year-old nurse walked into a shopping district on Jerusalem's Jaffa Road and detonated a bomb, killing herself as well as an Israeli, and injuring 150 others. In the Palestinian community, Idriss became a celebrity and was worshipped to the point that on July 24, 2003, Palestinian television broadcasted a glorious celebration of her life including an orchestra and song. Since her detonation in 2002 through the end of 2004, there were at least eight other Palestinian women who carried out suicide missions. These missions are not limited to Palestinian women. In November 2005,

**FIGURE 10.13**   Female suicide bomber garment.

a Belgian-born convert to Islam, Muriel Degauque, became the first European woman suicide bomber, killing herself in Iraq. An example of a female suicide garment is a "bra bomb" (Figure 10.13).

Use of females in attacks should not come as a surprise. Terrorists do their homework and, just like law enforcement should look to anticipate behaviors, they have found a well-noted weakness. Law enforcement personnel focus on men, as do military personnel. Terrorists have exploited this for nearly a half of a century, and it was noted in the film *Battle of Algiers*, a movie about the Algerian National Liberation Front (FLN) success over the French in the Algerian war for independence in the late 1950s.

When examining the use of suicide terrorism from a group perspective, the U.S. Army noted that there are several reasons that this tactic is employed by a group. Outlined below are some of these reasons[14]:

Suicide attacks can result in large numbers of casualties and extensive damage.
Success of the suicide mission is almost guaranteed once the attacker departs for the operation.
Suicide attacks usually have a large psychological effect on the public because of the sense of helplessness.
Suicide attacks are relatively inexpensive, yet very effective. Estimates are that it can cost as little as $150 to conduct a suicide attack.
Suicide attacks often result in large donations to support the cause of the group.
Suicide attacks are normally less complicated than other types of operations.
The use of suicide terrorism presents minimal security risks to the group.
Media coverage of a suicide attack is almost guaranteed.

## What Can You Look For?

Security or precautionary measures will not be sufficient in combating the potential problem posed by the suicide bomb threat. This was evident in the 2005 London attacks. Without a doubt, these types of events will continue to occur. Despite the shared willingness to die for their beliefs, there is no one unique profile for a suicide bomber that law enforcement can look for. However, suicide bombers do not act by themselves. There are handlers, motivators, spiritual advisors, and logistical and operational supporters. Someone must recruit and train these individuals. James Poland suggests that by taking proactive measures, it may be possible to interdict future suicide attacks. He suggests the following proactive measures[6]:

Family members may notice a change in the son or daughter's behavior patterns.
Successful counterstrategy requires comprehensive intelligence of the recruitment, selection, and training of the suicide bomber.
The person who recruits the potential suicide bomber usually follows that person throughout their military-type training and spiritual awakening.

- Operational groundwork for the attack includes preparation of the explosive device, locating a safe house, and the transport of the bomber and explosives to the target.
- Organizations that support and create an atmosphere for the use of suicide attacks must be identified.

Just like identifying a terrorist in a crowd, you will not be able to readily identify a suicide bomber. However, clothing is perhaps the most outwardly present observation. Items such as baggy clothes, clothing not consistent with the weather, and presence of heavy bags may give visual clues.

There are at least 15 terrorist organizations, including Hamas, Hezbollah, PIJ, and Partiya Karkerên Kurdistanê —Kurdistan Workers' Party (PKK), in at least 12 different countries that have utilized suicide terrorists, so there is no one clear-cut profile with which to work. However, according to Ganzor, there are some characteristic traits that have been observed in Middle Eastern suicide bombers. In the Anti-Defamation League publication, *Countering Suicide Terrorism*, Ganzor noted the following common characteristics of suicide bombers[17]:

Young—usually from 18 to 27 years of age.
Usually not married, unemployed, and from a poor family.
Usually the shahid completed high school.
Most were devoted students in the Islamic fundamentalist education centers in Gaza and the West Bank, directed and financed by Hamas.
Some of the shahids arrested by Israel in the past expressed the desire to avenge the death or injury of a relative or close friend at the hands of Israel.

Most suicide bombers feel a sense of patriotism and are promised eternal life in paradise, 72 virgins, and the privilege to promise life in heaven to 70 relatives. They may also believe that the social and economic status of their family may improve. The latter belief is realized when, as the Iraqi government once did, thousands of dollars were paid to the families of the suicide bomber.

## HOMEGROWN TERROR—LEARNING FROM OTHERS

There have been numerous individuals who could be classified as extremists or terrorists, both born and naturalized, who have roots in the United States. This is hard for some to believe or acknowledge, but nonetheless, it is true. Not every terrorist emanates from Europe, South America, Asia, or the Middle East. What is even tougher to comprehend is the fact that many of these individuals adopt the ideology of some of the most radical/extremist religion-based groups. We can comprehend that a citizen can belong to a "domestic terrorist group" but cannot fathom that he or she would join a "foreign terrorist group." This is a naïve approach. Terror is not restricted to a single country of origin. Just ask yourself one question. If you wanted to pull off an attack in a country, is it better to be a foreigner and try to assimilate into society or find someone who is a citizen, familiar with the surroundings and who "fits in"? Terrorists are not always from a particular ethnicity or culture. Just as terrorists from other lands may conduct operations in the United States, it is important to note that American citizens have supported terrorist operations abroad. An example of this would be Jaber Elbaneh, a U.S. citizen who was in custody in Yemen before escaping from prison with 23 other terrorists, and is wanted in Buffalo (Lackawanna), New York for a 2003 charge of providing material support to a terrorist organization. Others, who were not originally Muslims, have taken part in terrorist activities.

Outlined below is a sample of some of the more notable Americans who fought for the "enemy" or against members of the Western world:

Clement Rodney Hampton-El (aka Dr Rashid): A former New Jersey hospital technician, Hampton-El was wounded while fighting with Mujahideen fighters in Afghanistan in 1988.

Hampton-El eventually returned to the United States. It has been alleged that he became a bomb expert and had ties to Ramzi Yousef and Sheikh Omar Abdel Rahman. Clement Rodney Hampton-El was convicted of conspiring to blow up New York City landmarks in a 1993 terror plot linked to the World Trade Center bombing in February of that year.

John Walker Lindh: An American citizen who was born in Washington, DC, and lived in Marin County, California, Lindh was captured in 2001 while fighting for the Taliban in Afghanistan.

Adam Gadahn: Born in California and raised in Riverside County, Gadahn is suspected of being a member of al-Qaeda and is being investigated for being a spokesperson in video tapes from al-Qaeda against the United States. He is allegedly affiliated with the Wahhabi organization, the Islamic Society of North America (ISNA).

Iyman Faris: A truck driver from Ohio, Faris was born in Kashmir and entered the United States in the early 1990s, and became a citizen in the late 1990s. In 2003, Faris pled guilty to providing support to al-Qaeda. Faris allegedly met Khalid Sheikh Mohammad in 2002 and knows a suspect from the 2005 London bombings.

Jose Padilla: Born in Brooklyn, New York, Padilla, a street gang member, converted to Islam while in prison. He was arrested in Chicago in 2002 after traveling throughout the Middle East.

## EXPANDED DETAILS

### Adam Gadahn

Adam Yahiye Gadahn, an American citizen, has been publicly described as a homegrown terrorist and extremist. In May 2008, the United States Senate Committee on Homeland Security and Governmental Affairs prepared a report entitled *Violent Islamist Extremism, the Internet, and the Homegrown Terrorist Threat*. In this report, and numerous testimonials before the U.S. Congress, it has been highlighted that terrorist organizations are seeking to recruit American citizens to further their cause. Although not mentioned in this report, Gadahn's own writings highlight many aspects noted in the Committee report.

Gadahn, also known as Azzam al-Amriki, as well as several other aliases, was born Adam Pearlman on September 1, 1978, to parents of Jewish and Catholic heritage. Gadahn was raised in rural Riverside County, California, on a family farm. In the mid-1990s, Gadahn moved to Santa Ana in Orange County, California to live with his grandparents. According to an essay, *Becoming Muslim*, written by Gadahn in the 1990s while living with his grandparents and published on several Internet sites between 1995 and 2006, Gadahn outlines his upbringing and his self exposure to Islam on the Internet. At the age of 17, Gadahn converted to Islam while attending the Islamic Society of Orange County located in Garden Grove, California, and in the essay, Gadahn noted that it felt great to be a Muslim.

According to the FBI report, Gadahn moved to Pakistan in 1998 and attended al-Qaeda terrorist training camps in Afghanistan. Gadahn has become known as a propagandist for the terrorist organization, al-Qaeda. In 2004, Gadahn was one of seven individuals singled out by the FBI Director and the Attorney General as posing a danger to United States interests around the world. In October 2005, a grand jury in Santa Ana, California, indicted Gadahn for his alleged involvement in terrorist activities under violations of U.S. Code to include Treason and Providing Material Support to a Designated Foreign Terrorist Organization (al-Qaeda). This was a result of Gadahn making a series of propaganda video tapes for al-Qaeda. From 2004 to 2010, there have been at least a dozen videos where Gadahn has appeared in support of al-Qaeda promoting jihad against the United States and the West. The charges filed in the Central District of California say Gadahn "gave al-Qaeda aid and comfort ... with intent to betray the United States." Gadahn is the first person to be charged with treason against the United States since the World War II era.

According to the grand jury indictment, on September 2, 2006, al-Qaeda's second in command, Ayman al-Zawahiri, introduced Gadahn as "our brother Azzam the American" and he urged Americans to listen to Gadahn. As one of al-Qaeda's principal spokesmen, it has been noted that Gadahn's messages are targeted toward gaining support of English-speaking audiences in the United States and abroad. On October 11, 2006, the FBI added Gadahn to the Most Wanted Terrorists list and the U.S. Department of State began offering a reward of up to $1 million for information leading to Gadahn's arrest.

## Iyman Faris

Iyman Faris, also known as Mohammed Rauf, a naturalized U.S. citizen, was born in Kashmir in 1969. He lived in Ohio and was employed as a truck driver. Faris pled guilty in May 2003 for casing a New York City bridge and providing material support for al-Qaeda. Faris admitted to traveling to a training camp in Afghanistan in late 2000, where he was introduced to Osama bin Laden (Figure 10.14). He also admitted that during a meeting in late 2000, one of Osama bin Laden's men asked him about "ultralight" airplanes, and said al-Qaeda was looking to procure an "escape airplane." Faris admitted that about two months later, he performed an Internet search at a cafe in Karachi, Pakistan, and obtained information about ultralights, which he turned over to a friend for use by al-Qaeda.

During a visit to Karachi in early 2002, he was introduced to a senior operational leader in al-Qaeda. A few weeks later, the operational leader asked what he could do for al-Qaeda. Faris said

IN THE UNITED STATES DISTRICT COURT FOR THE
EASTER DISTRICT OF VIRGINIA

Alexandria Division

UNITED STATES OF AMERICA

v.                                           CRIMINAL NO.

IYMAN FARIS,
    a/k/a Mohammad Rauf,
        Defendant.

STATEMENT OF FACTS

Should this matter proceed to trial, the United States would prove the following beyond a reasonable doubt:

1. The defendant, Iyman Faris, a/k/a Mohammed Rauf, was born in Kashmir on June 4, 1969. The defendant entered the United States in May 1994 and became a United States citizen in December 1999. Defendant has been employed as an independent truck driver for several years.

2. In late 2000, the defendant traveled with a long-time friend, hereafter referred to as conspirator-1 (C-1), from pakistan to Afghanistan. (The defendant has known C-1 since the Soviet/Afghanistan war in the mid-1980's and has maintained a friendly relationship with him since that time.) After arriving in Afghanistan with C-1, the defendant was introduced to Osama bin Laden at an al Qaeda training camp. The camp had numerous tents and buildings, and there were several men present who wore black scarves and carried weapons. Since at least this meeting, the defendant knew that Osama bin Laden and C-1 were senior leaders in al Qaeda. The defendant understands C-1 to be Osama bin Laden's "right foot"—a man who serves a critical leadership role in providing supplies and materials needed by al Qaeda.

3. During this meeting in late 2000, one of Osama bin Laden's men asked the defendant.

**FIGURE 10.14** *United States v. Iyman Faris*, Statement of Facts.

he discussed his work as a truck driver in the United States, his trucking routes, and deliveries for airport cargo planes. The al-Qaeda leader said he was interested because cargo planes would hold "more weight and more fuel."

The al-Qaeda leader spoke with Faris about destroying a bridge in New York City by severing its suspension cables, and tasked Faris with obtaining the equipment needed for that operation. The leader also explained that al-Qaeda was planning to derail trains, and asked Faris to procure the tools for that plot as well.

### Jose Padilla—Aka The Dirty Bomber

It is unclear whether Jose Padilla, also known by his adopted Muslim name Abdullah al Muhajir, was using his gang affiliation to sponsor terrorism. Padilla, an admitted Latin Disciple gang member, was arrested at Chicago's O'Hare Airport as an associate member of the al-Qaeda terrorist network (Figure 10.15). The FBI reported that Padilla had changed his name, converted to Islam, and trained with the terrorist network after his last release from prison.

UNITED STATES DISTRICT COURT
SOUTHERN DISTRICT OF FLORIDA

CASE NO.  04-60001-CR-COOKE (s) (s) (s) (s) (s)

18 U.S.C. §956(a)(1)
18 U.S.C. §371
18 U.S.C. §2339A
18 U.S.C. §922(g)(5)(B)
18 U.S.C. §1001(a)
18 U.S.C. §1621(1)
18 U.S.C. §1505
18 U.S.C. §924(d)(1)
18 U.S.C. §2
21 U.S.C. §853

UNITED STATES OF AMERICA
v.
ADHAM AMIN HASSOUN,
      a/k/a "Abu Sayyaf,"
MOHAMED HESHAM YOUSSEF,
      a/k/a "Abu Turab,"
KIFAH WAEL JAYYOUSI,
      a/k/a "Abu Mohamed,"
KASSEM DAHER,
      a/k/a "Abu Zurr," and
JOSE PADILLA,
      a/k/a "Ibrahim,"
      a/k/a "Abu Abduallh the Puerto Rican,"
      a/k/a "Abu Abdullah Al Mujahir,"

Defendants.
_____/

SUPERSEDING INDICTMENT

The Grand Jury charges that:

INTRODUCTION

At times material to this Superseding Indictment:

**FIGURE 10.15**   Indictment of Jose Padilla, a.k.a. Abdullah al Muhajir.

Although street gangs are known for causing havoc on city streets through acts of "crime," Padilla was set to inflict major damage by conspiring to build and detonate a "dirty bomb" in the United States according to the FBI.

### William Morgan—Cuban Revolutionary

The aforementioned individuals were not the first and certainly will not be the last. One of the first modern era Americans to have left the United States to fight for someone else's beliefs was a man from Toledo, Ohio, William Alexander Morgan. Described by some as a troubled person, expelled from several schools, arrested, and removed from the U.S. Army, he was a recruiter's ideal candidate. According to the *Toledo Blade*, Morgan left his hometown to fight alongside Fidel Castro and Che Guevara and Castro's revolutionary forces in 1957. In Cuba, he was the Yanqui Comandante who was promoted to the rank of major. He was described as a charismatic tough man who stunned his family by leaving his home in Toledo to join the revolutionary forces—a soldier of fortune who vowed to fight for "freedom and democracy."[18]

Leading a band of young guerillas, he captured the town of Cienfuegos in 1958 in one of the last battles of the revolution. He was celebrated by many for his actions. However, his celebrity status diminished and he was eventually executed by Castro's government in March 1961.

Besides learning from others, individuals obtain and learn their ideology in many ways. One of the more prevalent is through radical or extremist teachings, some of which occur locally. Long-standing extremist-based groups are located in the United States.

### CASES FOR GROUPS FOUND IN THE UNITED STATES AND ABROAD

### Lackawanna Six

The Lackawanna Six, also known as the Buffalo Six, is a group of Yemeni-Americans, born and raised in the United States, who were charged with providing material support to al-Qaeda. They allegedly traveled to Pakistan and Afghanistan in early 2001. They were arrested in the Buffalo area in late 2002. In 2003, they pled guilty to the charges and were subsequently sentenced.

### Portland Seven

The group that came to be known in the media as the Portland Seven was a group of American Muslims from the Portland, Oregon area. In October 2002, the FBI began an operation that attempted to close down the suspected terrorist cell. The seven individuals were allegedly attempting to join al-Qaeda forces in their fight in Afghanistan after 9/11.

### Northern Virginia

In Northern Virginia, 11 men were indicted for conspiring to violate the Neutrality Act and firearm laws based on their participation in military-style training, including the use of paintballs, in the United States. Several of the defendants traveled to Lashkar-e-Taiba (LET) terrorist training camps in Pakistan in preparation for conducting violent jihad in Kashmir and elsewhere.

### Islamic Association for Palestine

Characterized by investigative reporter and terrorism expert Steven Emerson as Hamas' primary voice in the United States, the Islamic Association for Palestine (IAP) has established its North American Headquarters in Bridgeview, Illinois. In Emerson's documentary *Jihad in America*, the IAP was based and situated in Richardson, Texas. The IAP has been investigated by Emerson for their alleged ties to the first World Trade Center bombing. Emerson questioned a representative of the IAP as to their support for Hamas and their dislike for Jews. In this interview, there is little doubt of the representative's deception and attempt to avoid the truth. Emerson even noted in his February 1998 statement before the Senate Judiciary Committee's Subcommittee on Terrorism,

Technology, and Government Information that the IAP is a vehicle to recruit and train terrorists to attack the Israelis. Before being taken down, the IAP website proudly displayed an Israeli flag surrounded by a circle with a line through it and proclaimed "Jews Against Zionism."

The IAP was founded in 1981 by Mousa Mohammed Abu Marzook, a founder of the Holy Land Foundation, which was shut down because of its financial ties with terrorism. He is now an alleged political leader of Hamas and is located in Syria. A protégé of Marzook is Rafeeq Jaber, as of January 2006, the current president of the IAP. He is also a founder of the national office of the CAIR and a board member of the Mosque Foundation, also located in Bridgeview. The Mosque Foundation has been the focus of investigations for nearly 10 years for their alleged involvement related to raising funds for Palestinian terrorist organizations, primarily Hamas and the Muslim Brotherhood. Activities, financial and otherwise, of several members of the Bridgeview mosque and the Mosque Foundation, have brought this small town into the forefront of some of the more significant terrorist events and terrorist groups.

Situated in the Village of Bridgeview, Illinois, is a mosque with more than 2000 prayer attendees that has been on the terrorist-related radar screen of federal authorities for more than a decade. During the past several years, U.S. government officials have taken legal action against a number of former officials and other prominent members of the Bridgeview mosque for funding and participating in terrorist organizations, primarily Hamas affiliated. Membership of the mosque has allegedly poured hundreds of thousands of dollars into three charities that were closed shortly after 9/11 for financing terrorism: Global Relief Foundation, the Holy Land Foundation, and the Benevolence International Foundation.

On February 8, 2004, the *Chicago Tribune* published an investigative report titled *Struggle for the Soul of Islam, Hard-Liners Won Battle for Bridgeview Mosque*. This article provides explicit insight into one of the United States' largest Palestinian communities located in Cook County, Illinois—Bridgeview. Radical aspects of some of the membership as well as the aggressive fundraising efforts were highlighted.

Reporters and everyday citizens appear to have more insight into events that occur in this small village, Bridgeview, whose motto is "A Well Balanced Community," than local authorities who appear to view the aforementioned concerns as a matter for federal authorities. These local officials may also be concerned with political repercussions in a town whose political base once emanated from European descent and is now seen by some as "little Palestine." These officials are not alone in this mentality. Several small communities have experienced the reaches of radical, extreme, and terror groups, and they are totally unaware, fearful, or refuse to acknowledge it. At present, there is an active group in the United States, Jamaat al-Fuqra (JUF), which has extended its physical reaches in the same aggressive manner as the IAP. JUF has continued to stretch its reach across the United States, including extreme rural communities.

### Jamaat al-Fuqra and the Muslims of America

JUF, also referred to as al-Fuqra, and al-Faqra (The Poor, The Impoverished, and Community of the Poor), is a Sufi Islamic extremist sect consisting of predominately African American Muslims. Pakistani cleric Sheikh Mubarik Ali Gilani founded JUF in 1980 in Brooklyn, New York, but Gilani currently allegedly resides in the outskirts of Lahore, Pakistan. The group allegedly seeks to purify Islam through violence and was banned by the U.S. Department of State in 2000. Some refer to the group as Muslims of the United States (MOA). However, JUF and MOA are not necessarily one and the same; members of JUF are not necessarily members of MOA, and vice versa. MOA is a tax exempt, nonprofit organization registered in various locations in the United States, Caribbean, and Canada and may be used as a "front" for JUF activities. Both groups strictly adhere to the teachings, guidance, and orders of Sheikh Mubarik Ali Gilani from his base in Pakistan. Gilani is also the person who Daniel Pearl was seeking to visit and interview when he was abducted and murdered.

MOA is estimated to have as few as 3,000 and as many as 12,000 members in the United States alone who live in or around more than two dozen rural compounds called "jamaats," or villages.

These are in more than 10 locations across the United States: Coldwater, Michigan; Hancock, New York (alleged headquarters known as Islamberg); Jetersville, Meherrin, and Red House, Virginia; Commerce, Georgia; York, South Carolina (known as Islamville); Dover, Tennessee; Sweeny, Texas; Reidsville, North Carolina; and Fresno, California. MOA members have reportedly assimilated into society and hold positions in the public and the private sectors. However, assimilating may not be that far of a stretch because the group has focused efforts on recruiting black men and women from within the community. Several of the men have reportedly been brought to Pakistan by Gilani for the purposes of training.

## Coming to the Attention of Law Enforcement

MOA and JUF were virtually unknown names to many in the law enforcement community during their first 10 years of existence. However, in the late 1980s, the Colorado Attorney General's Office successfully prosecuted five members of JUF between 1993 and 1994. The investigation was initiated by Colorado Springs detectives who were investigating a series of burglaries. During subsequent investigations by Colorado law enforcement in the late 1980s, personnel discovered documents containing surveillance photos of many potential "targets." These included U.S. military installations such as Buckley Air Force Base in Denver, Rocky Mountain Arsenal in Commerce City, the U.S. Air Force Academy in Colorado Springs, two Wyoming National Guard armories in Cheyenne, and Cheyenne's Warren Air Force Base. They also located and seized a large weapons cache including bomb-making materials, explosives, military training manuals, and an array of "how to" publications.

The most damning items that helped secure the prosecutions were several workers' compensation claims, which led to a full-scale fraud investigation. This investigation revealed that members had defrauded the State of Colorado of approximately $350,000 during an 8-year period.[19]

## The Jamaat al-Fuqra and Muslims of the America Today

Gilani currently lives in the outskirts of Lahore, Pakistan. While in Pakistan, Gilani allegedly seeks to carry out a self-declared policy of jihad or holy war against enemies of the group. These include but are not limited to Muslims with whom they disagree, such as those in India who support the creation of an Islamic state in Kashmir, Hindus, Hare Krishna, Israel, the Jewish Defense League, and the Nation of Islam.

## Educating, Recruiting, and Funding

Gilani controls JUF and MOA, which allegedly has six branch offices in U.S. cities and Toronto, Canada. The International Quranic Open University, Inc., established in 1982 and operated by MOA, is their primary educational facility. The university has the alleged support of Pakistani authorities and is suspected of having ties to Pakistan's Inter-Services Intelligence Directorate (ISID).

Reflecting the doctrines of the organization, members of JUF refer to themselves as "Soldiers of Allah." They seek to recruit and expand their operations. One of the more prevalent recruiting grounds has been through the prison system. Many members of JUF have been convicted of criminal acts and have spent time in jails and prisons. Once released from incarceration, select members are welcome to live on one of the organization's remote rural compounds. However, recidivism appears not to dissipate once they join the group or move to a compound. There have been numerous criminal acts attributed to members of JUF and MOA during the past 25 years, many in the United States, including fire bombings and murders/assassinations. It is the criminal acts that appear to be funding much of the organization's activities including narcotics. There are also alleged nonprofit operations, educational initiatives, and businesses such as a security company.

JUF and MOA appear to have been around for more than two decades and show no signs of being eliminated, and it is incumbent on today's law enforcement community to be aware of their activities, as well as other similar groups. Even though JUF and MOA seem to be thriving in North America, they are not, and will not, be the last case of suspicion to come to the attention of law enforcement in North America or abroad.

## OTHER NOTABLE CASES

### Charlotte Hezbollah Case

Iredell County, North Carolina, appears to be a location far from the war on terror. However, in early 1995, it became the epicenter of one of the largest terrorist-related cases in the United States against members of Hezbollah (Figure 10.16). This case would also be one of the first tests of the 1996 enacted 18 U.S.C. §2339B, which prohibits providing material support and resources to designated foreign terrorist organizations.

FILED
CHARLOTTE, N. C.

UNITED STATES DISTRICT COURT
WESTERN DISTRICT OF NORTH CAROLINA
CHARLOTTE DIVISION

JUL 31 2000

U. S. DISTRICT COURT
W. DIST. OF N. C.

UNITED STATES OF AMERICA

v.

DOCKET NO.      3:00 CR-147-mu

BILL OF INDICTMENT

1. MOHAMAD YOUSSEF HAMMOUD
   a/k/a Ali A. A. Abousaleh
   a/k/a Ali A. A. Albousaleh
2. BASSAM YOUSSEF HAMOOD
   a/k/a Bassem Hammoud
   a/k/a Bassam Hammoud
3. CHAWKI YOUSSEF HAMMOUD
4. MOHAMAD ATEF DARWICHE
   a/k/a Mohamad Darwich
5. ALI HUSSEIN DARWICHE
   a/k/a Ali Hussein Darwich
6. ALI FAYEZ DARWICHE
   a/k/a Ali Darwich
   a/k/a Ali Darwieh
7. SAID MOHAMAD HARB
   a/k/a Mustapha Harb
   a/k/a Ahmad Al Alquam
   a/k/a Mohamad Dbouk
8. ANGELA GEORGIA TSIOUMAS
   a/k/a Angie Tsioumas
9. MEHDI HACHEM MOUSSAOUI
   a/k/a Mehdi Moussoui
   a/k/a Mehdi Masawi
10. FATME MOHAMAD HARB
    a/k/a Fatima Harb
    a/k/a Fahtme Harb
11. SAMIR MOHAMAD ALI DEBK
    a/k/a Samir Depk
12. HAISSAM MOHAMAD HARB
    a/k/a Mohamad Dbouk
13. TERRI JEANNE PISH
14. TONIA YVONNE MOORE
15. JESSICA YOLANDA FORTUNE

Violation(s): 8 U.S.C. §1324(ε)(1)(A)(v)(I)
8 U.S.C. §1325(c)
18 U.S.C. §201(b)(1)
18 U.S.C. §371
18 U.S.C. §982
18 U.S.C. §1546(a)
18 U.S.C. §1956(h)
18 U.S.C. §2342

**FIGURE 10.16**  Charlotte Hezbollah cell; *United States v. Mohamad Hammoud et al.* Bill of Indictment.

What was dubbed by some as Operation Smokescreen was initiated by Deputy Sheriff Robert Fromme who was working an off-duty detail for J. R. Tobacco in Statesville, North Carolina, for the purpose of apprehending shoplifters. His observations would eventually lead to a 4-year investigation, involvement of more than 15 local, state, federal, and international law enforcement agencies, and the arrest and conviction of more than 25 individuals.

## Birth of the Cell

Cell leader Mohamad Hammoud from Beirut, along with two relatives, entered the United States in 1992 after he purchased fraudulent U.S. visas in Venezuela after several attempts to obtain a visa in Syria through the U.S. Embassy. Once detained at JFK International Airport in New York, Hammoud claimed asylum, which was eventually denied in late 1993. He was ordered deported and then filed an appeal. In an attempt to remain in the United States while his appeal was pending, Hammoud entered into three fraudulent marriages between 1994 and 1997. During his efforts, which were found to be based on fraudulent documents, Hammoud was ordered to be deported at least once. Mohamad's brother, Chawki, and other relatives who were involved in the cell, engaged in similar behavior. The behavioral patterns of the cell members led them into entering into several bogus marriages. They even paid for at least one Charlotte, North Carolina man to travel to Lebanon for a marriage and bribery of an embassy official in Cyprus.

Once in the United States, cell members moved quickly to establish residency in the Charlotte area in modest rented apartments and took menial jobs including working at a pizza place. However, there was a need to assimilate into society and avoid detection by law enforcement officials. The cell's subjects assumed identities and established others in efforts to avoid officers, further criminal activity, and pursue initiatives designed to fund their operations. One of the codefendants, Said Harb, testified that he had many identities and made at least $150,000 per identity. It would ultimately be the cell's criminal activity that would be the basis for their demise.

*Making the case: After establishing their base in the United States, Hammoud's cell resorted to credit card schemes and cigarette smuggling in order to raise millions of dollars. Deputy Fromme initially observed what he thought were "Hispanic" men driving vans with out-of-state license plates and making large purchases with cash. His keen observation would lead to an investigation of a core group of eight Charlotte residents, including Hammoud, and the fact that they had purchased nearly $8 million worth of cigarettes. The profits reaped from their efforts were in the neighborhood of $2 million. These profits were eventually laundered through fraudulent shells and alias names, as well as reinvested into the cigarette smuggling operation.[20]*

The smuggling efforts were made attractive by the $7 per carton of cigarettes tax mark-up in Michigan compared with North Carolina. Expenses associated with the delivery of the cigarettes included rental vehicles, gas, and hotels, which were charged on credit cards. The profits derived from the cell's criminal activity enabled them to live large beyond their apparent means and to purchase many questionable items such as laser range finders and aviation software.

Law enforcement personnel ultimately did what they do best, investigate crime. There were many crimes that were available for investigation including fraud, visa violations, cigarette smuggling, stolen property, immigration violations, bribery, money laundering, bank fraud, and racketeering. In investigating the criminal activities of the group, law enforcement personnel employed traditional investigative techniques[20]:

Physical surveillance
Search warrants, subpoenas, and seizures
Cultivation of witnesses
Analysis of telephone records
Analysis of financial records
Pen registers and pole cameras

Investigators also found and reviewed correspondence indicating various members' involvement, books and pamphlets, and receipts, some with direct links to Hezbollah and its leadership. The aforementioned, coupled with cooperative police work such as that from their counterparts in Canada, and the execution of 18 search warrants in July 2000, enabled investigative personnel to put the puzzle together and successfully prosecute cell members.

After a five-week trial Hammoud was found guilty on all charges and sentenced to 155 years in prison.

## Bali Case

One of the locations in the world that has seen a rise in terrorism activities has been Indonesia. On August 6, 2003, a car bomb exploded outside a J.W. Marriott Hotel in Jakarta, killing 12, and on September 9, 2004, a truck packed with explosives detonated outside the Australian Embassy in Jakarta, killing 11 people. A second location in the region to feel the rage of terrorists has been Bali. Most recently, on October 1, 2005, bombs exploded near three restaurants, killing four people. However, the case we will focus on is the one that occurred on October 12, 2002, which killed more than 200 people at Sari Club and Paddy's Bar in Kuta (Figure 10.17). The 2005 nightclub bombings were the seventh major bombing in the region in a three-week time span. Indonesian police attributed the 2005 attack to the men behind the 2002 attack.

On October 12, 2002, a car bomb exploded outside the Sari nightclub in Bali, a popular tourist island in Indonesia. The attack was attributed to Jemaah Islamiah (JI), an Indonesian terrorist group with aims of creating an Islamic state composed of parts of Indonesia, Malaysia, and the Southern Philippines. However, according to U.S. and Asian intelligence authorities the attack was connected to al-Qaeda.

*Case specifics: In February 2002, a meeting was held in Thailand between the operational chief of JI, Nurjaman Riduan Ismuddin, also known as Hambali, and several other men including one known as Mukhlas, where the topic of bringing jihad to Southeast Asia was discussed. In April of the same year, Mukhlas returned home to the village of Tenggulun in Indonesia's East Java province to begin planning the attack with his younger brother Amrozi, when they allegedly decided to target Bali. Five months later, Amrozi reportedly bought the chemicals and van necessary for the attack. It has been suggested by some in the law enforcement community that the 2002 attack cost the terrorists somewhere in the neighborhood of just $30,000.*

**FIGURE 10.17**    Sari nightclub in Bali after car bomb explosion, October 12, 2002.

On October 12, 2002, a suicide bomber with a backpack bomb detonated himself inside Paddy's bar. A few minutes later, a van parked outside the Sari Club exploded. The combined explosions killed more than 200 people. A few miles away, a bomb exploded at the U.S. consulate about a minute after the van exploded. However, no one was injured. Seven days later, the purported radical spiritual leader of JI, Abu Bakar Bashir, was arrested by police.

A short time later on November 5, Amrozi was arrested in East Java where he confessed to owning the van responsible for the blast and also for buying the explosives used. He implicated his brother Mukhlas in the ownership of the van. Three days later al-Qaeda claimed responsibility for the Bali attacks.

Hambali, the purported organizer of the Bali bombings, was detained in Thailand by the U.S. government in August 2003. Hambali was also believed to have been involved in the 2003 J.W. Marriot Hotel bombings in Jakarta, as well as being a close associate of Khalid Sheikh Mohammed, the mastermind of the 9/11 attacks on the United States.

Throughout this chapter, several examples, such as the indictments that were illustrated, have been cited and illustrate what law enforcement will likely see again, only with different players. Access to such documents may make interesting reading and research for books such as this, but law enforcement must remember its potential impact on future terrorists. What value do "clearances" have if many aspects of a case are widely available through Freedom of Information Act or sunshine law requests? While you may not be able to legally seal every document, you must remain cognizant of what others can obtain and even learn from it in the future.

## CHAPTER CONCEPTS

The chapter concepts can be summarized as follows:

Modes of transportation have been used in terrorist attacks for over a century.

Transit systems are targets because they provide easy access and large concentrations of people, they are vital to the economy, a service disruption could affect millions, and they are a target-rich environment.

Aviation has been targeted by terrorists for decades. The masters of airline hijacking have been the PFLP terrorist group.

Transportation, especially buses and railways, have been targeted by terrorists for decades in an attempt to demonstrate that everyday citizens are not safe.

Most terrorist attacks involving transportation had pre-incident indicators before the actual attacks.

Suicide attacks have been largely used by LTTE and Hamas. A method to identify suicide bombers is not available, but there are potential indicators to identify.

Homegrown terrorists are a concern. There have been several from the United States including Faris, Padilla, Hampton-El, and Lindh.

There are groups that may pose a concern for law enforcement today in the United States, for example, IAP, JUF, and MOA.

## REFERENCES

1. Terrorism Knowledge Base. National Memorial Institute for the Prevention of Terrorism. http://www.tkb.org/GroupTargetModule.jsp (accessed February 26, 2006).
2. Jenkins, B. M., and L. N. Gersten. 2001. *Protecting Public Surface Transportation against Terrorism and Serious Crime: Continuing Research on Best Security Practices.* San Jose, CA: Mineta Transportation Institute, pp. 25–27.
3. U.S. Department of Justice Federal Bureau of Investigations. 2001. *The FBI's Counterterrorism Program Since September 2001.* Report to the National Commission on Terrorist Attacks upon the United States. pp. 14–15. (14 April 2004).

4. Dunham, S. 2002. *Mass Transit Defends Itself against Terrorism*. Homeland Security Institute. http://www. homelandsecurity.org/newjournal/articles/dunhammasstransit.htm (accessed March 12, 2006).

5. National Center for Transit Research. 2002. *Public Transportation Anti-Terrorism Research Guide*. Upper Tampa, FL: Center for Urban Transportation Research University of South Florida, p. 5.

6. Poland, J. M. 2005. *Understanding Terrorism Groups, Strategies, and Responses*. 2nd ed. Upper Saddle River, NJ: Prentice Hall, pp. 192, 202, 225.

7. Simonsen, C. E., and J. R. Spindlove. 2005. *Terrorism Today: The Past, the Players, the Future*. 2nd ed. Upper Saddle River, NJ: Prentice Hall, p. 371.

8. ICC Commercial Crime Services. 2006. International Chamber of Commerce. http://www.icc-ccs.org/main/ news.php?newsid=63 (accessed March 12, 2006).

9. Perl, R., and R. O'Rourke. 2001. *Terrorist Attack on USS* Cole: *Background and Issues for Congress*. CRS Report for Congress. Washington, D.C.: Congressional Research Service, p. 2.

10. Terrorism Knowledge Base. 2005. *Abu Hafs Al-Masri Brigade and Secret Organization of Al-Qaeda in Europe Attacked Transportation Target*. United Kingdom: MIPT. http://www.tkb.org/Incident.jsp? incID=24394 (accessed March 11, 2006).

11. Jenkins, B. M., and L. N. Gersten. 2001. *Protecting Public Surface Transportation and Serious Crime: Continuing Research on Best Security Practices*. San Jose, CA: Mineta Transportation Institute, College of Business, San Jose State University, pp. 49–51.

12. Wikipedia. 1998. United States embassy bombings. http://en.wikipedia.org/wiki/1998_U.S._embassy_ bombings#Pre-bombing_intelligence (accessed March 4, 2006).

13. Hudson, R. 1999. *The Sociology and Psychology of Terrorism: Who Becomes a Terrorist and Why?* Washington, D.C.: Federal Research Division, p. 29.

14. Deputy Chief of Staff for Intelligence. 2005. *Suicide Bombing in the COE*. Handbook No. 1.03. Fort Eustis, VA: U.S. Army Training and Doctrine Command, pp. 2–14.

15. Harel, A. 2001. Haaretz Daily. http://www.haaretzdaily.com/hasen/pages/ShArt.jhtml?itemNo= 80841 (accessed March 11, 2006).

16. Martin, G. 2006. *Understanding Terrorism*. 2nd ed. Thousand Oaks, CA: Sage, p. 366–367.

17. Ganzor, B. 2002. *Countering Suicide Terrorism*. Washington, D.C.: The Anti-Defamation League and The International Policy Institute for Counter Terrorism, p. 146.

18. Sallah, M. D. 2002. *Toledo Blade*. http://www.latinamericanstudies.org/cuban-rebels/morgan.htm (accessed February 25, 2006).

19. Colorado Department of Law. *Information Regarding Colorado's Investigation and Prosecution of Members of Jamaat Ul Fuqra*. http://www.ago.state.co.us/pr/121001_link.cfm (accessed March 11, 2006).

20. Broyles, D. S., and M. Rubio. 2004. *A Smoke Screen for Terrorism*. Washington, D.C.: The United States Attorney's Bulletin, Executive Office for United States Attorneys, Vol. 52, Number 1, p. 33.

# 11 What the Future May Hold

Law enforcement is heading toward uncharted waters. Besides dealing with criminal activity and enforcing state statutes, law enforcement personnel are at the time of writing in a war with a front line that has no defined latitude or longitude. The enemy is often faceless and leaderless. What does the future hold? Although no one can predict the future, one certainty is that technology will be at the forefront. International and domestic terrorist groups are here to stay, but they will no longer be treated as two distinct factions. There are no boundaries with terrorists or organized hate groups. Law enforcement has embarked on a new frontier that cannot be disregarded, and appears to be endless. Times have changed and so must law enforcement.

Chances are that the greatest terrorist impact will come from technology or science, such as cyber- or bioterrorism, rather than from conventional bombs. However, one must not underestimate the importance of conventional bombs or improvised explosive devices to the traditional terrorist. Of the tens of thousands of terrorist incidents based on tactics from 1968 through 2005, the number one tactic is bombing, coming in at around 60%. No matter what the source of the impact, agencies are cautioned against a simplistic approach. History demonstrates that most terrorist attacks are events that are planned well, often over the course of several months and years. Therefore, one must use extreme caution when gathering information and must avoid overlooking any seemingly harmless aspect of situations or events presented. The smallest, seemingly meaningless communication, transmission, purchase, or inquiry could be the missing component that links events. Agencies should take this information into account as well as all the categories mentioned in previous chapters when developing their database structures. Relegating minor items to a comments section or omitting them altogether may have adverse effects in the future. Also, database managers should include information on the various forms of terrorism, especially cyber and biological.

## FOREIGN-BASED TERRORIST INFLUENCE

Foreign terrorist organizations (FTOs) are foreign organizations that are designated by the secretary of state in accordance with section 219 of the Immigration and Nationality Act (INA), as amended. FTO designations play a critical role in our fight against terrorism and are an effective means of curtailing support for terrorist activities and pressuring groups to get out of the terrorism business. The official list of foreign terrorist organizations as identified by the U.S. Department of State on their state.gov website in November 2016 along with their respective date designated is as follows:

10/8/1997 Abu Nidal Organization (ANO)
10/8/1997 Abu Sayyaf Group (ASG)
10/8/1997 Aum Shinrikyo (AUM)
10/8/1997 Basque Fatherland and Liberty (ETA)
10/8/1997 Gama'a al-Islamiyya (Islamic Group) (IG)
10/8/1997 HAMAS
10/8/1997 Harakat ul-Mujahidin (HUM)
10/8/1997 Hizballah
10/8/1997 Kahane Chai (Kach)
10/8/1997 Kurdistan Workers Party (PKK) (Kongra-Gel)
10/8/1997 Liberation Tigers of Tamil Eelam (LTTE)
10/8/1997 National Liberation Army (ELN)
10/8/1997 Palestine Liberation Front (PLF)

10/8/1997 Palestinian Islamic Jihad (PIJ)
10/8/1997 Popular Front for the Liberation of Palestine (PFLF)
10/8/1997 PFLP-General Command (PFLP-GC)
10/8/1997 Revolutionary Armed Forces of Colombia (FARC)
10/8/1997 Revolutionary People's Liberation Party/Front (DHKP/C)
10/8/1997 Shining Path (SL)
10/8/1999 al-Qaida (AQ)
9/25/2000 Islamic Movement of Uzbekistan (IMU)
5/16/2001 Real Irish Republican Army (RIRA)
12/26/2001 Jaish-e-Mohammed (JEM)
12/26/2001 Lashkar-e Tayyiba (LeT)
3/27/2002 Al-Aqsa Martyrs Brigade (AAMB)
3/27/2002 Asbat al-Ansar (AAA)
3/27/2002 al-Qaida in the Islamic Maghreb (AQIM)
8/9/2002 Communist Party of the Philippines/New People's Army (CPP/NPA)
10/23/2002 Jemaah Islamiya (JI)
1/30/2003 Lashkar i Jhangvi (LJ)
3/22/2004 Ansar al-Islam (AAI)
7/13/2004 Continuity Irish Republican Army (CIRA)
12/17/2004 Islamic State of Iraq and the Levant (formerly al-Qa'ida in Iraq)
6/17/2005 Islamic Jihad Union (IJU)
3/5/2008 Harakat ul-Jihad-i-Islami/Bangladesh (HUJI-B)
3/18/2008 al-Shabaab
5/18/2009 Revolutionary Struggle (RS)
7/2/2009 Kata'ib Hizballah (KH)
1/19/2010 al-Qaida in the Arabian Peninsula (AQAP)
8/6/2010 Harakat ul-Jihad-i-Islami (HUJI)
9/1/2010 Tehrik-e Taliban Pakistan (TTP)
11/4/2010 Jundallah
5/23/2011 Army of Islam (AOI)
9/19/2011 Indian Mujahedeen (IM)
3/13/2012 Jemaah Anshorut Tauhid (JAT)
5/30/2012 Abdallah Azzam Brigades (AAB)
9/19/2012 Haqqani Network (HQN)
3/22/2013 Ansar al-Dine (AAD)
11/14/2013 Boko Haram
11/14/2013 Ansaru
12/19/2013 al-Mulathamun Battalion
1/13/2014 Ansar al-Shari'a in Benghazi
1/13/2014 Ansar al-Shari'a in Darnah
1/13/2014 Ansar al-Shari'a in Tunisia
4/10/2014 ISIL Sinai Province (formally Ansar Bayt al-Maqdis)
5/15/2014 al-Nusrah Front
8/20/2014 Mujahidin Shura Council in the Environs of Jerusalem (MSC)
9/30/2015 Jaysh Rijal al-Tariq al Naqshabandi (JRTN)
1/14/2016 ISIL-Khorasan (ISIL-K)
5/20/2016 Islamic State of Iraq and the Levant's Branch in Libya (ISIL-Libya)
6/30/2016 Al-Qa'ida in the Indian Subcontinent

Appendix D lists the U.S. Department of State's officially recognized foreign-based terrorist groups that are full of hate and have no limitations in their pursuit of fulfilling their beliefs.

Investigators and analysts should not be lulled into thinking that these are the only groups or factions dedicated to terrorism. The aforementioned list is merely the officially recognized listing.

### Identification

The Bureau of Counterterrorism in the State Department (CT) continually monitors the activities of terrorist groups active around the world to identify potential targets for designation. When reviewing potential targets, CT looks not only at the actual terrorist attacks that a group has carried out, but also at whether the group has engaged in planning and preparations for possible future acts of terrorism or retains the capability and intent to carry out such acts.

### Designation

Once a target is identified, CT prepares a detailed administrative record, which is a compilation of information, typically including both classified and open-source information, demonstrating that the statutory criteria for designation have been satisfied. If the secretary of state, in consultation with the attorney general and the secretary of the treasury, decides to make the designation, Congress is notified of the secretary's intent to designate the organization and given seven days to review the designation, as the INA requires. Upon the expiration of the seven-day waiting period and in the absence of Congressional action to block the designation, notice of the designation is published in the Federal Register, at which point the designation takes effect. By law an organization designated as an FTO may seek judicial review of the designation in the United States Court of Appeals for the District of Columbia Circuit not later than 30 days after the designation is published in the Federal Register.

Until recently the INA provided that FTOs must be redesignated every 2 years or the designation would lapse. Under the Intelligence Reform and Terrorism Prevention Act of 2004 (IRTPA), however, the redesignation requirement was replaced by certain review and revocation procedures. IRTPA provides that an FTO may file a petition for revocation 2 years after its designation date (or in the case of redesignated FTOs, its most recent redesignation date) or 2 years after the determination date on its most recent petition for revocation. In order to provide a basis for revocation, the petitioning FTO must provide evidence that the circumstances forming the basis for the designation are sufficiently different as to warrant revocation. If no such review has been conducted during a 5 year period with respect to a designation, then the secretary of state is required to review the designation to determine whether revocation would be appropriate. In addition, the secretary of state may at any time revoke a designation upon a finding that the circumstances forming the basis for the designation have changed in such a manner as to warrant revocation, or that the national security of the United States warrants a revocation. The same procedural requirements apply to revocations made by the secretary of state as apply to designations. A designation may be revoked by an Act of Congress, or set aside by a court order.

Legal Criteria for Designation under Section 219 of the INA as amended:

1. It must be a foreign organization.
2. The organization must engage in terrorist activity, as defined in section 212 (a)(3)(B) of the INA (8 U.S.C. § 1182(a)(3)(B)),* or terrorism, as defined in section 140(d)(2) of the Foreign Relations Authorization Act, Fiscal Years 1988 and 1989 (22 U.S.C. § 2656f(d)(2)),** or retain the capability and intent to engage in terrorist activity or terrorism.
3. The organization's terrorist activity or terrorism must threaten the security of U.S. nationals or the national security (national defense, foreign relations, or the economic interests) of the United States.

Legal Ramifications of Designation

1. It is unlawful for a person in the United States or subject to the jurisdiction of the United States to knowingly provide "material support or resources" to a designated FTO. (The term material support or resources is defined in 18 U.S.C. § 2339A(b)(1) as "any property, tangible or intangible, or service, including currency or monetary instruments or financial

securities, financial services, lodging, training, expert advice or assistance, safehouses, false documentation or identification, communications equipment, facilities. weapons, lethal substances, explosives, personnel (one or more individuals who may be, or include oneself), and transportation, except medicine or religious materials)." 18 U.S.C. § 2339A(b)(2) provides that for these purposes "the term 'training' means instruction or teaching designed to impart a specific skill, as opposed to general knowledge." 18 U.S.C. § 2339A(b)(3) further provides that for these purposes the term "expert advice or assistance" means advice or assistance derived from scientific, technical, or other specialized knowledge.

2. Representatives and members of a designated FTO, if they are aliens, are inadmissible to and, in certain circumstances, removable from the United States (see 8 U.S.C. §§ 1182 (a)(3)(B)(i)(IV)-(V), 1227 (a)(1)(A)).

3. Any U.S. financial institution that becomes aware that it has possession of or control over funds in which a designated FTO or its agent has an interest must retain possession of or control over the funds and report the funds to the Office of Foreign Assets Control of the U.S. Department of the Treasury.

### Other Effects of Designation

1. It supports our efforts to curb terrorism financing and to encourage other nations to do the same.
2. It stigmatizes and isolates designated terrorist organizations internationally.
3. It deters donations or contributions to and economic transactions with named organizations.
4. It heightens public awareness and knowledge of terrorist organizations.
5. It signals to other governments our concern about named organizations.

### Revocations of Foreign Terrorist Organizations

The INA sets out three possible bases for revoking a foreign terrorist organization designation:

1. The secretary of state must revoke a designation if the secretary finds that the circumstances that were the basis of the designation have changed in such a manner as to warrant a revocation.
2. The secretary of state must revoke a designation if the secretary finds that the national security of the United States warrants a revocation.
3. The secretary of state may revoke a designation at any time.

Any revocation shall take effect on the date specified in the revocation or upon publication in the Federal Register if no effective date is specified. The revocation of a designation shall not affect any action or proceeding based on conduct committed prior to the effective date of such revocation.

## GROUPS, MOVEMENTS, AND IDEOLOGIES WITH A PRESENCE IN THE UNITED STATES

Many groups have had a presence or a following, or have conducted business in the United States. According to the U.S. Department of State's designated foreign terrorist organization list for 2015, several groups have a confirmed presence in the United States:

al-Qaeda: Arabic for "the base" or "the formula," depending on the translation (worldwide); an Islamic extremist organization that opposes non-Islamic regimes and that has been linked to bombings throughout the world against U.S. government interests. An argument exists that although this is often classified as a group, al-Qaeda is more of a movement or an ideology when compared to other terrorist organizations.

Al-Gama'a al-Islamiyya (Egypt): An Islamic extremist group responsible for attacks on tourists in Egypt.

Hezbollah aka: Hizballah (Lebanon): An Islamic extremist group linked to the Iranian government and responsible for suicide truck bombings against U.S. interests.

Kahane Chai (Israel and the West Bank): A Jewish extremist group seeking to continue the founder's rejectionist agenda.

Hamas: A Palestinian fundamentalist group; an offshoot of the Muslim Brotherhood that came into existence in 1987; another group with an alleged presence in the United States.

Islamic State of Iraq and the Levant (aka: ISIL and ISIS): by its Arabic language acronym Daesh, this is a Salafi jihadist militant group that follows a fundamentalist, Wahhabi doctrine of Sunni Islam and is based in Syria.

Despite this reference to the Department of State's designated foreign terrorist listing, law enforcement personnel should not become complacent and merely focus on these or any one group for that matter. Many members of such groups have splintered away and the groups themselves have morphed their ideology to one some may consider as another group or faction. The fact remains that several groups, or remnants of groups, that is, active members, do remain within the United States. Groups such as the IRA, PKK, LTTE, and Jamaat al-Fuqra (JF) do have a presence within many countries although they are not on an official listing.

Although Appendix D outlines sufficient details on the aforementioned groups, more in-depth explanation is warranted. Therefore, three of the more prevalent groups, intentionally excluding al-Qaeda as it is viewed more as a movement, are outlined in the following subsections.

## HEZBOLLAH

Hezbollah, or Hizbollah, has continued to extend its international reach over the last quarter of a century. The word is Arabic for the "party of God"; Hezbollah is a pro-Iranian, Shia terrorist organization that grew out of the Iranian Revolution and the Iranian Revolutionary Guard between 1979 and 1982. There are several names associated with Hezbollah including Islamic Jihad, Revolutionary Justice Organization, and Organization of the Oppressed on Earth.

Since its inception, Hezbollah has become a sophisticated military and political network that reaches beyond Iran and Lebanon to virtually every continent in the world. With a multimillion dollar annual budget, fed by funding from Iran and Syria as well as illicit activities and donations, Hezbollah has become a formidable foe for any one government to address. The complexity of Hezbollah is evident in their hierarchal structure, which is comparable to that of a stand-alone government. Governed by a secretary general, the group has several councils with distinct areas of responsibility consisting of executive, judicial, political, and jihad (military) responsibilities.

## AL-GAMA'A AL-ISLAMIYYA

Organized in 1973 in the Upper Nile regions of Al-Minya, Asyu't, Qina, and Sohaj in Egypt, al-Gama'a al-Islamiyya came into being and became an active militant group in the late 1970s. Also known as the Islamic Group (IG), al-Gamma, or Jamaat al-Islamiyya, this group has been inspired by past generations of Egyptian Islamists, mainly Sayyid Qutb (spelling varies) of the Muslim Brotherhood. Qutb's writings, *Signposts and Milestones*, are, and continue to be, inspirational to many followers. Therefore, law enforcement personnel should review such literature and have a fundamental understanding of what the enemy may be following.

Around 1948 to 1949 Qutb studied in the United States (Greeley, Colorado) for at least six months, and his writings and views toward the United States were not favorable. Another leading voice associated with al-Gamma is that of Sheikh Omar abd al-Rahman who is also known as the "blind sheikh." He became widely known for his alleged affiliations with members of the first World Trade Center bombing in February 1993. Due to its ties with Afghanistan, there is also an alleged relationship of the group with Osama bin Laden.

## HAMAS (ISLAMIC RESISTANCE MOVEMENT)

Created in late 1987 in Gaza by Sheikh Ahmad Yassin as a Palestinian offshoot of the Muslim Brotherhood, Hamas is dedicated to the victory of Islam and eradication of the State of Israel. Hamas is an acronym in Arabic for Islamic Resistance Movement, which means "zeal"; it is both a terrorist organization and a social/religious movement. As of 2006, it is a political force to be reckoned with in Palestine.

Hamas allegedly receives millions of dollars in funding from Iran. They have also been recognized internationally for their fundraising ability, largely through alleged charities. To many Palestinians, Hamas members are not terrorists but liberators. Hamas-related activities have been identified in Illinois, Virginia, Michigan, Texas, and California. Two of the more notable Hamas affiliates in the United States are the Holy Land Foundation (HLF) and the Islamic Association for Palestine (IAP). The IAP currently notes its North American Headquarters to be in Bridgeview, Illinois.

Although the LTTE is associated with developing some of the first suicide vests and deploying suicide bombers, it is Hamas that has personified the use of suicide bombers. When analyzing approximately 545 terrorist incidents attributed to Hamas, the overwhelming majority of attacks, nearly 85%, are seen to have targeted private citizens and property.

### ISIS / ISIL /ISLAMIC STATE / DAIISH

The Islamic State of Iraq and Syria (ISIS) group was formed in 2013; its first publicly-known external plot against the West was in 2014. Since their emergence, many countries have spent tremendous resources studying, analyzing, and countering ISIS. There are also three other names cited when referencing ISIS. They are; ISIL, Islamic State, and DAIISH. With regards to the ISIL reference, the "L" stands for Levant which is a translation of "al-Sham" the word the group uses to refer to itself. The jihadists like to simply refer to themselves as the Islamic State which reflects their aspirations of creating a caliphate. The lesser known acronym is DAIISH. This is straight Arabic shorthand for the group known as al-Dawla al-Islamiya fi Iraq wa al-Sham. Some report that use of the acronym DAIISH is considered derogatory to the jihadists.

In July 2016, the United State's House Homeland Security Committee Majority Staff published a report titled *Terror Gone Viral*. This report highlighted many aspects of the shift in terrorism and highlighted what many report to be the greatest threat to the West—ISIS.

In the *Homeland Security Committee Terror Threat Snapshot* report from October 2016, Federal Bureau of Investigation (FBI) Director James Comey stated in September 2016 that the Bureau has about 1000 active homegrown terror investigations. He estimated in May 2016 that around 80% of active homegrown terror investigations are related to ISIS.

According to the July 2016 *Terror Gone Viral* report there have been at least 116 ISIS-linked plots to attack Western targets since 2014, including 36 inside the United States. The United States is not alone. Varying reports note that Europe is experiencing similar threats and concerns as the United States and some believe that the concerns in Europe are underreported since there are more "open" borders and travel from country to country is fairly simple.

The report goes on to note that at least 34 Islamist extremist groups have pledged their allegiance to ISIS. ISIS, its affiliates, and supporting groups have operated in approximately two dozen countries or territories, including Afghanistan, Algeria, Bangladesh, Brazil, Egypt, India, Indonesia, Iraq, Jordan, Libya, Lebanon, Nigeria, the Palestinian territories (Gaza), Pakistan, Philippines, Russia (North Caucasus region), Sudan, Syria, Tunisia, and Yemen. The group has established eight official branches.

In February 2016, before the U.S. Senate Armed Services Committee, Director of National Intelligence James Clapper noted that there are now more Sunni violent extremist groups, members, and safe havens than at any time in history … ISIL, including its eight established and several more emerging branches, has become the preeminent global terrorist threat ... ISIL's leaders are determined seek to strike the U.S. homeland—beyond inspiring homegrown violent extremist attacks.

ISIS attacks are getting deadlier and more destructive. The total number of casualties from the group's anti-Western attacks more than doubled in just the first half of this year. At least 875 people were killed or wounded in 2016 alone—more than the combined total from 2014 and 2015 (750 people)—and in just the past year the average number of casualties per attack jumped from 48 to 58. In all, ISIS-linked attacks against the West have been responsible for more than 1600 casualties since 2014. The three highest-casualty attacks all occurred within the past year, including the November assault in Paris (480 people), the attack in Brussels (335 people), and the recent truck massacre in Nice (286 people).

Most of the group's external operations are carried out by independent followers. ISIS is successfully "crowd-sourcing" its terrorism agenda. The majority of plots appear to have been masterminded by individuals who were inspired by ISIS, rather than those who worked with the terrorist organization directly or enlisted in one of its safe havens. For instance, this year during Ramadan, ISIS urged supporters around the world to conduct attacks in their homelands, and followers appear to have responded, such as the gunman in the Orlando 2016 attack. In a separate instance, a man in France killed a police chief and his wife in their home, citing ISIS's call for operations during the holy month.

But so-called lone wolves are not always operating alone, and ISIS is increasingly involved in directing plots. So far in 2016, 47% of ISIS-linked plots were likely "directed" by the group (and 53% "inspired")—a marked increase from 2015 (35% directed, 65% inspired). While many plots initially appear to only be motivated by the group, investigators are increasingly finding direct links. For instance, a 15-year-old girl who stabbed a police officer in Germany in April was later found to have met two ISIS "middlemen" in Istanbul who convinced her to carry out an operation when she returned home. Two other homegrown extremists were recently charged in the United States for planning separate terrorist attacks, one in Virginia and the other in Ohio. Authorities found that in both plots the suspects had actually been directed by ISIS operatives in Syria. In another case last year, passengers subdued a man on a train from Amsterdam to Paris while he attempted to launch a shooting rampage. The suspect was believed to have acted alone, but investigators now say he was in touch with a top ISIS plotter, Abdelhamid Abaaoud.

Foreign fighters and core ISIS operatives are playing a growing role in plots. In 2016, nearly half of ISIS-linked plots against the West involved an individual who trained in or was dispatched from a foreign terrorist safe haven, especially Syria and Iraq—up from one-third in 2015. Such individuals sometimes serve as lead plotters—as in the November 2015 Paris attack—but more often they inspire, recruit, or enable homegrown attackers. These fighters can provide guidance on targets, expertise about attack methods, and perceived legitimacy for aspiring jihadists. FBI Director James Comey has warned of an eventual "terrorist diaspora" out of Syria and Iraq, a prospect that is likely to increase the number of plots involving hardened ISIS fighters.

Terrorists are "going dark," making it harder to detect and disrupt attacks. ISIS urges its operatives and followers to mask their communications by using end-to-end encrypted messaging applications and encryption software, which is clearly impacting counterterrorism efforts. At a house committee on homeland security hearing in July, FBI Director James Comey said his agency faces a growing number of terrorism cases where the communications of suspects cannot be accessed, making it harder to stop plots. A number of ISIS-linked attacks—from the United States to Europe—were later found to have been plotted by operatives relying on encrypted communications.

Explosives are becoming a major part of the ISIS plotter's arsenal. In the past 2 years, there has been a four-fold increase in the number of ISIS-linked terror plots involving explosives—from 11% of plots (in 2014) to 47% (in 2016). After firearms were used in the Charlie Hebdo attacks, a known ISIS terrorist—arrested for his own plot against a train station in Rome—noted, "There's an easier way: to equip themselves and blow themselves up, that's the easiest way." Such methods have since been used in even deadlier attacks, including in the group's assault in Brussels.

Forty percent of ISIS plots against the West have targeted government, military, and law enforcement. ISIS propagandists have urged their followers to attack Western official buildings and government employees, especially law enforcement and military personnel—a call that has been heeded by supporters. In the United States, ISIS-linked terrorists have plotted to attack multiple military installations and to behead police officers and soldiers. The group's "kill lists," for instance, frequently include the names of police and members of the military. For example, ISIS released the contact information for 55 police officers from the New York and New Jersey area and asked its followers to carry out lone wolf attacks on these individuals. While this plot did not directly result in any known injuries, ISIS-inspired individuals in the United States have tried to attack police officers in several instances.

Refugee flows have become a key pathway for terrorists to expand their reach into Western countries. ISIS has advanced its operations by infiltrating operatives into the flow of refugees from the Middle East, including to plan attacks in Belgium, France, Germany, and Turkey. Lax border security and traveler screening has made it easier for the group to exploit these humanitarian programs. In Germany, for instance, four Syrians were arrested in June for plotting a terrorist attack and at least some are believed to have entered the country posing as refugees. Earlier this year, another ISIS operative managed to sneak into Turkey pretending to flee the Syrian civil war—and conducted a suicide bombing targeting Western tourists. Senior U.S. intelligence and law enforcement officials believe the group may also be attempting to infiltrate the U.S. refugee program, and authorities have already identified individuals tied to terrorism in Syria that have attempted to enter the United States as refugees.

Crowded places—especially public transit and entertainment venues—continue to be top terrorist targets. It comes as little surprise that ISIS is setting its sights on soft targets with large crowds of people. Such attacks have the highest death toll, including the massacres at the Bataclan Concert Hall in Paris, the airport and a metro station in Brussels, and a night club in Orlando. Additionally, police have tracked or disrupted multiple plots to attack sporting events, including the European soccer championship in France. Many of these public spaces are easy targets due to a perceived lack of security. In Tunisia, for instance, ISIS managed to conduct two high-profile attacks at a museum and a seaside beach resort, locations with relatively little security but which are frequented by Western tourists.

The majority of ISIS plotters continue to be young men. ISIS has tried to broaden its propaganda to appeal to all demographics, but the overwhelming bulk of its attack operatives still fit a similar profile. In cases where suspects were identified, almost 90% were male, and the average age was 26 years old. In fact, a clear majority (80%) were under the age of 30.

According to the same July 2016 House Homeland Security Committee Majority Staff Report titled *Terror Gone Viral Overview of the 100+ ISIS-Linked Plots Against the West*, the following listed plots against the West can be attributed to ISIS between 2014 and 2016. The following list of incidents has been adapted from the aforementioned report.

### July 2016 Germany
A 17-year-old Afghan refugee tied to ISIS stormed a train with an ax attacking passengers, before being shot by police.

### July 2016 France
A 31-year-old man drove a truck through a crowded promenade on Bastille Day in Nice, France, killing 84 and injuring over 200. He is believed to have been radicalized in part by ISIS propaganda.

### July 2016 South Africa
Two brothers were arrested for planning to attack the U.S. embassy in Pretoria, in addition to an unidentified "Jewish building," in the name of ISIS.

### July 2016 USA
An Ohio man pleaded guilty to attempting to kill law enforcement and military personnel after being directed to do so by a now-deceased ISIS operative in Syria.

**July 2016 USA**
An 18-year-old was arrested for planning terrorist attacks on government buildings in Phoenix and Tucson, Arizona. His classmate said he posted "calls for jihad" on Facebook.

**July 2016 USA**
A former member of the Army National Guard was arrested for providing material support and assisting with a plot to launch an attack on U.S. soil in the name of ISIS.

**July 2016 Bangladesh**
Bangladesh ISIS-linked terrorists killed two dozen people after holding hostages in a Dhaka café frequented by Western tourists and diplomats.

**June 2016 Belgium**
Belgium authorities arrested and charged three ISIS-linked operatives for plotting to attack the Euro 2016 soccer match between Belgium and Ireland.

**June 2016 France**
A 25-year-old attacker killed a local police official and his partner in their home in the name of ISIS.

**June 2016 USA**
An ISIS-radicalized shooter attacked a night club in Orlando, Florida, killing 49 people and injuring dozens more.

**June 2016 Online**
ISIS' so-called cyber caliphate released a "kill list" naming thousands of individuals for its supporters to target, mostly based in the United States.

**June 2016 Germany**
Four ISIS suspects from Syria were arrested for a plot to kill pedestrians using bombs and guns on the streets of Dusseldorf.

**May 2016 Australia**
An 18-year-old was arrested and charged with planning to launch a terrorist attack in Sydney, in addition to attempting to join ISIS in Syria.

**April 2016 Germany**
A 15-year-old girl attacked and stabbed a police officer at a train station in Hanover after the officer stopped to check her identity. She was reportedly urged by two ISIS middlemen to conduct an attack.

**April 2016 USA**
A 40-year-old man was arrested in South Florida for planning an explosive attack on a synagogue in the name of ISIS.

**April 2016 Australia**
A teenager communicating with an overseas ISIS operative was arrested for attempting to purchase a firearm in order to conduct a terrorist attack on Anzac Day.

**April 2016 Spain**
A Moroccan man and alleged ISIS recruiter were arrested for preparing an attack in Spain and attempting to join the terrorist group in Syria.

**March 2016 France**
Authorities arrested a man connected to the terrorist massacre in Brussels for plotting an additional attack.

**March 2016 Belgium**
ISIS operatives launched coordinated suicide bombings in Brussels, including against the airport and a metro station, killing dozens of civilians and injuring hundreds more.

**March 2016 USA**

A University of California – a Merced student stabbed a fellow student and attacked three others on campus. The suspect was reportedly inspired by ISIS and carried the group's flag during his attack.

**March 2016 France**

Authorities foiled a terrorist attack being plotted in the suburbs of Paris and arrested four suspects who were believed to be communicating with ISIS.

**March 2016 Belgium**

At least one terror suspect attacked authorities who were conducting a raid linked to the investigation into the November 2015 Paris attacks executed by ISIS.

**March 2016 Italy**

A Somali refugee in Italy was detained by police for allegedly planning an ISIS-linked attack at a train station in Rome.

**March 2016 USA**

An ISIS hacker group posted a "kill list" urging followers to carry out lone wolf attacks on 55 police officers from New York and New Jersey.

**February 2016 Sweden**

A 20-year-old man was arrested for plotting an ISIS-inspired suicide bombing after previously attempting to join ISIS in Syria.

**February 2016 USA**

A Michigan man was arrested by the FBI for planning to conduct a mass shooting at a nearby church, where he hoped to kill thousands of worshippers in the name of ISIS.

**February 2016 USA**

A Missouri woman was arrested by the FBI for making pro-ISIS threats of violence against government and military personnel through online postings which included personal and location information for some of the individuals.

**February 2016 Germany**

German police detained three suspects believed to be involved in an ISIS plot to conduct "severely violent attacks" in Berlin, possibly against two popular tourist locations. At least one of the suspects is believed to have trained with ISIS in Syria.

**January 2016 Denmark**

A teenage girl was arrested while plotting to bomb a Jewish school in Copenhagen with the help of an accomplice who had fought with ISIS in Syria.

**January 2016 France**

A teenage ISIS supporter was arrested on terror charges for attacking a Jewish teacher with a machete in Marseille.

**January 2016 France**

On the one year anniversary of the Paris Charlie Hebdo attacks, an ISIS-inspired knife-wielding man charged a Paris police station and was shot dead by authorities.

**January 2016 Turkey**

An ISIS suicide bomber struck a popular Istanbul tourist area killing 10, including nine German nationals, and wounding 15.

**January 2016 Indonesia**

A group of terrorists launched a complex attack in downtown Jakarta, targeting Westerners in a shopping district. ISIS took credit for the attack, which they said was targeted at foreigners and the "crusader alliance" fighting ISIS.

**December 2015 UK**
A knife-wielding man attacked passengers in a London tube station, reportedly yelling, "This is for Syria," and attempted to behead one individual. ISIS propaganda was found on his phone.

**December 2015 USA**
A New York man was arrested for plotting to attack civilians at a restaurant in Rochester, New York on New Year's Eve. The suspect claimed he received direction from an ISIS operative overseas and wanted to join the group in Syria.

**December 2015 USA**
An ISIS-inspired married couple opened fire at a holiday party at the Inland Regional Center in San Bernardino, killing 14. The suspects fled the scene but were later killed by police in a shootout.

**December 2015 Belgium**
Belgian authorities arrested two people on suspicion of being involved in a plot to attack "emblematic sites" in Belgium's capital during New Year's celebrations.

**December 2015 Turkey**
Turkey detained nearly a dozen suspected ISIS operatives for planning to conduct a suicide bomb attack on the U.S. consulate in Istanbul. A number of the suspects arrived in Turkey from Syria using fake passports.

**November 2015 Spain**
Three ISIS-linked Moroccans living in Spain were arrested in raids in Madrid and Rivas-Vacimadrid for planning a jihadist attack in the country's capital.

**November 2015 France**
ISIS operatives conducted a series of coordinated terrorist attacks in the French capital targeting a concert hall, restaurants, and cafes, killing 130 people and injuring more than 350. At least two operatives are believed to have entered Europe posing as refugees, and ISIS later released videos purportedly showing each of the attackers as having previously been in Syria.

**November 2015 Europe**
In a coordinated police sweep across Europe (Britain, Norway, Finland, and Italy), authorities detained 16 ISIS-linked suspects who were planning to attack and kidnap Western diplomats in the Middle East in a bid to free a jailed jihadist leader. Police were unable to detain some of the suspects, as they had already traveled to Syria to join groups like ISIS.

**September 2015 USA**
A Florida man who sympathized with ISIS was arrested for providing bombmaking advice to an informant for an intended terrorist attack on a 9/11 Anniversary ceremony in Kansas City, Missouri.

**August 2015 France**
A Moroccan man was subdued by passengers and later arrested after attempting to launch a mass shooting attack on a train traveling from Amsterdam to Paris. Several individuals were wounded by the suspect, who is believed to have been inspired by jihadist groups like ISIS and may have traveled to Syria.

**August 2015 USA**
A teenage boy was arrested outside Philadelphia for threatening to launch an ISIS-inspired assault on Pope Francis during his visit to the United States, including using firearms and explosives.

**August 2015 France**
A French citizen believed to have fought with ISIS was arrested by police for allegedly having returned from the group's stronghold in Syria with instructions to attack a concert.

**August 2015 USA**
An ISIS hacker group posted the personal information of hundreds of U.S. military and government personnel while urging followers to conduct attacks against such targets.

**July 2015 USA**
An ISIS-inspired Florida man was arrested for allegedly plotting to kill beachgoers using explosives hidden under the sand, a plot possibly timed around the Fourth of July.

**July 2015 USA**
A Massachusetts man was arrested for plotting to live-stream an ISIS-inspired terrorist rampage on a college campus, potentially timed around the Fourth of July.

**July 2015 Italy**
Two ISIS sympathizers were arrested after threatening to carry out a terrorist attack on a military base in Italy with a U.S. presence.

**July 2015 UK**
A British man was arrested and charged with plotting to attack U.S. troops in the United Kingdom as part of an ISIS-inspired plot.

**July 2015 France**
French authorities arrested four terror suspects who were plotting a shooting rampage at a French military base and planned to behead the base commander. Three of the suspects were believed to be in touch with ISIS operatives in Syria, including one who indicated he had been directed to strike France.

**July 2015 Kosovo**
Authorities in Kosovo arrested five ISIS-linked individuals for plotting to poison the water supply to Pristina, the country's 200,000 population capital. Two of the suspects are believed to have returned from Syria.

**July 2015 Egypt**
ISIS took credit for a car bomb attack against the Italian consulate in Cairo, killing one.

**June 2015 France**
A French individual believed to be inspired by ISIS beheaded his employer, planted jihadist banners near his victim, and rammed his car into the gas factory at which he had been employed, injuring two in the subsequent explosion.

**June 2015 Tunisia**
ISIS claimed responsibility for a shooting rampage at a Tunisian beach resort popular with Westerners, an attack that killed 38 individuals, all of which were European tourists. The suspect visited an ISIS training camp in Libya.

**June 2015 USA**
A 19-year-old North Carolina man was arrested and charged with "planning assassinations" and plotting to "kill a large number of U.S. citizens" in the name of ISIS.

**June 2015 UK**
Authorities disrupted an ISIS-linked bomb plot against an Armed Forces Day parade in London after a tip-off from a journalist, who had been in touch with an ISIS operative in Syria who directed the attack.

**June 2015 USA**
Two ISIS supporters were arrested and charged for assaulting law enforcement officers and were believed to be hatching a terrorist plot to set off explosives at New York City landmarks.

**June 2015 USA**
Police shot and killed a terror suspect in Boston after he charged authorities with a knife. The individual was inspired by ISIS, in touch with overseas operatives, and believed to be moving forward with an imminent plot to behead law enforcement officers.

**May 2015 USA**
Two Arizona men were killed while attempting to carry out a terrorist attack against a Prophet Mohammad "cartoon drawing" event in Garland, Texas. At least one of the attackers was in contact with a prominent ISIS operative overseas.

**April 2015 USA**
A Kansas man was arrested for plotting a suicide car bomb attack against Fort Riley military base in the name of ISIS.

**April 2015 France**
An Algerian man living in France was arrested after accidentally shooting himself in the leg, leading police to discover his plans to conduct a jihadist shooting attack against French churches. The suspect was in touch with at least one ISIS operative in Syria.

**April 2015 USA**
An Ohio resident with ties to ISIS—and who returned from fighting with jihadist groups in Syria—was arrested for plotting a terrorist attack against a U.S. military base.

**April 2015 USA**
Two ISIS-inspired women in New York were arrested after allegedly planning to build and detonate a homemade bomb in the United States. The suspects were reportedly in touch with terrorists overseas.

**April 2015 Saudi Arabia**
Saudi authorities arrested three individuals planning a car bomb attack against the U.S. Embassy in Riyadh. The individuals were part of a larger ISIS cell disrupted by authorities.

**April 2015 Australia**
Five Australian teens were arrested while planning a terrorist attack at a veteran's day event in Melbourne. At least one of the suspects received instructions from an ISIS operative in Syria.

**April 2015 Spain**
Authorities detained 10 individuals from an ISIS-linked group planning possible terrorist acts, including kidnappings, executions, attacks on Jewish shops, and attacks on public buildings.

**March 2015 Canada**
An ISIS-inspired Pakistani man was arrested for plotting to launch a terrorist attack against the U.S. consulate and other buildings in the financial district in Toronto using remote-controlled explosives.

**March 2015 Tunisia**
Terrorists shot and killed 21 people, primarily European tourists, at the National Bardo Museum in Tunisia. ISIS claimed responsibility for the attack.

**March 2015 USA**
A former U.S. National Guardsman and his cousin were arrested for an ISIS-inspired plot to conduct a terrorist attack against a military base in Illinois.

**March 2015 Spain**
Authorities arrested four individuals linked to ISIS militants for plotting a possible terrorist attack on Spanish soil.

**March 2015 Spain**
Authorities arrested multiple individuals who were part of an ISIS-linked terrorist cell believed to be preparing for attacks in Spain and beyond. The group's activities were reportedly coordinated by an ISIS operative in Syria.

**March 2015 USA**
A group claiming to be the ISIS hacking division released a hit list that included the names of over 100 U.S. military service members.

**February 2015 Denmark**
A gunman who pledged allegiance to ISIS opened fire at an event at a Copenhagen cultural center, killing one civilian and wounding three police officers. Authorities suspect the gunman was targeting Lars Vilks, a cartoonist who had caricatured the Prophet Muhammad; the suspect also shot and killed a security guard outside a synagogue later that evening.

**February 2015 France**
Two French soldiers were wounded in a knife attack outside a Jewish community center in Nice, France by a suspect recently expelled from Turkey under suspicion of heading to join ISIS.

**February 2015 Australia**
Australian police arrested two men for planning a public beheading in Sydney after discovering ISIS propaganda in their possession and a video detailing their plot.

**January 2015 Libya**
ISIS operatives detonated a car bomb at the Corinthia Hotel, a known residence of Westerners in Tripoli, and gunmen stormed the facility killing nine, including an American security contractor and a French national. The group said the attack was in retaliation against the U.S. capture of a Libyan jihadist.

**January 2015 France**
An associate of the Charlie Hebdo attackers in Paris held 15 hostages in a kosher market, killing four. The suspect pledged allegiance to ISIS and is also suspected of having killed a French police officer.

**January 2015 USA**
The FBI arrested an Ohio man inspired by ISIS for plotting a pipe bomb and shooting attack against the U.S. Capitol in Washington, DC.

**January 2015 Belgium**
Police killed two suspected ISIS operatives, who had recently returned from Syria and were believed to be plotting a major terrorist attack against police officers. A third suspect escaped.

**January 2015 Turkey**
Turkish authorities uncovered a plot by ISIS to attack U.S., French, and Belgian consulates in Istanbul.

**December 2014 Australia**
An Australian ISIS supporter took 17 people hostage in a downtown Sydney café. Three people died when police stormed the facility, including the suspect.

**December 2014 UAE**
Police arrested a woman allegedly inspired by ISIS and other jihadist groups for stabbing and killing an American teacher in a shopping mall bathroom.

**December 2014 France**
French police shot and killed a knife-wielding suspect who attacked and wounded three officers. The suspect had recently made ISIS-linked posts on social media.

**December 2014 UK**
UK authorities removed Royal guards from their public positions guarding the Queen's palace and place them in more secure positions after uncovering a potential ISIS-linked plot targeting the guards.

**November 2014 Saudi Arabia**
ISIS-linked militants reportedly shot and wounded a Danish citizen in Riyadh. A video claiming credit was later released by the group's supporters.

**November 2014 UK**
UK police arrested four ISIS-linked individuals on suspicion of planning a terrorist attack involving public beheadings timed during Britain's Remembrance Day events. One suspect was later released.

**November 2014 Egypt**
ISIS Egyptian branch took credit for the murder of a U.S. oil worker in Egypt.

**October 2014 Canada**
Canadian police killed a terrorist who shot a soldier at Canada's National War Memorial and then proceeded to attack the Canadian Parliament. The suspect was suspected to have been influenced by ISIS and other jihadist propaganda and reportedly sought to travel to Libya and Syria.

**October 2014 USA**
A hatchet-wielding man attacked four police officers in New York City, wounding two. Police killed the attacker, who was believed to have been inspired by ISIS and other jihadist groups.

**October 2014 Canada**
An ISIS-inspired extremist struck two Canadian soldiers with his car in Quebec, killing one and wounding the other. The suspect was killed by police in pursuit.

**October 2014 Denmark**
A Danish teenager radicalized by online ISIS propaganda was arrested after stabbing her mother to death, along with a 29-year-old Iraqi accomplice.

**October 2014 UK**
Several ISIS-inspired British residents were arrested plotting a potentially "significant" terrorist attack in London, reportedly public beheadings of civilians. One of the suspects had allegedly returned from Syria where he had been connected with ISIS.

**September 2014 Australia**
An ISIS-inspired teen stabbed two police officers in Australia after reportedly having his passport revoked over concerns he would try to join the group.

**September 2014 Australia**
Australian police arrested more than a dozen individuals in counterterrorism raids, including one who was reportedly in touch with an operative in Syria about planning a public beheading in Sydney.

**September 2014 Algeria**
A French citizen hiking in Algeria was kidnapped and beheaded by an ISIS affiliate, which later released a video claiming credit.

**May 2014 Belgium**
Four civilians were killed in a terrorist attack at a Jewish museum in Brussels. The shooting was perpetrated by an ISIS supported who had returned from Syria in 2013.

**May 2014 USA**
The FBI arrested an upstate New York man who sought to support ISIS and plotted to shoot and kill members of the U.S. military who returned from Iraq.

**March 2014 Switzerland**

Swiss authorities arrested four Iraqis suspected of planning a terrorist attack in Europe in the name of ISIS. The suspects had sought to purchase toxic gas and explosives for their attack.

**February 2014 France**

Police officials in the French Riviera arrested a French-Algerian extremist who fought with ISIS in Syria and was believed

## THE MUSLIM BROTHERHOOD MOVEMENT (HIZB AL-LKHWAN AL-MUSLIMUN)

Founded in Cairo, Egypt, between 1927 and 1928, the Muslim Brotherhood continues to have a tremendous following. It has allegedly been involved in Islamic revolutions in Egypt, Algeria, Syria, and the Sudan. Today, the Brotherhood, largely funded through Saudi Arabia, is banned in Egypt and has extended its reaches worldwide especially in Europe and North America through an array of organizations, many of which are student and youth based. The group is Sunni and doctrinally fundamentalist. There are many key or principal individuals associated with furthering the group's teachings and ideology. Among its alumni are Sayyid Qutb, Ayman Zawahiri (Osama bin Laden's deputy), and Omar Abdul Rahman. Prior to individuals like Sayyid Qutb coming to the forefront and initiating many writings, the Muslim Brotherhood had a strong presence and leadership.

The Brotherhood was founded by Hassan Al-Banna (1906–1949), a modest man from northern Egypt who was a sheikh's son born during the fall of the Ottoman Empire, the demise of the caliphate, and the rise of modernization/"de-Islamization" of Egypt and the Middle East (i.e., in social psychology a cathexis or significant emotional turning point for the Islamic civilization). At the age of 12 years, Al-Banna became the leader in his village of the Society for Moral Behavior and the Society for the Prevention of the Forbidden (*haram*). Al-Banna and other members imposed burdensome fines on Muslims who cursed their fellows and their families, or cursed in the name of religion. Al-Banna met his demise in February 1949 when he was shot by alleged secret agents of the Egyptian government shortly after he declared they were responsible for Arab weaknesses. Prior to his death the Brotherhood undertook what many would consider to be a radical form of Islam.

### WAHHABISM

Salafism or Wahhabism is a radical sect of Islam and is the ideological base of the Muslim Brotherhood. Salafis or Wahhabis claim to strictly follow the example of the Prophet and command a pure, unadulterated understanding of the Islamic religion. Al-Banna and his cofounders of the Muslim Brotherhood were steeped in the teachings of Muhammad Ibn Abdul al-Wahhab al-Tamimi (1703–1792), the leading scholar of Salafism or Wahhabism who was born in what is now Saudi Arabia. Wahhab was considered by many as a radical evangelist who believed Islam was corrupted by countless errors and innovations. He went as far as declaring most Islamic scholars, thinkers, and clerics as heretics. In 1736 he authored the *Book of Monotheism*, which became a reference text for the Wahhabi movement. Although he was accused of being devoid of intellectual creativity, Al-Wahhab nonetheless had some influence on the Brotherhood. Al-Wahhab taught that Islam had vanquished many earlier civilizations but had become corrupted by foreign influences and therefore had lost its sense of unity (*tawhid*). The concept of tawhid (unity of God) is the most important part of the Salafi ideology and most followers are fixated with the concept. From Al-Wahhab the term "Salafist" came into being, denoting a "pure" form of Islam believed to have been practiced by Muhammad and the early caliphs, the *al-salaf al-salihin*. Based on Wahhabi thinking, modern Wahhabis have transformed their radical religious reform into a political force. They have drawn heavily from modernist notions of nationalism and Marxist conceptions of class struggle, and world revolution. Many aspects of Islamic law are strict, for example, it forbids the uprising against

Muslim rulers. However, Wahhabbi doctrine allows scholars to declare leaders of countries like Egypt, Algeria, and Saudi Arabia as "unbelievers" in order to revolt against them. Scholars or Salafis are the primary nodes in the network and are responsible for many of the negative practices and terrorism. Salafiyya is not a unified movement, and there exists no single Salafi sect. Since its initial beginnings the Wahhabi sect continues to have a large following, especially in North America. In addition, its beliefs are regularly practiced in Saudi Arabia and Qatar.

## Wahhabi Organizations in North America

Many organizations exist in North America. Several of the most prevalent and widely known Wahhabi-based organizations believed to be in existence are outlined in this section. Just like with any other religious belief, law enforcement personnel should exercise caution when performing analysis or drawing relational conclusions regarding such groups:

Muslim World League (MWL), aka Rabita: Founded in 1962 and based in Saudi Arabia; headquarters in Herndon, Virginia; sister organization of the World Assembly of Muslim Youth

World Assembly of Muslim Youth (WAMY): Found in approximately 34 countries and based in Saudi Arabia; helps coordinate the work of domestic groups like the Muslim Student Association

Muslim Student Association (MSA): Established in 1963 by Muslim activists from the Muslim Brotherhood and Jamaat-e-Islami

Islamic Society of North America (ISNA): Established in 1981 by leaders of the MSA

North American Islamic Trust (NAIT): Founded by the MSA

Islamic Circle of North America (ICNA): Founded in 1971; North American arm of Jamaat-e-Islami

International Institute of Islamic Thought (IIIT): Established in 1980 by leaders of ISNA and WAMY

Council on American–Islamic Relations (CAIR), IAP, Mosque Foundation, and HLF: All allegedly founded by or affiliated with Hamas

Tabligi Jamaat (Missionary Party; TJ): Founded in 1926 in India

In addition to these organizations, several terrorist organizations follow Wahhabi beliefs. The groups outlined in the following list have some affiliations that would be considered Wahhabi, and some have been officially designated as terrorist groups.

al-Qaeda

Hizb ut-Tahrir (HT): Founded in Jerusalem in 1953

Jemaah Islamiah (Islamic Party): Ties to the Bali nightclub bombing

Hamas: Created in 1987 as a spin-off of the Palestinian branch of the Brotherhood

Islamic Jihad: Egyptian based and active since 1970

Hezbollah: Formed in 1982 in Iran

Ikhwan Al-Muslimin (Muslim Brotherhood): Founded in Egypt in the late 1920s

Al-Gama'a al-Islamiyya (The Islamic Group): Most powerful Egyptian group founded in 1970s

Jamaat al-Fuqra (The Poor): Formed in Hancock, New York, in 1980, with a base in Lahore, Pakistan. This group is also referred to as a cult by some. Many of its members are African-American (black) Muslim converts who live in rural compounds established by the organization in several states.

With any successful and long-lasting group or organization there is often a strong physical presence who leads or a history of strong thinkers. Wahhabis are no different.

## Wahhabi Thinkers

Many movements have a charismatic ideologue to establish their base of thought and lead interpretations of material for others to follow. Some of the leaders and thinkers associated with the Wahhabi movement are as follows:

Mohammed Ibn Abdul Wahhab

Osama bin Laden: Killed by United States Navy Seals in 2011 while living in a residential compound located in Abbottabad, Pakistan

Abdul A'La Mawdudi: Founded Jamaat-e-Islami in 1941 in Lahore, Pakistan; died in 1979

Sayyid Qutb (Syed Qutb): Chief ideologue of the Muslim Brotherhood after al-Banna's death in 1949; *Milestones and Signposts*; executed in 1966

Nasir Al-Albani: Author and not a religious scholar; died while under house arrest in Jordan in 1999

Abd Al-Aziz Ibn Abdullah Baz (aka Bin Baz): Saudi who died in 1999; material and pamphlets spread widely in the United States and Canada

Another individual who can be considered a leader is Sheikh Mubarak Ali Gilani, who calls himself the sixth Sultan Ul Faqr, and is the chief of JF. He currently resides in Lahore, Pakistan. *Wall Street Journal* reporter Daniel Pearl was allegedly on his way to meet Sheikh Gilani in Pakistan when he was kidnapped and later killed. Pearl was investigating the accusations that shoe-bomb suspect Richard C. Reid was one of Sheikh Gilani's followers. It is suspected that the 9/11 mastermind, Khalid Sheikh Mohammad (KSM), is responsible for Pearl's execution. It should be noted that KSM had attended Chowan College, a small Baptist school in Murfreesboro, North Carolina, in 1983 before transferring to the North Carolina Agricultural and Technical State University and completing a degree in mechanical engineering in 1986. He joined the Brotherhood when he was approximately 16 years old, prior to coming to the United States.

The Muslim Brotherhood and its alleged affiliates are no different from virtually any other extremist or terrorist-based organization, foreign or domestic. These groups have shown the propensity to target and recruit society's youth in order to bring them to their way of thinking. The Brotherhood just appears to be a bit more discrete in its tactics and has successfully utilized various student associations to promote its agenda. Sayyid Qutb, KSM, and even the suspected London bomber Magdy Asi el-Nashar, a chemical engineering student from North Carolina State University, all have had ties to American universities. Although there may be no direct confirmation of the aforementioned individuals to the Muslim Brotherhood while in the United States, one cannot dismiss the opportunities that may have existed for direct or indirect support.

## MEANS OF SUPPORT

In addition to the deep-seated concern over groups with confirmed and nonconfirmed official presences in the United States, six countries have been officially designated by the U.S. Department of State as being sponsors of terrorism: (1) Cuba (designated March 1982), (2) Iran (designated January 1984), (3) Libya (designated December 1979), (4) Sudan (designated August 1993), (5) North Korea (designated January 1988), and (6) Syria (designated December 1979). Although these are the officially recognized states, there is a strong likelihood that other locales also have terrorist bases. The potential for terrorist activities that threaten the security of the United States, its nationals, or its allied nations is greatly enhanced by the states that sponsor terrorism. However, these countries cannot be handled by local or state law enforcement agencies. This mission falls on the federal government and the military. The role of law enforcement agencies is to provide detailed local information and intelligence to the appropriate authorities on domestic matters, and on matters that involve international groups. Cyber activity is one component that may play key roles in future foreign-based terrorist endeavors and is handled largely by the law enforcement community. The cyber world provides a way for faceless operatives within terrorist organizations to attack key infrastructure systems from virtually anywhere in the world. Local law enforcement agencies likely encounter or investigate cyber-based operations dealing with terrorist recruiting, financing, and research.

## CYBERTERRORISM

The U.S. infrastructure is fragile, although it is perceived as secure. For every precaution in place, it is likely that there is an individual or group trying to compromise or access the system.

Technological growth has expanded the opportunities for penetrating vital commercial and financial computer systems, and for disabling a national computer infrastructure. Attacks on a nation's computer infrastructure to include their financial and government services can be characterized as a cyber or technical Pearl Harbor. Cyberterrorism probably does not have a body count associated with it, but it can cripple a nation, put corporations out of business, and cause huge financial losses. An example of financial loss was demonstrated in a survey of 611 companies doing business on the Internet in 2001. Results indicated that 83% of the companies experienced security breaches and 62% experienced some type of financial loss, with average damages of $47.8 million, compared to $26.6 million in 1999.[1] This is just a drop in the bucket compared to the potential for disaster if an entity like the stock market is targeted.

The aforementioned information is for one country, that is, the United States. A 2001 Dartmouth College Institute for Security Technology Studies[1] report reviewed four international cases. It demonstrated the correlation between conflict among countries and the rise in the number of website defacements that were experienced by one or both of the countries involved in physical conflicts.

The first case study examined the Pakistan–India–Kashmir region conflict. Pakistani hacker groups allegedly defaced hundreds of Indian websites between 1999 and the summer of 2001. By the end of summer in 2001, India experienced a 107% increase in the number of attacks compared to that for the entire year of 2000.

The second case study reviewed data from the Israel–Palestine conflict. A strong connection was realized between website defacements and key physical events between February 2000 and April 2001. It was evident that during the height of sustained violence there was a dramatic spike in the number of cyber attacks in the form of website defacements, denial of service, and use of worms and Trojan horses.

The third case reviewed was the Former Republic of Yugoslavia (FRY) and NATO conflict in Kosovo. During a NATO bombing campaign, hackers, allegedly employed by the FRY military, began a ping saturation campaign to keep legitimate users from accessing data. This was directed at servers hosting NATO's website and e-mail traffic.

The final case study involved the United States and China spy plane incident. After a midair collision in April 1, 2001, between a U.S. spy plane and a Chinese fighter aircraft, an online campaign of mutual cyber attacks and defacements took place on both sides. Between April and May of that year, over 1000 U.S. sites experienced denial of service attacks and defacements. Sites attacked included the White House, Department of Energy, and the U.S. Air Force.

Although only four case studies were reviewed, there is strong evidence supporting the connection between events and cyber attacks. For law enforcement personnel, this is another point to consider when identifying patterns or trends.

### DEFINING CYBERTERRORISM

Just as with every other component of terrorism, a working definition is needed for cyberterrorism. One of the first recognized working definitions came from the U.S. Air Force in the late 1970s. The problem associated with this definition was that it was broad-based and encompassed virtually anything dealing with information. Cyberterrorism was defined as "the use of information and information systems as weapons in a conflict where information and information systems are targets" (p. 21).[2]

Over time this definition, although not incorrect, has been modified. The National Defense Agency expanded upon the definition provided by the U.S. Air Force and readily modified it to fit the needs of most law enforcement agencies. The agency defines cyberterrorism as "any action to deny, exploit, corrupt, or destroy the enemy's information and its functions; protecting ourselves against those actions; and exploiting our own military information functions."[2] Although this definition mentions enemy and military information functions and warlike terms, it is just as applicable to law enforcement agencies now that these agencies are part of the war effort. Regardless of the definition, law enforcement personnel must remain cognizant of local, state, and federal laws governing cyber crimes.

## Spectrum of Cyber Conflict

The spectrum of cyber conflict can be used to understand the scale of activity associated with the cyberworld. Few agencies routinely deal with incidents of cyber crime. This, coupled with the in-depth knowledge needed to investigate crimes of this magnitude, has greatly limited proactive investigations into cyber crimes. Much of what is publicly mentioned about proactive cyber crime investigations is centered on child pornography and sexual predators.

Tracking violations of law or computer intrusions currently rests with law enforcement personnel, but this is not seen as a priority. Much of the information and evidence collection is done after the fact and this is often left to local law enforcement officials, or perhaps the FBI in the case of a large investigation. Unlike the U.S. Army's spectrum of conflict, the military or the Department of Defense (DOD) is not likely to participate in such actions. This is because many of the occurrences are of a domestic nature, and the traditional war-fighting military is prohibited from performing these duties. Its role is to provide national defense and to operate in an international theater.

Distinguishing between the two separate domains, domestic and international, requires coordination of the military and law enforcement communities, because cyber warfare provides the ability to attack infrastructures vital to national security from within or from outside the country. This is ironic, considering that the DOD has been the victim of numerous intrusion attempts since 1994. The total number of network attacks reported in 1994 throughout the DOD was 225. By 1999, the total reported events escalated to just over 22,000 and this number was anticipated to reach 24,000 by the end of 2001.[3] Examples of some of these attacks can be found in Figures 11.1 through 11.3. Information shown in Figure 11.1 is from the year 2000 from the U.S. Army website, which was hacked by a 16-year-old from Poland who referred to himself as "Terrorist of the New Age." It was reported that the U.S. Army's website was pinged three times per second in 1999. Figure 11.2 shows the result of a hack in 1999 by a 17-year-old from England into the U.S. Navy website. Navy personnel reported that their website experienced a hack attempt every 23 seconds in 1999. Figure 11.3 shows a hack into the official Pentagon website.[4] Cyber vulnerability of the armed services "is magnified by the fact that 95% of all U.S. military traffic moves over civilian telecommunications and computer systems."[5]

It has been stated that "Internet users now number 120 million—70 million of them in the United States. An estimated 1 billion people—one-sixth of humanity—will be online by 2005, two-thirds of them abroad" (p. 3).[6] These staggering figures demonstrate the tremendous tasks that lie ahead for law enforcement personnel. Although the number of attacks is dwarfed by the number of potential users, law enforcement personnel must remain vigilant when investigating cyber attacks because just one computer hard drive can contain over 50 million pages of data.

One of the primary cyber crimes that occurs and receives little media attention is often referred to as hacking. In 1998, the vulnerability of infrastructure systems was highlighted in an investigation into a Department of Energy laboratory that was shut down for a few weeks due to a breach of its systems by a hacker. Most hackers are thrill-seeking individuals driven to outdo each other with

**FIGURE 11.1** The U.S. Army's hacked web screen. (Courtesy of Sergeant Sean Holtz.)

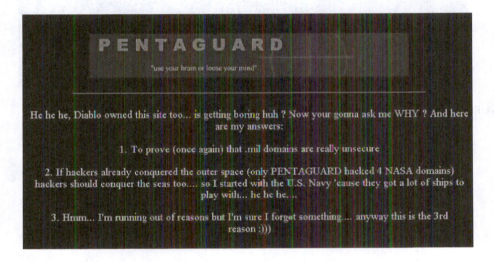

**FIGURE 11.2** The U.S. Navy's hacked web screen. (Courtesy of Sergeant Sean Holtz.)

their unique abilities and who generally do not damage data or systems. They will make it known that they gained access and leave their electronic signature or cyber tag after a successful hack. A cyber-terrorist, on the other hand, tries to avoid detection by using a Trojan horse and by phreaking (see Appendix I). This enables cyberterrorists to completely eliminate target records or systems while remaining anonymous and avoiding detection.

The spectrum of cyber conflict was discussed in a report prepared by a commanding member of the U.S. Air Force in 2001,[3] and law enforcement's role was explained in detail. It was noted that the spectrum consists of "various forms of cyber attack such as hacking, hacktivism (a form of computer-based civil disobedience), espionage, terrorism, and information warfare."[3] The level of escalation as it relates to the spectrum that was detailed in the report is demonstrated in Figure 11.4. A dashed vertical line divides the spectrum in order to differentiate between unintentional and intentional actors. The activity to the left of this line is seen as that by individuals who may be largely unaware or who do not truly understand the international ramifications of their actions. Activity to the right of the dashed line is viewed as that by people whose motive and intention is to inflict damage on national security interests.

Cyber crime on the spectrum is first on the level of escalation and is sometimes referred to as illegal exploration or hacking. Much of this activity comes in the form of illegal access into a company or

**FIGURE 11.3**   Pentagon's hacked web screen. (Courtesy of Sergeant Sean Holtz.)

**FIGURE 11.4**   Spectrum of cyber conflict.

government network system. Some hackers start out as outsiders who use various password attacks in order to gain access as a user of the network. Many begin as insiders, in the form of disgruntled or former employees. They use known weaknesses in the system to gain further access as an administrator or a super user. Once these privileges are attained, a hacker can then read or alter files, control a system, and insert a rogue code such as a virus to damage the infrastructure.

Hacktivism, the second step on the spectrum, is described as a form of electronic disobedience. The goal is to draw attention to a particular issue, such as human rights or political beliefs, by engaging in actions that are unusual in order to attract media attention. The motivation of a person committing an act of hacktivism differs from that of a hacker in that hacktivism represents a political motivation.

The next step on the spectrum is intentional actions in the form of cyber espionage. Although this may appear to be hacking, in reality the mission of a cyber espionage attack is to avoid detection and to gather as much information as possible from the targeted system. With the ability to perpetrate cyber attacks, terrorist organizations have a new arena in which to commit their acts and to gather valuable information about those they see as the enemy. Many organizations, especially organized hate groups, are technologically savvy. They know how to use computer-based systems to spread their messages, recruit, and attain illicit funds. The ability to commit acts of terrorism through non-lethal means, such as access to information, intelligence, and infrastructures, can cause detrimental effects on the general populace.

Reaching government infrastructures through cyberterrorism leaves only one step on the spectrum, cyber warfare. Cyber warfare is an intentional act designed to affect national security. It is an intensified extension of cyberterrorism.

No matter what level of the spectrum is used, law enforcement is involved. However, military involvement is generally limited to acts ranging from cyber espionage to cyber warfare, providing a third country is involved.

One way in which the law enforcement community may become involved is by becoming a victim of cyber crimes or hacking. For example, several agencies, including the Los Angeles Police Department, U.S. Department of Justice (DOJ), and the Central Intelligence Agency (CIA), were directly victimized in the past several years. Figure 11.5 illustrates an attack on the CIA website. Figure 11.6 is from the DOJ site, showing a symbol used by several organized hate groups. Hackers as well as terrorists are resilient, and no government agency is immune to their attack.

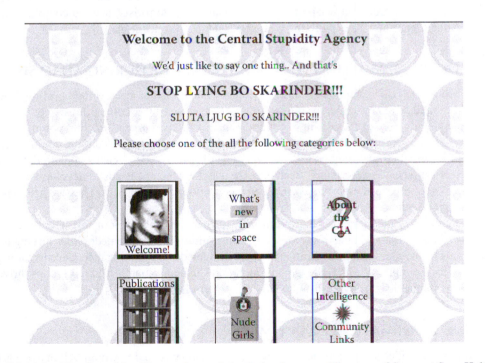

**FIGURE 11.5**    The Central Intelligence Agency's hacked web screen. (Courtesy of Sergeant Sean Holtz.)

**FIGURE 11.6**    The Department of Justice's hacked web screen. (Courtesy of Sergeant Sean Holtz.)

In order to enhance cyber security, law enforcement must partner with private sector corporations. More than 80% of all information systems in the United States are owned by the private sector.[7] Solutions for improving cyber security require joint initiatives between government and private entities as well as an understanding on how to read what one is viewing. Everyone is likely to be somewhat familiar with the Internet. However, one common piece of the puzzle may come from the use of Internet Protocol (IP) addresses and e-mail headers.

## USING IP ADDRESSES AND E-MAILS IN ANALYSIS

Increasingly, analysts and investigators in agencies throughout the world are being asked to deal with complaints from citizens about crimes committed against them by others who have discovered how to victimize people over the Internet. An even greater concern is the amount of correspondence being sent through e-mails or other electronic means by terrorists and their organizations. Therefore, it is essential that law enforcement personnel become aware of the terrorists' need to communicate in a covert manner, learn how to exploit this weakness, and use it in their analysis.

## SOME INTERNET PROBLEMS THAT MIGHT COME UP DURING ANALYSIS

What is brought to one's attention by someone might be an e-mail or a newsgroup posting. The problem with e-mails and newsgroup postings is that people can easily become offensive or even criminal. It is relatively easy to enclose, in a posting or an e-mail, vivid images of child pornography, for example, or to post a threat to a person's life. Issues that may arise from electronic communications are full of information that may be the missing piece to your puzzle. E-mails contain dates, times, machines, locations, and descriptors. Each of these may be what one needs to develop that association. One must not forget these when working on link analyses and databases. They are just as powerful as telephone numbers and addresses.

Chat rooms have their own problems, some of which are difficult for someone with little Internet experience to understand. Some of the most disgusting goings-on include pedophiles lurking in children's chat channels and children stumbling into adult-related chats. During recent events throughout the world, for example, World Trade Organization (WTO), many anarchist-based groups thrived on chat rooms. If anarchists can use them, then why not terrorists?

## FINDING INFORMATION IN AN E-MAIL

In most types of police work, personnel know what has happened and to whom. All one needs to do now is find out who did it, and prove it. It is amazing how much open-source information is available if one knows how to look for it. With electronic sources the opportunities to obtain information seem endless. The only requirement is one must know how to harvest the information and must remember to incorporate it into an analysis.

Many terrorists today are technology experts. Mobile and satellite telephones, instant messaging services, and e-mails are widely available and can be used by terrorists to communicate. These electronic media provide new challenges to law enforcement. While law enforcement personnel are still facing these challenges, terrorists continue to learn from the communication errors made by terror cells that are discovered by law enforcement personnel. Cells gain insight into law enforcement's ability to trace their telephone calls and e-mail correspondence. Therefore, they must embrace creative ideas such as sharing a common e-mail account. One subject would then create a message and leave it in the draft folder, instead of sending it over the Internet. A second subject would then sign in to the same account and read the message, thereby reducing the opportunities of being discovered. Although this option can transpire, the more likely scenario is that of the e-mail being sent. However, many in the law enforcement profession are not versed in the information available from an e-mail outside of the text body and many do not know how to retrieve it. Some basic information useful in exposing the information and other variables that can be used to develop relational links are outlined in this section.

Generally, an investigation starts from one of three points, an e-mail address, a web address, or an IP address:

1. E-mail address—xxxxx@xxxxxxx.com
2. web address—http://xxxxxxxxx.xxxxxxx.com/~sbunting/ or http://125.175.13.92/~43253/ (the latter is expressed using an IP address instead of a domain name format; both refer to the same address)
3. Internet Protocol address—125.175.13.92 (IP address of copsrus.mytown.com)

## E-MAIL ADDRESSES

If the information involves an e-mail or a newsgroup posting, one should obtain a printed copy of it. But one also needs a digital copy of what is on the machine, because it is only here that one can view what is called the "extended header" that reveals the IP address of the perpetrator. The IP address that law enforcement personnel eventually use in a search warrant discloses the name and address of the person using that account for criminal activity.

## What is a Header?

A header is a section of code that contains information about where the e-mail came from and how it reached its destination. It contains the e-mail address of the originator and/or the computer the perpetrator was using.

Revealing extended headers in different e-mail programs varies depending on the software product used. The majority of the more widely used packages provide sufficient information on their website or help menu to guide one through the process of viewing the e-mail's extended header. Other resources, primarily on the Internet, are a valuable source of information in translating an e-mail header.

Here is what a typical header looks like. What one is looking for in a header is the IP address, sometimes conveniently identified as the "originating IP." Personnel can trace and track someone by sending a search warrant to the Internet service provider (ISP) with the date and time of the offending e-mail, along with the IP address of the subject's computer. A sample e-mail header is outlined as follows:

From – Mon Mar 19 08:17:17 2006
Return-Path: < wsmith@xxxxxxxxxx.gov >

Received: from otma1.otm.xxxxxxxx.gov (votma1.xxxxxxxx.gov [167.21.1.115])
by xxxxxxxx@xxxxxx.com (8.9.3/8.9.3) with ESMTP id NAA06271
for <xxxxxxxx@xxxxxx.com>; Thu, 15 Mar 2006 13:10:40 -0500 (EST)
Received: from flcjnetmail1. xxxxxxxx.gov (email.flcjnet. xxxxxxxx.gov [172.20.66.11])
by otma1.otm. xxxxxxxx.gov (8.11.0/8.11.0) with ESMTP id f2FIA7t28739
for < xxxxxxxx@xxxxxx.com >; Thu, 15 Mar 2006 13:10:07 -0500 (EST)
Received: from xxxxxxxxxxxxxxx.gov [172.20.132.102] by flcjnetmail1.xxxxxxxx.gov with
    ESMTP
(SMTPD32-5.05) id A8B32701AE; Thu, 15 Mar 2006 13:23:47 -0500
Received: by STATEGOV with Internet Mail Service (5.5.1960.3)
id <FY66DSJT>; Thu, 15 Mar 2006 13:08:29 -0500
Message-ID: <777ED2AC6510D311BBB50000D11CB450167AAD@STATEGOV>
From: William Smith wsmith@xxxxxxxxxx.gov
To: "Jim Jones (E-mail)" xxxxxxxx@xxxxxx.com
Subject: Following My Brother
Date: Thu, 15 Mar 2006 13:08:28 -0500
MIME-Version: 1.0
X-Mailer: Internet Mail Service (5.5.1960.3)
Content-Type: text/plain
X-Mozilla-Status: 8003
X-Mozilla-Status2: 00000000

Headers also contain message identifiers (IDs). A message ID is a more or less unique identifier assigned to each message usually by the first mail server it encounters. Also, the date section of the header displays a time. The time information displayed in the aforementioned header (Date: Thu, 15 Mar 2001 13:08:28 -0500) is Greenwich mean time (GMT) or world time. This should be taken into consideration when performing temporal analysis. One must remember that not every location in the world observes daylight savings time and that machines are portable, which means that the time from a machine that originated in New York and is now in Los Angeles is likely to have a 3-hour difference.

## WHAT IS AN IP ADDRESS?

The reason one needs a printout and a digital copy is that even when someone has gone to some lengths to hide their identity, sometimes a clue is left behind. Personnel may find the IP address, which identifies a computer on the Internet. The IP address takes the form of a dotted quad number and looks something like 128.175.13.92.

### Understanding IP Addresses

Which of the IP addresses above should be traced and how is it read? Usually, the originating IP (in this case 172.20.132.102) is either called that and/or is closer to the bottom of the stack, nearer to the actual body of the message.

It is important to note that this source IP address (172.20.132.102) will not resolve on the Internet as it is within a block of IP addresses that are "reserved" private IP addresses. They are used behind corporate firewalls and proxy servers. They access the outside world through a network address translation (NAT) service. To find where this private IP address is located, personnel would have to contact the network administrator responsible for the IP address 167.21.1.115, which is a legitimate IP address, through which the private IP address passes on its way to the Internet.

Request for comments (RFC) 1918 describes IP addressing guidelines for private networks and for which the Internet Assigned Numbers Authority (IANA) has reserved for private networks. Several address ranges are reserved for special use. These addresses all have restrictions of some sort placed on their use, and in general they should not appear in normal use on the public Internet. They are the following:

10.0.0.0 to 10.255.255.255
172.16.0.0 to 172.31.255.255
192.168.0.0 to 192.168.255.255

According to IANA, these address blocks are reserved for use on private networks and should never appear in the public Internet. There are hundreds of thousands of such private networks (e.g., home firewalls sometimes make use of them). The IANA keeps no record of who uses these address blocks. Anyone may use these address blocks within their own network without any prior notification to IANA.

The point of there being a private address space is to allow many organizations in different places to use the same addresses, and as long as these disconnected or self-contained islands of IP-speaking computers (private intranets) are not connected there is no problem. If there is an apparent attack, or spam, coming from one of these address ranges, then either it is coming from one's local environment or the address has been "spoofed."

Users are assigned IP addresses by ISPs. The ISPs obtain allocations of IP addresses from a local Internet registry (LIR) or national Internet registry (NIR), or from their appropriate regional Internet registries (RIRs):

African Network Information Center (AfriNIC)—Africa region
Asia–Pacific Network Information Center (APNIC)—Asia–Pacific region
American Registry for Internet Numbers (ARIN)—North America region
Regional Latin-American and Caribbean IP Address Registry (LACNIC)—Latin America and
    some Caribbean islands
Réseaux IP Européens (RIPE NCC)—Europe, the Middle East, and Central Asia

The IANA's role is to allocate IP addresses from pools of unallocated addresses to the RIRs according to their established needs. When an RIR requires more IP addresses for allocation or assignment within its region, the IANA makes an additional allocation to the RIR. Remember, it is quite possible that an IP address in an e-mail header is fabricated. According to the IANA, e-mail protocols are not secure and anyone with the minor technical skills necessary can forge any part of an e-mail. Forgeries generally are difficult to identify. The IANA cannot locate individuals who forge e-mail headers. In fact, return addresses can be spoofed right down to the packet level. (Just like in postal mail, one can put pretty much anything as a return address, but if there is a problem with the "to" address, the letter cannot be delivered.) The IP addresses can be spoofed in protocols other than e-mail as well.

## More about IP Addresses

The reason why IP numbers are important is there are programs available on the Internet that translate these numbers into something approaching a readable language. One may get a web address or the details of an ISP.

One is likely to get an IP in an inquiry relating to Internet relay chat. People who chat can easily fake an e-mail address, but IP is the only thing that can be relied on as it positively identifies the computer that the offender is connected through at the time of commiting the offense.

It is very important once the IP address has been traced back to the ISP to contact that provider as soon as possible. A chat is live and there are few records of it, as ISPs tend to not keep records for very long (hours or possibly days). Personnel will need to know the time and date of the offense (they need to be careful with time zones—CST, EST, PDT, GMT, etc.). Armed with this information, the ISP should be able to identify which of its customers was accessing the Internet via that computer at that time.

## No Message, no Extended Header, no IP Address

If all the information personnel get on a subject is an e-mail address (no e-mail, no extended headers), then the next step is to find out to whom the address belongs. One way to do that is to look it up in "the book." The Internet contains white pages that are the Internet equivalent of a phone book. If the address is not there it does not necessarily mean that the address does not exist, but checking the white pages is worth a try.

It is important to note that there is no one-stop shop to search for a person's e-mail address to try to come up with a name.

## Tracing An E-Mail Address to an Owner

For e-mail investigations, providing the full e-mail headers is very helpful. However, this information is not always available. If it is not available, try changing the e-mail address to a web address, remove the xxxxx@, and replace it with www. One could well find the website of the user or the service provider. If the service provider is known, one can approach the provider for customer details.

Often, it is possible to identify someone with as little as an e-mail address. If the person being investigated has ever posted to a newsgroup, signed a guest book, or participated in a mailing list or forum, chances are the investigator can find a lot of information about the subject with just an e-mail address. Here are some methods that can be tried:

Go to http://www.google.com, click on Google Groups, and then select Advanced Groups Search. Here, one can search in one newsgroup or search all newsgroups (thousands of them) by words in the subject of the posting, by message ID, or by author. Type the e-mail address that the subject has used in the author box. This should bring up any articles that he or she has posted in the group. Pay close attention to this because often the author who has posted an article looking for teenage boys, illegal weapons, or drugs will have posted a few months prior trying to sell a peripheral or some other item. In this posting, the author will have included a home telephone number or an indication of what city he or she lives in. One may also find web page addresses, other e-mail addresses, an online résumé, the author's work location, or something that may help the investigator identify the subject.

An investigator can go to his or her favorite search engine and type in an e-mail address. This could show other places on the Internet where the subject has posted something using that e-mail address. Again, one may find a web page or some other important information.

If an investigator does happen to find a web page, it must be downloaded while he or she is there because it can be changed or deleted at any time. There are a number of utilities that can be used that will cache the web page with all its links intact so that one can browse them more easily when offline and save the digital evidence that was found.

Go to www.freeality.com and do a reverse e-mail search, which could pop the subject's real name. One can also use this site to do other searches such as reverse phone number searches and address searches.

If one would just like to know where the subject's ISP is located, go to Internic.com and type in the domain name of the website or the e-mail address. It will tell the investigator to whom that domain is registered. This, of course, is not of much help if the subject has a nationwide ISP such as AOL, Compuserve, or Earthlink.

Go to www.search.com, which is a "meta" search engine, and type in a name or an e-mail address. If that e-mail address has been used to post anything in the Internet, personnel should get some hits.

## Does the Target Have a Web Page?

If there is an e-mail address for a target, there is a chance that he or she has a web page that could give more information about the subject. Here are some things that may help in finding a target's web page:

If an e-mail address of a person, such as terrorist@onceuponatime.com, is available, one could check for it by going to http://www.onceuponatime.com/~terrorist. Of course one must replace the word "onceuponatime" with the name of the ISP he or she is using and the word "terrorist" with his username. The "~" character (found in the upper left-hand side of a computer keyboard) indicates that the website is likely put up by a person and not an organization.

Here are some places to look for a home page:

If the person is using AOL, try going to http://members.aol.com/username. Be sure to replace the word "username" with his or her screen name, or use the "Find" box to search by screen name. Teknion Tracker also has a specialty area to search AOL web pages.

If the person is using an AT&T account (user@worldnet.att.net), one can find out if he or she has a home page by going to http://home.att.net/ and searching for a member page or trying http://home.att.net/~username. Remember to replace the word "username" with the actual username of the suspect.

If the person is using an Earthlink account (user@earthlink.net), one can find out if he or she has a home page by going to http://www.earthlink.net and searching by username. Other national ISP accounts work pretty much the same way.

Once a web page is found, it is possible to check the source. Sometimes one will find real name information in the top part of the HTML code. With the mouse, right click on the center of the page and go down to "view page source." If there is any personal information, it will be included in the meta tags near the top. Some subjects also occasionally place passwords or instructions to operatives and coconspirators in the HTML coding and then alert them to come retrieve that information at a certain time and day, leaving law enforcement personnel none the wiser. So investigators might want to check this area for unusual information.

A lot of the HTML coding looks like gibberish, but it is necessary to scan through it anyway. Not everything that appears in the source code appears on the screen, and it may be that, intentionally or otherwise, the author has left some clues there. A simple example is if a subject wants to send a covert message to someone, he or she could hide the message in the page by making the text the same color as the background. The message would be unreadable when viewing the page itself but clear as day in the source code. Investigators can try opening two viewers side-by-side and have one display the source code and the other one open to the visual interface. When scrolling through both the viewers, one may observe discrepancies, if they are there.

One can also detect other things. Some of the code will give some clue as to what the software program is and, therefore, what type of computer the offender was using, his or her geographic location, etc.

## How Does One Trace a Web Address?

Connect to the Internet and go to the site. Most sites contain details of the owner's life, the person's hobbies, interests, location, phone, and the like. If a site does not contain details of its owner, it may provide some clue as to whom one is dealing with and where in the world the person might be.

Go to a multiple domain name server lookup engine such as http://www.bankes.com/nslookup.htm or http://www.samspade.com and type in the web page address. It will provide the ISP to contact and provide additional information. Two examples of information that was obtained from tracing web address data are illustrated in Figures 11.7 (Islamic Thinkers Society) and 11.8 (Taliyah). The Islamic Thinkers Society New York City (a group site that has been compared to al-Muhajiroun's, a

Registrant:
Domains by Proxy, Inc.

DomainsByProxy.com
15511 N. Hayden Rd., Ste 160, PMB 353
Scottsdale, Arizona 85260
United States

Registered through: GoDaddy.com (http://www.godaddy.com)
Domain Name: ISLAMICTHINKERS.COM
Created on: 06-Oct-04
Expires on: 06-Oct-06
Last Updated on: 04-May-05

Administrative Contact:
Private, Registration ISLAMICTHINKERS.COM@domainsbyproxy.com
Domains by Proxy, Inc.
DomainsByProxy.com
15511 N. Hayden Rd., Ste 160, PMB 353
Scottsdale, Arizona 85260
United States
(480) 624-2599
Technical Contact:
Private, Registration ISLAMICTHINKERS.COM@domainsbyproxy.com
Domains by Proxy, Inc.
DomainsByProxy.com
15511 N. Hayden Rd., Ste 160, PMB 353
Scottsdale, Arizona 85260
United States
(480) 624-2599

Domain servers in listed order:
NS7.SECURE-DNS.NET
NS8.SECURE-DNS.NET

**FIGURE 11.7**    Islamic Thinkers Society web address details.

**FIGURE 11.8**    Taliyah web address details.

radical group from the United Kingdom) provides some definitive detail including the time when the site was last updated. The Taliyah site provides some insight into what can be done in the electronic age from a prison cell, even death row. From the Taliyah site, enough information was gleaned to afford the opportunity to further expand open-source information, which, as can be seen from Figure 11.8, is quite detailed. When following sites such as these, it is important to note that the corresponding service providers may not be involved in a group's activities. Also, law enforcement personnel should be cognizant of the use of country codes as noted in the Taliyah illustration. In the website noted in the illustration, the individual has been posting to a website located in Germany, hence the ".de" in the address. Furthermore, some sites that appear to be overseas or in another country may actually be hosted from a web server located in a consulate or embassy right in the personnel's own backyard.

## BIOTERRORISM AND WEAPONS OF MASS DESTRUCTION

Biological and chemical weapons and their uses are receiving a great deal of media attention nowadays. Obtaining or making these weapons of mass destruction (WMDs) requires some level of expertise. Relatively few places in the world (approximately 17 states) have people with the skills necessary to develop a biological weapon or possess the radioactive material necessary to develop a nuclear weapon.[8] Although opportunities to use WMDs appear limited and results and the results of using them unpredictable, chemical and biological materials should not be overlooked. A report by the Center for Strategic and International Studies (CSIS) in 2000, referring to biological agents such as anthrax and plague, notes, "Ounce for ounce, the lethality of these agents is many times that of chemical agents or nuclear weapons."[9] There are five general categories of WMDs that can be used by analysts when tracking materials and investigative leads:

1. Biological
2. Chemical
3. Explosive
4. Incendiary
5. Nuclear

The WMDs that fall into these categories come in many deadly forms and devices. In the United States, Title 18 of the *U.S. Code* covers the legislative description for many of the destructive devices used as WMDs. A synopsis of what Title 18 encompasses is provided here:

Poison gas
Any weapon involving a disease organism
Any weapon designed to release radiation or radioactivity at a level dangerous to human life
Any destructive device as defined in section 921 of this title
The destructive devices defined in section 921 of Title 18 of the *U.S. Code* are as follows:
Any explosive, incendiary, or poison gas
Bomb
Grenade
Rocket having a propellant charge of more than four ounces
Missile having an explosive or incendiary charge of more than one-quarter ounce
Mine
Device similar to any of the devices described in the preceding clauses
Any type of weapon (other than a shotgun or a shotgun shell) that may be readily converted to
    expel a projectile ... with a bore of more than one-half inch in diameter
Any combination of parts ... from which a destructive device can be assembled

The FBI data reveal over 10,000 bombings resulting in 355 deaths and over 3,000 injuries between 1990 and 1995. Based on FBI data calculations, approximately 70% of domestic terrorist incidents involve some type of explosives. Analysts need to be aware that explosive devices can be composed of a wide variety of materials. A comprehensive list of explosive materials as listed by the Federal Bureau of Alcohol, Tobacco, and Firearms that should be added to all databases is provided in Appendix E.

The numbers of chemical, biological, and nuclear attack incidents are not as startling as those of the aforementioned conventional explosives. The Center for Nonproliferation Studies, in a 2000 CSIS report,[9] showed that in 1999 there were 175 reports of chemical, biological, and nuclear terrorist activities, 104 of which occurred in the United States. This points to a dramatic increase over the database findings in February 2000 of a total of 687 incidents since 1900.[9] Definitive numbers are difficult to attain. The center uses the media as its source of information, and it was noted that apparent increases might be attributed to hoaxes and different reporting methods. Regardless of the true numbers, there definitely appears to be an increase in the use or the perceived use of these agents.

There are numerous biological agents that can be employed by terrorists. The U.S. Army Medical Research Institute of Infectious Diseases lists the following diseases and biological toxins as potentially suitable for introduction into the population by deliberate dispersal:[10]

Bacterial infections—anthrax, cholera, plague, tularemia, and Q fever
Viruses—smallpox, Venezuelan equine encephalitis, and viral hemorrhagic fevers
Biological toxins—botulinum toxin, staphylococcal enterotoxin B, ricin, and T-2 mycotoxins

Chemical agents have been used in warfare for years even by law enforcement personnel in the form of riot-control agents. The following are among the commonly employed chemical agents:[10]

Nerve agents—sarin (GB)
Vesicants—mustard gas (HD, H), lewisite (L)
Lung-damaging agents—phosgene
Cyanide
Riot-control agents—CS and CN

Methods of exposure to the aforementioned biological and chemical agents include the following:

Absorption (through the skin)
Ingestion (swallowing or eating)
Inhalation (breathing)
Injection (usually through a hypodermic syringe)

The aforementioned chemical and biological concerns are critical when analyzing materials and data, but a greater concern exists for the first responder. It is the first responders of the world who will encounter, usually unsuspectingly, chemical and biological agents. Therefore, information must be made available to them immediately as it is discovered, and they must be properly trained in all aspects of this extremely dangerous situation.

Many how-to documents are available, some covering chemical and biological agents. In the terrorism training manual seized in Manchester, England, titled *Military Studies in the Jihad against the Tyrants*, several poisons are described in detail. Included in this compendium is information on extracts or derivatives of herbal and plant products that can be used to make substances such as ricin. Also included are the weights of each item needed and symptoms that can result from exposure. One method of poisoning that is mentioned in this manual that law enforcement personnel, especially those investigating deaths, should be aware of is poisoning from eating intentionally spoiled food. The method of spoiling food is explained in detail, including the symptoms and their timeline, and how to "cook" the poison is also mentioned. It is virtually a cookbook on the topic. The fact that this has been put into writing and made available to the general public means that law enforcement personnel must consider it a method of bioterrorism.

When it comes to WMDs there are variables that analysts can look for in order to expose potential weakness or to anticipate behavior. The key is to avoid looking for destruction. Instead, look for items associated with weapons of mass victimization, such as ideology, knowledge, management, audience, social distance, and symbolic value (IKMASS):

Ideology—intellectual or theoretical structure of the organization

Knowledge—tactical, technical, and strategic information within the group

Management—rules, etc., of a group; necessary to identify operational manager, for example, Aum Shinrikyo

Audience—important to know the group's message, where the audience is located, and for what purposes the attack would be taking place

Social distance—religious, ethnic, cultural, socioeconomic factors; analyze speeches to identify these factors

Symbolic value—both human and physical, for example, Yucca Mountain project in Nevada

Just like the acronym SKRAM, identification of IKMASS variables keep investigators and analysts alike focused on weaknesses and behaviors. Law enforcement personnel deal largely with victims and not destruction and they will excel in their duty by successfully analyzing those variables that can be verified, validated, and corroborated for the purpose of identifying a specific or grave threat.

Regardless of the threat, target, or tactic, one thing will more than remain consistent—bombs. Bombs have been the staple of nearly every terrorist group. It is essential to understand catchy acronyms and the meanings they represent. However, use of bombs has been and will continue to be the one weapon that law enforcement personnel strive to identify in the future, either physically or in the elements needed to construct one. Figure 11.9, a bomb blast distance guide, is provided as a reference for law enforcement and military personnel alike.

Bomb Threat Guidance

In 2015, the FBI and Department of Homeland Security (DHS) Office for Bombing Prevention (reviewed by the National Explosives Task Force (NETF)) jointly developed the *Bomb Threat Guidance*.

| | VEHICLE DESCRIPTION | MAXIMUM EXPLOSIVE CAPACITY | LETHAL AIR BLAST RANGE | MINIMUM EVACUATION DISTANCE | FALLING GLASS HAZARD |
|---|---|---|---|---|---|
| V E H I C L E   B O R N E   I M P R O V I S E D    E X P L O S I V E   D E V I C E S | COMPACT SEDAN | 500 Pounds 227 Kilos (In Trunk) | 100 Feet 30 Meters | 1,500 Feet 457 Meters | 1,250 Feet 381 Meters |
| | FULL SIZE SEDAN | 1,000 Pounds 455 Kilos (In Trunk) | 125 Feet 38 Meters | 1,750 Feet 534 Meters | 1,750 Feet 534 Meters |
| | PASSANGER VAN OR CARGO VAN | 4,000 Pounds 1,818 Kilos | 200 Feet 61 Meters | 2,750 Feet 838 Meters | 2,750 Feet 838 Meters |
| | SMALL BOX VAN (14 FT BOX) | 10,000 Pounds 4,545 Kilos | 300 Feet 91 Meters | 3,750 Feet 1,143 Meters | 3,750 Feet 1,143 Meters |
| | BOX VAN OR WATER/FULL TRUCK | 30,000 Pounds 13,636 Kilos | 450 Feet 137 Meters | 6,500 Feet 1,982 Meters | 6,500 Feet 1,982 Meters |
| | SEMI-TRAILER | 60,000 Pounds 27,273 Kilos | 600 Feet 183 Meters | 7,000 Feet 2,134 Meters | 7,000 Feet 2,134 Meters |

**FIGURE 11.9** Federal Bureau of Alcohol, Tobacco, and Firearms bomb-blast distance guide.

These guidelines are designed to help site decision makers of commercial facilities, schools, etc., respond to a bomb threat in an orderly and controlled manner with first responders and other stakeholders.

More detailed information can be found by going to the DHS Office for Bombing Prevention at OBP@dhs.gov.

Prior to threat:

1. Plan and prepare
2. Develop a bomb threat response plan
3. Provide bomb threat response plan training to all personnel

If a threat is received:

- Conduct threat assessment
- Execute appropriate actions outlined in bomb threat response plan
- Plan and prepare

Planning considerations

- Coordinate with local law enforcement and first responders to ensure smooth handling of a bomb threat
- Develop clear-cut primary and alternate levels of authority (referred to in this document as Site Decision Maker(s))
- Select evacuation teams and search teams
- Develop training plan
- Determine search procedures
- Designate control center locations
- Plan for emergency assistance (police, fire, etc.)
- Establish primary and alternate evacuation routes and assembly areas
- Establish evacuation signal(s)
- Develop a communications plan
- Determine procedures for accessing/shutting off and reactivating utilities

Preparation considerations

- Control building access
- Implement strict master key control
- Inspect incoming parcels
- Safeguard confidential material
- Keep exits unobstructed
- Ensure adequate internal/external emergency lighting
- Utilize electronic surveillance

Emergency toolkit contents

Items you may want to consider including in your emergency toolkit, which will be taken to the incident command post, are:

Building facility

- Complete set of master keys: coded to rooms and corresponding with a printed key list
- Blueprints and floor plans, or site map of building
- Video, photographs, or CD depicting building interior and exterior
- Emergency response plans

- Copies of the site crisis response plan, bomb threat plan, and crisis management plan
- A list of the following phone numbers:
  - Site decision maker(s)
  - Police/Fire/Emergency medical services (EMS)
  - Federal Bureau of Investigation (FBI)
  - Bureau of Alcohol, Tobacco Firearms and Explosives (ATF)
  - Postal inspector
  - Nearest hospital
  - Facility emergency names and phone numbers

Personnel information

- Building emergency response team member contact information and assignments
- List of personnel trained in CPR and/or first aid
- Updated list, with pictures if possible, of all staff/personnel
- Staff/visitors sign-in/out sheets that include names and dates; include provision for staff/visitors transported to medical facilities
- List of staff with special needs and description of need
- Contact information for neighboring/contiguous buildings

Additional emergency action resources

- Reflective vests for building emergency response team members with identifying marks
- Bullhorn with charged batteries
- AM/FM portable radio
- Flashlights and batteries
- Local street and zone maps
- Clipboards
- Writing materials (legal pads/pens/pencils/markers)
- Plastic red/yellow tape for cordoning off areas

Receiving a threat
Phoned threat

- Remain calm and DO NOT HANG UP.
- If possible, signal other staff members to listen and notify site decision maker(s) and authorities.
- If the phone has a display, copy the number and/or letters on the window display.
- Write down the exact wording of the threat.
- Keep the caller on for as long as possible and use the bomb threat checklist to gather as much information as possible.
- Record, if possible.
- Fill out the bomb threat checklist immediately.
- Be available for interviews with the building's emergency response team and law enforcement.

Verbal threat

- If the perpetrator leaves, note which direction they went.
- Notify the site decision maker(s) and authorities.
- Write down the threat exactly as it was communicated.

- Note the description of the person who made the threat:
  - Name (if known)
  - Race
  - Gender
  - Type/color of clothing
  - Body size (height/ weight)
  - Hair and eye color
  - Distinguishing features
  - Voice (loud, deep, accent, etc.).

Written threat

- Handle the document as little as possible.
- Notify the site decision maker(s) and authorities.
- Rewrite the threat exactly as is on another sheet of paper and note the following:
  - Date/time/location document was found
  - Any situations or conditions surrounding the discovery/delivery
  - Full names of any personnel who saw the threat
- Secure the original threat; DO NOT alter the item in any way
- If small/removable, place in a bag or envelope
- If large/stationary, secure the location

E-mailed threat

- Leave the message open on the computer.
- Notify the site decision maker(s) and authorities.
- Print, photograph, or copy the message and subject line; note the date and time.

Staff response
Site decision maker(s)

- Immediately contact local law enforcement if not done.
- Mobilize the building emergency response team(s).
- Communicate with personnel about bomb threat condition.
- Limit access to building.
- Evaluate authenticity of threat.
- Decide on appropriate action or combination of actions:
  - Lockdown: partial or full
  - Search: partial or full
  - Evacuation: partial or full

If search is initiated

- Assemble and deploy search teams.
- Search the entire building and grounds.
- Account for all personnel.

General search guidelines include:

- Start on the outside of the building and work inward.
- When inside, start at the bottom and work upward.

- Search personnel should always work toward one another.
- Listen for background noises.
- Clear evacuation routes and assembly areas.
- If suspicious item is located, leave indicators for emergency services.

Personnel

- If search is initiated by site decision maker(s), make a quick and complete visual scan of the workplace and any other common areas assigned.
- Divide room into various search levels.
- First sweep all objects resting on the floor or built into walls, up to your waist.
- Scan the room from waist to chin height.
- Scan room from top of head to the ceiling, including air ducts, window tops, and light fixtures.
- If anything unusual is noticed, move people away from the potential hazard and immediately report the location of the object to the site decision maker(s).
- Use of radio communications is NOT recommended unless the area has been cleared.

Suspicious item

A suspicious item is defined as any item (e.g., package, vehicle) identified as potentially containing explosives, an improvised explosive device (IED), or other hazardous material that requires bomb technician diagnostic skills and specialized equipment for further evaluatation. Suspicious indicators are based upon the prevailing and/or communicated threat, placement, and proximity of the item to people and valuable assets. More tangible aspects include, but are not limited to, unexplainable wires or electronics, other visible bomb-like components, unusual sounds, vapors, mists, or odors.

If a suspicious item is found:

- DO NOT touch, tamper with, or move the item.
- Immediately report item to site decision maker(s) and local law enforcement/first responders.

Site decision maker(s) must:

- Ensure area is secured and cleared of personnel.
- Notify search teams.
- Ensure emergency responders are briefed.
- Evacuation and search teams should remain available to assist and inform evacuees, media, staff, and others.

NOTE: The discovery of one device should not automatically mean the conclusion of a search. More devices may be present! The site decision maker(s) must take this into consideration during the planning and execution stages of the facility's bomb threat response plan.

Lockdown/evacuation

Considerations

- Threat assessment—is the threat credible?
- Search results—were any suspicious items located?
- What type of response is warranted considering the totality of the circumstances?
- Partial or full lockdown?
- Partial or full evacuation?
- No action?

If evacuation is initiated:

- Select evacuation routes and assembly areas that are not in the vicinity of the suspicious item; ensure these routes have been searched and cleared.
- Notify police/fire/EMS of evacuation and request assistance.
- Account for all personnel.
- Evacuation team must confirm the building is empty.
- Bring emergency kit and building trauma kits, if available.
- Advise all evacuees to remove all personal items (i.e., purses, backpacks).

Continuing actions after evacuation:

- Debrief emergency services and assist in coordinating further actions.
- Take accountability and report.
- Open media, medical, and family areas – brief regularly.
- As appropriate, determine reoccupy or dismiss action.
- Reoccupy when cleared and deemed appropriate.
- Dismiss in consultation with site administration.
- Notify all personnel of decision and ensure accountability.
- Site decision maker(s) remain(s) on the scene until the situation is resolved, or until relieved by another administrator.

A final note

Every bomb threat is unique and should be handled in accordance with the needs of the facility. Prior to any threat, site decision maker(s) and administrators should utilize this and other existing federal guidance to work with their local first responders to establish a bomb threat response plan that addresses each risk level appropriately, and is optimal for their building(s) and personnel. All threats should be carefully evaluated. One must consider the facts and the context, and then conclude whether there is a possible threat. The bomb guidance flow chart depicted in Figure 11.10 demonstrates a simple risk assessment flow that should be considered by personnel determining potential risk.

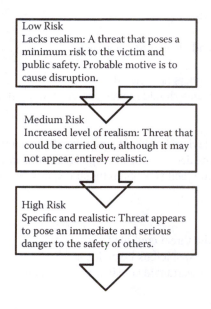

**FIGURE 11.10**    Bomb Guidance risk categories.

## THE PAST, PRESENT, AND FUTURE

The focus of this book is on circumstances surrounding the United States, but like many other subjects law enforcement topics are applicable to other locales and nations also. Past events demonstrate the violence and hatred associated with terrorist and organized hate groups and prove that rogue extremists know no borders. Thousands of events have taken place throughout the world over the past three centuries from which the law enforcement community can learn. Successful planning for the future requires an understanding of recent and distant past events. An example of this can be found in a 1999 Library of Congress Federal Research Division[11] report that studied and analyzed terrorists and their organizations. Events that were examined included the 1998 U.S. cruise missile attack against an al-Qaeda camp in Afghanistan, use of nuclear suitcase bombs, and the bombing of one or more airliners with time bombs. Spectacular retaliation methods against Americans were proposed. Apparently there were signs or some indicators present that elaborate methods of destruction existed, or these assumptions could not have been made 2 years before the 2001 deadly World Trade Center attack.

Current international terrorist threats against the United States and other countries can be divided into three categories:

1. State sponsors of terrorism
2. Formal terrorist organizations
3. Loosely affiliated rogue extremists

These three categories have been addressed in some manner throughout this book. Although there is tremendous concern regarding international or foreign-based terrorists, law enforcement must also remain aware of the numerous domestic-based terrorist and organized hate groups. The greatest danger at present is the occurrence of a mixture of international and domestic terrorism. Hate and terrorism have no borders. Future considerations should be directed toward opening lines of communication and sharing data.

Plans for the future are evolving. The chances of having a national law enforcement database have been viewed as remote for many years to come, but this perception is changing. If agencies are struggling simply to standardize methods and data entry within their own jurisdictions, can data be managed and overseen on a national level?

This is one question being answered today. Former U.S. Attorney General John Ashcroft unveiled the Gateway Information Sharing Project, a pilot program that integrates investigative data from federal, state, and local law enforcement agencies into one database. It will ultimately be accessible to all agencies participating via secure Internet. This program is the result of cooperation between numerous Illinois and Missouri local, county, and state agencies; the FBI; the U.S. Attorneys' Offices of the Southern District of Illinois; and the Eastern District of Missouri St. Louis Joint Terrorism Task Force.

No matter what the future holds, the three components that cannot be overlooked in any investigation are quality personnel, experience, and training. Training is probably the primary key to the future. The most important aspects to keep in mind are an understanding of the topic being analyzed, knowledge of what is being accomplished, and the importance of continually honing skills. Groups such as professional trade associations, private consultants, educators, and peers provide the best venues for future development.

## CHAPTER CONCEPTS

The chapter concepts can be summarized as follows:

Many foreign-based groups in the world are full of hate and are limitless in their pursuit of fulfilling their beliefs. Their influence is and will continue to be felt in the United States.
The Muslim Brotherhood's history and influence in the world have played an important role in the ideologies of terrorist groups like Hamas and al-Gamma.

There are many Wahhabi organizations in North America who play a role in the Islamic extremist movement.

The use of IP and e-mail in analysis is essential in today's era of technology. The information that can be gleaned using these analyses will likely aid in developing associations.

Cyberterrorism is one way by which foreign-based terrorists extend their reaches into other countries, and this is primarily handled by the law enforcement community.

The spectrum of cyber conflict demonstrates the five levels that law enforcement face: (1) cyber crime, (2) hacktivism, (3) cyber espionage, (4) cyber warfare, and (5) cyberterrorism.

WMDs include biological, chemical, explosive, incendiary, and nuclear devices. Chemical agents pose significant threats, and exposure is caused by absorption, ingestion, inhalation, and injection of such agents.

Current international terrorist threats against the United States, as well as against other countries, can be divided into three distinct categories: (1) state sponsors of terrorism, (2) formal terrorist organizations, and (3) loosely affiliated rogue extremists.

## REFERENCES

1. Vatis, M. A. 2001. *Cyber Attacks During the War on Terrorism: A Predictive Analysis*. 5–9. Hanover, NH: Institute for Security Technology Studies, Dartmouth College.
2. Holtz, S. 2003. *Cyber Terrorism*. Davie, FL: Florida Atlantic University. Photocopy.
3. Adkins, B. N. 2001. *The Spectrum of Cyber Conflict from Hacking to Information Warfare: What is Law Enforcement's Role?* vii, 1–2. U.S. Air Force.
4. Holtz, S. 2003. *Cyber Terrorism*. Miami: Miami-Dade Police Department. Presentation.
5. Cilluffo, F. et al. 2000. *Defending America in the 21st Century: New Challenges, New Organizations, and New Policies*. 3–4. Washington, DC: CSIS.
6. Webster, W., and A. de Borchgrave. 1998. *Cybercrime ... Cyberterrorism ... Cyberwarfare ...: Averting an Electronic Waterloo*. 3. Washington, DC: CSIS. http://www.csis.org/pubs/cyberfor .html (accessed February 28, 2003).
7. Rand. *Third Annual Report to the President and the Congress of the Advisory Panel to Assess Domestic Response Capabilities for Terrorism Involving Weapons of Mass Destruction*, 41. December 15, 2001. http://www.rand.org/nsrd/ terrpanel (accessed February 28, 2003).
8. Heymann, P. B. 2001/02. Dealing with terrorism: An overview, 24. http://mitpress.mit.edu/journals/pdf/isec_26_03_24_0.pdf, Int. Security, 26, 3, Winter 2001/02, MIT (accessed February 14, 2003).
9. Cordesman, A. H. 2000. *Defending America: Redefining the Conceptual Borders of Homeland Defense*. 66. Washington, DC: CSIS.
10. IACP Project Response Team. Leading from the Front: Project Response Terrorism, 6. Alexandria, VA: International Association of Chiefs of Police, October 23, 2001.
11. Library of Congress Federal Research Division. 1999. The sociology and psychology of terrorism: Who becomes a terrorist and why? 1–53. http://www.loc.gov/rr/frd/terrorism.htm (accessed March 7, 2003)

# 12 Conclusion

Many analysts began as clerical help and secretaries, working in back rooms and performing only administrative functions. Times have changed. They are now sought after and hired in large numbers. Their positions have come full circle, and they are now recognized as professional and vital to many law enforcement organizations. International professional trade associations such as the International Association of Crime Analysts (IACA) and the International Association of Law Enforcement Intelligence Analysts (IALEIA) have made great strides in the preceding decade in the areas of training and sharing of practices, but one component, national certification, still eludes the associations. However, certification looms on the horizon and will greatly standardize practices of analysts worldwide.

Information access is another analytical area that has been addressed by some agencies. Analysts should be granted access to all pertinent case information. If analysts are restricted, the quality and type of intelligence obtained will be deficient. Communication is consistently mentioned as the number one key to successful intelligence. Limiting an analyst is essentially the same as censoring them. Proactively working together and sharing information is the answer to addressing future incidents and combating issues that threaten homeland security worldwide.

The modern era of terrorism has a relatively short but devastating past. The federal government has undertaken initiatives toward terrorism since at least 1972. In 1985, President Ronald Reagan gave a speech on terrorism in Chicago. He noted that if there is no reaction to terrorism, it will spread like a cancer. He was right, and now the cancer has reached our shores. During that same period, the FBI and CIA created high-tech, state-of-the-art antiterrorism centers with the focus on cogent intelligence. The federal government has established numerous intelligence centers throughout the United States since 1985, but not all focus on terrorism. Many were established in high drug-trafficking areas and others in remote locales. How many are interconnected and share information? As learned in a post–9/11 world, the FBI and CIA collected in-depth intelligence on many groups but were prohibited by law from exchanging it. Reagan's speech is similar to today's rhetoric that the terrorist scourge has hit home. The same "importance of intelligence and communication" speeches from nearly 20 years ago are being replayed now. This is supported by the conclusions drawn in the 2000 Center for Strategic and International Studies (CSIS) working group reports on homeland defense that "U.S. homeland defense efforts have been reactive, disjointed, and focused on post facto consequence management."[1]

Technology is one way to overcome this. However, in order for technology to be effective, there must be a set of national standards for each agency to follow. Law enforcement agencies are going to continue to purchase records management and computer-aided dispatch (CAD) systems and develop proprietary databases designed to fit their needs and budgets, but with national standards the sharing of intelligence and data would be greatly enhanced. By establishing national standards, a designated agency such as the Department of Homeland Security has the opportunity to warehouse data from agencies throughout the nation. This could be achieved with little difficulty and minimal data conversion. The problem now being faced is that there are nearly 18,000 law enforcement agencies capturing data in 18,000 different formats. If we are ever to see continuous and effective sharing of information and intelligence, there must be national standards. Federal committees have been established in the arena of geographic information systems (GIS). Effective standards, formal and informal, designed for use by programmers, cartographers, and analysts using GIS, have made the sharing of GIS information routine among a wide variety of local, state, and federal agencies.

One method to effectively address information and intelligence sharing is by streamlining the process and consolidating resources into a "one-stop shop." The reorganization of the federal government's agencies under the Department of Homeland Security was perhaps the first step toward achieving this. One way to achieve a "one-stop shop" is to establish a national homeland security clearinghouse. Use of clearinghouses has proved to be an effective tool in law enforcement. In South Florida, a county-wide robbery clearinghouse was established over 20 years ago to analyze and process information on nearly 10,000 robbery cases from more than 30 different agencies. Since its inception, the clearinghouse has assisted in increasing the clearance rate well above the national average and decreasing the incidence of robbery. With the use of clearinghouses, detectives no longer have to rely on personal contacts and traveling around the county to check multiple databases. They have come to rely on the clearinghouse as their sole source of information and intelligence for coordinating county-wide robbery-related events. By establishing a national homeland security clearinghouse, agencies throughout the country would be able to standardize practices, expedite the intelligence process, and rely on a single source rather than pass information through a wide range of local, county, state, and federal agencies or individuals.

The public focus is still on excellent intelligence and information sharing, but little is done to enhance the capabilities of routine law enforcement on this front. All the intelligence in the world cannot always prevent a tragedy. Only the proactive moves of those in charge, armed with quality intelligence, can help control possible future events. The U.S. intelligence machine is primarily geared toward threats from foreign attacks. That is where law enforcement comes in. Federal agents and the military cannot be everywhere, but with the entire law enforcement community working together for a common goal, the combined effort and force will be able to deter the actions of terrorist organizations. In order for law enforcement to help in the war on terrorism, it must have an understanding of the mission at hand.

## EXPANDING HORIZONS THROUGH MEDIA OUTLETS

To help understand what has occurred and to gain insight, analysts and investigators must expand their horizons. One way to further this is by reviewing various news sources outside their respective country. Part of anticipating behaviors is the ability to identify the reality and truths that are likely to be hidden, intentionally or unintentionally, and published. Any investigator who has spent time perfecting interviews and interrogations will tell you that quite often there is some truth in any lie. Your job is to find it. Outlined below are some of the more prevalent Arabic/Islamic news websites. These sites provide information that may not be published in any other media outlet and help heighten law enforcement awareness.

## MUSLIM/ARAB INTERNET NEWS SITES AND RESOURCES

| | |
|---|---|
| http://middleeastdaily.com/ | Middle East Daily News |
| http://www.islam-online.net/ | Islam Online |
| http://www.ibn.net/ | Islamic Broadcasting Network |
| http://www.iviews.com/ | Muslim and Arabic news & views |
| http://menareport.com/ | Middle East News |
| http://www.musalman.com/ | Musalman newspaper |
| http://www.palestine-info.info/ | Palestine Info Center |
| http://www.palestinemonitor.org | Palestine Monitor |
| http://www.moheet.com/ | Moheet News Network—Arabic |
| http://www.dawn.com | Dawn Newspaper |
| http://www.islamicnews.org/ | International Islamic News Agency |
| http://www.khaleejtimes.com/index00.asp | Khaleej Times Online |
| http://www.informationtimes.com/ | Information Times |
| http://www.q-news.com/ | Q-News |
| http://eyoon.com/1/ | Arabic News and Media—Arabic |
| http://www.yementimes.com/ | Yemen Times |

| | |
|---|---|
| http://ptimes.org/ | Palestine Times |
| http://www.islamvision.org/ | Islam Vision |
| http://www.dailystar.com.lb/#axzz1BnbbLnUt | The Daily Star newspaper—Lebanon |
| http://www.mehrnews.com/ | Mehr News |
| http://www.menareport.com/ | North Africa Business Report |
| http://www.arabtop.net/ | Arabic Sites Directory |
| http://www.khilafah.com | Khilafah.com Daily News |
| http://www.middleeastdirectory.com/ | Middle East Directory |
| http://www.palestinechronicle.com | Palestine Chronicle |
| http://faridi.net/news | News from Pakistan |
| http://www1.albawaba.com/en/ | Middle East News |
| http://www.twf.org/News.html | The Wisdom Fund |
| http://www.arabia.com/english | Arabia.com |
| http://www.gulf-times.com | Gulf Times |
| http://www.gulfnews.com/ | Gulf News Online |
| http://www.jang.com.pk/thenews/ | The International News (Pakistan) |
| http://www.islamicvoice.com | Islamic Voice Monthly Newsletter |
| http://www.milligazette.com/ | Milli Gazette |
| http://www.salaam.co.uk/ | Salaam |
| http://www.mediamonitors.net/ | Media Monitors |
| http://www.muslimthai.com | Muslim Thai News |
| http://www.arabnews.com/ | Arab News |
| http://www.muslimobserver.com/ | The Muslim Observer |
| http://www.nation-online.com/ | The New Nation—Bangladesh |
| http://www.malaysiakini.com/ | Malaysiakini |
| http://www.thisiscyberia.com/ | Cyberia |
| http://www.al-moharer.com.au | Al-Moharer |
| http://pakobservercom.readyhosting.com | Pakistan Observer |
| http://www.newsofthegulf.com/ | News of the Gulf |
| http://www.cairotimes.com/ | Cairo Times |
| http://www.jang.com.pk/ | The International News |
| http://www.ameinfo.com/press/ | Middle East Business News |
| http://www.mediareviewnet.com/ | Media Review Network |
| http://www.kashmirobserver.com/ | Kashmir Observer |
| http://www.kmsnews.org/ | Kashmir Media Service |
| http://www.greaterkashmir.com/ | Greater Kashmir |
| http://www.alb-net.com/index.htm | Kosova Crisis Center |
| http://www.kurdishmedia.com/ | Kurdish Media |
| http://www.arabicnews.com/ | ArabicNews.com |
| http://www.jordantimes.com/ | Jordan Times |
| http://www.alhewar.com/ | Arabic and English papers online |
| http://www.sahafa.com/ | Sahafa Online |
| http://www.quran.net/qnet/news | Several news outlets here |
| http://metimes.com/ | Middle East Times—Egypt Edition |
| http://www.abdul.com/worldnews | A total of 99 news outlets here |
| http://news.pacificnews.org/news/ | Pacific News Service |
| http://www.islam.org/media/network.htm | More news outlets |
| http://www.muslimnews.co.uk | Muslim News |
| http://www.icna.com/main.shtml/ | Islamic Circle of North America (news items) |

| | |
|---|---|
| http://www.arab.net/ | ArabNet |
| http://www.alwafd.org/ | Al-Wafd |
| http://www.aljazeera.net/ | Al-Jazeera (Arabic) |
| http://english.aljazeera.net/ | Al-Jazeera English version home page |
| http://www.asharqalawsat.com/ | Asharqalawsat (Arabic) |
| http://www.sabiroon.org | Sabiroon |
| http://www.algeria-watch.org/ | Algeria Watch |

Awareness and an understanding of the topic are vital at all levels if law enforcement is to be successful in analysis, investigations, and proactive measures. Terrorism has been around for years. It may not be possible to eliminate it completely, but through comprehensive and thorough law enforcement efforts it can be controlled. Key to a successful endeavor is to maintain an awareness of current issues, have a fundamental understanding of the topic being faced, identify and exploit weaknesses, and be able to anticipate behavioral patterns. All the aforementioned measures will ultimately help prevent future catastrophic events and play an essential role in the war on terrorism. Other measures, such as tabletop exercises and on-the-job training scenarios, help ready personnel on an array of potential scenarios. However, one thing that tends to be missing is the intelligence process. Scenarios and tabletops do an excellent job in identifying weakness, equipment needs, and collaborative efforts among agencies, but most are designed to respond, react, and recover. Why not design and perform exercises that are proactive and based on intelligence? Lessons learned should not be void of the information and intelligence process.

Incidents and events, terrorist related or otherwise, do not occur in a vacuum. Traces and indicators are left by people and objects. With the use of databases, together with the ongoing collection of information and intelligence, terrorist groups can be located, assessed, traced, and their future activities predicted. Looking for and building the puzzle with skill, knowledge, resource, access(ibility), and motive (SKRAM) variables can assist in finding terrorist-related traces. You must be bold and locate pre-incident variables rather than analyzing past events. Anyone can analyze after the fact. Why wait when you can prevent an attack by being proactive? Success and victory in the war on terrorism will be achieved by working together, and analysis and intelligence will likely be there too.

## REFERENCE

1. Cilluffo, F. et al. 2000. *Defending America in the 21st Century: New Challenges, New Organizations, and New Policies.* 9. Washington, DC: CSIS.

# Appendix A: Domestic-Based Terrorist Organizations

This information comes from Jonathan R. White, *Terrorism: An Introduction,* Wadsworth Publishing, Florence, KY; MILNET website (http://www.milnet.com); SPLC website (http://www.splcenter.org); ADL website (http://www.adl.org); and the individual groups' websites.

1. **American Coalition for Life Activists:** Based in Oregon; founded by Andrew Burnett, a long-time antiabortionist activist whose group endorses the justifiable homicide of abortion clinic doctors.
2. **Animal Liberation Front:** Support groups are based throughout North America; in 1993, the group reportedly planted arson or incendiary devices in four Chicago stores; based on its website, it does not condone violence, and membership only carries out direct action by whatever means necessary.
3. **Army of God:** Highly militant antiabortion movement that believes God has given them the duty to kill abortionists; it allegedly claimed responsibility for a number of abortion clinic bombings in Georgia and Alabama; financially affiliated with Glory to Jesus Ministries in Virginia.
4. **Aryan Nation (a.k.a. Aryan Republican Army and Aryan National Alliance):** Base of operation is located in Hayden Lake, Idaho; categorized as white supremacists, Christian Identity group; founded by Richard Butler in the mid-1970s; believes that it is its duty to populate the country with member's progeny through polygamy; allegedly seeks to overthrow the American government using bank robberies as a means to an end; ideology follows Christian Identity, neo-Nazi, and paramilitary.
5. **Branch Davidians:** Thought to be an extinct operation; during their height of operation, they had bases of operation in Utah and Texas; considered by some to be a form of a cult, they are primarily firearms protestors.
6. **Christian Identity Movement:** Chapters are in approximately 18 states with an estimated 31 groups; alleged members were convicted of conspiracy to manufacture explosives; they are considered to be antiabortion and antibanking, and they depict Jews as biologically descended from Satan.
7. **Citizens of the Republic of Idaho:** Based in St. Maries, Idaho; founded by Hari Heath; members do not believe in the bureaucracy of the U.S. courts and government; therefore, they created their own; considered to be relatively docile.
8. **Colorado First Light Infantry:** Alleged members were charged with possessing and manufacturing illegal firearms; group publicly supports Timothy McVeigh's actions and the Oklahoma City bombing on April 19, 1995.
9. **Colorado Militia:** Based in Aurora, Colorado; professed goals are those of weapons rights.
10. **Covenant (a.k.a. Sword and Arm of the Lord):** Christian Identity group started in 1971 by James Ellison on the Arkansas/Missouri state line; based in Arkansas; considered to be a violent white supremacist group with close ties to members of the Ku Klux Klan.
11. **Earth Liberation Front (ELF; a.k.a. North American ELF):** Alleged members were linked to attacks against the U.S. Forest Service, logging companies, and bioengineering corporations; group is categorized as ecological activists.
12. **Evan Mecham Eco-Terrorist International Conspiracy (EMETIC):** Formed in 1985; satirically uses the name of an Arizona governor; the group is known for spiking trees and various forms of sabotage.

13. **Freeman:** Based in Montana; group members believe the U.S. legal system is not valid; supports an internal separatist government; alleged members were convicted of fraud and robbery; categorized as a right-wing group.

14. **Ku Klux Klan:** Categorized as a white supremacy group established during the Civil War era, December 1865; the group is primarily active in the South but allegedly has membership in approximately 28 different states, with an estimated membership base of 5500–6000 in just over 100 different groups; subgroups go by various names including Invisible Empire, Knights of the Klu Klux Klan, United Klans of America, and the National Knights of the Ku Klux Klan.

15. **Los Macheteros:** Marxist-Leninist group formed in 1976, but emerged publicly in 1978; it wants Puerto Rico to be an independent nation; name translation means "machete wielders" or "cane cutters"; Puerto Rican revolutionary group based in Puerto Rico and operating in several Northeastern states including New York; members allegedly detonated explosives in New York and committed homicides; members are also known for their many publicly claimed robberies in the early 1980s, including one for $7.1 million in Connecticut.

16. **Michigan Militia:** Formed in April 1994 by a firearm store owner named Norman Olson and real-estate agent Ray Southwell; categorized as a large weapons rights, survivalist, and militant antigovernment organization; no major illegal activity was directly traced to this group's membership; membership was reported as high as 12,000.

17. **Militia of Montana (MOM):** Founded in February 1994 by John, David, and Randy Trochmann; categorized as a weapons rights and militant antigovernment organization; encourages members to arm themselves with guns and knives; no major illegal activity has been directly traced to this group's membership; paramilitary militia.

18. **Mountaineer Militia:** Based in West Virginia; categorized as paramilitary, antigovernment, and weapons rights organization; alleged leader was convicted in August 1997 for conspiracy to engage in the manufacture of explosives.

19. **National Alliance:** Founded by William Pierce, author of *The Turner Diaries*, in Hillsboro (Mill Point), West Virginia in 1974; categorized as a white supremacist and neo-Nazi organization; leader is Erich Gliebe.

20. **North American Militia of Southwestern Michigan:** Categorized as a paramilitary, antigovernment, and weapons rights organization.

21. **Patriot's Council:** Based in Minnesota; categorized as a violent antigovernment and tax protest organization; the group allegedly created ricin, a toxic nerve agent.

22. **Phineas Priesthood:** Inspired by the book *The Vigilantes of Christendom* by Richard Hoskins; group membership opposes homosexuality, abortions, and interracial marriages; members have allegedly committed bank robberies and abortion clinic bombings.

23. **Posse Comitatus:** Founded by Henry Beach in the early 1970s; name is Latin for power of the county; categorized as anti-Semitic and as a white supremacist organization; chapters were established in almost every state of the union and have had ties with the Arizona Patriots.

24. **Reclaim the Seeds:** Categorized as an antibiotechnology organization; members allegedly claimed responsibility for a 2000 attack on crops at Seminis Vegetable Seeds Research Center and the Davis campus of the University of California.

25. **Republic of Texas:** Based in the Davis Mountains in West Texas; alleged leader is Richard McLaren; the organization contends that Texas was illegally annexed into the union in 1845 and that it remains an independent nation.

26. **Southern California Minuteman:** Group is allegedly against the influx of illegal aliens into the United States from Mexico and has used snipers to control them.

27. **The Order (a.k.a. The New Order):** Based in Oregon, Illinois, and Michigan; founded by the late Robert Mathews; categorized as a right-wing, white supremacist, neo-Nazi, racist,

and anti-Semitic group; followed by and affiliated with groups such as the Silent Brotherhood and Strike Force II.

28. **Viper Militia:** Based in Arizona; categorized as a paramilitary and antigovernment organization; allegedly had ties with Timothy McVeigh; trained to make illegal weapons, and construct and detonate fertilizer bombs.

29. **World Church of the Creator (Creativity Movement):** Founded in 1973 and headquartered in Riverton, Wyoming; also based in East Peoria, Illinois; alleged leader is Matt Hale; categorized as a white supremacist group.

# Appendix B: "Patriot" Groups in the United States

The Southern Poverty Law Center's Intelligence Project identified 158 "patriot" groups that were active in 2001. By 2009, they identified 512 groups as being active in the United States. Of the groups in 2001, 73 were militias, two were "common-law courts," and the remainder fit into a variety of categories, such as publishers, ministries, and citizens' groups. By 2004, the number of militias was 52, and the number of patriot groups was only 152, which was a decrease from 2003, when 171 were noted by the center. In 2009, they identified 127 as militias.

By 2016, the Intelligence Project reported 998 active extreme anti-government groups as of 2015. Of these groups, 276 were militias (noted by an asterisk), and the remainders include "common-law" courts, publishers, ministries, and citizens' groups (Figure B.1). Generally, such groups define themselves as opposed to the "New World Order," engage in groundless conspiracy theorizing, or advocate or adhere to extreme antigovernment doctrines.

Groups listed here are not implied to advocate or engage in violence or other criminal activities, or be racist. The list was compiled from field reports, patriot publications, the Internet, law enforcement sources, and news reports. Groups are identified by the city, county, or region where they are located. Within states, groups are listed alphabetically.

## ALABAMA (17)

Alabama Constitutional Militia,* Verbena
Bibb Rifles Militia,* Shelby County
Constitution Party of Alabama, Montgomery
Eagle Forum, Birmingham
Free Patriot Press, Birmingham
Freedom Yell, Ozark
Get Out Of Our House (GOOOH), Jefferson County
John Birch Society, Mobile
LewRockwell.com, Auburn
Oath Keepers, Bay Minette
Outlaw Militia,* Shelby County
Republic for the United States of America, Dothan
South Alabama Militia,* Dothan
Southeast Constitutional Militia,* Statewide
THREE%ER, Pinson
Three Percenters-III%ers, The Shelby County
Watchmen of Alabama,* Statewide

## ALASKA (11)

Alaska Citizens Militia,* Nikiski
Anchorage Municipality Defense Force,* Anchorage
Central Alaska Militia,* Delta Junction
Central Alaska Militia,* Fairbanks
Constitution Party of Alaska, Haines
Eagle Forum, Cordova
Get Out Of Our House (GOOOH), Statewide

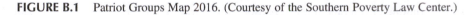

**FIGURE B.1**    Patriot Groups Map 2016. (Courtesy of the Southern Poverty Law Center.)

Kenai Peninsula Militia,* Kenai
Oath Keepers, Anchorage
South Central Patriots,* Wasilla
Three Percenters-III%ers, Statewide

## ARIZONA (31)

American Patriot Friends Network, Peoria
American Patriot Party, Statewide
Arizona Militia,* Glendale
Arizona State Militia,* Flagstaff
Arizona State Militia,* Kingman
Arizona State Militia,* Parker
Arizona State Militia,* Phoenix
Arizona State Militia,* Sierra Vista
Arizona State Militia,* Tucson
Committee of Safety, Mesa
Constitutional Sheriffs and Peace Officers Association, Higley
Constitution Party, Tempe
Eagle Forum, Glendale
Freedom's Phoenix, Glendale
Get Out Of Our House (GOOOH), Statewide
Hour of the Time, Eagar
Molon Labe, Phoenix
Oath Keepers, Chino Valley
Oath Keepers, Green Valley
Oath Keepers, Maricopa County
Oath Keepers, Pima County
Oath Keepers, Pinal County
Oath Keepers, Prescott Valley
Oath Keepers, Statewide

Outpost of Freedom, Tucson
Riders United for a Sovereign America, Corp., Phoenix
Surprise Tea Party Patriots, Surprise
Three Percenters-III%ers, The Navajo County
We the People, Phoenix
We the People, Scottsdale
You Have the Right, Statewide

## ARKANSAS (9)

Arkansas State Militia Corps,* Fayetteville
Constitution Party of Arkansas, Fayetteville
Eagle Forum, Little Rock
Get Out Of Our House (GOOOH), Statewide
Oath Keepers, Van Buren
Secure Arkansas, Little Rock
Three Percenters-III%ers, The Faulkner County
We the People, North Little Rock
We the People, Russellville

## CALIFORNIA (55)

III% United Patriots,* Sunnyvale
American Independent Party, Vacaville
Christian Exodus, Citrus Heights
Constitution Club, The Hemet
Constitution Party, Statewide
Democrats against U.N. Agenda 21, Santa Rosa
Dprogram.net, Sebastopol
Eagle Forum, Santa Rosa
Educate Yourself, Costa Mesa
Freedom Advocates, Santa Cruz
Freedom Law School, Phelan
Free Enterprise Society, Fresno
Free Republic, Fresno
Guardians of the Oath, Orange County
HISAdvocates.org, Costa Mesa
Jeremiah Films, Los Angeles
Liberty Under Fire Freedom Fighters, Taft
Oath Keepers, Anaheim
Oath Keepers, Apple Valley
Oath Keepers, Citrus Heights
Oath Keepers, Escondido
Oath Keepers, Huntington Beach
Oath Keepers, Merced
Oath Keepers, Orange County
Oath Keepers, Redding
Oath Keepers, Riverside
Oath Keepers, Roseville
Oath Keepers, Sacramento
Oath Keepers, San Diego County
Oath Keepers, San Luis Obispo

Oath Keepers, Victorville
Oath Keepers, West Sacramento
Post Sustainability Institute, Santa Rosa
Pro Trust Academy, Oakland
Radio Liberty, Soquel
Resistance—Mark Dice's Official Website, San Diego
Second Amendment Committee, Hanford
Southern California State Militia,* Riverside
Southern California State Militia,* San Diego
Tenth Amendment Center, Los Angeles
Three Percenters-III%ers, The Fresno County
Three Percenters Club,* Statewide
Truth Radio, Nipomo
United States Justice Foundation, Ramona
Ventura County Tea Party, Ventura County
Washitaw Empire de Dugdahmoundyah, San Pedro
Watchmen of California, Statewide
We Are Change, Bakersfield
We Are Change, Banning
We Are Change, Fresno
We Are Change, Orange County
We Are Change, Riverside
We Are Change, San Diego
We Are Change, San Francisco
We Are Change, San Leandro

## COLORADO (19)

American Constitution Party, Arvada
American Freedom Network, Johnstown
American Patriot Party, Statewide
Christian Exodus, Loveland
Discharge Debt, Broomfield
Eagle Forum, Brighton
Freedom First Society, Colorado Springs
Get Out Of Our House (GOOOH), Statewide
Oath Keepers, Aurora
SteveQuayle.com, Pueblo West
Team Law, Grand Junction
Three Percenters-III%ers, The Douglas County
We Are Change, Fort Collins
We Are Change, Lakewood
We Are Change, La Veta
We Are Change, Statewide
We Are Change, Walsenburg
We the People, Colorado Springs
We the People, Delta

## CONNECTICUT (9)

Connecticut Survivalist Alliance, Middlefield
Eagle Forum, Ridgefield

Get Out Of Our House (GOOOH), Statewide
John Birch Society, Statewide
Oath Keepers, Hartford
Post & Email, Stafford
Three Percenters-III%ers, The Hartford County
We Are Change, Wallingford
We Are Change, Waterbury

## DELAWARE (4)

Constitution Party of Delaware, Bear
Get Out Of Our House (GOOOH), Statewide
Oath Keepers, Statewide
Three Percenters-III%ers, The Kent County

## DISTRICT OF COLUMBIA (7)

Constitutional Rights PAC, Washington, DC
National Committee Against the U.N. Takeover, Washington, DC
Renew America, Washington, DC
Special Operations Speaks, Washington, DC
We Are Change, Washington, DC
WND Books, Washington, DC
WorldNetDaily, Washington, DC

## FLORIDA (33)

Agenda21Today, Shady Grove
American Coalition 4 Property Rights, Indian River
American Coalition 4 Property Rights, Martin
American Coalition 4 Property Rights, Palm Beach
American Coalition 4 Property Rights, St. Lucie
American Patriot Party, Statewide
Constitution Party of Florida, The Villages
Eagle Forum, Sanibel
Florida Militia,* Tampa
Freedom Law School, Brooksville
Get Out Of Our House (GOOOH), Statewide
John Birch Society, Pensacola
KrisAnne Hall, Wellborn
Now the End Begins, Jacksonville
Sarasota Patriots, Sarasota
Southeast Constitutional Militia,* Sarasota
Three Percenters-III%ers, The Orange County
Tri-County Tea Party, Oxford
We Are Change, Orlando
We Are Change, Palm Beach
We Are Change, Port Saint Lucie
We Are Change, Tampa
We the People, Cape Coral
We the People, Dunedin
We the People, Fort Lauderdale

We the People, Hudson
We the People, Jacksonville
We the People, Naples
We the People, New Port Richey
We the People, North Palm Beach
We the People, Sanford
We the People, Tampa
We the People, Tarpon Springs

## GEORGIA (22)

American Patriot Party, Statewide
Constitution Party of Georgia, Woodstock
Discount Book Distributors/The Patriot Depot, Powder Springs
Eagle Forum, Marietta
Freedom Fighter Radio, Martinez
Get Out Of Our House (GOOOH), Statewide
John Birch Society, Barnesville
Liberty Alliance, Powder Springs
Moorish Science Temple of America 1928, Atlanta
Oath Keepers, Duluth
Southeast Constitutional Militia,* Statewide
Sovereign Filing Solutions, Morrow
Three Percenters-III%ers, The Wilkinson County
True Patriots, Dallas
We the People, Atlanta
We the People, Cumming
We the People, Duluth
We the People, Gainesville
We the People, Jefferson
We the People, Marietta
We the People, Richmond Hill
We the People, Woodstock

## HAWAII (5)

Eagle Forum, Honolulu
Get Out Of Our House (GOOOH), Statewide
Three Percenters-III%ers, The Honolulu County
We Are Change, Maui
We Are Change, Pahoa

## IDAHO (20)

AVOW (Another Voice of Warning), Rigby
Constitution Party of Idaho, Coeur d'Alene
Eagle Forum, Ada County
Get Out Of Our House (GOOOH), Statewide
Idaho Light Foot Militia,* Ada County
Idaho Light Foot Militia,* Benewah County
Idaho Light Foot Militia,* Bonner County
Idaho Light Foot Militia,* Boundary County

Idaho Light Foot Militia,* Canyon County
Idaho Light Foot Militia,* Gem County
Idaho Light Foot Militia,* Kootenai County
Idaho Light Foot Militia,* Priest River
Idaho Light Foot Militia,* Shoshone County
Idaho Observer, Spirit Lake
Oath Keepers, Moyie Springs
Outlaw Militia,* Butte County
The Micro Effect, Kamiah
Three Percenters-III%ers, The Lemhi County
We Are Change, Lewiston
We the People, Parma

## ILLINOIS (36)

American Patriot Party, Statewide
Constitution Party of Illinois, Belleville
Eagle Forum, Arlington Heights
Get Out Of Our House (GOOOH), Statewide
Illinois Sons of Liberty,* Adams County
Illinois Sons of Liberty,* Brown County
Illinois Sons of Liberty,* Bureau County
Illinois Sons of Liberty,* Champaign
Illinois Sons of Liberty,* Clark County
Illinois Sons of Liberty,* Clay County
Illinois Sons of Liberty,* Cook County
Illinois Sons of Liberty,* Ford County
Illinois Sons of Liberty,* Hamilton County
Illinois Sons of Liberty,* Henry County
Illinois Sons of Liberty,* Jackson County
Illinois Sons of Liberty,* Kane County
Illinois Sons of Liberty,* Kankakee
Illinois Sons of Liberty,* Macoupin County
Illinois Sons of Liberty,* McHenry County
Illinois Sons of Liberty,* Peoria
Illinois Sons of Liberty,* Rockford
Illinois Sons of Liberty,* Saline County
Illinois Sons of Liberty,* Shelbyville
Illinois Sons of Liberty,* Statewide
Illinois Sons of Liberty,* St. Clair County
Illinois Sons of Liberty,* Warren County
Illinois Sons of Liberty,* Will County
Martial Law Survival, Thomson
Oath Keepers, Woodstock
Restore the Republic, Northbrook
Three Percenters-III%ers, The DeWitt County
Three Percenters Club,* Springfield
We Are Change, Chicago
We Are Change, Rockford
We the People, Chicago
We the People, Evanston

## INDIANA (26)

American Patriot Party, Statewide
Constitution Party of Indiana, Evansville
Constitution Preservation, Hammond
Eagle Forum, Indianapolis
Get Out Of Our House (GOOOH), Statewide
Indianapolis Baptist Temple, Indianapolis
Indiana Sons of Liberty,* Chandler
Indiana Sons of Liberty,* DeMotte
Indiana Sons of Liberty,* Garrett
Indiana Sons of Liberty,* Hardinsburg
Indiana Sons of Liberty,* Holton
Indiana Sons of Liberty,* Indianapolis
Indiana Sons of Liberty,* Kingman
Indiana Sons of Liberty,* Kokomo
Indiana Sons of Liberty,* Kurtz
Indiana Sons of Liberty,* Lyons
Indiana Sons of Liberty,* New Castle
Indiana Sons of Liberty,* Plymouth
Indiana Sons of Liberty,* Speedway
Indiana Sons of Liberty,* Warren
Oath Keepers, Bedford
Outlaw Militia,* Hamilton County
Three Percenters-III%ers, The Hamilton County
Three Percenters Club,* Statewide
Watchmen of Indiana,* Statewide
We Are Change, Lafayette

## IOWA (9)

American Patriot Party, Statewide
Constitution Party of Iowa, Eldon
Eagle Forum, Orange City
Get Out Of Our House (GOOOH), Statewide
Oath Keepers, Iowa
Three Percenters-III%ers, The Story County
Three Percenters Club,* Des Moines
We the People, Burlington
We the People, Davenport

## KANSAS (7)

American Patriot Party, Statewide
Eagle Forum, Olathe
Get Out Of Our House (GOOOH), Statewide
Oath Keepers, El Dorado
Patriot Freedom Alliance, Hutchinson
Prophecy Club Resources, Topeka
Three Percenters-III%ers, The Ellsworth County

## KENTUCKY (13)

Central-Kentucky Militia,* Lexington
Constitution Party of Kentucky, Lexington
Eagle Forum, Frankfort
Get Out Of Our House (GOOOH), Statewide
Kentucky Tea Party, Statewide
KY County Rangers,* Bath County
Oath Keepers, Ekron
Oath Keepers, Rowan County
PatriotResistance.com, Lexington
Take Back Kentucky, Clarkson
Three Percenters-III%ers, The Bullitt County
Watchmen of America, Lexington
We Are Change, Ashland

## LOUISIANA (11)

American Patriot Party, Statewide
Constitution Party of Louisiana, Minden
Eagle Forum, Shreveport
Get Out Of Our House (GOOOH), Statewide
Oath Keepers, Baton Rouge
Oath Keepers, Covington
Oath Keepers, Lake Charles
Oath Keepers, Ville Platte
Outlaw Militia,* Tangipahoa Parish
Three Percenters-III%ers, The Avoyelles Parish
Three Percenters Club,* Alexandria

## MAINE (12)

Citizens of the American Constitution, Bingham
Eagle Forum, South Portland
EPI—Environmental Perspectives Incorporated, Bangor
Get Out Of Our House (GOOOH), Statewide
Maine Militia,* Bangor
Oath Keepers, Gardiner
Three Percenters-III%ers, The Piscataquis County
Watchmen of Maine,* Kennebunkport
Watchmen of Maine,* Sanford
We Are Change, Bangor
We the People, Warren
We the People, York County

## MARYLAND (14)

III Percent Patriots, Gaithersburg
American Patriot Party, Statewide
America's Survival, Inc., Owings

Cecil County Patriots, Elkton
Constitution Party of Maryland, Rockville
Eagle Forum, Frederick
Get Out Of Our House (GOOOH), Statewide
Institute on the Constitution (aka American View), Pasadena
Kerodin.com, Gaithersburg
Oath Keepers, Statewide
Save-A-Patriot Fellowship, Westminster
Three Percenters-III%ers, Maryland
Three Percenters Club,* Baltimore
We the People, Frederick


## MASSACHUSETTS (8)

Constitution Party of Massachusetts, Framingham
Get Out Of Our House (GOOOH), Statewide
John Birch Society, Worcester
Oath Keepers, Ware
Three Percenters-III%ers, The Worcester County
Watchmen of Massachusetts,* Statewide
We Are Change, Springfield
We Are Change, Worcester County


## MICHIGAN (32)

American Patriot Party, Alger County
Constitution Party (U.S. Taxpayers Party of Michigan), Grand Rapids
Delta 5 Mobile Light Infantry Militia,* Calhoun County
Delta 5 Mobile Light Infantry Militia,* Eaton County
Eagle Forum, Birmingham
Heartland USA, Crystal Falls
Jack Van Impe Ministries International, Troy
Liberty Tree Radio, Dexter
Lost Horizons, Commerce Township
Michigan Downriver Volunteer Militia,* Wayne County
Oath Keepers, Jackson
Oath Keepers, Marquette County
Oath Keepers, Orion Charter Township
Southeast Michigan Volunteer Militia,* Genesee County
Southeast Michigan Volunteer Militia,* Livingston County
Southeast Michigan Volunteer Militia,* Monroe County
Southwest Michigan Volunteer Militia,* Ingham County
Southwest Michigan Volunteer Militia,* Lapeer County
Southwest Michigan Volunteer Militia,* Shiawassee County
Three Percenters-III%ers, The Isabella County
Three Percenters Club,* Lansing
We Are Change, Detroit
We Are Change, Grand Rapids
West Central Michigan Volunteer Militia,* Ionia County
West Central Michigan Volunteer Militia,* Kent County

West Central Michigan Volunteer Militia,* Montcalm County
West Michigan Volunteer Militia,* Kent County
West Michigan Volunteer Militia,* Muskegon County
West Michigan Volunteer Militia,* Newaygo County
West Michigan Volunteer Militia,* Oceana County
West Michigan Volunteer Militia,* Ottawa County
We the People, West Bloomfield

## MINNESOTA (11)

American Patriot Party, Statewide
Central Minnesota Tea Party, Central Minnesota
Constitution Party of Minnesota, Redwood Falls
Eagle Forum, St. Paul
Genesis Communications Network, Eagan
Oath Keepers, Aitkin
Oath Keepers, Hennepin County
Three Percenters-III%ers, The Crow Wing County
Three Percenters Club,* Saint Paul
We Are Change, Cedar Falls
We the People, Duluth

## MISSISSIPPI (27)

Citizens Militia of Mississippi,* Batesville
Citizens Militia of Mississippi,* Calhoun County
Citizens Militia of Mississippi,* DeSoto County
Citizens Militia of Mississippi,* Forrest County
Citizens Militia of Mississippi,* Hancock County
Citizens Militia of Mississippi,* Harrison County
Citizens Militia of Mississippi,* Itawamba County
Citizens Militia of Mississippi,* Webster County
Constitution Party of Mississippi, Seminary
Eagle Forum, Jackson
Get Out Of Our House (GOOOH), Statewide
Mississippi Militia,* Southaven
Mississippi Preparedness Project,* East Central
Mississippi Preparedness Project,* Northeast
Mississippi Preparedness Project,* Northwest
Mississippi Preparedness Project,* Southeast
Mississippi Preparedness Project,* Southwest
Mississippi Preparedness Project,* Statewide
Mississippi Preparedness Project,* West Central
Mississippi Tea Party, Jackson
Oath Keepers, Saucier
Outlaw Militia,* Leake County
Southeast Constitutional Militia,* Statewide
Three Percenters-III%ers, Petal
Three Percenters Club,* Jackson
We the People, Oxford
We the People, Perkinston

## MISSOURI (41)

2nd Amendment Patches.com, Halltown
Constitution Party of Missouri, Piedmont
Eagle Forum, Statewide
Get Out Of Our House (GOOOH), Statewide
Heal Our Land Ministries, Branson
John Birch Society, St. Louis
Missouri Citizen Militia,* Adair County
Missouri Citizen Militia,* Cooper County
Missouri Citizen Militia,* Crawford County
Missouri Citizen Militia,* Daviess County
Missouri Citizen Militia,* Greene County
Missouri Citizen Militia,* Johnson County
Missouri Citizen Militia,* Oregon County
Missouri Citizen Militia,* Ste. Genevieve County
Missouri Citizen Militia,* Texas County
Missouri Citizen Militia,* Warren County
Missouri Citizen Militia,* Washington County
Missouri Citizen Militia,* Wayne County
Oath Keepers, Clinton
Oath Keepers, Jackson County
Oath Keepers, Joplin
Oath Keepers, St. Louis
Power Hour, Versailles
Three Percenters-III%ers, The Cole County
We the People, Cedar Hill
We the People, High Ridge
William Lewis Films, Columbia

## MONTANA (11)

Eagle Forum, Billings
Get Out Of Our House (GOOOH), Missoula
John Birch Society, Great Falls
Liberty Defense League, Kalispell
Lincoln County Watch, Bozeman
Oath Keepers, Helena
Oath Keepers, Kalispell
Oath Keepers, Townsend
Stand Up America U.S., Bigfork
Three Percenters-III%ers, The Fergus County
We the People, Billings

## NEBRASKA (5)

III% United Patriots,* Comstock
American Patriot Party, Statewide
Eagle Forum, Bancroft
Oath Keepers, Omaha
Three Percenters-III%ers, The Custer County

## NEVADA (20)

Constitution Party (Independent American Party), Carson City
Eagle Forum, Elko
Get Out Of Our House (GOOOH), Statewide
Nevada Light Foot Militia,* Churchill County
Nevada Light Foot Militia,* Douglas County
Nevada Light Foot Militia,* Elko County
Nevada Light Foot Militia,* Eureka County
Nevada Light Foot Militia,* Humboldt County
Nevada Light Foot Militia,* Lander County
Nevada Light Foot Militia,* Lyon County
Nevada Light Foot Militia,* Pershing County
Nevada Light Foot Militia,* Storey County
Nevada Light Foot Militia,* Washoe County
Nevada Light Foot Militia,* White Pine County
Oath Keepers, Las Vegas
Save Our Sheriff, Las Vegas
Southern Nevada Militia,* Clark County
Three Percenters-III%ers, Statewide
We Are Change, Henderson
We Are Change, Las Vegas

## NEW HAMPSHIRE (9)

American Patriot Party, Statewide
Constitution Party of New Hampshire, Auburn
Eagle Forum, Merrimack
Get Out Of Our House (GOOOH), Statewide
John Birch Society, Conway
Oath Keepers, Alstead
Three Percenters-III%ers, The Belknap County
We Are Change, Manchester
What Really Happened, Concord

## NEW JERSEY (21)

Constitution Party of New Jersey, Palmyra
Eagle Forum, Bergenfield
Get Out Of Our House (GOOOH), Statewide
John Birch Society, Cranford
John Birch Society, Flemington
John Birch Society, Hainesport
John Birch Society, Holmdel
John Birch Society, Mantua Township
John Birch Society, Mercer County
John Birch Society, Ringwood
Oath Keepers, Cape May
Oath Keepers, Manville
Oath Keepers, Morristown
Oath Keepers, Newton

R.V. Bey Publications, Pleasantville
Southampton Township, Statewide
Three Percenters-III%ers, The Monmouth County
tomatobubble.com, Saddle Brook
We the People, Monmouth
We the People, Ocean Township

## NEW MEXICO (17)

Christian American Patriots Militia,* Bernalillo County
Constitution Party of New Mexico, Los Lunas
Eagle Forum, Alamogordo
Get Out Of Our House (GOOOH), Statewide
New Mexico Citizen's Militia,* Chaves County
New Mexico Citizen's Militia,* Doña Ana County
New Mexico Citizen's Militia,* Grant County
New Mexico Citizen's Militia,* Otero County
New Mexico Citizen's Militia,* Sandoval County
New Mexico Citizen's Militia,* San Juan County
Southern New Mexico Militia,* Doña Ana County
Southern New Mexico Militia,* Eddy County
Southern New Mexico Militia,* Grant County
Southern New Mexico Militia,* Lea County
Three Percenters-III%ers, The Torrance County
We the People, Albuquerque
We the People, Los Lunas

## NEW YORK (40)

American Patriot Party, Statewide
Constitution Party of New York, Buffalo
Get Out Of Our House (GOOOH), Statewide
John Birch Society, Nassau County
John Birch Society, New York
New York Mutual Assistance Group,* Suffolk County
Oath Keepers, Elmira
Oath Keepers, Erie County
Oath Keepers, Franklin County
Oath Keepers, Fulton County
Oath Keepers, Herkimer
Oath Keepers, Livingston County
Oath Keepers, Madison County
Oath Keepers, Malone
Oath Keepers, Marion County
Oath Keepers, Nassau County
Oath Keepers, New York County
Oath Keepers, Ontario County
Oath Keepers, Orange County
Oath Keepers, Otsego County
Oath Keepers, Rochester
Oath Keepers, Schenectady County
Oath Keepers, Staten Island

Oath Keepers, Statewide
Oath Keepers, Swan Lake
Oath Keepers, Thornwood
Oath Keepers, Warren County
Sovereign News, The Old Chelsea Station
Three Percenters-III%ers, The Herkimer County
We the People, Albany
We the People, Binghamton
We the People, Cooperstown
We the People, Lake Luzerne
We the People, Lewis
We the People, Middletown
We the People, New Baltimore
We the People, Pleasant Valley
We the People, Queensbury
We the People, Syracuse
We the People, Watertown

## NORTH CAROLINA (20)

American Patriot Party, Statewide
America's Remedy, Charlotte
Constitution Party of North Carolina, Charlotte
Eagle Forum, Statewide
Free North Carolina, Cape Carteret
Get Out Of Our House (GOOOH), Statewide
NCRenegade, Raleigh
NORTH-CAROLINA American Republic, Charlotte
NORTH-CAROLINA American Republic, Gaston County
NORTH-CAROLINA American Republic, Haywood County
NORTH-CAROLINA American Republic, Lincoln County
NORTH-CAROLINA American Republic, Rowan County
NORTH-CAROLINA American Republic, Rutherford County
NORTH-CAROLINA American Republic, Yadkin County
Oath Keepers, Faith
Oath Keepers, Mount Gilead
Oath Keepers, Statewide
Stokes County Militia,* Pinnacle
Three Percenters-III%ers, The Wake County
We the People, Winston-Salem

## NORTH DAKOTA (4)

Eagle Forum, Bismarck
Get Out Of Our House (GOOOH), Statewide
Oath Keepers, Fargo
Three Percenters-III%ers, The Sheridan County

## OHIO (52)

American Patriot Party, Statewide
Constitution Party, Eaton

Eagle Forum, Uniontown
Get Out Of Our House (GOOOH), Statewide
John Birch Society, Columbus
John Birch Society, Delaware
Oath Keepers, Akron
Oath Keepers, Columbus
Oath Keepers, Dayton
Oath Keepers, Marietta
Oath Keepers, Statewide
Oath Keepers, Toledo
Ohio Defense Force Home Guard,* Northeast
Ohio Defense Force Home Guard,* Northwest
Ohio Defense Force Home Guard,* Southeast
Ohio Defense Force Home Guard,* Southwest
Ohio Defense Force Home Guard,* Zanesville
Ohio Minutemen Militia,* Adams County
Ohio Minutemen Militia,* Ashtabula County
Ohio Minutemen Militia,* Athens County
Ohio Minutemen Militia,* Auglaize County
Ohio Minutemen Militia,* Belmont County
Ohio Minutemen Militia,* Clark County
Ohio Minutemen Militia,* Clinton
Ohio Minutemen Militia,* Coshocton County
Ohio Minutemen Militia,* Defiance County
Ohio Minutemen Militia,* Franklin County
Ohio Minutemen Militia,* Gallia County
Ohio Minutemen Militia,* Geauga County
Ohio Minutemen Militia,* Hamilton
Ohio Minutemen Militia,* Hardin County
Ohio Minutemen Militia,* Jefferson County
Ohio Minutemen Militia,* Licking County
Ohio Minutemen Militia,* Lorain County
Ohio Minutemen Militia,* Lucas
Ohio Minutemen Militia,* Morrow County
Ohio Minutemen Militia,* Perry County
Ohio Minutemen Militia,* Pike County
Ohio Minutemen Militia,* Preble County
Ohio Minutemen Militia,* Putnam County
Ohio Minutemen Militia,* Richland County
Ohio Minutemen Militia,* Sandusky
Ohio Minutemen Militia,* Stark County
Ohio Minutemen Militia,* Statewide
Ohio Minutemen Militia,* Union County
Ohio Minutemen Militia,* Washington County
Ohio Minutemen Militia,* Wyandot County
Silver Shield Xchange, Cleveland
Sons of Liberty Academy, Cleveland
Three Percenters-III%ers, The Knox County
Three Percenters Club,* Columbus
We the People, Lebanon

## OKLAHOMA (10)

American Patriot Party, Statewide
Constitution Party of Oklahoma, Chandler
Eagle Forum, Oklahoma City
Oath Keepers, Oklahoma City
Oklahoma Defense Force,* Inola
OK SAFE, Inc. (Oklahomans for Sovereignty and Free Enterprise), Tulsa
Outlaw Militia,* Creek County
Overpasses for America, Tecumseh
Three Percenters-III%ers, The Pottawatomie County
We the People, Tulsa

## OREGON (18)

American Patriot Party, Ashland
American Patriot Party, Statewide
Eagle Forum, Portland
Embassy of Heaven, Stayton
Get Out Of Our House (GOOOH), Statewide
McCutcheons Ink., Central Point
News With Views, Merlin
Oath Keepers, Douglas County
Oath Keepers, Josephine County
Oath Keepers, Portland
Oath Keepers, Redmond
Oregon Light Foot Militia,* Josephine County
Oregon Militia Alliance,* Bend
Three Percenters-III%ers, The Crook County
Three Percenters Club,* Bend
Voice of Freedom, The Klamath Falls
We the People, Grants Pass
We the People, Junction City

## PENNSYLVANIA (60)

Alt Market, Pittsburgh
American Patriot Party, Statewide
Constitution Party of Pennsylvania, Osceola
Eagle Forum, Pittsburgh
Eagle Forum, West Chester
Get Out Of Our House (GOOOH), Statewide
Liberty Dollar of Chambersburg, Marion
Oath Keepers, Allentown
Oath Keepers, Armstrong
Oath Keepers, Berks County
Oath Keepers, Bucks County
Oath Keepers, Cambria County
Oath Keepers, Carlisle
Oath Keepers, Chester
Oath Keepers, Clinton County

Oath Keepers, Crawford County
Oath Keepers, Girard
Oath Keepers, Greensburg
Oath Keepers, Huntingdon County
Oath Keepers, Hyndman
Oath Keepers, Jim Thorpe
Oath Keepers, Lackawanna County
Oath Keepers, Lake Ariel
Oath Keepers, Lancaster County
Oath Keepers, Lebanon County
Oath Keepers, Luzerne County
Oath Keepers, Lycoming County
Oath Keepers, Mifflin County
Oath Keepers, Millersburg
Oath Keepers, Monroe County
Oath Keepers, Montgomery
Oath Keepers, New Brighton
Oath Keepers, Northampton
Oath Keepers, Perry County
Oath Keepers, Pike County
Oath Keepers, Pittsburgh
Oath Keepers, Punxsutawney
Oath Keepers, Reading
Oath Keepers, Schuylkill County
Oath Keepers, Somerset County
Oath Keepers, Statewide
Oath Keepers, Sugar Grove
Oath Keepers, Susquehanna County
Oath Keepers, Tioga County
Oath Keepers, Union County
Oath Keepers, Uniontown
Oath Keepers, Washington County
Pennsylvania American Patriot Radio, Crawford County
Pennsylvania Light Foot Militia,* Cumberland County
Pennsylvania Light Foot Militia,* Jefferson County (2)
Pennsylvania Light Foot Militia,* Lackawanna County
Three Percenters-III%ers, The Northumberland County
Three Percenters Club,* State College
Unsolicited Opinion with Maggie, The Norristown
Western PA Liberty Forum, Grove City
We the People, Delaware County
We the People, Greensburg
We the People, New Kensington
WING TV, State College


## RHODE ISLAND (12)

American Patriot Party, Statewide
Oath Keepers, North Kingstown
Oath Keepers, Smithfield
Oath Keepers, Statewide

Rhode Island Citizen Militia,* East Providence
Rhode Island Citizen Militia,* Middletown
Rhode Island Citizen Militia,* North Smithfield
Rhode Island Citizen Militia,* Richmond
Rhode Island Citizen Militia,* Statewide
Rhode Island Citizen Militia,* West Warwick
Three Percenters-III%ers, Statewide
We Are Change, Providence

## SOUTH CAROLINA (14)

Christian Exodus, Fort Mill
Constitution Party of South Carolina, Taylors
Eagle Forum, Columbia
Get Out Of Our House (GOOOH), Statewide
Oath Keepers, Charleston
Outlaw Militia,* Horry County
South Carolina Light Foot Militia,* Horry County
Southeast Constitutional Militia,* Statewide
Three Percenters-III%ers, The Sumter County
Three Percenters Club,* Columbia
We Are Change, Columbia
We Are Change, Myrtle Beach
We the People, Fort Mill
We the People, Rock Hill

## SOUTH DAKOTA (6)

Constitution Party of South Dakota, Sioux Falls
Eagle Forum, Pierre
Get Out Of Our House (GOOOH), Statewide
Oath Keepers, Sioux Falls
Three Percenters-III%ers, The Stanley County
Three Percenters Club,* Kennebec

## TENNESSEE (18)

Black Robe Regiment, Springfield
Christian Exodus, Savannah
Eagle Forum, Nashville
East Tennessee Mountain Militia,* Knoxville
Get Out Of Our House (GOOOH), Statewide
Lawful Path, Lynnville
Oath Keepers, Knoxville
Outlaw Militia,* Davidson County
Salt and Light Institute, Nashville
Southeast Constitutional Militia,* Statewide
Three Percenters-III%ers, The Smith County
Three Percenters Club,* Nashville
United States Patriots Union, Hermitage
Veteran Defenders of America, Dickson
We the People, Etowah

We the People, Fayetteville
We the People, Maryville
We the People, Nashville

## TEXAS (54)

Adask's Law, Utopia
American Open Currency Standard, Frisco
American Patriot Party, Statewide
Anti-Shyster Magazine, Utopia
Brave New Books, Austin
Church of God Evangelistic Association, Waxahachie
Constitution Party of Texas, Princeton
Dallas City Troop (DCT),* Carrollton
Eagle Forum, Anderson
Freedom School, Austin
Get Out Of Our House (GOOOH), Liberty Hill
Golden Triangle Militia,* Orange
Groups Against Agenda 21, Sulphur Springs
Infowars.com, Austin
John Birch Society, Houston
John Birch Society, Temple
Oath Keepers, Dallas
Oath Keepers, Houston
Operation Patriot Rally Point,* Tarrant County
Outlaw Militia,* Hamilton County
Republic Broadcasting, Round Rock
Republic of Texas, Bastrop County
Rule of Law Radio, Austin
Silver Bear Café, Garland
Texas Eagle Forum, Dallas
Texas Lightfoot Militia,* Cherokee County
Texas Lightfoot Militia,* Smith County
Texas Militia,* Conroe
Texas Militia,* Corpus Christi
Texas Militia,* Dallas
Texas Militia,* Huntington
Texas Militia,* Lubbock
Texas Militia,* Midland
Texas Militia,* Statewide
Texas Militia,* Victory County
Texas Militia,* Waco
Three Percenters-III%ers, The Comanche County
Three Percenters Club,* Austin
TURF—Texans Uniting for Reform and Freedom, San Antonio
We Are Change, Dallas
We Are Change, El Paso
We Are Change, Fort Worth
We Are Change, Houston
We Are Change, Lubbock
We Are Change, Waco

We the People, Austin
We the People, Conroe
We the People, Dallas
We the People, Denton
We the People, Grapevine
We the People, Guyton
We the People, Hideaway
We the People, Point
We the People, Tyler

## UTAH (9)

American Patriot Party, Statewide
Constitution Party of Utah, Bountiful
Eagle Forum, South Jordan
Liberty RoundTable, Highland
Oath Keepers, Salt Lake City
Three Percenters-III%ers, The Sevier County
Three Percenters Club,* Gunnison
Utah Light Foot Militia,* Tooele County
We the People, Ogden

## VERMONT (6)

Eagle Forum, Burlington
John Birch Society, Statewide
Oath Keepers, Randolph
Three Percenters-III%ers, The Orange County
We Are Change, South Burlington
We the People, Williston

## VIRGINIA (41)

American Patriot Party, Statewide
American Policy Center, Remington
Constitution Party of Virginia, Vienna
Declaration Alliance, Herndon
Eagle Forum, Statewide
Get Out Of Our House (GOOOH), Statewide
GrassTopsUSA Inc., Lorton
Gun Owners of America, Springfield
IRS Zoom, Arlington
Oath Keepers, Accomac
Oath Keepers, Alleghany County
Oath Keepers, Bedford County
Oath Keepers, Botetourt County
Oath Keepers, Charlottesville
Oath Keepers, Chesterfield
Oath Keepers, Craig County
Oath Keepers, Culpeper
Oath Keepers, Forest
Oath Keepers, Franklin County

Oath Keepers, Fredericksburg
Oath Keepers, Goochland
Oath, Hampton
Oath Keepers, Madison
Oath Keepers, Mechanicsville
Oath Keepers, Mecklenburg County
Oath Keepers, Middlesex County
Oath Keepers, Montgomery County
Oath Keepers, Norfolk
Oath Keepers, Orange
Oath Keepers, Prince William County
Oath Keepers, Roanoke
Oath Keepers, Scottsville
Oath Keepers, Staunton
Oath Keepers, Vinton
Oath Keepers, Winchester
Outlaw Militia,* Albemarle County
Rappahannock Guard,* Fredericksburg
TAX-FREEDOM.com, Arlington
Three Percenters-III%ers, The Buckingham County
We Are Change, Blacksburg
We the People, Fredericksburg


## WASHINGTON (34)

American Patriot Party, Statewide
Church of Sovereigns: Sacred Family Temple of the Living Saint, Satsop
Citizen Review Online, Sequim
Constitution Party of Washington, Spokane Valley
DTM Enterprises, Ephrata
Get Out Of Our House (GOOOH), Statewide
John Birch Society, Lynden
National Association of Rural Landowners (NARLO), Fall City
National Association of Rural Landowners (NARLO), Issaquah
Oath Keepers, Colville
Sovereign-Citizenship.net, Satsop
Sovereign Project, The Clark County
Stevens County Assembly, Chewelah
Three Percenters-III%ers, The Pierce County
Three Percenters Club,* Yakima
Washington Lightfoot Militia,* Benton County
Washington Lightfoot Militia,* Clark County
Washington Lightfoot Militia,* Cowlitz County
Washington Lightfoot Militia,* Grant County
Washington Lightfoot Militia,* Skamania County
Washington Lightfoot Militia,* Spokane County
Washington Lightfoot Militia,* Yakima County
Washington State Militia,* Central Washington
Washington State Militia,* Northeast Washington
Washington State Militia,* Northwest Washington
Washington State Militia,* Southeast Washington

Washington State Militia,* Southwest Washington
We Are Change, Spokane
We the People, Bellevue
We the People, Camas
We the People, McKenna
We the People, Olalla
We the People, Onalaska
We the People, Prosser

## WEST VIRGINIA (4)

Constitution Party of West Virginia, Martinsburg
Oath Keepers, Statewide
Three Percenters-III%ers, Statewide
Three Percenters Club,* Sutton

## WISCONSIN (16)

American Opinion Foundation, Inc., Appleton
American Patriot Party, Statewide
Constitution Party of Wisconsin, Milwaukee
David-Wynn: Miller, Milwaukee
Eagle Forum, Milwaukee
John Birch Society, Appleton
John Birch Society Shop, Appleton
Oath Keepers, Port Washington
Three Percenters-III%ers, The Marathon County
Three Percenters Club,* Wausau
We Are Change, Marinette
We Are Change, Milwaukee
We the People, Janesville
We the People, Madison
We the People, Peshtigo
Wisconsin Light Foot Militia,* Wood County

## WYOMING (8)

American Patriot Party, Statewide
Constitution Party of Wyoming, Torrington
Get Out Of Our House (GOOOH), Statewide
Natural News, Cody
Oath Keepers, Cody
Three Percenters-III%ers, The Fremont County
Three Percenters Club,* Casper
We the People, Casper

# Appendix C: Symbols of Hate

White supremacists and other extremists have long been fond of signs, symbols, logos, and emblems, the meanings of which are not always obvious to the uninformed observer. Reproduced here are some of the most popular symbols currently used on the Internet, or in extremist publications, as displayed on the Southern Poverty Law Center's website (http://www.splcenter.org).

### KU KLUX KLAN BLOOD DROP

The blood drop is one of the Ku Klux Klan's best-known symbols. For Klan members, the drop represents the blood that Jesus Christ shed on the cross as a sacrifice for the white race.

### THE NIGHT RIDER

This depiction of the traditional robed Klansman on horseback signifies the Ku Klux Klan. Night riders originated in Ohio in the 1920s as a group of black-robed Klan terrorists who specialized in violent attacks on blacks and others.

### ZIONIST OCCUPIED GOVERNMENT

Zionist Occupied Government (ZOG), a phrase used by anti-Semitic and white supremacist groups to denote the federal government. These groups believe the government is secretly controlled by Jews.

### NAZI SWASTIKA

Adopted in 1935 as the official emblem of Germany's Nazi Party, the swastika is now widely used by neo-Nazi, skinhead, and other white supremacist groups. Dozens of variations on the swastika are common.

### WAR SKINS

This logo, incorporating a skull and crossbones, is used by the skinhead followers of the neo-Nazi group White Aryan Resistance (WAR).

### CELTIC CROSS

Originally a symbol for the Celts of ancient Ireland and Scotland, the Celtic cross was adopted by many American white supremacist groups. In modern times, it was first used by the far-right National Front in UK.

### THUNDERBOLT

This is a Nazi symbol signifying the Schutzstaffel (SS), the elite military arm of Adolf Hitler's Third Reich. The SS supervised Nazi Germany's network of death camps.

## NATIONAL ALLIANCE LIFE RUNE

This is the official symbol of the neo-Nazi National Alliance, based in Hillsboro, West Virginia. Originally, it was a character from a runic alphabet that signified life, creation, birth, rebirth, and renewal. Several runic alphabets were used by the Germanic peoples between the third and thirteenth centuries.

## WHITE PRIDE WORLD WIDE

Some groups incorporated this white supremacist slogan into the Celtic cross.

## WAR SWASTIKA

The symbol used by the neo-Nazi group White Aryan Resistance (WAR) incorporates the California-based group's acronym into a Nazi swastika.

## ARYAN NATIONS

This symbol is used by the neo-Nazi Aryan Nations, based in Hayden Lake, Idaho.

## CROSSED HAMMERS

Crossed hammers signify the many skinhead groups that use the word "hammer" as part of their names. Such groups exist in Australia, Europe, and the United States, and many incorporate the crossed hammers into their own symbols.

## THREE-BLADED SWASTIKA

This is a variation of the traditional swastika of Nazi Germany that is popular among some skinhead and other white supremacist groups. It has also been used by some South African extremist groups.

## SKINHEAD SKULL AND CROSSBONES

Many skinhead groups use variations of this symbol, which incorporates the Celtic cross into a skull and crossbones.

Two forms of text labeling are also common and are listed below.

## 14 WORDS

This is shorthand for a slogan coined by David Lane, an imprisoned member of The Order, or Silent Brotherhood: "We must secure the existence of our people and a future for White children." The Order was a revolutionary neo-Nazi group responsible for the theft of millions of dollars in armored car heists and the murder of a Jewish radio talk show host in the 1980s.

## 88

This number, widely used by neo-Nazis and others, is shorthand for "Heil Hitler." H is the eighth letter of the alphabet, and so the abbreviation HH is translated as 88.

# Appendix D: Foreign-Based Terrorist Organizations

The organization details listed here are from the U.S. Department of State. This report is now known as the Country Reports on Terrorism. These are not the only foreign-based terrorist organizations in existence; they are just the predominant and most active ones.

## ABU NIDAL ORGANIZATION (ANO)

### OTHER NAMES

Fatah Revolutionary Council
Arab Revolutionary Brigades
Black September
Revolutionary Organization of Socialist Muslims

### DESCRIPTION

This is an international terrorist organization led by Sabri al-Banna. Split from the Palestine Liberation organization (PLO) in 1974, the group is made up of various functional committees, including political, military, and financial.

### ACTIVITIES

The group has carried out terrorist attacks in 20 countries, killing or injuring almost 900 people. Targets include the United States, the United Kingdom, France, Israel, moderate Palestinians, the PLO, and some Arab countries. Major attacks included the Rome and Vienna airport attacks in December 1985, the Neve Shalom Synagogue in Istanbul, the Pan Am flight 73 hijacking in Karachi in September 1986, and the City of Poros day-excursion ship attack in Greece in July 1988. The group is suspected of assassinating the PLO deputy chief Abu Iyad and PLO security chief Abu Hul in Tunis in January 1991. ANO assassinated a Jordanian diplomat in Lebanon in January 1994 and was linked to the killing of the PLO representative there. The ANO has not attacked Western targets since the late 1980s.

### STRENGTH

A few hundred members, plus a limited overseas support structure.

### LOCATION/AREA OF OPERATION

Al-Banna relocated to Iraq in December 1998, where the group maintains a presence. It has an operational presence in Lebanon in the Bekaa Valley and has several Palestinian refugee camps in coastal areas of Lebanon. It also has a limited presence in Sudan and Syria, among others, although financial problems and internal disorganization reduced the group's activities and capabilities. Authorities shut down the ANO's operations in Libya and Egypt in 1999. The ANO has demonstrated the ability to operate over a wide area, including the Middle East, Asia, and Europe.

## EXTERNAL AID

It has received considerable support, including safe havens, training, logistical assistance, and financial aid from Iraq, Libya, and Syria (until 1987), in addition to close support for selected operations.

## ABU SAYYAF GROUP (ASG)

### DESCRIPTION

The ASG is the most violent of the Islamic separatist groups operating in the southern Philippines. Some ASG leaders studied or worked in the Middle East and allegedly fought in Afghanistan during the Soviet war. The group split from the Moro National Liberation Front in the early 1990s under the leadership of Abdurajak Abubakar Janjalani, who was killed in a clash with Philippine police on December 18, 1998. His younger brother, Khadaffy Janjalani, replaced him as the nominal leader of the group, which is composed of several semiautonomous factions.

### ACTIVITIES

The ASG engages in kidnappings for ransom, bombings, assassinations, and extortion. Although from time to time it claims that its motivation is to promote an independent Islamic state in western Mindanao and the Sulu Archipelago, areas in the southern Philippines heavily populated by Muslims, the ASG now appears to use terror mainly for financial profit. The group's first large-scale action was a raid on the town of Ipil in Mindanao in April 1995. In April of 2000, an ASG faction kidnapped 21 people, including 10 foreign tourists, from a resort in Malaysia. Separately in 2000, the group abducted several foreign journalists, three Malaysians, and a U.S. citizen. On May 27, 2001 the ASG kidnapped three U.S. citizens and 17 Filipinos from a tourist resort in Palawan, Philippines. Several of the hostages, including one U.S. citizen, were murdered.

### STRENGTH

The ASG is believed to have a few hundred core fighters, and at least 1000 individuals motivated by the prospect of receiving ransom payments for foreign hostages allegedly joined the group in 2000–2001.

### LOCATION/AREA OF OPERATION

The ASG was founded in Basilan Province and mainly operates there and in the neighboring provinces of Sulu and Tawi-Tawi in the Sulu Archipelago. It also operates in the Zamboanga Peninsula, and members occasionally travel to Manila and other parts of the country. The group expanded its operations to Malaysia in 2000 when it abducted foreigners from a tourist resort.

### EXTERNAL AID

The ASG is largely self-financed through ransom and extortion. The group may receive support from Islamic extremists in the Middle East and South Asia. Libya publicly paid millions of dollars for the release of the foreign hostages seized from Malaysia in 2000.

## AL-AQSA MARTYRS BRIGADE

### DESCRIPTION

The al-Aqsa Martyrs Brigade comprises an unknown number of small cells of Fatah-affiliated activists who emerged at the outset of the current intifada to attack Israeli targets. It aims to drive the

Israeli military and settlers from the West Bank, Gaza Strip, and Jerusalem, and to establish a Palestinian state.

## ACTIVITIES

The al-Aqsa Martyrs Brigade has carried out shootings and suicide operations against Israeli military personnel and civilians, and killed Palestinians whom the group believed were collaborating with Israel. At least five U.S. citizens, four of them dual Israeli-U.S. citizens, were killed in these attacks. The group probably did not attack them because of their U.S. citizenship. In January 2002, the group claimed responsibility for the first suicide bombing carried out by a woman.

## STRENGTH

Unknown

## LOCATION/AREA OF OPERATION

The al-Aqsa Martyrs Brigade operates mainly in the West Bank and has claimed attacks inside Israel and the Gaza Strip.

## EXTERNAL AID

Unknown

# ARMED ISLAMIC GROUP

## DESCRIPTION

An Islamic extremist group, the Armed Islamic Group (GIA) aims to overthrow the secular Algerian regime and replace it with an Islamic state. The GIA began its violent activities in early 1992 after Algiers voided the victory of the Islamic Salvation Front (FIS)—the largest Islamic party—in the first round of legislative elections in December 1991.

## ACTIVITIES

The GIA is responsible for frequent attacks against civilians, journalists, and foreign residents. In the past several years, the GIA conducted a terrorist campaign of civilian massacres, sometimes wiping out entire villages in its area of operations and frequently killing hundreds of civilians. Since announcing its terrorist campaign against foreigners living in Algeria in September 1993, the GIA killed more than 100 expatriate men and women—mostly Europeans—in the country. The GIA uses assassinations and bombings, including car bombs, and is known to kidnap victims and slit their throats. The GIA hijacked an Air France flight to Algiers in December 1994. In late 1999, several GIA members were convicted by a French court for conducting a series of bombings in France in 1995.

## STRENGTH

Precise numbers are unknown—probably about 200.

## LOCATION/AREA OF OPERATION

Algeria and France

## EXTERNAL AID

Algerian expatriates and Salafist Group for Call and Combat (GSPC) members abroad, many of whom reside in Western Europe, provide financial and logistical support. In addition, the Algerian government has accused Iran and Sudan of supporting Algerian extremists.

## 'ASBAT AL-ANSAR

### DESCRIPTION

'Asbat al-Ansar—the Partisans' League—is a Lebanon-based, Sunni extremist group composed primarily of Palestinians, which is associated with Osama bin Laden. The group follows an extremist interpretation of Islam that justifies violence against civilian targets to achieve political ends. Some of those goals include overthrowing the Lebanese government and thwarting perceived anti-Islamic influences in the country.

### ACTIVITIES

'Asbat al-Ansar has carried out several terrorist attacks in Lebanon since it first emerged in the early 1990s. The group carried out assassinations of Lebanese religious leaders and bombed several nightclubs, theaters, and liquor stores in the mid-1990s. The group raised its operational profile in 2000 with two dramatic attacks against Lebanese and international targets. The group was involved in clashes in northern Lebanon in late December 1999 and carried out a rocket-propelled grenade attack on the Russian Embassy in Beirut in January 2000.

### STRENGTH

The group commands about 300,000 fighters in Lebanon.

### LOCATION/AREA OF OPERATION

The group's primary base of operations is the 'Ayn al-Hilwah Palestinian refugee camp near Sidon in southern Lebanon.

### EXTERNAL AID

The group probably receives money through international Sunni extremist networks and bin Laden's al-Qaeda network.

## AUM SUPREME TRUTH (AUM)

### OTHER NAMES

Aum Shinrikyo

### DESCRIPTION

A cult established in 1987 by Shoko Asahara, the Aum aimed to take over Japan and then the world. Approved as a religious entity in 1989 under Japanese law, the cult ran candidates in a Japanese parliamentary election in 1990. Over time, the cult began to emphasize the imminence of the end of the world and stated that the United States would initiate Armageddon by starting World War III with Japan. The Japanese government revoked its recognition of the Aum as a religious organization in

October 1995, but in 1997 a government panel decided not to invoke the Anti-Subversive Law against the cult, which would have outlawed them. A 1999 law gave the Japanese government authorization to continue police surveillance of the cult due to concerns that the Aum might launch future terrorist attacks. Under the leadership of Fumihiro Joyu, the Aum changed its name to Aleph in January 2000 and claimed to have rejected the violent and apocalyptic teachings of its founder. (Joyu took formal control of the organization early in 2002 and remains its leader.)

## ACTIVITIES

On March 20, 1995, Aum members simultaneously released the chemical nerve agent sarin on several Tokyo subway trains, killing 12 persons and injuring up to 6000. The group was responsible for other mysterious chemical accidents in Japan in 1994. Its efforts to conduct attacks using biological agents have been unsuccessful. Japanese police arrested Asahara in May 1995, and he remained on trial facing charges of 13 crimes, including 7 counts of murder, at the end of 2001. Legal analysts say it will take several more years to conclude the trial. Since 1997, the cult has continued to recruit new members, engage in commercial enterprise, and acquire property, although it scaled back these activities significantly in 2001 in response to public outcry. The cult maintains an Internet home page. In July 2001, Russian authorities arrested a group of Russian Aum followers who planned to set off bombs near the Imperial Palace in Tokyo as part of an operation to free Asahara from jail and then smuggle him to Russia.

## STRENGTH

The Aum's current membership is estimated at 1500–2000 persons. At the time of the Tokyo subway attacks, the group claimed to have 9000 members in Japan and up to 40,000 worldwide.

## LOCATION/AREA OF OPERATION

The Aum's principal membership is located only in Japan, but a residual branch comprising an unknown number of followers surfaced in Russia.

## EXTERNAL AID

None

# AL-GAMA'A AL-ISLAMIYYA

## OTHER NAMES

Islamic Group (IG)

## DESCRIPTION

Egypt's largest militant group has been active since the late 1970s. The group appears loosely organized, having an external wing with supporters in several countries worldwide. The group issued a cease-fire in March 1999, but its spiritual leader, Shaykh Umar Abd al-Rahman, sentenced to life in prison in January 1996 for his involvement in the 1993 World Trade Center bombing and incarcerated in the United States, rescinded his support for the cease-fire in June 2000. The Gama'a has not conducted an attack inside Egypt since August 1998. A senior member signed Osama bin Laden's fatwa in February 1998 calling for attacks against the United States. The group unofficially split into two factions: one that supports the cease-fire led by Mustafa Hamza and one led by Rifa'i

Taha Musa, calling for a return to armed operations. In early 2001 Taha Musa published a book in which he attempted to justify terrorist attacks that would cause mass casualties. Musa disappeared several months later, and there are conflicting reports as to his current whereabouts. The group's primary goal is to overthrow the Egyptian government and replace it with an Islamic state, but disaffected IG members, such as those potentially inspired by Taha Musa or Abd al-Rahman, may be interested in carrying out attacks against U.S. and Israeli interests.

## ACTIVITIES

The group conducted armed attacks against Egyptian security and other government officials, Coptic Christians, and Egyptian opponents of Islamic extremism before the cease-fire. From 1993 until the cease-fire, al-Gama'a launched attacks on tourists in Egypt, most notably the attack in November 1997 at Luxor that killed 58 foreign tourists. Also, the group claimed responsibility for the attempt in June 1995 to assassinate Egyptian President Hosni Mubarak in Addis Ababa, Ethiopia. The Gama'a never specifically attacked a U.S. citizen or facility but has threatened U.S. interests.

## STRENGTH

Unknown—but at its peak, the IG probably commanded several thousand hard-core members and a like number of sympathizers. The 1999 cease-fire and security crackdowns following the attack in Luxor, Egypt in 1997, and more recently security efforts following September 11, probably resulted in a substantial decrease in the group's numbers.

## LOCATION/AREA OF OPERATION

The IG operates mainly in the Al-Minya, Asyu't, Qina, and Sohaj governorates of southern Egypt. The group also appears to have support in Cairo, Alexandria, and other urban locations, particularly among unemployed graduates and students. It has a worldwide presence, including in the United Kingdom, Afghanistan, Yemen, and Austria.

## EXTERNAL AID

Unknown—but the Egyptian government believes that Iran, bin Laden, and Afghan militant groups support the organization. The group may also obtain some funding through various Islamic nongovernmental organizations (NGOs).

## COMMUNIST PARTY OF THE PHILIPPINES—NEW PEOPLE'S ARMY

### DESCRIPTION

The military wing of the Communist Party of the Philippines (CPP), the New People's Army (NPA), is a Maoist group formed in March 1969 with the aim of overthrowing the government through protracted guerrilla warfare. The chairman of the CPP's Central Committee and the NPA's founder, Jose Maria Sison, directs all CPP and NPA activity from the Netherlands, where he lives in self-imposed exile. Fellow Central Committee member and director of the CPP's National Democratic Front (NDF) Luis Jalandoni also lives in the Netherlands and has become a Dutch citizen. Although primarily a rural-based guerrilla group, the NPA has an active urban infrastructure to conduct terrorism and uses city-based assassination squads. The NPA derives most of its funding from contributions of supporters in the Philippines, Europe, and elsewhere, and from so-called revolutionary taxes extorted from local businesses.

## ACTIVITIES

The NPA primarily targets Philippine security forces, politicians, judges, government informers, former rebels who wish to leave the NPA, and alleged criminals. The group opposes any U.S. military presence in the Philippines and attacked U.S. military interests before the U.S. base closures in 1992. Press reports in 1999 and in late 2001 indicated that the NPA is again targeting the U.S. troops participating in joint military exercises as well as U.S. Embassy personnel. The NPA claimed responsibility for the assassination of congressmen from Quezon (in May 2001) and Cagayan (in June 2001), and many other killings.

## STRENGTH

The strength of the NPA is slowly growing and is now estimated at more than 10,000.

## LOCATION/AREA OF OPERATIONS

The NPA operates in rural Luzon, Visayas, and parts of Mindanao. It has cells in Manila and other metropolitan centers.

## EXTERNAL AID

Unknown

# EUZKADI TA ASKATASUNA

## OTHER NAMES

Basque Fatherland and Liberty

## DESCRIPTION

Euzkadi Ta Askatasuna (ETA) was founded in 1959 with the aim of establishing an independent homeland based on Marxist principles in the northern Spanish provinces of Vizcaya, Guipuzcoa, Alava, and Navarra, and the southwestern French provinces of Labourd, Basse-Navarre, and Soule.

## ACTIVITIES

The group is primarily involved in bombings and assassinations of Spanish government officials, security and military forces, politicians, and judicial figures. ETA finances its activities through kidnappings, robberies, and extortion. The group has killed more than 800 people and injured hundreds since it began lethal attacks in the early 1960s. In November 1999, ETA broke its "unilateral and indefinite" cease-fire and began an assassination and bombing campaign that killed 38 individuals and wounded scores more by the end of 2001.

## STRENGTH

Unknown—the ETA may have hundreds of members, plus supporters.

## LOCATION/AREA OF OPERATION

The group operates primarily in the Basque autonomous regions of northern Spain and southwestern France but also bombed Spanish and French interests elsewhere.

## EXTERNAL AID

The ETA has received training at various times in the past in Libya, Lebanon, and Nicaragua. Some ETA members allegedly received sanctuary in Cuba, while others reside in South America.

# HAMAS (ISLAMIC RESISTANCE MOVEMENT)

## DESCRIPTION

Hamas was formed in late 1987 as an outgrowth of the Palestinian branch of the Muslim Brotherhood. Various Hamas elements used political and violent means, including terrorism, to pursue the goal of establishing an Islamic Palestinian state in place of Israel. Hamas is loosely structured, with some elements working clandestinely and others working openly through mosques and social service institutions to recruit members, raise money, organize activities, and distribute propaganda. Hamas' strength is concentrated in the Gaza Strip and a few areas of the West Bank. Hamas has also engaged in peaceful political activity, such as running candidates in West Bank Chamber of Commerce elections and winning a majority in the 2006 Palestinian general elections.

## ACTIVITIES

Hamas activists, especially those in the Izz el-Din al-Qassam Brigades, have conducted many attacks—including large-scale suicide bombings—against Israeli civilian and military targets. In the early 1990s, they also targeted Fatah rivals and began a practice of targeting suspected Palestinian collaborators, which continues. There was increased operational activity in 2001 during the intifada. Many attacks against Israeli government interests were claimed. The group has not targeted U.S. interests and continues to confine its attacks to Israelis inside Israel and the territories.

## STRENGTH

There are an unknown number of hard-core members and tens of thousands of supporters and sympathizers.

## LOCATION/AREA OF OPERATION

The group operates primarily in the West Bank, Gaza Strip, and Israel. In August 1999, Jordanian authorities closed the group's political bureau offices in Amman, arrested its leaders, and prohibited the group from operating on Jordanian territory. Hamas leaders are also present in other parts of the Middle East, including Syria, Lebanon, and Iran.

## EXTERNAL AID

The group receives funding from Palestinian expatriates, Iran, and private benefactors in Saudi Arabia and other moderate Arab states. Some fund-raising and propaganda activities take place in Western Europe and North America.

# HARAKAT UL-MUJAHIDIN

## DESCRIPTION

The Harakat ul-Mujahidin (HUM) is an Islamic militant group based in Pakistan that operates primarily in Kashmir. It is politically aligned with the radical political party Jamiat-i Ulema-i Islam Fazlur Rehman faction (JUI-F). The long-time leader of the group, Fazlur Rehman Khalil, stepped down as HUM emir in mid-February 2000, handing the reins over to the popular Kashmiri commander and his second-in-command, Farooq Kashmiri. Khalil, who was linked to bin Laden and signed his fatwa in February 1998 calling for attacks on the U.S. and Western interests, assumed the position of HUM secretary general. The HUM operated terrorist training camps in eastern Afghanistan until coalition airstrikes destroyed them during the fall of 2001.

## ACTIVITIES

The group conducted a number of operations against Indian troops and civilian targets in Kashmir. It is linked to the Kashmiri militant group al-Faran that kidnapped five Western tourists in Kashmir in July 1995: one was killed in August 1995 and the other four were reportedly killed in December of the same year. The HUM is responsible for the hijacking of an Indian airliner on December 24, 1999, which resulted in the release of Masood Azhar—an important leader in the former Harakat ul-Ansar imprisoned by the Indians in 1994—and Ahmad Omar Sheikh, who was arrested for the abduction/murder in January–February 2001 of the U.S. journalist Daniel Pearl.

## STRENGTH

The HUM has several thousand armed supporters located in Azad Kashmir, Pakistan, and India's southern Kashmir and Doda regions. Supporters are mostly Pakistanis and Kashmiris and also include Afghans and Arab veterans of the Afghan war. Supporters use light and heavy machine guns, assault rifles, mortars, explosives, and rockets. The HUM lost a significant share of its membership in defections to the Jaish-e-Mohammed (JEM) in 2000.

## LOCATION/AREA OF OPERATION

Although based in Muzaffarabad, Rawalpindi, and several other towns in Pakistan, members conduct insurgent and terrorist activities primarily in Kashmir. The HUM trained its militants in Afghanistan and Pakistan.

## EXTERNAL AID

The group collects donations from Saudi Arabia and other Gulf and Islamic states, as well as from Pakistan and Kashmir. The HUM's financial collection methods also include soliciting donations through magazine ads and pamphlets. The sources and amount of the HUM's military funding are unknown. In anticipation of asset seizures by the Pakistani government, the HUM withdrew funds from bank accounts and invested in legal businesses, such as commodity trading, real estate, and production of consumer goods. Its fund-raising in Pakistan was constrained since the government clamped down on extremist groups and froze terrorist assets.

# HIZBALLAH (PARTY OF GOD)

## OTHER NAMES

Islamic Jihad
Revolutionary Justice Organization

Organization of the Oppressed on Earth
Islamic Jihad for the Liberation of Palestine

## DESCRIPTION

Formed in 1982 in response to the Israeli invasion of Lebanon, this Lebanon-based radical Shi'a group takes its ideological inspiration from the Iranian revolution and the teachings of the Ayatollah Khomeini. The Majlis al-Shura, or Consultative Council, is the group's highest governing body and is led by Secretary General Hassan Nasrallah. Hizballah (alternately spelled Hezbollah) formally advocates ultimate establishment of Islamic rule in Lebanon and liberation of all occupied Arab lands, including Jerusalem. It expressed as a goal the elimination of Israel. The group expressed its unwillingness to work within the confines of Lebanon's established political system; however, this stance changed with the party's decision in 1992 to participate in parliamentary elections. Although closely allied with and often directed by Iran, the group may have conducted operations that were not approved by Tehran. While Hizballah does not share the Syrian regime's secular orientation, the group has been a strong tactical ally in helping Syria to advance its political objectives in the region.

## ACTIVITIES

The group is known or suspected to have been involved in numerous anti-U.S. terrorist attacks, including the suicide truck bombings of the U.S. Embassy in Beirut in April 1983, the U.S. Marine barracks in Beirut in October 1983, and the U.S. Embassy annex in Beirut in September 1984. Three members of Hizballah—Imad Mughniyah, Hasan Izz-al-Din, and Ali Atwa—are on the FBI's list of the 22 most wanted terrorists for the 1985 hijacking of TWA Flight 847, during which a U.S. Navy diver was murdered. Elements of the group were responsible for the kidnapping and detention of the U.S. and other Western hostages in Lebanon. The group also attacked the Israeli Embassy in Argentina in 1992 and is suspect in the 1994 bombing of the Israeli cultural center in Buenos Aires. In the fall of 2000, it captured three Israeli soldiers in the Shabaa Farms and kidnapped an Israeli noncombatant whom it may have lured to Lebanon under false pretenses.

## STRENGTH

There are several thousand supporters and a few hundred terrorist operatives.

## LOCATION/AREA OF OPERATION

The group operates in the Bekaa Valley, the southern suburbs of Beirut, and southern Lebanon. It has established cells in Europe, Africa, South America, North America, and Asia.

## EXTERNAL AID

The group receives substantial amounts of training, weapons, explosives, and financial, political, diplomatic, and organizational aid from Iran and received diplomatic, political, and logistical support from Syria.

# ISLAMIC MOVEMENT OF UZBEKISTAN (IMU)

## DESCRIPTION

This is a coalition of Islamic militants from Uzbekistan and other Central Asian states opposed to Uzbekistani President Islom Karimov's secular regime. Before the counterterrorism coalition began operations in Afghanistan in October 2001, the primary goal of the Islamic Movement of Uzbekistan (IMU) was the establishment of an Islamic state in Uzbekistan. If IMU political and ideological leader Tohir Yoldashev survives the counterterrorism campaign and can regroup the organization, however, he might widen the IMU's targets to include all those he perceives as fighting Islam. The group's propaganda has always included anti-Western and anti-Israeli rhetoric.

## ACTIVITIES

The IMU primarily targeted Uzbekistani interests before October 2001 and is believed to have been responsible for five car bombs in Tashkent in February 1999. Militants also took foreign hostages in 1999 and 2000, including four U.S. citizens who were mountain climbing in August 2000 and four Japanese geologists and eight Kyrgyzstani soldiers in August 1999. Since October the coalition captured, killed, and dispersed many of the militants who remained in Afghanistan to fight with the Taliban and al-Qaeda, severely degrading the IMU's ability to attack Uzbekistani or coalition interests in the near term. The IMU military leader Juma Namangani apparently was killed during an air strike in November. At the year's end, Yoldashev remained at large.

## STRENGTH

Militants probably number less than 2000.

## LOCATION/AREA OF OPERATION

Militants are scattered throughout South Asia and Tajikistan. The area of operations includes Afghanistan, Iran, Kyrgyzstan, Pakistan, Tajikistan, and Uzbekistan.

## EXTERNAL AID

The coalition has support from other Islamic extremist groups and patrons in the Middle East and Central and South Asia. IMU leadership broadcast statements over Iranian radio.

# JAISH-E-MOHAMMED

## OTHER NAMES

Army of Mohammed

## DESCRIPTION

The JEM is an Islamic extremist group based in Pakistan that was formed by Masood Azhar on his release from prison in India in early 2000. The group's aim is to unite Kashmir with Pakistan. It is politically aligned with the radical political party, Jamiat-i Ulema-i Islam Fazlur Rehman faction (JUI-F). The United States announced the addition of JEM to the U.S. Treasury Department's Office of Foreign Asset Control's (OFAC) list (which includes organizations that are believed to support terrorist groups and have assets in U.S. jurisdiction that can be frozen or controlled) in October and the Foreign Terrorist Organization list in December. The group was banned, and its assets were frozen by the Pakistani government in January 2002.

## ACTIVITIES

The JEM's leader, Masood Azhar, was released from Indian imprisonment in December 1999 in exchange for 155 hijacked Indian Airlines hostages. The 1994 HUA kidnappings by Omar Sheikh of U.S. and British nationals in New Delhi and the July 1995 HUA/Al-Faran kidnappings of Westerners in Kashmir were two of several previous HUA efforts to free Azhar. The JEM on October 1, 2001, claimed responsibility for a suicide attack on the Jammu and Kashmir legislative assembly building in Srinagar that killed at least 31 persons, but later denied the claim. The Indian government publicly implicated the JEM along with Lashkar-e-Tayyiba (LT) for the December 13, 2001, attack on the Indian Parliament that killed 9 and injured 18.

## STRENGTH

The JEM has several hundred armed supporters located in Azad Kashmir, Pakistan, and India's southern Kashmir and Doda regions, including a large cadre of former HUM members. Supporters are mostly Pakistanis and Kashmiris, and also Afghans and Arab veterans of the Afghan war. The group uses light and heavy machine guns, assault rifles, mortars, improvised explosive devices, and rocket grenades.

## LOCATION/AREA OF OPERATION

The group is based in Peshawar and Muzaffarabad, but members conduct terrorist activities primarily in Kashmir. The JEM maintained training camps in Afghanistan until the fall of 2001.

## EXTERNAL AID

Most of the JEM's cadre and material resources were drawn from the militant groups Harakat-ul Jihad al-Islami (HUJI) and the Harakat ul-Mujahedin (HUM). The JEM had close ties to Afghan Arabs and the Taliban. Osama bin Laden is suspected of providing funding to the JEM. The JEM also collects funds through donation requests in magazines and pamphlets. In anticipation of asset seizures by the Pakistani government, the JEM withdrew funds from bank accounts and invested in legal businesses such as commodity trading, real estate, and production of consumer goods.

## AL-JIHAD

### OTHER NAMES

Egyptian Islamic Jihad
Islamic Jihad
Jihad Group

### DESCRIPTION

This is an Egyptian Islamic extremist group active since the late 1970s. Al-Jihad merged with bin Laden's al-Qaeda organization in June 2001 but may retain some capability to conduct independent operations. The group continues to suffer setbacks worldwide, especially after the September 11, 2001, attacks. The primary goals are to overthrow the Egyptian government and replace it with an Islamic state and attack the U.S. and Israeli interests in Egypt and abroad.

## ACTIVITIES

The al-Jihad specializes in armed attacks against high-level Egyptian government personnel, including cabinet ministers, and car bombings against official U.S. and Egyptian facilities. The original Jihad was responsible for the assassination of Egyptian President Anwar Sadat in 1981. They claimed responsibility for the attempted assassinations of Interior Minister Hassan al-Alfi in August 1993 and Prime Minister Atef Sedky in November 1993. The al-Jihad has not conducted an attack inside Egypt since 1993 and has never targeted foreign tourists there. In 1995, the group was responsible for bombing the Egyptian Embassy in Islamabad; in 1998, a planned attack against the U.S. Embassy in Albania was thwarted.

## STRENGTH

Not known but probably has several hundred hard-core members.

## LOCATION/AREA OF OPERATION

The al-Jihad operates in the Cairo area, but most of its network is outside Egypt, including Yemen, Afghanistan, Pakistan, Lebanon, and the United Kingdom, and its activities for several years have been centered outside Egypt.

## EXTERNAL AID

Unknown, but the Egyptian government claims that Iran supports the al-Jihad. Its merger with al-Qaeda boosts bin Laden's support for the group. The group may obtain some funding through various Islamic NGOs, cover businesses, and criminal acts.

## JEMAAH ISLAMIYA ORGANIZATION

### DESCRIPTION

Jemaah Islamiya (JI) is an Islamic extremist group with cells operating throughout Southeast Asia. Recently arrested JI members in Singapore, Malaysia, and the Philippines revealed links with al-Qaeda. The JI's stated goal is to create an Islamic state comprising Malaysia, Singapore, Indonesia, and the southern Philippines. Three Indonesian extremists, one of whom is in custody in Malaysia, are the reputed leaders of the organization.

### ACTIVITIES

The JI began developing plans in 1997 to target U.S. interests in Singapore and in 1999 conducted videotaped casings of potential U.S. targets in preparation for multiple attacks in Singapore. A cell in Singapore acquired 4 tons of ammonium nitrate, which has not yet been found.

In December 2001, Singapore authorities arrested 15 JI members, some of whom had trained in al-Qaeda camps in Afghanistan, who planned to attack the U.S. and Israeli embassies and British and Australian diplomatic buildings in Singapore. In addition, the Singapore police discovered forged immigration stamps, bomb-making materials, and al-Qaeda-related material in several suspects' homes.

STRENGTH

Exact numbers are unknown, but press reports approximate that the Malaysian cells may comprise 200 members.

LOCATION/AREA OF OPERATION

The JI has cells in Singapore and Malaysia. Press reports indicate the JI is also present in Indonesia and possibly the Philippines.

EXTERNAL AID

Largely unknown, probably self-financed, possible al-Qaeda support

## KACH AND KAHANE CHAI

DESCRIPTION

Their stated goal is to restore the biblical state of Israel. Kach (founded by radical Israeli-American rabbi Meir Kahane) and its offshoot Kahane Chai, which means "Kahane Lives" (founded by Meir Kahane's son Binyamin following his father's assassination in the United States), were declared to be terrorist organizations in March 1994 by the Israeli Cabinet under the 1948 Terrorism Law. This followed the groups' statements in support of Baruch Goldstein's attack in February 1994 on the al-Ibrahimi Mosque—Goldstein was affiliated with Kach—and their verbal attacks on the Israeli government. Palestinian gunmen killed Binyamin Kahane and his wife in a drive-by shooting in December 2000 in the West Bank.

ACTIVITIES

The groups organize protests against the Israeli government and harass and threaten Palestinians in Hebron and the West Bank. They have threatened to attack Arabs, Palestinians, and Israeli government officials. The groups vowed revenge for the death of Binyamin Kahane and his wife.

STRENGTH

Unknown

LOCATION/AREA OF OPERATION

These groups have Israeli and West Bank settlements, particularly at Qiryat Arba in Hebron.

EXTERNAL AID

They receive support from sympathizers in the United States and Europe.

## KURDISTAN WORKERS PARTY

DESCRIPTION

This party was founded in 1974 as a Marxist-Leninist insurgent group primarily composed of Turkish Kurds. The group's goal is to establish an independent Kurdish state in southeastern Turkey, where the population is predominantly Kurdish. In the early 1990s, the Kurdistan Workers Party (PKK)

moved beyond rural-based insurgent activities to include urban terrorism. Turkish authorities captured Chairman Abdullah Ocalan in Kenya in early 1999; the Turkish State Security Court subsequently sentenced him to death. In August 1999, Ocalan announced a "peace initiative," ordering members to refrain from violence and withdraw from Turkey and requesting dialogue with Ankara on Kurdish issues. At a PKK Congress in January 2000, members supported Ocalan's initiative and claimed the group now would use only political means to achieve its new goal, improved rights for Kurds in Turkey.

## ACTIVITIES

The group's primary targets have been Turkish government security forces in Turkey. The group attacked Turkish diplomatic and commercial facilities in dozens of West European cities in 1993 and again in the spring of 1995. In an attempt to damage Turkey's tourist industry, the PKK bombed tourist sites and hotels and kidnapped foreign tourists in the early to mid-1990s.

## STRENGTH

The PKK has about 4000–5000 members, most of whom are currently located in northern Iraq. The group also has thousands of sympathizers in Turkey and Europe.

## LOCATION/AREA OF OPERATION

The PKK operates in Turkey, Europe, and the Middle East.

## EXTERNAL AID

The PKK received safe haven and modest aid from Syria, Iraq, and Iran. Damascus upheld its September 2000 antiterror agreement with Ankara, pledging not to support the PKK.

# LASHKAR-E-TAYYIBA

## OTHER NAMES

Army of the Righteous

## DESCRIPTION

The LT is the armed wing of the Pakistan-based religious organization, Markaz-ud-Dawa-wal-Irshad (MDI)—a Sunni anti-U.S. missionary organization formed in 1989. The LT is led by Abdul Wahid Kashmiri and is one of the three largest and best-trained groups fighting in Kashmir against India; it is not connected to a political party. In October 2001, the United States announced the addition of the LT to the U.S. Treasury Department's OFAC list—which includes organizations that are believed to support terrorist groups and have assets in U.S. jurisdiction that can be frozen or controlled. The group was banned, and its assets were frozen by the Pakistani government in January 2002.

## ACTIVITIES

The LT has conducted a number of operations against Indian troops and civilian targets in Kashmir since 1993. The LT claimed responsibility for many attacks in 2001, including an attack in January on Srinagar airport that killed five Indians along with six militants, an attack on a police station in Srinagar that killed at least eight officers and wounded several others, and an attack in April against

Indian border security forces that left at least four dead. The Indian government publicly implicated the LT along with JEM for the December 13, 2001, attack on the Indian Parliament.

## STRENGTH

The LT has several hundred members in Azad Kashmir, Pakistan, and the southern Kashmir and Doda regions of India. Almost all LT cadres are foreigners—mostly Pakistanis from seminaries across the country and Afghan veterans of the Afghan wars. Group members use assault rifles, light and heavy machine guns, mortars, explosives, and rocket-propelled grenades.

## LOCATION/AREA OF OPERATION

The LT is based in Muridke (near Lahore) and Muzaffarabad. The LT trains its militants in mobile training camps across Pakistan-administered Kashmir and trained in Afghanistan until the fall of 2001.

## EXTERNAL AID

The group collects donations from the Pakistani community in the Persian Gulf and the United Kingdom, Islamic NGOs, and Pakistani and Kashmiri businessmen. The LT also maintains a website (under the name of its parent organization Jamaat ud-Dawa), through which it solicits funds and provides information on the group's activities. The amount of LT funding is unknown. The LT maintains ties to religious and military groups around the world, ranging from the Philippines to the Middle East and Chechnya through the MDI fraternal network. In anticipation of asset seizures by the Pakistani government, the LT withdrew funds from bank accounts and invested in legal businesses such as commodity trading, real estate, and production of consumer goods.

## LASHKAR-I-JHANGVI

### DESCRIPTION

This group is a military wing of the Sipah-i-Sahaba-i-Pakistan, a Sunni-Deobandi terrorist outfit. Lashkar-i-Jhangvi means "army of Jhang," a region in Pakistan. Lashkar-i-Jhangvi (LJ) is an extremist organization that emerged in 1997.

### ACTIVITIES

While the LJ initially directed most of its attacks against the Pakistani Shia Muslim community, it also claimed responsibility for the killing of four workers of a U.S. oil company in 1997 in Karachi. LJ also attempted to assassinate then Pakistani Prime Minister Nawaz Sharif in 1999. The group is also responsible for the January 2002 kidnapping and killing of U.S. journalist Daniel Pearl and a March 2002 bus bombing that killed 15 people, including 11 French technicians. LJ is tied to the Islamabad Protestant church bombing in Karachi in March 2002, in which two U.S. citizens were killed. In July 2002, Pakistani police arrested four LJ members for the church attack.

### STRENGTH

Membership numbers are unknown. The LJ has ties to al-Qaeda and the Taliban, and received sanctuary from the Taliban in Afghanistan for its activity in Pakistan.

LOCATION/AREA OF OPERATION

Afghanistan and Pakistan


EXTERNAL AID

Unknown


## LIBERATION TIGERS OF TAMIL EELAM (LTTE)

### OTHER KNOWN FRONT ORGANIZATIONS

World Tamil Association (WTA)
World Tamil Movement (WTM)
Federation of Associations of Canadian Tamils (FACT)
The Ellalan Force
The Sangillan Force


### DESCRIPTION

Founded in 1976, the LTTE is the most powerful Tamil group in Sri Lanka and uses overt and illegal methods to raise funds, acquire weapons, and publicize its cause of establishing an independent Tamil state. The LTTE began its armed conflict with the Sri Lankan government in 1983 and relies on a guerrilla strategy that includes the use of terrorist tactics.


### ACTIVITIES

The Tigers integrated a battlefield insurgent strategy with a terrorist program that targets not only key personnel in the countryside, but also senior Sri Lankan political and military leaders in Colombo and other urban centers. The Tigers are notorious for their cadre of suicide bombers, the Black Tigers. Political assassinations and bombings are commonplace. The LTTE have refrained from targeting foreign diplomatic and commercial establishments.


### STRENGTH

The group's exact strength is unknown, but the LTTE is estimated to have 8,000–10,000 armed combatants in Sri Lanka, with a core of trained fighters of about 3,000–6,000. The LTTE also has a significant overseas support structure for fund-raising, weapons procurement, and propaganda activities.


### LOCATION/AREA OF OPERATION

The Tigers control most of the northern and eastern coastal areas of Sri Lanka but have conducted operations throughout the island. Headquartered in northern Sri Lanka, LTTE leader Velupillai Prabhakaran established an extensive network of checkpoints and informants to keep track of any outsiders who enter the group's area of control.


### EXTERNAL AID

The LTTE's overt organizations support Tamil separatism by lobbying foreign governments and the United Nations. The LTTE also uses its international contacts to procure weapons, communications, and any other equipment and supplies it needs. The LTTE exploits large Tamil communities in North America, Europe, and Asia to obtain funds and supplies for its fighters in Sri Lanka, often through false claims or extortion.

## MUJAHEDIN-E KHALQ ORGANIZATION

### OTHER NAMES

National Liberation Army of Iran (NLA, the militant wing of the MEK)
People's Mujahedin of Iran (PMOI)
National Council of Resistance (NCR)
Muslim Iranian Student's Society (front organization used to garner financial support)

### DESCRIPTION

The Mujahedin-e Khalq Organization (MEK or MKO) philosophy mixes Marxism and Islam. Formed in the 1960s, the organization was expelled from Iran after the Islamic Revolution in 1979, and its primary support used to come from the Iraqi regime of Saddam Hussein. Its history is studded with anti-Western attacks and terrorist attacks on the interests of the clerical regime in Iran and abroad. The MEK now advocates a secular Iranian regime.

### ACTIVITIES

The MEK worldwide campaign against the Iranian government stresses propaganda and occasionally uses terrorist violence. During the 1970s, the MEK killed several U.S. military personnel and U.S. civilians working on defense projects in Tehran. It supported the takeover in 1979 of the U.S. Embassy in Tehran. In 1981, the MEK planted bombs in the head office of the Islamic Republic Party and the premier's office, killing about 70 high-ranking Iranian officials, including Chief Justice Ayatollah Mohammad Beheshti, President Mohammad-Ali Rajaei, and Premier Mohammad-Javad Bahonar. In 1991, it assisted the government of Iraq in suppressing the Shia and Kurdish uprisings in northern and southern Iraq. Since then, the MEK has continued to perform internal security services for the government of Iraq. In April 1992, it conducted attacks on Iranian embassies in 13 different countries, demonstrating the group's ability to mount large-scale operations overseas. In recent years, the MEK targeted key military officers and assassinated the deputy chief of the Armed Forces General Staff in April 1999. In April 2000, the MEK attempted to assassinate the commander of the Nasr Headquarters—the interagency board responsible for coordinating policies on Iraq. The normal pace of anti-Iranian operations increased during Operation Great Bahman in February 2000 when the group launched a dozen attacks against Iran. In 2000 and 2001, the MEK was involved regularly in mortar attacks and hit-and-run raids on Iranian military and law enforcement units, and government buildings near the Iran–Iraq border. Since the end of the Iran–Iraq War, tactics along the border garnered few military gains and have become commonplace. MEK insurgent activities in Tehran constitute the biggest security concern for the Iranian leadership. In February 2000, for example, the MEK attacked the leadership complex in Tehran that houses the offices of the supreme leader and president.

### STRENGTH

The MEK has several thousand fighters located on bases scattered throughout Iraq and armed with tanks, infantry fighting vehicles, and artillery. The MEK also has an overseas support structure. Most of the fighters are organized in the MEK's NLA.

## Location/Area of Operation

In the 1980s, the MEK's leaders were forced by Iranian security forces to flee to France. When they resettled in Iraq in 1987, the group conducted internal security operations in support of the government of Iraq. In the mid-1980s, the group did not mount terrorist operations in Iran at a level similar to its activities in the 1970s, but by the 1990s, the MEK claimed credit for an increasing number of operations in Iran.

## External Aid

Beyond past support from Iraq, the MEK uses front organizations to solicit contributions from expatriate Iranian communities.

# NATIONAL LIBERATION ARMY (ELN)—COLOMBIA

## Description

The ELN is a Marxist insurgent group formed in 1965 by urban intellectuals inspired by Fidel Castro and Che Guevara. The group began a dialogue with Colombian officials in 1999 following a campaign of mass kidnappings—each involving at least one U.S. citizen—to demonstrate its strength and continuing viability, and to force the Pastrana administration to negotiate. Peace talks between Bogotá and the ELN, started in 1999, continued sporadically through 2001 until Bogotá broke them off in August. Talks resumed in Havana, Cuba, by year's end.

## Activities

ELN activities include kidnapping, hijacking, bombing, extortion, and guerrilla wars. The group has modest conventional military capability. It annually conducts hundreds of kidnappings for ransom, often targeting foreign employees of large corporations, especially in the petroleum industry. It frequently assaults the energy infrastructure and has inflicted major damage on pipelines and the electric distribution network.

## Strength

The ELN has about 3000–5000 armed combatants and an unknown number of active supporters.

## Location/Area of Operation

ELN members can mostly be found in rural and mountainous areas of north, northeast, and southwest Colombia and Venezuela border regions.

## External Aid

Cuba provides some medical care and political consultation.

# PALESTINE ISLAMIC JIHAD

## Description

The Palestine Islamic Jihad (PIJ) originated among militant Palestinians in the Gaza Strip during the 1970s. The PIJ-Shiqaqi faction, currently led by Ramadan Shallah in Damascus, is the most active. The group is committed to the creation of an Islamic Palestinian state and the destruction of Israel through holy war. It also opposes moderate Arab governments that it believes were tainted by Western secularism.

## ACTIVITIES

PIJ activists conducted many attacks, including large-scale suicide bombings against Israeli civilian and military targets. The group increased its operational activity in 2001 during the intifada, claiming numerous attacks against Israeli interests. The group has not targeted U.S. interests and continues to confine its attacks to Israelis inside Israel and the territories.

## STRENGTH

Unknown

## LOCATION/AREA OF OPERATION

The group is located and operates primarily in Israel, the West Bank, Gaza Strip, and other parts of the Middle East including Lebanon and Syria, where the leadership is based.

## EXTERNAL AID

The PIJ receives financial assistance from Iran and limited logistic assistance from Syria.

## PALESTINE LIBERATION FRONT

### DESCRIPTION

The Palestine Liberation Front (PLF) broke away from the PFLP-GC in the mid-1970s. It later split again into pro-PLO, pro-Syrian, and pro-Libyan factions. The pro-PLO faction is led by Muhammad Abbas (Abu Abbas), who became a member of the PLO Executive Committee in 1984 but left it in 1991.

### ACTIVITIES

The Abu Abbas-led faction is known for aerial attacks against Israel. Abbas's group also was responsible for the attack in 1985 on the cruise ship *Achille Lauro* and the murder of U.S. citizen Leon Klinghoffer. A warrant for Abu Abbas's arrest is outstanding in Italy.

### STRENGTH

Unknown

### LOCATION/AREA OF OPERATION

The PLO faction was based in Tunisia until the *Achille Lauro* attack. Now, it is based in Iraq.

### EXTERNAL AID

The group receives support from a variety of Middle Eastern factions. In the past, it received support from Libya and Iraq.

# POPULAR FRONT FOR THE LIBERATION OF PALESTINE

## DESCRIPTION

The Popular Front for the Liberation of Palestine (PFLP) is a Marxist–Leninist group founded in 1967 by George Habash as a member of the PLO. He joined the Alliance of Palestinian Forces (APF) to oppose the Declaration of Principles signed in 1993 and suspended participation in the PLO. He then broke away from the APF, along with the Democratic Front for the Liberation of Palestine (DFLP), in 1996 over ideological differences. Then, he took part in meetings with Arafat's Fatah party and PLO representatives in 1999 to discuss national unity and the reinvigoration of the PLO, but continues to oppose current negotiations with Israel.

## ACTIVITIES

The PFLP committed many international terrorist attacks during the 1970s. Since 1978, the group has conducted attacks against Israeli or moderate Arab targets, including killing a settler and her son in December 1996. The PFLP stepped up operational activity in 2001, highlighted by the shooting death of the Israeli tourism minister in October to retaliate for Israel's killing of the PFLP leader in August.

## STRENGTH

The group has about 800 members.

## LOCATION/AREA OF OPERATION

Syria, Lebanon, Israel, the West Bank, and Gaza Strip

## EXTERNAL AID

The PFLP receives safe haven and some logistic assistance from Syria.

# POPULAR FRONT FOR THE LIBERATION OF PALESTINE-GENERAL COMMAND

## DESCRIPTION

The Popular Front for the Liberation of Palestine-General Command (PFLP-GC) split from the PFLP in 1968, claiming it wanted to focus more on fighting and less on politics. The group is violently opposed to Arafat's PLO. Led by Ahmad Jabril, a former captain in the Syrian Army, the PFLP-GC is closely tied to Syria and Iran.

## ACTIVITIES

The group carried out dozens of attacks in Europe and the Middle East during 1970–1980. The PFLP-GC is known for cross-border terrorist attacks into Israel using unusual means, such as hot-air balloons and motorized hang gliders. Now the primary focus is on guerrilla operations in southern Lebanon, and small-scale attacks in Israel, the West Bank, and Gaza Strip.

## STRENGTH

Several hundred members

LOCATION/AREA OF OPERATION

The PFLP-GC is headquartered in Damascus with bases in Lebanon.

EXTERNAL AID

The group receives support from Syria and financial support from Iran.

## AL-QAEDA

DESCRIPTION

Al-Qaeda was established by Osama bin Laden in the late 1980s to bring together Arabs who fought in Afghanistan against the Soviet Union. The group helped finance, recruit, transport, and train Sunni Islamic extremists for the Afghan resistance. The group's current goal is to establish a pan-Islamic caliphate throughout the world by working with allied Islamic extremist groups to overthrow regimes it deems "non-Islamic," and expel Westerners and non-Muslims from Muslim countries. Al-Qaeda issued a statement under the banner of "The World Islamic Front for Jihad Against the Jews and Crusaders" in February 1998, saying it was the duty of all Muslims to kill U.S. citizens—civilian or military—and their allies everywhere. The group merged with Egyptian Islamic Jihad (Al-Jihad) in June 2001.

ACTIVITIES

On September 11, 2001, 19 al-Qaeda suicide attackers hijacked and crashed four U.S. commercial jets, two into the World Trade Center in New York City, one into the Pentagon near Washington, DC, and the other one into a field in Shanksville, Pennsylvania, leaving about 3000 individuals dead or missing. The October 12, 2000 attack on the USS *Cole* in the port of Aden, Yemen, killing 17 U.S. Navy personnel and injuring another 39 was conducted by al-Qaeda. The group also conducted bombings in August 1998 of the U.S. embassies in Nairobi, Kenya, and Dar es Salaam, Tanzania, that killed at least 301 people and injured more than 5000 others. The group claimed to have shot down U.S. helicopters and killed U.S. servicemen in Somalia in 1993 and to have conducted three bombings that targeted U.S. troops in Aden, Yemen, in December 1992.

Al-Qaeda is linked to the following plans that were not carried out: to assassinate Pope John Paul II during his visit to Manila in late 1994, to kill President Clinton during a visit to the Philippines in early 1995, to conduct the midair bombing of a dozen U.S. transpacific flights in 1995, and to set off a bomb at Los Angeles International Airport in 1999. Al-Qaeda also plotted to carry out terrorist operations against U.S. and Israeli tourists visiting Jordan for millennial celebrations in late 1999. (Jordanian authorities thwarted the planned attacks and put 28 suspects on trial.) In December 2001, suspected al-Qaeda associate Richard Colvin Reid attempted to ignite a shoe bomb on a transatlantic flight from Paris to Miami.

STRENGTH

Al-Qaeda may have several thousand members and associates. The group also serves as a focal point or umbrella organization for a worldwide network that includes many Sunni Islamic extremist groups, some members of al-Gama'a al-Islamiyya, the Islamic Movement of Uzbekistan, and the Harakat ul-Mujahidin.

LOCATION/AREA OF OPERATION

Al-Qaeda has cells worldwide and is reinforced by its ties to Sunni extremist networks. Coalition attacks on Afghanistan since October 2001 dismantled the Taliban—al-Qaeda's protectors—and led to the capture, death, or dispersal of al-Qaeda operatives. Some al-Qaeda members at large probably will attempt to carry out future attacks against U.S. interests.

## EXTERNAL AID

Osama bin Laden, member of a billionaire family that owns the bin Laden Group construction empire, is said to have inherited tens of millions of dollars that he uses to help finance the group. Al-Qaeda also maintains money-making front businesses, solicits donations from like-minded supporters, and illicitly siphons funds from donations to Muslim charitable organizations. The efforts of the United States to block al-Qaeda funding have hampered al-Qaeda's ability to obtain money.

# REAL IRA

## OTHER NAMES

True IRA

## DESCRIPTION

Formed in early 1998 as a clandestine armed wing of the 32-County Sovereignty Movement, the Real IRA (RIRA) is a "political pressure group" dedicated to removing British forces from Northern Ireland and unifying Ireland. The 32-County Sovereignty Movement opposed Sinn Fein's adoption in September 1997 of the Mitchell principles of democracy and nonviolence, and opposed the amendment in December 1999 of Articles 2 and 3 of the Irish Constitution, which laid claim to Northern Ireland. Michael "Mickey" McKevitt, who left the IRA to protest its cease-fire, leads the group; Bernadette Sands-McKevitt, his wife, is a founder-member of the 32-County Sovereignty Movement, the political wing of the RIRA.

## ACTIVITIES

The RIRA conducts bombings, assassinations, and robberies. Many RIRA members are former IRA members who left that organization following the IRA's cease-fire, and they bring to the RIRA a wealth of experience in terrorist tactics and bomb making. Targets include British military and police in Northern Ireland, and Northern Ireland Protestant communities. The RIRA is linked to and understood to be responsible for the car bomb attack in Omagh, Northern Ireland on August 15, 1998, that killed 29 and injured 220 people. The group began to observe a cease-fire following Omagh but in 2000 and 2001 resumed attacks in Northern Ireland and on the UK mainland against targets such as the MI6 headquarters and the BBC.

## STRENGTH

The group has 100–200 activists plus possible limited support from IRA hardliners dissatisfied with the IRA's cease-fire and other republican sympathizers. British and Irish authorities arrested at least 40 members in the spring and summer of 2001 including leader McKevitt, who at the time of this writing is in prison in the Irish Republic awaiting trial for being a member of a terrorist organization and directing terrorist attacks.

## LOCATION/AREA OF OPERATION

Northern Ireland, Irish Republic, and Great Britain

## EXTERNAL AID

RIRA is suspected of receiving funds from sympathizers in the United States and of attempting to buy weapons from U.S. gun dealers. RIRA also is reported to have purchased sophisticated weapons from the Balkans. Three Irish nationals associated with RIRA were extradited from Slovenia to the United Kingdom and are awaiting trial on weapons procurement charges.

# REVOLUTIONARY ARMED FORCES OF COLOMBIA

## DESCRIPTION

Established in 1964 as the military wing of the Colombian Communist Party, the Revolutionary Armed Forces of Colombia (FARC) is Colombia's oldest, largest, most capable, and best-equipped Marxist insurgency. The FARC is governed by a secretariat, led by septuagenarian Manuel Marulanda, aka "Tirofijo," and six others, including senior military commander Jorge Briceno, aka "Mono Jojoy." The group is organized along military lines and includes several urban fronts. In 2001, the group continued a slow-moving peace negotiation process with the Pastrana administration that gained the group several concessions, including a demilitarized zone used as a venue for negotiations.

## ACTIVITIES

The FARC is responsible for bombings, murders, kidnapping, extortion, and hijacking, as well as guerrilla and conventional military actions against Colombian political, military, and economic targets. In March 1999, the FARC executed three U.S. Indian rights activists on Venezuelan territory after it kidnapped them in Colombia. Foreign citizens are often targets of FARC kidnapping for ransom. FARC has well-documented ties to narcotics traffickers, principally through the provision of armed protection.

## STRENGTH

FARC has about 9,000–12,000 armed combatants and an unknown number of supporters, mostly in rural areas.

## LOCATION/AREA OF OPERATION

FARC operates in Colombia with some activities—extortion, kidnapping, logistics, and R&R—and in Venezuela, Panama, and Ecuador.

## EXTERNAL AID

Cuba provides some medical care and political consultation.

# REVOLUTIONARY NUCLEI (FORMERLY ELA)

## OTHER NAMES

Revolutionary Cells

## DESCRIPTION

Revolutionary Nuclei (RN) emerged from a broad range of antiestablishment and anti-U.S./NATO/ European Union (EU) leftist groups active in Greece between 1995 and 1998. The group is believed to be the successor to or offshoot of Greece's most prolific terrorist group, Revolutionary People's Struggle (ELA), which has not claimed an attack since January 1995. Indeed, RN appeared to fill the void left by ELA, particularly as lesser groups faded from the scene. RN's few communiqués show strong similarities in rhetoric, tone, and theme to ELA proclamations. RN has not claimed an attack since November 2000.

## ACTIVITIES

Beginning operations in January 1995, the group claimed responsibility for some two dozen arson attacks and explosive low-level bombings targeting a range of U.S., Greek, and other European targets in Greece. In its most infamous and lethal attack to date, the group claimed responsibility for a bomb it detonated at the Intercontinental Hotel in April 1999 that killed a Greek woman and injured a Greek man. Its modus operandi includes warning calls of impending attacks, use of rudimentary timing devices, and strikes during the late evening-early morning hours. RN last attacked U.S. interests in Greece in November 2000 with two separate bombings against the Athens offices of Citigroup and the studio of a Greek–American sculptor. The group also detonated an explosive device outside the Athens offices of Texaco in December 1999. Greek targets included court and other government office buildings, private vehicles, and the offices of Greek firms involved in NATO-related defense contracts in Greece. Similarly, the group attacked European interests in Athens, including Barclays Bank in December 1998 and November 2000.

## STRENGTH

Group membership is believed to be small, probably drawing from the Greek militant leftist or anarchist milieu.

## LOCATION/AREA OF OPERATION

The primary area of operation is in the Athens metropolitan area.

## EXTERNAL AID

Unknown, but believed to be self-sustaining

# REVOLUTIONARY ORGANIZATION 17 NOVEMBER (17 NOVEMBER)

## DESCRIPTION

This is a radical leftist group established in 1975 and named for the student uprising in Greece in November 1973 that protested the military regime. It is anti-Greek, anti-United States, anti-Turkey, and anti-NATO and is committed to the ousting of U.S. bases, removal of Turkish military presence from Cyprus, and severing of Greece's ties to NATO and the EU.

## ACTIVITIES

Initial attacks were assassinations of senior U.S. officials and Greek public figures. The group added bombings in the 1980s. Since 1990, the group expanded targets to include EU facilities and foreign firms investing in Greece and added improvised rocket attacks to its methods. The most recent attack claimed was the murder of British Defense Attaché Stephen Saunders in June 2000.

STRENGTH

Unknown, but presumed to be small

LOCATION/AREA OF OPERATION

Athens, Greece

EXTERNAL AID

Unknown

# REVOLUTIONARY PEOPLE'S LIBERATION PARTY/FRONT (DHKP/C)

OTHER NAMES

Devrimci Sol (Revolutionary Left)
Dev Sol

DESCRIPTION

The group was originally formed in 1978 as Devrimci Sol, or Dev Sol, a splinter faction of the Turkish People's Liberation Party/Front. Renamed in 1994 after factional infighting, it espouses a Marxist ideology and is virulently anti-United States and anti-NATO. The group finances its activities chiefly through armed robberies and extortion.

ACTIVITIES

Since the late 1980s, the group has concentrated its attacks against current and retired Turkish security and military officials. The group began a new campaign against foreign interests in 1990. Members assassinated two U.S. military contractors and wounded a U.S. Air Force Officer to protest the Gulf War. It launched rockets at the U.S. Consulate in Istanbul in 1992. It assassinated a prominent Turkish businessman and two others in early 1996, its first significant terrorist act as DHKP/C. Turkish authorities thwarted a DHKP/C attempt in June 1999 to fire a light antitank weapon at the U.S. Consulate in Istanbul. The DHKP/C conducted its first suicide bombings, targeting Turkish police, in January and September 2001. A series of safe-house raids and arrests by Turkish police since 2000 has weakened the group significantly.

STRENGTH

Unknown

LOCATION/AREA OF OPERATION

The DHKP/C conducts attacks in Turkey, primarily in Istanbul. It raises funds in Western Europe.

EXTERNAL AID

Unknown

# SALAFIST GROUP FOR CALL AND COMBAT

## DESCRIPTION

The Salafist Group for Call and Combat (GSPC) splinter faction that began in 1996 eclipsed the GIA since approximately 1998 and is currently assessed to be the most effective remaining armed group inside Algeria. In contrast to the GIA, the GSPC gained popular support through its pledge to avoid civilian attacks inside Algeria (although, in fact, civilians have been attacked). Its adherents abroad appear to have largely co-opted the external networks of the GIA, active particularly throughout Europe, Africa, and the Middle East.

## ACTIVITIES

The GSPC continues to conduct operations aimed at government and military targets, primarily in rural areas. Such operations include false roadblocks and attacks against convoys transporting military, police, or other government personnel. According to press reporting, some GSPC members in Europe maintain contacts with other North African extremists sympathetic to al-Qaeda, a number of whom were implicated in terrorist plots during 2001.

## STRENGTH

Strength is generally unknown; there are probably several hundreds to several thousands inside Algeria.

## LOCATION/AREA OF OPERATION

Algeria

## EXTERNAL AID

Algerian expatriates and GSPC members abroad, many residing in Western Europe, provide financial and logistics support. In addition, the Algerian government accused Iran and Sudan of supporting Algerian extremists in previous years.

# SENDERO LUMINOSO

## OTHER NAMES

Shining Path

## DESCRIPTION

Former university professor Abimael Guzman formed Sendero Luminoso (SL) in the late 1960s, and his teachings created the foundation of SL's militant Maoist doctrine. In the 1980s, SL became one of the most ruthless terrorist groups in the western hemisphere—about 30,000 people have died since Shining Path took up arms in 1980. Its stated goal is to destroy existing Peruvian institutions and replace them with a communist peasant revolutionary regime. It also opposes any influence by foreign governments as well as by other Latin American guerrilla groups, especially the Tupac Amaru Revolutionary Movement (MRTA).

In 2001, the Peruvian National Police thwarted an SL attack against "an American objective," possibly the U.S. Embassy, when they arrested two Lima SL cell members. In addition, government authorities continued to arrest and prosecute active SL members, including Ruller Mazombite, aka

"Camarada Cayo," chief of the protection team of SL leader Macario Ala, aka "Artemio," and Evorcio Ascencios, aka "Camarada Canale," logistics chief of the Huallaga Regional Committee. Counterterrorist operations targeted pockets of terrorist activity in the Upper Huallaga River Valley and the Apurimac/Ene River Valley, where SL columns continued to conduct periodic attacks.

## ACTIVITIES

The SL has conducted indiscriminate bombing campaigns and selective assassinations. The group detonated explosives at diplomatic missions of several countries in Peru in 1990, which included an attempt to car bomb the U.S. Embassy in December. Peruvian authorities continued operations against the SL in 2001 in the countryside, where the SL conducted periodic raids on villages.

## STRENGTH

Membership is unknown but estimated to be 100–200 armed militants. SL's strength was vastly diminished by arrests and desertions.

## LOCATION/AREA OF OPERATION

Peru, with most activity in rural areas

## EXTERNAL AID

None

# UNITED SELF-DEFENSE FORCES OF COLOMBIA

## DESCRIPTION

The United Self-Defense Forces of Colombia (AUC)—commonly referred to as the paramilitaries—is an umbrella organization formed in April 1997 to consolidate most local and regional paramilitary groups, each with the mission to protect economic interests and combat insurgents locally. The AUC—supported by economic elites, drug traffickers, and local communities lacking effective government security—claims its primary objective is to protect its sponsors from insurgents. The AUC now asserts itself as a regional and national counterinsurgent force. It is adequately equipped and armed, and reportedly pays its members a monthly salary. AUC political leader Carlos Castaño claimed that 70% of the AUC's operational costs are financed with drug-related earnings, the rest from "donations" from its sponsors.

## ACTIVITIES

AUC operations vary from assassinating suspected insurgent supporters to engaging guerrilla combat units. Colombian National Combat operations generally consist of raids and ambushes directed against suspected insurgents. The AUC generally avoids engagements with government security forces and actions against U.S. personnel or interests.

## STRENGTH

The strength of the AUC is estimated to be 6000–8150, including former military and insurgent personnel.

## Location/Area of Operation

AUC forces are strongest in the northwest in the Antioquia, Córdoba, Sucre, and Bolívar departments. Since 1999, the group has shown a growing presence in other northern and southwestern departments. Clashes between the AUC and the FARC insurgents in Putumayo in 2000 demonstrated the range of the AUC to contest insurgents throughout Colombia.

## External Aid

None

# Appendix E: Explosive Materials

The Bureau of Alcohol, Tobacco, Firearms, and Explosives (ATF) published a notice in the Federal Register in January 2010 containing the list of 237 explosive materials that are subject to federal law and implementing regulations.

This list covers not only explosives but also blasting agents and detonators, all of which are defined as explosive materials in the United States Code chapter regulating the importation, manufacture, distribution, receipt, and storage of explosive materials. The Department of Justice must publish and revise the explosives list annually, pursuant to 18 U.S.C. 841.

The 2009 list does not contain any new terms. However, ammonium perchlorate composite propellant (APCP) has been removed. As a result of a court decision in March 2009, APCP is no longer regulated under federal explosive laws.

The list is comprehensive, but is not all-inclusive. Therefore, an explosive material may not be on the list but may still be within the coverage of the law if it meets the statutory definitions. Some of the explosive materials on the list include dynamite, black powder, pellet powder, safety fuses, squibs, detonating cord, display fireworks, igniter cord, and igniters.

ATF has jurisdiction for enforcement in Title 18 U.S. Code, chapter 40, as amended by the Safe Explosives Act in 2002. As such, ATF is the federal agency primarily responsible for administrating and enforcing the regulatory and criminal provisions of federal laws pertaining to destructive devices (e.g., bombs) and explosives.

ATF has the experience and ability to detect, prevent, protect against, and respond to explosives incidents resulting from improvised explosive devices (IEDs). Since 1978, ATF has investigated more than 25,000 bombings and attempted bombings, more than 1000 accidental explosions, and more than 22,000 incidents involving recovered explosives or explosive devices. The majority of these bombings involved the use of IEDs. ATF is the primary source of explosives investigative and training support throughout the world.

As of January 2, 2011, the 2009 List of Explosive Materials can be viewed at http://www.atf.gov/regulations-rulings/rulemakings/general-notices.html.[*]

## COMMERCE IN EXPLOSIVES

Pursuant to 18 U.S.C. 841(d) and 27 CFR 555.23, the department must publish and revise at least annually in the Federal Register a list of explosives determined to be within the coverage of 18 U.S.C. 841 et seq. The list covers not only explosives but also blasting agents and detonators, all of which are defined as explosive materials in 18 U.S.C. 841(c). As a result of a recent court decision, APCP is no longer regulated under the federal explosives laws. Therefore, APCP has been removed from the list of explosives. In addition, the department is revising the list to include a parenthetical text after "ammonium perchlorate explosive mixtures" to clarify that this term excludes APCP.

The list is intended to include any and all mixtures containing any of the materials on the list. Materials constituting blasting agents are marked by an asterisk. While the list is comprehensive, it is not all-inclusive. The fact that an explosive material is not on the list does not mean that it is not within the coverage of the law if it otherwise meets the statutory definitions in 18 U.S.C. 841. Explosive materials are listed alphabetically by their common names followed, where applicable, by chemical names and synonyms in brackets.

---

[*] For further information, contact Arson and Explosives Programs Division, Bureau of Alcohol, Tobacco and Firearms, 650 Massachusetts Avenue, NW, Washington, DC, 20226.

The department has not added any new terms to the list of explosive materials. However, APCP has been removed from the list of explosive materials. On March 16, 2009, the United States District Court for the District of Columbia vacated the ATF classification of APCP as an explosive as defined under 18 U.S.C. 841(d), Tripoli Rocketry Ass'n, Inc. v. ATF, No. 00-0273 (March 16, 2009 Order). As a result of the court's decision, APCP is no longer regulated under the federal explosives laws at 18 U.S.C., chapter 40. Accordingly, APCP has been removed from the list of explosive materials. In addition, the department is revising the list to include a parenthetical text after "ammonium perchlorate explosive mixtures" to clarify that the term excludes APCP.

# A

Acetylides of heavy metals
Aluminum-containing polymeric propellant
Aluminum ophorite explosive
Amatex
Amatol
Ammonal
*Ammonium nitrate explosive mixtures
Ammonium perchlorate explosive mixtures (excluding ammonium perchlorate composite propellant [APCP])
Ammonium perchlorate having particle size less than 15 microns
Ammonium picrate [picrate of ammonia, Explosive D]
Ammonium salt lattice with isomorphously substituted inorganic salts
*ANFO [ammonium nitrate-fuel oil]
Aromatic nitro-compound explosive mixtures
Azide explosives

# B

Baranol
Baratol
BEAF [1,2-bis (2,2-difluoro-2-nitroacetoxyethane)]
Black powder
Black powder–based explosive mixtures
*Blasting agents, nitro-carbo-nitrates, including non-cap-sensitive slurry and water gel explosives
Blasting caps
Blasting gelatin
Blasting powder
BTNEC [bis (trinitroethyl) carbonate]
BTNEN [bis (trinitroethyl) nitramine]
BTTN [1,2,4-butanetriol trinitrate]
Bulk salutes
Butyl tetryl

# C

Calcium nitrate explosive mixture
Cellulose hexanitrate explosive mixture
Chlorate explosive mixtures
Composition A and variations
Composition B and variations

Explosive organic nitrate mixtures
Explosive powders

## F

Flash powder
Fulminate of mercury
Fulminate of silver
Fulminating gold
Fulminating mercury
Fulminating platinum
Fulminating silver

## G

Gelatinized nitrocellulose
Gem-dinitro aliphatic explosive mixtures
Guanyl nitrosamino guanyl tetrazene
Guanyl nitrosamino guanylidene hydrazine
Guncotton

## H

Heavy metal azides
Hexanite
Hexanitrodiphenylamine
Hexanitrostilbene
Hexogen [RDX]
Hexogene or octogene and a nitrated N-methylaniline
Hexolites
HMTD [hexamethylenetriperoxidediamine]
HMX [cyclo-1,3,5,7-tetramethylene 2,4,6,8-tetranitramine; octogen]
Hydrazinium nitrate/hydrazine/aluminum explosive system
Hydrazoic acid

## I

Igniter cord
Igniters
Initiating tube systems

## K

KDNBF [potassium dinitrobenzo-furoxane]

## L

Lead azide
Lead mannite
Lead mononitroresorcinate
Lead picrate
Lead salts, explosive
Lead styphnate [styphnate of lead, lead trinitroresorcinate]

Liquid nitrated polyol and trimethylolethane
Liquid oxygen explosives

# M

Magnesium ophorite explosives
Mannitol hexanitrate
MDNP [methyl 4,4-dinitropentanoate]
MEAN [monoethanolamine nitrate]
Mercuric fulminate
Mercury oxalate
Mercury tartrate
Metriol trinitrate
Minol-2 [40% TNT, 40% ammonium nitrate, 20% aluminum]
MMAN [monomethylamine nitrate]; methylamine nitrate
Mononitrotoluene-nitroglycerin mixture
Monopropellants

# N

NIBTN [nitroisobutametriol trinitrate]
Nitrate explosive mixtures
Nitrate sensitized with gelled nitroparaffin
Nitrated carbohydrate explosive
Nitrated glucoside explosive
Nitrated polyhydric alcohol explosives
Nitric acid and a nitro aromatic compound explosive
Nitric acid and carboxylic fuel explosive
Nitric acid explosive mixtures
Nitro aromatic explosive mixtures
Nitro compounds of furane explosive mixtures
Nitrocellulose explosive
Nitroderivative of urea explosive mixture
Nitrogelatin explosive
Nitrogen trichloride
Nitrogen tri-iodide
Nitroglycerine [NG, RNG, nitro, glyceryl trinitrate, trinitroglycerine]
Nitroglycide
Nitroglycol [ethylene glycol dinitrate, EGDN]
Nitroguanidine explosives
Nitronium perchlorate propellant mixtures
Nitroparaffins explosive grade and ammonium nitrate mixtures
Nitrostarch
Nitro-substituted carboxylic acids
Nitrourea

# O

Octogen [HMX]
Octol [75% HMX, 25% TNT]
Organic amine nitrates
Organic nitramines

# P

PBX [plastic-bonded explosives]
Pellet powder
Penthrinite composition
Pentolite
Perchlorate explosive mixtures
Peroxide-based explosive mixtures
PETN [nitropentaerythrite, pentaerythrite tetranitrate, pentaerythritol tetranitrate]
Picramic acid and its salts
Picramide
Picrate explosives
Picrate of potassium explosive mixtures
Picratol
Picric acid (manufactured as an explosive)
Picryl chloride
Picryl fluoride
PLX [95% nitromethane, 5% ethylenediamine]
Polynitro aliphatic compounds
Polyolpolynitrate-nitrocellulose explosive gels
Potassium chlorate and lead sulfocyanate explosive
Potassium nitrate explosive mixtures
Potassium nitroaminotetrazole
Pyrotechnic compositions
PYX [2,6-bis(picrylamino)] 3,5-dinitropyridine

# R

RDX [cyclonite, hexogen, T4, cyclo-1,3,5-trimethylene-2,4,6-trinitramine; hexahydro-1,3,5-trinitro-
    S-triazine]

# S

Safety fuse
Salts of organic amino sulfonic acid explosive mixture
Salutes (bulk)
Silver acetylide
Silver azide
Silver fulminate
Silver oxalate explosive mixtures
Silver styphnate
Silver tartrate explosive mixtures
Silver tetrazene
Slurried explosive mixtures of water, inorganic oxidizing salt, gelling agent, fuel, and sensitizer
    (cap sensitive)
Smokeless powder
Sodatol
Sodium amatol
Sodium azide explosive mixture
Sodium dinitro-ortho-cresolate
Sodium nitrate explosive mixtures
Sodium nitrate-potassium nitrate explosive mixture

Sodium picramate
Special fireworks
Squibs
Styphnic acid explosives

## T

Tacot [tetranitro-2,3,5,6-dibenzo-1,3a,4,6a tetrazapentalene]
TATB [triaminotrinitrobenzene]
TATP [triacetonetriperoxide]
TEGDN [triethylene glycol dinitrate]
Tetranitrocarbazole
Tetrazene [tetracene, tetrazine, 1(5-tetrazolyl)-4-guanyl tetrazene hydrate]
Tetrazole explosives
Tetryl [2,4,6-tetranitro-N-methylaniline]
Tetrytol
Thickened inorganic oxidizer salt slurried explosive mixture
TMETN [trimethylolethane trinitrate]
TNEF [trinitroethyl formal]
TNEOC [trinitroethylorthocarbonate]
TNEOF [trinitroethylorthoformate]
TNT [trinitrotoluene, trotyl, trilite, triton]
Torpex
Tridite
Trimethylol ethyl methane trinitrate composition
Trimethylolthane trinitrate-nitrocellulose
Trimonite
Trinitroanisole
Trinitrobenzene
Trinitrobenzoic acid
Trinitrocresol
Trinitro-meta-cresol
Trinitronaphthalene
Trinitrophenetol
Trinitrophloroglucinol
Trinitroresorcinol
Tritonal

## U

Urea nitrate

## W

Water-bearing explosives having salts of oxidizing acids and nitrogen bases, sulfates, or sulfamates
Water-in-oil emulsion explosive compositions

## X

Xanthomonas hydrophilic colloid explosive mixture

# Appendix F: Homeland Security State Contact List

Contact information, telephone numbers, and Internet website details are primarily from the official White House website as of January 9, 2011. It should be noted that many states have consolidated intelligence or fusion centers for the purposes of homeland security as well as Joint Terrorism Task Forces (JTTF). The contact information outlined below may not be an investigative point-of-contact.

## STATE HOMELAND SECURITY CONTACTS

*Alabama*
James M. Walker Jr.
Director of Homeland Security
Alabama Department of Homeland Security
PO Box 304115
Montgomery, AL 36130-4115
334-956-7250
Main fax: 334-223-1120
http://www.dhs.alabama.gov

*Alaska*
John Madden
Deputy Director
Office of Homeland Security
Department of Military and Veteran Affairs
PO Box 5750
Bldg 4900, Suite B-214
Fort Richardson, AK 99505
907-428-7062
www.ak-prepared.com/homelandsecurity

*Arizona*
Gilbert M. Orrantia
Director
Arizona Department of Homeland Security
1700 West Washington St, #210
Phoenix, AZ 85007
602-542-7030

*Arkansas*
Dave Maxwell
Director
Department of Emergency Management
Bldg 9501
Camp Joseph
North Little Rock, AR 72119-9600
Conway, AR 72033

501-730-6700
www.adem.arkansas.gov

*California*
Matt Bettenhausen
Director of Office of Homeland Security
State Capitol, 1st Floor
Sacramento, CA 95814
916-324-8908
http://www.homeland.ca.gov

*Colorado*
Larry D. Trujillo
State Homeland Security Coordinator
9195 East Mineral Ave, #200
Centennial, CO 80112
720-852-6602
http://www.colorado.gov

*Connecticut*
Peter Boynton, Commissioner
Department of Emergency Management and Homeland Security
25 Sigourney St., 6th Floor
Hartford, CT 06106-5042
860-256-0800 or 800-397-8876
http://www.ct.gov/demhs/

*Delaware*
Kurt Reuther
Delaware Homeland Security Advisor
Department of Safety and Homeland Security
303 Transportation Circle
PO Box 818
Dover, DE 19903
302-744-2680
http://dshs.delaware.gov/

*District of Columbia*
Millicent Williams, Director
Homeland Security & Emergency Management Agency
2720 Martin Luther King Jr Ave, SE
Washington, DC, 20032
202-727-4036
http://www.dcema.dc.gov/dcema/site/default.asp

*Florida*
Mark Perez, Homeland Security Advisor
PO Box 1489
Tallahassee, FL 32302-1489
850-410-8300
www.fdle.state.fl.us/osi/DomesticSecurity/

*Georgia*
Charlie English, Homeland Security Director
PO Box 18055, Bldg 2
Atlanta, GA 30316-0055
404-635-7000
www.gema.state.ga.us

*Hawaii*
MG Robert Lee, Adjutant General
3949 Diamond Head Rd.
Honolulu, HI 96816-4495
808-733-4246
www.scd.state.hi.us

*Idaho*
COL Bill Shawver
Director
Bureau of Homeland Security
4040 West Guard St, Bldg 600
Boise, ID 83705-5004
208-422-3040
www.state.id.us/government/executive.html

*Illinois*
Joseph Klinger
Director
Illinois Emergency Management Agency
2200 South Dirksen Pkwy
Springfield, IL 62703
217-557-6225

*Indiana*
Joe Wainscott
Executive Director
Indiana Department of Homeland Security
302 W. Washington St, Rm. E-208
Indianapolis, IN 46204
317-232-3986
http://www.in.gov/sema/

*Iowa*
Lt. Gov. Patty Judge, Homeland Security Advisor
Hoover State Office Bldg
1305 E Walnut St
Des Moines, IA 50319
515-725-3231
www.iowahomelandsecurity.org

*Kansas*
MG Tod Bunting
Homeland Security Advisor

2800 SW Topeka Blvd
Topeka, KS 66611-1287
785-274-1001

*Kentucky*
Thomas L. Preston
Director
Office of Homeland Security
200 Metro St
Frankfort, KY 40622
502-564-2081
http://homelandsecurity.ky.gov/

*Louisiana*
Mark Cooper
Director
Governor's Office of Homeland Security and Emergency Preparedness
7667 Independence Blvd
Baton Rouge, LA 70806
225-925-7500
www.ohsep.louisiana.gov

*Maine*
BG John Libby, Adjutant General
Department of Defense, Veterans & Emergency Management
33 State House Station, Camp Keyes
Augusta, ME 04333-0001
Normal working hours: 207-626-4205

*Maryland*
Andrew Lauland
Homeland Security Advisor
The Jeffrey Building
16 Francis St
Annapolis, MD 21401
www.gov.state.md.us/homelandsecurity.html

*Massachusetts*
Kurt Schwartz
Undersecretary of Homeland Security
Executive Office of Public Safety
1 Ashburton Place, Rm. 2133
Boston, MA 02108
617-727-7775

*Michigan*
Kyle Bowman
Homeland Security Advisor
713 South Harrison Rd.
E. Lansing, MI 48823
517-336-2686
www.michigan.gov/homeland/

*Minnesota*
Michael Campion
Commissioner of Public Safety, Director, Homeland Security
DPS, North Central Life Tower
445 Minnesota St., St. 1000
St. Paul, MN 55101
651-215-1527
http://www.hsem.state.mn.us/

*Mississippi*
Jay Ledbetter
Director
Office of Homeland Security
PO Box 958
Jackson, MS 39296-4501
601-346-1499
www.homelandsecurity.ms.gov

*Missouri*
John Britt
Director
Missouri Office of Homeland Security
PO Box 749
Jefferson City, MO 65102
573-522-3007
www.dps.mo.gov/homelandsecurity/

*Montana*
Ed Tinsley
Homeland Security Advisor
MT Disaster & Emergency Services Division
1956 MT Majo St
PO Box 4789
Fort Harrison, MT 59636
406-841-3911
http://dma.mt.gov

*Nebraska*
Lt. Gov. Rick Sheehy
PO Box 94848
Lincoln, NE 68509-4848
402-471-2256
rick.sheehy@email.state.ne.us

*Nevada*
Frank Siracusa
Homeland Security Advisor
2478 Fairview Drive
Carson City, NV 89711
775-684-5678

*New Hampshire*
Christopher Pope
State Homeland Security Advisor
Director, Office of Emergency Management
10 Hazen Drive
Concord, NH 03305
603-271-6911

*New Jersey*
Charlie McKenna
Director
New Jersey Homeland Security and Preparedness
PO Box 091
Trenton, NJ 08625
609-584-4000
www.njhomelandsecurity.gov

*New Mexico*
John Wheeler, Secretary
New Mexico Department of Homeland Security & Emergency Management
PO Box 1628
Santa Fe, NM 87507-1628
505-476-1051

*New York*
Deputy Secretary for Public Safety
Governor's Office
State of New York
Executive Chamber
State Capitol
Room 229
Albany, NY 12224
Phone: 518-474-3522
Fax: 518-473-9932

*North Carolina*
Reuben Young, Secretary
Department of Crime Control and Public Safety
4701 Mail Service Center
Raleigh, NC 27699
919-733-2126
www.nccrimecontrol.org

*North Dakota*
Greg Wilz
Director
Division of Homeland Security
Department of Emergency Services
PO Box 5511
Bismarck, ND 58506
701-328-8100
www.nd.gov/des/

*Ohio*
Bill Vedra Jr.
Director of Homeland Security
1970 W. Broad St.
Columbus, OH 43223-1102
614-466-3383
www.homelandsecurity.ohio.gov

*Oklahoma*
Kerry Pettingill
Director
Oklahoma Office of Homeland Security
PO Box 11415
Oklahoma City, OK 73136-0415
405-425-7296
okohs@dps.state.ok.us
www.homelandsecurity.ok.gov/

*Oregon*
MG Raymond F. Rees
The Adjutant General, Oregon Homeland Security Advisor
Oregon Military Department
PO Box 14350
Salem, OR 97309-5047
503-584-3991
http://www.oregon.gov/OMD/

*Pennsylvania*
Robert French
Director
Pennsylvania Emergency Management Agency/Homeland Security Advisor
2605 Interstate Drive
Harrisburg, PA 17110
717-651-2715
www.homelandsecurity.state.pa.us

*Puerto Rico*
Max Perez-Bouret
Homeland Security Advisor
La Fortaleza
PO Box 9020082
San Juan, PR 00902-0082
787-977-7730/7731

*Rhode Island*
Robert Bray, Homeland Security Advisor
645 New London Ave
Cranston, RI 02920
Phone: 401-275-4333
Fax: 401-944-1891
Robert.bray@us.army.mil

*South Carolina*
Reginald Lloyd
Chief
S.C. Law Enforcement Division (SLED)
4400 Broad River Run Rd.
Columbia, SC 29210
803-896-7001

*South Dakota*
James Carpenter
Director
Office of Homeland Security
118 West Capitol Ave
Pierre, SD 57501
605-773-3450

*Tennessee*
Dave Mitchell
Commissioner of Safety and Homeland Security
1150 Foster Ave
Nashville, TN 37243
615-251-5166
dave.mitchell@state.tn.us

*Texas*
Steve McCraw
Director
Office of Homeland Security
PO Box 12428
Austin, TX 78711
512-475-0645

*Utah*
Keith D. Squires
Deputy Commissioner
Department of Public Safety
4501 South 2700 West
PO Box 1411775
Salt Lake City, UT 84114-1775
801-965-4498
www.cem.utah.gov

*Vermont*
CAPT Christopher Reinfurt
Director
Department of Public Safety
103 South Main St
Waterbury, VT 05671-2101
802-241-5357
http://www.dps.state.vt.us/homeland/home_main.html

*Virginia*
Terri Suit
Assistant to the Governor for Commonwealth Preparedness
Patrick Henry Building
1111 East Broad St
Richmond, VA 23219
804-692-2595
Fax: 804-225-3882
For regular U.S. mail, please use the following address:
PO Box 1475
Richmond, VA 23218
http://www.ocp.virginia.gov/

*Washington*
MG Timothy J. Lowenberg
Adjutant General and Director
State Military Department
Washington Military Dept., Bldg 1
Camp Murray, WA 98430-5000
253-512-8201

*West Virginia*
James Spears, Secretary, Dept. of Military Affairs and Public Safety
State Capitol Complex, Bldg 6, Rm B-122
Charleston, WV 25305
304-558-3795

*Wisconsin*
BG Donald Dunbar
Homeland Security Advisor
PO Box 8111
Madison, WI 53707-8111
608-242-3000
homelandsecurity.wi.gov

*Wyoming*
Joe Moore
Director
Wyoming Office of Homeland Security
Herschler Bldg 1st Floor E
122 W. 25th St
Cheyenne, WY 82002-0001
307-777-4663
wyohomelandsecurity.state.wy.us/main.aspx

*Guam*
Frank T. Ishizaki
Homeland Security Advisor
PO Box 2950
Hagatna, GU 96932
671-475-9600/9602

*Northern Mariana Islands*
Patrick J. Tenorio
Special Advisor for Homeland Security
Caller Box 10007
Saipan, MP 96950
670-664-2280

*Virgin Islands*
Noel Smith
Homeland Security Advisor
USVI Emergency Management Agency
2 C Content, AQ Building
St. Thomas, VI 00802
340-774-2231

*American Samoa*
Mike Sala
Director
Department of Homeland Security
American Somoa Government
Pago Pago, AS 96799
011-684-633-2827

# Appendix G: Publication References

107th Congress, HR 3162
  Uniting and Strengthening America by Providing Appropriate Tools Required to Intercept and Obstruct Terrorism Act of 2001 (also known as the PATRIOT ACT of 2001).

Presidential Decision Directive-39
  This directive provides an unclassified synopsis of the U.S. national policy on terrorism and counterterrorism as laid out in Presidential Decision Directive-39 (PDD-39).

Presidential Decision Directive-62
  "Protection Against Unconventional Threats to the Homeland and Americans Overseas," dated May 22, 1998.

The National Strategy for Homeland Security: Office of Homeland Security (PDF)
  Office of Homeland Security, July 2002
  This document is the first national strategy for addressing homeland security issues in the United States. Topical material includes threats and vulnerability, organizing for a secure homeland, critical mission areas such as intelligence and warning, border and transportation security, domestic counterterrorism, protecting critical infrastructures and key assets, defending against catastrophic threats, and emergency preparedness and response.

The Country Report on Terrorism (formerly Patterns of Global Terrorism)
  United States Department of State, published each year since 1993
  This document provides a chronological breakdown and dates of significant terrorist incidents as well as excerpts of the terrorist activity that took place and the locations.

The National Strategy for the Physical Protection of Critical Infrastructures and Key Assets (PDF)
  White House, published in February 2003
  This document identifies the road ahead for a core mission area identified in the President's National Strategy for Homeland Security. It covers cross-sector priorities, securing critical infrastructures and protecting key assets.

National Strategy for Combating Terrorism (PDF)
  White House, published February 2003
  This publication looks at the nature of the terrorist threat today and the availability of weapons of mass destruction. Reviewed are the goals and objectives of defeating, denying, and diminishing terrorist activities.

Project Megiddo—Federal Bureau of Investigation (FBI)
  "Project Megiddo" is the culmination of an FBI research initiative that analyzed the potential for extremist criminal activity in the United States by individuals or domestic groups who attach special significance to the year 2000.

The Directory of Homeland Security
  This directory provides contact information for more than 500 states and federal agencies. The following is provided: more than 150 pages of contacts, key local and federal personnel of each office, information on national organizations working on homeland security, agency-specific procurement information and contacts, helpful resources on selling products to the federal government, and a listing of selected companies, including names of homeland security directors, number of employees, homeland security products/services, and key personnel.

The documents listed below are readily available on various websites, but the majority can be found on the government's counterterrorism training website www.counterterrorismtraining.gov, which was based on a workgroup convened by the Department of Justice's Bureau of Justice Assistance.

Assessing the Threats (PDF)
   Center for Defense Information, 2002
   Examined in this document are threats to security and stability as perceived from four per-
      spectives: American, West European, Russian, and Northeast Asian. Chapters include
      information focusing on current security problems, weapons of mass destruction, and
      various terrorist activities.
Assessing Threats of Targeted Group Violence: Contributions from Social Psychology (PDF)
   National Threat Assessment Center, 1999
   Recent increases in domestic and international acts of extremist violence perpetrated against
      American citizens prompted an increased need for information. To help understand and
      evaluate the threat posed to U.S. targets by extremist groups and their individual mem-
      bers, this article summarizes research on group behavior and effects of group member-
      ship on individual behavior, proposes specific questions to consider in evaluating the
      risk for violence by groups and by individuals influenced by groups, and suggests further
      research needs.
Bioterrorism in the United States: Threat, Preparedness, and Response (PDF)
   Chemical and Biological Arms Control Institute, 2000
   Reviewed in this report are current programs that address the health and medical dimensions
      of the national response to bioterrorism in the United States.
Combating Terrorism: Assessing the Threat of Biological Terrorism (PDF)
   Rand, October 2001
   Presented in this report is testimony before the House Subcommittee on national security,
      veterans affairs, and international relations on biological terrorism, the feasibility and
      likelihood of terrorist groups using biological or chemical weapons, and what the govern-
      ment can and should do to deal with biological or chemical threats.
Combating Terrorism: Assessing Threats, Risk Management, and Establishing Priorities
   Center for Nonproliferation Studies, July 2000
   Presented in this report is testimony before the House Subcommittee on national security,
      veterans affairs, and international relations on terrorism threat assessments and risk-
      management strategies.
Cyber Protests: The Threat to the U.S. Information Infrastructure (PDF)
   National Infrastructure Protection Center, 2001
   Discussed in this report is the growing threat of cyber protests. Examples of recent events are
      provided.
Defending America: Asymmetric and Terrorist Attacks with Biological Weapons (PDF)
   Center for Strategic and International Studies, February 2001
   Explored in this report are various aspects of bioterrorism, including possible avenues of
      attack, potential threats, and possible solutions and preventative measures.
Defending America: Redefining the Conceptual Borders of Homeland Defense: The Risks and
   Effects of Indirect, Covert, Terrorist, and Extremist Attacks with Weapons of Mass
   Destruction (Final Draft) (PDF)
   Center for Strategic and International Studies, February 2001
   Examined in this report are the threat of terrorist attacks as well as more conventional means
      of attack (including how the two might overlap), the impact of technological change on
      homeland defense, and challenges for response planning.
Domestic Terrorism: Resources for Local Governments (PDF)
   National League of Cities, 2000
   This guidebook helps local decision makers to develop and implement domestic terrorism
      preparedness plans. It surveys national strategy and describes the resources available
      to state and local governments for planning, training and exercises, equipment, intelli-
      gence, and medical services.

Homeland Security: Key Elements of a Risk Management Approach (PDF)

    U.S. General Accounting Office, October 2001

    Described in this report are the key elements of a good risk-management approach, including assessment of threat, vulnerability, and criticality.

International Crime Threat Assessment

    President's International Crime Control Strategy, 1998

    This global assessment examines the threat posed by international crime to Americans and their communities, U.S. business and financial institutions, and global security and stability. It was prepared by a U.S. federal interagency working group in support of the President's International Crime Control Strategy.

Protective Intelligence and Threat Assessment Investigations: A Guide for State and Local Law Enforcement Officials (ASCII or PDF)

    National Institute of Justice, January 2000

    Described in this report are protective intelligence and threat-assessment investigations, focusing on protocols and procedures for law enforcement and security agencies responsible for protecting public persons and others who are vulnerable to targeted violence.

The Sociology and Psychology of Terrorism: Who Becomes a Terrorist and Why?

    Federal Research Division, Library of Congress, September 1999

    In an effort to help improve U.S. counterterrorism methods and policies, this study examines the types of individuals and groups that are prone to terrorism. The relevant literature with which to assess the current knowledge of the subject is examined, and psychological and sociological profiles of foreign terrorist individuals and selected groups are developed to use as case studies in assessing trends, motivations, and likely behavior, as well as in revealing vulnerabilities that would aid in combating terrorist groups and individuals.

The World Factbook

    Central Intelligence Agency

    The first classified factbook was published in August 1962, and the first unclassified version was published in June 1971. The 1975 Factbook was the first to be made available to the public with sales through the U.S. Government Printing Office (GPO). This publication provides statistical information on all the countries in the world, including data on populations, militaries, geography, governments, and transnational issues.

Patterns of Global Terrorism

    U.S. Department of State

    Examined in this report is the danger that terrorism poses to the world and efforts of the United States and international partners to defeat it. Aspects of the war on terrorism include diplomatic actions to form a global coalition against terror, cooperation among intelligence agencies, enhanced and cooperative law enforcement efforts, economic actions to deny financial support to terrorism, and military operations and assistance. The report is issued annually per congressional mandate. See the archive for reports from 1995 to 1993.

Political Violence Against Americans, 1998 (PDF)

    U.S. Department of State, 1998

    An overview of the political violence that American citizens and interests encountered abroad in 1998 is provided in this report. Incidents included were selected based on their seriousness, the use of unusual tactics or weapons, or the specific targeting of representatives of the United States.

Significant Incidents of Political Violence against Americans, 1997 (PDF)

    U.S. Department of State, 1997

    Provided in this report is an overview of the political violence that American citizens and interests encountered abroad in 1997.

The Sociology and Psychology of Terrorism: Who Becomes a Terrorist and Why?
Library of Congress, Federal Research Division, 1999
This report was prepared under an interagency agreement, and it provides approaches to terrorism analysis, general hypotheses of terrorism, psychology of the terrorist, and terrorist profiling based on research.

Terrorism in the United States, 1999 (PDF)
Federal Bureau of Investigation, 1999
This annual publication reviews the year's terrorist incidents, suspected terrorist incidents, arrests that prevented terrorist attacks, and other significant events. The report also describes 30-year feuds in domestic and international terrorism and the FBI's response.

1997 Bombing Incidents (PDF)
FBI Bomb Data Center
This bulletin provides statistics on criminal bombing incidents that occurred in the United States in 1997. Bombing data are presented by state, region, target, time of occurrence, and time of year.

Office for Domestic Preparedness (ODP) Information Clearinghouse
The ODP Information Clearinghouse is a searchable virtual library of publications and other resources on domestic preparedness, counterterrorism, and weapons of mass destruction. The clearinghouse also offers an electronic newsletter that provides e-updates on domestic preparedness news, such as conference or training events, new ODP programs, and new publications.

Homeland Security Act of 2002 (H.R. 5005)
Signed into law on November 25, 2002, this act restructures and strengthens the executive branch of the federal government to better meet the threat posed by terrorism. In establishing a new Department of Homeland Security, the act, for the first time, created a federal department with a primary mission that is to help prevent, protect against, and respond to acts of terrorism.

Protecting Democracy: States Respond to Terrorism
The National Conference of State Legislatures created web pages for counterterrorism legal issues of interest on the state level. Its state legislation database is updated monthly and is searchable by state, category, date/range, status, bill number/type, and keyword.

In addition to publications produced by governmental entities or those funded through the government, many leading authorities have authored a variety of crime/intelligence-based books. Below is a listing of analytical and intelligence publications that can be found through a variety of sources. This list is by no means complete but will enable one to obtain a firmer understanding of many of the tools and techniques available to analysts.

## CRIME/INTELLIGENCE ANALYSIS PUBLICATIONS

*The Enemy Within: Intelligence Gathering, Law Enforcement, and Civil Liberties in the Wake of September 11*, Stephen Schulhofer, Twentieth Century Fund, 2002, ISBN 0-87078-482-X.

*Defending the Homeland: Domestic Intelligence, Law Enforcement, and Security*, Dr. Jonathan White, Thomson/Wadsworth, 2004, ISBN 0-534-62169-4.

*Psychology of Intelligence Analysis*, Richards Heuer, Center for the Study of Intelligence (CIA), 1999, ISBN 1-929667-00-0.

*Applications in Criminal Analysis*, Marilyn Peterson, Praeger, 1998, ISBN 0-275-96468-X.

*Criminal Intelligence Analysis*, Paul Andrews and Marilyn Peterson, Palmer Enterprises, 1990, ISBN 0-912479-08-8.

*Crime Analysis: From First Report to Final Arrest*, Steven Gottlieb, Sheldon Arenberg, and Raj Singh, Alpha Publishing, 1998, ISBN 0-9634773-0-7.

*Introduction to Crime Analysis: Basic Resources for Criminal Justice Practice*, Deborah Osborne and Susan Wernicke, The Haworth Press, 2003, ISBN 0-7890-1867-3.

*Using Microsoft Office to Improve Law Enforcement Operations: Crime Analysis, Community Policing, and Investigations*, Mark Stallo, Analysis Consulting & Training Now, Inc., 2003, ISBN 1-59109-886-6.

*Mapping Crime: Principle and Practice*, Keith Harries, Ph.D, National Institute of Justice, December 1999, NCJ 178919.

*Applied Crime Analysis*, Karim Vellani and Joel Nahoun, Butterworth-Heinemann, 2001, ISBN 0750672951.

*Intelligence Analysis: A Target-Centric Approach*, Robert Clark, CQ Press, 2004, ISBN 1-56802-830-X.

*Law Enforcement Counterintelligence*, Lawrence Sulc, Varro Press, 1996, ISBN 1-888644-74-5.

*Geographical Profiling*, D. Kim Rossmo, CRC Press, 1999, ISBN 0849381290.

*Advanced Crime Mapping Topics*, National Law Enforcement and Corrections Technology Center (NLECTC), www.nlect.org/cmap/cmap_adv_topics_symposium.pdf.

The following books can be obtained through the Police Executive Research Forum:

*Crime Mapping Case Studies: Success in the Field* (Volume 1), Nancy LaVigne and Julie Wartell, eds., 1998, ISBN 1-878734-61-X, 150 pp.

*Problem-Oriented Policing: Crime-Specific Problems, Critical Issues and Making POP Work* (Volume 1), Anne Grant and Tara O'Conner Shelley, eds., 1998, ISBN 0-878734-60-1, 430 pp.

*Problem-Oriented Policing: Crime-Specific Problems, Critical Issues and Making POP Work* (Volume 2), Corina Solé Brito and Tracy Allan, eds., 1999, ISBN 0-878734-70-9, 412 pp.

*Mapping Across Boundaries: Regional Crime Analysis*, Nancy LaVigne and Julie Wartell, 2001, ISBN 1-878734-74-1, 130 pp.

*Crime Mapping Case Studies: Success in the Field* (Volume 2), Nancy LaVigne and Julie Wartell, eds., 2000, ISBN 1-878734-71-1, 140 pp.

*Police Crime Analysis Unit Handbook*, LEAA, National Institute of Law Enforcement and Criminal Justice 1973, 100 pp.

*Intelligence 2000: Revising the Basic Elements*, Marilyn B. Peterson, Bob Morehouse, and Richard Wright, eds. (LEIU), 2000, ISBN 0-970-6887-0-9, 245 pp.

*Information Management and Crime Analysis: Practitioner's Recipes for Success*, Melissa Miller Reuland, ed., 1997, ISBN 1-878734-48-2, 152 pp.

*Crime Analysis Through Computer Mapping*, Carolyn Rebecca Block, Margaret Dabdoub, and Suzanne Fregly, eds., 1995, ISBN 1-878734-34-2, 297 pp.

*Solving Crime and Disorder Problems: Current Issues, Police Strategies and Organizational Tactics*, Melissa Reuland, Corina Solé Brito, and Lisa Carroll, eds., 2001, ISBN 1-878734-75-x, 208 pp.

The following are free government publications available online in .pdf format:

Crime Analysis in the United States – 1/28/2002 (www.cops.usdoj.gov/mime/open.pdf?Item=790)

This is the final report of a COPS-funded study conducted by the University of South Alabama concerning the nation's law enforcement crime analysis units. Researchers conducted national telephone interviews, mail surveys, and site visits in order to develop a comprehensive understanding of the state of crime analysis in the United States. The researchers also provide recommendations on ways the local law enforcement agencies can enhance and develop their own crime analysis capabilities.

Crime Analysis in the United States: Findings and Recommendations–4/1/2003 (www.cops. usdoj.gov/mime/open.pdf?Item=855)

Although crime analysts have traditionally emphasized tactical analysis activities like iden- tifying offenders, community policing encourages more focus on strategic and problem analysis functions. This includes identifying the underlying conditions that give rise to community problems, developing responses to them that are linked to these analyses, assessing the effectiveness of responses, and developing long-term organizational opera- tional plans. This guide is a product of the findings of a study conducted by the University of South Alabama documenting the state of crime analysis in the nation's law enforce- ment agencies. These findings and recommendations are intended to inform police man- agers of the structural issues to address when considering a crime analysis function within a community policing context. They are also intended to expose the current limitations of crime analysis and the policies that those findings imply.

Problem Analysis in Policing–4/21/2003 (www.cops.usdoj.gov/mime/open.pdf?Item=847)

This report introduces and defines problem analysis and provides guidance on how problem ana- lysis can be integrated and institutionalized into modern policing practices. The 64-page report is not a "how-to" guide on conducting problem analysis, but is a summary of what problem analysis is, what skills and knowledge are necessary to conduct it, and how it can be advanced by the law enforcement community, academia, the federal government, and other institutions. The ideas and recommendations in this report come primarily from a 2-day forum conducted in February 2002 by the Police Foundation and the COPS Office that brought a group of aca- demics, practitioners, and policy makers together to discuss problem analysis and make recommendations for its progress. This report is a culmination of the concepts and ideas dis- cussed in the forum and it includes specific, relevant statements made by participants.

Problem-Solving Tips: A Guide to Reducing Crime and Disorder through Problem-Solving Partnerships–7/29/2002 (www.cops.usdoj.gov/mime/open.pdf?Item=441)

This guide is intended to serve as a reference for those in all stages of implementing the problem-solving approach. It contains insights into every stage of the process, most of which are drawn from the experience of law enforcement officers in the field, and relies on the SARA model: scanning, analyzing, response, and assessment of problems.

Tackling Crime and Other Public-Safety Problems: Case Studies in Problem-Solving (www.cops.usdoj.gov/default.asp?Item=583)

This compilation provides detailed descriptions of nearly 50 problem-oriented policing efforts dealing with a wide variety of specific crime and social disorder problems. Editor's notes are included after each section, detailing the noteworthy aspects of each effort.

The Law Enforcement Tech Guide: How to Plan, Purchase and Manage Technology (Successfully!)–9/1/2002 (www.cops.usdoj.gov/default.asp?Item=512)

The Law Enforcement Tech Guide presents best practices in strategic IT planning and procurement, reveals pitfalls to avoid, consolidates and expands on various sources of relevant information currently available, and reviews best practices to help create a user-friendly product that will provide law enforcement with the tools they need to suc- cessfully achieve their IT goals. Contact the U.S. Department of Justice Response Center at 800-421-6770 to obtain hard copies.

Using Analysis for Problem-Solving: A Guide Book for Law Enforcement–9/14/2001 (www.cops.usdoj.gov/mime/open.pdf?Item=342)

This guide provides law enforcement practitioners with a resource for conducting problem analysis. It summarizes many challenges of the analysis phase of the problem-solving process, identifies tools for analysis, and proposes tips for using each tool effectively. This book builds on the foundation presented in "Problem-Solving Tips: A Guide to Reducing Crime and Disorder Through Problem-Solving Partnerships," and comple- ments the "Problem-Oriented Guides for Police Series."

# Appendix H: Government Legislative References

The origins of the listed documents are from the http://www.counterterrorismtraining.gov website (unless otherwise noted). The counterterrorism training website documents are based on recommendations made by the Counter-Terrorism Training Coordination Working Group convened by the U.S. Department of Justice's (DOJ) Office of Justice Programs to examine the counterterrorism tools available to law enforcement and first responder communities.

Working group participants included the Bureau of Justice Assistance, the Executive Office for U.S. Attorneys, the Federal Bureau of Investigation, the Federal Emergency Management Agency, the Federal Law Enforcement Training Center, the National Institute of Justice, the Office for Domestic Preparedness, the Office of Community Oriented Policing Services, the Office of Homeland Security, the Office of Justice Programs, the Office of the Police Corps and Law Enforcement Education, the U.S. Customs Service, and the U.S. Department of Labor. Working group membership will expand to include other federal agencies and nongovernmental organizations that represent affected constituencies.

National Security Institute: Counter-Terrorism Legislation
> http://nsi.org/terrorism.html
> > This is a one-stop shop for links to counterterrorism legislation, executive orders, terrorism facts, terrorism precautions, and related sites.

Code of Federal Regulation-28 CFR Part 23
> http://www.iir.com/28cfr/guideline.htm and www.iir.com/28cfr
> > This provides complete text and guidelines from the Institute for Intergovernmental Research.

United States Code Title 18—Crimes and Criminal Procedure
> http://www.access.gpo.gov/uscode/title18/title18.html and http://uscode.house.gov/usc.htm
> > A complete detailed listing of guidelines and procedures for a wide array of crimes in five parts: (1) covering crimes, (2) criminal procedures, (3) prisons and prisoners, (4) correction of youthful offenders, and (5) immunity of witnesses. Chapters cover a wide range of material, including biological and chemical weapons, terrorism, and sabotage.

Cyber Security Research and Development Act (H.R. 3394, Public Law 107–305)
> Signed into law on November 27, 2002, this legislation will establish computer security research centers and fellowship programs through the National Science Foundation and the National Institute of Standards and Technology.

Effective Counterterrorism Act of 1996 (H.R. 3071)
> Signed into law on April 24, 1996 (as S.735, Public Law No. 104–132), this bill sets penalties for providing terrorist organizations with material support, expands federal jurisdiction over bomb threats, adds terrorism offenses to the money laundering statute, and establishes or increases other penalties related to acts of terrorism. It also authorizes funding for specialized training or equipment to enhance the capability of metropolitan fire and emergency service departments to respond to terrorist attacks.

Foreign Intelligence Surveillance Act of 1978 (FISA) (U.S. Code Title 50, Chapter 36)
> Under a November 18, 2002, FISA ruling by an appeals panel of the U.S. Foreign Intelligence Surveillance Court of Review, police were given broader power in the use of surveillance against terror and espionage suspects. This action affirms the implementation of new U.S.

Department of Justice procedures that allow easier information access between federal domestic police agencies and intelligence agencies.

Homeland Security Act of 2002 (H.R. 5005)

Signed into law on November 25, 2002, this act restructures and strengthens the executive branch of the federal government to better meet the threat posed by terrorism. In establishing a new Department of Homeland Security, the act, for the first time, creates a federal department with a primary mission that will be to help prevent, protect against, and respond to acts of terrorism.

Illegal Immigration Reform and Immigrant Responsibility Act of 1996. Program to Collect Information Relating to Nonimmigrant Foreign Students and Other Exchange Program Participants (Public Law No. 104–208, Section 641)

A final rule promulgated under this law established the Student and Exchange Visitor Information System (SEVIS), an Internet reporting and tracking system that will track "F," "M," and "J" visa participants from the time they receive their documentation until they graduate or leave school, or conclude or leave their programs. Schools had until January 30, 2003, to enter data on new, nonimmigrant students and until August 1, 2003, to complete entries on current students. This information will be available to law enforcement, school officials, and certain U.S. State Department, and Immigration and Naturalization Service (INS) personnel.

Immigration and Nationality Act of 1952 (U.S. Code Title 8)

The U.S. INS asked state and local police to voluntarily arrest aliens who violated criminal provisions of the U.S. Immigration and Nationality Act, or civil provisions that render an alien deportable and who are wanted as recorded by the National Crime Information Center. The National Security Entry-Exit Registration System Fact Sheet details the purpose and procedures called for by the INS National Security Entry-Exit Registration System. On December 6, 2002, the INS issued a statement emphasizing the registration requirements for visiting foreign nationals from the 18 countries affected. On December 18, 2002, the INS updated special registration requirements to include certain nonimmigrants from Pakistan and Saudi Arabia.

Maritime Transportation Security Act of 2002 (Public Law 107–295) (PDF)

Signed into law on November 25, 2002, this bill amends the Merchant Marine Act of 1936 to establish a program to ensure greater security for U.S. seaports. The act directs the Secretary of Transportation to assess port vulnerability and to prepare a National Maritime Transportation Antiterrorism Plan for deterring catastrophic emergencies.

Preparedness against Terrorism Act of 2000 (H.R. 4210)

Referred to the Senate committee on July 26, 2000, this bill requires the president to ensure that federal emergency preparedness plans and programs are adequate and carried out in the event of an act of terrorism, or other catastrophic event.

Safe Explosives Act (Homeland Security Act of 2002, Public Law No. 107–296, Section 1121)

Included as part of the Homeland Security Act of 2002 and signed by President George W. Bush on November 25, 2002, the Safe Explosives Act empowers the Bureau of Alcohol, Tobacco and Firearms (ATF) to apply stricter controls on the purchase of explosives. Effective May 24, 2002, any person who wants to transport, ship, cause to be transported, or receive explosive materials must first obtain a federal permit. ATF prepared a special online reference page to keep the public informed of resulting regulations.

Terrorist Bombings Convention Implementation Act of 2002 (Title I) and Suppression of the Financing of Terrorism Convention Implementation Act of 2002 (Title II; H.R. 3275, Public Law No. 107–197)

This bill was enacted as Public Law No. 107–197 on June 25, 2002. Title I implements the International Convention for the Suppression of Terrorist Bombings, which was signed by the United States on January 12, 1998. This convention imposes legal obligations on state parties to submit for prosecution or to extradite any person within their jurisdiction who unlawfully and intentionally delivers, places, discharges, or detonates an explosive or other lethal device in, into, or against a place of public use, a state or government facility, a public transportation system, or an infrastructure facility. Title II implements the International Convention for the Suppression of the Financing of Terrorism, which was signed by the United States on January 10, 2000. This convention imposes legal obligations on state parties to submit for prosecution or to extradite any person within their jurisdiction who unlawfully and willfully provides or collects funds with the intention that they should be used to carry out various terrorist activities. State parties are subject to the obligations of these conventions without regard to the place where the alleged acts included in these conventions take place.

The below-listed legislative hate crime references can be located on the Department of Justice's National Criminal Justice Reference Service website at http://www.ncjrs.org/hate_crimes/legislation.html.

Hate Crimes Prevention Act of 1999 Bill (H.R. 1082)
    This act amends 18 U.S.C. 245 that prohibits persons from interfering with an individual's federal rights (e.g., voting or employment) by violence or threat of violence due to his or her race, color, religion, or national origin. This act allows for more authority for the federal government to investigate and prosecute hate crime offenders who committed their crime because of perceived sexual orientation, gender, or disability of the victim. It also permits the federal government to prosecute without having to prove that the victim was attacked because he or she was performing a federally protected activity.

Church Arson Prevention Act of 1996 (18 U.S.C. 247)
    This act created the National Church Arson Task Force (NCATF) in June 1996 to oversee the investigation and prosecution of arson at houses of worship around the country. The NCATF brought together the FBI, the ATF, and Department of Justice prosecutors in partnership with state and local law enforcement officers and prosecutors. In addition to the NCATF's creation, the law allowed for a broader federal criminal jurisdiction to aid criminal prosecutions and established a loan guarantee recovery fund for rebuilding.

Hate Crimes Sentencing Enhancement Act (Section 280003 of the Violent Crime Control and Law Enforcement Act of 1994)
    As a part of the 1994 Crime Act, the Hate Crimes Sentencing Enhancement Act provides for longer sentences when the offense is determined to be a hate crime. A longer sentence may be imposed if it is proved that a crime against a person or property was motivated by "race, color, religion, national origin, ethnicity, gender, disability, or sexual orientation."

Hate Crime Statistics Act of 1990 (28 U.S.C. 534)
    This act requires the Department of Justice to collect data on hate crimes. Hate crimes are defined as "manifest prejudice based on race, religion, sexual orientation, or ethnicity." The FBI, using the Uniform Crime Reporting system, compiles these statistics. The Crime Act of 1994 also requires the FBI to collect data on hate crimes involving disability.

# Appendix I: Glossary of Terminology

## CYBER TERMINOLOGY

**back door**. A hole in the security of a computer system deliberately left in place by designers or programmers or maliciously established by manipulating a computer system.

**code master**. An individual who epitomizes the art of computer usage, programming, and in the case of cyber terror, malicious activity.

**denial of service (DOS)**. A malicious activity that renders a server, or a service, useless. This is often done through transmission of a virus or a repetitive electronic attack.

**domain name service (DNS)**. A distributed Internet directory service. DNS is used mostly to translate between domain names and IP addresses, and to control e-mail delivery. Most Internet services rely on DNS to work.

**hacker**. An individual who gains unauthorized access to a computer system.

**pharming**. The misdirecting of users to fraudulent sites or proxy servers, typically through DNS hijacking or poisoning.

**phishing**. Use of "spoofed" e-mails to lead consumers to counterfeit websites designed to trick recipients into divulging financial data such as credit card numbers, account usernames, passwords, and social security numbers.

**phreak**. A technologically savvy individual who understands the inner workings of communication and phone systems and uses that knowledge to exploit illicit cyber activity (phreaking, verb).

**Ping**. A networking computer program that verifies Internet Protocol (IP).

**script kiddie**. Individuals who break security on computer systems without truly understanding the exploit they are using.

**Trojan horse**. A hidden script attached to a program that appears legitimate but contains code allowing unauthorized collection, exploitation, falsification, or destruction of data on a host computer.

**worm**. A type of virus that acts as an independent program that replicates itself from machine to machine across network connections in an effort to cause a denial of service.

## GENERAL TERRORIST-RELATED TERMINOLOGY

**berserker**. Term considered and posed by Jonathan White in 2000 to better explain actions of a single-event terrorist. These individuals are crazed true believers who went too far and possibly crazy for their cause.

**hard target**. A well-fortified and secure location that is extremely difficult to penetrate, for example, a military installation, government facility, or nuclear site.

**lone wolf**. Considered a one-hit wonder and an extremist. This type of terrorist is often leaderless, acts on his own, and once he commits the violent act, will vanish.

**militia**. Any number of American paramilitary right-wing groups that focus their beliefs and issues on taxes, white supremacy, gun control, abortion, and antigovernment.

**soft target**. A less-fortified and often more attractive target for a terrorist because of its relative ease of accessibility, for example, a hotel, market, or an arena.

**wolf packs**. American right-wing extremist term for small groups of activists operating below a militia.

## ISLAMIC TERMINOLOGY

It is important to note that depending on the source or translation, there may be variations of some terms. Also, this listing is not all-inclusive but merely represents some of the more common terms seen in publications or writings.

## CELL LEADERSHIP STRUCTURE TERMS

**Al Awlani.** The leader.
**Al Hakeem**. Medic/doctor.
**Al Jare**. Courier; infantryman.
**Al Kannas**. Sniper/killer with one shot.
**Al Mukabir**. Communications/intelligence.

## GENERAL ISLAMIC TERMS

**Adhan.** (1) The Islamic way of calling Muslims to the five obligatory prayers.
**Allah**. (2) The Muslim name for the one and only God—there are no others.
**Allahu akbar**. Statement said by Muslims numerous times—means Allah is the greatest
**Amin**. Custodian or guardian—one who is loyal or faithful.
**Asr**. The late-afternoon prayer.
**Ayatullah**. Title of the major Shi'a cleric; translation means "Sign of God."
**Barakat**. Blessings.
**Barakate**. Reference to Osama bin Laden used at Guantanamo Bay, Cuba.
**Barzakh**. Translation means "The Partition": the time between death and resurrection.
**Bayaat**. Allegiance to
**Dajjal**. The anti-Christ.
**Eid**. Festivity, a celebration, a recurring happiness, and a feast. In Islam, there are two major 'Eids, namely the feast of Ramadan ('Eid Al-Fitr) and the feast of sacrifice ('Eid Al-Adha).
**'Eid Al-Adha**. Islamic holiday at the end of the Hajj.
**'Eid Al-Fitr**. Islamic holiday at the end of the Ramadan fast.
**Esa**. Islamic name for Jesus.
**Fajr**. The dawn prayer.
**Fatwa**. Legal ruling or opinion issued by an Islamic scholar.
**Hadith**. Sayings and practices of the Prophet Mohammed that were collected after his death.
**Hajj**. Annual pilgrimage to Mecca that takes place in the twelfth month of the Islamic calendar.
**Hajji**. Translation means "Pilgrim"; the title given to a person who completes Islamic pilgrimage.
**Halaqa**. Study circle.
**Hijab**. Head scarf worn over the hair.
**Imam**. Sunni Islamic leader; a person who leads congregational prayers.
**Iman**. Faith and trust in Allah.
**Isha**. The night prayer.
**Jihad**. Arabic term for the "struggle."
**Khalifa**. Supreme leader of the Muslim community; translation means the "caretaker."
**Maghrib**. The sunset prayer.
**Masjid**. Proper name for a Muslim house of worship; also referred to as a mosque.
**Mecca**. Southwestern Arabian city founded by Abraham's wife Hagar and their son; the birthplace of Muhammad.
**Medina**. First capital city of Islam in AD 622 when Muhammad fled Mecca.
**Muslim**. Follower of the religion of Islam.
**Nabi**. A prophet from God.
**Nika**. Islamic marriage ceremony.
**Qiblah**. Direction of Mecca toward which all Muslims face when they pray.
**Quran**. Islamic Holy Book.
**Ramadan**. Ninth month of the Islamic lunar calendar.
**Sadaqa**. Islamic term for charity.
**Sayyid**. A leader or chief.

**Shahadah**. The Creed of Islam.
**Shaheed (Shahid)**. Islamic term for martyr.
**Shari'ah**. The term for Islamic Law.
**Shi'a**. Second largest sect of Islam.
**Surah**. The Quran is composed of 114 chapters, each of which is called a Surah.
**Sunni**. Largest sect of Islam.
**Ummah**. Muslim community or motherland.
**Wudu**. Islamic practice of washing the face, hands, and feet with water.
**Yahudi**. Arabic term for a Jew.
**Zakat**. Charitable contribution (donation) part of five pillars.
**Zuhr**. The afternoon prayer.

## KLANSPEAK TERMINOLOGY

The culture and makeup of many domestic groups has led to them developing their own terminology and lingo. In his book *Blood in the Face*, James Ridgeway provides an example of what is referred to as "Klanspeak." The following terms and definitions are shown as represented in his work and are provided as an example of just one group's use of distinct terms.

**Dominion**. Five or more counties of a Realm.
**Empire**. The national Ku Klux Klan organization.
**Exalted**. Cyclops Head of a Klanton.
**Giant**. Head of a Province.
**Grand Dragon**. Head of a Realm.
**Great Titan**. Head of a Dominion.
**Imperial Wizard**. Head of national Ku Klux Klan.
**Kladd**. Assistant to Exalted Cyclops.
**Klaliff**. Vice president to Exalted Cyclops.
**Klanton or Den**. Local chapter.
**Klavern**. Local meeting place.
**Kleagle**. An organizer.
**Klokard**. National lecturer.
**Kludd**. Chaplain.
**Realm**. The Klan in a particular state.

## LAW ENFORCEMENT AND CRIMINAL INTELLIGENCE TERMINOLOGY

The definitions contained herein are provided from the perspective of *law enforcement intelligence*. It is recognized that some words and phrases will have alternate or additional meanings when used in the context of national security intelligence, the military, or business. The definitions are intended to be merely descriptive of an entity, issue, or process that may be encountered by those working with the law enforcement intelligence function.

**access (to sensitive or confidential information)**. Sensitive or confidential information and/or intelligence may be released by a law enforcement agency when at least one of four prescribed circumstances applies to the person(s) receiving the information.
**actionable**. Intelligence and information with sufficient specificity and detail that explicit responses to prevent a crime or terrorist attack can be implemented.
**administrative analysis**. The analysis of economic, geographic, demographic, census, or behavioral data to identify trends and conditions useful to aid administrators in making policy and/or resource allocation decisions.

**allocation**. The long-term assignment of personnel by function, geography, and shift/duty tour along with the commitment of required supporting resources to deal with crime and law enforcement service demands in the most efficient and effective manner.

**analysis**. An activity whereby meaning, actual or suggested, is derived through organizing and systematically examining diverse information and applying inductive or deductive logic in order to arrive at the meaning.

**Anti-Terrorism Information Exchange (ATIX)**. Operated by the Regional Information Sharing Systems, ATIX is a secure means to disseminate national security or terrorist threat information to law enforcement and other first responders through the ATIX electronic bulletin board, secure website, and secure e-mail.

**archiving (records)**. The maintenance of records in remote storage after a case has been closed or disposed of, as a matter of contingency should the records be needed for later reference.

**association analysis**. The entry of critical investigative and/or assessment variables into a two-axis matrix to examine the relationships and patterns that emerge as the variables are correlated in the matrix.

**bias/hate crime**. Any criminal act directed toward any person or group as a result of that person's race, ethnicity, religious affiliation, or sexual preference.

**black chamber**. One of the earliest (1919) scientific applications to intelligence, wherein a working group responsible for deciphering codes used to encrypt communications between foreign powers' diplomatic posts.

**C3**. An intelligence applications concept initially used by military intelligence which means command, control, and communications as the hallmarks for effective intelligence operations.

**clandestine activities**. Activities that are usually extensive and goal-oriented, planned and executed to conceal the existence of the operation. Only participants and the agency sponsoring the activity are intended to know about the operation. "Storefront" operations, "stings," and certain concentrated undercover investigations (such as ABSCAM) can be classified as clandestine collection.

**classified information/intelligence**. A uniform system for classifying, safeguarding, and declassifying national security information, including information relating to defense against transnational terrorism, to ensure certain information be maintained in confidence in order to protect citizens, U.S. democratic institutions, U.S. homeland security, and U.S. interactions with foreign nations and entities.

1. **Top secret classification** Applied to information, the unauthorized disclosure of which reasonably could be expected to cause exceptionally grave damage to the national security that the original classification authority is able to identify or describe (Executive Order 12958, March 25, 2003).
2. **Secret classification** Applied to information, the unauthorized disclosure of which reasonably could be expected to cause serious damage to the national security that the original classification authority is able to identify or describe (Executive Order 12958. March 25, 2003).
3. **Confidential classification** Applied to information, the unauthorized disclosure of which reasonably could be expected to cause damage to the national security that the original classification authority is able to identify or describe (Executive Order 12958. March 25, 2003).

**collation (of information)**. A review of collected and evaluated information to determine its substantive applicability to a case or problem at issue and the placement of useful information into a form or system that permits easy and rapid access and retrieval.

**collection (of information)**. The identification, location, and recording/storage of unanalyzed information, typically from an original source and using both human and technological means, for input into the intelligence cycle to determine its usefulness in meeting a defined tactical or strategic intelligence goal.

**collection plan**. The preliminary step toward completing an assessment of intelligence requires the determination of what type of information needs to be collected, alternatives for how to collect the information, and a time line for collecting the information.

**command and control**. Command and control functions are performed through an arrangement of personnel, equipment, communications, facilities, and procedures used by a commander in planning, directing, coordinating, and controlling forces and operations in the accomplishment of a mission.

**commodity**. Any item or substance which is inherently unlawful to possess (contraband), or materials that, if not contraband, are themselves being distributed, transacted, or marketed in an unlawful manner.

**commodity flow**. Graphic depictions and descriptions of transactions, shipment, and distribution of contraband goods and money derived from unlawful activities in order to aid in the disruption of the unlawful activities and apprehend those persons involved in all aspects of the unlawful activities.

**communications intelligence (COMINT)**. The capture of information—either encrypted or in "plaintext"—exchanged between intelligence targets or transmitted by a known or suspected intelligence target for the purposes of tracking communications patterns and protocols (traffic analysis), establishing links between intercommunicating parties or groups, and/or analysis of the substantive meaning of the communication.

**computer virus**. Programs which were written to perform a desired function but have a hidden code introduced into the command sequence which, when triggered, performs an unwanted or destructive function; it "infects" the computer by spreading through its memory and/or operating system and can "infect" other computers if introduced through shared data media or through a communications medium.

**conclusion**. A definitive statement about a suspect, action, or state of nature based on the analysis of information.

**confidential**. *See* Classification, Confidential Classification.

**continuing criminal enterprise**. Any individual, partnership, corporation, association, or other legal entity, and any union or group of individuals associated, in fact although not a legal entity, which are involved in a continuing or perpetuating criminal event.

**controlled unclassified information (CUI)**. Information that has not been federally classified which pertains to significant investigations or inquiries that require confidentiality for the security of the inquiry and/or for the protection of civil rights.

**coordination**. The processes of interrelating work functions, responsibilities, duties, resources, and initiatives directed toward goal attainment.

**counterintelligence**. A national security intelligence activity that involves blocking or developing a strategic response to other groups, governments, or individuals through the identification, neutralization, and manipulation of their intelligence services.

**covert intelligence**. A covert activity is planned and executed to conceal the collection of information and/or the identity of any officer or agent participating in the activity. Undercover operations, electronic eavesdropping, and "closed" surveillance of an intelligence target would fall within this category.

**cracker**. A person who accesses a computer system without consent with the intent to steal, destroy information, disrupt the system, plant a virus, alter the system and/or its processes from the configuration managed by the system manager, or otherwise alter information in the system or its processes.

**crime analysis**. The process of analyzing information collected on crimes and police service delivery variables in order to give direction for police officer deployment, resource allocation, and policing strategies as a means to maximize crime prevention activities and the cost-effective operation of the police department.

**crime pattern analysis**. An assessment of the nature, extent, and changes of crime based on the characteristics of the criminal incident including modus operandi, temporal, and geographic variables.

**criminal history record information (CHRI).** Information collected by criminal justice agencies on individuals consisting of identifiable descriptions and notations of arrests, detentions, indictments, information, or other formal criminal charges, and any disposition arising there from sentencing, correctional supervision, and/or release. The term does *not* include identification information such as fingerprint records to the extent that such information does not indicate involvement of the individual in the criminal justice system.

**criminal investigative analysis.** An analytic process that studies serial offenders, victims, and crime scenes in order to assess characteristics and behaviors of offender(s) with the intent to identify or aid in the identification of the offender(s).

**criminal predicate.** Information about an individual or about his or her behavior that may only be collected and stored in a law enforcement intelligence records system, when there is reasonable suspicion that the individual is involved in criminal conduct or activity and the information is relevant to that criminal conduct or activity.

**cryptanalysis.** The process of deciphering encrypted communications of an intelligence target.

**cryptography.** The creation of a communications code/encryption system for communication transmission with the intent of precluding the consumption and interpretation of one's own messages.

**cryptology.** The study of communications encryption methods which deal with the development of "codes" and the "scrambling" of communications in order to prevent the interception of the communications by an unauthorized or unintended party.

**data owner.** The agency or analyst that originally enters information or data into a law enforcement records' system.

**data quality.** Controls implemented to ensure all information in a law enforcement agency's records system is complete, accurate, and secure.

**deconfliction.** The process or system used to determine if multiple law enforcement agencies are investigating the same person or crime and providing notification to each agency involved of the shared interest in the case as well as providing contact information. This is an information- and intelligence-sharing process that seeks to minimize conflicts between agencies and maximize the effectiveness of an investigation.

**deployment.** The short-term assignment of personnel to address specific crime problems or police service demands.

**designated state and/or major urban area fusion center.** The fusion center in each state designated as the primary or lead fusion center for the information-sharing environment.

**discrete intelligence.** A collection activity that must be conducted cautiously to avoid undue curiosity and public interest, to minimize interference with the collection activity, and to minimize the suspicions of the intelligence target. Discrete activities may be acknowledged by and attributed to their agency/sponsor.

**dissemination (of intelligence).** The process of effectively distributing analyzed intelligence in the most appropriate format to those in need of the information to facilitate their accomplishment of organizational goals.

**division of labor.** Tasks within the organization which require close supervision and/or security and which are divided among personnel based on expertise, performance expectations, demand, and/or the inherent nature of the tasks; specialization of duties is part of the division of labor.

**due process.** Fundamental fairness during the course of the criminal justice process, includes adherence to legal standards and the civil rights of the police constituency; the adherence to principles which are fundamental to justice.

**effective.** Doing the *right job*. It is performing the tasks and expending the effort to accomplish the specifically defined goal of the task(s) at hand.

**efficient.** Doing the *job right*. It is concerned with the judicious use of resources and effort to accomplish the intended tasks without expending undue time, money, or effort.

**El Paso Intelligence Center (EPIC).** Operated by the Drug Enforcement Administration; a cooperative intelligence center serving as a clearinghouse and intelligence resource for local, state, and federal law enforcement agencies. Primary concern is drug trafficking, however, intelligence on other crimes is also managed by EPIC.

**enterprise**. Any individual, partnership, corporation, association, or other legal entity, and any union or group of individuals associated in fact although not a legal entity.

**evaluation (of information)**. All information collected for the intelligence cycle is reviewed for its *quality* with an assessment of the validity and reliability of the information.

**event flow analysis**. Graphic depictions and descriptions of incidents, behaviors, and people involved in an unlawful event intended to help understand how an event occurred as a tool to aid in prosecution as well as prevention of future unlawful events.

**exemptions (to the Freedom of Information Act [FOIA])**. Circumstances wherein a law enforcement agency is not required to disclose information from a FOIA request.

**Field Intelligence Group (FIG)**. The centralized intelligence component in a Federal Bureau of Investigation (FBI) Field Office that is responsible for the management, execution, and coordination of intelligence functions within the Field Office region.

**financial analysis**. The use of forensic accounting techniques to review monetary transactions (i.e., "the paper trail") for evidence of funding for criminal enterprises and terrorism, as well as money laundering criminal activity.

**forecast (as related to criminal intelligence)**. The product of an analytic process which provides a probability of future crimes and crime patterns based on a comprehensive analysis of current trends integrated with analysis of developing or likely trends.

**Freedom of Information Act (FOIA)**. The Freedom of Information Act, 5 U.S.C. 552, enacted in 1966 statutorily provides that any person has a right, enforceable in court, of access to federal agency records, except to the extent that such records (or portions thereof) are protected from disclosure by one of nine exemptions.

**fusion center**. The physical location of the law enforcement intelligence fusion process.

**fusion center guidelines**. A series of nationally recognized standards developed by law enforcement intelligence subject matter experts designed for the good practice of developing and managing an intelligence fusion center.

**fusion process**. The overarching process of managing the flow of information and intelligence across levels and sectors of government.

**goal**. The end to which all activity in the unit is directed.

**granularity**. Considers the specific details and pieces of information, including nuances and situational inferences, which constitute the elements on which intelligence is developed through analysis.

**hacker**. A person who has expertise and skills to penetrate computer systems and alter such systems, processes, and/or information/data in files, but he or she does no damage or commits no theft or crime. Although a hacker may enter files or systems without authorization, the action is more akin to a trespass and no theft or damage results.

**Homeland Security Advisory System**. An information and communications structure designed by the U.S. Government for disseminating information to all levels of government and the American people regarding the risk of terrorist attacks and for providing a framework to assess the risk at five levels: low, guarded, elevated, high, and severe.

**human intelligence (HUMINT)**. Intelligence gathering methods that require human interaction or observation of the target or targeted environment. The intelligence is collected through the use of one's direct senses or the optical and/or audio enhancement of the senses.

**hypothesis (from criminal intelligence analysis)**. A proposed relationship between persons, events, and/or commodities based on the accumulation and analysis of intelligence information.

**imagery**. The representation of an object or locale produced on any medium by optical or electronic means. The nature of the image will be dependent on the sensing media and sensing platform.

**indicator**. Generally defined and observable actions which, based on an analysis of past known behaviors and characteristics, collectively suggest that a person may be committing, preparing to commit, or has committed an unlawful act.

**inductive logic**. The reasoning process of taking diverse pieces of specific information and inferring to a broader meaning of the information through the course of hypothesis development.

**inference development**. The creation of a probabilistic conclusion, estimate, or prediction related to an intelligence target based on the use of inductive or deductive logic in the analysis of raw information related to the target.

**informant**. An individual not affiliated with a law enforcement agency who provides information about criminal behavior to a law enforcement agency. An informant may be a community member, a businessperson, or a criminal informant who seeks to protect himself or herself from prosecution and/or provide the information in exchange for payment.

**information**. Pieces of raw, unanalyzed data that identify persons, evidence, events, or illustrate processes that indicate the incidence of a criminal event or witnesses or evidence of a criminal event.

**information/intelligence sharing**. *See* National Intelligence Sharing Plan.

**information sharing environment**. An environment for the sharing of terrorism information in a manner consistent with national security and with applicable legal standards relating to privacy and civil liberties.

**information sharing system**. An integrated and secure methodology, whether computerized or manual, designed to efficiently and effectively distribute critical information about offenders, crimes, and/or events in order to enhance prevention and apprehension activities by law enforcement.

**information system**. An organized means, whether manual or electronic, of collecting, processing, storing, and retrieving information on *individual entities* for purposes of record and reference.

**information warfare**. Information warfare is the offensive and defensive use of information and information systems to deny, exploit, corrupt, or destroy an adversary's information, information-based processes, information systems, and computer-based networks while protecting one's own. Such actions are designed to achieve advantages over military or business adversaries. Synonymous with cyber warfare.

**intelligence (criminal)**. The product of the analysis of raw information related to crimes or crime patterns to ascertain offenders and trends.

**intelligence assessment**. A comprehensive FBI Office of Intelligence SBU report on an intelligence issue related to criminal or national security threats within the service territory of an FBI Field Office and available to state, local, and tribal law enforcement agencies. Distribution will be through LEO, RISS.net, JREIS, and the FBI Field Intelligence Groups.

**intelligence bulletins**. An FBI Office of Intelligence finished intelligence product in article format that describes new developments and evolving trends. The bulletins are typically SBU and available for distribution to state, local, and tribal law enforcement. Distribution will be through LEO, RISS.net, JREIS, and the FBI Field Intelligence Groups.

**intelligence community**. The agencies of the U.S. Government, including the military, which have the responsibility of preventing breaches to U.S. national security and responding to national security threats.

**intelligence cycle**. An organized process by which information is *gathered, assessed,* and *distributed* in order to fulfill the goals of the intelligence function—it is a method of performing analytic activities and placing the analysis in a useable form.

**intelligence estimate**. The appraisal, expressed in writing or orally, of available intelligence relating to a specific situation or condition with a view to determine the courses of action open to criminal offenders and terrorists and the order of probability of their adoption. It includes strategic projections on the economic, human, and/or quantitative criminal impact of the crime or issue that is subject to analysis.

**intelligence function**. The activity within a law enforcement agency responsible for some aspect of law enforcement intelligence, whether collection, analysis, and/or dissemination.

**intelligence gap**. An unanswered question about a cyber, criminal, or national security issue or threat.

**intelligence information reports**. Raw, unevaluated intelligence concerning "perishable" or time-limited information concerning criminal or national security issues in a report prepared by the

FBI Office of Intelligence. Although the full IIR may be classified, state, local, and tribal law enforcement agencies will have access to SBU information in the report under the tear line. Distribution will be through LEO, RISS.net, JREIS, and the FBI Field Intelligence Groups.

**intelligence-led policing**. The dynamic use of intelligence to guide operational law enforcement activities to targets, commodities, or threats for both tactical responses and strategic decision-making for resource allocation and/or strategic responses.

**intelligence mission**. The *role* that the intelligence function of a law enforcement agency fulfills in support of the overall mission of the agency—it specifies in general language *what* the function is intended to accomplish.

**Intelligence Mutual Aid Pact (IMAP)**. A formal agreement between law enforcement agencies designed to expedite the process of sharing information in intelligence records.

**intelligence officer**. A sworn law enforcement officer assigned to an agency's intelligence function for purposes of investigation, liaison, or other intelligence-related activity that requires or benefits from having a sworn officer perform the activity.

**intelligence products**. Reports or documents that contain assessments, forecasts, associations, links, and other outputs from the analytic process that may be disseminated for use by law enforcement agencies for prevention of crimes, target hardening, apprehension of offenders, and prosecution.

**intelligence records (files)**. Stored information on the activities and associations of individuals, organizations, businesses, and groups who are suspected of being or having been involved in the actual or attempted planning, organizing, financing, or commission of criminal acts; or are suspected of being or having been involved in criminal activities with known or suspected crime figures (LEIU Guidelines).

**intelligence records guidelines**. Derived from federal regulation 28 CFR Part 23, these are guidelines/standards for the development of records management policies and procedures used by law enforcement agencies that have federally funded multijurisdictional criminal intelligence systems.

**International Criminal Police Organization (INTERPOL)**. INTERPOL is a worldwide association of national police forces established for mutual assistance in the detection and deterrence of international crimes; it is an information clearinghouse for nonpolitical, international criminals, international transportation of stolen properties, and international trade of contraband.

**investigatory value**. Intelligence or information is disseminated in the law enforcement community for surveillance or apprehension.

**joint intelligenced**. Fundamental principles that guide the preparation of intelligence and the subsequent provision of intelligence to support military forces of two or more services used in coordinated action.

**key word in context (KWIC)**. An automated system that indexes selected key words that represent the evidence or information being stored.

**law enforcement intelligence (LEI)**. The end product (output) of an analytic process which collects and assesses information about crimes and/or criminal enterprises with the purpose of making judgments and inferences about community conditions, potential problems, and criminal activity with the intent to pursue criminal prosecution or project crime trends.

**money laundering**. The practice of using multiple unlawful transactions of money and/or negotiable instruments gained through illegal activities with the intent of hiding the origin of the income, those who have been "paid" from the income, and/or the location of the unlawful income.

**motion sensing**. Various methods exist to detect the presence, direction, and nature of moving people, vehicles, or objects. Motion sensors may be on either a fixed or mobile platform and include acoustic, seismic, and disturbance sensors.

**National Central Bureau (NCB or USNCB)**. The United States Headquarters of INTERPOL located in Washington, DC.

**National Criminal Intelligence Resource Center**. An Internet website designed to provide information, model policies, and a wide variety of resources to help law enforcement agencies develop, implement, and retain a lawful and effective intelligence capacity.

**National Criminal Intelligence Sharing Plan**. A formal intelligence sharing initiative, supported by the U.S. Department of Justice, Office of Justice Programs, that securely links local, state, tribal, and federal law enforcement agencies, facilitating the exchange of critical intelligence information. The plan contains model policies and standards and is a blueprint for law enforcement administrators to follow when enhancing or building an intelligence function. It describes a nationwide communications capability that will link all levels of law enforcement personnel, including officers on the street, intelligence analysts, unit commanders, and police executives.

**national security intelligence**. The collection and analysis of information concerned with the relationship and homeostasis of the United States with foreign powers, organizations, and persons with regard to political and economic factors, as well as the maintenance of the United States' sovereign principles.

**need-to-know**. As a result of jurisdictional, organizational, or operational necessities, intelligence or information is disseminated to further an investigation.

**network**. A structure of interconnecting components designed to communicate with each other and perform a function or functions as a unit in a specified manner.

**open communications (OPCOM)**. The collection of open or publicly available communications, broadcasts, audio or video recordings, propaganda, published statements, and other distributed written or recorded material for purposes of analyzing the information.

**open source information (or intelligence)**. Individual data, records, reports, and assessments that may shed light on an investigatory target or event which does not require any legal process or any type of clandestine collection techniques for a law enforcement agency to obtain, rather it is obtained through means that meet copyright and commercial requirements of vendors, as well as being free of legal restrictions to access by anyone who seeks that information.

**operational analysis**. An assessment of the methodology of a criminal enterprise or terrorist organization that depicts how the enterprise performs its activities including communications, philosophy, compensation, security, and other variables that are essential for the enterprise to exist.

**operational intelligence**. Information is evaluated and systematically organized on an active or potential target. This process is developmental in nature, wherein there are sufficient articulated reasons to suspect criminal activity. Intelligence activities explore the basis of those reasons and newly developed information in order to develop a case for arrest or indictment.

**organizing**. The rational coordination of the activities of a number of people for the achievement of some common explicit purpose or goal through division of labor and function and through a hierarchy of authority and responsibility.

**outcome evaluation**. The process of determining the value or amount of success in achieving a predetermined objective through defining the objective in some qualitative or quantitative measurable terms; identifying the proper criteria (or variables) to be used in measuring the success toward attaining the objective; determining and explaining the degree of success; and recommending further program actions to attain the desired objectives/outcomes.

**planning**. The preparation for future situations, estimating organizational demands and resources needed to attend to those situations, and initiating strategies to respond to those situations.

**prediction**. Projection of future criminal actions or changes in the nature of crime trends or a criminal enterprise based on an analysis of information depicting historical trends from which a forecast is based.

**preventive intelligence**. Intelligence that can be used to interdict or forestall a crime or terrorist attack.

**privacy (information)**. The assurance that legal and constitutional restrictions on the collection, maintenance, use, and disclosure of personally identifiable information will be adhered to by criminal justice agencies with use of such information to be strictly limited to circumstances where lawful legal process permits the use of the personally identifiable information.

**privacy (personal)**. The assurance that legal and constitutional restrictions on the collection, maintenance, use, and disclosure of behaviors of an individual, including his or her communications, associations, and transactions, will be adhered to by criminal justice agencies with the use of such information to be strictly limited to circumstances where a lawful legal process authorizes surveillance and investigation.

**Privacy Act.** Legislation that allows an individual to review almost all federal files (and state files under the auspices of the respective state privacy acts) pertaining to him or her; places restrictions on the disclosure of personally identifiable information; specifies that there be no secret records systems on individuals; and compels the government to reveal its information sources.

**proactive.** Taking action that is anticipatory to a problem or situation with the intent to eliminate or mitigate the effect of the incident.

**procedural due process.** Mandates and guarantees of law that ensure that the procedures used to deprive a person of life, liberty, or property during the course of the criminal justice process meet constitutional standards.

**procedures.** A method of performing an operation or a manner of proceeding on a course of action. It differs from policy in that it directs action in a particular situation to perform a specific task within the guidelines of policy. Both policies and procedures are goal oriented. However, policy establishes limits to action while procedure *directs responses* within those limits.

**process evaluation.** The assessment of procedures used to attain objectives within the criteria of substantive contribution, effectiveness of resources, coordination with other activities, and properly trained staff.

**process hypothesis.** Represents a hypothesized link, procedure, or behavior throughout a criminal enterprise that is the basis for the logic to make summary hypotheses, conclusions, estimates, and/or prediction.

**profile/criminal profile.** An investigative technique to identify and define the major personality and behavioral characteristics of the (criminal) offender based on an analysis of the crime(s) he or she has committed.

**protocol (of intelligence collection).** Information collection *procedures* used to obtain verbal and written information, actions of people, and physical evidence required for strategic and tactical intelligence analysis.

**public value.** Intelligence or information is released to the public because of the value that may be derived from public dissemination to (1) aid in locating targets/suspects and (2) for public safety purposes (i.e., hardening targets, taking precautions).

**purging (records).** The removal and/or destruction of records because they are deemed to be of no further value or further access to the records would serve no legitimate government interest.

**qualitative (methods).** Research methods that collect and analyze information that are described in narrative or rhetorical form and conclusions drawn based on the cumulative interpreted meaning of that information.

**quantitative (methods).** Research methods that collect and analyze information that can be "counted" or placed on a scale of measurement that can be statistically analyzed.

**racketeering activity.** State felonies involving murder, robbery, extortion, and several other serious offenses, and more than 30 serious federal offenses including extortion, interstate theft offenses, narcotics violations, mail fraud, and securities fraud.

**Racketeering-Influenced Corrupt Organization (RICO).** Title IX of the Organized Crime Control Act of 1970 (18 U.S.C. Sections 1961–1968), which provides civil and criminal penalties for persons who engage in a "pattern of racketeering activity" or "collection of an unlawful debt" that has a specified relationship to an "enterprise" that affects interstate commerce.

**reasonable grounds/suspicion.** When a police officer, based on his or her experience, has an articulable reason to believe that a person has committed, is committing, or is about to commit a crime.

**recommendations.** Suggestions for actions to be taken based on the findings of an analysis.

**records system.** A group of records from which information is retrieved by reference to a name or other personal identifier such as a social security number.

**red team**. A technique for assessing vulnerability that involves viewing a potential target from the perspective of an attacker to identify its hidden vulnerabilities and to anticipate possible modes of attack.

**Regional Information Sharing System (RISS)**. RISS projects consist of six regionally grouped states from which state and local law enforcement agencies can become members to share intelligence information and have a clearinghouse for information and resources for targeted crimes. A member-based intelligence sharing network and clearinghouse for information and resources for targeted crimes. Local and state law enforcement agencies can become members of one of the six regional centers.

**regional intelligence centers**. Multijurisdiction centers cooperatively developed within a logical geographical area that coordinate federal, state, and local law enforcement information, with other information sources to track and assess criminal and terrorist threats that are operating in or interacting with the region.

**reliability**. Asks the question, "Is the *source* of the information consistent and dependable?"

**remote sensing (REMSEN)**. The collection of information which is typically not communications but can be viewed or interpreted by intelligence personnel to learn more about the intelligence target and provide support for case preparation.

**reporting**. Depending on the type of intelligence, the process of placing analyzed information into the proper form to ensure the most effective consumption.

**requirements (intelligence)**. The types of intelligence operational law enforcement elements need from the intelligence function within an agency or other intelligence—producing organizations in order for law enforcement officers to maximize protection and preventive efforts, as well as identify and arrest persons who are criminally liable.

**responsibility**. Responsibility reflects how the authority of a unit or individual is used and determining if goals have been accomplished and the mission fulfilled in a manner that is consistent with the defined limits of authority.

**right-to-know**. Based on one's official position, legal mandates, or official agreements, the individual may receive intelligence reports.

**risk assessment**. An analysis of a target, commodity, or victim intended to identify the probability of being attacked or criminally compromised.

**risk management–based intelligence**. An approach to intelligence analysis that has as its object the calculation of the risk attributable to a threat source or acts threatened by a threat source; a means of providing strategic intelligence for planning and policy making especially regarding vulnerabilities and countermeasures designed to prevent criminal acts; a means of providing tactical or operational intelligence in support of operations against a specific threat source, capability or modality; can be quantitative if a proper database exists to measure likelihood, impact, and calculate risk; can be qualitative, subjective, and still deliver a reasonably reliable ranking of risk for resource allocation and other decision making in strategic planning and for operations in tactical situations.

**sealing (records)**. Records are stored by the agency but cannot be accessed, referenced, or used without a court order based on a showing of evidence that there is a legitimate government interest to review the sealed information.

**security**. A series of procedures and measures which, when combined, provide protection to people from harm; information from improper disclosure or alteration; and assets from theft or damage.

**sensitive but unclassified (SBU) information**. Information that has not been classified by a federal law enforcement agency that pertain to significant law enforcement cases under investigation and criminal intelligence reports that require dissemination criteria to only those persons necessary to further the investigation or to prevent a crime or terrorist act.

**sensitive compartmented information (SCI)**. Classified information concerning or derived from intelligence sources, methods, or analytical processes, which is required to be handled within formal access control systems established by the Director of Central Intelligence.

**sensitive compartmented information facility (SCIF).** An accredited area, room, group of rooms, buildings, or an installation where SCI may be stored, used, discussed, and/or processed.

**signal intelligence (SIGINT).** The interception of various radio frequency signals, microwave signals, satellite audio communications, nonimagery infrared and coherent light signals, and transmissions from surreptitiously placed audio micro-transmitters in support of the communications intelligence activity.

**social capital.** Consists of the stock of active connections among people: the trust, mutual understanding, and shared values and behaviors that bind the members of human networks and communities and make cooperative action possible.

**sources.** From an intelligence perspective, these are persons (human intelligence or HUMINT) who collect or possess critical information needed for intelligence analysis.

**spatial analysis.** The process of using a geographic information system in combination with crime analysis techniques to assess the geographic context of offenders, crimes, and other law enforcement activity.

**statistical system.** An organized means of collecting, processing, storing, and retrieving *aggregate* information for purposes of analysis, research, and reference. No individual records are stored in a statistical system.

**strategic intelligence.** An assessment of targeted crime patterns, crime trends, criminal organizations, and/or unlawful commodity transactions for purposes of planning, decision making, and resource allocation; and the focused examination of unique, pervasive, and/or complex crime problems.

**substantive due process.** Guarantees persons against arbitrary, unreasonable, or capricious laws, and it acts as a limitation against arbitrary governmental actions so that no government agency may exercise powers beyond those authorized by the constitution.

**surveillance.** The observation of activities, behaviors, and associations of a LAWINT target (individual or group) with the intent to gather incriminating information or "lead" information, which is used for the furtherance of a criminal investigation.

**tactical intelligence.** Evaluated information on which immediate enforcement action can be based; intelligence activity focused specifically on developing an active case.

**target.** Any person, organization, group, crime or criminal series, or commodity being subject to investigation and intelligence analysis.

**target profile.** A profile that is person-specific and contains sufficient detail to initiate a target operation or support an ongoing operation against an individual or networked group of individuals.

**targeting.** The identification of crimes, crime trends, and crime patterns which have discernable characteristics that make collection and analysis of intelligence information an efficient and effective method for identifying, apprehending, and prosecuting those who are criminally responsible.

**tear-line report.** A report containing classified intelligence or information that is prepared in such a manner that data relating to intelligence sources and methods are easily removed from the report to protect sources and methods from disclosure. Typically, the information below the "tear line" can be released as "Sensitive but Unclassified."

**telemetry.** The collection and processing of information derived from noncommunications electromagnetic radiations emitting from sources such as radio navigation systems (e.g., transponders), radar systems, and information/data signals emitted from monitoring equipment in a vehicle or device.

**telephone record (toll) analysis.** An assessment of telephone call activity associated with investigatory targets to include telephone numbers called and/or received, the frequency of calls between numbers, the dates of calls, length of calls, and patterns of use.

**third agency rule.** An agreement wherein a source agency releases information under the condition that the receiving agency *does not* release the information to any other agency—that is, a "third agency."

**threat assessment**. An assessment of the criminal or terrorist presence within a jurisdiction integrated with an assessment of potential targets of that presence and a statement of probability that the criminal or terrorist will commit an unlawful act. The assessment focuses on the group's opportunity, capability, and willingness to fulfill the threat.

**threat inventory**. An information and intelligence-based survey within the region of a law enforcement agency to identify potential individuals or groups that pose criminal or terrorist threats without a judgment of the kind of threat they pose. The inventory is simply to determine their presence.

**undercover investigation**. Active infiltration (or attempting to infiltrate) a group believed to be involved in criminal activity and/or the interaction with a LAWINT target with the intent to gather incriminating information or "lead" information that is used for the furtherance of a criminal investigation.

**variable**. Any characteristic on which individuals, groups, items, or incidents differ.

**vet**. To subject a proposal, work product, or concept to an appraisal by command personnel and/or experts to ascertain the product's accuracy, consistence with philosophy, and or feasibility before proceeding.

**Violent Criminal Apprehension Program (VICAP)**. A nationwide data information center operated by the FBI's National Center for the Analysis of Violent Crime, designed to collect, collate, and analyze specific crimes of violence.

**vulnerability assessment**. An assessment of possible criminal or terrorist group targets within a jurisdiction integrated with an assessment of the target's weaknesses, the likelihood of being attacked, and the ability to withstand an attack.

**warning**. To notify in advance of possible harm or victimization as a result of information and intelligence gain concerned with the probability of a crime or terrorist attack.

## DOMESTIC EXTREMISM LEXICON

In March 26, 2009, the Department of Homeland Security, Office of Intelligence and Analysis, Strategic Analysis Group and Extremism and Radicalization Branch, Homeland Environment Threat Analysis Division published the Domestic Extremism Lexicon. The following terms and their respective definitions are derived from this document, which can be found in public Internet forums.

**aboveground**. A term used to describe extremist groups or individuals who operate overtly and portray themselves as law-abiding.

**alternative media**. A term used to describe various information sources that provide a forum for interpretations of events and issues that differ radically from those presented in mass media products and outlets.

**anarchist extremism**. A movement of groups or individuals who advocate a society devoid of government structure or ownership of individual property. Many embrace some of the radical philosophical components of anticapitalist, antiglobalization, communist, socialist, and other movements.

**animal rights extremism**. A movement of groups or individuals who ascribe equal value to all living organisms and seek to end the perceived abuse and suffering of animals. These groups have been known to advocate or engage in criminal activity and ploy acts of violence and terrorism in an attempt to advance their extremism goals.

**antiabortion extremism**. A movement of groups or individuals who are virulently antiabortion and advocate violence against providers of abortion-related services, their employees, and their facilities.

**anti-immigration extremism**. A movement of groups or individuals who are vehemently opposed to illegal immigration, particularly along the U.S. southwest border with Mexico, and who have been known to advocate or engage in criminal activity and plot acts of violence and terrorism to advance their extremist goals.

**antitechnology extremism**. A movement of groups or individuals who are opposed to technology. They have targeted college and university laboratories, scholars, biotechnology industries, U.S. corporations involved in the computer or airline industry, and others.

**Aryan prison gangs**. Individuals who form organized groups while in prison and advocate white supremacist views.

**Black bloc**. An organized collection of violent anarchists and anarchist affinity groups that band together for illegal acts of civil disturbance and use tactics that destroy property or strain law enforcement resources. Black blocs operate in autonomous cells that infiltrate nonviolent protests, often without knowledge of the organizers of the event.

**Black nationalism**. A term used by black separatists to promote the unification and separate identity of persons of black or African American descent and who advocate the establishment of a separate nation within the United States.

**Black power**. A term used by black separatists to describe their pride in and the perceived superiority of the black race.

**Black separatism**. A movement of groups or individuals of black or African American descent who advocate the separation of the races or the separation of specific geographic regions from the rest of the United States; some advocate forming their own political system within a separate nation.

**Christian identity**. A racist religious philosophy that maintains non-Jewish whites are "God's Chosen People" and the true descendants of the Twelve Tribes of Israel. Groups or individuals can be followers of either the Covenant or Dual Seedline doctrine; all believe that Jews are conspiring with Satan to control world affairs and that the world is on the verge of the Biblical apocalypse.

**Cuban independence extremism**. A movement of groups or individuals who do not recognize the legitimacy of the Communist Cuban Government and who attempt to subvert it through acts of violence, mainly in the United States.

**decentralized terrorist movement**. A movement of groups or individuals who pursue shared ideological goals through tactics of leaderless resistance independent of any larger terrorist organization.

**direct action**. Lawful or unlawful acts of civil disobedience ranging from protests to property destruction or acts of violence. The term is most often used by single-issue or anarchist extremists to describe their activities.

**environmental extremism**. A movement of groups or individuals who use violence to end what they perceive as the degradation of the natural environment by humans.

**ethnic-based extremism**. A movement of groups or individuals who are drawn together and form extremist beliefs based on their ethnic or cultural background.

**extremist group**. An ideologically driven organization that advocates or attempts to bring about political, religious, economic, or social change through the use of force, violence, or ideologically motivated criminal activity.

**green anarchism**. A movement of groups or individuals who combine anarchist ideology with an environmental focus. They advocate a return to a preindustrial, agrarian society, often through acts of violence or terrorism.

**Jewish extremism**. A movement of groups or individuals of the Jewish faith who are willing to use violence or commit other criminal acts to protect themselves against perceived affronts to their religious or ethnic identity.

**leaderless resistance**. A strategy that stresses the importance of individuals and small cells acting independently and anonymously outside formalized organizational structures to enhance operational security avoid detection.

**left-wing extremism**. A movement of groups or individuals who embrace anticapitalist, communist, or socialist doctrines and seek to bring about change through violent revolution rather than through established political processes.

**Mexican separatism**. A movement of groups or individuals of Mexican descent who advocate the secession of southwestern U.S. states to join Mexico through armed struggle. Members do not recognize the legitimacy of these U.S. states.

**militia movement**. A right-wing extremist movement composed of groups or individuals who adhere to antigovernment ideology often incorporating various conspiracy theories. Members oppose most federal and state laws, regulations, and authority.

**Neo-Nazis**. Groups or individuals who adhere to and promote Adolph Hitler's beliefs and use Nazi symbols and ideology.

**patriot movement**. A term used by right-wing extremists to link their beliefs to those commonly associated with the American Revolution.

**primary targeting**. Plans or attacks directed by extremists against parties that are the focus of an organized campaign.

**Puerto Rican independence extremists**. Groups or individuals who engage in criminal activity and advocate the use of violence to achieve Puerto Rican independence.

**racial nordic mysticism**. An ideology adopted by many white supremacist prison gangs who embrace a Norse mythological religion such as Odinism or Asatru.

**racialist**. A term used by white supremacists intended to minimize their extreme views or racial issues.

**racist skinheads**. Groups or individuals who combine white supremacist ideology with a skinhead ethos in which "white power" music plays a central role. Dress may include a shaved head or very short hair, jeans, thin suspenders, combat boots or Doc Martens, a bomber jacket, and tattoos of Nazi-like symbols.

**radicalization**. The process by which an individual adopts an extremist belief system leading to his or her willingness to advocate or bring about political, religious, economic, or social change through the use of force, violence, or ideologically motivated criminal activity.

**right-wing extremism**. A movement of right-wing groups or individuals who can be broadly divided into those who are primarily hate-oriented, and those who are mainly antigovernment and reject federal authority in favor of state or local authority.

**secondary targeting**. Plans or attacks directed against parties that provide direct financial, logistic, or physical support to the primary target of an organized campaign, with the goal of coercing those parties to end their engagement with a primary target. Secondary targets can include customers of or suppliers to a primary target or employees of a primary target organization.

**single-issue extremist groups**. Groups or individuals who focus on a single issue or cause—such as animal rights, environmental, or anti-abortion extremism—and often use criminal acts.

**skinheads**. A subculture composed primarily of working-class, white youth who embrace shaved heads for males, substance abuse, and violence.

**sovereign citizen movement**. A right-wing extremist movement composed of groups or individuals who reject the notion of U.S. citizenship. They claim to follow only what they believe to be God's law or common law and the original 10 amendments (Bill of Rights) to the U.S. Constitution.

**tax resistance movement**. Groups or individuals who vehemently believe taxes violate their constitutional rights. Among their beliefs are that wages are not income, that paying income taxes is voluntary, and that the 16th Amendment to the U.S. Constitution was not properly ratified.

**tertiary targeting**. Plans or attacks against parties with indirect links to the primary target of an organized campaign.

**underground**. A term used to describe clandestine extremist groups, individuals, or their activities.

**violent antiwar extremism**. A movement of groups or individuals who advocate or engage in criminal activity and plot acts of violence and terrorism in an attempt to voice their opposition to U.S. involvement in war-related activities.

**violent religious sects**. Religious extremist groups predisposed toward violence. These groups often stockpile weapons, conduct paramilitary training, and share a paranoid interpretation of current world events, which they often associate with the end of the world.

**white nationalism**. A term used by white supremacists to emphasize what they perceive as the uniquely white (European) heritage of the United States.

**white power**. A term used by white supremacists to describe their pride in and the perceived superiority of the white race.

**white separatism**. A movement of groups or individuals who believe in the separation of races and reject interracial marriages. Some advocate the secession of specific geographic regions from the rest of the United States.

**white supremacist movement**. Groups or individuals who believe that whites—Caucasians—are intellectually and morally superior to other races and use their racist ideology to justify committing crimes, acts of violence, and terrorism to advance their cause.

## ACRONYMS USED IN CRIMINAL INTELLIGENCE

| | |
|---|---|
| AAR | After Action Report |
| ACS | Automated Case System (FBI) |
| ADNET | Anti-Drug Network |
| AFIS | Automated Fingerprint Identification System |
| AFIWC | Air Force Information Warfare Center |
| AGILE | Advanced Generation of Interoperability for Law Enforcement |
| AOR | Area of Responsibility |
| ARJIS | Automated Regional Justice Information System |
| ASAC | Assistant Special Agent in Charge |
| ATAC | Anti-Terrorism Advisory Council |
| ATF | Bureau of Alcohol, Tobacco, Firearms and Explosives |
| ATIX | Automated Trusted Information Exchange |
| ATPA | Auto Theft Prevention Authority |
| BATIC | Border Auto Theft Information Center |
| BATS | Bombing and Arson Tracking System (ATF) |
| BJA | Bureau of Justice Assistance |
| BLS | As used by ODP and DHS, Blended Learning Strategy |
| BLS | As used by the Department of Commerce, Bureau of Labor Statistics |
| BRTC | Border Research Technology Center |
| BSA | Bank Secrecy Act (FinCEN related) |
| C3 | Command, Control, and Communications |
| C3I | Command, Control, Communications, and Information |
| CAD | Computer-Assisted Dispatch |
| CATIC | California Anti-Terrorism Information Center |
| CBP | Customs and Border Protection of DHS |
| CBRNE | Chemical, Biological, Radiological, Nuclear, and Explosive |
| CDICG | Counterdrug Intelligence Coordination Group |
| CDX | Counterdrug Intelligence Executive Secretariat |
| CERT | Computer Emergency Response Team |
| CFI | Certified Firearms Instructor |
| CFR | Code of Federal Regulations |
| CHRI | Criminal History Record Information |
| CI | Counterintelligence |
| CIA | Central Intelligence Agency |
| CICC | Criminal Intelligence Coordinating Council |
| CIO | Chief Information Officer |
| CIP | Critical Infrastructure Protection |
| CIPA | Classified Information Procedures Act |

| | |
|---|---|
| CIPWG | Critical Infrastructure Protection Working Group |
| CIRT | Computer Incident Response Team |
| CISAnet | Criminal Information Sharing Alliance Network |
| CITAC | Computer Investigation and Infrastructure Threat Assessment Center |
| CJIS | Criminal Justice Information Services |
| CLE | Criminal Law Enforcement |
| CLEAR | Chicago Citizen and Law Enforcement Analysis and Reporting |
| CODIS | Combined DNA Indexing System |
| COMINT | Communications Intelligence |
| COMSEC | Communications Security |
| CONOPS | Concept of Operations |
| CONUS | Continental United States |
| COPS | Office of Community-Oriented Policing Services |
| CP | Command Post |
| CPTED | Crime Prevention Through Environmental Design |
| CSDN | Customs Secure Data Network |
| CST | Civil Support Team (Regional National Guard WMB Teams) |
| CT | Counterterrorism |
| CTAC | Counter-Drug Technology Assessment Center |
| CTC | Counter-Terrorism Center |
| CTO | Chief Technology Officer |
| CTTWG | Counter-Terrorism Training Working Group |
| CVNIP | Commercial Vehicle Narcotics Interdiction Program |
| DCI | Director of Central Intelligence |
| DEA | U.S. Drug Enforcement Administration |
| DHS | U.S. Department of Homeland Security |
| DIA | Defense Intelligence Agency |
| DISA | Defense Information Systems Agency |
| DISN | Defense Information System Network |
| DL | Driver's License |
| DNS | Domain Name Servers |
| DoD | U.S. Department of Defense |
| DoJ | U.S. Department of Justice |
| DoS | U.S. Department of State |
| DoT | Department of Transportation |
| EMS | Emergency Medical Services, fire, and ambulance |
| EOC | Emergency Operations Center |
| EOP | Executive Office of the President |
| EPIC | El Paso Intelligence Center |
| ERT | Evidence Response Team (FBI) |
| FAS | Federation of American Scientists |
| FBI | Federal Bureau of Investigation |
| FEMA | Federal Emergency Management Agency |
| FI | Field Interview/Field Interview Card |
| FIG | Field Intelligence Group of the FBI Field Offices |
| FinCEN | Financial Crimes Enforcement Network |
| FLETC | Federal Law Enforcement Training Center |
| FOIA | Freedom of Information Act |
| FOUO | For Official Use Only |
| FTTTF | Foreign Terrorist Tracking Task Force |
| FY | Fiscal Year |

| | |
|---|---|
| GAC | Global Justice Information Sharing Initiative Advisory Committee |
| GAO | General Accountability Office |
| GIWG | Global Intelligence Working Group |
| Global | Global Justice Information Sharing Initiative |
| GSA | General Services Administration |
| HazMat | Hazardous Materials |
| HEAT | Help End Auto Theft Program |
| HIDTA | High-Intensity Drug Trafficking Area |
| HIFCA | High-Intensity Financial Crime Area |
| HIVA | Hazard Identification and Vulnerability Assessment |
| HQ | Headquarters |
| HSAS | Homeland Security Advisory System |
| HSDN | Homeland Secure Data Network |
| HSIN | Homeland Security Information Network |
| HSOC | Homeland Security Operations Center |
| HSPD | Homeland Security Presidential Directive |
| HUMINT | Human Intelligence |
| IACP | International Association of Chiefs of Police |
| IAD | Internal Affairs Division |
| IADLEST | International Association of Directors of Law Enforcement Standards and Training |
| IAFIS | Integrated Automated Fingerprint Identification System |
| IAIPDHS | Information Analysis and Infrastructure Protection Directorate |
| IALEIA | International Association of Law Enforcement Intelligence Analysts |
| IC | Intelligence Community |
| ICE | Immigration and Customs Enforcement of DHS |
| ICS | Incident Command System |
| IED | Improvised Explosive Device |
| III | Interstate Identification Index |
| ILP | Intelligence-Led Policing |
| IMINT | Imagery Intelligence |
| INFOSEC | Information Systems Security |
| INTERPOL | International Criminal Police Organization |
| IP | Internet Protocol |
| IRS | Intelligence Resource Specialist and Internal Revenue Service |
| ISI | Gateway Information Sharing Initiative |
| ISR | Intelligence, Surveillance, and Reconnaissance |
| IT | Information Technology |
| ITCWG | Intelligence Training Coordination Working Group |
| IW | Information Warfare |
| JCON | Justice Consolidated Office Network |
| JITF–CT | Joint Intelligence Task Force–Combating Terrorism |
| JTTF | Joint Terrorism Task Force |
| JRIES | Joint Regional Information Exchange System |
| LEA | Law Enforcement Agency |
| LECC | Law Enforcement Community Coordinator |
| LEI | Law Enforcement Intelligence |
| LEIN | Law Enforcement Information Network |
| LEIU | Law Enforcement Intelligence Unit |
| LEO | Law Enforcement Online (operated by the FBI) |
| LES | Law Enforcement Sensitive |

| | |
|---|---|
| MAGLOCLEN | Middle Atlantic-Great Lakes Organized Crime Law Enforcement Network (a RISS center) |
| MAP | Mutual Aid Pact |
| MATRIX | Multi-State Anti-Terrorism Information Exchange |
| MCC | Major City Chiefs Association |
| MOA | Memorandum of Agreement |
| MOCIC | Mid-States Organized Crime Information Center (a RISS center) |
| MOU | Memorandum of Understanding |
| NCB | National Central Bureau (of INTERPOL) |
| NCIC | National Crime Information Center |
| NCIS | Naval Criminal Investigative Service |
| NCISP | National Criminal Intelligence Sharing Plan |
| NCJRS | National Criminal Justice Reference Service |
| NCTC | National Counterterrorism Center |
| NDIC | National Drug Intelligence Center |
| NDPIX | National Drug Pointer Index |
| NESPIN | New England State Police Information Network (a RISS center) |
| NICS | National Instant Criminal Background Check System |
| NIJ | National Institute of Justice |
| NIMA | National Imagery and Mapping Agency |
| NIMS | National Incident Management System |
| NIPC | National Infrastructure Protection Center |
| NIPRNET | Non-classified Internet Protocol Router Network |
| NISP | National Industrial Security Program |
| NIST | National Institute of Standards and Technology |
| NLECTC | National Law Enforcement and Corrections Technology Centers |
| NLETS | National Law Enforcement Telecommunications System |
| NOC | National Operations Center |
| NSA | National Security Agency |
| NSA | National Sheriffs' Association |
| NSD | National Security Directive |
| NTAC | United States Secret Service National Threat Assessment Center |
| NVPS | National Virtual Pointer System |
| NW3C | National White Collar Crime Center |
| OCONUS | Outside the Continental United States |
| ODP | Office for Domestic Preparedness of DHS |
| OIG | Office of Inspector General |
| OJP | Office of Justice Programs |
| OMB | Office of Management and Budget |
| OPSEC | Operations Security |
| OSI | Open Source Intelligence |
| OSIS | Open Source Information System |
| PCII | Protecting Critical Infrastructure Information |
| PPE | Personal Protective Equipment |
| RAC | Resident Agent in Charge |
| RCPI | Regional Community Policing Institute (of COPS) |
| RFI | Request for Information |
| RFS | Request for Service |
| RICO | Racketeering-Influenced Corrupt Organization |
| RISS | Regional Information Sharing System |
| RISS.NET | Regional Information Sharing Systems secure intranet |

| | |
|---|---|
| RMIN | Rocky Mountain Information Network (a RISS center) |
| RMS | Records Management System |
| ROCIC | Regional Organized Crime Information Center (a RISS center) |
| SAC | Special Agent in Charge (FBI, DEA, ATF) |
| SAR | Suspicious Activity Report |
| SATINT | Satellite Intelligence |
| SBU | Sensitive But Unclassified |
| SCI | Sensitive Compartmentalized Information |
| SCIF | Secret Compartmentalized Information Facility |
| SHSI | Sensitive Homeland Security Information |
| SIG | Special Interest Groups |
| SIGINT | Signal Intelligence |
| SLATT | State and Local Anti-Terrorism Training program of BJA |
| SLGCP | Office of State and Local Government Coordination and Preparedness of DHS |
| SLTLE | State, Local, and Tribal Law Enforcement |
| SOP | Standard Operating Procedure (directives at the division/unit level) |
| SPPADS | State and Provincial Police Academy Directors Section |
| SWBSADIS | Southwest Border States Anti-Drug Information System |
| TCL | Targeted Capabilities List of ODP/DHS |
| TEWG | Terrorism Early Warning Group |
| TIP | Department of State Terrorist Interdiction Program |
| TSA | Transportation Security Act and Transportation Security Administration |
| TSC | Terrorist Screening Center |
| TTIC | Terrorist Threat Integration Center |
| UCR | Uniform Crime Reports |
| USAO | United States Attorney's Office |
| VBIED | Vehicle-Based Improvised Explosive Device |
| VICAP | Violent Criminal Apprehension Program |
| VIN | Vehicle Identification NumberNumber |
| VPN | Virtual Private Network |
| WMD | Weapons of Mass Destruction |
| WSIN | Western States Information Network (a RISS center) |
| XML | Extensible Markup Language |

# Appendix J: Department of Homeland Security–Recognized Fusion Centers

Federally funded and supported fusion centers can be found in nearly every state in the United States. The Department of Homeland Security (DHS) has officially recognized 72 fusion centers. Outlined below is a representative list of the DHS-recognized centers. It should be noted that the information is derived from an array of sources and should be verified for accuracy before official use. There are also many law enforcement agencies that partner with the lead agencies noted below as well as many agencies that have developed and established their own fusion centers, which are not reflected herein.

Alabama Fusion Center
Montgomery, Alabama
Phone: (334) 517-2660
Fax: (334) 517-2746
Toll-Free: (866) 229-6220
fusioncenter@alacop.gov
fusion.alabama.gov

Alaska Information and Analysis Center
Anchorage, Alaska
Phone: (907) 269-8900
Toll-Free: (855) 692-5425
AKIAC@alaska.gov

Arizona Counter Terrorism Information Center
Phoenix, Arizona
Phone: (602) 644-5805
Toll-Free: (877) 272-8329
actic@azdps.gov
www.azdps.gov

Arkansas State Fusion Center
Little Rock, Arkansas
Phone: (501) 618-8001
Toll-Free: (866) 787-2332
arfusioncenter@asp.arkansas.gov

Austin Regional Intelligence Center; Austin, TX
Austin, Texas
Phone: (512) 974-2742
aric@austintexas.gov
www.arictexas.org

Boston Regional Intelligence Center; Boston, MA
Boston, Massachusetts
Phone: (617) 343-4328
bric.bpd@cityofboston.gov
www.mbhsr.org/

California State Threat Assessment Center
Mather, California
Phone: (916) 874-1100
STAC@CalOES.ca.gov
www.calstac.org

Central California Intelligence Center; Sacramento, CA
McClellan, California
Phone: (916) 808-8383
Toll-Free: (888) 884-8383
info@sacrtac.org
www.sacrtac.org

Central Florida Intelligence Exchange (CFIX)
Orlando, Florida
Phone: (407) 858-3950
cfix@ocfl.net
www.ocso.com/cfix

Chicago Crime Prevention and Information Center; Chicago, IL
Chicago, Illinois
Phone: (312) 745-5669
cpic@chicagopolice.org

Colorado Information Analysis Center
Lakewood, Colorado
Phone: (877) 509-2422
ciac@ciac.co.gov
dhsem.state.co.us

Connecticut Intelligence Center
Hartford, Connecticut
Phone: (860) 706-5500
Fax: (806) 706-5535
ctic@ct.gov
www.ct.gov/demhs

Dallas Fusion Center; Dallas, TX
Dallas, Texas
Phone: (214) 671-3482
dallas.fusion@dpd.ci.dallas.tx.us

Delaware Information and Analysis Center
Dover, Delaware
Fax: (302) 739-1609
Alternate Phone: (302) 739-5996
Toll-Free: (800) 367-2312
diac@state.de.us
www.dediac.org

Delaware Valley Intelligence Center; Philadelphia, PA
Philadelphia, Pennsylvania
Phone: (215) 897-0800
Fax: (215) 683-2794
dvic@phila.gov
dvicphila.org

Detroit and Southeast Michigan Information and Intelligence Center; Detroit, MI
Detroit, Michigan
Phone: (313) 967-4600
DSEMIIC@michigan.gov

El Paso Multi-Agency Tactical Response Information eXchange (MATRIX); El Paso, TX
El Paso, Texas
Phone: (915) 212-4200
Fax: (915) 212-0280
pdfusion@elpasotexas.gov

Florida Fusion Center
Tallahassee, Florida
Phone: (850) 410-7645
Toll-Free: (800) 342-0820
FloridaFusionCenter@fdle.state.fl.us
www.fdle.state.fl.us

Georgia Information Sharing and Analysis Center
Atlanta, Georgia
Phone: (404) 486-6420
generalinfo@gisac.gbi.ga.gov

Greater Cincinnati Fusion Center
Cincinnati, Ohio
Phone: (513) 263-8000
Fax: (513) 263-8225
GCFC@GCFC.org
www.GCFC.org

Hawaii Fusion Center
Honolulu, Hawaii
Phone: (916) 356-4467
hsfc@dod.hawaii.gov
www.pacclear.org

Houston Regional Intelligence Service Center; Houston, TX
Houston, Texas
Phone: (713) 884-4710
HRISC-Fusioncenter@houstonpolice.org

Idaho Criminal Intelligence Center
Meridian, Idaho
Phone: (208) 846-7676
ICIC@fusion.idaho.gov
www.isp.idaho.gov/icic

Illinois Statewide Terrorism and Intelligence Center
Springfield, Illinois
Phone: (877) 455-7842
stic@isp.state.il.us

Indiana Intelligence Fusion Center
Indianapolis, Indiana
Phone: (866) 400-4432
iifc@iifc.in.gov
www.in.gov/iifc

Iowa Intelligence Fusion Center
Des Moines, Iowa
Phone: (800) 308-5983
intel@dps.state.ia.us
www.dps.state.is.us/intell/index.shtml

Kansas City Terrorism Early Warning Fusion Center; Kansas City, MO
Kansas City, Missouri
Phone: (816) 413-3601
kctew@kcpd.org
www.kctew.org

Kansas Intelligence Fusion Center
Topeka, Kansas
Phone: (785) 274-1805
intelligence.fusion@ksag.org

Kentucky Intelligence Fusion Center
Frankfort, Kentucky
Phone: (502) 564-2081
fusioncenter@ky.gov
www.homelandsecurity.ky.gov

Los Angeles Joint Regional Intelligence Center; Los Angeles, CA
Norwalk, California
Phone: (562) 345-1100
Fax: (562) 345-1766
jric@jric.org
www.jric.org

Louisiana State Analytical & Fusion Exchange
Baton Rouge, Louisiana
Phone: (225) 925-4192
Toll-Free: (800) 434-8007
lafusion.center@dps.la.gov
www.la-safe.org

Maine Information and Analysis Center
Augusta, Maine 04330-0164
Phone: (207) 624-7280
Toll-Free: (877) 786-3636
intel.msp@maine.gov

Mariana Regional Fusion Center (Guam)
Agana Heights, Guam
info@mlrin.org

Maryland Coordination and Analysis Center
Woodlawn, Maryland
Phone: (800) 492-8477
mdwatch@leo.gov
www.mcac.maryland.gov

Massachusetts Commonwealth Fusion Center
Maynard, Massachusetts
Phone: (978) 451-3711
Alternate Phone: (978) 451-3700
fusion@massmail.state.ma.us

Michigan Intelligence Operations Center
Lansing, Michigan
Phone: (517) 241-8000
Toll-Free: (877) 616-4677
mioc@michigan.gov
www.michigan.gov/mioc

Minnesota Fusion Center
St. Paul, Minnesota
Phone: (651) 793-3730
Fax: (651) 793-3731
Toll-Free: (800) 422-0798
info@icefishx.org
www.icefishx.org

Mississippi Analysis and Information Center
Pearl, Mississippi
Phone: (601) 933-7200
MSAIC@dps.ms.gov
www.homelandsecurity.ms.gov/msaic.html

Missouri Information Analysis Center
Jefferson City, Missouri
Phone: (866) 362-6422
miac@mshp.dps.mo.gov
www.miacx.org

Montana Analysis & Technical Information Center
Helena, Montana
Phone: (406) 444-1330
dojintel@mt.gov
doj.mt.gov

Nebraska Information Analysis Center
Lincoln, Nebraska
Phone: (402) 479-4049
Fax: (402) 479-4950
nefusioncenter@nebraska.gov

Nevada Threat Analysis Center; Carson City, NV
Carson City, Nevada
Phone: (775) 687-0450
ntac@dps.state.nv.us

New Hampshire Information and Analysis Center
Concord, New Hampshire
Phone: (603) 271-0300
nh.iac@dos.nh.gov
www.nh.gov/safety/information-analysis-center

New Jersey Regional Operations Intelligence Center
West Trenton, New Jersey
Phone: (609) 963-6900
roic@gw.njsp.org

New Mexico All Source Intelligence Center
Santa Fe, New Mexico
Phone: (505) 476-9600
intelligence.fusion@state.nm.us
www.nmdhsem.org

New York State Intelligence Center
East Greenbush, New York
Phone: (866) 723-3697
ciu@nysic.ny.gov

North Carolina Information Sharing and Analysis Center
Raleigh, North Carolina
Phone: (919) 716-1111
Toll-Free: (888) 624-7222
ncisaac@ncdoj.gov

North Central Texas Fusion Center; McKinney, TX
McKinney, Texas
Phone: (972) 548-5537
NCTFC@co.collin.tx.us
www.co.collin.tx.us

North Dakota State and Local Information Center
Bismarck, North Dakota
Phone: (866) 885-8295
ndslic@nd.gov
www.nd.gov/des/homeland/fusion-center

Northeast Ohio Regional Fusion Center; Cleveland, OH
Cleveland, Ohio
Phone: (216) 515-8477
Toll-Free: (877) 515-8477
info@neorfc.us
neorfc.us

Northern California Regional Intelligence Center; San Francisco, CA
San Francisco, California
Phone: (866) 367-8847
dutyofficer@ncric.org
www.ncric.org

Northern Virginia Regional Intelligence Center; Fairfax, VA
Fairfax, Virginia
Phone: (703) 212-4590
fcpdnvric@fairfaxcounty.gov

Ohio Strategic Analysis and Information Center
Columbus, Ohio
Phone: (614) 799-3555
saic@dps.state.oh.us
www.homelandsecurity.ohio.gov/index.stm

Oklahoma Information Fusion Center
Oklahoma City, Oklahoma
Phone: (405) 842-8547
Alternate Phone: (405) 848-6724
fusion@osbi.ok.gov
www.okfusion.ok.gov

Orange County Intelligence Assessment Center; Orange County, CA
Santa Ana, California
Phone: (714) 289-3949
Fax: (714) 289-1025
ociac@ociac.org
www.ociac.org

Oregon Terrorism Information Threat Assessment Network
Salem, Oregon
Phone: (503) 378-6347
oregonfusioncenter@doj.state.or.us
www.oregonfusioncenter@doj.state.or.us

Pennsylvania Criminal Intelligence Center
Harrisburg, Pennsylvania
Phone: (877) 777-6835
sp-intelligence@pa.gov
www.psp.pa.gov

Puerto Rico National Security State Information Center
Hato Rey, Puerto Rico
Phone: (787) 793-1234
nssic@policia.pr.gov

Rhode Island State Fusion Center
Providence, Rhode Island
Phone: (866) 490-8477
Fax: (401) 458-1173
fusion@risp.dps.ri.gov

San Diego Law Enforcement Coordination Center; San Diego, CA
San Diego, California
Phone: (858) 495-5730
info@sd-lecc.org

South Carolina Information and Intelligence Center
Columbia, South Carolina
Phone: (866) 472-8477
Toll-Free: (803) 896-7133
sciic@sled.sc.gov
www.sled.sc.gov

South Dakota Fusion Center
Sioux Falls, South Dakota
Phone: (605) 367-5940
sdfusioncenter@state.sd.us

Southeast Florida Fusion Center; Miami, FL
Miami, Florida
Phone: (305) 470-3900
ioc@mdpd.com
www.mdpd.com

Southeastern Wisconsin Threat Analysis Center; Milwaukee, WI
Milwaukee, Wisconsin
Phone: (414) 935-7741
stac@milwaukee.gov
WiWATCH.org

Southern Nevada Counter-Terrorism Center (Las Vegas, Nevada)
Las Vegas, Nevada
Phone: (702) 828-2200
ansec@lvmpd.com
www.snctc.org

Southwest Texas Fusion Center; San Antonio, TX
San Antonio, Texas
Phone: (210) 207-7680
swtxfusion@sanantonio.gov

Southwestern PA Region 13 Fusion Center; Pittsburgh, PA
Pittsburgh, Pennsylvania
Phone: (412) 473-2550

St. Louis Fusion Center; St. Louis, MO
St. Louis, Missouri
Phone: (314) 615-4839
info@sltew.org
www.sltew.org

Tennessee Fusion Center
Nashville, Tennessee
Phone: (877) 250-2333
tfc@tn.gov
www.tennessee.gov/homelandsecurity

Texas Joint Crime Information Center
Austin, Texas
Phone: (866) 786-5972
TXJCIC@dps.texas.gov

U.S. Virgin Islands Fusion Center
St. Thomas, Virgin Islands
Phone: (340) 776-3013
fusioncenter@vitema.vi.gov

Utah Statewide Information and Analysis Center
Sandy, Utah
Phone: (801) 256-2360
SIAC@utah.gov
www.publicsafety.utah.gov/investigations/siac.html

Vermont Intelligence Center
Williston, Vermont
Phone: (802) 872-6110
VIC@listserv.dps.state.vt.us
www.dps.state.vt.us

Virginia Fusion Center
North Chesterfield, Virginia
Phone: (804) 674-2196
vfc@vsp.virginia.gov
www.vsp.state.va.us/FusionCenter

Washington Regional Threat and Analysis Center (Washington, D.C.)
Washington, DC, Washington DC
Phone: (202) 481-3075
wrtac@dc.gov

Washington State Fusion Center
Seattle, Washington
Phone: (877) 843-9522
intake@wsfc.wa.gov

West Virginia Intelligence Fusion Center
Charleston, West Virginia
Phone: (304) 558-4831
wvfusion@wv.gov
www.fusioncenter.wv.gov

Wisconsin Statewide Information Center
Madison, Wisconsin
Phone: (608) 242-5393
wsic@doj.state.wi.us
www.doj.state.wi.us/dci/division-criminal-investigation-dci

# Appendix K: Sources of Information References for Investigators

Resources, and access to them, are vital to nearly all criminal investigations and intelligence products. One document that gathers information on many resources is *The Guide to Sources of Information for Intelligence Officers, Analysts, and Investigators*. Many resources cited below have been compiled and updated by Michael Chesbro who operates the website www.chesbro.tech. Dr Michael Chesbro is a security researcher and technologist, specializing in cyber intelligence and counterintelligence threat analysis. He is a Board Certified Forensic Examiner, Certified Forensic Consultant with a background in digital forensics, and a Fellow of the American College of Forensic Examiners. He also has an extensive and distinguished military intelligence background. Compiled from multiple and various open sources over the past decade, the information found in the guide was obtained from the organizations listed herein or from other open sources and may not have been fully validated.

The guide is not intended to be an exhaustive compilation of all sources of information available to intelligence officers, analysts, and investigators. There are many other sources of valuable information that may be useful for intelligence, analytical, and investigative purposes. The specific sources of information identified in the guide exemplify the types of information available, and that which may have proved useful in the past. The guide was originally compiled and produced in October 2009. The guide is a living document to which changes and updates are continually made and those agencies listed below are not at all inclusive.

## FEDERAL AGENCIES

ATF Field Operations Offices
Bureau of Diplomatic Security – Diplomatic Security Service
Central Intelligence Agency
Crime Records Center (U.S. Army – USACIDC)
Customs and Border Protection (CBP)
DEA Field Offices
Defense Advanced Research Projects Agency (DARPA)
FBI Field Offices
FBI – Joint Terrorism Task Forces
Federal Protective Service (FPS)
High Intensity Drug Trafficking Areas
Homeland Security Points of Contact (by state)
Immigration & Customs Enforcement (ICE) Detention and Removal Operations Offices
Marine Corps Intelligence Activity
Military Law Enforcement/Investigative Agencies

- Naval Criminal Investigative Service (NCIS)
- U.S. Air Force Office of Special Investigations (AFOSI)
- U.S. Army Criminal Investigation Command

National Drug Intelligence Center (NDIC)
National Gang Intelligence Center (NGIC)
National Nuclear Security Administration
Postal Inspection Service
Secret Service Field Offices

Terrorist Screening Center (TSC)
Transportation Security Administration (TSA)
United States Attorneys Offices
United States Citizenship and Immigration (USCIS) Offices
United States Intelligence Community
U.S. Marshals District Offices

## INFORMATION SHARING NETWORKS & RESOURCES

American Board for Certification in Homeland Security (ABCHS)
Bomb Arson Tracking System (BATS)
Consumer Sentinel
Cybercop (Secure Portal)
El Paso Intelligence Center
DHS Recognized Fusion Centers
DOD Issuances
DOD Social Media Hub
FBI Citizens Academy
FBI Law Enforcement Online (LEO)
Federal Protective Service Portal
First Observer
Foreign Military Studies Office – Joint Reserve Intelligence Center (FMSO-JRIC)
High Tech Crime Consortium
High Technology Crime Investigation Association
Homeland Security Information Network (HSIN)
Information Assurance Support Environment – Defense Information Systems Agency (DISA)
Information Sharing Environment
Infragard
IntelCenter
Intelink
Intelligence Is The Future: Intelligence Applications & Analysis for Law Enforcement
Intelligence Knowledge Network
International Association of Crime Analysts (IACA)
International Association of Law Enforcement Intelligence Analysts (IALEIA)
Internet Fraud Alert Program
Law Enforcement Intelligence Unit (LEIU)
Lessons Learned Information Sharing Network
Multi-State Information Sharing and Analysis Center (MS-ISAC)
National Counter-Terrorism Center
National Criminal Intelligence Resource Center (NCIRC)
National Defense Intelligence College (NDIC) Press
National Equipment Register, Inc. (NER)
National Insurance Crime Bureau
National Missing and Unidentified Persons System (NamUs)
National Technical Investigators' Association
National White Collar Crime Center (NW3C)
Office of the National Counterintelligence Executive
Open Source Center
Overseas Security Advisory Council (OSAC)
Protective Design Center – U.S. Army Corps of Engineers
Regional Information Sharing System (RISS)

Regional and State Online Resource for Emergency Management
SENTRY system
State and Local Antiterrorism Training (SLATT)
Strategic Studies Institute – United States Army War College
TRIPwire
United States Private and Public Partnership (USP3)

In addition to the living document compiled by Chesbro, the Government Accountability Office (GAO) originally produced the *Investigators' Guide to Sources of Information* which was published in 1988, and revised in 1992 and 1997. This was done as a service to the investigative community by GAO's Office of Special Investigations. It was intended to be a useful investigative tool for identifying sources of information about people, property, business, and finance. Outlined below are some substantive resources that can add value to an investigation and may be overlooked by some investigators.

## LOCAL AND STATE GOVERNMENTS

### LOCAL GOVERNMENT

### Building Inspector

The following information is available from a building inspector's office:

- Building permits, which generally show the name of the applicant, the address of construction, the estimated cost of construction, and the name of the builder or contractor
- Blueprints and plans, which show construction details and are often submitted with applications for building permits
- Building inspectors' reports, which contain information regarding compliance with construction specifications

### Coroner/Medical Examiner

Coroner registers generally contain the name or description of the deceased; date of inquest, if any; property found on the deceased and its disposition; and the cause of death.

### Court Clerk

Court clerks often maintain court files on such civil actions as liens, name changes, and divorces. These files generally include the complaint (identifying the plaintiff(s), the defendant(s), and the cause of action); the answer to the complaint; and the judgment rendered. Also, depositions introduced as exhibits become part of the court records. The court clerk's minutes or the file jacket may indicate whether a transcript of the proceedings was taken.

Divorce case complaints usually identify the plaintiff and defendant; place and date of marriage (which points to the appropriate county recorder's records); date of separation, if applicable; names, ages, and birthdates of any children; community property; and grounds or charges, if any; and the attorneys retained by the parties. The plaintiff's signature is usually on the complaint and the defendant's signature can be found on the cross-complaint or answer.

Probate indexes will list probate actions alphabetically, by name of the estate or petitioner, and will give the filing date and the docket number. Individual case files often list causes of action and rulings regarding the estate, and status of potential beneficiaries who may be minors, adopted, incompetent, or insane.

Court clerks also maintain criminal court files, which may contain information describing the crime and the charges in an indictment. These files may also contain the complainant's signature (exemplar); a transcript of the preliminary hearing (usually consisting of testimony of the complainant, defendant, witnesses, and arresting officer); the names of the prosecuting and defense attorneys; the probation officer's report, with complete background investigation of the defendant; and any subpoenas issued in the case.

## Health Department

Health departments often license and inspect properties, identify and investigate local health problems, educate businesses on local health issues, and provide direct emergency services. Death certificates are usually available at health departments. A death certificate provides the decedent's name; address; sex; age; race; social security number; birthplace; birthdates; and date, place, and time of death. Additionally, a death certificate generally provides the medical and coroner's certificate and information about the decedent's parents, including their occupations.

## Personnel Department

Personnel departments maintain the following information:

- Personal history statements on employees and political leaders
- Employment records, efficiency reports, and records of salary liens on employees

Public schools maintain the following information:

- Student records showing grades, disciplinary actions, and, in some school districts, biographies
- Teacher biographies showing personal background, education, and former employment

Recorder offices maintain the following information:

- Documents pertaining to real estate transactions, including deeds, grants, transfers, mortgages, releases of mortgages, powers of attorney, and leases that have been acknowledged or approved
- Mortgages on personal property
- Wills admitted to probate
- Uniform Commercial Code filings
- Official bonds
- Notices of mechanics' liens
- Transcripts of judgments that are made on real estate liens
- Notices of attachment of real estate
- Papers pertaining to bankruptcy
- Certified copies of decrees and judgments of courts of record
- Department of Defense DD 214 forms that are recorded by some veterans as evidence of veteran status, particularly in those states that grant veterans reduced property tax rates
- Marriage licenses and certificates that can provide the names, ages, cities of residence, and places of birth of the licensees; date and place of marriage; names of witnesses to the marriage and their residence; and names of the cleric, judge, or justice of the peace who performed the ceremony.

Registrar of Voters Registrars of voters may maintain the following:

- Affidavit of registration, which includes the registrant's name and age, occupation, and address at the time of registration
- Nomination papers of candidates for public office

## Regulatory Agencies

Applications for business licenses, which are filed by local regulatory agencies, have valuable information on certain types of businesses and professions. Also, such applications often have useful information about individuals engaged in those businesses or professions. In many cities, the following types of businesses and professions would be regulated and their owners and/or practitioners would be required to apply for licenses:

- Businesses seeking liquor licenses
- Professionals, including those trained as certified public accountants, dentists, doctors, plumbers, electricians, and optometrists
- Businesses that health and fire departments periodically inspect, including restaurants, bars, and nightclubs
- Businesses operating under names other than the owners' names (such businesses must register under assumed names and are included in the "doing business as" files).

Surveyor offices maintain maps of elevations, baselines, landmarks, important sites, roads, rights of way, and easements.

## Tax Assessor

Tax assessor offices maintain maps of real property, including information on a property's dimensions, address, owner, taxable value, and improvements.

## Tax Collector

Tax collector offices maintain the following information:

- Names and addresses of payers of property taxes, including payers who are not the apparent owners
- Legal descriptions of property
- Amounts of taxes paid on real and personal property
- Delinquency status of taxes
- Names of former owners of property

## Welfare Commission

Information filed by welfare commissions is gathered by social workers, psychologists, and physicians. Generally, the information gathered—frequently provided by welfare recipients—is not verified. Welfare commission files contain such information as the recipient's address, previous employment, prior earnings, and property owned. Welfare files also contain information on the property owned by the recipient's relatives and the relatives' health and criminal records.

## STATE GOVERNMENT

## Attorney General

State attorneys general are good sources of information on efforts made in the areas of statewide criminal justice, civil enforcement, and consumer protection and the functions—or administrative structure—of the state offices responsible for these areas.

## Bureau of Vital Statistics

Bureaus of Vital Statistics have birth certificates on file and are an excellent source of information about people. Birth certificates can provide a child's name, sex, date of birth, and address of place of birth; the names of the attending physician, midwife, and/or other assistants; the parents' names, ages, addresses, race, places of birth, and occupations; the mother's maiden name; and the number of siblings. (In some states, birth certificates may be found at the local level, such as at the health department.)

## Department of Motor Vehicles

The Department of Motor Vehicles maintains information on driver's licenses, vehicle registrations, titles, automobile transfers and sales, car dealers, car salespersons, emission inspection facilities, and, in some states, auto repair businesses as well as voter's records and concealed weapon permits. Of those states requiring that photographs of licensed drivers appear on their licenses, most maintain the photographs. Many states are changing to digital photographs.

## Regulatory Agencies

Departments and agencies that regulate individual and business activities within a particular state can be valuable sources of information. Individuals obtain licenses for activities such as driving, hunting, and fishing, and for such professions as medical, legal, and public accounting. Businesses are also often required to obtain licenses and permits to operate and file periodic reports such as for workers and unemployment compensation, sales tax, and state income tax. The following state regulatory departments and agencies maintain information valuable to investigators:

- Bureau of Professional and Vocational Standards or Department of Licensing
- Controller/Treasurer
- Department of Agriculture
- Department of Industrial Relations
- Department of Natural Resources
- Gambling Commission/Horse Racing Board
- Secretary of State
- Department of Corrections
- Liquor Commission
- Lottery Commission
- Securities Commission
- Utility Commission

# FEDERAL AGENCIES

## DEPARTMENT OF AGRICULTURE (USDA)

Various USDA agencies maintain information on:

- Meat or poultry companies
- Feedlot owners or operators, livestock brokers, and meat packers or canners; rural electric or telephone cooperatives
- Logging (tree harvesting) companies that remove timber from national forests
- Certain improvements to farmland
- The import or export of agricultural commodities, animals, or plants; and current or former USDA employees

Some USDA agencies maintain—or have access to—financial records at the state and local levels concerning:

- Contracts with the agency
- Recipients of various benefits, such as food stamps

- Retail grocery stores authorized to accept food stamps
- Free or reduced-price school lunch meals

Other USDA agencies maintain data on applicants/recipients of agriculture loans, such as:

- Loan applications and financial statements
- Bank account particulars
- Crop yields and business profits
- Applications for and indemnities paid by federal crop insurance
- Plats of property and location of other assets

In addition, USDA has information including certain financial data concerning the ownership, management, and operation of farms and ranches that participate in various USDA programs.

The Department of Commerce has information on international trade, social and economic statistics, patents, trademarks, ocean studies, domestic economic development, and minority businesses.

## DEPARTMENT OF DEFENSE (DOD)

To obtain information concerning military pay, dependents, allotments, deposits, and other financial information, contact Defense Joint Military Pay System; Director, Military Pay Directorate, Room 404; Defense Finance and Accounting Service Headquarters; Crystal Mall #3; 1931 Jefferson Davis Highway; Arlington, VA 22202 or at (703) 607-1373.

Records that survived a July 1973 fire concerning the personnel and medical histories of former military personnel are located at the Military Personnel Records Center; General Services Administration; 9700 Page Boulevard; St. Louis, MO 63132-5100. To obtain such information, contact the Army at (314) 538-4122; the Air Force at (314) 538-4218; and the Navy, Marine Corps, and Coast Guard at (314) 538-4200. Records destroyed in the fire may be reconstructed. If you wish to have a record reconstructed, call (314) 538-4144.

## DEPARTMENT OF ENERGY

### Federal Energy Regulatory Commission (FERC)

Electric utility and natural gas companies are required to file annual reports with FERC. The reports provide excellent financial pictures of the companies as well as other information, for example, names of officers, directors, and stockholders who own more than 10% of the company. FERC also maintain license and permit information concerning companies within its regulatory control.

## DEPARTMENT OF HEALTH AND HUMAN SERVICES (HHS)/FOOD AND DRUG ADMINISTRATION (FDA)

The FDA is an enforcement agency of HHS. FDA investigators in the field conduct investigations of drug firms under the jurisdiction of the FDA.

## DEPARTMENT OF JUSTICE (DOJ)

### DRUG ENFORCEMENT ADMINISTRATION (DEA)

DEA maintains information on individuals and businesses licensed to handle narcotics obtained under the Controlled Substances Act and persons in violation of federal drug laws and regulations. DEA administers the El Paso Intelligence Center and the Narcotics and Dangerous Drugs Information System.

## Federal Bureau of Investigation (FBI)

The FBI can provide information on criminal records and fingerprints, as well as nonrestricted information pertaining to criminal offenses and subversive activities. It also can provide information about foreign fugitives and wanted, missing, and unidentified persons. FBI administers the National Crime Information Center which maintains information on a variety of subjects, such as stolen vehicles, license plates, and guns.

FBI also maintains the following indexes:

- State Criminal History Records
- Criminal History Records of Federal Offenders
- National Stolen Property Index (stolen government property)
- National Fraudulent Check Index

## U.S. Citizenship and Immigration Services (USCIS)

USCIS retains the following information: alien registration records in effect since August 27, 1940 (from July 1, 1920, to August 27, 1940, immigrants were given identification cards); lists of passengers and crew on vessels from foreign ports; passenger manifests and declarations (ship, date, and point of entry); naturalization records (names of witnesses to naturalization proceedings and acquaintances of the individual); records of deportation proceedings; and financial statements of aliens and persons sponsoring their entry.

## U.S. Marshal's Service (USMS)

USMS maintains information on individuals wanted as fugitives by the federal government and records on the seizing, managing, and selling of assets forfeited by drug traffickers and other criminals.

## U.S. National Central Bureau for the International Criminal Police Organization (USNCB-INTERPOL)

USNCB represents the United States in INTERPOL, operating continuously to provide international support for U.S. law enforcement. USNCB provides an essential communications link between the U.S. police community and its counterparts in over 176 foreign member countries. USNCB, therefore, can request information regarding ownership, previous investigations, vessels possibly involved in narcotics trafficking, cultural property and artwork that might have been stolen, and any other information legally releasable from any of the INTERPOL member countries around the world. The degree of information available is determined by the laws of the countries from which the information is requested. USNCB can place an INTERPOL international lookout for persons who have committed an extraditable offense in the United States and are believed to have fled to another country.

Seventeen federal and state law enforcement agencies are part of USNCB, and all fifty states have established INTERPOL liaison offices. The following agencies are part of USNCB: Bureau of Alcohol, Tobacco and Firearms; Criminal Division, DOJ; Environmental Protection Agency; Office of the Inspector General, USDA; Diplomatic Security Service, Department of State; DEA; FBI; Federal Law Enforcement Training Center; Massachusetts State Police; Immigration and Naturalization Services (INS); Internal Revenue Service; Naval Criminal Investigative Service; Office of the Comptroller of the Currency; U.S. Customs Service; USMS; U.S. Postal Inspection Service; and the U.S. Secret Service.

## DEPARTMENT OF LABOR

The Department of Labor has information about the Federal Employees Compensation Act, Job Partnership Training Act, Occupational Safety Health Act, and Mine Safety Health Act. The

Department conducts programs under these acts and retains substantial data on businesses that participate in special work programs with the agency. Labor organizations must submit to the Department annual financial reports, which include statements of assets and liabilities and statements of receipts and disbursements. They must also complete supporting schedules: loans receivable; other investments; other assets; other liabilities; fixed assets; loans payable; sales of investment and fixed assets; disbursement to officers; disbursement to employees; purchases of investment and fixed assets; benefits; and contributions, gifts, and grants.

## DEPARTMENT OF STATE

The Department of State maintains information on passport records, and import and export licenses. The Department's Bureau of Diplomatic Security has information on previous investigations conducted by that office.

## DEPARTMENT OF TRANSPORTATION

### Federal Aviation Administration (FAA)

FAA maintains records reflecting the chain of ownership of all civil aircraft in the United States. These records include documents relative to the manufacture, sale, transfer, inspection, and modification of an aircraft, for example, bill of sale, sales contract, mortgage, and liens. FAA also maintains records on pilots, aircraft mechanics, flight engineers, and other individuals that it certifies for flight safety positions. These records include information on certificates held by airmen and the medical and law enforcement histories of airmen. The FAA Compliance Enforcement Program will provide a microfiche listing of registrants and their aircraft tail numbers (N number). This office can provide the registration history of a given aircraft using the aircraft tail number, serial number, or registrant's name. It can also provide airworthiness information, and lien and previous owner data.

### U.S. Coast Guard

The Coast Guard is the primary federal agency with maritime authority for the United States. It is a complex organization of people, ships, aircraft, boats, and shore stations that responds to tasks in several mission and program areas, including interdiction of drug smugglers and illegal immigrants.

The U.S. Coast Guard maintains the following information:

- Records on documented U.S. vessels
- Names of merchant mariners on U.S. vessels and investigative records pertaining to them
- Records relating to maritime drug smuggling
- Records on criminal investigations

### Federal Highway Administration (FHWA)

FHWA—Office of Motor Carriers—licenses, regulates, inspects, and registers all motor carriers operating in interstate commerce. It keeps records of its inspections of motor carriers and a history of violations of each carrier.

## DEPARTMENT OF THE TREASURY

### Bureau of Alcohol, Tobacco and Firearms (ATF)

ATF retains data on distilleries, wineries, breweries, manufacturers of tobacco products, wholesale and retail dealers of alcoholic beverages, and certain other manufacturers, dealers, and users of alcohol; investigative reports on alleged violations under its jurisdiction; data on federally licensed firearms manufacturers, importers, and dealers; and data on federally licensed explosive manufacturers, importers, and dealers.

ATF can trace firearms that have a serial number and that were manufactured or imported from the manufacturer or importer to the retailer after 1968. It can trace explosives materials from the manufacturer to the distributor and/or user. ATF also maintains records on federal firearms and explosive license holders, including manufacturers, importers, and dealers.

## Bureau of Engraving and Printing

The Bureau of Engraving and Printing can assist law enforcement with tracking currency from its printing offices to Federal Reserve banks. The bureau maintains computer files on all currency research that is done at the request of law enforcement agencies. If a match is made, for example, by serial numbers, the bureau will notify the law enforcement agency of the match.

Currency search requests should be sent to the Office of Security, Investigative Branch; Bureau of Engraving and Printing; Room 510-A; 301 14th Street, S.W.; Washington, DC 20228.

## Bureau of the Public Debt

The Bureau of the Public Debt maintains information on purchased and redeemed U.S. savings bonds (registered bonds), marketable securities, and special securities. Information maintained includes the series of bonds involved and the surname, given name, middle name or initial, and address of each person in whose name bonds were purchased.

## Financial Crimes Enforcement Network (FinCEN)

FinCEN is an organization established by the Department of the Treasury that collects, analyzes, and disseminates intelligence on financial crimes. Its mission is to provide a government-wide, multisource intelligence and analytical network to support law enforcement agencies in the detection, investigation, and prosecution of financial crimes. FinCEN uses the majority of its resources to assist agencies in their investigations of financial aspects of the illegal narcotics trade. FinCEN then prioritizes investigations of such non-narcotic crimes as money laundering offenses, Bank Secrecy Act violations, and other offenses of a financial nature, for example, tax and tariff violations; corruption; treason; and bankruptcy, financial institution, and government contract fraud. In both the narcotic and non-narcotic areas, FinCEN concentrates on investigations of national or international criminal organizations. FinCEN produces two types of products—tactical support and strategic analysis. Its tactical support reports either provide information and leads on criminal organizations and activities that are under investigation by law enforcement organizations or proactively identify previously undetected criminal organizations and activities so that investigations can be initiated. These FinCEN reports will assist agencies in identifying assets for seizure and forfeiture purposes, and in supporting ongoing investigations. During its strategic analyses, FinCEN collects, processes, analyzes, and develops intelligence on the emerging trends, patterns, and issues related to activities such as financial crimes and money laundering. FinCEN's financial database has information from reports that are required to be filed under the Bank Secrecy Act, including the Currency Transaction Report, Report of International Transportation of Currency or Monetary Instruments, Currency Transaction Report by Casinos, and Reports of Foreign Bank and Financial Accounts. Furthermore, FinCEN has access to data from Internal Revenue Service Form 8300 (Reports of Cash Payments Over $10,000 Received in a Trade or Business). FinCEN can be contacted at (800) SOS-BUCK (767-2825) or (703) 905-3520.

## Financial Management Service (FMS)

FMS reconciles all government checks paid by the U.S. Treasury and processes all subsequent claims of forgery and nonreceipt. It maintains photocopies of canceled U.S. government checks. However, original checks that have been determined to be forgeries are maintained by the U.S. Secret Service, also a Treasury bureau. When information must be obtained for the issuing disbursing office, the investigation may be expedited by asking that office to obtain the photocopy of the original check.

In lieu of the original check, FMS' Check Claims Branch can provide a certified microfilm copy of the check which is recognized and accepted in most courts of law. FMS charges a nominal fee for providing check copies.

## Internal Revenue Service (IRS)

There are two distinct law enforcement functions within the IRS: the Criminal Investigation Division and Internal Security. The Criminal Investigation Division investigates allegations of violations of the Internal Revenue Code as it relates to income tax, the Bank Secrecy Act, and money laundering statutes. The division's special agents possess financial investigative abilities that enable them to solve crimes by following the money trail. Armed with these financial investigative skills and clearly defined statutory jurisdiction, this IRS division works closely with federal, state, and local law enforcement organizations to solve crimes such as public corruption, telemarketing fraud, health care fraud, income tax evasion, and those that are narcotics related.

IRS internal security inspectors work for the chief inspector. Their mission is to protect the integrity of the IRS, its system, and its employees. They do this by investigating allegations of attempts to bribe IRS employees and allegations of employee misconduct.

## Office of the Comptroller of the Currency

The Office of the Comptroller of the Currency regulates national banks and maintains information concerning them. National bank examinations are made to determine banks' financial position and to evaluate bank assets. Bank examiners' reports contain information about bank records, loans, and operations. In view of their purpose and the basis on which they are obtained, reports of national bank examinations and related correspondence and papers are considered confidential. Requests for these documents should include the subject's name and address, the information desired, the reason it is needed, and the intended use.

## U.S. Customs and Border Protection Service

Customs retains the following data:

- Names of businesses that are involved in imports and exports
- Lists/records of importers and exporters
- Lists of suspects
- Records of seized smuggled property
- Declaration forms

Customs Office of Investigations investigates alleged violations of import and export practices. The office's special agents participate in the organized crime drug enforcement task force.

## U.S. Secret Service

The Secret Service is responsible for investigating the counterfeiting of currency and securities; forgery and altering of government checks and bonds; thefts and fraud relating to Treasury electronic funds transfers; financial access, telecommunications, computer, and telemarketing fraud; fraud concerning federally insured financial institutions; and other criminal and noncriminal cases.

The Secret Service investigates financial systems crimes, including bank fraud; access device fraud; telemarketing and telecommunications fraud (cellular and hard wire); computer fraud; crimes involving automated payment systems, teller machines, and direct deposits; forgery; alteration, false personation, or false claims involving U.S. Treasury checks, U.S. savings bonds, U.S. Treasury notes, bonds, and bills. The Secret Service also investigates electronic funds transfers, including Treasury disbursements and fraud within Treasury payment systems; fraud involving U.S. Department of Agriculture food coupons and Authority to Participate cards; Federal Deposit Insurance Corporation investigations; Farm Credit Administration violations; and fraud and related activity in connection with identification and seizure. Further, the Secret Service coordinates the activities of the U.S. Secret Service Organized Crimes Program and oversees money laundering investigations. The Secret Service has concurrent jurisdiction with DOJ to investigate fraud against any federally insured financial institution. Agents of the Secret Service review thousands of criminal referrals submitted by regulators of the Department of the Treasury. The Secret Service maintains records pertaining to counterfeit, forgery, and U.S. security violation cases. The Secret Service's central files in Washington, DC contain about 100,000 handwriting specimens from known forgers. An electronic information retrieval system facilitates the comparison of questioned handwriting with the examples on file, for identification purposes.

As part of the 1995 Crime Bill, Congress mandated the Secret Service to provide forensic/technical assistance—to federal, state, and local law enforcement agencies, the Morgan P. Hardiman Task Force, and the National Center for Missing and Exploited Children—in matters involving missing and sexually exploited children. Much of the forensic assistance is used in the United States by the Secret Service's Forensic Services Division. The forensic technology allows the document examiner to scan and digitize text and writings, and later search that material against previously recorded writings. As a result, the Secret Service created a national handwriting repository for comparison purposes for handwritten letters in these types of cases.

The Forensic Services Division also operates a hybrid automated fingerprint identification system, the largest of its kind, which is composed of remote latent fingerprint terminals providing connection to fingerprint databases with access to more than 25 million fingerprints. Division staff can search latent fingerprints, developed in cases involving missing and sexually exploited children, through this system for identification purposes. Other services offered by this program are polygraph consultation or assistance; photographic, graphic, age progression/regression; and voice and image enhancement technology.

## Department of Veterans Affairs (VA)

VA retains records of loans, tuition payments, insurance payments, and nonrestricted medical data related to disability pensions. These records are available at regional offices in several specific large metropolitan areas throughout the country. The data, including photocopies, may be obtained by writing or visiting the appropriate regional office. All requests should include a statement covering the need and intended use of the information. The statement should clearly identify the veteran and, if available, include the veteran's VA claim number, date of birth, branch of service, and enlistment and discharge dates.

## Financial Institutions and Related Federal Administrations and Corporations Banks

The relationship between banks and their customers is confidential and privileged. Generally, information from banks may be obtained only by subpoena. The release of information may be subject to the Right to Financial Privacy Act (12 U.S.C. 3401-3422). The following types of records and information are available from banks:

- Central master files of customers (depositors, debtors, and safe-deposit box holders) are maintained by the bank. The bank usually requires the customer's consent, a search warrant, or a court order before an authorized bank official can open a safe-deposit box. A record of entry to a safe-deposit box can be obtained by subpoena.
- Bank account applications can provide handwriting samples and certain personal information about the customer, depending on the type of account. Bank account records reflect date of deposit, amounts of currency and checks, and dates and amounts of withdrawals.
- When currency in excess of $10,000 is deposited in a bank account, the customer is required to complete a Department of the Treasury Form 4789, Currency Transaction Report (CTR).

The CTR specifies the depositor's name, address, social security number, and birth date, and records the total amount of the transaction and various other information. The bank is to retain CTRs and forward copies to the Department of the Treasury.

## Export-Import Bank of the United States (EXIM Bank)

Export-Import Bank is an independent self-sustaining agency that helps finance the overseas sales of U.S. goods and services. Its mission is to create jobs through exports. It provides guarantees of working capital loans for U.S. exporters and it guarantees the repayment of loans or makes loans to foreign purchasers of U.S. goods and services. Ex-Im Bank maintains information about U.S exporters and foreign buyers who are in good standing or who have defaulted on payments.

## FARM CREDIT ADMINISTRATION

The Farm Credit Administration is the independent federal regulator responsible for examining and ensuring the safety and soundness of all Farm Credit System institutions. The agency is funded by the lending institutions it regulates. The Farm Credit System is a nationwide financial cooperative that lends to agriculture and rural America, providing more than $60 billion in loans to some 500,000 borrowers, including farmers, ranchers, rural homeowners, agricultural cooperatives, rural utility systems, and agribusinesses.

## Federal Deposit Insurance Corporation (FDIC)

FDIC is a federally chartered corporation with two major functions: to determine the safety and soundness of financial institutions, and to solve the problems created by insolvent institutions and recover funds through the management and ultimate sale of the institutions' assets. FDIC maintains information on FDIC-regulated banks and failed FDIC-insured banks, including their ownership and officers, the identities of loan borrowers, and previous investigations. In addition, FDIC is the successor organization and custodian of records for the former Resolution Trust Corporation, a similarly chartered corporation that liquidated the assets of failed savings institutions from August, 1989 until December 31, 1995.

FDIC-insured banks and FDIC savings associations are examined periodically by FDIC examiners. Each examination includes an appraisal of management, directors, officers, and staff. The reports of examination contain an alphabetical list of all directors, officers, and principal employees. The examiner also comments on the capabilities of each individual, gives his/her approximate age, and cites other business affiliations. Additionally, the examiner completes a form on each individual, setting forth his/her estimated net worth, par value of stock owned, and salary.

Inquiries regarding types of records available to the public (including records available under the Freedom of Information Act) should be directed to the appropriate FDIC regional office or to the Office of the Executive Secretary, which can be contacted at (202) 898-3687.

## Federal Reserve System

The Federal Reserve System is a valuable source of information on banks and bank holding companies. The Federal Reserve has supervisory responsibility over domestic and international operations of all member banks, Edge Act and agreement corporations, U.S. bank holding companies, and over many of the U.S. activities of foreign banking organizations. The Federal Reserve conducts joint examinations with state agencies or alternates annual examinations with those agencies and cooperates with the states in other areas to reduce duplication and overlap in the examination and supervision of state-chartered banks. The examination of a depository institution generally entails:

1. An appraisal of the soundness of the institution's assets
2. An evaluation of internal operations, policies, and management
3. An analysis of key financial factors such as capital, earnings, liquidity, and interest rate sensitivity

4. A review for compliance with all banking laws and regulations
5. An overall determination of the institution's solvency

In addition to these examinations for the general safety and soundness of state member banks and bank holding companies, the Federal Reserve conducts special examinations of state member banks in certain areas such as consumer affairs; activities of trust departments, stock transfer agents, and municipal securities dealers; and electronic data processing. The Federal Reserve also is the primary supervisor for bank holding companies. In addition to quarterly reports on condition (which are available to the public), banks and bank holding companies examination reports may be requested for official agency use under the Federal Reserve Board of Governor's rules regarding availability of information.

## National Credit Union Administration (NCUA)

NCUA regulates, insures, and supervises all federal credit unions, as well as state-chartered credit unions that apply for its insurance. NCUA has two reporting requirements: federally insured credit unions with more than $50 million in assets must file quarterly reports and those with assets totaling less than $50 million must file semiannually.

## Independent Agencies and Government Corporations Commodity Futures Trading Commission (CFTC)

CFTC maintains the following information:

- Registration information concerning firms and individuals
- Administrative and injunctive actions filed by CFTC against firms and individuals
- Financial reports filed by CFTC registrants
- Consumer complaints filed against CFTC registrants

The National Futures Association, a self-regulatory organization authorized by the Commodity Exchange Act, operates under the supervision of the CFTC and is a one-stop information source for registration and disciplinary information regarding firms and individuals in the futures industry. This information includes registration status and employment history; disciplinary actions filed by the association, the CFTC, and the commodity exchanges; and customer complaints filed under the CFTC's reparations program. The association's information center can be contacted at (800) 621-3570 or, in Illinois, at (312) 781-1410.

## FEDERAL COMMUNICATIONS COMMISSION (FCC)

FCC regulates interstate and international communications by radio, television, wire, satellite, and cable. It investigates and studies all phases of communication problems and the best methods of obtaining the cooperation and coordination of radio and wire communication systems, including those relative to police, fire, and forestry.

The FCC staff is organized, by function, into six operating bureaus: mass media, cable services, common carrier, compliance and information, wireless telecommunications, and international. The various bureaus maintain data on licensees and users of communication frequencies that include the licensing of radio/telephone circuits and their assigned frequencies for operations.

## FEDERAL MARITIME COMMISSION

The Federal Maritime Commission investigates applicants for licenses to engage in oceangoing freight-forwarding activities. Applicants provide information to the Commission covering many aspects of their history, including the names and residences of all corporate officers and directors, names of partnership members or individual proprietors, names of direct holders of 5% or more of company stock, names of stockholders with beneficial interest in shipments moving in U.S. foreign export commerce, and employment history of license applicants.

## GENERAL SERVICES ADMINISTRATION (GSA)

GSA has considerable information on architects, engineers, personal property auctioneers, real estate appraisers, construction contractors, sales brokers, and businesses that contract with GSA. GSA also maintains a computerized list of parties excluded from federal procurement and non-procurement programs.

## NATIONAL AERONAUTICS AND SPACE ADMINISTRATION (NASA)

Over 85% of NASA's multibillion dollar budget goes to NASA's contractors. Procurement files maintained by its procurement office contain information about individual firms and their employees. NASA requires that contractors submit with the proposals their qualifications and résumés of the personnel who will be directly assigned to the project. The résumés should include each person's educational background, work experience, length of service with the firm, and work projects.

## NATIONAL ARCHIVES AND RECORDS ADMINISTRATION

The National Archives and Records Administration operate federal records centers throughout the country, including the National Personnel Records Center in St. Louis, Missouri, and the Office of the Federal Register in Washington, DC. It also operates regional archives and the presidential libraries.

The Federal Register is the medium for notifying the public of official agency actions; all federal regulations must be published in it. The Office of the Federal Register provides a periodic workshop on the use of the Federal Register as an information source. A handbook on the uses of the Federal Register is also available. For information, call (202) 523-5240.

## NATIONAL RAILROAD PASSENGER CORPORATION (AMTRAK)

Amtrak maintains information on passenger reservation histories, method of payment, and dates of travel; the railroad industry; railroad contractors, subcontractors, and vendors; train routes and schedules. Amtrak police have access to records of all Amtrak employees. To contact Amtrak police regarding the Amtrak National Communications Center or investigation and police report records, call 1-800-331-0008.

## NUCLEAR REGULATORY COMMISSION (NRC)

NRC regulates commercial nuclear power reactors; nonpower research reactors; fuel cycle facilities; medical, academic, and industrial uses of nuclear materials; and the transport, storage, and disposal of nuclear materials and waste. NRC also maintains applications and licenses of persons and companies that export nuclear material and equipment from the United States.

## SECURITIES AND EXCHANGE COMMISSION (SEC)

SEC maintains public records of corporations with stock and securities sold to the public. These records include the following:

- Financial statements
- Identification of officers and directors
- Identification of owners of more than 10% of a corporation's stock

- A description of the registrant's properties and businesses
- A description of the significant provisions of the security to be offered for sale and its relationship to the registrant's other capital securities
- Identification of events of interest to investors
- Identification of accountants and attorneys, and
- A history of the business

SEC maintains files on individuals and firms that have been reported to it as having violated federal or state securities laws. The information contained in these files pertains to official actions taken against such persons and firms, including denials, refusals, suspensions, and revocations of registrations; injunctions, fraud orders, stop orders, and cease and desist orders; and arrests, indictments, convictions, sentences, and other official actions.

The Securities and Exchange Commission Summary lists the changes in beneficial ownership by officers, directors, and principal stockholders of securities listed and registered on a national securities exchange or those relating to public utility companies, and certain closed-end investment companies.

Copies of the documents maintained by SEC are available at its regional or branch offices in the following cities: Atlanta, Georgia; Miami, Florida; Boston, Massachusetts; Chicago, Illinois; Cleveland, Ohio; Detroit, Michigan; St. Louis, Missouri; Denver, Colorado; Salt Lake City, Utah; Fort Worth, Texas; Los Angeles, California; San Francisco, California; New York, New York; Seattle, Washington; Washington, DC; and Philadelphia, Pennsylvania.

Corporate filings include the following:

- Annual Report of Publicly Traded Company (Form 10-K)—excerpts or complete report via DIALOG or LEXIS databases
- Quarterly Report of Publicly Traded Company (Form 10-Q)—same as Form 10-K
- Special Events Re Publicly Traded Company (Form 8-K)—transactions resulting in change of controlling interest
- Registration of Security (Form 8-A)—prospectus, data relative to the issuer
- Registration of Security by the Successor to (Form 8-B)—name of issuer, relationship to primary registrant/issuer
- Special Events Re Foreign Security (Form 6-K)—information similar to Forms 10-K and 8-K, except the security is registered under other U.S. law
- Report of Acquisition of Beneficial Ownership of 5% or More of Capital Stock of Public Company (Form 13-D)—identity of each person or firm acquiring beneficial ownership of 5% or more of capital stock or constituting a group that acquires such beneficial ownership; description of security; agreements or other undertakings by reporting entity; whether acquisition results in change of control; background on each person reporting; and sources of funds for acquisition, purpose of acquisition, and relationship of parties

## SMALL BUSINESS ADMINISTRATION (SBA)

SBA guarantees loans made by commercial lenders to eligible small businesses; makes loans to businesses and individuals following federally-declared disasters; and licenses investment companies to provide venture capital to eligible small businesses. SBA also connects small firms owned by socially and economically disadvantaged Americans with contracts set aside by other federal agencies and seeks to increase federal contract opportunities for small businesses in general. SBA-guaranteed loans are made by private sector lenders, with SBA promising to reimburse a specified percentage of any amounts lost by the lender. By law, the amount of SBA's guaranty under its most popular and least restricted lending program is limited to $750,000 and the loan maturity to 25 years.

SBA may be the best source of financial and other information about the small businesses (and their principals) to which it provides assistance; many of them are exempt from public disclosure laws because of their small size. Records on businesses and individuals that have received SBA assistance are maintained by the division that administers the program involved. The local SBA district office maintains most records. Contact the local office of SBA's Office of Inspector General, Investigations Division, for assistance in obtaining records and other information.

## Social Security Administration (SSA)

SSA retains original applications for social security numbers. Applications list an applicant's name (maiden and married names for a female), birth date, birthplace, sex, race, parents' names, and address at time of application.

## U.S. Postal Service and U.S. Postal Inspection Service

The U.S. Postal Service maintains the names and addresses of post office box holders and change of address information. It can verify that an individual is receiving mail at a particular address.

Requests for photocopies of postal money orders may be made through the local office of the U.S. Postal Inspection Service. Information concerning the mailing addresses, telephone numbers, and fax numbers of U.S. Postal Inspection Service offices nationwide is available on the U.S. Postal Inspection Service home page on the Internet. Information concerning missing U.S. and Canadian money order forms, counterfeit Canadian money order forms, and invalid express mail accounts can be found on the U.S. Postal Service home page on the Internet.

The Postal Inspection Service, through the judicial officer, is empowered under 39 U.S.C. 3005 to issue false presentation orders and cease and desist orders in cases where the mail is being used to obtain money from the public by means of false and fraudulent statements. The orders require mail to be returned to the sender, they forbid payment of postal money orders connected to the scheme, require the return of money to those who purchased the money orders, and require that cited schemes cease.

Postal regulations require commercial mail-receiving agencies to complete a PS Form 1583, Application for Delivery of Mail Through an Agent. The data from that form, which includes personal identification information and references for a specific individual, can be made available to federal, state, and local law enforcement agencies. The mailing addresses, telephone numbers, and fax numbers of Postal Inspection Service offices nationwide are available on the Internet.

# Index